ETHICS and the Human Community

ETHICS
and the Human
Community

90972

MELVIN RADER
University of Washington

HOLT, RINEHART AND WINSTON
New York · Chicago · San Francisco · Toronto · London

PREFACE

Some of my readers will saye, seeing that I graunte that I have gathered this booke of so many writers, that I offer unto you an heape of other mennis labourers, and nothing of mine owne. . . . To whom I answere that if the honeye that the bees gather out of so many floure of herbes, shrubbes, and trees, that are growing in other mennis meadows, feldes, and closes may justelye be called the bee's honeye . . . so maye I call that I have learned and gathered of so many autoures . . . my booke.

So wrote William Turner, philosopher, botanist, and keeper of bees, in the preface to one of his books (1551). I have also gathered the honey of other men's thoughts, but I like to think that this book is mine. I have tried to look at ethical problems afresh and to exercise independent judgment. The result may be unique enough to justify my effort.

My concern has been with the basic issues: What is the essential value of human life? What is right action? What is the nature of a good social order? Unless we can find reasonable answers to these questions, we shall fritter away our energies in senseless, inconsistent, whimsical strivings. This book tries to answer these questions and, by so doing, to clarify the ideals that can guide us in an uncertain world.

I have used the title *Ethics and the Human Community* because it emphasizes the humanistic spirit of my argument. By "humanism" I mean the view that ethics should be based upon human nature and its potentialities. Opposed to humanism are the relativist and subjective theories that deny the possibility of universal and objective standards of value, and also the intuitional and a priori theories that reject an empirical basis for ethics. Although I cling to humanism, I believe that each of the great theories of ethics, humanist and nonhumanist alike, makes an indispensable contribution to sound moral philosophy. These theories I try to present as fairly as possible; when I differ, I give my reasons.

A dominant theme in this book is the tension between individualism and collectivism. This problem divides and bedevils the world. Its resolution, I believe, requires an intermediate position, "the ideal of the human community." A community exists when the experience of personal interdependence

v

is the voluntary basis of group coherence. The bond of community is a person-taken-as-person relation among free individuals, an uncoerced relation of mutuality. This book explores, among various themes, the meaning and implications of community as an ethical concept.

Far more than most writers on ethics, I have reckoned with social ideals, such as liberalism and democracy, aristocracy and communism. The ultimate locus of goodness is, I believe, the individual, but it is difficult for any person to live a good life in a bad social order. An adequate ethics is concerned with the total human personality in the context of a well-functioning society.

Much of the argument of my *Ethics and Society*, published in 1950 by Holt, Rinehart and Winston, has been incorporated in this volume, but I have added and revised far more than I have repeated. I have also used portions of articles that I have written: "Toward a Definition of Cultural Crisis," *Kenyon Review*, Spring 1945; "Crisis and the Spirit of Community," *Proceedings and Addresses of the American Philosophical Association*, 1954; "The Artist as Outsider," *Journal of Aesthetics and Art Criticism*, March 1958; and "Community in Time of Stress," *University of Colorado Studies: Series in Philosophy*, August 1961. I thank the editors of these publications for their kind permission to reproduce this material. My friends and colleagues, Arval Morris of the School of Law, Charles A. Valentine of the Department of Anthropology, and Karl A. Wittfogel of the Far Eastern and Russian Institute, have given very generously of their critical advice. I am greatly indebted to my colleagues in the Department of Philosophy, University of Washington, and our departmental librarian, Marion Stanton, for their help and stimulation. Most of all I am indebted to Charner Perry of the Department of Philosophy, University of Chicago, for invaluable advice and criticism. I also wish to thank the Rockefeller Foundation for a grant-in-aid (1948–1949) for work on crisis and community, and the Graduate School of the University of Washington for financial assistance toward the preparation of the manuscript. My indebtedness to authors, titles, and publishers is indicated by the many notes that appear at the conclusion of each chapter.

Seattle, Washington   M. R.
1964

CONTENTS

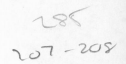

Preface   v
Introduction   1

Part One: FACT AND VALUE

   I The Laws of Nature   15
  II Human Excellence   56
 III Enjoyment   85
 IV Interest   111

Part Two: RIGHT AND OBLIGATION

   V The Laws of God   127
  VI Duty   136
 VII Utilitarianism   164
VIII Bias and Obligation   197

Part Three: SKEPTICAL THEORIES

  IX Cultural Relativism   227
   X Subjectivism, Old and New   247

Part Four: SOCIAL IDEALS

  XI The Group and the Individual   279
 XII The Communist Ideal   306
XIII The Democratic Ideal   343
XIV Crisis   372
 XV The Basis of Renewal   385
XVI The Spirit of Community   408

Conclusion   435
Appendix   443
Bibliography   448
Index   459

ETHICS and the Human Community

Introduction

TWO CONCEPTIONS OF ETHICS

Living is a kind of experiment. Since no one can live twice, it is an "experiment" that cannot be repeated. But some details of living can recur and much can be foreseen. Gradually one can learn the principles of wise choice. Ethics is a critical study of the principles or standards for conducting this experiment.

Ethics differs from morality as theory differs from practice. Both ethics and morality are concerned with judgments of approval and disapproval, judgments of the rightness or wrongness, the goodness or badness, of actions, dispositions, ends, and means. Both spring from the human desire to narrow the gap between things as they are and things as they ought to be. But ethical wisdom consists in knowing how to frame the ideal, and moral sagacity consists in knowing how to put the ideal to work and realize it in practice. We may therefore define morality as the practice, and ethics as the theory, of wisdom in conduct. But neither can flourish in artificial separation from the other.

We can distinguish two main conceptions of ethics in the history of Western civilization: the study of the good and the study of the moral law.

The Study of the Good. According to the Platonic and Aristotelian view, which is that of Greek philosophy generally, the primary subject of ethical investigation is what is good in and for man. The first task of ethics is to discover what is good as an end—good for its own sake—ultimately and intrinsically good. Then the task is to determine what is good as a means to this end—good instrumentally.

The distinction between *intrinsic* and *instrumental* good is basic. If your teeth need repair, it is good for you to go to a dentist and to submit to his painful operations. But it is good as a *means* and not as an end—good instrumentally. You do not seek out the dentist because you enjoy the experience for its own sake. But there are some things, for example, happiness, which seem to be good in their own right and not merely because they produce something else which is good. They are good as *ends*—good intrinsically.

Now the term *intrinsic goodness* can be understood more or less strictly. For example, one can speak of a vacation as intrinsically good, meaning that the vacation is worth having for its own sake—in other words, that it is good even if the consequences are indifferent or even if it is considered quite apart from any consequences. But many aspects or incidents of the vacation are intrinsically bad or indifferent; hence we cannot say that the vacation is intrinsically good throughout.

We can use the term *intrinsic good* more strictly. We can mean by it, for example, that ingredient in the vacation which *makes* it worth having for its own sake, namely, that ultimate goodness which is good through and through, so that no part of it is bad or indifferent. A hedonist, for example, would maintain that the vacation is intrinsically good (in the less strict sense of the term) because it contains pleasure, and that, in the last analysis, it is pleasure and pleasure alone that is good for its own sake—ultimately good, or good throughout, or intrinsically good in the strict sense of the term. As G. E. Moore declares:

> We may, in short, divide intrinsically good things into two classes: namely (1) those which, while as wholes they are intrinsically good, nevertheless contain some parts which are not intrinsically good; and (2) those which either have no parts at all, or, if they have any, have none but what are themselves intrinsically good.[1]

The ethics of goals tries to discover the meaning of ultimate good. Morality is the effectuating of purposes—it is action to realize an end—and the ethical problem is to find out the nature of ultimate goodness and the means to its attainment. Well-doing is the promotion of well-being.

Such an ethics will be subdivided in accordance with various conceptions of well-being. Hedonistic ethics maintains that the good is pleasure; voluntaristic ethics maintains that the good is the satisfaction of desire; intellectualistic ethics maintains that the good is wisdom; and so forth. But all of these varieties agree that right action promotes goodness or diminishes evil. This type of ethics we shall call "teleological" (from the Greek word *telesis,* meaning purpose), or, in the wide sense of the word, "utilitarian." Derived from Greek philosophy, teleological ethics runs like a guiding thread through the intellectual history of the Western world.

The Study of Moral Law. The religious and ethical imperatives of the Bible have proved even more influential for the ethical conduct and aspirations of Western society than the Greek tradition. Although there are many different strands in our Biblical heritage, the most prominent theme is the idea of moral law. It appears, for example, in the stories of God's command to Adam, His covenant with Abraham, and His dictation to Moses of the Ten Commandments. The laws or commandments thus "God-given" are held to be sacred and enforced by divine decree. In the words of the Old Testament, "Righteousness exalts a nation, but sin is the shame of peoples" (*Proverbs* 14:34); and in the words of the New Testament, "The wages of sin is death" (*Romans* 6:23). Righteousness is obedience to God's law; sin is disobedience. The idea of "the gods' unwritten and unfaltering law," as set forth in Sophocles' play *Antigone*, is likewise present in the moral reflection of the Greeks; but the concept of moral law was not dominant in Greek ethical philosophy, and its prominence in modern thought is more the result of the Hebrew and Christian influence than of the Greek.

Thus we arrive at a second conception of ethics, which emphasizes the general rules of duty or laws of right action. This type of ethics, when sharply distinguished from the utilitarian view, maintains that the moral code is binding on every man regardless of the consequences. Moral law is accepted as ultimate; there is no attempt to penetrate behind it to determine whether it is useful or conducive to welfare. The law declares what is right, and one ought to do what is right irrespective of consequences. According to ethics of this type, the basis of right conduct is to be found in the moral "ought." Its fundamental concepts are right, duty, and law as prescribing the content of obligation.

In its original Hebrew-Christian form, it is primarily theological, seeking the foundations of ethics in the laws of God. Among many modern philosophers, the theological element has been shorn away—the moral laws are interpreted as the dictates of conscience, intuition, or pure reason. What unites these divergent interpretations are their antiutilitarian approach—they maintain that the moral quality of acts depends upon conformity to laws, rules, or principles of action rather than upon goals and consequences. Ethics of this type is called by philosophers "deontological," a term that I shall adopt.

I do not wish to imply that there is necessarily a sharp dualism between utilitarian and deontological ethics. Even in the Bible the ethics of moral righteousness was supplemented and enriched by the ethics of fulfillment. In the Middle Ages many streams intermingled. The Greek way of life, as reinterpreted by St. Thomas Aquinas, was accepted as the ethics of man's natural affairs, while Christian principles were required at the level of man's spiritual life. A number of recent philosophers, such as W. D. Ross, have sought to combine the utilitarian and deontological strains in ethics.

Another kind of dualism, the sharp distinction between personal morality and social policy, was no original part of either the teleological or the deontological traditions. The split between individual ethics and social theory is primarily a modern phenomenon. It did not exist for Plato and Aristotle, who regarded "ethics" and "politics" as divisions of the same subject. The ancient Hebrews knew nothing of the split: religion and morality and social righteousness for them were bound together. It is mainly in the postmedieval world that the bifurcation has occurred—an unpolitical ethics and an amoral politics have gone their separate ways. The sorry state of the world is partly a result of this fact.

In this book, I shall deliberately avoid the modern bifurcation. I shall not artificially separate the two questions, first, the nature of the good life for the individual, and second, the standards that should govern the association of individuals in societies. A man's life is inevitably bound up with his fellows, and moral values tend of necessity to be expressed in social terms. Also economic and political theory, if it is to avoid superficiality, must come to grips with ethical considerations. "The economist, like everyone else," declared Alfred Marshall, "must concern himself with the ultimate aims of man."[2] An identical statement applies to the statesman or political theorist. The focus of my discussion will be ethics, but I shall heed its social dimensions, bearings, and implications.

THE SUBJECT MATTER OF ETHICS

Whether ethics be utilitarian or deontological, its subject matter is human conduct. By "conduct" I mean voluntary activity. Ethics has meaning only for free and responsible agents. It is concerned with the principles of choice, but there can be no choice unless there is a measure of freedom. The concept of *ought* has an implicit reference to free acts. I *ought* implies *can* and excludes *must*. There is no sense in saying that a hopeless cripple ought to run a race.

When a man makes a choice, he comes to a decision. Some decisions are better than others—hence there must be some standards whereby decisions can be judged. Men apply standards in making decisions and in judging decisions already made. Not all decisions are moral, for the standards may be esthetic, or technical, or of some other nonmoral type. Moral issues are most likely to arise when there are conflicts; for example, when an artist must choose between devotion to his work and obligation to his family.

For an act to be subject to moral judgment, it need not be *completely* voluntary. Men are morally praised or condemned for their habits, and habits are not easy to shake off. But if habitual acts are involuntary, how can they be subject to moral judgments? The answer is that, to a degree, a man *is* responsible for his habits. When a habit is starting, he can avoid it; and even when established, it can be broken, or controlled and corrected. Some habits become addictions, and if they are then completely involuntary, they are not subject to moral censure, unless the victim of habit is being blamed for his *past* voluntary acts. A confirmed drug addict, alcoholic, or sexual pervert should be treated by a physician, psychiatrist, or clinical psychologist rather than condemned by a moralist. For a similar reason, an insane person who can no longer distinguish between right and wrong should be treated medically rather than judged morally. But a man may be *partly* responsible for his acts, since insanity or drug addiction may be a matter of degree. To help a person recover his freedom and responsibility is an important factor in curing him.

The idea of moral freedom and responsibility is closely related to the ancient metaphysical problem of free will. This problem is so intricate and vexing that I hesitate to discuss it in detail, and there is scarcely any need to do so. The concept of free action is accepted by everybody in common speech and in all except the most mechanistic of psychologies. It is a verifiable fact that men act purposefully, that they deliberate and decide, that they pursue ideals and make choices, that they praise and blame and hold one another responsible, and that they judge acts and motives in the light of moral criteria. We constantly use expressions, such as "I could do it, but I would rather not," or "You should not have done that," which involve the notion of free acts. It is impossible to divest ourselves of all such modes of thought and speech; and even if it were possible, the effect would be to eliminate the moral realm of discourse. So long as we think in ethical terms at all, we must suppose that there are open alternatives. Freedom is the condition of morality, and morality is the best evidence for freedom. An unfree morality is a contradiction in terms.

This does not mean that an indeterministic theory of human behavior is necessarily correct. The indeterminist is too inclined to assume that freedom can have only one meaning, *his* meaning, and that we should leap from the valid premise that morality presupposes freedom to the doubtful conclusion that free acts are uncaused. Human freedom consists neither in the blind operation of lifeless, unthinking forces, as in a landslide, nor in sheer indeterminism, which is equally blind. Nothing is so fatal as an accident, and nothing is more accidental than an undetermined event. As Santayana has said:

The notion that . . . the intervention of groundless movements would tend towards a happy issue rests upon a complete confusion. It is the gambler's fallacy. Empty possibility seems to him full of promise; but in fact sheer chance, throwing dice, would seldom throw sixes. The only force that really tends towards happy results is the innate force of the soul herself.[3]

Freedom, I believe, consists of self-determination, involving the causal efficacy of intelligence, purpose, imagination, and character. This conception of free personality, as a part of nature, and yet a power in its own right, is compatible with causal explanation; it simply insists that human nature, as creative and teleological, is a force to be reckoned with. If we distinguish between mechanistic and teleological causation, we can work out a theory of self-determination that admits foresight and intelligent choice. We can thus avoid a doctrine of mechanistic determination, which seems to be the chief bugbear feared by the indeterminists.

Some such reconciliation of freedom and determinism is required to make sense out of our lives. As Carl Rogers, the distinguished American psychologist, has written:

Behavior, when it is examined scientifically, is surely best understood as determined by prior causation. This is one great fact of science. But responsible personal choice, which is the most essential element in being a person, which is the core experience in psychotherapy, which exists prior to any scientific endeavor, is an equally prominent fact in our lives. To deny the experience of responsible choice is, to me, as restricted a view as to deny the possibility of a behavioral science. That these two important elements of our experience appear to be in contradiction has perhaps the same significance as the contradiction between the wave theory and the corpuscular theory of light, both of which can be shown to be true, even though incompatible.[4]

If we avoid the extreme doctrine of materialistic mechanism, it is possible, I believe, to resolve the conflict between freedom and determinism. But it would lead us too far astray to thresh out this issue in a prolonged argument. The dispute will continue as a genuine issue for metaphysicians and theologians; but at the level of normal experience and ordinary language, the reality of free action must be taken for granted. So will it be in the present book.

THE METHODS OF ETHICS

As a rational activity, ethics is based upon method rather than upon prejudice and hearsay. There are only two methods that seem to me applicable to ethics—the method of experience and the method of intuition. Other so-called methods—deduction, analysis, or the use of authority—are no substitutes. The deductive or a priori method, except as a phase of a larger pattern of reasoning, is ill adapted to the practical concerns of ethics. I shall have something to say about this method when we consider the ethics of Kant in Chapter V. Linguistic analysis, if it can be called a method, is not coordinate with the empirical and intuitional methods; the latter are directed to determining which ethical judgments are correct whereas linguistic analysis is directed to the clarification of meanings. Some contemporary writers maintain that clarification is the *only* philosophical task, but I do not accept this milk-and-water conception of philosophy, and what is more to the point, neither have the great analytical philosophers. The best of them would agree with J. L. Austin, that clarification is not just an end in itself. "We are looking . . . not merely at words . . ." declared Austin, "but also at the realities we use words to talk about. We are using a sharpened awareness of words to sharpen our perception of . . . the phenomena."[5] The citation of authority, invoking a famous name in support of one's doctrine, is not properly considered an independent method. If we cite an authority, what makes the authority reliable? If every "authority" should depend upon some previous "authority," there would be an infinite regress and no ultimate justification. It is only because authority has some basis *other* than authority (for example, experience or reason) that it has any claim upon us. If we are to discriminate wisely between conflicting authorities, moreover, we need some insight of our own. This insight, it would appear, must be based upon either empirical reasoning or intuition.

The Method of Experience. The empirical method is illustrated in the recommendation of Aristotle that we should rely more upon the facts of life than upon the authority of wise men:

> The opinions of the wise seem . . . to harmonize with our arguments. But while even such things carry some conviction, the truth in practical matters is discerned from the facts of life; for these are the decisive factor. We must therefore survey what we have already said, bringing it to the test of the facts of life, and if it harmonizes with the facts we must accept it, but if it clashes with them we must suppose it to be mere theory.[6]

According to the method of experience, the human good must be studied in terms of human nature—its needs, faculties, potentialities, and environmental conditions. The sufferings and enjoyments, the frustrations and fulfillments, the obstacles and opportunities of life, can be studied like any set of facts. Human conscience is a fact of human nature, and it, too, must be studied. If the moralist is to do more than beat the air with vague exhortations, he must understand the structure and workings of our moral faculties, the more thoroughly and accurately, the better. He must know human beings in their concrete relationships—as they function in the family, the neighborhood, the workshop or cultural association, the nation or the international tribunal.

I shall say no more about the method of experience, for I mean by it nothing unusual—just the use of ordinary inductive logic, as in any empirical science. I am very sympathetic with this method, but I am aware of its limitations and difficulties when applied to ethical inquiry. Ethics is not a descriptive science like psychology. There is a difference between describing what is the case and deciding what ought to exist or what we ought to do. The problem of the relation between the "is" and the "ought," between facts and ideals, is one of the basic questions of ethics. We shall return to it again and again.

The Method of Intuition. Among philosophers who emphasize the contrast between *what is* and *what ought to be,* there is a tendency to reject the method of experience. Ethics, they say, is a "normative" science, and a "norm" is not a natural fact to be empirically studied. We cannot use an empirical method, which is adapted to the study of facts, in the determination of duties. "Good," "right," or "obligation" are not "natural" or empirically observable properties. The term "ought" takes us out of the observational and experimental field. Facts are one thing, ethical imperatives are quite another. The method of experience is suitable for the sciences; the method of intuition is required for ethics.

The implications of this "non-naturalistic" view, with its reliance upon intuition, will become clearer as the argument of this book unfolds. At this point, an initial clarification is all that is required. By "intuition" is meant direct apprehension that a proposition is true, or that something is the case. In intuitive knowledge, as John Locke wrote, "the mind is at no pains of proving or examining, but perceives the truth as the eye doth the light, only by being directed towards it. Thus, the mind perceives that white is not black, that a circle is not a triangle, that three is more than two, and equal to one and two."[7]

The words of Locke indicate that intuition is not confined to ethics. Some intuitions are presupposed in all reasoning. The fundamental "laws of thought"—the principle of identity ("if any statement is true, then it is true"), the principle of contradiction ("no statement can be both true and false"), and the principle of excluded middle ("any statement is either true or false")—are known intuitively rather than demonstratively, since they have to be taken for granted in all reasoning. Moreover, in any chain of reasoning, each step must be recognized as valid. Suppose I argue A (the premise), *therefore* B, *therefore* C. The argument is invalid unless B really follows from A, and C really follows from B. That it does follow I must see directly, and direct insight is intuition.

Many philosophers have argued that certain ethical truths must be known intuitively if they are to be known at all. G. E. Moore maintained that we intuit the goodness of certain objects (love, knowledge, virtue, happiness, and beauty), and Sir David Ross contended that we intuit the rightness of certain acts (promise-keeping, truth-telling, restitution for harm done, and so forth). Ultimately all of us have certain moral convictions that we cannot prove—for example, that it is wrong to torture an innocent man simply for torture's sake. We can hold that these convictions are simply baseless prejudices—and in that case, we can scarcely say that we have much conviction. Or we can say that we have some immediate insights—that we "see" directly that wanton torture is wrong. This principle may be derived from some more general principle—for example, that unhappiness is intrinsically bad—but this more general principle must then rest upon intuition. So an intuitionist would argue.

Intuition has often been attacked as an uncritical "begging of the question." If a man says, "I know this by intuition," the effect is to cut off the argument. This objection to begging the question is often valid, but it may not be a valid objection to a judicious and critical employment of intuition.

The intuitionist need not claim infallibility. The mark of intuition is its directness, not its certainty. I have said that intuition is required at each step in a chain of inferential reasoning, yet it is well known that one may make mistakes in inference. Likewise in the case of ethical insight, one may *seem* to know something directly and still be mistaken.

My own opinion is that the method of experience should be our main reliance, but that *some* intuitions are indispensable. We cannot hope to prove
everything, since something must be taken for granted, even in the first
proof. The "laws of thought," as we have already said, underlie all reasoning.
Similarly, there can be no ethics unless men recognize that there *are* values,
that some experiences are better or worse than others. We need to discern
what *is* good and evil, and that values lay obligations upon us. These are insights that, in my opinion, cannot be *demonstrated* by inductive or deductive
reasoning, although reasoning can help to clarify and sharpen our intuitions.
When it comes to these very ultimate questions, rationally persuasive but
not demonstrative arguments are possible.

As a result of modern criticism, some of which has been based upon misunderstanding, the word "intuition" has fallen into disrepute. Hence it may
be preferable, as A. C. Ewing has suggested, to substitute "direct cognition"
in place of "intuition." I shall continue to use the latter term, but I shall
mean by it nothing more than immediate insight. To quote Ewing:

> To say that we sometimes see by "intuition" what constitutes a good or bad
> reason in ethics is only to say that we can sometimes know what is a good
> reason without having to give another reason why it is a good reason, a not very
> extravagant suggestion.[8]

So understood, the contention that some ethical truths can be known intuitively is modest enough.

ON FINDING THE ANSWER
BEFORE KNOWING THE QUESTION

I shall not outline in detail the questions that we shall seek to answer. Philosophy is no cut-and-dried affair in which the specifications can be laid down
in advance.

There is an apocryphal story about the death of Gertrude Stein that illustrates this point. As Gertrude neared the end, she appeared to be wrestling
with some profound problem. A friend sitting beside her bed heard her
mumble, "What is the *answer?*" She turned and tossed in deep thought, until
finally her face lit up and she appeared more relaxed. But soon her agitation
returned and she was heard to murmur, "What, then, is the *question?*"

It may appear silly to search for an answer before the question is clearly
known—but is it really as silly as it appears? Just as the painter, struggling
with his pigments, is engaged in an act of discovery, so the philosopher,
struggling with his concepts, is adventuring into the unknown. An artist does
not know in detail what he wants to do until he has done it. As Croce has
said, the intuition of what he wishes to express is formulated in the very act
of expression. The philosopher likewise clarifies his intent as he works; the

question becomes clear to him only as he gropes for the answer. If, at the end, he can very clearly formulate the question, this is often a sign that the answer has been found. Likewise, the reader of a book on philosophy cannot be expected to understand the questions in advance. They become intelligible only as the answers take shape.

What I have just said appears to be in contradiction with the very first words in G. E. Moore's *Principia Ethica:*

It appears to me that in Ethics, as in all other philosophical studies, the difficulties and disagreements, of which its history is full, are mainly due to a very simple cause: namely to the attempt to answer questions, without first discovering precisely *what* question it is which you desire to answer.[9]

This sentence strikes the keynote of the strongly analytical character of twentieth-century ethics. But, valid as it is within limits, Moore's statement expresses only one side of the truth; the other side is suggested by the story about Gertrude Stein. The fact is that the asking and answering of questions are dialectically interdependent. The mind of the philosopher works back and forth like a shuttle from question to answer, the tentative question clarifying the answer and the tentative answer illuminating the nature of the question. It is only at the end of the quest that both question and answer are clear and definitive.

Hence I shall not try in the beginning to define the detailed questions that will be considered in this book. It should suffice at this point to indicate the very broad divisions of the argument. In Part One, "Fact and Value," we shall consider the natural basis of human ideals, as found in "the laws of nature" and the constitution of man. The emphasis will be upon good rather than right. In Part Two, "Right and Obligation," this emphasis will be reversed. The meaning of obligation, and the contrast between formalistic and teleological interpretations of right, will be explored. After developing in Parts One and Two the main outlines of a humanistic ethics, we shall turn to objections in Part Three, "Sceptical Theories." Here we shall critically examine the relativist and subjective doctrines that deny the objective basis of a universal ethics. In Part Four, "Social Ideals," we shall turn to the clash between individualism and collectivism and aristocracy and democracy, probing the great conflicts that divide and bedevil mankind, and exploring the meaning of human community—its import in terms of values and ideas. Finally, in a Conclusion, I shall draw together some of the diverse threads of my argument.

NOTES

1. G. E. Moore, *Ethics.* New York: Oxford University Press, 1912, p. 75.
2. Quoted by John Kenneth Galbraith, *The Affluent Society.* Boston: Houghton Mifflin Company, 1958, title page.
3. George Santayana, *The Genteel Tradition at Bay.* New York: Charles Scribner's Sons, 1931, p. 39.
4. Carl R. Rogers and B. F. Skinner, "Some Issues Concerning the Control

of Human Behavior: A Symposium," *Science*, vol. 124 (Nov. 30, 1956), p. 1064.

5. J. L. Austin, "A Plea for Excuses," *Proceedings of the Aristotelian Society*, vol. 57 (1956–1957), p. 8.

6. Aristotle, *Ethics* (translated by W. D. Ross). New York: Oxford University Press, 1942, 1179a.

7. John Locke, *An Essay Concerning Human Understanding*, Book IV, Chap. 2.

8. A. C. Ewing, "Recent Developments in British Ethical Thought," in C. A. Mace (ed.), *British Philosophy in the Mid-Century*. London: George Allen and Unwin, Ltd., 1957, p. 95.

9. G. E. Moore, *Principia Ethica*. New York and Cambridge: Cambridge University Press, 1903, p. vii.

PART ONE

Fact and value

CHAPTER I

The laws of nature

I. THE COMMON FEATURES OF NATURAL-LAW THEORIES

A few years ago, there was a popular song to the effect that we ought to keep on doing "what comes naturally." This point of view has evidently been prevalent as long as man has existed on our planet. In its most permissive version, it amounts to no more than William Blake's maxim: "Damn braces. Bless relaxes."[1] But there are other versions, and among these are the theories of "natural law." We shall examine a number of natural-law doctrines, which hold the following convictions in common.

Morality should be based on something more objective than whimsy and prejudice and more universal than custom and governmental law. In addition to the rules an individual may make for himself, or the laws a state may impose on its citizens, there are principles of moral conduct that apply to *all* men.

These universal principles have a realistic basis. Man's basic nature and environment provide the ultimate standard of right conduct, whether of individuals or states. Human beings have fundamental needs and tendencies; their fulfillment is good; their frustration is evil. To fulfill these requirements of a good life and to harmonize with the basic forces of the universe is the realistic goal of human ideals.

This conception of ethics has certain implications. It implies that nature determines the characteristic tendencies of a species, and that these tendencies require fulfillment if good is to be achieved. A bear, a rabbit, or a human being possesses a certain nature which it shares with others of its kind. The good for a human being is both like and unlike the good for a rabbit or a bear. It is like insofar as man shares in a common animal nature; it is unlike insofar as man is distinguished by human nature.

The laws of nature are the patterns of action required to fulfill the essential tendencies of man both as animal and human, and, beyond this, to harmonize with the basic forces of the universe. These laws are enforced by natural sanctions: those who violate them suffer harm, those who obey them achieve happiness.

A law of nature, in this, its *ethical* sense, must be distinguished from a physical law, such as "the law of gravity." The latter (which is "natural law" in the *scientific* sense of that ambiguous term) is purely descriptive and non-moral. It connotes no more than observed uniformity of action. Because it is imposed by physical necessity without regard to will or reason, it is just as binding upon a clod as it is upon a human being. Even the actions of men, insofar as they are uniform, are subject to laws of this descriptive type—as, for example, when we speak of the laws of psychology. These are laws stating not what men ought to do, but what they do. Quite different is "natural law" in the ethical sense. It orders conduct only as approved by reason and imposed by moral will. It is law that ought to prevail, although in practice it may not. A man by the prerogative of free choice may turn from it and follow his own desires. As a law of human fulfillment, it is both natural and moral—*natural* because the good for man depends upon the nature of man and his universe, *moral* because it binds by conscience rather than by necessity.

A very important corollary is the concept of *natural rights*. A natural right is a moral right that is justified by the laws of nature, although it may conflict with the customs and enacted laws of society. It is reasonable in view of the essential characteristics of human nature and its environment. That a man has a natural right to something means that it is naturally right that he should have it. If he has a natural right to liberty, for example, this means that liberty is essential to the rightful fulfillment of his nature.

A right and a duty are correlative terms. If you have a right to be un-molested then I have a duty not to molest you. If you have a right to freedom of speech then I have a duty not to abridge your freedom. In this sense, we can speak of natural duties as well as natural rights.

When a person has a right, and insists upon its being observed, he is mak-ing a claim. But he may have a right which, in virtue of particular circum-stances, he may not be justified in claiming. His right may conflict with the rights of others, or conditions may be unfavorable to the exercise of the right. But if its exercise is *never* justifiable, it should not be called a "right." The word "right" implies justifiability, and "natural right" implies justifiability in terms of natural law.

We shall now review a number of historical examples of the natural-law theory, which will indicate the variety and range of this type of ethics.

2. NATURAL LAW IN THE STOICS AND CICERO

The foundations of the natural-law theory can be traced back to various Greek thinkers, such as Heraclitus, the Sophists, Plato, and Aristotle. But it was among the Stoics that the theory first emerged as a characteristic and easily identifiable doctrine of "natural law."

Stoicism sprang up in a time of troubles. After the Peloponnesian War, Greece was so weakened and rent by internal strife that it fell an easy prey to the imperialistic designs of Macedonia. In the words of the Book of Maccabees, "Alexander son of Philip, the Macedonian, . . . made many wars, and won many strongholds, and went through to the ends of the earth, and took spoils of many nations." After the breakdown of the Macedonian empire, the political scene exhibited only despotic monarchies and warring city-states. Through gradual conquest, Rome subsequently achieved peace and a wide dominion.

Originating in Athens and spreading throughout the Roman empire, Stoicism reflected these stormy events. It was a philosophy of refuge, finding salvation not in vigorous political and social reconstruction, which men no longer had the courage or vision to undertake, but in individual self-manage-ment—the deliberate cultivation of mental tranquillity raised above the storms and vicissitudes of life. In its cosmopolitanism, it reflected the age of im-perialism, an age of the uprooting and migration and mixture of peoples, in which the little city-state was dissolving and the great empires of Macedonia and Rome were demanding new concepts of universal citizenship. Stoicism became strong and flourished because it marched with the times, in pace with the mood of an expansive but declining civilization.

Its leadership indicates something of its cosmopolitan and varied character. Its founder was Zeno (circa 336–264 B.C.), a Phoenician from Cyprus, who lived in Athens as a resident alien and gave lectures in a building known as the Stoa Poikile, or Painted Porch, whence the name Stoic was derived. The early Stoics were recruited from many places, especially from Syria; the later Stoics were mostly Romans. Their leaders came from high and low station; for example, Epictetus (born circa A.D. 60) was originally a penniless slave and Marcus Aurelius (A.D. 121–180) was a mighty emperor.

The Stoics were interested in two questions: what to believe, and how to live. Some of them exhibited a real and independent interest in the first question, but most of them were mainly interested in the second. They be-lieved, however, that the second question could be answered only if the first could be resolved. We must know what is real, they contended, before we can judge what we ought to do.

In giving an account of reality, Stoicism, as Zeno formulated it, started with what appears to be an uncompromising materialism. Everything is ma-terial; even God and the soul are bodies; the divine reason is a kind of fire. This is a bit hard to make sense of; it is difficult to see the consistency of a doctrine that identifies reason with a material substance. The Stoics, however, were hylozoists: they believed that all matter is endowed with life. If we grant this premise, it no longer seems so strange to say that the material uni-verse is a living being and that matter is shot through with reason. Just as soul or life force animates the human body, so a spiritual force rolls through all things. This soul or life force can be called God, Nature, Reason—syno-

nyms for the inner essence and animating principle of the world. It is the
productive, formative power, the natural spontaneity, the force that makes
for movement and growth. It is divine reason, all-pervasive and all-powerful;
hence there is no sheer evil in the world, and nothing is left to chance. From
this standpoint, it is also fate—not a blind mechanical necessity but a purposive, providential force, the living activity of the whole expressing itself
through every natural event.

The divine fire is in every man: reason is his governing principle, the core
and center of his being. What corresponds to his reason and expresses his
nature also corresponds to the world soul and expresses the universal nature.
To "live according to nature" is to express our rational nature and, at the same
time, to be in harmony with the rational order of the world. This means that
one should not merely submit to fate but approve and welcome it.

At this point we meet a serious difficulty. If nature is fate, it seems that we
have no choice—it is not that we had "better" accept it; we *must* accept it.
The Stoics met this difficulty by making an exception. They said that all *outward* occurrences, all matters of fortune, are fated, but in his inner attitudes
man is free. To quote Epictetus:

> Of all existing things, some are in our power, and others are not in our power.
> In our power are thought, impulse, will to get and will to avoid, and, in a word,
> everything which is our own doing. Things not in our power include the body,
> property, reputation, office, and, in a word, everything which is not our own
> doing.[2]

The essence of morality is to make the "things in our power"—our inner
attitudes—harmonize with the "things not in our power"—the outward course
of events. "Ask not that events should happen as you will," Epictetus advised,
"but let your will be that events should happen as they do, and you shall
have peace."[3] The logic here is rather simple: if you want what you get, you
will get what you want.

What *really* matters is one's attitude. External "goods" of property, physical
"goods" of the body, are not truly good. Only goodness is good, and it is a
state of mind. If a man loses health or wealth, this should be a matter of indifference to him; if he is laid upon the rack, this too should be indifferent.
In the face of every vicissitude, he should preserve his inner tranquillity.
"Remember . . . on every occasion which leads thee to vexation to apply this
principle," admonished Marcus Aurelius: "not that this is a misfortune, but
that to bear it nobly is good fortune."[4] In practice, this means to live a simple,
austere, meditative life, concentrating upon the inner man rather than upon
outward endowments. Individual self-management, not social action, resig-
nation, not vigorous social reconstruction, are dominant notes of Stoic ethics.

The conservative and individualistic implications of this philosophy are
somewhat counterbalanced by the Stoic doctrine of human brotherhood and
natural law. All men, they taught, are parts of the whole: they are all bound

together by "the natural law of fellowship," the kinship of all men as children of nature and citizens of the universe, that "highest city of which all other cities are like families."[5] Marcus Aurelius declared:

If our intellectual part is common, the reason also, in respect of which we are rational beings, is common; if this is so, common also is the reason which commands us what to do, and what not to do; if this is so, there is a common law also; if this is so, we are fellow-citizens; if this is so, we are members of some political community; if this is so, the world is in a manner a state. For of what other common political community will any one say that the whole human race are members? And from thence, from this common political community comes also our very intellectual faculty and reasoning faculty and our capacity for law. . . .[6]

Reasoning similarly, Epictetus pointed out the ethical implications.

Every matter has two handles, one of which will bear taking hold of, the other not. If thy brother sin against thee, lay not hold of the matter by this, that he sins against thee; for by this handle the matter will not bear taking hold of. But rather lay hold of it by this, that he is thy brother, thy born mate; and thou wilt take hold of it by what will bear handling.[7]

This noble profession of human brotherhood differs from Christianity mainly in its coolness, its intellectual detachment. The Stoic is restrained by his aloofness from any passionate commitment. He must retain an unruffled inner composure.

The Stoic doctrine of natural law was expressed most eloquently by Marcus Tullius Cicero (106–43 B.C.), the famous statesman, philosopher, and man of letters. Although he was something of an eclectic, he emphasized the Stoic theory of a harmonious natural order of which man is an integral part. Like Marcus Aurelius, he maintained that "this whole universe" is "one commonwealth of which both gods and men are members," and "that no single thing is so like another, so exactly its counterpart, as all of us are to one another."[8] All men have received from nature the gift of reason, the sense of justice, and the propensity to associate with their fellows. The highest good is to live in accordance with human nature as well as the nature of the universe.

If the whole world is a sort of state or commonwealth, then there is a common law, the law of nature, which as fellow citizens and brothers we are morally bound to observe. Declared Cicero:

Law is the distinction between things just and unjust, made in agreement with that primal and most ancient of all things, Nature; and in conformity to Nature's standards are framed those human laws which inflict punishment upon the wicked but defend and protect the good.[9]

Whereas human law is relative to time and place, is the law of a specific state, and is enacted at one time and repealed at another, natural law is of universal application, unchanging and everlasting. Cicero continued:

True law is right reason in agreement with nature; it is of universal application, unchanging and everlasting; it summons to duty by its commands, and averts from wrongdoing by its prohibitions. . . . We cannot be freed from its obligations by senate or people, and we need not look outside ourselves for an expounder or interpreter of it. And there will not be different laws at Rome and at Athens, or different laws now and in the future, but one eternal and unchangeable law will be valid for all nations and all times, and there will be one master and ruler, that is, God, over us all, for he is the author of this law, its promulgator, and its enforcing judge. Whoever is disobedient is fleeing from himself and denying his human nature, and by reason of this very fact he will suffer the worst penalities, even if he escapes what is commonly considered punishment. . . .[10]

No man, Cicero declared, is morally bound to obey human law unless it conforms to the law of nature, for the natural law represents absolute and immutable principles and should be followed whenever it conflicts with human laws. As for "the many deadly, the many pestilential statutes which nations put into force," "these no more deserve to be called laws than the rules a band of robbers might pass in their assembly."[11] Here in essence is the revolutionary doctrine that men owe supreme allegiance to nature and nature's God rather than to any temporal state, and that they have the inalienable right to revolt against an unnatural and tyrannical government.

It may be illuminating to compare this doctrine with that of Aristotle. According to Cicero, men belong to two "societies"—first, the natural society of the universe, governed by natural laws; second, the particular state with its positive laws. When the positive laws conflict with the natural laws, a man's duty is to reject the former. All men are part of this natural society, and thus are joined together in a universal human community. Aristotle, in contrast, admitted a "natural justice" that is best, but he thought that only *some* men are prepared to recognize it, and he conceived it as a standard of speculative judgment, not as an imperative more binding upon conscience than positive law. He also rejected the doctrine, later espoused by Cicero, of the natural equality and fraternity of men, and maintained the natural inferiority of women to men, of barbarians to Greeks, of slaves to freeborn. In the transition from Aristotelianism to Roman Stoicism, Aristotle's polis became Cicero's cosmopolis.

In his theory of natural law, Cicero did not assert a perfect identity between *what is* and *what ought to be*. He recognized that there are bad men and bad states. The laws of nature, in the ethical sense, represent not what men actually do in all cases, but what they should do. These laws express the rational order that governs the universe, not brute physical necessity. Whatever role fate may play in the total scheme of things, there is an indefeasible area of choice within the human soul. It is here that one, as a citizen of the universe, can choose to accept or reject the common laws of all humanity. Here one may freely embrace the natural laws of reason, equity, justice, and inborn rights.

The Stoic interpretation of ethics, to a greater extent than Cicero's eclectic doctrine, tends to be inconsistent, with its paradoxical combinations of fate and free will, cosmopolitanism and self-sufficiency, tacit admission that certain things are preferable, and yet explicit teaching that all happens for the best. In writers such as Marcus Aurelius and Epictetus, there is too much concentration upon the inward man and too little concern for outward circumstances. As Cicero, who recognized some of the weaknesses in Stoicism, declared:

To maintain that the only good is moral worth [in the sense of cultivation of the inner man] is to do away with the care of one's health, the management of one's estate, participation in politics, the conduct of affairs, the duties of life; nay to abandon that moral worth itself.[12]

Yet there is much to admire in Stoicism: the courage, the tranquillity, the cosmopolitanism, the sense of universal fellowship, the attempt to see the rational connections and necessity of things, the poise and magnanimity of outlook that result from identifying oneself with the whole frame of nature. Most valuable of all, judged in terms of its enduring influence, was the Stoic doctrine of natural law. This conception not only deeply affected Roman lawmakers and jurists but persisted, with various transmutations, throughout the Dark Ages and the Middle Ages into modern times. Transmitted to posterity in the great codification of laws and legal principles under the Emperor Justinian (the *Corpus Juris Civilis*, 533 A.D.), it is still a very potent and living reality. At present, almost 900 million people live under systems traceable to Roman law. Its philosophical premise is that law, being grounded on the nature of men as men, is the common patrimony of all men everywhere. This is one of the greatest ideas of human culture.

3. THE THOMISTIC THEORY OF NATURAL LAW

In the Middle Ages, the humanistic ethics of Plato and Aristotle and the natural-law tradition of the Stoics were blended with the evangelical ethics of Christianity. The medieval philosophers emphasized the same factors as did Plato and Aristotle: qualities, not quantities; universals, not particulars; values, not bare facts; teleological interpretations, not mechanistic explanations; social responsibilities, not individualistic rights. But their culture was more intensely religious than was the Graeco-Roman. For them, nature was enveloped in the supernatural order, which sustained it and gave it meaning. Theology was conceived as the supreme science and the highest pursuit of man, and the Church was the dominant institution.

Inspired in this manner, the Middle Ages created a "universal" culture. It was based upon a universal religion, the Catholic; a universal law, the Roman; a universal scholarly language, the Medieval Latin; a universal art, the Gothic; a universal philosophy, the Scholastic; and a universal ethic, the

Christian. The University of Paris, which was the main center of thought at the height of the Middle Ages, typified the the universal character of medieval civilization. Not only Frenchmen, but Germans, Englishmen, Italians, Spaniards, Belgians, and Scandinavians congregated here. Although this body of learned men furiously debated with one another, they accepted "the old Greek principle, that unity is better than multiplicity."[13] St. Thomas' teaching that "universals are real" and Dante's dream of a world-wide commonwealth express the essence of this culture. It may be objected that medieval civilization was not really as universal as it supposed. This is unquestionably true, but the intent was to achieve values and institutions of universal range.

In the field of ethics, universalism found expression in the doctrine of natural law. The medieval philosophers sought to base morality upon the normal functioning of human nature in the kind of universe in which man finds himself. This theory was meant to apply to all humanity in all ages and in all climes. Its classic expression is to be found in the *Summa Theologica* of St. Thomas Aquinas (1225?–1274). I shall now sketch its main tenets.

Its basis is a fourfold conception of law. First, the *eternal law* is the plan of divine wisdom by which the whole creation is governed. It is eternal, for God is everlasting; but man, as a temporal being, can grasp it only imperfectly. Second, the *natural law* is the reflection of divine reason in created things. It is a reflection that man's unaided reason can discern in his own nature and in his natural environment. Third, the *divine law* is the revelation of God's laws through scripture or the church. The will of God is revealed to remedy the weakness of human judgment and to lead man to his heavenly destination. Fourth, the *human law* is promulgated by the representatives of the community. Its function is to adapt the natural law to specific circumstances.

The eternal law is the foundation of the three other types of law. It is rational in its basis. God is bound by His own reason to will what He knows to be good. He cannot by His will make good that which is not good (just as He cannot make a square, round). Even for Almighty God, moral distinctions are objective, not arbitrary. Finite human beings grasp the eternal law, not as God grasps it, but as embodied in the natural order or as revealed by God's grace.

When the eternal law shows itself in nature, it is called the natural law. Every entity is characterized by a certain essence that constitutes *its* nature and determines that it will act in a certain way. Flowers naturally bloom, fish swim, birds fly, men think. What is good for any entity is to exist and to act and to fulfill itself according to its own proper mode. Human beings are the only animals that can discern the natural law by the light of reason and direct their actions freely toward their natural fulfillment. This law obliges us because it is not based on any whim or guesswork, but on the very nature of man and of the universe he inhabits.

Now it is the nature of man to be a rational animal. This means that he is, first, a material substance like every other temporal being; second, an animal; and third, a rational spirit. The law of his nature is to realize himself in this threefold sense.

For there is in man, first of all, an inclination to good in accordance with the nature which he has in common with all substances, inasmuch, namely, as every substance seeks the preservation of its own being, according to nature; and by reason of this inclination, whatever is a means of preserving human life, and of warding off its obstacles, belongs to natural law. Secondly, there is in man an inclination to things that pertain to him more specially, according to that nature which he has in common with other animals; and in virtue of this inclination, those things are said to belong to natural law which nature has taught to all animals, such as sexual intercourse, the education of offspring, and so forth. Thirdly, there is in man an inclination to good according to the nature of his reason, which nature is proper to him. Thus man has a natural inclination to know the truth about God and to live in society; and in this respect, whatever pertains to this inclination belongs to the natural law: e.g., to shun ignorance, to avoid offending those among whom one has to live, and other such things regarding the above inclination.[14]

In this passage, St. Thomas expounds the natural law of human life. It can be discovered in all its richness of detail only by a never-ending investigation of human nature and its environment. We must learn to distinguish between the essential human inclinations and the superficial or perverted inclinations that mingle with the basic ones. But even now we can know that man is an animal gifted with reason. He shares with all beings, according to St. Thomas, the need and tendency to exist. He shares with all other animals the need for warmth, light, air, food, rest, and sexual intercourse—all that is required for the normal and healthy functioning of his body. But he lives in a dimension that no other animal shares—the intellectual dimension that is open to him as a rational being. He can thus explore the whole world of culture—he can know the moral law and live as a civic being, he can be lifted up and transformed by the intellectual love of God. The good for man is to realize all of these human powers.

In his emphasis upon the development of natural capacities St. Thomas resembles a modern humanist, but he insists that there is another side to ethics corresponding to a different dimension of human existence. Man is not only a rational animal with natural proclivities, but an immortal soul with a heavenly destination. The divine law revealed in scripture and illuminated by supernatural grace is requisite to guide man heavenward. This law and the natural law are harmonious. Both emanate from God: reason as God's supreme gift to the natural man, revelation or grace as a gift from God to supplement the light of reason. Grace does not abolish nature, nor nature abolish grace.

The theological virtues continue where the natural virtues leave off. The virtues set forth by Aristotle—prudence, justice, courage, and temperance—are habits engendered by respect for the natural law. But the theological virtues —faith, hope, and charity—are based on the Christian revelation. They order man's actions to God and eternal blessedness; the natural virtues order man's actions to fulfillment in this life. As Aristotle maintained, the natural virtues should tend toward a mean; the theological virtues are properly an extreme. "Never can man love God as much as he ought to be loved; nor believe or hope in him as much as is his due."[15]

The divine law supplements the natural law by being superior; the human law supplements the natural law by being inferior. It is necessary for human beings to promulgate specific laws and to enforce them, but the *moral* sanction of these laws lies in their rationality, not in extraneous force. As St. Thomas says:

> That which is not just seems to be no law at all. Hence the force of a law depends on the extent of its justice. Now in human affairs a thing is said to be just from being right, according to the rule of reason. But the first rule of reason is the law of nature. . . . Consequently, every human law has just so much of the nature of law as it is derived from the law of nature. But if in any point it departs from the law of nature, it is no longer a law but a perversion of law.[16]

Thus, natural law is more ultimate and authoritative than positive law; and the moral obligation to obey the state is conditional. Disobedience may even be a duty.

All laws—eternal, natural, divine, and human—are linked together in a coherent system. This vision of a harmonious universe with its fourfold hierarchy of laws is the essence of the ethical and metaphysical hypothesis of St. Thomas. It is a sublime and daring vision, but its truth is subject to dispute. Modern naturalistic philosophers reject its supernaturalistic components.

According to these critics, St. Thomas was trying, with ingenuity and genius, to mix oil and water. His attempt to achieve a harmonious blend of Aristotelian naturalism and Christian mysticism was bound to fail. He agreed with Aristotle that the soul and body are not two substances but one substance, yet as a good Christian he was not willing to accept the inevitable consequence, that when death dissolves the union of soul and body, the individual personality must perish. Although he embraced Aristotle's doctrine of the inseparability of matter and form in the natural world, he was forced by his Christian theology to reject Aristotle's corollary of this doctrine, the eternity of the natural universe, and to maintain that the forms of nature preexisted in the mind of God before the creation of the universe *ex nihilo*. His retention of such theological concepts as original sin, the grace of God, and the supreme value of supernatural salvation accorded but ill with the more purely humanistic ethics that he inherited from Aristotle and tried to incorporate in his system. The virtue of the system is its inclusiveness, not consistency or scientific rigor. Someone has quipped, "St. Thomas officiated at the marriage of Catholic Faith and Hellenic Reason, a union in which it was Reason that had to promise to love, honor, and obey."

This quip is not altogether just, for there is a great deal of sound reason and profound moral insight in the Thomistic system. The problem for a modern reader is to determine what remains valid after every proper criticism is given its due. One's opinion in this matter will be swayed by religious and moral convictions. Those who believe in a supernatural order are bound to be more sympathetic to the Thomist argument than those who do not. For the "true believer," supernaturalism provides the only adequate foundation for the sense of human dignity. Jacques Maritain, a modern Thomist, has written:

Man . . . exists not merely physically; there is in him a richer and nobler existence; he has spiritual superexistence through knowledge and through love. . . . In the flesh and bones of man there lives a soul which is a spirit and which has a greater value than the whole physical universe. However dependent it may be on the slightest accidents of matter, the human person exists by virtue of the existence of its soul, which dominates time and death. It is the spirit which is the root of personality.[17]

For a person who shares this faith, the emphasis upon the supernatural order appears entirely justified.

There is one other point to evaluate in the Thomistic theory. Both Cicero and St. Thomas insisted that positive law has no moral binding force if it conflicts with natural law, a naturally unjust law being no valid law at all. This belief, surviving until the present time, has inspired democratic revolutions and impugned tyrannies. But it causes confusion if understood in too absolute a sense. For example, the idea has been put forward that natural law ought to be freely invocable in courts and take precedence over positive laws. This would mean that a judge would decide a case contrary to the established laws of society whenever he deemed them inconsistent with natural justice. To give judges this power to nullify precedent and statute and constitution would not be consistent with democratic government. It would expose us to the judge's whims and private dogmas. Imperfect though the positive law may be, it is a necessary safeguard against subjectivism and individual fallibility.

4. THE MODERN THEORY OF NATURAL LAW

The theory of natural law has been profoundly influenced by the transition from the medieval to the modern age. The nature of this great transition has been summarized by Jacob Burckhardt:

In the Middle Ages both sides of human consciousness—that which was turned within as that which was turned without—lay dreaming or half awake beneath a common veil. The veil was woven of faith, illusion, and childish prepossession, through which the world and history were seen clad in strange hues. Man was conscious of himself only as member of a race, people, party, family, or corporation—only through some general category. In Italy this veil first melted into air; an *objective* treatment and consideration of the state and of all things of this world became possible. The *subjective* side at the same time asserted itself with corresponding emphasis; man became a spiritual *individual*, and recognized himself as such.[18]

Burckhardt's classic interpretation has been challenged by scholars who maintain that the characteristics of the Renaissance were present in the Middle Ages and that the traits of the Middle Ages lingered in the Renaissance. Such criticisms serve to qualify the thesis of Burckhardt but not to invalidate it. Although the contrast between the two periods is not as sharp as he depicted it, he has recognized the essential differences between medieval and Renaissance culture.

Modern history has been mainly the development of the two tendencies distinguished by Burckhardt: the objective treatment of man and nature, and the discovery and cultivation of man's subjective, individualistic being. The first of these tendencies resulted in a more secular and scientific interpretation of natural law; the second tendency resulted in a strong emphasis upon the "natural rights" of the individual. In the present section we shall consider the objective interpretation of natural law, and in the next section we shall discuss the theory of natural rights.

The medieval conception of the law of nature was closely bound to theology, but the germ of a more secular interpretation was already present in the Thomistic philosophy. As we have already remarked, St. Thomas maintained that moral distinctions are objective and that even God is bound by His reason to recognize them. The objective laws of morality as embodied in nature can be grasped by the natural light of reason residing in each human being. From these premises, some of the successors to St. Thomas drew a revolutionary conclusion—that the natural law would exist and be valid, God or no God.

The founder of the modern doctrine of international law, the Dutchman Hugo Grotius (1583–1645), prepared the way for this secular interpretation. He repeated the contention of St. Thomas that moral distinctions cannot be negated by God's will:

> The law of nature . . . is unchangeable—even in the sense that it cannot be changed by God. Measureless as is the power of God, nevertheless it can be said that there are certain things over which that power does not extend. . . . Just as even God . . . cannot cause that two times two should not make four, so He cannot cause that that which is intrinsically evil be not evil.[19]

Since the principles of natural law have an independent binding force, Grotius concluded that they would still retain "a degree of validity even if we should concede that which cannot be conceded without the utmost wickedness, that there is no God, or that the affairs of men are of no concern to Him."[20] This statement is carefully qualified so as to avoid any suggestion of atheism, but it implies the possibility of constructing a theory of natural law independent of theological presuppositions.

In the ensuing centuries, the primary appeal was to nature, not to theology. The laws of nature, declared Jefferson, are the laws of nature's God; but although the existence of God was inferred from nature, the laws of nature were not deduced from God. The principles of natural law were discovered by "the light of reason" alone. God was invoked as the remote creator of the natural order rather than as the source of divine revelation or supernatural grace. The work of secularization was carried on in even more pronounced fashion by Hobbes, Pufendorf, and Spinoza. They heralded the application to the study of law and morality of the methods of mathematics and natural science.

The first phase of this secular approach to natural law was rationalistic. The appeal was to first principles analogous to the axioms of mathematics. The American Declaration of Independence held "these truths to be self-evident"; the French Declaration of the Rights of Man subscribed to "simple and indisputable principles." This rationalistic temper can be traced back to earlier thinkers. Grotius explicitly rejected an empirical, and adopted an a priori method. ". . . Just as the mathematicians treat their figures as abstracted from bodies," he declared, "so in treating law I have withdrawn my mind from every particular fact."[21] The law of nature rests upon "certain fundamental conceptions which are beyond question; so that no one can deny them without doing violence to himself. For the principles of that law, if only you pay strict heed to them, are in themselves manifest and clear. . . ."[22] John Locke maintained that mathematics and morality are alike in that both are capable of demonstration, and Spinoza and Leibniz attempted such deduction. The a priori strain in Kant's ethics and jurisprudence can be considered a continuation of this sort of rationalism.

But the extreme a priori method constitutes a break with the moral realism of the natural law tradition. That tradition maintains that the good for man is the realization of human nature in the world as we find it. One may argue that human nature can be known by a priori reason alone, but the more plausible view is that man's nature can be known by empirical means. Such an empirical study may be either historical or psychological.

The herald of the historical approach was the great Italian humanist, Giambattista Vico (1668–1744). Although his ideas were embedded in scholastic modes of expression, his method was new and farsighted. He rejected the antihistorical rationalism that constructs an abstract concept of man and "timeless" moral axioms, and he insisted that the historical record of what man has done is the plainest manifestation of what man is. His great book was The New Science, in which he studied the "common nature" of nations as disclosed in their cultural history. "Now since this world of nations has been made by men," he declared, "let us see in what things all men agree and have always agreed. For these things will be able to give us the universal and eternal principles . . . on which all nations were founded and still preserve themselves."[23] Vico traced the characteristic stages of development through which, in his opinion, every civilization passes. These parallel forms of culture are not the result of imitation of one people by another or diffusion from a single center—they are independent expressions of the common nature of man. "The natural law of nations," Vico concluded, "is coeval with the customs of the nations, conforming one with another in virtue of a common human sense, without any reflection and without one nation following the example of another."[24] I shall not recount the details of Vico's historical interpretation. What is significant is the main concept—that the real character of mankind can reveal itself, and be known, only through its history.

Vico's point of view was much in advance of his age, but it has gradually made headway. Few recent proponents of natural-law philosophy would deny the relevance of historical insights. To cite an example, the prominent Catholic theologian, John Courtney Murray, denies that natural law "can be constructed in geometric fashion" apart from historical evidence. We must come to grips, he declares, with "the real man who grows in history, . . . only gradually exploring the potentialities and demands and dignities of his own nature." The law of nature must have "changing and progressive applications, as the evolution of human life brings to light new necessities in human nature that are struggling for expression and form."[25] The full meaning of natural law, according to Father Courtney, is revealed in the long travail and upward ascent of humanity. I would suggest a more radical view: not only does the *knowledge* of natural law change, but *natural law itself changes*. It is neither necessary nor desirable to conceive of the natural law as unchanging. The nature of man may change, and therewith the moral law that applies to it.

The study of psychology is another empirical approach to natural-law ethics. At present I shall barely mention the essential tenets involved in this approach, namely, that mankind has a common human nature to fulfill, that this nature can be discovered by psychological research, and that the good for man is the fulfillment of the nature thus disclosed.

5. THE THEORY OF NATURAL RIGHTS

The second characteristic of the modern age that Burckhardt pointed out was the discovery and cultivation of individuality. The typical man of the Middle Ages was hardly conscious of himself as an individual: he was essentially a member of the family, guild, feudal manor, church, university, or village community. Toward the end of the Middle Ages a great change in social relations and in men's thoughts about human associations made itself felt. With the gradual breaking down of the corporate life of the medieval guild and manor and the rise of a commercial and industrial economy, men tended to think and act individualistically.

In the classical and medieval theories, the predominant emphasis was upon the *social* nature of man. Not so in the theories of individualistic philosophers from Machiavelli to Bentham. For example, Thomas Hobbes declared that man is a selfish animal impelled by his nature to war with his fellows. John Locke conceived of man as less predatory and more gregarious, but even he defined the self in terms of self-concern. "The self," he said, "is that conscious thinking being . . . which is sensible or conscious of happiness or misery, and so is concerned for itself so far as that consciousness extends."[26] Adam Smith maintained that each man normally pursues "his own advantage," and that liberty and economic well-being are attained when "every man, as long as he does not violate the laws of justice, is left perfectly free to pursue his own interest his own way."[27] Influenced by this current of thought, the theory of natural law suffered a profound change.

The classical and medieval doctrine was that man is a political animal and cannot live by and for himself. The later doctrine maintained that the "social contract" is a deliberate artifice for uniting men who, by original nature, are separate. In the precivil "state of nature," declared Locke, every man is "absolute lord of his own person and possessions, equal to the greatest and subject to nobody."[28] But self-interest impelled men to join in a political covenant. According to Hobbes, the motive was the desire for self-preservation. According to Locke, it was the desire to be secure in one's life and possessions. "The great and chief end of men uniting into commonwealths . . . is the preservation of their property."[29] This includes the goal of self-preservation, since Locke contended that each man's life is part of his "property."

Locke used the theory of the social contract as a defense of "natural rights." The individual, as "absolute lord," had certain rights in the state of nature. He had the right to preserve his own life, to own his own person, and to enjoy the fruits of his own labor, including the right to private property. Declared Locke:

The state of nature has a law of nature to govern it, which obliges everyone; and reason, which is that law, teaches all mankind, who will but consult it, that being all equal and independent, no one ought to harm another in his life, health, liberty, or possessions.[30]

The main defect of the state of nature was insecurity, which resulted from the lack of any written law, any impartial judge, and any civil authority to enforce the law. Hence government, resting upon the consent of the governed, was set up to protect natural rights. "The end of law," Locke contended, "is not to abolish and restrain but to preserve and enlarge freedom."[31] If the sovereign should signally fail to respect the natural rights of the citizens, he is guilty of a breach of contract, and the people have the right to revolt. For no one ought to be "subject to the inconstant, uncertain, unknown, arbitrary will of another man."[32] The dissolution of government, which may occur in the event of revolt, is not the dissolution of moral responsibility, which is antecedent to, and independent of, the political institutions of mankind. "Truth and keeping of faith belongs to men as men, and not as members of society."[33]

It has often been pointed out that Locke was far from an unqualified libertarian. In his *Letter Concerning Toleration,* he advocated severe limitations on freedom of speech. "No opinions contrary to human society," he declared, "are to be tolerated," and "those are not at all to be tolerated who deny the being of a God." In his *Thoughts on Education,* he advocated a narrow vocational training for working-class children, and referred contemptuously to "the abhorred rascality" of the common people. Even in his *Second Treatise of Civil Government,* he was more intent upon defending the rights of the middle class, as represented by Parliament, than in defending the poor and disfranchised or the solitary individual. Nevertheless, his version of the natural-rights theory had an enormous impact, especially in the rebellious American colonies.

Rephrasing Locke's doctrine, Jefferson wrote the solemn words of the Declaration of Independence:

We hold these truths to be self-evident, that all men are created equal, that they are endowed by their Creator with certain unalienable Rights, that among these are Life, Liberty and the Pursuit of Happiness. That to secure these rights, Governments are instituted among Men, deriving their just powers from the consent of the governed. That whenever any form of Government becomes destructive of these ends, it is the Right of the People to alter or abolish it, and to institute new Government, laying its foundation on such principles and organizing its power in such form, as to them shall seem most likely to effect their Safety and Happiness.

In this Declaration, Locke's phrase "life, liberty, and property" has been changed to "life, liberty, and the pursuit of happiness." By implication, the right to happiness takes precedence over the right to property. But even in the theory of Locke, property rights were by no means unmitigated or absolute. In his *Second Treatise of Civil Government,* he argued that property rights to land and its product are lodged in those who labor on that land to satisfy life's needs. Property rights cannot be fixed on idle or wasted land and products. These, not being properly used, rightfully belong to others. When the phrase "the pursuit of happiness" was substituted for the term "property" in the Declaration of Independence, Jefferson and his colleagues made explicit what was already implicit in the argument of Locke.

Jefferson's insistence upon "the consent of the governed" was combined with an equal insistence upon the rights of the minority. "The will of the majority . . . ," he declared, "to be rightful must be reasonable," and "the minority possess their equal rights which law must protect, and to violate would be oppression."[34]

Respect for individuals and minorities is likewise apparent in the Bill of Rights. Liberty is conceived as the immunity of groups and individuals from oppression. The Bill protects the right to privacy, the right to free speech, free assembly, free and independent worship, fair trial and "due process." It safeguards the lone individual or unpopular minority against the overweening power of army and police and the arbitrary action of judges, magistrates, and legislators. The rights stated in the Bill, at first binding only upon the federal government, have with certain exceptions been extended to the states through the Fourteenth Amendment and judicial interpretations.

It would be difficult to exaggerate the importance of these rights. They are indispensable to the life of a free people. But there is another conception of right implicit in Jefferson's phrase, "the pursuit of happiness." No man is really free if he is unable to pursue happiness—if he is insecure, hungry, diseased, ignorant, the victim of hate and prejudice. Rights imply not only *being allowed,* the concept of immunity, but *being able,* the concept of power and opportunity. This is a point to which we shall return in Chapter XIII, "The Democratic Ideal."

In the nineteenth century, the individualistic conception of human rights —the doctrine of immunities—was supplemented by an affirmative and social conception of rights—the doctrine of claims to the assistance of government. Perhaps no one has more clearly expressed this idea of freedom than the Victorian philosopher, Thomas Hill Green (1836–1882), in the following characteristic passage:

We shall probably all agree that freedom, rightly understood, is the greatest of blessings . . . But when we thus speak of freedom, we should consider carefully what we mean by it. We do not mean by it merely freedom from restraint or compulsion. We do not mean merely freedom to do as we like irrespectively of what it is that we like. We do not mean a freedom that can be enjoyed by one man or set of men at the cost of a loss of freedom to others. When we speak of freedom as something to be so highly prized, we mean a positive power or capacity of doing or enjoying something worth doing or enjoying, and that, too, something that we do or enjoy in common with others. We mean by it a power which each man exercises through the help or security given him by his fellow-men, and which he in turn helps to secure for them.[35]

Freedom so conceived requires cooperation among individuals and vigorous action by social agencies.

At the present time, human rights are interpreted as dual in character: they include not only the immunities and privacies of the older liberal tradition but also the affirmative claims and powers implied by the newer conception of freedom. Both are combined, for example, in the Universal Declaration of Human Rights adopted by the United Nations Assembly on December 10, 1948. In the language of the natural-law tradition, the Preamble reaffirms "the dignity and worth of the human person" and "the equal and inalienable rights of all members of the human family." The Articles delineate the civil and political liberties already embodied in the American Constitution, such as freedom of speech, assembly, worship, association, and the press; the protection from arbitrary arrest, unfair trial, and unjust punishment; the right to take part in the government directly or through freely chosen representatives. But the Articles also include a new set of social, economic, and cultural rights, such as the right to work and to a decent livelihood, the right to the protection of health, the right to education, and the right to share in the culture and progress of civilization. Included are the so-called "civil rights"—the right to freedom from discrimination based on color, race, religion, national origin, or minority status. This kind of right is now involved in the struggle for freedom all over the world. It is absolutely basic, because it demands "the freedom to be free"—the freedom to participate as a first-class citizen in the freedom and opportunities of the whole society. Without *all* of these rights, as a UNESCO Committee has declared, "men cannot give the best of themselves as active members of the community because they are deprived of the means to fulfill themselves as human beings."[36] In this sense these rights can be called natural rights. An inclusive liberalism seeks to realize the full gamut of rights, and thus to combine a catalog of immunities with a schedule of claims.

Thus the theory of natural law has come full circle. It began with the classical doctrine that the human animal is both social and rational, and this conception was reaffirmed in the medieval doctrine of the rational and corporate nature of man. But the Renaissance brought a new sense of individuality, and in the course of time this led to an individualistic, although still a predominantly rational, theory of natural rights. Now we have returned to the social conception of man, but our idea of rights has been broadened and enriched by a recognition of the emotional components of human personality, and by a fusion of the individualistic and the social interpretation of rights.

As we glance at the historical development of the natural rights theory, we find that its proponents have been mistaken about various matters. They have conceived natural rights as absolute and inviolable. In practice, however, the courts have discovered that all such rights must be hedged by qualifications and exceptions. (For example, a group may not have the right to "free assembly" if, under the given circumstances, the meeting would lead to a bloody riot.) The advocates of natural rights have sometimes assumed that their principles are "self-evident," that there is, consequently, some easy method of insight or immediate intuition whereby rights can be determined; but, in truth, long investigation and deep reflection are required to ascertain the nature, limits, and conditions of human rights. The proponents of natural rights tend to conceive these rights abstractly, each independently of the others and independently of concrete historical circumstances, whereas rights are profoundly conditioned by their interrelations and historical circumstances. They tend to connect these rights with mythical history—a primitive "state of nature"—whereas rights, far from being complete in some mythical golden age, are achieved only by the long, hard, difficult ascent of man out of barbarism. They tend to conceive these rights too negatively and individualistically, as inherent in the individual apart from positive social action, whereas freedom is positive and not merely negative—it is the presence of opportunity rather than the mere absence of constraint. There is no liberty of the "natural man," inherent in the isolated individual, to be uncovered merely by stripping away the "yoke" of social relations. The individual, apart from society, lacks the opportunity for significant choice; he is ineluctably social in his nature, and he can never achieve real and substantial freedom except by mastering social forces.

Having made these criticisms of the individualistic theory of natural rights, we must turn to the basic truth that it expresses. As defenders of natural rights, Locke and Jefferson were maintaining, in effect, that there is a higher and more ultimate court of appeals than ordinary human conventions and laws; that there are rights that inhere in the very nature of things; that whenever government violates these rights, it stands condemned before men's reason and conscience; that the individual is consequently more than a creature of social convention or government, and that he can never wholly surrender his independence; that the state does not simply create morality but must be judged by it; and that the citizens owe obedience to the state only insofar as it is, on the whole, a guarantor of basic human rights. When properly interpreted and qualified, these contentions seem to me to be true and extremely salutary. Even if one should conclude that the objective existence of natural laws and rights has not been proved, one can scarcely deny the perennial vitality of this set of premises in the Western ethical dialogue.

Despite innumerable polemics to the contrary, most of us believe that there are relatively constant characteristics of human nature, of the physical environment, of the conditions of social existence, which have been and will continue to be fundamental factors in the pursuit of happiness. Natural laws, so far as they define natural rights, are these permanent and general conditions of human happiness; and natural rights are the claims that human beings, whether as groups or individuals, can legitimately make in view of these natural laws. It is not fantastic to say, for example, that the Nazis, with their callous disregard of human sympathy, reason, and the fundamental conditions of happiness, violated the natural rights of man and therefore forfeited all moral claim to remain in power. To insist upon natural rights is to deny that all values are merely relative, merely the creations of the government in power or the existing society. These rights, far from being unfounded or obsolete, are antitotalitarian and have never been more timely than in the present century when political totalitarianism has encroached so greatly upon freedom. They are, I believe, the necessary defenses against tyranny.

6. THE CONFLICT BETWEEN TWO CONCEPTS OF NATURAL LAW

The interpretation of natural law and rights that I have been sketching suffered a sharp reversal in the nineteenth century. Actually, the adverse currents of thought had set in much earlier. Beginning with the rapid progress of physical science in the seventeenth century, the orthodox theory of natural law was conjoined with another conception of nature to which it was in latent opposition—an opposition that eventually became overt. As a result of the great strides in physics and astronomy, the formulation of nonteleological scientific laws of nature made difficult, if not impossible, the fusion of descriptive and moral law that had been utilized by the natural law theorists. Finally, when the conflict between these two interpretations of natural law— the normative, teleological conception and the descriptive, nonteleological conception—became shockingly apparent, the older traditional doctrine, on which the structure of Western civilization largely rested, appeared to be irretrievably doomed.

To explain what happened, it will be helpful to retrace the transition from the medieval to the modern age. There is an eloquent passage in the *Inferno* which illuminates the nature of this transformation. Addressing Dante in the midst of hell, the spirit of Ulysses tells of his final journey beyond the Pillars of Hercules. Not even years of wandering and tribulation, nor love for his "sweet son," old father, and long-sought wife could conquer Ulysses' inward hunger

> To master earth's experiences, and to attain
> Knowledge of man's mind, both the good and bad.

So he and his crew set sail once again, but when they approached the Pillars, the courage of his mariners faltered and they wished to turn back. Whereupon Ulysses spoke to them:

> "Brother," I said, "who manfully, despite
> Ten thousand perils, have attained the West,
> In the brief vigil that remains of light
> To feel in, stoop not to renounce the quest
> Of what may in the sun's path be essayed,
> The world that never mankind hath possessed.
> Think ye on the seed ye spring from! Ye were made
> Not to live life of brute beasts of the field
> But follow virtue and knowledge unafraid."

These words seem to epitomize the very spirit of adventure and scientific inquiry that burst forth in the Renaissance, but they are intended by Dante to illustrate the presumption and impiety that led Ulysses to his place among the damned. Concluding his narrative, Ulysses relates how God's punishment was visited upon the rash mariners. They pushed on into the unknown until

> there arose a mountain in the sea,
> Dimm'd by the distance: loftier than aught
> That ever I beheld, it seemed to be.
> Then we rejoiced; but soon to grief were brought.
> A storm came out of the strange land, and found
> The ship, and violently the forepart caught.
> Three times it made her to spin round and round
> With all the waves; and, as Another chose
> The fourth time, heaved the poop up, the prow drowned,
> Till over us we heard the waters close.[37]

The contrast between the author's stern judgment and his character's unfettered spirit aptly characterizes the difference between the medieval and the modern age. That Dante depicts Ulysses as a very noble and courageous figure, the herald of discovery, is evident enough. But he also and principally regards his character as a transgressor. For Dante, with his eyes fixed upon the medieval synthesis, theology is the queen of the sciences, and earthly ambitions must be subordinated to the mandates of heaven. It seems to him, as it had to Aeschylus, that God

> . . . is a chastener of froward wills
> And he correcteth with a heavy hand.[38]

Since nature is the handiwork of God, its laws and processes, including the storm that engulfed Ulysses and his mariners, must serve the divine will. Hence the doctrine of St. Thomas, that natural laws reflect and embody the moral wisdom of God, appears to Dante altogether obvious. But, unlike the optimistic Thomas, he senses the emerging conflict between the new discoveries of natural science and the old moral-religious doctrine of natural law.

The determination of Ulysses "to master earth's experience" and to "follow virtue and knowledge unafraid" became the master impulse of the Renaissance and Enlightenment. Boldly reinterpreting the meaning of nature, the post medieval thinkers gradually substituted quantitative and mechanistic "descriptions" in place of the qualitative and teleological "explanations" of the earlier philosophers and theologians. Scientists were the leaders of this revolution in thought—a revolution not merely in the content of science itself but in the philosophy and ideology that accompanied it. Initially the scientists, such as Copernicus, Kepler, and Newton, retained many vestiges of the old teleological interpretation of nature, but gradually the nonteleological view emerged with painful clarity.

The Renaissance physicists and astronomers seized upon a notion that had figured centrally in ancient Pythagorean speculation—that the world is made of numbers—and gave to it a new meaning and application. Plato, in the tradition of Pythagoras, had called attention to the mathematical character of astronomical motions, and had suggested that the ultimate elements of the cosmos are geometrically describable. When such ideas were revived by Renaissance thinkers, they assumed that the cosmos is a mathematical harmony.

Nicolaus Copernicus (1473–1543), who adopted this neo-Platonic faith, could present no *facts* that were inexplicable upon the basis of Ptolemaic astronomy. Medieval astronomy, however, had become incredibly complicated with its cycles and epicycles. By abandoning the geocentric scheme of Ptolemy, the Copernican system reduced this complex mathematical labyrinth into a beautifully simple and orderly system. But the theory of Copernicus, in many respects transitional, was far from the modern conception of the universe. He taught that the universe is heliocentric, with a fixed sun enthroned at the center and a fixed outermost sphere beyond which nothing else exists; that the harmonious motions of the planets are a sign of their divine origin; that the spherical form of the universe is the most noble; that the sun at the center does not move because immobility is better than movement; and that gravity represents the striving of bodies to unite in the form of a sphere. His universe was still small and cozy like that of Aristotle: simpler, more stable, more synoptic, than our universe of countless solar systems and infinite distances. Although he suggested the possibility that space might be infinite, he was unprepared to advocate so fearsome a doctrine.

Giordano Bruno (1548–1600) was the principal Renaissance thinker boldly to advance the doctrine of infinity. He was intoxicated with the vision of the boundless cosmos: everywhere there were worlds, everywhere there was the center of things, everywhere and nowhere. "There is a double sort of infinity," he declared, "in size of the universe and in number of worlds."[39] God also is infinite, not as a being apart from the universe, but as its animating force. This conception of the deity is a big step toward a purely naturalistic philosophy. On the basis of its own premises, the Inquisition had some excuse for burning Bruno at the stake.

With the world now regarded as a mere speck in an infinite cosmos, it was far more difficult to believe that God was akin to man, that he had sent His only begotten Son to the earth, or that merely human values had any *cosmic* metaphysical significance. I do not mean that the scientists explicitly drew these conclusions. But inevitably the soul of man, when confronted by an *infinite* universe, was forced radically to reorient itself. Pascal, contemplating the staggering change, cried out: "The eternal silence of these infinite spaces terrifies me."

The great German astronomer, Johannes Kepler (1571–1630), was another transitional figure. In certain respects, he was very superstitious: He cast horoscopes, worshipped the sun, and tried to correlate planetary motions and distances with musical scales. Assuming that the universe was created by God, he attempted to show that it was constructed in accordance with the principles of mathematical harmony, and his famous three laws of astronomical motion seemed to him a vindication of this view.[40] The mystical theories he entertained, however, were not really substantiated by his discoveries, for it turned out that the motions of the planetary bodies could be described in purely quantitative terms. Although he began with different premises, he helped to substitute quantitative and mechanistic descriptions in place of the qualitative and teleological theories of the Greek and medieval syntheses. "Just as the eye was made to see colors, and the ear to hear sounds," he declared, "so was the human mind made to understand, not whatever you please, but quantity."[41]

Galileo (1564–1641) was more hardheaded and modern than Kepler. He believed that nature is a simple, orderly system whose processes are inexorably necessary. Physical nature, it seemed to him, could be reduced to purely mathematical functions—the position, motion, shape, and size of atomic particles, and the measurable spaces and times within which they move. All other qualities—color, odor, sound, taste, and texture—were thought to be effects *in the human organism* of the varied motions of atoms somehow operating upon the senses. He compared these qualities to the tickle which a person feels when a feather grazes his hand: the tickle is not in the feather but in the human reaction to the feather. Galileo's mind, however, was not washed clear of teleological concepts: he still retained traces of the Pythagorean doctrine of the beauty and sacredness of the mathematical harmonies found in nature. Rejecting this point of view, Francis Bacon, his English contemporary, represented the more advanced outlook. Bacon dryly remarked that "final causes" (ends, purposes, or values as explanatory principles) are like virgins, attractive but barren.

In the work of Isaac Newton (1642–1727), the scientific revolution of the Enlightenment was brought to its culmination. Like Galileo, he supposed that matter could be analysed into "solid, massy, hard, impenetrable, movable particles" and that "the changes of corporeal things are to be placed only in the various separations and new associations and motions of these permanent particles. . . ."[42] His famous theories of gravitation and astronomy made nature appear a huge, uniform machine, the laws of which could be expressed mathematically. He was somewhat embarrassed by his own conclusions. As a religious man, he was worried lest God should have nothing to do except to maintain the mechanical regularity of nature. He suggested, therefore, that irregularities may arise through the reciprocal action of comets and planets, and that God must correct these irregularities. Leibniz scornfully compared Newton's God to a tinkering watchmaker who makes such a poor watch that it must often be repaired. Newton also sought to reconcile religion with science by contending that time and space are the sense organs of God. But space and time as he *scientifically* conceived them are mathematical abstractions, mere extrinsic and indifferent receptacles for physical forces and moving bodies, to which no esthetic, religious, or moral qualities can relevantly be ascribed.

The initial effect of the scientific synthesis upon religion and morals was to confirm orthodoxy, since nature as the great machine presupposes the divine inventor and mechanic. "Cosmic Toryism," to employ Professor Basil Willey's apt term, became the prevalent form of metaphysical optimism.[43] Since nature, including man's life, was regarded as Gods' mechanically perfect plan, the *status quo,* morally and politically, was conceived to be divinely fixed.

The more critical and dynamic personalities rebelled against a doctrine so smug and yet so hopeless. In the eighteenth century, men like Voltaire, Rousseau, Diderot, and Holbach in France, and Swift, Mandeville, and Hume in England, each in his own way, undermined the Tory Cosmos. Finally the rise of evolutionary doctrines in the nineteenth century, culminating in the work of Darwin, removed any "scientific" basis for the theory of special creation and a static universe.

The main tenets of the Darwinian theory had been anticipated by earlier thinkers, such as the French mathematician and scientist, Pierre Louis Maupertius (1698–1759). In his *Essai de Cosmologie* (1756), Maupertius stated the theory of natural selection:

In the fortuitous combination of the productions of Nature . . . only those with certain adaptive relationships could survive. . . . In the other, infinitely greater part, there was neither adaptation nor order. All these last have perished . . . and the species we see today are only the smallest part of those which a blind destiny produced.[44]

Darwin developed the theory with great acumen and an immense body of empirical data. Although he had no intention of undermining orthodox religion, his doctrine of evolution by fortuitous variations and blind struggle was opposed to traditional theology. The intense crisis in Victorian religious thought, reflected in such poems as Arnold's "Dover Beach" and Tennyson's "In Memoriam," was primarily caused by the shocking implications of the Darwinian theory.

Although the transition was gradual, the cumulative sweep of these scientific ideas, from Copernicus to Darwin, undermined the normative conception of nature. In Greece, in Rome, in the Middle Ages—as well as in other advanced cultures the world over—the dominant faith has been that the world is a moral order. But thanks to the scientific revolution, modern civilization, particularly in the West, has come more and more to hold the opposite view, that the world is *not* a moral order. The universe, as revealed in modern science, appears to be indifferent to values, not only to human values, but to any values whatsoever. To suppose that nature aims at noble ends is now considered naive.

The new "scientific" view of the world has had very disturbing results. Moral values, having lost their traditional foundations, seem merely subjective and arbitrary. The idea of natural law in the normative sense, which has so long been the intellectual foundation of civilization, now appears to be an obscurantist doctrine, not only nonsense but, as Bentham characteristically put it, "nonsense upon stilts." Our sense of duty seems little more than a human prejudice, and morality appears to have no firm foundation at all. As a consequence, our value systems have become so terribly shaken that they cannot minimize anxiety and give meaning and direction to our lives, and the dark powers of the subconscious have usurped controls that should be exercised in the clear light of humanistic insight. Herein lies the intellectual misery of our age.

7. PHILOSOPHICAL REACTIONS
TO THE FACT-VALUE DICHOTOMY

We have been tracing the historical origin of the great schism of the modern world. As C. P. Snow has pointed out so provocatively, Western culture has been divided into two camps, the scientific and the humanistic.[45] Science has been equated with the study of facts, the humanities (including ethics) have been equated with the appreciation of values. In the sciences, supposedly, we are dealing with questions that are potentially and theoretically answerable by an appeal to evidence; in ethics and the humanities, we are wrestling with questions that cannot be resolved by any empirical method. This profound schism between the sciences and the humanities is tied to the whole grand historical movement of the rise and development of science from the Renaissance to the present day. The crucial problem of modern philosophy is whether this fact-value dichotomy is valid.

It may be instructive to recall some of the typical answers to this question among philosophers. René Descartes (1596–1650) and Thomas Hobbes (1588–1679) represent two different reactions, which have persisted down to the present. Hobbes sought to avoid the dichotomy between value and fact by extending materialistic explanations to man. Human thought, as he conceived it, is but a pale wraith in a universe of physical forces. He was determined that the teleological mode of explanation, abandoned by the physical sciences, should also be excluded by the psychologist; hence he regarded the human organism as mechanistically determined and materialistically constructed. In his political theory, he was not always mindful of his materialistic metaphysics, but his analysis dissolved social wholes into egoistic human beings, analogous to atomic isolates. Organizations were thought to be, in a sense, fictions, and the reality to consist of aggregated individuals whose fierce competitive nature must be held in check.

Descartes decided to surrender the physical world to the scientists, but hoped to retain a separate commerce between God and man by means of innate ideas divinely implanted in the human mind. This attempt was soon frustrated by Locke's polemic against innate ideas, but the Cartesian dualism, in modified form, persisted as one of the principal interpretations of reality. There is, on the one hand, the realm of extension—the world of space and physical objects—and on the other hand, the realm of thought—the world of understanding, willing, feeling, perceiving, and imagining. All concrete sensuous qualities (the so-called secondary qualities), such as the tickle caused by Galileo's feather, belong wholly to this latter realm. Descartes thus made the outer world an infinite machine consisting wholly of mathematically measurable characteristics, such as extension and motion (the so-called primary qualities), whereas color, sound, fragrance, beauty, and purposiveness became merely subjective, illusory.

The mechanistic trend of his thought is indicated by his interpretation of animals, which he conceived to be mere physical automatons, with sensations of a sort but without thoughts or feelings. This theory of the "beast-machine" became immensely influential, and was embraced by such leading thinkers as Pascal, Arnauld, Malebranche, and Bossuet. The famous school of Port Royal, according to La Fontaine, maintained the doctrine with ostentatious imperturbability:

> They administered beatings to dogs with perfect indifference, and made fun of those who pitied the creatures as if they had felt pain. They said that the animals were clocks; that the cries they emitted when struck were only the noise of a little spring which had been touched, but that the whole body was without feeling.[46]

For a time Descartes speculated about the possibility of likewise reducing human functions to a mechanistic basis, and proposed the invention of a man-machine to be activated by magnets. It remained for La Mettrie, however, to advance the doctrine of human mechanism in his famous book, *L'Homme-Machine*, published in 1748. The "soul," he maintained, is a function of the body. The essential difference between man and beast is that the body of the former is more complexly organized than that of the latter, and consequently thought reaches a higher stage in man. But since La Mettrie's theory recognized mental qualities and different levels of organization, his somewhat ambiguous "mechanism" was apparently not so reductive as that of Hobbes.

Gilbert Ryle's derisive characterization of Cartesian dualism as "the dogma of the Ghost in the Machine" is illustrative of the recent revolt against a dualistic metaphysics.[47] Nevertheless, the more mechanistic elements of Descartes' theory, along with the materialism of Hobbes and La Mettrie, are echoed in many contemporary doctrines. No one in touch with recent thought, especially in England and America, can doubt that physical science has tended to set the pattern of belief, and that nature is usually conceived as purposeless, qualityless, deterministic. Moral, religious, and metaphysical questions have been frequently dismissed as "nonsensical," especially among the more positivistic philosophers, such as Vilfredo Pareto and A. J. Ayer. The mechanistic conception of life is still prevalent in the attempt to interpret animals and human beings as "stimulus-response mechanisms." The statement of J. B. Watson, the American psychologist, may be cited: "Psychology, as the behaviorist views it, is a purely objective, experimental branch of natural science which needs consciousness as little as do the sciences of chemistry and physics."[48] Although the brash self-confidence of the early behaviorists is no longer prevalent, the behavioristic method and viewpoint have won general acceptance among psychologists, at least in America and Great Britain. With the development of electronic computers, it has become fashionable to liken the human mind to an "electronic brain," a very complicated physical system rather than a moral agent. To thinkers of this persuasion, the old teleological doctrine of natural law has seemed to be only a quaint superstition.

Another reaction to modern science, which emerged quite clearly in the nineteenth century, is to give the old "natural law" tradition a new antihumanitarian twist. This way of coping with "nature" appeared most clearly in the attempt to interpret the data of biological science. Writers such as Thomas Robert Malthus (1766–1834) and Herbert Spencer (1820–1903) declared, in effect, that if human beings break with nature, nature will break them. Merciless as nature's ways may appear, it behooves human beings to conform.

Malthus, a pious clergyman, believed that he had discovered the natural limits of progress in the laws of population. He contended that the human birthrate, if unrestrained by natural checks, would double about every twenty-five years, increasing in geometrical proportion (2, 4, 8, 16, 32 . . .), while the food supply would increase only arithmetically (1, 2, 3, 4, 5 . . .). In the past, the population has been kept down by wars, epidemics, and famines; even so, the bulk of mankind has always hovered at the edge of starvation. In the future, any increase in the supply of food will only bring an increase in the number of people to consume it, so that no betterment, on the average, will occur. Declared Malthus:

> I see no way by which man can escape the weight of this law which pervades all animated nature. No fancied equality, no agrarian regulations, in their utmost extent, could remove the pressure of it even for a single century. . . . Were I to propose a palliative; and palliatives are all that the nature of the case will admit; it should be, the total abolition of all the present parish-laws [providing public charity and relief]. . . . To prevent the recurrence of misery, is, alas! beyond the power of man. In the vain endeavor to obtain what in the nature of things is impossible, we now sacrifice not only possible but certain benefits.[49]

In later editions of his *Essay on Population,* Malthus hedged somewhat, suggesting that population pressure might be tempered by "moral restraints," such as postponement of marriage and sexual chastity. "Vice," he darkly hinted, might also be of some avail, whether by the spread of venereal diseases or deliberate contraception. But the note of gloom remained predominant even in the later editions, and this note was reinforced by Ricardo's "iron law of wages," which applied Malthusian ideas to economics. The living hell of the early industrial revolution was thus sanctified as part of God's natural order.

Charles Darwin, influenced by Malthus in formulating his theory of natural selection, arrived at somewhat similar conclusions:

> Man, like every other animal, has no doubt advanced to his present high condition through a struggle for existence consequent on his rapid multiplication; and if he is to advance still higher, it is to be feared that he must remain subject to a severe struggle. Otherwise he would sink into indolence, and the more gifted men would not be more successful in the battle of life than the less gifted. Hence, our natural rate of increase, though leading to many and obvious evils, must not be greatly diminished by any means. There should be open competition for all men.[50]

If this be the substance of Darwinism, Darwin was not always a Darwinian. In a number of interesting passages, he pointed out that cooperation often helps animals to survive, and that culture and morality play a decisive role in human evolution. But these remarks made little impression on his contemporaries. "Darwinism," as commonly interpreted, meant that pitiless competition is the law of life.

It was Herbert Spencer, not Darwin, who coined the phrase "the survival of the fittest." Human progress, he maintained, results from the stern discipline of nature which eliminates the unfit. The rigors of the human struggle for survival are therefore blessings in disguise. Spencer went so far as to declare:

> The poverty of the incapable, the distresses that come upon the imprudent, the starvation of the idle, and those shoulderings aside of the weak by the strong, which leave so many "in shallows and in miseries," are the decrees of a large, far-seeing benevolence.[51]

Therefore no regulation of industry, no poor relief, no program of public sanitation or health care, no social legislation to soften the struggle for survival, should ever be permitted. Any such measure can only impair the natural selective process which insures progress. "What can be a more extreme absurdity," Spencer asked, "than that of proposing to improve social life by breaking the fundamental law of social life?"[52]

Despite his advocacy of *laissez faire,* Spencer was opposed to war and in favor of voluntary cooperation. Others, with more belligerent tendencies, used evolutionary theory to justify racial, class, and nationalistic conflict. For example, the Austrian sociologist, Ludwig Gumplowicz, viewed history as a succession of tribal, racial, national, and class struggles, in which the fittest individuals and groups survive. In Germany, militarists such as Marshal von Moltke and General von Bernhardi exalted war as a means of "natural selection" and therefore as one of the prime conditions of human progress. Oswald Spengler, the famous German historian, insisted that "man is a beast of prey," and denounced as unnatural "the toothless feelings of sympathy and reconciliation."[53] Mussolini, Hitler, and the Nazi philosopher Alfred Rosenberg similarly argued that throughout nature there is a ceaseless struggle for survival and that the strong and fit survive. Man, they said, is a fighting animal; in strife, mankind has become great. The nation, or the state, is the natural fighting unit; its combative force depends upon its rejection of humanitarian and democratic principles as unnatural. Even in democratic England, the theory of evolution has been used as a defense of carnage. Sir Arthur Keith, in a famous lecture delivered after World War I, told his English audience: "Nature keeps her orchard healthy by pruning; war is her pruning-hook. We cannot dispense with her services."[54]

Ethical Darwinism has been popular among the American defenders of economic *laissez faire*. For example, the popular American sociologist, William Graham Sumner, was lecturing as follows during the severe economic depression of 1879:

If we do not like the survival of the fittest, we have only one possible alternative, and that is the survival of the unfittest. The former is the law of civilization; the latter is the law of anti-civilization.[55]

Such views were absorbed into the "folklore" of American business civilization. "You can't make the world all planned and soft," says the typical businessman of "Middletown." "The strongest and best survive—that's the law of nature after all—always has been and always will be."[56] This is the comment of a small businessman, but it differs little from the remark of a great tycoon. Listen to the words of John D. Rockefeller:

The growth of a large business is merely the survival of the fittest. . . . The American Beauty rose can be produced in the splendor and fragrance which brings cheer to its beholder only by sacrificing the early buds which grow up around it. This is not an evil tendency in business. It is merely the working out of a law of nature and a law of God.[57]

In the early part of the twentieth century, the normative theory of natural law survived mainly in this form. It was a far cry from the doctrine of Cicero, St. Thomas, Locke, or Jefferson.

8. DISSONANCE AND HARMONY IN NATURE

Turning now to criticism, I shall make a few remarks about "Ethical Darwinism" and the Malthusian creed. The Ethical Darwinists depicted nature as a war of each against all, with the fittest animals living to fight another day and to breed warriors like themselves. The Darwinists announced that man, too, is a beast of prey, and that he does well to follow nature's pattern.

The nature of animals is misconceived by these theorists. Animals are violent, but they are also placid; they kill, but they also live by mutual aid. Those who have known and loved animals, such as St. Francis and W. H. Hudson, have discovered much in them besides carnivorousness and ferocity. Referring to the famous dictum of Hobbes, *Homo homini lupus,* Lord Shaftesbury observed, "To say in disparagement of man 'that he is to man a wolf' appears somewhat absurd when one considers that wolves are to wolves very kind and loving creatures."[58] The defenders of the "beast of prey" as typical of "nature" are interpreting all life in terms of their own predatory impulses.

I will not deny that there is some truth in this point of view. Any well-balanced presentation of the facts—such as we find in Charles S. Sherrington's chapter on "Altruism" in his wise and erudite book, *Man on His Nature*—must grant that there is terrible waste and conflict among animals. There is both harmony and dissonance in nature, and a careful scientist will deny neither.

It may be objected that cooperation is derivative from the conditions of struggle. Individuals *within* a species cooperate among themselves in order to *compete* more successfully against *other* species. Wolves are loving toward their own kind, but fierce toward their enemies. Although there is truth in this objection, it does not change the fact that cooperation is a potent factor in evolutionary development. The Ethical Darwinists have thought too exclusively in terms of the struggle of individuals, as distinguished from the struggle of groups and species, for survival. At the human level, moreover, the development of scientific warfare has eliminated the distinction, because the fate of man, both as individual and species, depends upon curbing the impulses of aggression. Your life, like mine, will be safe only if the vision of Micah is realized: "Nation shall not lift up a sword against nation, neither shall they learn war any more."

Most of the proponents of "Evolutionary Ethics" have committed the genetic fallacy, the fallacy of identifying something in its developed form with its origins. They have argued that since man's moral life flows out of nature, it must exhibit the same characteristics as the nature out of which it flows. Because he evolved from lower animals, man must abide by the same "law" of survival that holds for ape and tiger. But development or evolution, if it means anything, must mean change. Various characteristics must exist at the end of the process that were not present in the beginning. Man evolved from apelike ancestors, but he is not an ape. Human beings alone have the capacity to think out a plan of life and to live according to a plan. They alone have the capacity to substitute rational persuasion in place of force and they are the most inventive species among all forms of animate nature.

As Alfred North Whitehead has pointed out, we can distinguish two different aspects of the evolutionary process, adaptation and creative power. "On one side, there is a given environment with organisms adapting themselves to it." Darwin emphasized this factor of adaptation, and herein lies the enduring truth of his theory. But it is a one-sided emphasis.

The other side of the evolutionary machinery, the neglected side, is expressed by the word *creativeness*. The organisms can create their own environment. For this purpose, the single organism is almost helpless. The adequate forces require societies of cooperating organisms. But with such cooperation and in proportion to the effort put forward, the environment has a plasticity which alters the whole ethical aspect of evolution.[59]

In producing man, nature has at last created an animal that exhibits this creative capacity in a preeminent degree. If he looks to subhuman nature as a fixed model to imitate, he fails to use his greatest natural gift—his creative intelligence.

Most of the proponents of Evolutionary Ethics have committed the "fallacy of factualism." This fallacy consists in supposing that *what is,* is synonymous with *what ought to be.* Given the factual proposition, *x is the case,* we are asked to infer the normative proposition, *x is good* or *x ought to be.* We cannot thus leap from a factual proposition to a normative proposition unless we *assume* that whatever exists is good—surely a dubious assumption.

The fact that this fallacy is involved in Ethical Darwinism tends to be concealed by the equivocal meaning of the word *fittest.* If we fail to distinguish between the biological and the ethical meaning of *fittest,* it is easy to commit this fallacy: we will assume that the biologically fit are the ethically fit; that what survives *ought* to survive. But the fittest, from the standpoint of biological survival, may be merely the cunning or the cruel or a combination of the weak. What is fittest depends upon the environmental conditions and is wholly relative to them. If the earth were to cool again in a new ice age, the "survival of the fittest" might bring about more and more stunted and humbler organisms, such as lichens. Within a gang of human cutthroats, perhaps only the most ruthless cutthroat can survive.

The plain truth is that neither survival nor adaptation attests to high ethical character or goodness of any kind. Tapeworms are well adapted to their environments. Flies are more plentiful than human beings, and bacteria more plentiful than flies. But we do not conclude that flies or bacteria or tapeworms are a higher species.

It may be argued that evolution *on the whole* means progress. This position avoids the untenable notion that *all* evolution is for the better. But how can we judge that certain trends *are* progressive unless we have an independent criterion of good? By judging that they are *main* trends? Yet the mere fact that something is a main trend does not make it good. One of the main trends in human development has been the increasing destructiveness of war. Does it follow that it would be good for this process to continue? If so, "good" may consist in the clean extinction of the human race.

Even if we were to assume that the *end* of evolutionary development is always good, we would have no right to conclude that the natural *means* to the natural *end* are best. There may be a blind proliferating and indiscriminate eliminating process in nature that brings about real progress, but at terrible cost. Man, with his power of reason, can achieve the *end* of evolutionary advance by far more economical *means* than nature ordinarily employs. As Tennyson said of nature, "Of fifty seeds she often brings but one to bear."[60] Why should man be so spendthrift merely because nature is?

I have been criticizing the theory of Ethical Darwinism, but I do not intend my criticism to extend, *in toto,* to the earlier theory of Malthus. His sweeping condemnation of humanitarianism was callous and narrow-minded; but his main theory, that population tends to increase faster than the means of subsistence, cannot be brushed aside.

In a recent essay, Aldous Huxley has summarized the relevant facts. "Thanks to modern science," he points out, "death rates have been halved but, except in the most highly industrialized, contraceptive-using countries, birth rates remain as high as ever." The result has been a spectacular increase in human numbers:

At the beginning of the Christian era, so demographers assure us, our planet supported a human population of about two hundred and fifty millions. When the Pilgrim Fathers stepped ashore, the figure had risen to about five hundred millions. We see, then, that in the relatively recent past it took sixteen hundred years for the human species to double its numbers. Today world population stands at three thousand millions. By the year 2000, unless something appallingly bad or miraculously good should happen in the interval, six thousand millions of us will be sitting down to breakfast every morning. In a word, twelve times as many people are destined to double their number in one-fortieth of the time.[61]

The explosive pace of multiplication poses a very serious problem for mankind. The present rate of population growth cannot continue indefinitely, for it would rapidly exhaust the physical resources and limits of our world.

An underdeveloped and overpopulated country, such as India or Brazil, faces the grimmest prospect. The danger is that all the nation's available resources will be absorbed in the task of supplying the primary needs of its new members.

The situation of these nations with such rapidly increasing populations reminds one of Lewis Carroll's parable in *Through the Looking Glass,* where Alice and the Red Queen start running at full speed and run for a long time until Alice is completely out of breath. When they stop, Alice is amazed to see that they are still at their starting point. In the looking glass world, if you wish to retain your present position, you must run as fast as you can. If you wish to get ahead, you must run at least twice as fast as you can.[62]

The result is profound frustration and unrest. The road is short from this unrest, through chaos, to dictatorship.

The moral of this story is pointed out by Huxley:

Committing that sin of overweening bumptiousness, which the Greeks called *hubris,* we behave as though we were not members of earth's ecological community, as though we were privileged and, in some sort, supernatural beings and could throw our weight around like gods. But in fact we are, among other things, animals—emergent parts of the natural order.[63]

Willy-nilly, we have to dwell on this earth if we are to live at all. If the future is to be tolerable, we must bring human breeding under sensible control, and we must conserve our natural resources. We must learn how to live in symbiotic harmony with nature.

9. THE RESIDUAL TRUTH IN THE CLASSICAL DOCTRINE OF NATURAL LAW

Let us now turn back to the older tradition of natural law. Although we have noted variations within this tradition, certain fundamentals are common to all the schools. Whether they be naturalists or supernaturalists, empiricists or rationalists, the proponents of the classical doctrine have emphasized the interdependence of law and morals and the dependence of both upon nature. They have agreed that there are valid moral laws embedded in the nature of things. They have denied a sharp dualism between fact and value, between what is and what ought to be. They have rejected the notion that human norms represent blind force, or blind faith, or mere subjective preference. Looking beyond the relativities of time and place, they have agreed that the good is a common good inasmuch as men have a common human nature and live in a common universe.

In the nineteenth century this creed fell into disfavor. The ancient books of natural law theory lay dusty and neglected on library shelves. The development of science convinced men that the world is not a spiritual order and that there is no vital link between nature and law and morals. Nevertheless, the idea of natural law was not so easily put to rest. "The undying spirit of that law," wrote Otto Gierke, "can never be extinguished. If it is denied entry into the body of positive law, it flutters about the room like a ghost."[64] The ghost has recently taken on a pretty substantial body. The idea of the unity of mankind under the universal laws of nature has been revived by such neo-scholastic philosophers as Jacques Maritain and Etienne Gilson, and such non-Catholic humanists as Erich Kahler, Ernest Barker, and Walter Lippmann.[65] It has found practical expression in the United Nations Declaration of Human Rights and the revolutionary drive for Negro emancipation in the United States and Africa.

This initial chapter shall not attempt to answer in detail the voices of scepticism. This entire book, in a sense, is an attempt to answer these voices. It will suffice, in the beginning, to identify the opposition and suggest the tenor of my answers. If opinions already expressed should be repeated, the repetition will serve the purposes of summary.

Legal positivism, as a doctrine counter to natural-law theory, conceives of positive law as a self-contained body of statutes and precedents tested and interpreted exclusively in terms of juristic premises and inner logical consistency, and enforced by the police-powers of the state rather than by moral suasion. Whereas natural-law theory links together positive law and morals, the legal positivists insist upon a clear and sharp separation. This positivistic theory has been immensely influential in Great Britain and America, and, to a lesser extent, on the European continent. Austin and Maine in England, Gray and Holmes in the United States, Pareto and Kelsen on the Continent, are among the jurists and philosophers who have proclaimed it.

We must admit to a modicum of good sense in the positivistic doctrine. As Morris Cohen has remarked, the "distinction between what is in fact law and what on ethical grounds we think ought to be the law is not a pleasant one to face," but it is, nevertheless, a "clear distinction" that intellectual honesty requires us to acknowledge.[66] It is a distinction that, in a certain sense, natural-law theorists themselves are prepared to grant, or even to emphasize. It is implicit in Cicero's doctrine that the laws of the state often violate the natural law; in St. Thomas' distinction between natural law and human law; and in Locke's and Jefferson's theory of the right of revolution against tyrannical laws. If not pushed too far, the distinction between moral and positive law is realistic and salutary.

The main bone of the contention is to be found, not in this realistic distinction between law as it is and law as it ought to be, but in the denial of *any* essential connection between the two. It seems to me, as it does to many legal theorists, that the positivists have been too sharply dualistic in their approach. Lon L. Fuller, Professor of Jurisprudence at Harvard University, has argued with great cogency that there is a kind of "internal morality" of positive law itself.[67] This morality requires that like cases should be treated alike; that there should be consistency and impartiality; that the law should be public and not secret; that "due process" and fair play should be respected. When these principles are spurned, so that the "wild beast" in man prevails, law itself ceases to exist. Such was nearly the condition of Nazi Germany when, as a result of unprincipled nihilism and lust for power, the whole legal system was on the point of breaking down. As Franz Neumann, in *Behemoth*, described German National Socialism, it was "a non-state, a chaos, a rule of lawlessness and anarchy," which had " 'swallowed' the rights and dignity of man," and was "out to transform the world into a chaos. . . ."[68] The Gestapo and judges were told, "Do not worry about legal precedents or principles; deal with each case as Nazi expediency requires." Of an outrageous Nazi practice that thus wore the trappings of law, it is realistic to say, "This thing is the product of a system so oblivious to the morality of law that it is not entitled to be called law."[69]

When positive law is thus seen as having its own inner morality, the *sine qua non* of its very existence, it becomes farfetched to insist, as the legal positivists do, upon the absolute distinction between law as it is and law as it ought to be. A relative distinction there is; but a sharp cleavage is an evil to be regretted, and it should not be raised to the level of an absolute principle.

Even the most hardy positivists, such as John Austin, have not always maintained a consistent opposition to the natural-law theory. In an essay, "The Uses of the Study of Jurisprudence," Austin remarks that there are certain "subjects and ends of Law that are common to all systems," and notes "those resemblances between different systems which are bottomed in the common nature of man."[70] Here the language belongs to the tradition of natural law rather than to the theory of positivism. Likewise in the case of Hobbes and Hume, despite their strong tendency toward positivism, there is a residual ethics of natural law based on the primordial human need to survive. As Hume wrote:

Human nature cannot by any means subsist without the association of individuals: and that association never could have place were no regard paid to the laws of equity and justice.[71]

The state, as H. L. A. Hart has remarked, is by its very nature not a suicide club, and we are committed to life by some of the deepest forces of human nature.[72]

If we choose to live rather than die, why should we not choose to live well, and to make law our instrument? There are good laws and bad laws, wise laws and foolish laws; and it makes a great deal of difference what kind of laws we have. Whenever well-being and human rights can be served best by altering or abolishing the law, it should be altered or abolished. The Declaration of Independence, in ringing sentences, affirms this great truth.

I would not deny for a moment that there are generally excellent reasons for respecting and maintaining the law. The rule of law is necessary, especially in a complex society, if criminals are to be restrained and anarchy is to be avoided. Legal order is the only substitute for private war, and even irrational rules are ordinarily better than no rules at all. Law also provides a necessary protection against the fallibility and abuse of power among the rulers of the state, and the judicial following of precedent is a reasonable protection against individual whim and unpredictable miscarriages of justice. As Aristotle points out, law is a necessary safeguard against the subjectivism and irrationalism that eschews precedents and depends upon the momentary decree.

He who bids the law rule, may be deemed to bid God and reason alone rule, but he who bids man rule adds an element of the beast; for desire is a wild beast, and passion perverts the minds of rulers, even when they are the best of men. The law is reason unaffected by desire.[73]

These considerations, far from being arguments for the sharp separation between law and morals, indicate the overlapping of the two realms. That such overlapping exists is one of the abiding truths of natural law thinking. Whether we are speaking of "the duty of the executive to administer the law, the duty of the legislature to abide by constitutional limitations," or "the duty of courts to abide by precedent and the holdings of courts of superior jurisdiction," all of "these important duties are both legal and moral, and it follows, therefore, that the existence of a legal system, as distinct from the existence of an effective regime of coercion, presupposes and rests upon the acceptance of a more than rudimentary system of moral ideas."[74] If human "law" should cease to be moral, and should become a mere engine of oppression, the right, nay the *duty,* of civil disobedience becomes paramount.

Distinguishing between legal and ethical positivism, we can define the latter as the contention that ethical statements and moral judgments cannot be established by reason and evidence, as statements of fact can be. This sceptical thesis has been very widely asserted by philosophers in recent years. It is obviously opposed to the classical doctrine of natural law.

As this sceptical doctrine will be discussed in Part Three, little need be said about it at this point. I am willing to go a certain distance with the positivists, and no farther. We should distinguish, as they insist we should, between fact and ideal, and between descriptive and normative discourse. If we fail to make this distinction and interpret descriptive laws as if they were normative principles, we are guilty of "the fallacy of factualism." To make this point clear let us consider some of the meanings of nature.

First, *nature* is sometimes used to refer to the typical, common, or usual. Nature, so understood, is not necessarily good or right. We have no duty to be typical if the type is mediocre or bad. The advice, "When in Rome do as the Romans do," is a counsel of prudence and not of morality. It is not always our duty to be on the winning side. The majority may be wrong. High attainment, by virtue of its height, is unusual. As Spinoza said in the concluding sentence of his *Ethics,* "All excellent things are as difficult as they are rare."

Second, *nature* may mean the primitive. Here, too, there is no reliable basis for ethical choice. The primitive may have a pristine vitality or unspoiled simplicity that we rightly admire, but it may also be "poor, nasty, brutish, and short." The mere fact that something occurs early in a developmental process does not make it good.

Third, *nature* may mean the innate rather than the acquired, as when we contrast it with *nurture.* But unless we are to abandon all education, all training and cultivation, we cannot assert that nature, in this sense, is always to be preferred to nurture.

Fourth, *nature* may mean that which exists apart from human control or contrivance, as when we speak of nature as wild and untended and spontaneous. Here, again, we have no basis for an ethical norm, because all of man's arts and sciences consist in interfering with nature, so understood. Without such an interference, human life would be impossible. There can be no sound reason for excluding control on the ground that it is "unnatural."

Fifth, *nature* may be used to denote *all that is*—the entire system of things. But the mere fact that something exists gives it no special claim to value. Using "nature" in this sense, W. Macneile Dixon has pertinently asked:

> Is nature concerned whether we wash or not, have good manners or not, keep our promises or not? Is nature . . . concerned whether we are ambitious or not, musical or not, humorous or not? . . . Is she concerned whether we live by thieving or honest toil, are pitiful or cruel, have many love affairs, few, or none, prefer sport to study, delight in war, hunting, adventure, or shudder at them? She makes men of every pattern, and sends her rain upon the just and unjust alike. People talk as if nature should be better pleased with good than with bad men, as we judge good and bad. But they are equally her children, as are the fish of the sea and the fowls of the air.[75]

So construed, nature provides no basis for selection. Anything and everything is natural; hence the injunction, "Follow nature," is meaningless, for one could never do anything else.

If we are asked to live according to *nature* in any of these five meanings of the word, we are being asked to commit the fallacy of factualism. We are being asked to take some merely factual characteristic—all-inclusiveness, or typicality, or primitiveness, or innateness, or lack of cultivation—and to turn it into a norm for conduct. But the factual is not the ideal: physics and ethics are distinct. "What is" is not identical with "what ought to be." Valid ideals sometimes come true: the good and the actual overlap, yet they do not coincide.

The natural-law philosophers have not always kept in mind the distinction between the normative and the purely descriptive meaning of law. They have interpreted the *goals* of law as a kind of *actual* law, or the *actual* as the *goal*. They have glossed over the defects of institutions on the ground that they are natural. Instead of realizing the ideal, they have idealized the real. Nothing but confusion results from obliteration of the distinction between what is and what ought to be.

The failure clearly to distinguish between fact and ideal accounts in part for the inconsistent character of the natural-law tradition. The theory of natural law is a common parent of both teleological and deontological theories. "To live according to nature" may be interpreted as obedience to self-evident laws or the *actual* patterns of nature, whatever these may be. Here the emphasis is formalistic or deontological. To live in accordance with nature may also be interpreted as the realization of basic human needs and capacities. Man has natural drives and goal-seeking propensities, and his good is the fulfillment of these native bents. Here the emphasis is teleological or utilitarian. I sympathize with the latter view rather than with the former.

If by *nature* we do not mean the actual but the ideal, it may indeed serve as a basis for conduct. Sometimes the word is used in this sense, as when Aristotle speaks of "natural" as the fully realized, the ideal fulfillment of the type. An ethics based upon such a concept is essentially purposive: it does not ask us to imitate a given pattern; it is forward-looking, end-seeking, open-minded, and adventurous.

Such an ethics is not indifferent to, or independent of, fact. It recognizes that actuality—the factually real world—supplies us with the materials with which we must work and sets limits upon what we can do. Although we cannot identify fact with norm, we can determine what is ideal only in the light of real needs and tendencies. Human life, to paraphrase Santayana, has both actual basis and ideal fulfillment. The identification of its basis with fulfillment or the separation of fulfillment from its basis is equally fallacious. I maintain that morals have an objective basis in the nature of man and his world, and in this crucial respect, agree with the philosophers of natural law.

To find this objective basis we must look to science. It is primarily by means of science that we can discover the strange and compelling harmony of the natural order. It is by means of science, through its technological consequences, that we can marvellously increase our powers, and thus tap the infinite bounties of nature for the enhancement of life. It is also by means of psychology and social science that we can discover the basic needs of man. But to do so, we must be careful not to combat mechanism by an uncritical acceptance of spiritualistic doctrines. I am inclined to think that the tendency to interpret matter idealistically is as wrong-headed as the tendency to interpret human beings and animals mechanically. Whatever may be our conclusions about these abstruse epistemological and metaphysical questions, we must insist that biological, mental, and social qualities, with the values and purposes to be found at the higher levels, are quite as indefeasibly real, although not as widely dispersed, as any physical and chemical processes. The interpretation of nature should be based upon the whole variegated range of our experience and not upon a dehumanized fragment of it.

NOTES

1. "The Marriage of Heaven and Hell," in *Poetry and Prose of William Blake*. New York: Random House, Inc., 1927, p. 194.
2. *The Manual of Epictetus*, in Whitney J. Oates, *The Stoic and Epi-
curean Philosophers*. New York: Random House, Inc., 1940, p. 468.
3. *Ibid.*, p. 470.
4. Marcus Aurelius, *Meditations*, in *ibid.*, p. 516.
5. *Ibid.*, p. 506.

6. *Ibid.*, p. 509.
7. Quoted by Matthew Arnold, "An Essay on Marcus Aurelius," in *ibid.*, p. 594.
8. Cicero, *De Legibus* (translated by Clinton Walker Keyes). Cambridge, Mass: Harvard University Press, 1943, pp. 323, 329.
9. *Ibid.*, pp. 385–386.
10. Cicero, *De Re Publica* (translated by Keyes). Cambridge, Mass.: Harvard University Press, 1943, p. 211.
11. *De Legibus, op. cit.*, p. 385.
12. Cicero, *De Finibus* (translated by H. Rackham). Cambridge, Mass.: Harvard University Press, 1914, p. 375.
13. Etienne Gilson, *Medieval Universalism and Its Present Value*. New York: Sheed and Ward, Inc., 1937, p. 16.
14. Thomas Aquinas, *Summa Theologica*, I–II, question 94, article 2. Anton C. Pegis (editor), *Basic Writings of Saint Thomas Aquinas*. New York: Random House, Inc., 1945, Vol. II, p. 775.
15. *Ibid.*, I–II, question 64, article 4.
16. *Ibid.*, I–II, 95, 2; Pegis, *op. cit.*, II, p. 784.
17. Jacques Maritain, *The Rights of Man and Natural Law*. New York: Charles Scribner's Sons, 1943, p. 3.
18. Jacob Burckhardt, *The Civilization of the Renaissance in Italy*. London: George Allen & Unwin, Ltd., 1921, p. 129.
19. Hugo Grotius, *The Law of War and Peace* (translated by Francis W. Kelsey). New York: Oxford University Press, 1925, p. 40.
20. *Ibid.*, p. 13.
21. *Ibid.*, p. 30.
22. *Ibid.*, p. 23.
23. Giambattista Vico, *The New Science* (translated by Thomas Goddard Bergin and Max Harold Fisch). Ithaca, N.Y.: Cornell University Press, 1948, p. 86.
24. *Ibid.*, p. 82. For a recent survey of the relevant evidence, see Clyde Kluckhohn, "Universal Categories of Culture," in A. L. Kroeber (editor), *Anthropology Today*. Chicago: University of Chicago Press, 1953, pp. 507–523.
25. John Courtney Murray, "The Natural Law," in R. M. MacIver (editor), *Great Expressions of Human Rights*. New York: Harper & Row, Publishers, Inc., 1950, pp. 98–99.
26. John Locke, *Essay on Human Understanding*, Vol. II, Ch. 29, para. 17.
27. Adam Smith, *The Wealth of Nations*. New York: Modern Library, 1937, pp. 421, 423, 651.
28. John Locke, *Second Treatise on Civil Government*, Ch. IX, section 123.
29. *Ibid.*, section 124.
30. *Ibid.*, II, 6.
31. *Ibid.*, VI, 57.
32. *Ibid.*, IV, 22.
33. *Ibid.*, II, 14.
34. Thomas Jefferson, *First Inaugural Address*.
35. Thomas Hill Green, "Liberal Legislation and Freedom of Contract" (lecture), 1880.
36. *Human Rights: A Symposium Edited by UNESCO*. London: Allan Wingate, Ltd., 1949, p. 263.
37. Dante, *Inferno* (translated by Lawrence Binyon). London: Macmillan & Co., Ltd., 1952, Canto XXVI, pp. 303, 305. Quoted by permission of the Society of Authors. For a more complete analysis of this passage, see Sir Ernest Barker, "Dante and the Last Voyage of Ulysses," in *Traditions of Civility*. Cambridge: Cambridge University Press, 1948.
38. Aeschylus, *The Persians* (translated by G. M. Cookson). New York: E. P. Dutton & Co., Inc., 1906, lines 999–1000.
39. Giorgio de Santillana (editor), *The Age of Adventure: The Renaissance Philosophers*. New York: The New American Library of World Literature, Inc., 1956, p. 250.
40. His three laws of motion are as follows: First, the planets move in elliptical orbits, in which the sun occupies one focus. Second, the line joining a planet to the sun sweeps out equal areas in equal times. Third, the square

of the period of revolution of a planet in its movement around the sun is proportional to the cube of its average distance from the sun.

41. Johannes Kepler, *Opera* (edited by Frisch). Frankfurt: Heyder and Zimmer, 1858, I, p. 21.

42. Isaac Newton, *Optics*, in H. S. Thayer (editor), *Newton's Philosophy of Nature: Selections from his Writings.* New York: Hafner Publishing Company, 1953, pp. 175–176.

43. *Cf.* Basil Willey, *The Eighteenth Century Background.* New York: Columbia University Press, 1941.

44. Quoted by A. C. Crombie, "The Idea of Organic Evolution," *Discovery,* vol. 14 (March 1953), p. 95.

45. *Cf.* C. P. Snow, *The Two Cultures and the Scientific Revolution.* London and New York: Cambridge University Press, 1959.

46. Jean de La Fontaine, *Memoires Pour Servir à l'Histoire de Port Royal,* 1738, II, pp. 52–53. Quoted by Leonora Cohen Rosenfield, *From Beast-Machine to Man-Machine.* London and New York: Oxford University Press, 1941, p. 54.

47. *Cf.* Gilbert Ryle, *The Concept of Mind.* London: Hutchinson & Co., Ltd., 1949.

48. John B. Watson, *Behavior.* New York: Holt, Rinehart and Winston, Inc., 1914, p. 27.

49. Thomas Robert Malthus, *An Essay on the Principles of Population,* 1798 edition. London: J. Johnson, 1798, Chs. I, V.

50. Charles Darwin, *The Descent of Man.* London: John Murray, Ltd., 1871, Chapter 21.

51. Herbert Spencer, *Social Statics.* New York: Appleton-Century-Crofts, 1888, p. 354.

52. Herbert Spencer, *Principles of Ethics.* New York: Appleton-Century-Crofts, 1897, II, p. 260.

53. Oswald Spengler, *The Hour of Decision.* New York: Alfred A. Knopf, Inc., 1934, p. 21. And *Man and Technics.* New York: Alfred A. Knopf, Inc., 1932, p. 43.

54. Sir Arthur Keith, *The Place of Prejudice in Modern Civilization.* London: Williams & Norgate, Ltd., 1931, p. 49.

55. William Graham Sumner, *Essays.* New Haven: Yale University Press, 1934, II, p. 56.

56. Robert and Helen Lynd, *Middletown in Transition.* New York: Harcourt, Brace & World, Inc., 1937, p. 500.

57. Cited by Richard Hofstadter, *Social Darwinism in American Thought.* London and New York: Oxford University Press, 1944, p. 31.

58. Quoted by Havelock Ellis, *The Dance of Life.* Boston and New York: Houghton Mifflin Company, 1923, p. 250.

59. Alfred North Whitehead, *Science and the Modern World.* New York: The Macmillan Company, 1925, pp. 163–164.

60. "In Memoriam," LV.

61. Aldous Huxley, *The Politics of Ecology* (pamphlet). New York: The Fund for the Republic, Inc., 1963, p. 2.

62. *Ibid.,* p. 3.

63. *Ibid.,* p. 6.

64. Otto Gierke, *Natural Law and the Theory of Society.* Boston: Beacon Press, 1957, p. 226.

65. See Bibliography on "Natural Law and Rights" at the end of this volume.

66. Morris Cohen, *A Critical Sketch of Legal Philosophy in America.* New York: New York University Press, 1937, pp. 266, 285.

67. Lon L. Fuller, "Positivism and Fidelity to Law," *Harvard Law Review,* vol. 71 (1958), pp. 630–672.

68. Franz Neumann, *Behemoth.* London and New York: Oxford University Press, 1942, p. vii. This interpretation is abundantly confirmed by William L. Shirer, *The Rise and Fall of the Third Reich.* New York: Simon and Schuster, Inc., 1960.

69. Fuller, "Positivism and Fidelity to Law," *op. cit.,* p. 661.

70. John Austin, *The Province of Juris-prudence Determined Etc.* London: Weidenfeld and Nicolson, Ltd., 1954, p. 373.
71. David Hume, *An Enquiry Concerning the Principles of Morals* (edited by L. A. Selby-Bigge). London and New York: Oxford University Press, 1902, p. 206.
72. *Cf.* H. L. A. Hart, *The Concept of Law.* London and New York: Ox-ford University Press, Chapter IX.
73. Aristotle, *Politics* (Jowett's translation). London and New York: Oxford University Press, 1921, 1287a.
74. Marcus G. Singer, "Hart's Concept of Law," *Journal of Philosophy*, vol. 60 (1963), p. 208.
75. W. Macneile Dixon, *The Human Situation*. New York: David McKay Company, Inc., no date, pp. 288–289.

CHAPTER II

Human excellence

I. THE CONFUCIAN ETHICS OF FULFILLMENT

According to the more metaphysical versions of the natural-law tradition, the universe is in some sense a moral order, and human morality reflects the cosmic order of things. This chapter will not discuss these large metaphysical issues, but rather the more limited humanistic thesis of the natural-law philosophy. This is the doctrine that the good is the cultivation and fulfillment of human nature, whether in the individual or in the race. It is not only natural but morally right for human beings to fulfill their essential needs and tendencies. Goodness is human excellence, the perfection of human kind.

An objection advanced by nearly all critics of this type of ethics is the vagueness or ambiguity of its principal concepts. The idea of human fulfillment, according to these critics, is too general and hazy to be useful. This objection is not necessarily valid. A humanist who bases his ethics on contemporary theories of psychological dispositions and personality structure may achieve a high degree of precision. But even some of the older theories, such as those of Aristotle and Spinoza, are reasonably clear and exact. The following pages will review a number of typical theories, old and recent.

To understand a doctrine it is helpful to grasp it in its pure and simple form. The ethics of human fulfillment was stated in a simple way by Confucius (551–479 B.C.), or as he is known in China, Master K'ung. I shall begin with the teachings of this ancient sage.

Born of humble parents, he became Secretary of Justice and later Chief Minister of the little kingdom of Chou, in what is now the province of Shantung. He was eventually forced into exile by political intrigue and spent thirteen years wandering from state to state, hoping to persuade the rulers to practice virtue. Finally he returned, a disappointed old man, to his original homeland, where he died three years later. The compilation of his "works" took place long after his death, and it is impossible to know how authentic they are.

Living in a period of social disunity and decline, he tried to reintroduce unity on a moral basis. His basic concept was "human-heartedness" or "true manhood." By this he meant the principle of cultivating one's own humanity and respecting the like humanity in others. In the words of a Confucian classic: "From the Son of Heaven down to the mass of the people, all must consider the cultivation of the person the root of everything besides."[1] His ethical goal was the full and harmonious development of human nature.

Every person, he believed, has fundamentally the same nature. Men obviously have mouths, ears, and eyes alike, they have similar digestive systems, they are alike in their basic physical and mental faculties. Some things fit in with this nature and other things do not. Hay is good food for an ox but not for a man, because it does not suit human nature. Similarly a life without proper rest, without exercise of the mind as well as the body, without satisfaction of basic instincts and cultivation of fundamental talents, is not in accordance with human needs.

Because human nature is complex, the cultivation of the person is no one-sided affair. Confucius was a scholar and had a deep respect for wisdom, but he realized that intellectual cultivation, if unaccompanied by emotional balance and esthetic refinement, produces only a distorted human being. The "true man" achieves a profound emotional rapport with his environment—a natural harmony between himself and earth and heaven.

Once when Confucius was sitting with several of his disciples, he asked each to express his wishes. One replied that he would like to be a minister of war, a second to be a minister of finances, and a third to be a master of ceremonies. Turning to the fourth, Confucius asked, "Tien, what are your wishes?"

Tien, pausing as he was playing on his lute, while it was yet twanging, laid the instrument aside, and rose. "My wishes," he said, "are different from the cherished purposes of these three gentlemen." "What harm is there in that?" said the Master; "do you also, as well as they, speak out your wishes." Tien then said, "In this, the last month of spring, with the dress of the season all complete, along with five or six young men . . . ., and six or seven boys, I would wash in the river Yi, enjoy the breezes among the rain altars, and return home singing." The Master heaved a sigh and said, "I give my approval to Tien."[2]

The "true man" is like Tien—his spirit is molded by the esthetic element in nature and the human environment. He is not only a scholar, but a poet, a musician, a master of decorum. The ideal is that of man in equipoise—his intellect alert and cultivated and his spirit harmonized by art and ceremony.

Inward grace is not to be confused with outward show. Art and ritual are meaningless without sincerity. "If a man is not a true man," Confucius asked, "what is the use of rituals? If a man is not a true man, what is the use of music?"[3] In the same spirit he declared:

I hate things that resemble the real things but are not the real things. . . . I hate the ingratiating fellows, because they get mixed up with the good men. I

hate the glib-talkers because they confuse us about honest people. . . . I hate the
goody-goodies because they confuse us about the virtuous people. . . .[4]

"Fine words and an insinuating appearance," he said, "are seldom associated
with true virtue."[5]

The person who sincerely cultivates his own nature has a "measuring
square" for regulating his conduct toward others. Drawing from his own self
a measure for the treatment of other men, he lives according to the Golden
Rule. A disciple asked Confucius, "Is there one word which may serve as a
rule of practice for all one's life?" The Master answered, "Is not Reciprocity
such a word? What you do not want done to yourself, do not do to others."[6]
Here the rule is stated negatively, but elsewhere in the sayings of Confucius
it is stated positively, as in the Christian version. Among the duties implied
are these:

> To serve my father, as I would require my son to serve me . . .; to serve my
> prince, as I would require my minister to serve me . . .; to serve my elder
> brother, as I would require my younger brother to serve me . . .; to set the
> example in behaving to a friend, as I would require him to behave to me. . . .[7]

The final test for any civilization is whether it produces friends, relatives, and
citizens who practice reciprocity toward one another.

The ruler should ask himself how he would like to be treated by some one
near and dear to him; then he should treat his subjects in the same considerate way. When both ruler and subjects cling to this principle, disputes
are resolved by friendly agreement rather than by force or litigation. "In
presiding over lawsuits, I am as good as anybody," declared Confucius. "The
thing is so to aim that there be no lawsuits."[8] Politics should be subordinated
to morals, and morals based upon respect for the human person. "Guide the
people by law, keep them in line by punishment," said Confucius, "and they
may shun crime, but they will be shameless. Guide them by mind, keep them
in line by courtesy, and they will learn shame and grow good."[9] This view
reflects the primacy of family life in the Chinese scheme of things. Confucius
taught that the state is the family writ large, just as Plato taught that the
state is the magnified soul. "Rule a big country as one would fry small fish,"[10]
advised Lao-Tse; and Confucius agreed that statemanship requires the
delicacy that one learns in the intimate concerns of life.

Love, in one sense of the word, is the fundamental principle of Confucian
ethics, but it is not the impersonal, all-embracing love advocated by another
Chinese philosopher, Mo Ti (circa 468–390 B.C.). According to the latter,
everyone should love all humanity without discrimination and equally. To
the follower of Confucius, this kind of indiscriminate love is too cold and
impersonal. There must be discrimination and degrees in loving—else it cannot be warm. The fire of love is first kindled in the intimate community, and
its warmth radiates out from this point.

Confucius distinguished between good men, who deserve love, and bad men, who do not.

Someone said, "What do you say concerning the principle that injury should be recompensed with kindness?" The Master said, "With what then will you recompense kindness? Recompense injury with justice and recompense kindness with kindness."[11]

This is a discriminating person-to-person approach, neither the universal love of Mo Ti nor the impersonal law of the West.

The subordination of rules to persons and occasions is illustrated by Confucius' formulation of the Principle of the Mean. Long before Aristotle advocated a similar doctrine, Confucius taught that virtue tends to be a mean between extremes. On a certain occasion, a disciple, Tsze-Kung, asked Confucius which of two individuals, Shih or Shang, was the superior. The Master said, "Shih goes beyond the due mean, and Shang does not come up to it." "Then," said Tsze-Kung, "the superiority is with Shih, I suppose." The Master replied, "To go beyond is as wrong as to fall short."[12] This principle is adjustable to the particularities of time and place. For instance, gaiety that would be moderate enough for some informal occasion would be excessive under more formal circumstances. Flexible though it be, the principle is still too strict to include all the situations of life. When his favorite disciple Yen Yüan died, Confucius bewailed him exceedingly, and the disciples who were with him said, "Master, your grief is excessive?" "Is it excessive?" said he. "If I am not to mourn bitterly for this man, for whom should I mourn?"[13] There are spontaneous responses that cannot be evaluated even by the flexible criterion of the mean. This lack of definiteness may offend the abstract reasoner but it is in the spirit of a humanistic ethics.

After dominating Chinese culture for 2500 years, the humanism of Confucius has been submerged by communism. Perhaps it could have withstood the communist flood if it had incorporated more of the scientific, technological, and organizational skills of Western civilization. But Confucius saw some things quite clearly. His most important insight was the ideal of human-heartedness—"the cultivation of the human person as the root of all things besides."

2. ARISTOTLE AND THE LIFE OF REASON

One of the classic expressions of humanism is to be found in the ethics of Aristotle (384–322 B.C.). Son of the physician to the Macedonian king, Aristotle acquired the empirical interests of the medical profession; he regarded ethics as an art, like medicine, although the former was concerned with the health of the soul rather than the body. He was also greatly influenced in his ethical concepts by Plato, whose student and assistant he was for twenty years. Like his master, he believed that the good is the harmonious development of human capacities, above all the capacity to reason. After the death of Plato, Aristotle spent four years on the coast of Asia Minor, engaged in biological research; then for several years he acted as tutor to prince Alexander of Macedon. In 335 he returned to Athens, where he spent twelve very productive years as head of a school of his own founding, the Lyceum. Finally he was accused of impiety, and fled to the island of Euboea, where he died a year later. His ethics reflected the love of philosophy, to which he devoted his life.

His conception of ethics was essentially humanistic. The knowledge of man, he believed, is the basis of establishing norms and values. Ethics is based upon psychology and not upon theology or transcendental metaphysics. It is a branch of practical science and a part of politics. The business of the ethical philosopher is to determine the qualities in human life that the educator and the statesman should cultivate in the people. Its principal object is to find out what is man's highest good.

In the opening paragraphs of *The Nicomachean Ethics,* Aristotle pointed out that the various practical arts are to be distinguished by the ends they serve. Health is the aim of medicine, vessels of shipbuilding, victory of military strategy, and wealth of economics. The ends and corresponding arts form a hierarchy, some being subordinate to others. Bridle-making is subservient to horsemanship, horsemanship to strategy, and so on. Finally we arrive at some ultimate end and the art corresponding to it. This is the art of arts—the art whose function it is to harmonize and control all the other arts and whose end, therefore, is not this or that particular good but the good for man. Aristotle called this highest art the art of politics, of which ethics, since it defines the ultimate good, is an integral part.

What is this good? Aristotle answered that, so far as the name is concerned, there is general agreement to call it "happiness." The real question, however, is one of fact. What kind of life deserves to be called happy?

He laid down three criteria for determining happiness. First, it must be desirable for its own sake—an end, and not just a means. Hence it cannot consist of merely external goods, such as wealth. Second, it must be self-sufficient; it must be adequate in itself to satisfy us. Hence it cannot be pleasure or honor, because these, he believed, are not sufficient. Third, it must be found in the life and work peculiar to man. Every creature has a characteristic function, and the good for that creature is to exercise that function. A bear, for example, should be a bear: it should express a bear's function. A man should likewise be a man: he should so far as possible express his specifically human function. The function of anything is that which it can do best, and which expresses its essential and distinctive characteristics. In performing the human function we are being most truly ourselves and doing what it is our nature to do.

Beginning with the last criterion, what is it that *only* man can do? The capacity for growth and reproduction we share even with plants; the capacity for feeling, sensation, and impulse we share with animals; these cannot be the differentiating function and characteristic work of man. In human beings there is superimposed upon these faculties a higher faculty, the capacity to reason. This is man's distinctive gift, his essential attribute, his differentiating characteristic. Reason is the power to calculate, reflect, and know, to understand relations and universal qualities, to live by rule instead of being swayed by appetite.

Happiness is the life of reason—not the mere potentiality of reasoning, which a man may possess when he is fast asleep, but the active exercise of intelligence. It must also, Aristotle added, be in accordance with virtue, or, if there is more than one virtue, with the best and most perfect of them. (The word "virtue" here means the peculiar excellence of a faculty that enables it to perform its function well.) Happiness, to deserve the name, must be manifested not merely for short periods but in a complete life; one swallow does not make a summer, nor does a snatch of happiness make a happy life. To sum up, happiness is an active, virtuous, and sustained mode of living that calls into play the specifically human capacities, above all, man's rational nature.

When thus defined, happiness satisfies not only the third criterion, but the other two as well. It is desirable for its own sake—an end or ultimate good, and not merely a means. It is also self-sufficient and preferable to any other kind of life. It is the only life that can permanently satisfy man.

This conception has the merit of including other common conceptions of happiness. Some say that happiness is virtue; others say that it is pleasure; still others say it is external prosperity. Now virtue is the spring from which happiness flows, pleasure is its natural accompaniment, and prosperity is its normal precondition.

Aristotle was not a hedonist, but he believed that pleasure is intrinsically good. It is good, but not the supreme good. Animals also experience pleasure, and Aristotle was confident that the good for man must be higher than the good for lower animals. But pleasure is the result and sign of the fulfillment of our capacities, and thus, as it were, puts a crown on our activities. It attains its maximum with the freest and healthiest functioning of the soul. We would not be completely satisfied with our activity unless it resulted in pleasure, but the pleasure is not separable from the activity or to be desired apart from it. Pleasures differ in kind, and some kinds are unworthy of man. In the activity proper to our own nature we find the finest and greatest pleasure. The life of reason is therefore not only the best and noblest but the most pleasant of all lives.

External goods, although not good for their own sakes, are the necessary conditions of the good life. A certain amount of wealth, security, and comfort are essential for the noble employment of leisure, without which man's highest nature cannot find expression. In Aristotle's ethics there is no disparagement of external goods such as we find in the Stoics.

There are two forms of goodness corresponding to the two main divisions of man's personality, the rational and the subrational. The first form is intellectual goodness, corresponding to the rational part. It consists in the exercise of reason for its own sake. The second is moral goodness, corresponding to the subrational part. This part Aristotle subdivided into the "vegetative," which consists of the elementary vital functions of nourishment, growth, and reproduction, and the "appetitive," which consists of perception, emotion, pleasure and pain, desire and aversion. The vegetative part is beyond the pale of reason (except as subject to the art of medicine), but the appetitive part is rational to the degree that it obeys the dictates of reason. Moral goodness consists in the guidance of the appetitive part by reason.

Let us first consider moral goodness, which is a kind of excellence or virtue. We inherit little more than a capacity for virtue, and the actualization of this capacity requires much practice. A man may know what is right, and yet he may succumb to desires or impulses to do what is wrong. Moral weakness, which results in doing wrong knowingly, is not, as Socrates supposed, an illusion. Man's nature is complex, and if he is to guard against incontinence, he must strengthen his character by practice and insight. As a result of habit and education, the mere capacity for right action becomes a developed disposition; and this disposition is what we mean by moral virtue.

Moral goodness is the disposition to choose moderation rather than some extreme. It is destroyed equally by excess or deficiency.

This is plain in the case of strength and health. Too much and too little exercise alike destroy strength, and to take too much meat and drink, or to take too little, is equally ruinous to health, but the fitting amount produces and increases and preserves them. Just so, then, is it with temperance also, and courage, and the other virtues. The man who shuns and fears everything and never makes a stand, becomes a coward; while the man who fears nothing at all, but will face anything, becomes foolhardy. So, too, the man who takes his fill of any kind of pleasure, and abstains from none, is a profligate, but the man who shuns all (like him whom we call a "boor") is devoid of sensibility. For temperance and courage are destroyed both by excess and defect, but preserved by moderation.[14]

Aristotle gave many examples of virtue as a mean: dignified self-respect is a mean between humility and vanity; generosity, between stinginess and prodigality; friendliness, between quarrelsomeness and obsequiousness; and so on. This principle of moderation is not limited to actions, but also applies to emotions.

For instance, it is possible to feel fear, confidence, desire, anger, pity, and generally to be affected pleasantly and painfully, either too much or too little, in either case wrongly; but to be thus affected at the right times, and on the right occasions, and towards the right persons, and with the right object, and in the right fashion, is the mean course and the best course, and these are characteristics of virtue.[15]

This latter quotation implies that the right mean is not a fixed point between extremes but a sliding, adjustable mean relative to the time, the place, the circumstances, the person who acts, and the persons affected. Moral choice deals with particulars, and cannot be reduced to rote. It is easy to miss the bull's-eye and hard to hit it—there are many ways of going wrong and only one way of going right. Such a conception pushes aside rigid moral laws, like those of Kant, and makes morality a subtle intellectual art governed by a feeling for proportion and harmony and by a nice calculation of consequences.

One part of the life of reason is the practical wisdom involved in moral virtue, which we have just discussed. This involves instrumental goods and not simply intrinsic. Another part is the exercise of reason for its own sake. Because man's chief intrinsic good is the perfect development of his rational nature, it must be found primarily in intellectual virtue, or in the free exercise of reason. Such virtue requires leisure, which Aristotle distinguished from amusement. Leisurely activities are those worth performing for their own sake, because in them man realizes and expresses his true nature.

The life of the statesman and of the soldier, though they surpass all other [morally] virtuous exercises in nobility and grandeur, are not leisurely occupations, and aim at some ulterior end, and are not desired merely for themselves. But the exercise of reason seems to be superior in seriousness (since it contemplates truth), and to aim at no end besides itself, and to have its proper pleasure (which also helps to increase the exercise); and its exercise seems further to be self-sufficient, and leisurely, and inexhaustible (as far as anything human can be), and to have all the other characteristics that are ascribed to happiness. . . . For every being, that is best and pleasantest which is naturally proper to it. Since, then, it is the reason that in the truest sense is the man, the life that consists in the exercise of the reason is the best and pleasantest for man—and therefore the happiest.[16]

The highest law of ethics is the love of intellectual virtue. Satisfaction of this love means the life of intellectual contemplation—the life that finds godlike expression in science and philosophy.

3. A CRITICISM OF ARISTOTELIAN ETHICS

Aristotle's contention that reason is exclusively man's attribute, and that it must therefore constitute man's chief good, is questionable. As the psychologist Wolfgang Köhler has proved in a number of experiments, chimpanzees also have the capacity of reason. They can figure out ways of piling and mounting boxes, for example, so as to reach bananas hanging high from the ceiling of their cage. Aristotle would reply that this is practical, not theoretical, reason, and that only man can possess the latter. But it appears that both monkeys and dogs have curiosity and enjoy satisfying it. It is not at all obvious that reason, even in the sense of disinterested wonder, is exclusively human.

What fundamentally distinguishes man is the whole remarkable development of culture, expressing his capacity for creativity and self-transcendence. Bach, the man of art, is as profoundly human as Kant, the man of reason. Jesus, the man of religion, towers as high above the brutes as Aristotle, the man of science and philosophy. Moreover, what truly matters is the *worth* of a faculty at the human level; that a faculty has its origins in subhuman life does not detract from its worth. Is love, for example, any less valuable because dogs display affection? I think no one would say so.

The valuable is not necessarily the distinctively human: it is what is *worthy* of being human. Apparently only man among the animals knows the difference between right and wrong. Only man, therefore, can act immorally—fiendish immorality is a distinctively human trait—yet it is not the good Aristotle sought. He asked, "What is man's proper function?" But if "proper" means distinctively human, it is not necessarily relevant to the moral ideal of happiness. On the other hand, if "proper" means *morally* proper, the attempt to get at its nature by reference to a purely human function constitutes a begging of the question: the assumption, which begs the question, is that the human *is* the morally proper. This assumption is unwarranted. If all human beings were like other animals except that they alone had bowlegs, this would not prove that human good is bowleggedness. Goodness does not reside in whatever is distinctively human: it resides in the *part* of human nature that is intrinsically valuable, whether this part is distinctively human or not. Aristotle assumed that man *is* superior to other animals and that this superiority must lie in what man alone possesses. But it is quite possible that all of man's faculties have their evolutionary beginnings in the animal world, and that the human good is the full development and realization of these common traits.

Aristotle may be right in contending that happiness is the fullest actualization of human potentialities, but he conceived these potentialities too narrowly. Our human good is the free functioning and full development of our many-sided nature, including emotion, imagination, and will. Aristotle's rather exclusive emphasis upon reason betrays the natural bias of the philosopher. Although Confucius likewise advocated a humanistic ethics, he expressed a more inclusive and well-balanced conception of fulfillment.

In his strong emphasis upon the generic nature of man, Aristotle neglected the importance of individuality. Only in rare passages did he speak of self-realization in individualistic terms. He would probably have admitted, for example, that a person with very great musical talent should develop his special gift. But his emphasis is upon the reason that all men share, and there is too little respect for the matchless individuality that is the core of every human life.

In making these criticisms, I do not wish to disparage the value of reason. Without judgment, or practical wisdom, life would not be distinguished from madness. The main *practical* function of reason, as Aristotle realized, is to govern our feelings and appetites. If it does not do so, the human personality cannot function in a normal, satisfactory, healthful, and harmonious way. It is only when reason maintains a working harmony among our faculties, that each will interfere least with the others, and all can be developed with minimal conflict and frustration. The ultimate value of a rational harmony is that it is better for our nature to be fully rather than partially fulfilled.

The value of reason, according to Aristotle, is not merely instrumental but also intrinsic. Again and again he pointed out that the life of reason is what men are really interested in—what they fundamentally want and crave—what fully and deeply satisfies them. There is much truth in this point of view. Most men dread insanity, especially if it should be permanent. Admittedly, a person, such as a mad genius, may be remarkably rational in certain respects even though he is insane. Yet there is a radical impairment of reason in the insane person, an impairment that almost no one would choose. The explanation of this aversion surely is that rationality is one of the things we most value and the loss of rationality one of the things we most dread. Moreover, curiosity, the desire to know, is a basic human trait. It may be observed in young children, who ask innumerable questions and have an unquenchable curiosity about animals, machines, people, and such natural objects as stars and thunderstorms. Lucky is the man who retains this curiosity and whose sense of wonder develops into wide and deep intellectual interests!

Aristotle's conception of science is primarily intellectual contemplation rather than active experiment. He exalts pure rather than applied science. His point of view contrasts sharply with Francis Bacon's aphorism that "knowledge is power" and with Robert Boyle's contention that true science is such knowledge "as hath a tendency to use." It is closely connected with his contempt for physical labor and his aristocratic predilection for "the noble employment of leisure." His bias in favor of pure science is condemned by a democrat such as John Dewey, who has pointed out that it is typical of aristocrats in a slave-owning society.

In defense of Aristotle, it can be urged that the love of knowledge for its own sake is one of the great sources of happiness, and that the applications of knowledge to life have very frequently been unsatisfactory or positively mischievous. In modern times, applied science has multiplied trivial amusements, rendered much labor monotonous, made war diabolical and has produced, among other things, a vast quantity of ill-distributed and shoddy commodities. If it is to be wholly a boon to mankind, men must change their ideals and direct it to better uses.

Despite Aristotle's fine appreciation of pure science and philosophy, his outlook in certain other respects was narrow. One may scan the pages of his *Ethics* in the vain attempt to find more than a cursory mention of esthetic values. In his *Poetics*, it is true, he displayed keen insight into the qualities of great poetry, and in his *Politics* he showed some understanding of the educational function of music and other forms of art. But he ranked art far below science and philosophy, and he exhibited little awareness of the immense contribution that beauty and art can make to happiness. In his discussion of moral virtue, he was almost exclusively concerned with pointing out the value of "the golden mean." This value, however, is instrumental and relative; there is a golden mean of the villain as well as the virtuous. "Be cautious; avoid extremes; follow the mean" is a counsel of prudence and not necessarily of morality—the wicked and crafty can find it useful. The main value for a good man in observing the mean is that it promotes the harmony and hence the maximum realization of the various interests of the personality; but this value is negligible unless the interests thus harmonized are themselves rich in quality. Taken by itself, moderation makes for tameness and insipidity; it contributes greatly to happiness only when it is counterbalanced by a relish for adventure and the careless rapture of intense moments of experience. Although Aristotle discussed friendship at length, his remarks never rose above the level of common sense nor indicated any realization of the value of passion. Also he showed very little appreciation of the importance of sympathy; and like other aristocratic Greeks, he condoned slavery and regarded manual workers with considerable disdain.

As we reflect upon his ethics, we find that most of it is sensible, but that it is marred by a too-exclusive intellectualism. "The life of reason," as Santayana remarked, "will mark a real progress whenever it gives fuller expression to the interests that prompt its gropings."[17] Apart from this vital background of interests, it is too dry and abstract to speak for the human heart. No man would choose a life of mere intellectual activity devoid of feeling and satisfied desire.

4. LIFE ENHANCEMENT
IN SPINOZA'S ETHICS

A more comprehensive conception of human fulfillment is to be found in the ethics of Baruch Spinoza (1632–1677). Born and reared in Amsterdam where his Iberian-Jewish family had sought refuge from the Inquisition, Spinoza departed early from Jewish orthodoxy and was solemnly cursed and excommunicated by the synagogue. He lived most of the remainder of his life in The Hague, eking out a living as a grinder of optical lenses. The dust from the grinding probably aggravated the tuberculosis from which he died at the age of forty-four. Living a studious and austere life, he left an estate of priceless value for mankind—the manuscript of his *Ethics*.

To discuss and criticize fully his ethical doctrines would require a searching examination of the metaphysical system of which his ethics is a part. For reasons of space and emphasis this is here impossible, and we shall therefore note only some of the main tenets of his metaphysics. Having defined God as a being utterly infinite, Spinoza sought to prove that God is the sum and system of all that exists. Everything is logically derivative from the whole, and it is what it is because of the nature of the totality. God and nature are one and the same, and a particular man is a finite mode of this single reality. Although infinite in an infinite number of ways, God manifests Himself to man only in thought and matter. The human mind-body is a completely determined expression of the cosmic being, and the belief in free will arises only from ignorance of the causes that determine us. Man's good is to understand his position in nature and to accept this role.

The essence of every human being is a *conatus* or volitional drive, a propensity for self-conservation and self-enhancement, an urge to increase the plenitude of his being. When related to the mind alone, it is called "will"; when related to both the mind and the body, it is called "appetite"; and when a man is conscious of his appetite, it is called "desire." Volition, so interpreted, is the basis of all our evaluations: "We neither strive for, wish, seek, nor desire anything because we think it to be good, but, on the contrary, we adjudge a thing to be good because we strive for, wish, seek, or desire it."[18] Thus, good springs from desire and not desire from good.

Since man's basic urge is life enhancement, to be good means to facilitate human powers. "A thing is called by us good or evil," Spinoza declared, "as it increases or diminishes, helps or restrains, our power of action."[19] Thus he built his ethics upon the distinction between descending and ascending life. The ethical problem is to make the transition to heightened vitality—to become more and more energized, projective, alive, and integrated—because triumphant vitality is what we fundamentally desire.

Spinoza interpreted this doctrine in terms of his theory of mind-body identity. He maintained that "the mind and the body are one and the same thing, conceived at one time under the attribute of thought, and at another under that of extension. . . . Consequently the order of the actions and passions of our body is coincident in nature with the order of the actions and passions of the mind."[20] Viewed on its physical side the *conatus* is the tendency of the physical organism to maintain its equilibrium and to increase the physical energies within its system. On the psychical side, it is the tendency of the human mind to maintain its characteristic unity and to heighten its joy and intellectual mastery.

The fulfillment of appetite, desire, and will has its accompaniment of thought. Intellectually, it means replacing muddle and confusion with order and rational arrangement by an ascent through three levels of knowledge. The first level is *imagination,* which includes both sensation and imagery: it gives us separate, fragmentary, superficial glimpses of reality. It fails to grasp the true order of causes in nature, and leaves men the victims of illusion and error. *Reason,* or the second level, is more adequate: it gives us science; its effect is to facilitate and to unify our understanding. Mathematics in general, and geometry in particular, is the science Spinoza chiefly admired, and he expected that physics and psychology would eventually attain to the beautiful rigor and harmony of Euclid's geometry. No one has ever believed more fervently than he that the truth will make us free. But intellectual mastery is not attained until we reach the third kind of knowledge, *intuition,* an "intellectual vision" that starts with the whole of things in order to understand the part, since the part is implicated in the whole. At this level, the certainty and necessity of scientific demonstration unite with a concrete, immediate, spiritual sense of the whole. At the summit of his intellectual development, man grasps the unity of the whole of being: he achieves his health and freedom by living consciously as a whole man within a cosmic all-embracing whole.

Keeping pace with the fulfillment of desire and the widening of thought is the transformation of our emotional life, a transition from passive to active emotions. A passive emotion is localized, disengaged, unfused with the personality as a whole—a mere response to external forces dominating us—not an expression of individuality and integrity, not the result of organic fulfillment. Such passive emotions include panic fears, overmastering loves and hates and jealousies, and every immoderate passion. They correspond to the confused and inadequate ideas of the first kind of knowledge: detached sensory impressions, popular opinions, conventions, and superstitions. They arise when the mind is not aware of the causes of its ideas and when it is consequently the victim of external forces. In contrast, the active emotions spring from the integral expression of the whole man, and are correlated with reason and intuition. Insofar as the mind has adequate ideas, it experiences active emotions; and insofar as it has inadequate ideas, it necessarily suffers. Human freedom, in the only true sense, consists in the predominance of clear ideas and active emotions.

In general, pain is a sign of the depression of vitality and the frustration of *conatus,* and pleasure is a sign of organic efficiency and fulfillment. The greatest delight is not a passive response to local stimulation, such as the pleasure of scratching one's back, but the joy of total organic vitality. Although Spinoza was no mere hedonist, he was opposed to puritanical repression and relished both intellectual and sensuous pleasures.

Nothing but a gloomy and sad superstition forbids enjoyment. For why is it more seemly to extinguish hunger and thirst than to drive away melancholy? My reasons and my conclusions are these:—No God and no human being, except an envious one, is delighted by my impotence or my trouble, or esteems as any virtue in us tears, sighs, fears and other things of this kind, which are signs of mental impotence; on the contrary, the greater the joy with which we are affected, the greater the perfection to which we pass thereby, that is to say, the more do we necessarily partake of the divine nature. To make use of things, therefore, and to delight in them as much as possible (provided we do not disgust ourselves with them, which is not delighting in them), is the part of a wise man. It is the part of a wise man, I say, to refresh and invigorate himself with moderate and pleasant eating and drinking, with sweet scents and the beauty of green plants, with ornament, with music, with sports, with the theater, and with all things of this kind which one man can enjoy without hurting another.[21]

There is no such thing as an excess of happiness; but a pleasure is instrumentally bad if it hinders the activity of the mind-body as a whole, and a pain is instrumentally good if it restores the balance and harmony. Although life should be lived and enjoyed to the utmost, a particular pleasure may have to be checked and moderated by reason.

Spinoza's emphasis upon *self*-fulfillment appears egoistic, but his is a "higher egoism" that does not exclude love. By self-transcendence and identification with the human community men achieve their highest blessedness.

Above all things is it profitable to men to form communities and to unite themselves to one another by bonds which may make all of them as one man; and absolutely, it is profitable for them to do whatever may tend to strengthen their friendships.[22]

The wise man is incapable of hatred and returns good for evil.

All emotions of hatred are evil, and, therefore, the man who lives according to the guidance of reason will strive as much as possible to keep himself from being agitated by the emotions of hatred and, consequently, will strive to keep others from being subject to the same emotions. But hatred is increased by reciprocal hatred, and, on the other hand, can be extinguished by love, so that hatred passes into love. Therefore he who lives according to the guidance of reason will strive to repay the hatred of another, etc., with love, that is to say, with generosity. He who wishes to avenge injuries by hating in return does indeed live miserably. But he who, on the contrary, strives to drive out hatred by love, fights joyfully and confidently, with equal ease resisting one man or a number of men, and needing scarcely any assistance from fortune. Those whom he conquers yield gladly, not from defect of strength, but from an increase of it.[23]

Happiness depends upon the quality of the objects upon which love is fixed, and love toward the greatest of objects, God or nature, feeds the mind with a profound joy. He who loves God in this intellectual way is a free man. His life is a communion with that sublime and marvellous order that reveals itself in the world of thought. Detached from all petty concerns, he escapes the fears that beset the slave of circumstance. He grasps, so far as a mortal man can, the eternal order and necessity of things.

> For to bear all naked truths,
> And to envisage circumstance, all calm,
> That is the top of sovereignty.[24]

There is no better prophylactic against hate and misery and fanaticism.

Such was Spinoza's view of the transition from human bondage to human freedom—a transition motivated and propelled by volition, but including both intellectual and emotional fulfillment within its wide arc.

5. A BRIEF APPRAISAL OF SPINOZISTIC ETHICS

The part of Spinoza's theory that is most vulnerable to criticism is the dependence of his ethics upon his metaphysics. We can no longer accept the confident rationalism of his seventeenth-century outlook. As Santayana remarked in a famous essay:

> Nature was dominated, [Spinoza] assumed, by unquestionable scientific and dialectical principles; so that while the forces of nature might often put our bodily existence in jeopardy, they always formed a decidedly friendly and faithful object for the mind. There was no essential mystery. The human soul from her humble station might salute the eternal and the infinite with complete composure and with a certain vicarious pride. Every man had a true and adequate idea of God; and this saying, technically justified as it may be by Spinoza's definition of terms, cannot help surprising us: it reveals such a virgin sense of familiarity with the absolute.[25]

Few philosophers at the present time believe in Spinoza's doctrine of a single all-inclusive system of logically necessitated events; few would attempt to work out a deductive metaphysics, or would dismiss "free will" as meaningless nonsense. Some schools of contemporary psychiatry strongly emphasize free choice, and even physics is indeterministic. Among philosophers, an antideterminist such as Charles Peirce or William James is closer to the realities of contemporary science than Spinoza.

The ethics of Spinoza, with its basis in nature as a deterministic system, is Stoical in cast, and part of my criticism of Stoicism in Chapter I is applicable to him. But he was a greater philosophical genius than any of the Stoics, and there is profound originality and wisdom in his works. As Stuart Hampshire has pointed out, Spinoza anticipated some of the most important insights of modern dynamic psychology.[26] The unity of the psychophysical organism, one of his main tenets, is now generally accepted in psychology, psychiatry, and medicine.

I have discussed Spinoza mainly because he represents a very broad concept of self-realization. His ethics, although voluntarist in basis, involves the fulfillment of man's whole being. A man's personality has three fundamental sides or capacities: knowing, feeling, and striving—or, in more academic language, cognition, affection, and volition. For Spinoza, human welfare consists in the fulfillment of all these capacities, and in addition, he recognizes the importance of physical and subconscious and low conscious levels in the healthful functioning of the human organism. His is a broader concept than the intellectualism of Aristotle. Although Spinoza was more rationalistic and less empirical in his idea of method than Aristotle, he had a more ample interpretation of the human organism and its well-being. His ideas were likewise more adequate than, for example, the voluntarism of Nietzsche and Schopenhauer. For Schopenhauer, will is the captain, reason is the obedient steersman: will determines the ends sought, reason merely discovers or invents the means. Nietzsche maintained that the will to power is the fundamental driving force of life; and that it not only is, but ought to be, the ruling faculty within the personality. He exalted, above all other types, the strong, proud, self-assertive, domineering aristocrat, whose ideal is to master and exploit—not the happy man, not the man of reason, not the man of love. Spinoza, in contrast, believed that no ethics is adequate that slights the values of feeling and thought. He was a realist in emphasizing the interrelatedness of mental functions.

6. THE FREUDIAN IMAGE OF MAN

Between Spinoza and Freud there is a considerable leap in time but a narrower leap in doctrine. Among the basic ideas that the two men held in common are the following: the conception of man as part of nature and governed by nature's laws; the rejection of mind-body dualism and the ethics of asceticism; the belief that free will is an illusion, and that real freedom can be based only on knowledge; the idea that mental activity extends far below the level of consciousness; and the recognition of an instinctive drive toward life-preservation and life-enhancement (the conatus of Spinoza, the libido of Freud).

Sigmund Freud (1856–1939) was, like Spinoza, a heterodox Jew with the courage and independence of the ancient Jewish prophets. Studying medicine at the University of Vienna, he became interested in the structure of nerve cells and the treatment of neuroses. In 1885 he went to Paris, where he investigated hysteria and the effects of hypnosis under Jean Charcot, the great French neurologist. After his return to Vienna, he spent years in clinical work with mental patients, using his own techniques of free association of ideas and dream interpretation. With a daring and speculative turn of mind, he gathered about him a brilliant group of intellectuals, who formed the nucleus of the psychoanalytical movement. In 1938 he escaped from the Nazis and fled to London, where he died, after a brave bout with cancer of the jaw, a year later. By the time of his death, his name had become a household word. No other thinker of the twentieth century has had such a profound impact upon laymen and learned alike. Although he was not a philosopher, almost every branch of philosophy has felt his influence.

The key Freudian concepts are such common intellectual coinage nowadays that they scarcely need explanation. But it may help to see Freudian theory afresh if we regard it as primarily a reinterpretation of the great ethical concepts of Western civilization—*hubris*, self-knowledge, catharsis, Eros, polarity, and self-realization.

One of the main themes of classical tragedy is the danger of that over-weening human pride and arrogance that the Greeks called *hubris*. Closely related is the idea of self-love, as symbolized by the myth of Narcissus, who fell in love with his own image in a pool. Ideas of this sort reappear in the Christian doctrine that "pride goeth before a fall." Conceit is not confined to the individual—mankind has beguiled itself with inflated estimates of its own cosmic importance.

Freud describes how human pride and self-love has suffered three severe blows from the researches of science. Originally, man believed that his earthly abode was the center of the whole universe. This geocentric view was finally demolished by Copernicus and other Renaissance scientists. The self-love of mankind suffered its first great blow, the *cosmological* one. Still puffed up with pride, man conceived himself as set apart from the entire animal kingdom, having been created separately by God. But the researches of Charles Darwin and other biologists destroyed this illusion, and dealt the second, the *biological,* blow to human narcissism. Humbled in his external relations, man still took pride in self-mastery. His highest faculty, reason, was sovereign over his appetites and instincts. By direct introspection, he could know himself, and by critical intelligence, sensibly guide the course of his life. But psychoanalysts—Freud first and foremost—have revealed how shallow is this view. The two great discoveries of psychoanalysis—"that the life of our sexual instincts cannot be wholly tamed, and that mental proc-esses are in themselves unconscious and only reach the ego and come under its control through incomplete and untrustworthy perceptions—these two discoveries amount to the statement that *the ego is not master in its own house.*"[27] Together they constitute the third, the *psychological,* blow to man's conceit and self-love.

Freud believed that true humility lies in science, not in religion. The re-ligions of the world belong in the category of dreams or fantasies. They correspond to the childhood of the human mind, being dramatizations, on a cosmic plane, of the child's relation to his parents. God has been invented by the human imagination to satisfy the craving for an authoritative father-image. We should grow up, put away such childish illusions, and trust to science.

The attainment of intellectual maturity requires, above all, self-knowledge. Freud revived the ancient Greek injunction, "Know thyself." Like a modern Socrates, he undertook to search his own mind and the minds of his fellows in an attempt to discover the essence of man and the means to his fulfill-ment. But he interpreted self-discovery in a radical new way: "Know thy *hidden* self," he enjoined, for that is the real self. Gone is the old simple account of man's mind as governed by conscious thought and deliberate pur-pose: the hidden portion, the well of the unconscious, is by far the greater part of the psyche. Freud tried to explore these depths with the the help of the "free association" of ideas, a method of encouraging the patient to recall, in random fashion, his long-forgotten experiences; by the analysis of verbal slips and other inadvertent mistakes that betray what is going on in the unconscious; by the interpretation of dreams, myths, and other works of the imagination; and by the analysis of neurotic symptoms.

The human personality is seen to have a threefold structure, represented by three Latin terms, "id," "ego," and "superego." The id is the bearer of the libido, the energy of the life-preservative instincts, of which sex is the dynamic core. This part of the self is called the id (Latin for "it") because we regard its manifestations as foreign to ourselves—as when we say, "That was not what I meant," or "I was carried away by my emotions." The id is the most unruly and irrational part of the psyche: it knows no values, no good or evil; it is unmoral, illogical; it has immense driving power but no unity of purpose, no conscious intent. Arising from the id, but never completely differentiated, is a second part of the personality—the "ego" (Latin for "I"). This is the more conscious self, concerned with the perception of outer reality, and one's adjustment to it. The function of the ego is not only to regulate itself but to curb and discipline the id. There is an almost constant struggle between the repressive force of the ego—which Freud calls the "censor"—and the wishes seething in the unconscious. To circumvent the censor, the wishes assume various disguises, such as dream symbols or neurotic symptoms. The superego, as its name implies, is a kind of "higher self" imposed on the conscious ego. It is the seat of our deeply ingrained ideals and moral standards, which have been built up in the individual mainly during early childhood, and have become so habitual as to be largely unconscious. The censor acts mainly at the behest of the superego, whose demands are more archaic and severe than those of the conscious ego. Hence the normal person is not only far more immoral than he believes (referring to the naughty repressed wishes in the unconscious id), but also far more straightlaced than he realizes (referring to the unconscious scruples in the superego).

In this analysis, Freud reverses the popular conception of evil. Mephistopheles, in folk legends, is depicted as having a very definite shape and set of characteristics, with horns, a tail, a pitchfork, and a quaint, ironical sense of humor. For Freud, on the contrary, the devil appears an an all-enveloping fog, without definite lineaments. He is dangerous and oppressive because he is so cloudy. As soon as we can give him a true and authentic form, we can cast him out. The therapeutic function of art, as Freud divined, is to give evil an imaginative form, whereby the mind is purged of its vague terrors. "Art," as Picasso said, "is a lie that reveals." The therapeutic function of psychoanalysis is more severe—it is to expose the naked truth, even the most ugly and repulsive. But the devil is full of guile and wears many disguises;

it is not until these are stripped away, and he is correctly identified, that he can be cast out forever.

Freud demands an ethics of absolute honesty, which, in spirit, is the opposite of neurosis. "The neurotic turns away from reality because he finds it unbearable."[28] In repressing his wishes into the unconscious, he provides for them a hiding place, where they fester and infect the mind. The fantasies, fixations, and regressions of neurosis are the sick disguises of the unconscious.

The psychoneuroses are substitutive satisfactions of some instinct the presence of which one is obliged to deny to oneself and others. Their capacity to exist depends on this distortion and lack of recognition. When the riddle they present is solved and the solution is accepted by the patients these diseases cease to be able to exist.[29]

The remedy is to probe down beneath the layers of falsehood and fantasy to the realities of our mental life.

The process of casting out the devil was known to the ancients by the name of "catharsis." As interpreted by the Greeks, the rites and music of Bacchic festivals and the profound stirrings of tragic drama cleanse the mind through the overflow of powerful feelings. Goethe, expressing a similar thought, related in his memoirs how, when lacerated by suicidal thoughts, he resorted to the remedy of writing down his sufferings, until he could again feel free and joyful. The "talking cure" of psychoanalysis is similarly a psychic catharsis—a way of getting hidden morbidities out of one's system—but it is distinguished from Dionysian art in aiming at *clarity*, rather than merely *intensity*, of expression. But clarity alone is not enough—Freud discovered that the morbid ideas are laden with powerful emotions, and these emotions must also be brought to the surface and cast out.

The ideas and feelings that are to be purged go back to the very beginning of life. "The little human being," remarks Freud, "is frequently a finished product in his fourth or fifth year, and only gradually reveals in later years what lies buried in him."[30] This emphasis upon the crucial importance of early childhood is expressed in the famous theory of the "Oedipus complex" (named after the king in Sophocles' play who unknowingly killed his father and married his mother). Early in the child's development, its unconscious desire for sexual gratification becomes focused upon the parent of the opposite sex. The little boy falls in love with his mother, and becomes jealous of his rival, the father; the little girl similarly loves her father and is jealous of her mother. The child will unconsciously harbor incestuous desires toward the one parent, and death wishes toward the other. A "castration complex" arises late in the infancy period through fear of parental punishment. The boy is afraid that he will be castrated; the girl, disappointed over her lack of a penis and feeling as though she were a castrated male, is intensely envious. These two emotions, penis envy and castration fear, may continue to rankle in the unconscious, causing psychic disturbances in later life. Normally, the child outgrows the Oedipus and castration complexes, but the regressions, fixations, and anxieties of the adult indicate that this process of maturation is not always successful. Arrested or regressive development is the sign of mental illness, and the achievement of maturity is the sign of mental health.

It is instructive to compare Freud's ideas of the tripartite psyche and role of sex with the ideas of Plato, who likewise speaks of love and the division of the soul. In the language of the *Phaedrus,* Plato's charioteer (reason) is akin to the ego, the unruly black horse (appetite) is akin to the id, and the noble white horse (spirit) is akin to the superego. Both in this dialogue and in the *Symposium,* the instinct of love, personified as the god Eros, is depicted as the supreme motivating force of the human soul. The similarity with Freudian concepts is obvious, but there are also important differences. As Raphael Demos has pointed out:

> Both Plato and Freud agree that love is the root impulse of life; but whereas Freud would represent all idealistic impulses—such as those of religion, affection, poetry—as "sublimations" of physical desire, Plato would represent physical desire as a distorted manifestation of a spiritual impulse. If it is legitimate for Freud to go behind the apparent content of an impulse, so it is for Plato; and the question whether the "lower" or the "higher" impulses should be taken as fundamental cannot be settled except by reference to a general metaphysical standpoint.[31]

Plato thinks of reason as the source of moral judgment, whereas Freud's view is more complicated. The id is totally unmoral, the ego strives to be moral in a realistic way, and the superego is hypermoral, often in a cruelly repressive way.

During his later period, Freud concentrated more and more upon the psychology of death, and linked the hypothesis of a universal death instinct with the psychological phenomena of masochism and sadism. Using the symbolism of Greek mythology, he asserted an irreconcilable conflict between Eros, seeking to preserve and enhance life, and Thanatos, seeking to return life to death and nothingness. In *Beyond the Pleasure Principle,* he contended that this dualism infects all organic life; and in *Civilization and its Discontents,* he maintained that it is the ultimate basis of neurosis.

The notion of bipolarity permeates all of Freud's thinking and appears in other concepts than Eros and Thanatos. Earlier he had pitted the "ego instincts," preservative of the self, against the "sexual instincts," preservative of the race; also he pitted the ego against the id. In characterizing the latter polarity, he contrasted "the pleasure principle," which governs the id, and "the reality principle," which governs the ego. The pleasure principle is the tendency to strive for pleasure and the avoidance of pain; the reality principle is the tendency to adapt oneself to the requirements of the objective world. The pleasure and reality principles are both based upon the life drive, and, in this sense, they stand in opposition to the death instinct.

Freud's friends, noting the dualistic cast of his thought, jokingly declared that "he had never learned to count beyond the number two." But, far from repeating a stale and simple-minded idea, he enriched the concept of polarity by interpreting it as "ambivalence"—the simultaneity, or quick alternation, of opposite states. For example, we love and hate the same thing, we are attracted and yet repelled, we want something and yet we do not want it. The result is tension and conflict, providing the dynamics of growth and development.

From the standpoint of morality, the most significant of all dualisms is that of culture and recalcitrant human nature. The libido, driven by its "pleasure principle," is too blind and wild to harmonize with the requirements of social existence. Even more antagonistic to social order is the death instinct, with its destructive bent. Freud maintains "that men are not gentle creatures who want to be loved, and who at the most can defend themselves if they are attacked; they are, on the contrary, creatures among whose instinctual endowments are to be reckoned a powerful share of aggression."[32] To make civilization possible, the ego and superego have been forced to erect powerful barriers against the libidinal and aggressive instincts. One result is that society has so narrowed the range of erotic satisfaction that the sexual life has been seriously disabled. ". . . The life of present-day civilized peoples leaves no room for the simple natural love of two human beings."[33] A second result is that the death instinct, thwarted in its primary expressions, is "internalized" as self-hatred, thus heightening the sense of sin and guilt. In consequence, "some civilizations, or some epochs of civilization—possibly the whole of mankind—have become 'neurotic.' "[34] Even at this great cost, civilization has not succeeded in quelling the Old Adam. "The primitive, savage and evil impulses of mankind have not vanished in any individual, but continue their existence, although in a repressed state . . . and . . . wait for opportunities to display their activity."[35] Military atrocities, such as the horrible sack of Jerusalem by the medieval Crusaders, or the hyperbolic wars of the twentieth century, confirm this view of man.

Despite the seemingly pessimistic tenor of his argument, Freud holds out considerable hope for human betterment.

We may expect gradually to carry through such alterations in our civilization as will better satisfy our needs and will escape our criticisms. But perhaps we may also familiarize ourselves with the idea that there are difficulties attaching to the nature of civilization which will not yield to any attempt at reform.[36]

Because evils, when comprehended, lose half their sting, an understanding of the limits of reform is itself a powerful defense.

Science, directed not only toward the exploration of mind and culture but also toward the mastery of external nature, offers the greatest hope for mankind:

Against the dreaded external world one can only defend oneself by some kind of turning away from it, if one intends to solve the task by oneself. There is, indeed, another and better path: that of becoming a member of the human community, and, with the help of a technique guided by science, going over to the attack against nature and subjecting her to the human will. Then one is working with all for the good of all.[37]

Admitting that mankind craves an "enemy," Freud proposes that we should direct our enmity against the evils of our human estate. Mankind should unite in the scientific war against ignorance, poverty, disease, and oppression.

This directing of a drive or instinct, which may otherwise have an undesirable outlet, to a less primitive and culturally higher expression, Freud calls "sublimation." It is the normal modification of impulses not adapted to social needs and realities. If not overly repressive, it is a healthy and constructive way of dealing with harmful impulses. Aggressive drives may be sublimated in this manner, as, for example, in competitive sports, or in the imaginative wish fulfillment of art and literature.

But sublimation, Freud believes, seldom results in complete satisfaction: there are residual tensions that are partly responsible for the nervousness of civilized man. The cure may be a more direct satisfaction of instinct. Freud is convinced that modern society is overly repressive, imposing unnecessary amounts of instinctual renunciation. "Psychoanalysis . . . proposes that there should be a reduction in the strictness with which instincts are repressed."[38] Child rearing, for example, should be based upon love and understanding, with more use of rewards and less use of punishments, and with frank sexual enlightenment of children. "From the very beginning everything sexual should be treated like everything else that is worth knowing about."[39] Parents should avoid creating the impression in the child's mind that anything and everything connected with sex is despicable and abhorrent. There should also be more natural and spontaneous sexual relations among adults. In a more puritanical generation than our own, Freud defended the values of free and joyous relations between the sexes. He did not mean that we should renounce all control over our instincts, but rather that we should steer "between the Scylla of giving the instincts free play and the Charybdis of frustrating them."[40]

He spoke of "far-reaching modifications" that our contemporary civilization will have to undergo if people are "to live in accordance with psychological truth."[41] Although he did not explain in detail what modifications he had in mind, he insisted that life must be enhanced and transformed by love:

The fateful question of the human species seems to me to be whether and to what extent their cultural development will succeed in mastering the disturbance of their communal life caused by the human instinct of aggression and self-destruction. . . . Men have gained control over the forces of nature to such an extent that with their help they would have no difficulty exterminating one another to the last man. They know this, and hence comes a large part of their current unrest, their unhappiness and their mood of anxiety. And now it is to be expected that the other of the two "Heavenly Powers," eternal Eros, will make an effort to assert himself in the struggle with his equally immortal adversary.[42]

7. SOME CRITICAL REMARKS ABOUT THE FREUDIAN THEORY

The ethical significance of Freudian psychology is to be found primarily in its dynamic character. As Gardner Murphy has said, its most general proposition is "that all psychological activity is motivated, driven, guided, directed by life tensions seeking resolution. . . . Every idle fancy, every quick calculation, every odd remark, every whim and every great decision alike spring basically from the tensions of the tissues within us."[43] This means that life is not lived for ends external to man. Life is a process: its motion is forward: its driving power comes from the wishes that are in us. It is a short step from this dynamic view of the human personality to an ethical conclusion. We shall live well if, instead of suppressing these wishes, we find ways to minimize their destructive impact and to maximize their fulfillment. Such is clearly the intent of Freudian therapy.

This intent is in accord with the humanism of the natural-law tradition. The end of any creature, according to Marcus Aurelius, "is in that towards which it is carried; and where the end is, there also is the advantage and the good of each thing."[44] A similar thought was recently expressed by Philip Blair Rice: "All living beings are loaded and cocked when they come into existence. . . . It is of their nature that men—not to mention children—are trying to go somewhere."[45] Hence normativeness is part of the very make-up of the human animal; it is this "vectorial character of existence" that provides a natural basis for ethics. Or to quote D. W. Gotshalk: "The life of the individual . . . is a field of activity with a telic structure, and its principle of value, furnishing its standard for judging items, is embedded in it. Indeed, its principle of value is simply its telic or purpose structure, conceived as developed congenially and effectively."[46]

The implication is that ethical theory should be based upon psychological insight. As the knowledge of human nature is deepened and clarified, our understanding of good and evil will be correspondingly enriched. This does not mean that we should reduce ethics to a kind of descriptive psychology. The distinction between facts and norms will remain; we will first discover what man *is* and then decide what he ought to become. Like bees gathering honey, we will take from real things their sweetest essences and thus construct the honeycomb of our ideals. It follows from this point of view that any hope for a renascence of ethics lies in an interdisciplinary cooperation between philosophy and psychology. But since real man, ethical man, is the person *in relation to his fellows,* the nature of the social order must enter heavily into the reckoning.

One issue that is fundamental to the logic of inquiry is whether Freud is too reductionist in his explanations of human behavior. The psychoanalyst may argue, for example, that the scientific urge to know and understand the world is "nothing but" a deviate of sexual curiosity. This kind of explanation tends to be not only too simple but too generalized. Freud, to take another example, finds the Oedipus complex almost ubiquitous in the life of the child, and its effects almost everywhere in the life of the adult. "With boys the wish to beget a child from their mother is never absent," he declares, "with girls the wish to have a child by their father is equally constant."[47] He then tries to make this wish the key to a great many psychological riddles.

How could one verify such a sweeping generalization? How useful would it be even if it could be verified? The scientific value of this sort of proposition is questioned by C. D. Broad:

Suppose we are told that a taste for music is due to suppressed sexual desire or to Dr. Ernest Jones's family pet, "infantile anal-erotic sensations." What is the precise cash-value of such a statement? It cannot mean that this is a *sufficient* condition of a taste for music, since the psychoanalyst would be the first to assure us that suppressed sexual desire can exist in people who show no taste for music but an excessive fondness for pet animals. Thus other factors must be needed to account for the taste for music in one person and the mania for keeping cats in the other. And these other factors will plainly be the more characteristic cause-factors, since the suppressed sexual desire is supposed to be the *common* condition of *both,* whilst the other factors determine *which of the two* shall result. So the most that can be said is that the suppressed sexual desire is a *necessary* condition of a taste for music. Now it is obvious that the more different states the psychoanalyst ascribes to suppressed sexual desire the more trivial his statement becomes about any one of them. If this desire be a necessary condition of fifty different tastes, accomplishments, diseases, and crotchets, it is of extremely little interest to say of any one of them that it is "due to" suppressed sexual desire. It is about as useful to say that committing a murder is "due to" being born. This is true, since you could not commit a murder without being born. But it is not very interesting or important, since it is equally true that being born is a necessary condition of saving another man's life at the risk of your own.[48]

My impression is that a good deal of Freud's reasoning is subject to Broad's criticism.

What is partly at stake in the Freudian type of explanation is the nature and importance of human instincts. Freud would trace the dynamics of human behavior back to instinctive bases—hunger, the libido, the death instinct. We may understand by the word "instinct" a specific and fixed reaction pattern that is determined by the congenital structure of the species (such as the automatic tendency of the human eyelid to close when the eye is threatened by a moving object). Most of the behavior of insects, but comparatively little of the behavior of human beings, can be explained in terms of these specific reactions. But Freud, using the word "instinct" in a different way, refers to biological needs or drives, such as hunger. Just as hunger shows itself in unrest and seeking, leading finally to action which brings the unrest to a close, so the sexual instinct arouses unrest and tension, driving the organism toward sexual fulfillment and quiescence.

It is characteristic of the instinctive reaction patterns of insects that they can be modified by learning only to a minor degree; but human biological needs, such as sex, hunger, thirst, and sleep, are influenced by learning to a much greater extent. That men possess certain needs is a biological fact, but the manner in which they satisfy these needs is a *social* fact. Men biologically need a place to sleep and protection from the cold and the rain, but the varied forms of shelter, with all their artistic elaborations, are the creation of human culture. Men likewise instinctively need sexual fulfillment, but the varied forms of love, with all their romantic embellishments and institutional expressions, are the products of culture. There is a tendency in Freud to overrate the biological factors and to underrate the cultural, or to seek, reductively, to derive the latter from the former.

This tendency is most clear in the case of the "death instinct." That man has an "instinct" to kill and destroy, as Freud maintains, is a proposition that needs to be very carefully analyzed. The researches of Walter B. Cannon demonstrate that aggression is accompanied by bodily changes, such as the secretion of adrenalin and the increase of blood pressure.[49] It would be naive to leap to the conclusion that these bodily changes, as somehow instinctive, are the *cause* of the aggression. On the contrary, emotions such as fear and rage, which motivate aggressive behavior, are responses to the environment. They serve the function of emotional reinforcement, injecting fresh energy into a drive that may otherwise be insufficient for its task. Except when neurosis has deranged these primary functions, rage and fear generally serve useful purposes, summoning the reserve energies of the organism to meet *real* dangers or obstacles. The bodily changes investigated by Cannon are the physical aspects of this process of reinforcement.

If this be the correct analysis, the use of the term "death instinct" by Freud is extremely misleading. The word "instinct" suggests that the tendency to destroy, as in the case of war, is fixed and underivative, that the most we can hope to accomplish is to sublimate it. The fact is that fear and rage spring from conditions of frustration and insecurity. Hence we can expect them to be excessive during crises of insecurity and frustration, such as in afflicted Germany during the period of Hitler's rise and ascendancy. This is exactly what we find. Extensive researches, such as the University of California Public Opinion Study of prejudice, bear out the theory that aggressive impulses spring from insecurity, surplus repression, and the obstacles to human fulfillment.[50] Hate, far from being an innate tendency to destruction, is a reaction to environmental situations in which some basic value is threatened or obstructed. In developing the concept of a death instinct, Freud is putting the psychological cart in front of the sociological horse. This mistake has led him to be quite unnecessarily pessimistic about human nature.

His error in method is to seek to reduce virtually all social phenomena to a psychological basis. He explains war largely in terms of instinctive aggression, religion in terms of father fixation, the state in terms of instinct repression, and so forth. This is to underestimate or neglect the vast influence of cultural factors and institutional molds. Man has indeed an original biological nature, but this nature is transformed by society and culture. There emerges a kind of second human nature: cultural man is superimposed upon biological man. As a result, human beings do not express merely raw biological drives such as hunger and sex; they express innumerable social ways of feeling, culturally acquired needs, tastes, and ideas. Language, for example, is a product of human culture; without language men would be utterly different than they are. Mature arts and sciences, the educational and technological resources of civilization, provide means of remolding human existence in a quite radical way. Even the human body and its biological make-up can be profoundly altered by nutritional advances and disease elimination, or by eugenics and birth control. We can thus speak of the creation of new human environments and even new human natures; we can look forward to the realization of human potentialities that can today hardly be glimpsed.

Freud, of course, was keenly aware of certain cultural factors, especially the depth and subtlety of the family's influence upon the growing child. But his attitude toward culture tends to be adverse. He sees very clearly its repressive force, but has little confidence in its regenerative power. He underestimates the extent to which it can reconstitute human nature, creating new needs, drives, capacities. He also fails to realize the extent to which human actions are explicable in terms of the social situations in which they occur. As Karl Popper has declared, the psychological part of the explanation may be trivial as compared with the detailed determination of the action by what we may call the logic of the situation.[51]

The remedy for the one-sidedness in Freud is not to emphasize cultural factors exclusively. This sort of cultural determinism is not only as lopsided as biological determinism—it leads into the morass of extreme cultural relativism, with its nihilistic and totalitarian implications. If we are to have some independent basis for criticizing totalitarian systems, we must find an objective touchstone for judging social orders, and the only touchstone that exists is *nature*—above all, the rock-bottom nature of man. As Lionel Trilling has said:

> Now Freud may be right or he may be wrong in the place he gives to biology in human fate, but I think we must stop to consider whether this emphasis on biology, whether correct or incorrect, is not so far from being a reactionary idea that it is actually a liberating idea. It proposes to us that culture is not all-powerful. It suggests that there is a residue of human quality beyond the reach of cultural

control, and that this residue of human quality, elemental as it may be, serves to bring culture itself under criticism and keeps it from being absolute. . . . Somewhere in the child, somewhere in the adult, there is a hard, irreducible, stubborn core of biological urgency, and biological necessity, and biological *reason,* which culture cannot reach and which reserves the right, which sooner or later it will exercise, to judge the culture and resist and revise it.[52]

To conclude, I find much in Freud to question, but I do not doubt the greatness of his achievement. Is his analysis of human motivation too narrow? Does his theory do justice to the more enlightened and less authoritarian aspects of the human conscience? To the meaning of love? To the values of religion and art? Does he rely too exclusively upon science for the redemption of man? To what extent is it possible to verify his doctrines? These and other questions will linger in the mind of the critical reader. But no one can study his works without feeling the impact of a genius. Such books as *The Interpretation of Dreams* and *The Psychopathology of Everyday Life* are wonderful representations, if not entirely cogent explanations, of "the labyrinthine ways" of the human mind. As students of ethics, we have good reason to cherish the humanistic insights that abound in his pages.

We have now reviewed a number of "human-nature theories"—Confucian, Aristotelian, Spinozistic, Freudian—as a basis for ethics. Before we leave this type of theory, we should note its connection with the next two chapters. There are, as we have previously noted, three main sides of the human personality, the cognitive, the affective, and the volitional. In Confucianism these three sides are not clearly differentiated, although there is considerable emphasis upon intellectual and aesthetic development. The cognitive side is strongly reflected in the ethics of Aristotle; the volitional in the ethics of Spinoza, although the other sides are by no means neglected in his theory. The affective has characteristically found expression in hedonistic psychology and ethics, such as we find in the works of Jeremy Bentham. There is both a hedonistic and a volitional emphasis in the psychology of Freud. From the very beginning of life, he declares, the human organism aims at pleasure and the avoidance of pain. But "wish" is an even more fundamental concept in the Freudian system than "the pleasure principle." The role of pleasure in the good life will be examined in Chapter III, and wish or desire, as it finds expression in the "interest theory," will be the subject of Chapter IV.

NOTES

1. *The Great Learning* (translated by James Legge). *The Chinese Classics.* Hong Kong: Hong Kong University Press, 1960, I, p. 359.
2. Confucius, *Analects* (XI, 25), in *ibid.,* p. 248.
3. Lin Yutang, *The Wisdom of China and India.* New York: Random House, Inc., 1942, p. 833 (*Analects,* III, 3).
4. *Ibid.,* p. 838.
5. *Analects* (Legge), op. cit. (I, 4), p. 139.

6. *Ibid.* (XV, 25), p. 301.

7. *The Doctrine of the Mean*, in *ibid.*, p. 394.

8. Lin Yutang, *op. cit.*, p. 571 (*Analects*, XII, 13).

9. L. A. Lyall, *The Sayings of Confucius*. New York: David McKay Company, Inc., 1935, p. 4 (*Analects*, II, 3).

10. Lao-Tse, *The Book of Tao*, LX, in Lin Yutang, *op. cit.*, p. 614.

11. *Analects* (Legge), *op. cit.* (XIV, 36), p. 288.

12. *Ibid.* (XI, 15), p. 242.

13. *Ibid.* (XI, 9), p. 240.

14. Aristotle, *The Nicomachean Ethics* (translated by F. H. Peters). London: Kegan Paul, Trench, Trübner & Co., 1891, II, 2.

15. *Ibid.*, II, 6.

16. *Ibid.*, X, 7.

17. George Santayana, *The Life of Reason*. New York: Charles Scribner's Sons, 1927, Vol. I, p. x.

18. Benedict Spinoza, *Ethics* (translated by W. Hale White and Amelia H. Stirling). London and New York: Oxford University Press, 1930, p. 116.

19. *Ibid.*, p. 186.

20. *Ibid.*, p. 108.

21. *Ibid.*, pp. 217–218.

22. *Ibid.*, p. 243.

23. *Ibid.*, pp. 218–219.

24. John Keats, "Hyperion."

25. George Santayana, "Ultimate Religion," in *The Works of George Santayana*. New York: Charles Scribner's Sons, 1937, vol. X, p. 246.

26. *Cf.*, Stuart Hampshire, *Spinoza*. Harmondsworth: Penguin Books, 1951, pp. 141–144.

27. Sigmund Freud, "A Difficulty in the Path of Psychoanalysis," *The Complete Psychological Works of Sigmund Freud*. London: Hogarth Press, Ltd., 1953–1962, XVII, pp. 140–141.

28. Freud, "Formulations Regarding the Two Principles in Mental Functioning," *Collected Papers*. London: Hogarth Press, Ltd., 1948–1950, IV, p. 13.

29. Freud, "The Future Prospects of Psychoanalytic Therapy," *The Complete Psychological Works of Sigmund Freud, op. cit.*, XI, p. 148.

30. Freud, *Introductory Lectures on Psychoanalysis*. London: George Allen & Unwin Ltd., 1919, p. 298.

31. Raphael Demos, *Plato: Selections*. New York: Charles Scribner's Sons, 1927, p. xxiii.

32. Freud, *Civilization and Its Discontents* in *The Complete Psychological Works of Sigmund Freud*. (Standard Edition, edited by James Strachey). London: Hogarth Press, Ltd., 1961; New York: W. W. Norton & Co., Inc., 1962, Vol. XXI, p. 111.

33. *Ibid.*, p. 105.

34. *Ibid.*, p. 144.

35. Freud, Letter of December 28, 1914, in Ernest Jones, *The Life and Work of Sigmund Freud*. New York: Basic Books, Inc., 1955, II, pp. 368–369.

36. Freud, *Civilization and Its Discontents, op. cit.*, p. 66.

37. *Ibid.*, p. 18.

38. Freud, *Collected Papers, op. cit.*, V, p. 171.

39. Freud, "The Sexual Enlightenment of Children" (1907), quoted by Stanley Edgar Hyman, *The Tangled Bank*. New York: Atheneum Publishers, 1962, p. 350.

40. Freud, *New Introductory Lectures on Psychoanalysis*. London: Hogarth Press, Ltd., 1933, pp. 191–192.

41. Freud, "Thoughts for the Times on War and Death," *Collected Papers, op. cit.*, IV, p. 300.

42. Freud, *Civilization and Its Discontents, op. cit.*, p. 145.

43. Gardner Murphy, "The Current Impact of Freud on American Psychology," in Benjamin Nelson (editor), *Freud and the Twentieth Century*. Cleveland: The World Publishing Company, 1957, p. 105.

44. Marcus Aurelius, *Meditations*, in Whitney J. Oates (editor), *The Stoic and Epicurean Philosophers*. New York: Random House, Inc., 1940, p. 521.

45. Philip Blair Rice, *On the Knowledge of Good and Evil*. New York: Random House, Inc., 1955, pp. 178–179.

46. D. W. Gotshalk, *Patterns of Good and Evil*. Urbana: University of Illinois Press, 1963, p. 127.

47. Sigmund Freud, *Collected Papers, op. cit.*, II, p. 182.

48. C. D. Broad, *The Mind and Its Place in Nature*. London: Routledge & Kegan Paul Ltd., 1925, pp. 13–14. For similar criticism, see the discussion of the "Atavistic Fallacy" in Ralph Barton Perry, *Realms of Value*. Cambridge, Mass.: Harvard University Press, 1954, pp. 22–24, 27.

49. See Walter B. Cannon, *Bodily Changes in Pain, Hunger, Fear and Rage*. New York: Appleton-Century-Crofts, 1929.

50. See the summary of this and similar studies in Jerome Himelhoch, "Is There a Bigot Personality?" *Commentary*, vol. 3 (March 1947), pp. 277–284.

51. See Karl Popper, *The Open Society and Its Enemies*. Princeton: Princeton University Press, 1950, Chapter 14, especially pp. 289–290.

52. Lionel Trilling, *Freud and the Crisis of Our Culture*. Boston: The Beacon Press, 1955, pp. 48, 54.

CHAPTER III

Enjoyment

I. INTRODUCTORY COMMENTS

In considering the foundation of ethics in human nature, we have distinguished between affective and volitional theories—the first being represented by hedonism, the second by the "interest theory." We shall examine the argument for hedonism in the present chapter. According to the hedonistic doctrine, *pleasure,* and this alone, has positive ultimate value; *displeasure,* and this alone, has negative ultimate value. The intrinsic value or disvalue of anything else, such as intellectual activity or esthetic experience, is to be found solely in the pleasures or displeasures they contain.

Historically, hedonism has been associated with utilitarianism. The most prominent hedonists in modern times, such as Bentham and Mill, have been both hedonists and utilitarians. The movement to which they have been attached has generally been called "utilitarianism," interpreted as a doctrine about the nature of good as well as a doctrine about the nature of right. So defined, utilitarianism is the view that the right act, among all the acts open to the agent, is that which will produce the maximum quantity of pleasure and the minimum quantity of pain or displeasure. This usage is misleading, since it does not clearly distinguish between utilitarianism and hedonism.

As I use the term "utilitarianism," it designates a theory about the nature of right. It states that the right must be determined in the light of good consequences—*whatever the good may be.* The good as conceived by the utilitarian might be pleasure, or the fulfillment of desire, or the actualization of potentialities, or almost anything else. The theory is thus logically independent of any particular interpretation of good, such as hedonism. Bentham and Mill misleadingly speak as if the test of consequences is necessarily linked to the sole end of pleasure; but this is manifestly not the case. Hastings Rashdall and G. E. Moore, for example, have combined the utilitarian principle that ethics is teleological with a nonhedonistic interpretation of the ethical end. In the present chapter, the emphasis will be upon hedonism as a theory of good; in Chapter VII, on utilitarianism as a theory of right.

Hedonism has flourished from the time of Democritus (*circa* 460–362 B.C.) until the present day. In the early part of the fourth century B.C., Aristippus of Cyrene, a pupil of Socrates, founded a school of hedonism which maintained that the pleasure of the moment is alone worthy of consideration. Epicurus, who went to Athens in 306 B.C., established a far more famous school of hedonism, which flourished for nearly nine centuries. Unlike Aristippus, whose motto was, "Eat, drink, and be merry, for tomorrow we die," Epicurus believed that pleasure and the avoidance of pain could best be attained by a simple, austere, intellectual life, in which more emphasis is put upon the avoidance of evil than the attainment of good. Typical of his viewpoint are these words from one of his letters:

By pleasure we mean the absence of pain in the body and of trouble in the soul. It is not an unbroken succession of drinking-bouts and of revelry, not sexual love, not the enjoyment of the fish and other delicacies of a luxurious table, which produce a pleasant life; it is sober reasoning, searching out the grounds of every choice and avoidance, and banishing those beliefs through which the greatest tumults take possession of the soul.[1]

In the Middle Ages, hedonism suffered an eclipse, but it reappeared with the revival of classical learning in the Renaissance. In England, where it enjoyed its greatest vogue, it was represented in various degrees and in divers manners by a great succession of philosophers, including Thomas Hobbes, John Locke, David Hume, Jeremy Bentham, James Mill, John Stuart Mill, and Henry Sidgwick. It is less widely held today than it was in the nineteenth century, but it has been represented in this century by men of great ability, and it still requires a hearing.

2. THE QUANTITATIVE HEDONISM OF BENTHAM

Some of the authors I have mentioned, such as Locke and Hume, were not altogether committed to hedonism. For our present purpose, it is best to select as an example a hedonist of a more consistent type. None is more important or typical than Jeremy Bentham (1748–1832).

He was born into a well-to-do London family and enjoyed the advantages of a good education and an independent income. As a very precocious lad, he entered Oxford University at the age of twelve and graduated at the age of fifteen. His father, an attorney, prescribed the study of Blackstone, the leading teacher of jurisprudence. But Bentham was shocked by Blackstone's praise of the British legal system, and devoted his acute mind to exposing its faults and abuses. Encountering Hume's *Treatise of Human Nature* at an early age, he felt as if scales had fallen from his eyes and the truth had been revealed. He decided that "utility was the test and measure of all virtue," and formulated the hedonistic and utilitarian philosophy that he espoused all the rest of his life. Among his innumerable projects were prison reform, prevention of cruelty to animals, establishment of savings banks, invention of an international language, and the emancipation of women. In politics, he became the leader of an influential group known as the Radicals, and his ideas greatly influenced the political and social development of Europe. Among his voluminous writings, *An Introduction to the Principles of Morals and Legislation* (1789) is the most important source of his ethical doctrine. I shall now expound his main theories, inserting a few critical comments.

His Basic Hedonism. The keynote to his philosophy was struck in the opening sentences of his book:

> Nature has placed mankind under the governance of two sovereign masters, *pain* and *pleasure*. It is for them alone to point out what we ought to do, as well as to determine what we shall do. On the one hand the standard of right and wrong, on the other hand the chain of causes and effects, are fastened to their throne.[2]

Bentham is here stating two quite distinct doctrines, one psychological and the other ethical. The psychological doctrine states that every man is so constituted that he always seeks his own pleasure, or the avoidance of his own pain, in every action. The ethical doctrine states that happiness, consisting in the maximum surplus of pleasure over pain, is the sole standard of welfare and the goal of right action. The first doctrine is called psychological hedonism. It is formulated by Bentham as follows:

> On the occasion of every act he exercises, every human being is led to pursue that line of conduct which, according to his view of the case, taken by him at the moment, will be in the highest degree contributory to his own greatest happiness.[3]

The second doctrine is called ethical hedonism. It maintains that pleasure always is good for its own sake, and that nothing else is ever good for its own sake. Similarly pain, and nothing else, is bad for its own sake. Bentham believed that ethical hedonism is the only sensible basis of morals, but he admitted that it cannot be proved.

The two doctrines, psychological hedonism and ethical hedonism, are logically quite separate. Bentham believed that ethical hedonism rests upon psychological hedonism: that pleasure must be good because it is always desired; but it is possible that something may be good even though it is not desired, and desired even though it is not good. Indeed, in recent years psychological hedonism has been almost universally rejected by psychologists and philosophers, whereas ethical hedonism is still widely maintained. Moreover, if we agree with the psychological hedonist that each man *must*, by the compulsion of his nature, pursue his own pleasure, we cannot logically agree with the ethical hedonist that he *ought* to pursue pleasure. He has no obligation to aim at what he cannot aim at (the good of others), and he also has no obligation to aim at what he cannot help but aim at (his own good). "Ought," as Kant maintained, implies free choice, not necessity. Hence there is a logical incompatibility between psychological and ethical hedonism.

Bentham has formulated ethical hedonism inaccurately. The real opposite of pleasure is not pain, as he maintains, but displeasure. Pain is usually displeasurable, but it may be pleasant. A youngster with a loose tooth, for example, may put his tongue to his tooth and wiggle it, finding pleasure in the interesting painful sensation that he thus derives. The masochist's enjoyment of pain is a well-known psychological fact. As the psychologist Edward Titchener remarks: "Pain . . . is a sensation, and it is a sensation that at different intensities and under different circumstances, may be pleasant, indifferent, or unpleasant."[4] Bentham should have defined "happiness" as the maximum surplus of pleasure over displeasure. This is not to deny that most pain, especially when intense, is displeasurable. (In the present chapter, I shall ordinarily use the term "pain" rather than "displeasure," since this is the practice of the writers I am discussing.)

Adverse Principles. To sharpen the meaning of his ethical theory, Bentham contrasted his hedonism with "adverse" doctrines. These he listed under two headings, "asceticism" and "sympathy and antipathy."

By the principle of asceticism, he meant "that principle, which, like the principle of utility, approves or disapproves of any action, according to the tendency which it appears to have to augment or diminish the happiness of the party whose interest is in question; but in an inverse manner: approving of actions in as far as they tend to diminish his happiness; disapproving of them in as far as they tend to augment it."[5] Bentham correctly observed that asceticism, so defined, "never was, nor ever can be consistently pursued by any living creature," for its effect would be to turn one's life "into a hell."[6]

An ascetic, whether a Hindu yoga, a Christian saint, or some other type, would object to Bentham's definition. No one has ever maintained that the end of life is to get as little pleasure and as much pain as possible. The aim of the typical ascetic is to transcend the pleasures of the flesh in order to prepare for heavenly beatitude, Nirvana, or some other state of spiritual bliss. The relevant attack upon the ascetic is not to caricature his doctrine, as Bentham does, but to criticize his dualism, the pitting of spirit against flesh. It was no sensualist who wrote, "The Word was made flesh, and dwelt among us . . . full of grace and truth."

Bentham was more successful in characterizing "the principle of sympathy and antipathy," or as he later called it, "the principle of caprice." It is, he said, a principle in name rather than in reality, the subjective reliance upon *feeling* rather than upon any objective standard of good or right. To conclude that something is good merely because it is *felt* to be good is the negation of all principle. Such reliance upon feeling, rather than upon objective calculations of pleasure and pain, leads inevitably to vagueness and caprice.

Subjectivism appears in many forms, some not easy to recognize. One man says that a thing is good or right becaues his "moral sense" tells him so; another appeals to "common sense," conveniently leaving out "the sense of those whose sense is not the same" as his own; a third will prate about "eternal and immutable principles" of right, but his feelings will dictate what principles he regards as everlasting and immutable; others invoke "the law of nature," or "natural justice," or "natural rights," but in so doing they merely reflect their own sentiments.

The dismissal of natural law as a merely subjective principle may seem peculiar, but it is one of Bentham's most strongly held positions. In his detailed criticism of Blackstone's theory of natural law, he maintained that the concept is so vague and undemonstrable that it amounts to no more than a reliance upon sentiments. His criticism of the theory of natural rights was no less withering:

> *Natural rights* is simply nonsense: natural and imprescriptable rights, rhetorical nonsense—nonsense upon stilts. . . . What is the language of reason and plain sense upon this same subject? That in proportion as it is *right* and *proper*, i.e., advantageous to the society in question, that this or that right . . . should be established and maintained, in that same proportion it is *wrong* that it should be abrogated: but as there is no *right*, which ought not to be maintained so long as it is on the whole advantageous to society that it should be maintained, so there is no right which, when the abolition of it is advantageous to society, should not be abolished.[7]

According to Bentham, the only rule of action that is unconditionally true is that which bids us maximize the surplus of pleasure over pain. Only in so far as, and as long as, "rights" and "liberties" have this effect, are they justified.

On Intentions and Motives. In rejecting the principle of sympathy and antipathy, Bentham opposed every type of ethics that puts primary stress upon motives and intentions. Apart from pleasure or pain, what a person intends, or what motivates him, is ethically unimportant. If motives are good or bad, it is only on account of their hedonic effects. Hence no motive is "either constantly good or constantly bad."

Bentham took sharp issue with Kant. According to the latter, good will alone is unconditionally good, and pleasure is bad if combined with ill will. The pleasure of a sadist in torturing his victim is bad through and through. In contrast, Bentham declared:

> Let a man's motive be ill-will; call it even malice, envy, cruelty; it is still a kind of pleasure that is his motive: the pleasure he takes at the thought of the pain which he sees, or expects to see, his adversary undergo. Now even this wretched pleasure, taken by itself, is good: it may be faint; it may be short: it must at any rate be impure [that is to say, followed by pain]: yet while it lasts, and before any bad consequences arrive, it is as good as any other that is not more intense.[8]

Bentham does not deny that there are, in a sense, bad pleasures. The pleasures of cruelty generally produce, in the long run, an overbalance of pain—their instrumental badness outweighs their intrinsic goodness. Viewed in isolation from the consequences, however, the pleasure of the sadist is as good as any other pleasure of equal intensity and duration. Nothing but pleasure is ultimately good, and it is *always* good in itself.

Moral Arithmetic. The proper business of the legislator or moralist is to calculate the hedonic consequences of alternative acts. To do this it is necessary to know how pleasures vary in value. Bentham maintained that, apart from consequences, pleasures should be judged solely in terms of quantity. All that matters is that we should get the greatest possible amount of pleasure: not that we should get any certain *kind* of pleasure, nor that we should get it in any particular way—for "quantity of pleasure being equal, pushpin [a very simple game] is as good as poetry."[9] Quantity is determined by two factors: duration, or the length of time the pleasure lasts, and intensity, or the relative strength of the pleasure at any one moment.

If a *future* pleasure or pain is to be considered, we must add its certainty or uncertainty and its propinquity or remoteness. If, in addition, we wish to consider the *consequences* of a pleasure or pain, we must calculate two other factors: first, its "fecundity" (that is, the likelihood that the pleasure will be followed by more pleasure, or the pain by more pain), and, second, its "purity" (that is, the freedom of a pleasure from subsequent pain, and of a pain from subsequent pleasure). Finally, if we are considering an action affecting a group of individuals, we must consider the number of persons who will experience pleasure or pain.

Bentham summed up his advice in a little ditty:

> Intense, long, certain, speedy, fruitful, pure—
> Such marks in pleasures and in pains endure.
> Such pleasures seek if private be thy end:
> If it be public, let them wide extend.
> Such pains avoid whatever be thy view;
> If pains must come, let them extend to few.[10]

He proposed to calculate the worth of action in terms of all the plus values in way of pleasure and all the minus values in way of pain, subtracting the latter from the former. An act is right to the extent that it produces a total balance of pleasure over pain. Since each man seeks pleasure, vice is simply a "miscalculation," either in forecasting or in estimating the value of pleasures and pains. Virtue is correct moral arithmetic.

"The Greatest Happiness Principle." Bentham's formulation of his hedonistic doctrine was ambiguous. He originally called it "the principle of utility," but this phrasing left unspecified his hedonistic goal. To clarify his meaning,

he changed his phrasing to "the greatest happiness of the greatest number," defining happiness as the surplus of pleasure over pain. But this formula also is ambiguous. Does it mean the greatest amount of happiness among men, or the greatest number of men who are happy? In a group of one hundred people, for example, one alternative might make *all* of them happy; another alternative might make only eighty of them happy, but this happiness might be great enough to exceed the less intense or durable happiness of the entire group. Should we choose the first alternative, and sacrifice the greatest happiness to the greatest number; or should we choose the second alternative, and sacrifice the greatest number to the greatest happiness? Bentham's formula does not provide an answer, because it joins together "the greatest happiness criterion" and "the greatest number criterion," indicating no priority in the event of conflict. Apparently Bentham became aware of this ambiguity, for he came to refer to his doctrine as "the greatest happiness principle," thus avoiding the ambiguity of his earlier phrasing.

But, even so, the ambiguities were not entirely eliminated. Each person, he continued to say, should count as one, and no person as more than one. This formula can be interpreted as meaning that the pleasure of any man is as intrinsically good as the quantitatively equal pleasure of any other man. The formula can also be interpreted as meaning that a smaller amount of pleasure *equally* distributed may be morally preferable to a greater amount of pleasure *unequally* distributed. If this latter view was Bentham's real conviction, he made some exception to his greatest happiness principle and thereby deviated from strict hedonism. On this interpretation, he subordinated hedonistic considerations to a democratic sense of justice.

Egoistic Versus Universalistic Hedonism. Whether Bentham phrased his goal as "the greatest happiness," or "the greatest happiness of the greatest number," it was a social, rather than a narrowly egoistic, objective. "The greatest happiness of all those whose interest is in question," he declared, is "the right and proper, and the only right and proper and universally desirable end of human action."[11] In applying his hedonistic principle to the social order, he used highly altruistic language:

The science of which the basis has been investigated in this work can be pleasing only to elevated souls who are warmed with a passion for the public good. . . . We are here employed upon the greatest interests of humanity; the art of forming the manners and the character of nations; of raising to its highest point the security of individuals; and of deriving results equally beneficial from different forms of government. Such is the object of this science; frank and generous; asking only for light; wishing nothing exclusive; and finding no means so sure to perpetuate the benefits it confers as to share them with the whole family of nations.[12]

At the same time, Bentham avowed that each person necessarily pursues his own happiness as an end, and that "the constantly proper end of action on the part of any individual at the moment of action is his real greatest happiness from that moment to the end of his life."[13] He scoffed at the "illusory" view that men are unselfish:

Dream not that men will move their little finger to serve you, unless their advantage in doing so is obvious to them. Men never did so, and never will. . . . But they will desire to serve you, when by so doing they can serve themselves.[14]

It would appear that Bentham inconsistently combined an altruistic ethical point of view with an egoistic psychological hedonism.

In his *Deontology*, he tried to resolve the conflict by insisting that the individual's true interest is always to act in a way most conducive to the general happiness of the community.[15] There is, he argued, a natural coincidence of duty and self-interest; even within "altruistic" motives we can detect self-regard, if we are searching enough in our analysis. The enlightened egoist says to himself, "Be benevolent, behave charitably," realizing that altruism serves his own interests directly or indirectly.

Nevertheless, Bentham did not propose to leave the conjunction of benevolence and prudence entirely to chance. In order "to join interest with duty and that by the strongest cement,"[16] he advocated the establishment of sanctions in the form of rewards and punishments. A sanction, as he defined it, is some force or power or inducement that tends to make a person conclude that his own greatest happiness coincides with the greatest happiness of others. Punishment or reward at the hands of public opinion constitutes the "popular" sanction; at the hands of the state, it is the "legal" or "political" sanction; at the hands of God, it is the "divine" sanction; at the "hands" of nature, through causes independent of human agency, it is the "physical" or "natural" sanction. The divine and natural sanctions cannot be controlled by the judge, legislator, or moralist, but the other sanctions can, and Bentham proposed ingenious methods of perfecting them. The end he had in view, whether in rewarding or punishing, was always to increase pleasure and diminish pain.

3. THE QUALITATIVE HEDONISM OF MILL

The ethics of John Stuart Mill (1806–1873) grew out of the philosophical problems and perplexities created by Bentham. The latter was an intimate friend of the Mill family, and the young John was thoroughly indoctrinated in his philosophy. If teaching could entirely determine a person's convictions, Mill should have grown up to be the perfect Benthamite, but his own bent was too strong to be curbed.

John was the son of James Mill, himself a philosopher and the principal disciple of Bentham. Under his father's tutelage, the boy received an astonishing education. He learned Greek at the age of three; Latin, algebra, and geometry at the age of eight; logic at twelve; and political economy at thir-teen. By the time he was nine, he had read the whole of Herodotus, two books by Xenophon, much of Diogenes Laertius, and six dialogues of Plato— all in the original Greek! This education was capped by a complete indoctri-nation in Benthamism. The effect was tragic as well as amazing. As Mill later wrote to Carlyle:

> I, a schoolboy, fresh from the logic school, had never conversed with a reality, never seen one, knew not what manner of thing it was, had only spun, first other people's and then my own deductions from assumed premises.[17]

In his twenty-first year, Mill fell into a profound nervous depression, evi-dently caused by his unnatural childhood. He finally emerged from his mental crisis a changed man. Through his suffering, he had gained a deeper appreciation of the value of poetry, especially Wordsworth's, and a conviction of Bentham's inadequacy as man and thinker. He later commented on the shortcomings of Bentham:

> In many of the most natural and strongest feelings of human nature he had no sympathy; from many of its graver experiences he was altogether cut off; and the faculty by which one mind understands a mind different from itself, and throws itself into the feelings of that other mind, was denied him by his deficiency of imagination. . . . He never knew prosperity and adversity, passion nor satiety. . . . His own lot was cast in a generation of the leanest and barrenest men whom England had yet produced.[18]

Although not intentionally, the comment is generally applicable to his father, James Mill.

At the susceptible age of twenty-four, John fell deeply in love with Harriet Taylor, the beautiful and cultivated wife of a London merchant. Their Platonic love lasted for many years, until the death of Mr. Taylor enabled them to marry in 1851. After seven happy years of wedlock Harriet suddenly died of bronchitis. Her death, said Mill, was "the most unexpected and bitter calamity" that he ever experienced.

From an early age, he had worked in the East India Company, where he was employed for thirty-five years, rising to the highest post in his depart-ment. This employment permitted considerable leisure, and he devoted it to philosophical research and writing. In his latter years, he became the acknowl-edged spokesman for liberalism, serving a term in parliament. Among his most important books, *Utilitarianism* (1863) is the chief source of his ethics. I shall now briefly summarize its tenets.

The Goal of Happiness. Up to a point Mill agreed with Bentham. "Nothing is a good to human beings," he declared, "but in so far as it is either itself pleasureable or a means of attaining pleasure or averting pain."[19] The happi-ness that is the end of life is not "the agent's own greatest happiness, but the greatest amount of happiness altogether." When Mill worked out the implications of Bentham's quantitative hedonism, however, it led to a conclusion from which he recoiled.

To illustrate the issue at stake, let us suppose that a highly cultivated human being should encounter a death-dealing alligator. Which should survive, man or alligator? It is quite possible that a comfortable and long-lived alligator would experience in the normal course of life more pleasure and less pain than would the human being. Judged by Bentham's quantitative standard, the alligator's life would be intrinsically more precious. The human dimensions of living—knowledge, beauty, love, and moral character—would count for nothing apart from pleasure. Mill was dissatisfied with this view and introduced a new criterion, which he called *quality* of pleasure. He maintained that the higher quality of a cultivated man's pleasure outweighs the greater quantity of a beast's or a moron's pleasure. When he reflected, he was convinced that there is a dignity and manifoldness in human nature that are ignored in Bentham's quantitative measure for all value.

Almost everyone, he contended, would prefer to be a wise man than a fool, even if the fool finds life more pleasant, and almost no one would choose to be changed into a lower animal even for the fullest allowance of a beast's pleasures. Nevertheless, Mill tried to rescue hedonism by his distinction between quantity and quality of pleasure, and by an emphasis upon quality:

> It would be absurd that while, in estimating all other things, quality is to be considered as well as quantity, the estimation of pleasures should be supposed to depend on quantity alone. If I am asked, what I mean by difference of quality in pleasures, or what makes one pleasure more valuable than another merely as a pleasure, except its being greater in amount, there is but one possible answer. Of two pleasures, if there be one to which all or almost all who have experience of both give a decided preference, irrespective of any feeling of moral obligation to prefer it, that is the more desirable pleasure. If one of the two is, by those who are competently acquainted with both, placed so far above the other that they prefer it, even though knowing it to be attended with a greater amount of discontent, and would not resign it for any amount of the other pleasure which their nature is capable of, we are justified in ascribing to the preferred enjoyment a superiority in quality, so far outweighing quantity as to render it, in comparison, of small account.[20]

Mill went so far as to argue that there are pleasures so qualitatively superior as to outweigh any quantity of inferior pleasures. This is preeminently true of the pleasures connected with the higher human faculties, the intellect, the esthetic imagination, the moral will, and the capacity for spiritual friendship.

The test of superior quality, as the above quotation indicates, is the well-considered preference of those best acquainted with the qualities being compared. The wise man, with a broader range of experience and a greater capacity for introspective analysis, is better able to discriminate and judge the qualities of pleasure than is a more limited type of being.

And if the fool, or the pig, are of a different opinion, it is because they only know their own side of the question. The other party to the comparison knows both sides. . . . From this verdict of the only competent judges, I apprehend there can be no appeal.[21]

To sum up, the ultimate goal of life "is an existence exempt as far as possible from pain, and as rich as possible in enjoyments, both in point of quantity and quality; the test of quality and the rule for measuring it against quantity being the preference felt by those who, in their opportunities of experience, to which must be added their habits of self-consciousness and self-observation, are best furnished with the means of comparison."[22]

The Question of Proof. In the first chapter of *Utilitarianism,* Mill declared that, strictly speaking, no proof of ultimate goodness is possible. "Questions of ultimate ends," he declared, "are not amenable to direct proof. Whatever can be proved to be good, must be so by being shown to be a means to something admitted to be good without proof."[23] This contention was reinforced by remarks in the final chapter of Mill's *Logic.* There he distinguished between ethics as an "art" (analogous to "the art of medicine") and science as descriptive of matters of fact.

Now, the imperative mood is the characteristic of art, as distinguished from science. Whatever speaks in rules or precepts, not in assertions respecting matters of fact, is art; and ethics, or morality, is properly a portion of the art corresponding to the sciences of human nature and society.[24]

Like Hare and a number of present-day philosophers, Mill contended that the art of ethics is essentially prescriptive, being concerned with the "ought" as an imperative. He clearly distinguished the "ought" of prescription from the "is" of description. "A proposition of which the predicate is expressed by the words *ought* or *should be,*" he pointed out, "is generically different from one expressed by is or will be."[25] Good, in the sense of what ought to be, and right, in the sense of what ought to be done, are therefore not provable by the inductive methods of empirical science. As an empiricist, Mill likewise rejected the possibility of any deductive justification. Hence the proof of ultimate ethical principles, in the ordinary meaning of "proof," is impossible.

This position was not essentially different from that of Bentham, who declared:

Is [the principle of utility] susceptible of any direct proof? It should seem not: for that which is used to prove everything else, cannot itself be proved: a chain of proofs must have their commencement somewhere. To give such proof is as impossible as it is needless.[26]

Bentham also distinguished ethical hedonism, as a standard to judge the "ought," from psychological hedonism, as a description of "causes and effects." Neither Mill nor Bentham committed "the factualist fallacy" of reducing the "ought" of prescription to the "is" of description.

But they were not satisfied with leaving the question of justification at this point. Bentham argued that the motive of attaining happiness is the only one that makes sense, contending that hedonism, and it alone of all ethical theories, squares with our common-sense moral judgments, and sets up a goal which, by the basic law of human motivation, is sought by all people. Psychological hedonism, as he interpreted it, does not *prove* but strongly *supports* ethical hedonism. Similarly Mill maintained that his ethics squares with the actual motives of human beings.[27]

Having remarked that questions of ultimate ends do not admit of proof, Mill nevertheless contended that a persuasive argument can be given. Unfortunately his language was careless, and it has exposed him to the charge of committing some egregious fallacies:

> The only proof capable of being given that an object is visible, is that people actually see it. The only proof that a sound is audible, is that people hear it: and so of the other sources of our experience. In like manner, I apprehend, the sole evidence it is possible to produce that anything is desirable, is that people do actually desire it.[28]

Mill went on to argue, in the spirit of psychological hedonism, that all men desire what they think will be pleasant and nothing else. Hence ethical hedonism is justifiable by the test of psychological realism; it squares with the actual desires of human beings as no other ethical theory does.

The criticism of Mill's argument turns upon the peculiarities of his language. The analogy in the above quotation between the visible and the desirable is said to be misleading. "Visible" means "capable of being seen"; and from the fact that something *is* seen, it really does follow that it is visible. But "desirable," in its *ethical* import, does not mean "capable of being desired"—it means *"worthy* of being desired." From the mere fact that I desire something it does not follow that it is worth desiring, any more than, from the mere fact that I see something, it follows that it is worth seeing. Mill's argument seems to depend upon the failure to distinguish between two meanings of "desirable"—the psychological meaning, "capable of being desired," and the ethical meaning, "worthy of being desired." When we make this distinction, the argument is seen to be fallacious.

This interpretation is not a necessary one. Assuming the truth of psychological hedonism (as both Mill and Bentham do), it follows that hedonism is the only ethical doctrine that men *actually* practice. It would be foolish, Mill is implying, to reject the one doctrine that squares with the psychological realities of men's behavior in favor of some doctrine that no one ever followed outside of the philosopher's ivory tower. The analogy with "visible" is indeed misleading, but at least it ties meaning to psychological facts, the point that Mill was trying to emphasize.

The next step in his argument appears obviously fallacious:

> The sole evidence . . . that anything is desirable is that people do actually desire it. . . . No reason can be given why the general happiness is desirable ex-

cept that each person . . . desires his own happiness. . . . This, however, being a fact, we have . . . all the proof . . . which it is possible to require, that happiness is a good: that each person's happiness is a good to that person, and the general happiness, therefore, a good to the aggregate of all persons.[29]

We have already noted the ambiguity of the word "desirable," and it would appear that Mill is here trading upon this ambiguity. But there is an additional fallacy. Since each person desires *his own* happiness, Mill concludes that the *general happiness* is desired by all. Now it may be true that all men desire the general happiness in the sense that each and every one desires his own happiness, but it does not follow that all men desire the general happiness in the sense that each desires the happiness of himself and of all others. As Professor Thomas E. Hill has remarked, this "is like saying that because each child in a family wants a stick of candy for himself, all of them want all the others to have one. Any observant parent knows that this is not so."[30]

But it may be that we are again misinterpreting Mill. Commenting on this passage in a letter, he remarked:

When I said that the general happiness is a good to the aggregate of all persons I did not mean that every human being's happiness is a good to every other human being. . . . I merely meant . . . to argue that since A's happiness is a good, B's is a good, C's is a good, etc., the sum of all these goods must be a good.[31]

If we grant that goods can be added, and that the additive sum of goods is "a good," then there would be nothing fallacious in the argument as interpreted in Mill's letter.

Yet the argument seems to involve more than this. It seems to be an attempt to infer *universalistic* ethical hedonism from *egoistic* psychological hedonism. If so, the argument is invalid, for we cannot leap from the proposition that each man's happiness is desired by him to the proposition that every man wishes to promote, or should promote, the happiness of the community. On the contrary, it would follow from the premise that no one can desire anything but his own happiness, that he can *not* desire the happiness of the community at large. So far as Mill accepts Bentham's egoistic psychological hedonism—and this he here appears to do—he has no sound basis for his own ethical universalism.

The Question of Motives. At times, Mill seems to be arguing from wider premises than psychological hedonism. In an early essay, he had criticized Bentham's theory of "the springs of action":

Man is never recognized by him as a being capable of pursuing spiritual perfection as an end; of desiring, for its own sake, the conformity of his own character to his standard of excellence, without hope of good or fear of evil, from other source than his own inward consciousness.[32]

It is difficult to see what either psychological or ethical hedonism has to do with this selfless pursuit of spiritual perfection. Mill elsewhere admitted nonhedonistic motives, for example, when he spoke of "the desire to be in unity with our fellow men" as a "powerful natural sentiment" that tends to become stronger as civilization advances.[33] In his *Autobiography,* he recognized impersonal interests in other things than pleasure, and he even recommended these self-transcending interests as the secret of happiness "for the great majority of mankind":

Those only are happy (I thought) who have their minds fixed on some object other than their own happiness. . . . Ask yourself whether you are happy, and you cease to be so. . . . Treat not happiness, but some end external to it, as the purpose of life. . . . And if otherwise fortunately circumstanced you will inhale happiness with the air you breathe.[34]

This contention, that the way to *get* happiness is to *forget* it, expresses a profound truth (known as "the hedonistic paradox"), but it does not accord with psychological hedonism.

In his interpretation of human motives, Mill was dissatisfied with Bentham's doctrine that virtue is only a means to an end outside itself. He pointed out that the hedonists "place virtue at the very head of the things that are good as means to the ultimate end," but he also claimed that virtue becomes a part of the end itself. A practice initially adopted as a means by association with the end of pleasure may itself become pleasant and desired as an end. Virtue, according to Mill, is a good of this description.

There was no original desire of it, or motive to it, save its conduciveness to pleasure, and especially to protection from pain. But through the association thus formed, it may be felt to be a good in itself, and desired with as great intensity as any other good.[35]

Mill is expressing an important truth, that a practice initially adopted as a means may come eventually to acquire intrinsic value. But the truth as he expresses it is not wholly consistent with hedonism. However strongly associated with pleasure, virtue has an essence of its own, and it is impossible for a consistent hedonist to consider it good for its own sake. Furthermore, one may question whether there is *never* an original desire for virtue, or motive to it, save its conduciveness to pleasure or absence of pain. Both Mill's conception of human motivation and his ethical ideal are too broad to be supported by the narrow foundation of psychological hedonism.

4. A CRITICAL COMPARISON OF BENTHAM AND MILL

Mill and Bentham differed about a number of very fundamental questions. This divergence points to some of the most important issues in the whole field of ethics.

The Question of Psychological Hedonism. Both philosophers espoused psychological hedonism, Bentham more consistently than Mill. Even though psychological hedonism is not wholly false, the truth is on the side of Mill's revision, except that the revision is not drastic enough.

That men frequently desire pleasure no one can deny. For example, a person may yearn for the pleasure of sexual love; in fact, he likes many kinds of pleasure. The anticipated pleasantness of the gratification of a desire does not always explain the desire (which, as in the case of sex, may have various physiological and psychological causes), but it can greatly add to its strength and durability, and the pleasure, once aroused, may *then* become the object of a desire to prolong or renew it. But it would be a mistake to maintain, as the psychological hedonist does, that pleasure, or the avoidance of displeasure, is the *sole* object of liking or desire. Actually, there is much more that people desire, such as knowledge, security, honor, or power.

To suppose that pleasure alone is *always* the object of desire is the result of a confusion of thought—the failure to distinguish between the desire for pleasure and the pleasure of fulfilled desire. I always get some pleasure from realization of my desire, but this does not mean that the pleasure is necessarily the object of my desire. Because pleasure arises when we get what we want, we mistakenly suppose that it is pleasure alone that we want. For example, when I am lonely, I desire companionship, and when I satisfy this desire, I get pleasure. But the craving for companionship comes first, and the pleasure is a *consequence* of the satisfaction of this craving rather than the object of the craving. Actually, we often forget all pleasure, and strive for other things; and, as Mill noted, we are very apt to obtain more pleasure if we do forget it. The secret of happiness is the power of impersonal interests, such as selfless devotion to a cause or absorption in creative work, to lift men out of their petty personal concerns and thereby make them happy.

Bishop Joseph Butler (1692–1752), in a famous criticism of psychological hedonism, distinguished between a man's "general desire for his own happiness," and "a variety of particular affections, passions, and appetites to external objects." The object of the "general desire" is one's own enjoyment, but this is not true of the particular wants. They are directed outwardly toward things, not inwardly toward feeling. A person often concentrates upon the external object for which he has a particular appetite, thinking not at all about any effect upon himself.

That all particular appetites and passions are toward *external things themselves*, distinct from the *pleasure arising from them*, is manifested from hence: that there could not be this pleasure, were it not for that prior suitableness between the object and the passion: there could be no enjoyment or delight from one thing more than another, from eating food more than from swallowing a stone, if there were not an affection or appetite to one thing more than another.[36]

Most current philosophers and psychologists agree with Butler that many of our desires are for objective things or processes, the effect upon ourselves not being the end in view.

The psychological hedonist might reply by invoking the theory of unconscious motivation. Even when a person appears unconcerned with pleasure, he may be unconsciously motivated by hedonic impulses. A husband who is cruel toward his wife, for example, may not seek pleasure *consciously*, but still be motivated *unconsciously* by sadistic delight. Even in this amended version, psychological hedonism is not tenable. The whole theory of what happens at the unconscious level is notoriously slippery, and it provides no firm ground for psychological hedonism. In *Beyond the Pleasure Principle* Freud contends that there are some actions that are not done, consciously or unconsciously, for the sake of pleasure. Most non-Freudians are even less inclined to stress the unconscious desire for pleasure.

I would not deny that there is a close relation between pleasure and the satisfaction of desire. As my former teacher, William Savery, tersely noted:

A realization of a desire, as such, is pleasant. . . . A failure to realize a desire, as such, is unpleasant. A pleasant experience is accompanied or followed by a desire to retain it if possible, and on occasion to renew it. An unpleasant experience is accompanied or followed by a desire to remove it, and on occasion to avoid a similar unpleasant experience.[37]

However, the psychological hedonist has gone too far. All too easily he has slid from the true proposition, that the fulfillment of desire brings pleasure, to the false proposition, that pleasure or pain-avoidance is *all* that we ever desire. In general, enjoyment is *not* a goal; it is a feeling that accompanies on-going activity; pleasure is dependent on function. As W. B. Wolfe declares:

If you observe a really happy man you will find him building a boat, writing a symphony, educating his son, growing double dahlias in his garden, or looking for dinosaur eggs in the Gobi Desert. He will not be searching for happiness as if it were a collar button that has rolled under a radiator. He will not be striving for it as a goal in itself.[38]

Quantities versus Qualities of Pleasure. Mill's qualitative hedonism is more adequate but less consistent and, in some respects, less correct than Bentham's pure quantitative hedonism. In the first place, it is questionable if pleasures, taken by themselves, differ in kind or quality. An authority in the field, Edward Titchener, in his *Textbook on Psychology,* denies that there are any such differences. He suggests that the apparent difference in kind is really a difference, not in the pleasures themselves but in the very different *contents* of consciousness that have the common property of pleasing. According to this interpretation, the pleasure of swimming in the ocean is no different qualitatively than the pleasure of reading a book by the fire; but otherwise the two experiences differ greatly.

On the other hand, it is questionable if we can thus sharply separate the pleasure from the content to which it is attached. "Pure pleasure," it would seem, is an unreal abstraction. No doubt we can mentally abstract the pleasantness of an experience, but what we can thus *consider* separately is, in fact, not separated. What occurs in real life is pleasant experience and not bare pleasure. We never find pleasures "flocking all alone"; we find them as constituents of emotions, or intertwined with desires, or fused with ideas, images, or sensations. Such pleasant experiences do have qualitative differences. There is a difference in quality, for example, between the pleasant experiences of listening to a symphony, of playing a fast game of tennis, of reading a philosophical argument, of wriggling one's toes while sun-bathing. The feelings involved in each experience are subtly interfused with the total content. As Felix Krueger, an eminent German psychologist, has written:

> Never are the differentiable parts or sides of real experience as isolated from one another as the parts of physical substance, i.e., its molecules or its atoms. All things that we can differentiate there, by comparison, always grip into one another and around one another in the greatest elaboration. And every time it is, without exception, imbedded within a total whole, by which it is penetrated and more or less completely enclosed. Feelings are the qualities of experiences of this total-whole.[39]

If by a pleasure is meant not a pleasure abstracted from all content but a pleasant state of experience, then Mill was right in maintaining that pleasures differ in kind. This is because the experience contains more than pleasure and the pleasure is fused with the other constituents of the experience. Mill's language inadvertently bears witness to these facts. He speaks, for example, of the greater "dignity" or "intellectuality" of the pleasures that he prefers. This implies that not only is pleasure good, but also the dignity or intellectuality that serves to differentiate one pleasant experience from another. Mill appears to be advocating hedonism, but he is really maintaining, albeit unclearly and inconsistently, that the good is the *pleasant development* of the personality. His view, a kind of synthesis of hedonism and self-realizationism, is no more like that of Bentham than like that of Aristotle. In his essay *On Liberty* Mill quoted approvingly the statement of a German philosopher, Wilhelm von Humboldt, that "the end of man . . . is the highest and most harmonious development of his powers to a complete and consistent whole."[40] This doctrine, not mere hedonism, represents his basic conviction. For reasons that I shall state later, his view is more adequate, although less consistent, then unadulterated hedonism.

The Question of the Hedonistic Calculus. Bentham believed the legislator or moralist should calculate the hedonic effects of alternative acts. This entails the "moral arithmetic" or quantitative assessment of pleasures and pains already described. By abandoning quantitative hedonism, Mill greatly restricted the applicability of this hedonistic calculus. His final test is the preference, not of the pig or the fool or the average man, but of the moral connoisseur or wise man.

This clash of doctrine raises a number of questions. Is it possible to measure pleasures and pains? Is intensity of pleasure commensurable with its duration? Is pain commensurable with pleasure? Is the preference of the wise a better guide than quantitative assessment?

There are inescapable difficulties in Bentham's calculus. Although we can sometimes measure the duration of pleasure by means of a clock, intensities of pleasure resist precise calculation. There is no unit of intensity which goes six times into one pleasure and ten times into another. Also, it is impossible to judge precisely when the greater intensity of one pleasure is offset by the greater duration of another. No one can exactly balance pleasures against pains, judging precisely the net gain or loss when we subtract the latter from the former. As John Dewey remarked, "How can one weigh the amount of pain in a jumping and long-continued toothache against, say, the pleasure of some charitable deed?"[41]

The hedonist can reply that similar difficulties beset any teleological theory of ethics. Every teleological system, even if nonhedonistic, holds that *some* alternatives are better than others, that some yield more and others less good. In all these systems, estimation of good is necessary, and it is no less difficult to determine, for example, the quantity of "satisfaction of desire," or the degree of "self-realization," or the extent of "interest-fulfillment," than to estimate the amount of pleasure. It is likewise difficult to forecast the future and to calculate probabilities—but again this difficulty applies not only to hedonism. The plain fact is that moral choice is often very difficult and exact determination impossible.

This does not mean that we cannot make rough-and-ready comparisons. As Walter Stace has written:

Even if you cannot measure pleasures and pains, this does not prevent you from knowing that some pleasures or pains are greater than others. A man does not need a thermometer to know that he is being frozen to death or boiled alive. And without any such instrument he can detect the difference between a hot day and a cold one. So too a man knows that some pains are terrible, some slight; that some pleasures are great, some small; although he cannot measure either the pleasures or the pains.[42]

Bentham may have been naive about his "moral arithmetic," but we should not leap to the opposite extreme view, that all estimations or comparisons are impossible.

Mill's qualitative criterion introduces new complications. In judging best results, we must consider not only the quantity but the quality of intrinsic goods, and somehow relate the two. Nevertheless, there is, in principle, no insuperable difficulty. If we can distinguish the good, or what ought to exist, from the good-making properties of pleasureable experience, we can hold that the amount of good depends on the quality as well as on the quantity of these properties. The question, Who is an expert connoisseur of such qualities? may be puzzling, but no more puzzling than the parallel question, Who is an expert connoisseur of esthetic qualities? The question of quality will be further discussed later in this chapter.

There are other difficult issues raised by the clash between Bentham and Mill, such as the question of the social distribution of good and the intrinsic worth of virtue. These can best be considered in Chapter VII in connection with utilitarianism.

Most of the errors in Mill and Bentham are absent in the reformulation of Henry Sidgwick (1828–1900), the greatest hedonist of the late nineteenth century. Sidgwick rejected psychological hedonism, returned to quantitative ethical hedonism, pointed out the difficulties in Bentham's calculus, and discussed the conflict between egoistic and universalistic hedonism. The principle of hedonism, he maintained, cannot be established by induction from experience or deductive proof. We must intuit the nature of the good if we are to know it at all. It seemed self-evident to Sidgwick, when he carefully reflected, that nothing has ultimate value except experiences, and that this value is wholly determined by the pleasure and/or pain in the experience. It is this main contention, rather than the intricacies of hedonistic theory as set forth by Bentham and Mill, that we must now try to evaluate.

5. CRITICISM OF HEDONISM

Is pleasure always ultimately good (or good for its own sake), and nothing else ever ultimately good? To answer this question, we must first be sure that we understand the meaning of pleasure. If by "definition" we intend analysis into simpler parts, "pleasure" cannot be defined; but this is true of a great many unambiguous words. We all know the meaning of "yellow" even though we cannot analyze it into parts. In the same way we know the meaning of pleasure. We know that it is a feeling-state and that it is agreeable. If there is any doubt about its meaning, we can clarify it by examples. Are you fond of wine? Do you like a brisk swim? Do you enjoy dancing, music, poetry? The word "pleasure" stands for the feeling-state that all these experiences share in common.

I do not deny that there may be misunderstandings. In certain contexts, "pleasure" denotes the enjoyments of the body rather than the delights of the mind. The tendency of both sensualists and Puritans to think of pleasure as bodily accounts for the widespread denunciation of hedonism as a "pig-philosophy." But this restricted interpretation of "pleasure" is by no means necessary. Most hedonists have included enjoyments of every sort—esthetic, intellectual, moral, religious, and so forth.

It is possible to think of pleasures not only too narrowly but too abstractly. Strictly speaking, what occurs are pleasant experiences, not just bare pleasures. There is no pleasure as an entirely separate thing. It is not pleasure in the abstract that is good, but rather pleasures in the concrete—specific experiences with hedonic tones. When pleasures are understood in this way it is more plausible to argue that they vary in quality, as Mill maintained. For a pleasant experience always has specific qualities in addition to generic pleasantness. We must decide whether these qualities count in terms of ultimate value—for if we do so decide, we will have abandoned a strict and exclusive hedonism.

Many of the criticisms of hedonism are based upon confusions or mis-understandings. Ethical hedonism is neither psychological hedonism, nor egoism, nor sensualism, nor the theory that hedonic states are measureable. The hedonist does not deny that there are morally bad pleasures and morally good pains—he is quite willing to grant that the intrinsic goodness of a pleasure or the intrinsic badness of a pain may be outweighed by its consequences. He does not necessarily depreciate the values of beauty, knowledge, love, or virtue—though he thinks these values are extrinsic or, if intrinsic, reducible to their constituent pleasures. Certain other objections need not be taken seriously—as when a man says, "A constant heaven of pleasures would be intolerable boredom." Clearly boredom and pleasure are opposites, and the pleasure ceases when the boredom sets in. If all such confusions are cleared up, most of the objections to hedonism vanish.

Still we have not yet come to the nub of the question—the intuitive "moment of truth." It seemed to Sidgwick self-evident that pleasure, and nothing else that he could discover, is ultimately good. Similarly William Savery declared:

I maintain that it is self-evident that pleasure is good. I do not find it self-evident that everything good is pleasant, but I have never found anything good which was not. Nor have I ever found anything which added to the value of a good unless it increased its pleasureableness.[43]

Now I agree that no theory of ultimate goodness can be proved, and that we must ultimately rely upon a kind of critical intuition.

It goes without saying that one should be very careful in reaching the point of decision. A person should rid himself of misunderstandings, prejudices, irrelevant considerations and inadequacies in his own experience of values. He should not confuse an intuition or immediate insight with an inference or a confirmed prejudice. He should not confuse what is good as a means with what is good as an end. He should not attribute existence to unreal abstractions, such as a bare pleasure, apart from some further content. He should not overlook diverse qualities if these qualities are really present.

Insofar as possible, he should isolate the factor he regards as good to see if it is good when considered by itself or whether the good depends upon some associated factor. He should ask himself whether his supposed insights are consistent with one another, or whether inconsistencies indicate that he has made some mistake. He should check his conclusion against the judgment of other careful thinkers to reduce the likelihood of error. In the last resort, however, he must himself decide. He must reflect very carefully upon the possible ends of life, and judge what is ultimately good by whatever insight he can muster. When in such a reflective state, I disagree with the hedonist, not so much in what he includes as in what he excludes. In this respect, I think I am in accord with the reflective judgment of most of my fellowmen.

It seems to me true that sanity is one thing that men judge to be good even when they carefully reflect. There are some forms of insanity involving delusions of grandeur that are pleasant; yet most thoughtful persons would not want to go insane, even if they could be positively assured that they would thereby achieve more pleasure and less displeasure than they would otherwise experience.

There are other goods that men desire when they reflect. To determine whether this is the case, let us try a mental experiment. Imagine two worlds *equal in amount of pleasure* but otherwise different. In the first world, the only creatures that exist are just sufficiently conscious to feel pleasure, but they are not conscious of one another or of what kind of world they live in. They have no love, imagination, awareness of beauty, insight into truth, or excellence of character. In the second world, there are human beings who not only experience pleasure but achieve knowledge, love, beauty, virtue, and the full expression of human capacities. Is not the second world, though equal in amount of pleasure, more desirable than the first? Most reflective persons would probably say yes.

Or let us consider a single life. If someone could prove that a certain drug would put a man's faculties permanently to sleep except for the capacity to feel pleasure, this loss of varied human capacities would not be a matter of sheer indifference, even if the total amount of his pleasure would remain the same. In saying this, I am thinking of the *intrinsic* values of the person's life and not the instrumental values which would, of course, be reduced or eliminated.

The reply of the hedonist is that love, knowledge, beauty, and so forth, are indeed good, but good as sources of pleasure. This answer seems to me inadequate, because it is not simply desirable that one should feel pleasure, but that one should feel pleasure in certain ways and with certain accompaniments. In all of the foregoing examples, we have supposed that the less attractive alternative is equal or greater in amount of pleasure, but it lacks certain other things that men want when they reflect carefully.

The meaning of good can perhaps best be understood in contrast with evil. Let us take a familiar example from literature: the terrible moment when

Macbeth realizes the utter futility and meaninglessness and misery of his own existence. Disaster after disaster has come upon him; Lady Macbeth is dead; all his hopes and dreams lie in ruins; he knows at last that the witches have betrayed him, that defeat and death are fast approaching. With the merciless candor of despair, he then sums up the evil of life:

> Tomorrow, and tomorrow, and tomorrow,
> Creeps in this petty pace from day to day
> To the last syllable of recorded time,
> And all our yesterdays have lighted fools
> The way to dusty death. Out, out, brief candle!
> Life's but a walking shadow, a poor player
> That struts and frets his hour upon the stage
> And then is heard no more: it is a tale
> Told by an idiot, full of sound and fury,
> Signifying nothing.

What is this appalling realization of evil? It is not, as the hedonist would say, that life is simply unpleasant. The displeasure might be more intense if Macbeth had hit his thumbnail a sharp blow with a hammer, but there would have been lacking that deeper and wider realization of evil—the sense that all meaning, all dignity, all worth has dropped out of existence; the sense that life is nothing but a noisy, idiotic tale. It is in this mood, when one's life seems to be an affair of absolute inconsequence with no pattern for the intelligence, no attraction for the will, and no delight for the feelings and emotions, that a man commits suicide.

It might be objected by a hedonist that Macbeth, in mental retrospect, is realizing the evil of a great span of life, whereas a man with a crushed fingernail is experiencing only a transient displeasure, and that the relative insignificance of his displeasure is due entirely to its evanescence. However, my point is that, *at any one moment,* Macbeth is experiencing a more comprehensive and massive evil, a more pervasive soul-sickness, enveloping his whole personality and gnawing into the innermost vitals of his being. Given an equal duration and taken alone, the specific physical displeasure is less damaging because of its singleness, its peripheral and localized character, its failure to envelop all dimensions of one's being, and to strike at the soul of life's plot. A personality that is defeated in every essential respect and in its innermost nature *loathes* itself more profoundly than a personality that is injured in only one respect, as for example, hedonically.

The evil of life is better expressed by the word "depression" than by the word "pain" or "displeasure." If a person's spirit is robust enough, if his vital energies remain strong, if he still has the rewarding sense of achievement, he can stand a good deal of hedonic suffering. The morale of some men in Nazi concentration camps remained high despite a great deal of pain. But when a person experiences a total depression, when there is a complete enervation and failure of nerve, the pain or displeasure may not be so excessive, but the evil is substantial and strikes at the core of his being.

Likewise when we turn to the good of life, we need a word that is more ample in its connotations than "pleasure." "Happiness" is a more adequate term, perhaps because of its very ambiguity. As Aristotle remarked, we can agree that the good of life is happiness, but we differ as to what it means. We generally know when we are happy, but we are baffled when we are asked to define happiness. But it can be described as what we like and want in the way of immediate experience, just as unhappiness is what we dislike and do not want. What we want is activity that is free from irreconcilable conflicts and frustrations, enjoyable and emotionally gratifying, satisfying without loss of interest or satiety. "Pleasure" as the sole word to apply to such experiences will always seem inadequate to many people. So at least it seems to me for the reasons I have given.

The word "enjoyment," rather than pleasure, is less restrictive, but even this is inadequate. C. I. Lewis has pointed out the disadvantage in clinging to a single word:

> If "pleasure" or any other name is to serve as synonym for the immediately and intrinsically valuable, then it must be adequate to the wide variety of what is found directly good in life. It must cover the active and self-forgetting satisfactions as well as the passive and self-conscious ones; the sense of integrity in fronting the "unpleasant" as well as "pleasure"; the gratification in having one's own way, and also the benediction which may come to the defeated in having finished the faith. It must cover innocent satisfactions as well as those of cultivation; that which is found in consistency and also that of perversity and caprice; the enjoyment of sheer good fortune, and that which adds itself to dogged achievement. All this in addition to the whole range of the sensuously pleasing and the emotionally gratifying. And the immediately disvaluable has its equal and corresponding variety. Such immediate goods and bads are ill compressed into any single term or pair of them. . . . The variety of our adjectives of prizing is better taken as indicative than would be any one of them, which might well be too narrow.[44]

Lewis concludes that the good might best be conceived a "dimensionlike mode" or "range" of qualities.

I agree with Lewis that no single word such as "enjoyment" or "pleasure," unless we stretch its meaning unmercifully, can denote the various specific qualities that we find intrinsically good. The cardinal mistake of hedonists is to reduce all the varieties of goodness to a least common denominator assessed *only* quantitatively. Mill had a sounder impulse when he seized upon the idea of qualitatively higher and lower pleasures, but he tried to cling to hedonism and ended in inconsistency. It is better frankly to abandon hedonism, while recognizing the qualitative diversity of human goods. As W. T. Stace has written:

> Whether a particular kind of satisfaction contributes much or little to the happiness of human beings depends . . . upon its specific nature. This is no different

from saying that certain specific kinds of satisfaction contribute more to happiness than do certain other specific satisfactions; and that this is so independently of "quantities" or intensities of the several satisfactions. Satisfactions are therefore "high" or "low" by virtue of their specific natures (their qualities) and not by virtue of any quantitative aspect which they may possess.[45]

I believe that these higher and lower qualities are related to comparative fulfillments of human needs and capacities. The higher qualities are more accurately and fully expressive of our human nature, both the generic nature that all men share in common and the unique nature of each individual. This is the underlying truth of ethical humanism and its theory of natural law.

I shall express the same thought in other words. In the happiest and most successful life, there is a blend of enjoyment and achievement—achievement corresponding to the conative side of our nature, enjoyment corresponding to the affective side. The good, in the sense of the life worth living, is the *enjoyable* fulfillment and satisfaction of our deep-seated interests and desires. These desires and interests arise because we are the kind of being we are—they correspond to the main telic or purposive structure of our nature. A person's aims should be adjusted to his powers and resources—then his life will combine enjoyment and achievement, congeniality and effectiveness. We are estranged from our true selves and we are at odds with the world so long as we are living any other kind of life, for the same reason that a fish is unhappy out of water.

In asserting that the good of human life includes more than pleasure, I am not maintaining that pleasure is neutral in value. Although it is not exhaustive of intrinsic goodness, it *is* intrinsically good. When I try critically to introspect, it does not seem to me that any experience *wholly* lacking in pleasure is ever intrinsically good, even though other factors add to and heighten the value. Pleasure all by itself is not the good, but the good consists of complex states of experience which contain pleasure as an essential ingredient. Moreover, I am inclined to believe that pleasant experience is *always* intrinsically good. Kant's attempt to prove the contrary seems to me fallacious. He argued that pleasure must be combined with good will to be intrinsically good; that the pleasure taken in an act of torture, for example, is bad for its own sake. It is certainly true that pleasure of this sort is bad; but it is bad, not because it is pleasure, but because it is symptomatic of an immoral disposition and entails more evil than good. Its bad effects and accompaniments vastly outweigh its intrinsic goodness, but it is, *as pleasant*, intrinsically good. But I am not *certain* that I am right in this contention. It is possible that the pleasure is so infected through and through by its morally evil accompaniments, and so violates the deeper conative nature of man, that it is intrinsically evil.

In this chapter, we have reviewed hedonism, the most common form of the affective theory of value. We have examined, first, the doctrine of Jeremy Bentham, the most consistent of the classical hedonists, and second, the theory of John Stuart Mill, a less consistent, but in my judgment, a more adequate ethical philosopher. Pleasure, we have concluded, is not the only object of reflective desire. Men want love, beauty, knowledge, and other substantial goods, even when they carefully reflect. The answer of the hedonist, that these goods are valuable only for the sake of pleasure and pain-avoidance, seems to me untrue. The result of our study has been to confirm the conclusion of the preceding chapters, that the norm of wellbeing is the comprehensive fulfillment of the human personality. Its basis is both affective and volitional—hence I have spoken of life's goal as including the volitional as well as the affective dimension, achievement as well as enjoyment. In the interest theory, which we shall examine in the next chapter, there will be greater stress upon this volitional side.

NOTES

1. Epicurus, *Letter to Menoeceus* (Hick's translation in the Loeb Library), in Gordon H. Clark and T. V. Smith, *Readings in Ethics.* New York: Appleton-Century-Crofts, 1935, p. 91.
2. Jeremy Bentham, *An Introduction to the Principles of Morals and Legislation.* New York: Hafner Publishing Company, 1948, p. 1. (Hereafter referred to as *Introduction.*)
3. *The Works of Jeremy Bentham,* Vol. IX. Edinburgh: W. Tait, 1843, p. 5.
4. Edward Titchener, *Textbook of Psychology.* New York: The Macmillan Company, 1910, p. 227.
5. Bentham, *Introduction, op. cit.,* Ch. II, sec. 3.
6. *Ibid.,* sec. 10.
7. Bentham, *Anarchical Fallacies,* in *Works, op. cit.,* II, p. 501.
8. Bentham, *Introduction, op. cit.,* Ch. X, sec. 10 footnote.
9. Bentham, *The Rationale of Reward.* London: Hunt, 1825, p. 206.
10. Bentham, *Introduction, op. cit.,* Ch. III, sec. 12.
11. *Ibid.,* Ch. I, sec. 1 footnote.
12. Bentham, *The Theory of Legislation* (edited by C. K. Ogden). New York:

Harcourt, Brace & World, Inc., 1931, p. 472.
13. Bentham, *Memoirs,* in *Works, op. cit.,* X, p. 560.
14. Bentham, *Deontology,* in *Works, op. cit.,* II, p. 133.
15. See also Bentham, *Works, op. cit.,* X, pp. 560–561.
16. Quoted from Bentham, "Management of the Poor," 1796, p. 363, by David Baumgardt, *Bentham and the Ethics of Today.* Princeton: Princeton University Press, 1952, p. 423.
17. Quoted by Thomas Woods, *Poetry and Philosophy: A Study in the Thought of John Stuart Mill.* London: Hutchinson & Co., Ltd., 1961, p. 37.
18. John Stuart Mill, "Bentham," in *Dissertations and Discussions.* Boston: Spencer, 1865, I, pp. 378–380.
19. Mill, *Utilitarianism.* New York: E. P. Dutton & Co., Inc., 1910, p. 38.
20. *Ibid.,* pp. 7–8.
21. *Ibid.,* pp. 9–10.
22. *Ibid.,* p. 11.
23. *Ibid.,* p. 4.
24. Mill, *A System of Logic,* 8th ed. New York and London: Harper & Row, Publishers, Inc., 1904, p. 653.

25. *Ibid.*, p. 6.
26. Bentham, *Introduction, op. cit.*, I, sec. 11.
27. *Cf.*, Everett W. Hall, "The 'Proof' of Utility in Bentham and Mill," *Ethics,* vol. 60 (1949), pp. 1–18.
28. Mill, *Utilitarianism, op. cit.*, p. 32.
29. *Ibid.*, pp. 32–33.
30. Thomas E. Hill, *Ethics in Theory and Practice.* New York: Thomas Y. Crowell Company, 1956, p. 165.
31. Hugh S. R. Elliot (editor), *The Letters of John Stuart Mill.* London: Longmans, Green & Co., Ltd., 1910, II, p. 116.
32. Mill, "Bentham," *op. cit.*, pp. 384–385.
33. Mill, *Utilitarianism, op. cit.*, p. 29.
34. Mill, *Autobiography.* New York: Columbia University Press, 1924, p. 100.
35. Mill, *Utilitarianism, op. cit.*, pp. 34–35.
36. *The Works of Joseph Butler,* Vol. II. London and New York: Oxford University Press, 1897, p. 158. Criticizing Butler's doctrine, C. D. Broad, in his *Five Types of Ethical Theory,* remarks that the object of an impulse is never a static thing, but is always a *change* in the state of a person or thing. This correction does not affect Butler's argument, that many impulses are directed outwardly toward a variety of objectives, rather than inwardly towards the agent's subjective feeling.
37. William Savery, "A Defense of Hedonism," *Ethics,* vol. 45 (1934), p. 14. For an excellent discussion of the extent to which psychological hedonism is true, see Stephen C. Pepper, *Ethics.* New York: Appleton-Century-Crofts, 1960, especially pp. 77–84.
38. W. B. Wolfe, *How to Be Happy Though Human.* New York: Holt, Rinehart and Winston, Inc., 1931, pp. 5–6.
39. Felix Krueger, "The Essence of Feeling," in Martin L. Reymert (editor), *Feelings and Emotions.* Worcester, Mass.: Clark University Press, 1928, p. 67.
40. Mill, *On Liberty.* New York: E. P. Dutton & Co., Inc., 1910, p. 115.
41. John Dewey and James H. Tufts, *Ethics.* New York: Holt, Rinehart and Winston, Inc., 1908, p. 277.
42. W. T. Stace, *The Concept of Morals.* New York: The Macmillan Company, 1937, pp. 131–132.
43. William Savery, "A Defense of Hedonism," *op. cit.*, p. 14.
44. C. I. Lewis, *An Analysis of Knowledge and Valuation.* La Salle, Ill.: The Open Court Publishing Company, 1946, p. 405.
45. W. T. Stace, *The Concept of Morals, op. cit.*, p. 158.

CHAPTER IV

Interest

I. DESIRE AND INTEREST

Whereas the theories we have been considering in Chapter III emphasize pleasure, the theory now to be considered puts greater stress upon desire, not in artificial isolation from other psychological factors, but in vital connection with thought, feeling, and bodily movement. The following analysis may clarify the components in the expression and fulfillment of desire:

Impulse or Drive. Volition is the dynamic element in personality: it is impulse, drive, movement, or tendency. A living organism, whether because of instinctive or acquired characteristics, has appetitions and governing propensities—physiological drives, such as hunger, thirst, sex appetite, and the urge to rest or sleep; and psychical dispositions, such as curiosity, desire to play, interest in security, and artistic impulse. The values of our bodies and minds are primarily the fulfillments of these needs, urges, and tendencies.

Thought. If there is not to be mere blind impulse but conscious desire, thought must become aware of the impulse, or drive, and must envisage, truly or falsely, the supposed goal of the activity—either an immediate or more remote goal. In the case of hunger, for example, the eating of food is the conscious goal of the impulse. The goal may be critically scrutinized by intelligence and judged worthy or unworthy. Such an act of judgment frequently involves choice, and sometimes thoughtful reorientation of desire.

Striving. Between the inception of an impulse and its appeasement, there is usually an interval of tension, unrest, and seeking. It is often, but not invariably, accompanied by unpleasure, which is a sign of lack and restlessness. As the seeking passes over into consummation, the unpleasure and accompanying negative emotions change to pleasure and positive emotions. But sometimes, as in the case of an agreeable appetite for food, there is no painful sense of deficiency, and the phase of seeking is pleasant throughout.

Anticipation and Memory. The consummation of desire is not instantaneous: there is a foretaste of satisfaction in anticipation and an aftertaste of satisfaction in memory. Each new satisfaction may revive the memory of similar past satisfactions and may evoke the yearning for possible future renewals. As Professor DeWitt H. Parker pointed out:

> Every value contains . . . echoes out of the past, and itself provides new overtones of new values in the future. A value is a harmonic system, like a tone sounding with all its partials. Through the imaginative anticipation of satisfaction, we enjoy before we have enjoyed; through memory we enjoy after we have enjoyed; and every joy contains a before and after joy. It follows from the role played by imagination in value—by anticipation and memory—that value does not pertain to the terminus of the experience, to consummation alone, but to the entire process of desire-seeking-fulfillment.[1]

Consummation or Frustration. If the desire is consummated, the result is satisfaction; conversely, if it is frustrated, the result is dissatisfaction. Satisfaction brings relief from tension, pleasure, and positive emotions such as love and joy; dissatisfaction brings aversion, unpleasure, and negative emotions such as hate and disgust. Occasionally we fulfill a wish, but do not like the result. For instance, we may wish to taste an unfamiliar fruit, but we find, when we bite into it, that it has a bitter flavor that we do not enjoy. The bitter taste is not what we really want, and we would not seek it if we had accurate foreknowledge. Genuine consummation occurs when we are not thus disappointed.

The experience of value consists in this whole complex process of satisfying desire. As we have pointed out, it involves impulse, thought, imagination, emotion, and pleasure or unpleasure. The good is mainly the total satisfaction, with its emotional and hedonic ingredients; the evil is mainly the dissatisfaction, with its corresponding ingredients. When desire is analyzed in this inclusive way, it contains intellectual, hedonic, and emotional factors. It is only when desire is thus broadly conceived that it may properly be called the basis and content of value. Abstract desire, apart from all thought, emotion, and feeling, is unreal and is therefore not the content of value experience.

Since *desire* is very often conceived abstractly and narrowly, it is better, in indicating the psychological basis of value, to use the word "interest." This word implies an attitude of volition or striving, but it also suggests an element of feeling and does not exclude thought (note that we often speak of an intelligent interest). I shall now turn to a recent theory that interprets human fulfillment in these terms.

2. THE INTEREST THEORY OF RALPH BARTON PERRY

The most comprehensive analysis of interest as the basis of value is to be found in the works of Ralph Barton Perry (1876–1957), a distinguished Harvard philosopher. In two remarkable works, the *General Theory of Value*

(1926) and *Realms of Value* (1954), he formulates an inclusive theory of value, unifying such various domains as ethics, political theory, economics, and esthetics. An earlier work, *The Moral Economy* (1909), is devoted more exclusively to ethics, and represents a somewhat different point of view. I shall now very briefly state the interest theory as Perry construes it.

Interest is any attitude of liking or disliking, of prizing or disprizing, of preference, appreciation, or appraisal. It involves feeling, emotion, desire, will, or some similar attitude, and in Perry's version the accompanying bodily movements. To consider an example, let us suppose that we have a white rock and a black rock, and let us ask which one should be to the right of the other. Does it really matter? It does not matter to the *rocks*. They have no consciousness, no feelings, no desires, and therefore nothing that could be called an interest; and where there is no interest, there is no distinction between better and worse, or good and bad. A universe made up of nothing but rocks would be without value.

Suppose we ask some person whether the white rock should be to the right of the black, or vice versa? He might reply, "I do not care the least bit one way or the other." He would be conscious of the rocks but totally indifferent. Now suppose *all* conscious states were of this type. In a universe devoid of all but indifferent conscious states, there would be no more value than in a universe made up of unconscious objects, because in both there would not be the slightest interest.

But let us suppose that the person replies, "I like the black rock to the right of the white one. It looks better that way." He is conscious of the alternatives and is not indifferent. He likes or favors one rather than the other. Positive interest is just such a state of liking or favoring; negative interest is the opposite state of disliking or disfavoring; and both are distinguished from states of indifference. But Perry does not limit interest to *mental* factors. Influenced by behavioristic psychologists, he includes the overt actions that accompany the play of desire. "A thing," he says, "is an object of interest when its being expected induces actions looking to its realization or non-realization."[2] Expectancy triggers motor responses: these, with the bodily sets which they involve, are included in interest. In brief, interest is an act, attitude or disposition of favor or disfavor that is outwardly visible in approach or withdrawal.

The question can now be asked, *How shall we define value?* An interest, we have said, is a state distinguishable from indifference, and wherever there are interests there are values. But is the value to be identified with the *interest,* or with the *object* of interest? For example, is it my liking for an apple, or is it the apple, or some quality thereof, as the object of my liking? Perry chooses the second alternative. To the question, What is value? he answers, "any object of any interest." Or, less tersely, ". . . a thing—*anything* —has value, or is valuable, in the original and generic sense, when it is the object of an interest—any interest."[3]

The word *"anything"* is to be understood quite literally. Any object of experience, introspective or extrospective—anything whatsoever that can be perceived, conceived, or imagined in any way—a tint of pink, a twinge of pain, a dream image, or a handshake—is a value so long as it is "the object of an interest." Since we are often interested in interests, even an interest can function as an object and therefore as a value, but *qua* object and not *qua* interest. Just as Perry in no way restricts value to certain kinds of things, so he in no way restricts interest to certain kinds of favor or disfavor.

Value is a *relational* property that exists if and only if someone is interested in the object. It is interest that *confers* value upon the object. Perry accepts Spinoza's famous dictum "that in no case do we strive for, wish for, long for or desire anything because we deem it to be good, but on the other hand we deem a thing to be good, because we strive for it, wish for it, long for it, or desire it."[4] Hence it is quite mistaken to think of values as somehow present in the world before anyone is interested. "The silence of the desert is without value, until some wanderer finds it lonely and terrifying; the cataract, until some human sensibility finds it sublime, or until it is harnessed to satisfy human needs."[5] But once the interest is present, there is always a corresponding value.

Good, in its widest sense, is defined by Perry as "the character which anything derives from being the object of any positive interest; whatever is desired, liked, enjoyed, willed, or hoped for, is *thereby* good."[6] Evil, in its general meaning, is similarly the character which anything derives from being the object of a *negative* interest. But the concept of "morally good" is less broad: it is "the character imparted to objects by interests harmoniously organized."[7] Similarly, morality is "the harmonization of interests for the sake of the interests harmonized," and the good life, morally speaking, is "a condition of *harmonious* happiness—a condition in which, through the increase and cooperation of its members, all interests tend to be positive," thus conferring positive value upon their objects.[8] The essence of the moral task is the achievement of a more inclusive and harmonious integration of interests, so that impulse will no longer war with impulse, or individual with individual, or group with group.

Moral principles define the adjustment of interest to interest, for the saving of each and the strengthening of both against failure and death. Morality is only the method of carrying on the affair of life beyond a certain point of complexity. It is the method of concerted cumulative living, through which interests are brought from a doubtful condition of being tolerated by the cosmos, to a condition of security and confidence.[9]

Taken in isolation, no particular interests or values have priority over any others. It is only when the values or interests are in conflict that judgments of comparative goodness must be made.

To say that one value is better than another may mean (a) that it is the object of a more enlightened interest (since error is apt to prove harmful in the long run), or (b) that it is the object of a more intense interest, or (c) that the object is preferred to a comparable object by an interested party (as when one prefers a painting by Cézanne to one by Matisse), or (d) that the object will foster a greater number of interests. Similarly, we can say of an interest that it is better if it is (a) more enlightened, (b) more intense, (c) more preferred, or (d) more inclusive. When these criteria conflict, it is (d) the criterion of inclusiveness, that should be decisive. The most inclusive and harmonious integration of enlightened, intense, and preferred interests within a single personality produces a good life, and a similar integration of interests among the individuals in a community produces a good social order. The principal means to such an all-inclusive harmonious system of interests is enlightened love. When intelligent individuals are united by friendship or love, each tends to make the other person's interests his own, so that the several interests avoid collision and achieve mutual reinforcement. Of all forms of political organization, democracy is the friendliest.

In its fundamental meaning a democracy is a society of persons who so manage their relations and their affairs as to escape the evils of isolation, frustration, and violence, and achieve the good of living innocently and fruitfully together. It is a harmony of wills by which to achieve the maximum fulfillment of the interests of all concerned. So defined the democratic society is the ideal society, and in proportion as this ideal is achieved a society merits the name of "democracy."[10]

Admitting that democracy has never been fully realized, Perry regards it as the only political ideal that is fully consonant with the imperatives of morality.

3. AN ALTERNATIVE ANALYSIS OF INTEREST AND VALUE

Although I think Perry's theory is close to the truth, I disagree with him on several counts. I shall devote the remainder of this chapter to an alternative analysis that seems to me more nearly correct.

Perry is mistaken in supposing that the value-situation always has a twofold character: an *interest* in an object and an *object* of interest. If we are speaking of instrumental values (means to ends), there is no necessity that an interest should always be present. Before the development of organic chemistry, there were many unknown properties of food, such as vitamins, that were highly valuable to the human organism; but since no one knew about them, no one had an interest in them. There must be many factors that contribute to human health and happiness that we still know nothing about. These factors are instrumentally valuable quite apart from any interest in them.

There are also good or bad subjective attitudes without corresponding objects. We may awake in the morning with an objectless grouch: we do not as yet know *what* we are angry at but we are angry. Similarly anxiety, especially if neurotic in origin, may be a kind of free-floating state, unattached to any object. In many cases, however, psychoanalysts have discovered that there is a real subconscious object. In these cases, if we eventually pick an inoffensive thing or person upon which we focus our fear or vent our spleen, we are making a substitution and are thus sublimating the fear or anger that otherwise would be pent up. The process of sublimation, however, proves that an interest, without being completely altered, can be detached from an object and attached to another. It may thus be relatively independent of any specific object.

In analyzing the meaning of value, DeWitt Parker has pointed out that there may be desires or emotions without any corresponding objects:

It is notable . . . that there exist rare cases of value without corresponding valuable objects. One of the most interesting examples is music. When we listen to music desires are now aroused, now satisfied, but the desires are not desires *for* anything or the satisfactions, satisfactions *in* anything. The sounds heard are not the objects of these desires any more than words that express longing are the objects longed for; they are expressions, embodiments of desire, not objects of desire. In music desires are objectless; we desire, but desire nothing, and are satisfied, but satisfied over nothing. In the musical experience, there are also no explicit objectives or goals; desire has not formulated whither it is tending or what would satisfy it.[11]

Is this an adequate analysis? When we hear and remember the initial phases of a musical composition, the mind is set vibrating with expectation and desire; certain tones demand and naturally lead into other tones. Dissonances must be "resolved"; there are "upleader" or "downleader" notes which naturally lead into the tonic; and the finale may be an answer to much premonition and desire. Hence we can be said to desire what satisfactorily completes and fulfills the cravings earlier aroused; and if so, the later phases of the music may be said, in some measure, to be the *objects* of the desires evoked by the earlier phases. Yet we cannot be said to desire the *exact* tones we hear, because these particular tones are unexpected, and indeed their delightfulness depends partly upon their novelty. Music is partly an object, but partly an expression, of desire.

Let us suppose that it is merely the expression of desire and emotion. Even so, by stretching our terms a little, we can still speak of an "interest" and an "object." The emotion or desire felt in the presence of the music *is* a state of psychological nonindifference, a value that *moves* the mind, and in this sense an *interest*, even when it is not an interest in anything specific. Moreover, the word "object" can be retained if we mean by it either that which we are interested in, *or* that which is an expression of an interest. The music, as a free creation of the imagination, illustrates this latter type of object. We often use the term "esthetic object" in this way, so we are not violating English idiom when we extend the term "object" to cover instances of this type —to denote, in other words, *expressive* objects—objects that are the expressions and embodiments of emotions, desires, or feelings.

It would seem possible, moreover, to use the term "potential interest" to designate a subjective emotion such as an "objectless" grouch or state of euphoria. An emotion of this sort is not an actualized interest in the sense of being directed toward a definite object, but it is a potential interest in the sense that it tends to become attached to an object. We could thus use "interest" as a convenient blanket term to include all feelings, emotions, and volitions, whether they are actually or only potentially attached to objects. Such broad usage is necessary if we are to have an "interest theory" that will be inclusive enough to cover all the phases of ethical life.

4. THE ANALYSIS OF INTRINSIC VALUES

Does the value, to repeat our question, lie in the interest or in the object? In trying to answer this question, philosophers do not always agree. Some declare that the value is the *interest* in the object; some (including Perry) say it is the *object* of the interest; others say it is the *relation* between the interest and the object; and still others say it is a character of the *entire interest-object situation*. The full discussion of these alternatives requires an intricate analysis that would be out of place in this book.

I shall try merely to clarify the issue with a few remarks. By "intrinsic value" I mean that which is an end in itself or good for its own sake. An object of interest may, in an inexact sense, possess intrinsic value. It may be said, for example, that I am treating a piece of candy as an "end in itself" when I eat it, not for the sake of some future consequences, but simply because it is delicious. When I say that a personality has intrinsic value, however, I am using the terms in a different way. I do not mean that he acquires such value, for example, when a cannibal decides to eat him! He has intrinsic value in a more inward and essential sense. Intrinsic value, in this stricter meaning, seems to me to attach to the inner quality of experience, and the outward object seems to me valuable *not* intrinsically but instrumentally, as a means of arousing or expressing this experience.

I may, for example, desire a book, but the book is not good in itself. It may be called, in a manner of speaking, the object of my desire, but my real objective is *reading* the book, with the satisfactions that accrue therefrom. Suppose the book is painfully desired and not secured. Then it is instrumentally bad in the sense that it causes me suffering. Or suppose I obtain the book and read its contents. It would still be instrumentally bad if it displeases me. Suppose I enjoy its contents. It would then be instrumentally good—good as a means to the end of instructing or delighting me. But it is never, so far as I can see, good in itself, good intrinsically. So it is with other objects. Of course, when the object itself is an interest, it possesses intrinsic value, but *qua* interest and not *qua* object.

Intrinsic value, therefore, is interest, and not, as Perry declares, the object of interest. If the interest is positive, a state of liking, the value is positive, good rather than evil. If the interest is negative, a state of disliking, the value is negative, evil rather than good. These remarks need to be qualified. Positive interest may involve moments of uneasiness and painful tension—the pangs of desire. To this extent, it involves evil and is therefore not an unqualified good. Unalloyed goodness consists primarily in the *fulfillment* of interests, whereby desire, in the process of being satisfied, becomes enjoyment. More inclusively stated, the human ideal is not only the fulfillment but the *cultivation* of interests. It is important not merely to fulfill interests but to get more interests to fulfill: to pass from a narrower to a wider range of interests and to fulfill this wider range. As John Stuart Mill remarked, "The cultivated mind . . . finds sources of inexhaustible interest in all that surrounds it; in the objects of nature, the achievements of art, the imaginations of poetry, the incidents of history, the ways of mankind, past, present and their prospects in the future."[12] The truly happy life is experienced by the man who responds with positive interests to a great range of objects and who fulfills these interests in activity that brings the full flavor of enjoyment. If we were to sum up the good in terms of an interest theory, we would say that it is *the cultivation and fulfillment of positive interests.* Conversely, the sign of an unhappy or intrinsically evil life is the predominance of negative interests, and the noncultivation and frustration of such interests as are positive.

Although intrinsic value seems to me to reside in interests rather than in their objects, these interests are not blind and directionless and isolated, with an esoteric ghostly abstration from the real world; they find expression *in* objects and are directed *toward* objects and are publicly describable in terms of their objective references and behavioral manifestations. I enjoy *this* painting. I love *this* person. I admire *this* act. The objects can still be spoken of as values in the light of their capacity to evoke and express interests, and even if they do not possess intrinsic value in the strict essential meaning of the term, they may still possess *terminal* value (or in the words of C. I. Lewis, "inherent value") in the sense that interest is consummated in and through them. The fact that an object *immediately* contributes to a person's interest and satisfaction does not make it *intrinsically* good. It is the *satisfaction* of interest, and not the *object* of the satisfaction, that possesses intrinsic value.

5. VALUE AND WORTHINESS

Even in the limited sense in which objects can accurately be conceived as values, I cannot agree with Perry's doctrine that value "attaches promiscuously to all objects of all interest." This doctrine is subject to a very fundamental criticism. Before an object of interest can be considered a trustworthy value, we must determine whether it is merely "liked" or is genuinely "like-able," merely "desired" or is really "desirable," merely "admired" or is truly "admirable." There may be a vast difference between what is prized and what is prizeworthy and between thoughtless prizing and thoughtful appraising. Unless we recognize these distinctions, our lives will be thoroughly anarchic. As John Dewey has said:

> There is nothing in which a person so completely reveals himself as in the things which he judges enjoyable and desirable. Such judgments are the sole alternative to the dominion of belief by impulse, chance, blind habit and self-interest. The formation of a cultivated and effectively operative good judgment or taste with respect to what is esthetically admirable, intellectually acceptable and morally approvable is the supreme task set to human beings by the incidents of experience.[13]

Perry was not unaware of Dewey's point, and in his own way, he distinguished between thoughtful and thoughtless prizing. For him, the question whether something is good on the whole, or on balance, is the question whether in the long run the pro-interests (liking and the objects liked) predominate over the anti-interests (disliking and the objects disliked). But as Brand Blanshard has remarked:

> We seem to have a stubborn conviction that whatever may be the facts of men's interest, some things are worth their devotion and others not, and therefore that our interests should be adjusted to, and appraised by, the goodness, not the other way about. We are not prepared to admit even that if the race generally should come to favor something, that would settle the question of its goodness. Suppose that in the next world war our "proud and angry dust" were to raise such effective dust-storms as to force the gibbering remnant of us that remained into a troglodyte existence, where science and art had lost their interest, moral sensitiveness was sneered at as effeminacy, and love derided in any but its animal forms. Would the fact that these things, formerly prized so highly, were now regarded with indifference or aversion, settle anything about their value?[14]

Perry's theory, in insisting that pro-interest *ipso facto* confers goodness upon its object, has the questionable implication that the objects of even the most depraved desires are good—not only good momentarily, or in a limited sense, but good "on the whole" if such desires should become sufficiently common.

A more satisfactory way of phrasing the interest theory is to discriminate qualitatively between the worth of various objects, on the one hand, and of various interests on the other. In a situation in which an object is related to an interest, the basis of the value is not wholly in the interest or wholly in the object, but in the *worthiness* of each to contribute to the value situation. The object is fit, as it were, to excite a favorable attitude in the subject, and the subject is fit to prize the object. Hence the goodness is the result of a felt harmony between the mind and its object, each being fit or worthy for the other. A great work of art, for example, is more worthy of being enjoyed than trash, and a gifted art-lover is better fitted to enjoy it than an insensitive beholder. The object deserves to be favored, and the appreciator is well prepared to favor it. If the value is not realized, the fault may be in the object, or the subject, or both.

This way of phrasing the theory has the incidental advantage of escaping from "the naturalistic fallacy" (or, as I have preferred to call it, "the factualist fallacy"). It recognizes an implicit "oughtness" in value judgments, for a worthy object is the sort that ought to excite a pro-interest, and a worthy interest is the kind that ought to be cultivated. Goodness, in the sense of what ought to exist, lies in the fitting congruity of the object and the interest, each being worthy of the other. We would commit the naturalistic fallacy if we should simply define goodness as the object of interest or the interest in an object, without any reference to worth. One of the central questions for an interest theory of values is whether goodness is to be construed in terms of unqualified or qualified interests. Perry argued for the former alternative, and I have been arguing for the latter.

This way of putting the matter does not mean that I have abandoned the humanist standpoint. Every ideal fulfillment has its natural basis and every natural tendency has its ideal fulfillment. The human personality, in its fundamental dynamic character, is an organization of interests, and the enrichment and fulfillment of these interests constitutes its welfare. As an organization of interests, it differs from a mere collection; it is more like a miniature community. Plato, in *The Republic*, wanted his ideal state to be a real community, with genuine interdependence and mutuality among its components; analagously, he wanted the individual soul to be a kind of "community" of its parts, with a harmonious interplay of all its faculties. One may restate Plato's point of view in modern psychological terminology: the good personality is the well-organized personality, in which all the sides of a man's nature—the volitional, intellectual, hedonic, and passional—form a community, an organic unity in which part is harmoniously related to part and part to whole, and in which all these interrelated parts, expressing themselves in manifold interests, are cultivated and fulfilled. "Cultivation of interests," as I employ it, is a normative term, implying not just *more* but *better* interests and *fitter* objects of interest.

If we are morally wise, so it would seem to me, this is what we value as a proper goal. We are interested in interests; we have a commanding interest in the cultivation and fulfillment of interests; we have a supreme interest in personality, as the sole locus and dynamic center of interests. To the living being, therefore, all values must be contributory. The whole of human culture—science, art, religion, morality—must serve and facilitate life. The basic human aspiration, to quote D. H. Lawrence, is to awaken "the unborn body of life hidden within the body of this half death which we call life."[15]

I do not mean to deny that we should be interested in more than man. Nothing contributes more to happiness than impersonal interests, self-transcending and even life-transcending, such as the astronomer's interest in probing the mysterious universe or the ordinary man's sense of the beauty and fascination of nature. Yet these interests are valuable to us because they enrich life. When we are thus engrossed, we open wide the windows of our minds and let fresh winds play upon our spirits from the far corners of the universe. We fulfill life by transcending life; the effect, as Spinoza so eloquently maintained, is life-enhancement. If the enrichment of life is indeed our goal, it is found in the realization of the whole man: not in reason alone, nor the will, nor the emotions, but in the full expression and realization of human nature as a dynamic organization of interests.

6. THE HUMAN GOAL

The valid theory of interest is one which admits that the whole personality is sometimes brought into play in the act of being interested *and* as an object of interest. When a person looks at his life and finds it truly glorious, he is expressing and valuing all sides of his nature—the volitional, intellectual, hedonic, and passional. But these "sides," although they must be separated for purposes of analysis, are not realized separately: in actuality they interpenetrate and enrich one another within the organic unity of the personality. The highest good, I believe, is the exhilaration of the whole organism, the joy of total organic fulfillment. The intellectual, the volitional, the hedonic, and the passional merge in a core of unity or self-identity; the man becomes one and relatively complete. He is not just a bundle of changing states, but a continuing and evolving I. This I becomes the master of change; it expresses itself through what it does, through its acts and thoughts. Such a personality is well integrated, and the elements thus unified are rich and various. They form a kind of "community," characterized by the interdependence and mutual enhancement of its members. The psychological core of interests is affective-volitional states, but these cannot be sharply separated from other "sides" of the personality.

So far I have described the fulfillment of the personality in terms of its conscious faculties—feeling and emotion, volition, and intellect—and of their interpenetration in the organic unity of the purposive self. This account is incomplete unless we include physical and subconscious and low conscious levels. Every person is a psychophysical organism with body and "subconscious mind" and conscious mind so intimately connected as to constitute a single system. As a result of the work of innumerable physiologists, such as Jacques Loeb and Walter Cannon, and of the work of many psychologists, such as Pierre Janet and Sigmund Freud, we can now assert the close linkage of body and mind and consciousness and "subconsciousness" in almost every aspect of life. Just as the physical hormones, for example, have a decisive influence upon man's temperament, so psychic conflict may profoundly disturb physical functions. Even though intrinsic value is to be found only in conscious states of interest, we must bear in mind the interdependence of mind and body if we are adequately to interpret physical and mental health.

I am pleading for an ethics of the whole human organism rather than an ethics of a mere fragment of it. From the standpoint of such an integral humanism, the fundamental biological values, such as good nutritious food, rest, decent shelter, warm clothing, exercise and physical play, sex expression, and health care, must be considered basic to the personality and therefore to the good life. But the more "ideal values" of man, such as beauty, knowledge, love and cooperation, security, adventure, and creative work, are, if less basal, no less indispensable to the human organism. The two sets of values—the biological and the psychological—must be regarded as interactive, interdependent, and often coalescent. They are elements in the total organic fulfillment—the complete physiological and psychological health of the personality—which is the norm of human welfare.

The detailed definition of that norm requires the cooperative insight of many "experts"—the physician, the hygienist, the dietitian, the psychologist, the esthetician, the philosopher, the educator, the social welfare worker, and the community planner. The human arts and sciences must pool their wisdom in defining the human goal—the total health and welfare of the personality. This is not a task for quacks or vague "idealists." It is possible to employ the methods of empirical science in finding out what human drives are so basic that their satisfaction leads to happiness and fulfillment and their denial to physical disease, insanity, suicide, or, in society, to war, economic collapse, and mass sadism. It is not true that the table of values is eternally fixed—it is necessary for man to extend and deepen his acquaintance with values, and by informed insight and critical judgment to test and improve the table. For the present, however, I wish to insist only upon the central concept: that the norm of aspiration is the health and happiness of the *total* personality, emerging in the harmonious cooperation of interrelated physical and mental activities.

No supernatural oracle reveals that such total fulfillment is the highest good. The only witness to value is man himself. The *"summum bonum"* is defined by man's most careful judgment *after all the available evidence is in.* The *highest* good—not the *"bonum"* but the *"summum bonum"*—is what morally wise men crave when they sit down in a cool hour, reflect upon a full gamut of experience, consider the alternatives as defined by science and vivified by art, and decide what it is that they basically and truly want. Value judgment should rest upon all the insight that a man can muster, upon science, imaginative sensitivity, practical experience, and critical introspection. I believe that morally sensitive people, if they thus reflect, want a life that is well integrated and rich and various in experienced quality. They want the comprehensive and harmonious realization of their potentialities, not pleasure or passion if it means insanity, not intellectuality if it means emotional frigidity, not cultivation of the mind to the neglect of the body or the body to the neglect of the mind. When "wants" and "interests" are construed in this inclusive way, they imply the residual truth of the "natural law" theory, and form the basis of a viable interpretation of human well-being.

NOTES

1. DeWitt H. Parker, *Human Values*. New York: Harper & Row, Publishers, Inc., 1931, pp. 25–26.
2. Ralph Barton Perry, *Realms of Value*. Cambridge, Mass.: Harvard University Press, 1954, p. 3.
3. *Ibid.*, pp. 2–3.
4. Benedict de Spinoza, *Ethics*, Part III, Prop. IX. Quoted by Perry, *General Theory of Value*. New York: David McKay Company, Inc., 1926, p. 43.
5. Perry, *ibid.*, p. 125.
6. Perry, *Realms of Value, op. cit.*, p. 101.
7. *Ibid.*
8. *Ibid.*, p. 104.
9. Perry, *The Moral Economy*. New York: Charles Scribner's Sons, 1909, p. 19.
10. Perry, *Realms of Value, op. cit.*, p. 274.
11. DeWitt H. Parker, *Human Values, op. cit.*, p. 23.
12. John Stuart Mill, *Utilitarianism*. New York: E. P. Dutton & Co., Inc., 1910, p. 13.
13. John Dewey, *The Quest for Certainty*. New York: Minton, Balch & Co., 1929, p. 262.
14. Brand Blanshard, *Reason and Goodness*. New York: The Macmillan Company, 1961, pp. 278–279.
15. D. H. Lawrence, "Glad Ghosts," *Dial*, vol. 81 (July 1926), p. 2.

PART TWO

Right and obligation

CHAPTER V

The laws of God

I. GOD AS MORAL LAWGIVER

In Part One our emphasis was on the goals of human conduct, and the primary concept has been that of good rather than right. In Part Two we shall reverse this emphasis. Our main concern will be the meaning of right and the nature of moral obligation.

As pointed out in the Introduction, there are two principal interpretations of right, utilitarian and deontological. According to utilitarianism, the rightness of actions is to be judged by their consequences. The deontological doctrine, on the other hand, is that the nature of right is set forth in a rule of law, which is either self-evident, or a priori, or derived from some authoritative and unchallengeable source. Right is not primarily determined by consequences. I shall begin with the deontological type of theory, first in its theological guise (Chapter V), and then in its intuitional and a priori versions (Chapter VI).

In the spontaneous effort to invest moral customs and laws with an awesome authority, ancient civilizations have conceived these customs and laws as godgiven and enforced by a divine concern. It will be instructive to glance at a few examples.

The oldest written code of law known to historians until recently is that promulgated by Hammurabi, King of Babylon, in 1704–1662 B.C. On a great pillar of black diorite, almost eight feet high, a code setting forth the moral and legal concepts of Babylon is inscribed. Carved into the same rock is a representation of the king receiving his laws from the seated figure of Shamas, the sun god, "the judge of heaven and earth."

Similar representations are to be found in other ancient civilizations. In the Old Testament, for example, we have the stories of God's command to Adam, his covenant with Abraham, and his dictation to Moses of the Ten Commandments. The Book of Manu (*circa* 250 B.C.), an authoritative source of moral law for Hindus, is declared to be an emanation from the Supreme God. The moral teachings of Islam are likewise represented as a direct revelation from God, communicated word for word to Mohammed by the Angel Gabriel. The opening passage of Plato's dialogue, *The Laws,* reads:

ATHENIAN STRANGER. Tell me, Strangers, is a God or some man supposed to be the author of your laws?

CLEINIAS. A God, Stranger; in very truth a God: among us Cretans he is said to have been Zeus, but in Lacedaemon, whence our friend here comes, I believe they would say that Apollo is their lawgiver: would they not, Megillus?

MEGILLUS. Certainly.[1]

Such illustrations could be multiplied.

The laws or commandments thus "God-given" are held to be sacred and enforced by divine decree. According to the purely formalistic interpretation, these divine laws are right simply because God commands them. An influential Protestant theologian, Emil Brunner, has stated this doctrine succinctly: ". . . There is no intrinsic good. What God does and wills is good; and all that opposes the will of God is bad. The good has its basis and its existence solely in the will of God." It is to be chosen "because He wills it."[2] The opposite point of view maintains that the right and good have a validity independent of God's commands.

The issue involved in this clash of opinion is set forth clearly in Plato's *Euthyphro.* This dialogue raises the whole question of the relation between holiness and virtue, between duty toward God and duty toward man. It also presents the dramatic conflict between two figures, Euthyphro and Socrates, each representing a different orientation toward religion and morality. I shall now briefly summarize the dialogue.

A soothsayer named Euthyphro, impelled by his sense of religious duty, has come to the Athenian hall of justice to file a charge of murder against his father, whose cruel negligence has caused the death of a slave. He happens to meet Socrates, who has come to the hall to respond to the charge of "introducing false divinities and corrupting the youth," for which "crime" he will be sentenced to die.

The contrast between Euthyphro and Socrates symbolizes much of the history of mankind. Euthyphro represents the age of mythology, when life was regulated by dreams and images, the mythical figures and legends of religious tradition. The values for which he stands are substantial: the world of myth has a real glory and fascination, a power to enchant the emotions and dissolve the reason. In Athens, the mythical picture of the universe has begun to fade; but most men still cling to the old, and the new has not yet found its norm, its rational expression. Socrates, with his critical and questing spirit, represents the strange, dangerous, enigmatic future. He is a great dissolver of myth, and in this sense, he is "guilty."

Socrates, as is his habit, draws Euthyphro into philosophical conversation. The latter declares that the killing of the slave was a religious offense, and that his act in charging his father with murder is holy. Socrates asks him to explain what he means by holiness, and after reciting some stories of the gods Euthyphro replies: "What is pleasing to the gods is holy, and what is not pleasing to them is unholy." Socrates then counters with a profound question: "Do the gods love holiness because it is holy, or is it holy because they love it?"

This question brings us to the whole rationale of theological ethics. Why, for example, should we obey the Ten Commandments? Let us suppose—what many Christians and Jews believe—that God has laid down these commandments. Are they right *because* God has commanded them, or has he commanded them because, in their own independent and essential nature, they are right? Socrates is asking a similar question: Is an act pleasing to the gods because it *is* holy, or is it holy merely because it is pleasing to the gods? It is the latter view that Euthyphro favors and that Socrates questions.

Drawing out the implications of Euthyphro's definition, Socrates explains that when we use a passive participle, such as "being carried," "being led," or "being seen," we are not indicating the *inner essence* of something but only its *external relations*. To say that an object is "being seen" is not so much to characterize the quality that is visible as to indicate that this quality is related to an external observer. The question remains, what *is* it that is visible? Its visibility depends upon its nature, its nature does not depend upon its visibility. Similarly with holiness: its being loved depends upon its being holy, its holiness does not depend upon its being loved, even though the love is divine. Implied is the thought that a god is no merely capricious being: he loves objects that are *worthy* of being loved.

Euthyphro would prefer to abandon the attempt to find a satisfactory definition, but Socrates prods him and takes a new tack. He asks how holiness is related to justice? Is all holiness just? And if so, is all justice holy? Or is only a part of justice holy, and the rest of it something else?

Again, Socrates is asking a fundamental question. To appreciate its import, we must realize that the Greek word for "justice" has a very broad meaning: it is practically equivalent to "virtue" or "right conduct." Hence Socrates, in effect, is asking Euthyphro, "What is the relation between holiness and virtue?" Are we to divide morality into two sharply distinguished parts, such as duty to man and duty to God? Or shall we say that we serve God in the very act of serving man?

Euthyphro misses the deeper import of the question, and after a certain amount of perplexity and fumbling, gives a superficial and quite traditional answer. He replies that holiness is "that part of justice which has to do with the attention that is due to the gods; and that what has to do with the attention due to men, is the remaining part of justice." Thus he would split life into two distinct parts, the sacred and the secular.

Socrates, as we may infer by reading between the lines, rejects this dualism of the sacred and the secular. Love of justice and wisdom is service to God; unswerving devotion to truth is faithfulness to the divine trust. To understand the nature of goodness and to seek it at risk of one's very life is to be united with the divinity which shines through all goodness.

In the centuries since this dialogue was written, many people have agreed with Euthyphro that morality depends, in whole or in part, upon arbitrary divine will. So influential was this theory in the Middle Ages that St. Thomas took especial care to combat it. As explained in Chapter I, he interpreted good and right as having their own inherent character. Even for God, moral distinctions are objective, and He is bound by his reason to will what He knows to be good. Yet St. Thomas' antiformalistic doctrine was fiercely contested, and the formalistic point of view bobbed up again and again among a number of late medieval thinkers. For example, William of Ockham, in his *Commentary on the Sentences of Peter Lombard,* maintained that murder, fornication, robbery, and other vices could be stripped of their evil and made right by a reversal of the divine decree. To murder, to rob, and to fornicate would be meritorious "if they were to agree with the divine precept just as now, *de facto,* their opposites agree with that precept." The reason for this is that our duty is to obey God, and God, being omnipotent, "is obliged to the causing of no act."[3]

Many Protestants as well as Catholics have subsequently maintained this position. The question is reviewed, for example, in Sören Kierkegaard's *Fear and Trembling,* based upon the Biblical story of God's command to Abraham that he sacrifice Isaac, his dearly beloved son. Does evil become good simply because God commands it? "But what then is duty?" asks Kierkegaard. "Duty is, to be sure, just a synonym for God's will!" Even quite recently, the neo-orthodox theologians, such as Barth and Brunner, have lent support to this doctrine.

If we examine the formalistic theory, we are confronted by a point of view that few reflective persons would espouse without qualification. Even the neo-orthodox theologians that I have mentioned shrink from a pure and unadulterated formalism—there is at least the suggestion that God is not entirely arbitrary in what He commands. But for the sake of clarity let us consider the theory in its pure and unmitigated state.

It asserts that moral distinctions depend solely upon the decree of God. God cannot command anything *because* it is right, since it would be right only after and because He commanded it. This would mean that His commands would be based upon no ethical reason whatever. He might just as reasonably command that we should hate and kill one another as that we should follow the golden rule.

Such views make God's power and not His goodness basic to His essence; but if God is to be regarded as merely the most powerful being in the universe, there would be no valid *moral* reason for obeying Him. Might does not make right, not even the might of God. Promethean defiance might be very imprudent, but it would be *morally* quite as justifiable as obedience. If the reply be made that "morality" simply *means* obedience to supreme power, we can object that this does violence to our moral sense. The worship of power *merely* because it is power is incompatible with ethical and religious maturity. Although religion may begin with fear, it rises to a reverence for goodness and wisdom, which Bertrand Russell has described as "the free man's worship."

If it be maintained that God is not only powerful but also good, the formalistic interpretation of ethics is no longer tenable. On this view, since God is good and goodness has a certain actual character, the good is not determined by some extrinsic factor, such as an arbitrary command. In reply, one might argue that right is entirely independent of goodness, and that right, if not goodness, is determined by mere decree. If God is good, however, His decrees are not arbitrary; they must reflect and express His goodness, and therefore right as formulated in these decrees is not independent of goodness. We are told in the First Epistle of John that God is good will, is love. If so, the right as embodied in His aims must be directed to the good, for surely God would not capriciously disregard and violate His own goodness. Because good has a character of its own, God by His mere will could not make that good which is not good, any more than He could make that round which is not round. Even God cannot do that which is contradictory: even He cannot make a round square or a good evil.

In addition to pointing out such difficulties, we can criticize formalistic religious ethics for its naïveté. It depends upon a highly anthropomorphic conception of the deity. God is thought of as a sort of king or lawmaker, handing down arbitrary decrees from on high. As Walter Lippmann has pointed out in his *Preface to Morals*, it is difficult for modern educated men to take such views seriously. Gone are the old certainty and vivid imagery that once made "God and His plan seem as real as the lamp-post." We can no longer picture "his throne, his crown, his scepter, his seraphic retinue, his laws, rewards, and punishments."[4] This concrete visualization was always poetry in a measure, but it made the scheme very much more vivid and therefore far more profound in its influence. The modern tendency is to banish all this vivid spectacle: God is abstract; hell is unreal; heaven is inconceivable.

This change in men's outlook is an inevitable accompaniment of the growth of science and knowledge. Modern man has become aware of many religions each claiming authoritativeness and of many ways of reading and interpreting the Bible. He thus has discovered that much is conjectural that once was regarded as certain, that the so-called "revealed" ethics of his own religion is paralleled by other "revealed" ethical systems, and that basic moral concepts such as the "golden rule" are to be found in these other religions. The development of science has dispelled many supernaturalistic beliefs and has instilled a spirit of tentativeness opposed to religious dogma. Also modern critical philosophy, represented, for example, by the writings of Hume, Kant, and McTaggart, has very effectively questioned the arguments for traditional theism. Responding to these various influences, modern man finds it impossible to believe that God, acting like a despotic king, has imposed a specific code of morals by arbitrary fiat.

If we are to have a united nation or a world order, we cannot build it upon the basis of attitudes that have so largely crumbled or that represent only a minority of mankind. In our country, there are secularists, humanists, and theists of many kinds. All of these groups can make moral judgments and can do so rationally. To insist upon a single authoritarian creed is to violate the spirit of a democratic society. It is also to undercut world unity. Nothing is less conducive to international understanding than a holier-than-thou attitude toward creeds other than our own.

2. A HISTORICAL EXAMPLE OF THE TRANSITION
TO A PURPOSIVE RELIGIOUS MORALITY

As soon as we escape from the bounds of a narrow intolerant outlook, we either flounder in moral anarchy or advance to a broader view of things. The Bible is the record of such a transition from a narrow formalism to a broad and purposive morality.

In the parts of the Old Testament that are most primitive, the lawgiver to the Jewish people is conceived to be Yahweh (translated Jehovah in the King James' version), a tribal god, jealous and revengeful, whose power, according to Abraham, is greater than the combined strength of all the other gods. The doctrine is not monotheism but henotheism, devotion to one god while recognizing others. This view is implied by such admonitions as "Thou shalt not revile the gods" and "Thou shalt have no other gods before me."[5]

Yahweh lays down a commandment code, in which rituals and taboos are prescribed along with moral customs.

Never carve yourselves any metal gods. Hold the festival of unleavened cakes. . . . All the first-born belong to me, with the firstlings of your cattle, both oxen and sheep; you may buy back a firstling ass with a lamb or a kid; but if you do not choose to buy it back, you must break its neck. Any first-born boy you must buy back. . . . For six days you shall labour, but on the seventh day you shall desist from work. . . . You must hold the festival of Weeks . . . and the festival of ingathering. . . . You must never present the blood of any sacrifice with leavened cakes, and no part of the sacrifice at the passover festival must be left over all night. . . . You must not boil a kid in its mother's milk.[6]

If a man is moral, he follows the law as thus prescribed; if he is immoral, he violates the law. Yahweh, who enforces these decrees, is relentless against His enemies, merciless against the unrepentant sinner, exacting an eye for an eye, a tooth for a tooth.

Yet very early in the religious development of the Jews, other conceptions crept in. God was sometimes conceived as kind and forgiving, slow to anger, rich in love. Tribal rituals and taboos were supplemented by the admonition of Leviticus, "Love thy neighbor as thyself."⁷ Morality, moreover, was broadened: it transcended the tribe and embraced the stranger: "The alien who settles beside you shall be treated like a native, and you must love him as you love yourself; for you were aliens yourselves in the land of Egypt."⁸ A similar statement is to be found in the twenty-third chapter of Exodus, which dates from the ninth century B.C. and perhaps is retained from a much earlier period. Gradually primitive polytheism, with its tribal exclusiveness, passed over into monotheism. The doctrine that the Jews are a "chosen people" was retained, but this particularistic emphasis was paradoxically combined with a universal trend. The chosen people, according to this new and sublime interpretation, would prepare the way for a realm of true brotherhood among all human beings, a united humanity under a universal God.

Two types of religious leaders, the priests and the prophets, appeared among the Jewish people. The priests were the formalists, generally insisting upon the ritual observance and the letter of the law, such as circumcision, the dietary taboos, the keeping of the Sabbath, and the observance of religious ceremonies. They became scribes and scholars of the Torah, codifying, interpreting, and sanctifying the law. The prophets were the seers and the idealists, often rejecting the traditional rules and laws, not for the sake of being above moral law but for the sake of better principles and laws. Criticizing the past and anticipating the future, they insisted upon the active pursuit of ideals—righteousness and justice, loving kindness and mercy. Among the great prophets, such as Amos, Hosea, Micah, Isaiah, and Jeremiah, we find utterances with revolutionary social implications—the condemnation of the rich, the praise of the poor, and the vision of peace and justice:

And He shall judge among many people, and rebuke strong nations afar off; and they shall beat their swords into plough-shares, and their spears into pruning-hooks: nation shall not lift up a sword against nation, neither shall they learn war any more.⁹

God is no longer a tribal deity enforcing ritual law or demanding sacrifice, but a universal, loving Father-God:

He hath showed thee, O man, what is good; and what doth the Lord require of thee, but to do justly, and to love mercy, and to walk humbly with thy God.¹⁰

In the time of Jesus, the intense vision of the prophets had somewhat faded, and there was considerable moral laxity. The Jewish people, by that time in subjection to Rome, could not sustain the lofty idealism of the prophets. Their lives were dominated by the traditional Jewish law, conceived largely in terms of strict ritual, dietary taboos, and petty or repressive regulations. Fanatical sects, such as the Zealots and the Pharisees, insisted upon the literal observance of the law. A priestly class, jealous and intolerant, imposed itself upon the masses. At the same time, the old Messianic hope of

the people, the doctrine that a God-given leader would deliver the Jews from
bondage, was being widely agitated. It was a time of transition; the culture
of Greece and Rome was declining; the old Jewish culture was decaying; it
was high time for a beginning of the new.

There is no good evidence that Jesus was the intellectually "emancipated"
thinker that modern liberal theology has conceived him to be. As Albert
Schweitzer maintained in *The Quest of the Historical Jesus,* he shared with
his time the strange and intense vision of a supernatural Messianic Kingdom
and conceived of himself as the Messiah, with the end of the world near.
This apocalyptic creed did not prevent him from reviving the ethical idealism
of the prophets. Without love, he maintained, no man can enter into the
Kingdom, and this love is not to be bound by formal rules.

His nonformalistic attitude is most clearly illustrated in his remarks about
the Sabbath. The law that the Sabbath must be kept—one of the Ten Commandments—was perhaps the most strictly guarded of all the traditional religious rules. In *Exodus* 31:12–17, God is represented as declaring to Moses
that the Sabbath "is a sacred day for you, and anyone who desecrates it shall
be put to death. For whoever does any business on the Sabbath, that man
shall be outlawed."[11] Many of the acts prohibited on the Sabbath were entirely harmless, such as lighting a fire, sewing two stitches, or tying and un-
tying a knot. Reaping was also forbidden, and even the gathering of a few
heads of grain was classified as reaping. One Sabbath when Jesus and his
disciples were passing through a field of grain a number of Pharisees rebuked
them for pulling some heads of grain. Jesus replied: "The Sabbath was
made for man, and not man for the Sabbath."[12] If we generalize this remark,
it means that the law is made for man, not man for the law. This is a central
thesis of teleological ethics.

Jesus was thoroughly familiar with the Jewish moral and religious law,
and he did not intend to overthrow it. "Never imagine I have come to destroy
the law or the prophets;" he said, "I have not come to destroy, but to fulfill."[13]
Yet he interpreted the old law with a new flexibility. Again and again he used
the phraseology: "You have heard it said of old. . . . But I say to you. . . ."
He insisted not upon a moral code but upon a spiritual community, the
brotherhood of man under the fatherhood of God. When he was asked the
question, "What is the greatest commandment?" he replied:

> You must love the Lord your God with your whole heart, with your whole
> soul, and with your whole mind. This is the greatest and chief command. There is
> a second like it: you must love your neighbor as yourself. The whole Law and
> the prophets hang upon these two commands.[14]

As we can judge from the story of the good Samaritan, moreover, one's
"neighbor" is every man. His special concern was for those "beyond the
pale": the poor, the lowly, the stranger, the outcast, the prostitute, the prodi-

gal son. Like the prophets of the Old Testament, he enunciated a moral ideal, not a set of formal rules.

When religion reaches maturity, it divests itself of formalism, as did the religion of Jesus and the prophets. It no longer conceives morality as imposed arbitrarily from on high but as immanent in men's purposes and deeds. It emphasizes not the letter of the law but the inner spirit and the consequences of action. In some of its modern forms, it is essentially humanistic: a consecration to life-enriching ideals. It does not confine men's gaze to heaven but leads them to see more clearly what is to be done here on earth. If its mood is optimistic, its optimism is qualified by the realization that

> The very source and fount of day
> Is dash'd with wandering isles of night.[15]

A religion that glosses over the injustices and suffering in the world can do little to realize the old, old ideal of human brotherhood that so many great religions and moral systems have advocated.

NOTES

1. Plato, *The Laws* (translated by Benjamin Jowett). London and New York: Oxford University Press, 1924, p. 1.
2. Emil Brunner, *The Divine Imperative*. Philadelphia: The Westminster Press, 1947, pp. 53, 58.
3. William of Ockham, *Super Quatuor Libros Sententiarum*, Lyons, 1495, II, qu. 19. Cited by Francis Oakley, "Medieval Theories of Natural Law," *Natural Law Forum*, vol. 6 (1961), p. 69. Professor Oakley argues that this formalistic doctrine represents Ockham's basic conviction, and that certain other statements of Ockham which appear to be contrary to this doctrine are not really opposed to it when they are correctly interpreted.
4. Walter Lippmann, *Preface to Morals*.

New York: The Macmillan Company, 1929, p. 22.
5. *Exodus* 22:28 and 20:3 (King James' translation).
6. *Exodus* 34:18–27. From *The Bible: A New Translation*, by James Moffat. New York: Harper & Row, Publishers, Inc., 1935. I have used whichever version seems to be better for the specific passage.
7. *Leviticus* 19:18 (King James).
8. *Leviticus* 19:34 (Moffat).
9. *Micah* 4:3 (King James).
10. *Ibid.*, 6:8.
11. *Exodus* 31:12–17 (Moffat).
12. *Mark* 2:27 (Moffat).
13. *Matthew* 5:17 (King James).
14. *Matthew* 22:36–40 (Moffat).
15. Alfred Lord Tennyson, *In Memoriam*, XXIV, 3.

CHAPTER VI

Duty

I. THE ETHICS OF CONSCIENCE

Men have sought to find moral law in two ways: by looking beyond themselves or by looking within. Seeking an authority external to the individual mind, they have looked to society or God or nature; seeking the direct witness of their own minds, they have looked to some inner source, such as conscience, intuition, or a priori reason.

In the preceding chapter, I have criticized formalistic theological ethics. In this chapter, I shall examine "deontological" theories which seek moral guidance from an inner faculty. That faculty may be conceived variously and may receive various names. The term most often employed in everyday usage is *conscience*.

I wish first to consider a particular interpretation of conscience, namely, that it distinguishes the rightness or wrongness of acts or motives without consideration of the value of their consequences. According to this view, conscience is a kind of innate, intuitive faculty that prompts us to certain beliefs and attitudes, and it does so in an immediate, unreasoned manner.

Some people, usually the least philosophical, think of conscience as providing a ready-made decision for each moral occasion. It operates almost instantaneously like a sense organ or instinctive prompting without regard to rules or principles. Such an interpretation scarcely requires an extended discussion. It supposes that the injunctions of conscience are so unrational and capricious that they are based upon no principles whatever. This view would leave us with nothing but a chaos of emotional attitudes; all idea of objective morality would be lost. If we are to have moral objectivity rather than whimsy we must take the view that similar cases should be treated similarly and identical cases treated identically. As Hastings Rashdall, in *The Theory of Good and Evil*, points out:

We do not say to a child who asks whether he may pick a flower in somebody else's garden, "My good child, that depends entirely upon the circumstances of the particular case . . . consult your own conscience, as each case arises, and all will be well." On the contrary, we say at once: "You must not pick the flower: *because* that would be stealing, and stealing is wrong." Make any reserves you please as to the inadequacy of the rule, its want of definiteness, its inability to meet many problems of life, the necessity for exceptions and the like; yet it must be admitted that if there be any one point about morality as to which there is a consensus alike among all plain men and nearly all philosophers it is surely this— that general rules of conduct do exist.[1]

To discard all such guiding considerations and to allow subrational impulses dubbed "conscience" to determine action in the light of the moment only, is to rely so completely upon caprice as to destroy morality entirely.

By *conscience*, however, one may mean something different, namely, the immediate insight that certain kinds of acts are right or wrong. According to this point of view, there are self-evident rules for determining right action in the different departments of conduct. Certain classes of acts, such as theft or murder, are to be disapproved upon the basis of rules intuited by conscience; certain other classes of acts, such as telling the truth or keeping promises, are to be approved upon the same basis. This doctrine has had such a wide acceptance that Henry Sidgwick, writing at the end of the nineteenth century, called it the point of view of "common sense morality."[2] His criticism of this theory in his *Methods of Ethics* is a classic of reasoning. Although my remarks are much briefer, they differ little from the considerations he advances.

First, the rules enjoined by conscience are not really self-evident. What is meant by self-evidence was clearly stated by Thomas Reid (1710–1796), a proponent of the view that we are now criticizing. Self-evident propositions, he declared, are those "which are no sooner understood than they are believed. . . . There is no searching for evidence, no weighing of arguments: the proposition is not deduced or inferred from another; it has the light of truth in itself, and has no occasion to borrow it from another."[3] The simple propositions of mathematics or logic may be said to have this character. That "two and two make four," for example, will be assented to by anyone who understands the proposition: its denial would be logically contradictory. Or to take another illustration, we know independently of observation or proof that "if x implies y, and if x is true, y is true" (where x and y symbolize propositions). To say that the proposition y is false when it is implied by a true proposition (namely x) is clearly contradictory. On the other hand, the denial of an ethical rule, for example, that "a person ought not to steal," is not logically contradictory; and indeed the rule has not always been maintained. The children of ancient Sparta, for example, were taught to steal; and Polish or French children, during World War II, were taught that stealing from the Nazis was a meritorious, although dangerous, act.

Second, the supposedly self-evident moral rule turns out upon examination to be ambiguous. Let us consider, for example, the rule that one should not murder. What is murder? Quakers have condemned war and capital punishment as forms of murder. Most people have disagreed, but we can scarcely decide such a question by merely counting the number of proponents or opponents of the belief. In practice, murder is hard to define; it is often difficult to distinguish between justifiable homicide, manslaughter, and murder; juries have deliberated such questions for many hours. Or consider the rule that one should not lie. Is the literal truth, if its effect is to deceive, a lie? Is deceit by look, gesture, or silence a lie? Is it a lie when one tells a falsehood to a child if he cannot understand the real truth or if the truth would hurt his feelings? Every such moral rule is ambiguous when applied to certain borderline cases.

Third, the moral rules may conflict. One rule, for example, may say, "Do not lie," but another rule may say, "Do not inflict suffering"; and the two rules, as applied to a given situation, may be in conflict. When the duty of veracity conflicts with the duty of benevolence, which should take precedence? The old question, "Should a physician ever lie to the sick?" involves this moral dilemma. Or suppose that at a dinner party someone deliberately slanders a friend of yours. Should you act on the injunction, "Be loyal to your host and do not make a scene by challenging or denouncing the slanderer?" Or should you act on the principle, "Be loyal to your friend and defend him even at the cost of precipitating an embarrassing argument?" A more poignant illustration of the conflict of duties is to be found in Mark Twain's *Huckleberry Finn*. This novel about pre-Civil War life pictures "Huck" as torn between the duty to lie to save his friend the runaway slave, Jim, from his pursuers, and the duty to tell the truth and thus abide by the law. In the torment of moral confusion Huck cries out:

It don't make no difference whether you do right or wrong, a person's conscience ain't got no sense and goes for him anyway. If I had a yaller dog and he had no more sense than my conscience I would poison him. It takes up more room than a person's insides and ain't no good nohow. Tom Sawyer says so too.

The moral perplexities of life arise in this way: one principle impels us to act contrary to another principle. When we are confronted by these perplexities, the apparent self-evidence of the moral rule disappears, and in practice we cannot decide what to do without a consideration of the consequences of our actions.

Fourth, the injunctions of conscience vary from time to time and from place to place, and this fact implies that they are not really infallible or self-evident. For example, the ancient Greeks believed that the exposure and fatal abandonment of unwanted infants was morally permissible. Even Plato, a morally conscientious man, believed in such exposure when it would serve a eugenic purpose. Homosexuality was likewise approved among many Greeks. Or, to cite another period in history, very strait-laced and conscientious Christians engaged in slave traffic, and there seemed nothing morally reprehensible to them in the terrible suffering and huge death toll among the Negroes they transported from Africa. The burning of "witches" was also practiced by Christian communities. Indeed, this practice was carried to fantastic extremes; altogether, many hundreds of women were burned. Almost invariably they confessed to being witches when tortured and retortured; and the good Christians of the community thereupon burned them with the most conscientious of scruples. It is difficult to find any practice, however cruel or reprehensible, that has not been accounted virtuous in some time or place. Almost everything morally condemned by any one community has been morally approved by some other.

In view of such differences, it is impossible to regard the "intuitive" promptings of conscience, which usually coincide with the mores of the given society, as genuinely objective and universal. Modern psychologists, such as Freud, have explained conscience as the "internalization" of the commands of the external authorities within the individual's environment, especially his childhood environment. Erich Fromm, a contemporary psychologist, has written:

> In the formation of conscience . . . such authorities as the parents, the church, the state, public opinion are either consciously or unconsciously accepted as ethical and moral legislators whose laws and sanctions one adopts, thus internalizing them. The laws and sanctions of external authority become part of oneself, as it were, and instead of feeling responsible to something outside oneself, one feels responsible to something inside, to one's conscience. Conscience is a more effective regulator of conduct than fear of external authorities; for, while one can run away from the latter, one can not escape from oneself nor, therefore, from the internalized authority which has become part of oneself.[4]

The prescriptions of nonreflective conscience are the voice of custom or traditional authority, so deeply ingrained in the human mind as to appear self-evident.

2. THE REHABILITATION OF CONSCIENCE

It would be a great mistake to conclude that the concepts of *conscience* and *duty* are illegitimate. A man's proudest boast is that "I have been true to my own conscience." In the name of conscience Socrates drank the hemlock, Joan of Arc burned at the stake, and many a nameless hero braved the worst tortures that the Nazis could devise. Conscience has inspired the best in human conduct; without it, man is no better than a beast.

Conscience involves a combination of several factors: first, convictions about right and wrong; second, emotional attitudes of approval or disapproval; and third, a sense of duty or obligation. If the convictions are irrational, then conscience is irrational. If they are authoritarian, then conscience is authoritarian. But if they are reasonable and sound, the fact that they are reinforced by emotions and a sense of obligation is all to the good. The business of ethics is not to supplant emotion by intelligence. As Francis Bacon has said, ethics should so compose the passions that they fight on the side of intelligence rather than against it.

So many people associate *conscience* and *duty* with a puritanical, authoritarian, or superstitious ethics that the liberal meaning of these terms is obscured. But we must distinguish between the authoritarian and reflective level of conscience. Authoritarian conscience seems to involve immediate unreasoned knowledge of ethical truths, but actually these "self-evident truths," as we have said, are the mandates of custom or traditional authority which have become so much a part of oneself that they seem self-evident. Quite different is the reflective level of conscience, present for example in a person like Socrates. Although he often spoke of his "inner voice," he insisted that "the unexamined life is not worth living." He realized that the conscience of every individual must be deeply informed by the norms of cultural tradition, but he subjected these norms to the habit of reflection and unfettered discussion. In fulfilling the philosopher's mission, he strengthened rather than weakened the force of his own conscience.

Today we are in great need of such a reflective yet forceful conscience. The ethics of formal rules and authority seems rapidly to be crumbling. We have become aware of many conflicting traditions and many "moral worlds," and we are aware of too many contrasting standards to rest comfortably in the illusion that our own are necessarily the right ones. To many people there no longer seems to be any reasonable course of action; there is merely a babble of voices, each calling without justification to some divergent path. Amid all this confusion, we need something more than the internalized voice of authority, however self-evident its dictates may appear.

Reflection is especially necessary in respect to social ethics in our modern age. Authoritarian conscience is quick to condemn the old familiar personal crimes, such as undisguised murder or theft; but it is not nearly so quick to condemn the new *social* forms of wrong-doing. Deliberate overcapitalization of an industry is a form of theft, but it is very likely to be accepted as shrewd business practice. Misleading advertising or "slanted" newspaper reporting are forms of lying, but they have become so common as to be downright respectable. Employment of workers under unsafe or unhealthful conditions may be a form of murder, but since the effects are not immediate, violent, or obvious, it usually escapes without punishment.

There is an increasing distance, both physically and psychologically, between the agent and the patient. In the old-fashioned neighborhood, the effects of actions were immediate and palpable: robbery or murder was a person-to-person operation. In our complex business system, on the other hand, a high executive is able from his office chair to pick a thousand pockets without knowing a single one of his victims. Similarly, a laboratory technician or a factory worker may be preparing the death of a soldier or a civilian on the other side of the world months or years hence. Even the flyer who drops his bomb from high in the air cannot clearly witness the hideous results of his action. Men can now rob and kill "sight unseen." As an Austrian philosopher, Günther Anders, has written:

War . . . has assumed an uncannily indirect character, since enemies do not see each other any longer, and since the magnitude of the effects of one's deeds definitely surpasses one's psychological capacities. We can *do* more . . . than we can visualize, produce more than we can mentally reproduce, and there exists a strange inverse relation between inhibition and the magnitude of the deed, because the mechanism of inhibition is silenced if the effects of our deeds definitely transcend the capacity of our fantasy—in short, we can become *guiltlessly guilty*.[5]

The moral responsibility of the ordinary citizen is obscured by the anonymity of collective decisions. The issues are so complex, the information at hand is so inadequate, and the individual's voice is such a tiny part of an immense historical process, that the "little man" naturally considers that *his* moral choice is of no importance. He feels that he can neither understand nor influence the events upon which his happiness and very life may depend. Under these circumstances, it is easy to feel guiltless and to dismiss moral considerations with a shrug. Yet in a democracy the attitudes of millions of "little men" have a decisive importance.

Even among the "big men" in public life, it is the exceptional individual who realizes keenly the moral issues involved in large-scale collective actions. Robert Oppenheimer is a person of such rare stature. As director of the great scientific laboratories at Los Alamos during World War II, he was profoundly moved by the moral implications of the atomic research in which he was engaged.

When the first bomb was exploded in New Mexico his first thought was a line from the Bhagavad-gita (he reads Sanskrit and five other languages): "I am become death, the shatterer of worlds." One of his constant anxieties has been the moral problem of the creators of the bomb. "The physicists have known sin," he said, "and this is a knowledge which they cannot lose." His former mentor at Harvard, Dr. Bridgman, answered him, "Scientists aren't responsible for the facts that are in nature. It's their job to find the facts. There is no sin connected with it, no morals."[6]

The issue here stated goes to the heart of the scientist's moral dilemma. As a decent human being, Bridgman must have been shocked by Nazi cruelty; but the attitude of the Nazi doctors who experimented on human beings as if they were guinea pigs, seems to carry his thesis to its logical conclusion.[7] He appears to leap from the defensible premise that natural *science* is ethically neutral to the indefensible conclusion that *scientists* are likewise amoral. Natural science *is* neutral in the sense that no values enter into the data. To talk of naughty atoms, or to think of gravitation as moral, is nonsensical. But this is not the whole story. In reaching a *practical* scientific conclusion, as for example in judging the human tolerance limit for strontium 90, science must take account of the worth of human life and the moral issues at stake. The amount of evidence demanded to justify a decision that can have *no* deleterious effects upon human life may be quite different than the amount required to justify a decision that may doom innumerable children in future generations to death by leukemia. However "neutral" science is in itself, it can be put to devilish uses, and if scientists lend themselves to these practices, they can be just as morally culpable as anyone else. Oppenheimer's awareness that scientists cannot escape moral responsibility helped to make him suspect. The text that formed the basis for denying him "security clearance" contained the following passage: "It was further reported that in the autumn of 1949, and subsequently, you strongly opposed the development of the hydrogen bomb on (1) moral grounds. . . ."[8]

The issues here involved are not simple. The Cold War has forced good men to make very distasteful choices. But surely we have every reason to look morally askance at a superbomb which has been described by the scientists themselves as "no longer a weapon of war but a means of extermination of whole populations," whose use "would be a betrayal of all standards of morality. . . ."[9] The moral sensitivity of such men as Robert Oppenheimer and Albert Schweitzer offers far more hope for mankind than the insensitivity so common today. It is also more practical. No one should suppose that if we let the djinn of atomic violence out of the bottle, he will be a well-behaved djinn toward everyone except "our enemy."

Science and technology have so prodigiously increased human power, both for good and for ill, that the issue "What shall we do?" has acquired a terrible urgency. The problems of our age are too acute and unprecedented to be resolved in terms of the old static formal rules, and these problems confront not only scientists and statesmen but all mankind.

There are two possible reactions to these new issues—first, to shirk individual responsibility, and second, to recognize that the individual is responsible even in the case of "collective guilt."

The first type of reaction is illustrated by the case of Adolf Eichmann, who meticulously fulfilled the orders of his Nazi superiors to exterminate millions of Jews. Although his role was not as subordinate as he wished it to appear, he pleaded that he was nothing but a tool in a vast bureaucratic system. "In actual fact," he declared, "I was merely a little cog in the machinery that carried out the directives and orders of the German Reich."[10]

The second type of reaction is illustrated by Major Claude Eatherly, the pilot who led the Hiroshima A-bomb mission in World War II. For a less sensitive person, it would have been easy to shrug off all responsibility for this comparatively innocent participation in a military operation. But the horrendous nature of the event preyed on his mind night and day, convincing him that "we have to answer not only for our own individual acts, but also for the team acts in which we just participate or are made to participate."[11] His sense of "guilt" drove him to mental illness and acts of desperation, but it finally impelled him to dedicate his life to the cause of peace.

As he wrote to Günther Anders: "In the past it has sometimes been possible for men to 'coast along' without posing to themselves too many searching questions about the way they are accustomed to think and to act—but it is reasonably clear that our age is not one of these."[12]

As Anders has said, it is not sufficient to examine "the innermost voices and the most hidden motives" of our minds; it is necessary also to examine "the secret voices, motives, and maxims" of our *instruments*—to look upon these scientific devices as extensions of ourselves, and to accept moral responsibility for them. The responsibility belongs to us all. Perhaps we can never get rid of war until we take to heart the words of Father Zossima in Dostoevsky's *The Brothers Karamazov*. "Little heart of mine, my joy," he said to Alyosha, "believe me, everyone is really responsible to all men for all men and for everything. I don't know how to explain it to you, but I feel it so, painfully even." We also need sober realism and deep thought to cope with the intricate moral perplexities of a scientific age, and we must therefore seek the rehabilitation of conscience on a reflective basis.

3. A PRIORI REASON AND GOOD WILL

If we reject an authoritarian ethics and seek a more reflective approach, we must still reckon with Immanuel Kant (1724–1804). He believed that the rightness of single acts must always be judged by their relation to rules, and that the many ethical rules advocated by "common sense morality" can ultimately be reduced to a very few general principles or laws apprehended by a priori reason. His ethics, in a sense, is reflective, and it may offer us the guidance that we need in the rehabilitation of conscience. We should therefore examine it with care.

The ethical philosophy of Kant has been frequently misunderstood. One reason for the misunderstanding is that he has been traditionally depicted as some sort of intellectual machine, without spontaneity or emotional resilience. Unquestionably there is some basis for this characterization, but it is a caricature that leaves out the more human side of Kant's nature. He was, for example, fond of and remarkably good at cards, though often impatient at the slowness of his partner's playing. He loved good company, especially at dinner, and never thought of dining without guests. As a teacher at the university, he was popular with his students and had the power to excite them both to laughter and to tears. "Even when he was old and withered," according to H. J. Paton, "he did not lose his simple and kindly and courteous character. When he was so weak that he fell in the street and could not rise till two unknown ladies helped him up, he presented one of them with the rose which he happened to be carrying."[13] Despite his addiction to routine and system-building, there was a touch of the true romantic in him and a great deal of emotional warmth. Those who overlook this side of his nature are inclined to interpret his ethics as coldly formalistic and purely intellectual. Such an interpretation is one sided.

In terms of the historical background of his thought, Kant was a child of the Protestant Reformation, the Enlightenment, and the American and French Revolutions. Reared in a pious family, he was deeply imbued with the spirit of Protestant ethics and religion. One of his main ambitions as a philosopher was to vindicate the belief in God, freedom, and immortality, not as the dogmas of an authoritarian Church but as the articles of a reasonable moral faith. In his insistence that every human being is an end in himself, he expressed in philosophical terms the Christian doctrine of the infinite intrinsic worth of the individual human soul and also the revolutionary doctrine of the Rights of Man. He sympathized with the French Revolution until the Reign of Terror and admired the new American republic; and he believed that freedom is basic to all morality and all social progress. He was also greatly influenced by the Enlightenment, the great critical movement in European thought that markedly inspired the French and American Revolutions. Like many of the apostles of this movement, he had a strong confidence in reason. This confidence was strengthened by his early cultivation of mathematics and astronomy (to which he contributed "the nebular hypothesis"). But like Rousseau, one of his favorite authors, he wished to vindicate the "heart" as well as the "head." He combined, in a complex way, rigor and kindness, reason and faith, belief in freedom and respect for authority.

I shall trace Kant's argument as it appears in *The Fundamental Principles of the Metaphysics of Morals*, a book small in size but great in scope. The details cannot be expounded in the limited space of this chapter, and I recommend that the reader not only study the original but a good commentary, such as *Kant's Ethical Theory* by Sir David Ross.

In a short introduction Kant insisted that ethics must be based upon a priori rather than merely empirical principles. A priori knowledge was defined by Kant as universal and necessary, and hence not derived from the changing content of experience. Pure mathematics, such as geometry, is entirely a priori. That two plus three equals five, or that the sum of the angles of a triangle are 180 degrees, is true universally; its denial is logically contradictory. In addition to pure mathematics, there is natural science, which studies the laws of nature, and ethics, which studies the laws of moral choice. Here, too, there is an a priori element, but this is combined with an empirical content. All sensible experience, from which natural science draws its data, has necessary forms and categories (for example, that everything must have a cause)—and these, in the sense of being universal and necessary—are a priori. So, similarly, morality has certain universal and necessary features, but the detailed application of moral principles requires a great deal of empirical knowledge. The part of ethics that studies these a priori principles Kant called "the metaphysics of morals."

After explaining the meaning of a priori ethics in his introduction, Kant began his ethical argument by maintaining that nothing is unconditionally and unqualifiedly good except a good will. Knowledge, wealth, health, or any talent of mind or body is not good if employed for villainous ends. Even pleasure is bad if malicious. For example, the pleasure that a sadist might obtain in torturing an innocent child is thoroughly bad. Good will is the sole exception: it is good intrinsically and absolutely. Like a jewel, it shines by its own light.

This doctrine does not mean that good will is the whole good or the only noninstrumental good. For Kant there are two goods: the good will, which is unconditionally good, and happiness, which is good for its own sake only when combined with good will. He believed that virtue merits reward, that good will should be crowned with happiness. By happiness he frequently means a maximum of pleasure, but sometimes he uses the term more broadly to denote the maximum satisfaction of a man's needs and inclinations.

To realize one's own happiness is the principal aim of prudence. Every man has the right to pursue his own happiness in his own way so long as the effort does not conflict with the moral law. It may even be one's indirect duty to pursue one's own happiness, since an unhappy man is so fettered by his misery that he finds it difficult to fulfill his duty, whereas a happy man may find it relatively easy. Nevertheless, Kant felt that there is a fundamental difference between a life of prudence and one of moral goodness, and that love for oneself, or striving for one's own happiness, is not directly virtuous.

Since a virtuous will is absolutely and unconditionally good, it must have its full worth in itself, apart from any consequences that may ensue. In holding this doctrine, Kant rejected all forms of utilitarianism. He did not mean that a good man ignores consequences; to act intelligently a person must have in mind the intended effects of his actions. He will aim at certain consequences because it is his duty to do so, but his duty is determined by universal moral law rather than the specific consequences of an act. Kant would allow us to take account of particular consequences to *apply* a moral law, but not to establish its *validity,* or to make ourselves an exception.

Inclination is likewise not the determining ground of a moral act. The good man acts upon the maxim, "I will do my duty whatever my inclination may be." He does not say, "I will do my duty if I happen to be so inclined." He does what he ought to do simply because it is morally right to do it, and not for any consideration external to his duty. This does not mean that he must always act *contrary* to his inclination. Kant has often been criticized for holding that duty must always be disagreeable, but this objection is based upon a misunderstanding. It is no sign of moral imperfection to do one's duty with a cheerful heart. Kant believed that the highest type of will is the "holy will," in which duty and inclination perfectly agree. Such a will, unfortunately, is superhuman, and the call of duty for human beings is not only distinguishable from inclination but often contrary to it. Also men are freely choosing agents and are not psychologically bound to obey the moral law.

A good will is one that wills rightly. If the criterion of right volition is neither consequences nor inclination, what is it? Kant answers that the rightness of the volition depends upon two factors: *right incentive* and *right maxim*.

The *right incentive* is respect and reverence for the moral law. This incentive sets men apart from all the rest of nature, and gives to the inner life a unique and unconditional value. A person with this incentive acts *because* of duty, and not merely *in accordance* with duty. A moral act must be done for duty's sake. If a person's inclination happens to conform to duty, so much the better, but it is still incumbent upon him to recognize his duty and to act out of respect for it.

The *right maxim* is the principle of "the categorical imperative." An imperative is an injunction or command: it says that a person ought to do so and so. There are two kinds of imperatives: hypothetical and categorical. A hypothetical imperative always takes a conditional form: "*If* you wish to achieve *x*, then you ought to do *y*." It is based upon the fact that "whoever wills the end, wills also (so far as reason decides his conduct) the means in his power which are indispensably necessary thereto."[14] Ordinary rules of skill and counsels of prudence are hypothetical imperatives: they tell us what we ought to do—"ought" in the sense of what we would be well advised to do —*if* we desire certain ends. They may be entirely legitimate but they are not moral. A categorical imperative, on the other hand, asserts simply and unconditionally, "You ought to act thus and thus." There is no "if" in front of the "ought." Obligation is not determined by wish or expediency but by objective moral necessity, which can be stated in a universal rule. When I say, for example, that a man ought to respect the rights of others, or that he ought not to murder, I do not mean that the "ought" is conditional upon the man's wish or is merely a matter of prudence. Such an "ought"—objective, necessary, unconditional, absolute—is a categorical imperative. Every such imperative and no other kind of imperative is moral.

Kant's usage of the term, "categorical imperative," is a little confusing. It will be helpful to distinguish between three levels of categorical requirements. First, there is the particular act that is one's duty—this can be called a "moral act." Second, there is the rule that defines one's duty in the particular case—for example, the rule that one ought not to murder, or that one should keep one's promises. Such a rule can be called "*a* categorical imperative" or "moral law." Third, there is the general formula for deriving the rules. Kant called it "*the* categorical imperative," or "the formula of the categorical imperative." As an example of such a formula, every person should refrain from conduct that he would not be willing to have made the universal rule. In addition to the formula of universal law, Kant advocated the formula of humanity as an end in itself and the formula of freedom and responsibility. All three of these formulas will be explained in the pages that follow.

The kind of necessity and universality involved in a categorical imperative was explained by Kant as follows:

Everyone must admit that if a law is to have moral force, i.e., to be the basis of an obligation, it must carry with it absolute necessity; that, for example, the precept, "Thou shalt not lie," is not valid for men alone, as if other rational beings had no need to observe it; and so with all the other moral laws properly so called; that, therefore, the basis of obligation must not be sought in the nature of man, or in the circumstances in the world in which he is placed, but a priori simply in the conceptions of pure reason; and although any other precept which is founded on principles of mere experience may be in certain respects universal, yet, in as far as it rests even in the least degree on an empirical basis, perhaps only as to a motive, such a precept, while it may be a practical rule, can never be called a moral law.[15]

Kant is here stating the position of ethical absolutism: that moral laws admit of no exceptions and hold universally without regard to differing circumstances or inclinations. He is not even willing to base morality upon human nature or apply it specifically to man. It must rest upon abstract reason and apply uniformly to all rational creatures—even to angels, if they exist and are rational. The categorical imperative is necessary in the sense of being morally obligatory upon all rational beings.

This kind of necessity is quite different from physical necessity. It means strict obligation: it does not mean any kind of physical compulsion. Indeed, when I am compelled to do something, there is no sense in saying that I ought to do it; I can only say that I *must* do it. Empirical science, in describing or causally explaining a succession of events, is simply concerned with what is, not with what ought to be; whereas ethics expresses the ideal rather than the factual. Since moral judgments are not judgments of fact, since they are not empirical generalizations, they must be derived a priori—that is, independently of experience.

They can be so derived and will exhibit a kind of necessity if they are akin to mathematical propositions. As I have already remarked, there is an absolute, unconditional necessity about the proposition that two and three equal five. We do not mean that two and three sometimes or usually equal five but that they always and necessarily do. It is contradictory and therefore impossible for the sum of two and three to be anything but five. This we can know by pure reason without considering any particular case. According to Kant, the moral law is likewise necessary and universal because its denial involves a contradiction. Assuming as he does that moral laws are universal a priori propositions, the sign of their validity is that they can be willed without contradiction, whereas immoral principles cannot be so willed. But the analogy with mathematics is not perfect—unlike a mathematical falsehood, an immoral principle does not necessarily involve a *logical* contradiction. Contradictory it is, but it may be either a "contradiction in ideas" or a "contradiction in will." As an example of the latter, one may *try* to will a certain rule as absolutely universal, and yet inevitably wish oneself an exception. In this wide sense, an immoral principle is *always* inconsistent.

4. THE FORMULAS OF THE CATEGORICAL IMPERATIVE

The first formula. When we are considering some type of action, such as telling a lie, we should formulate the principle manifested in it and see if we can consistently will it as universal. If not, it is inconsistent and immoral. In this way, Kant derived his first formula of the categorical imperative: "Act only on that maxim which you can will as a universal law." This formula expresses the very conception of the categorical imperative, namely, that it be independent of empirical and hypothetical grounds, that is, strictly universal and formal.

Consider, as an example of how the formula is applied, the above-mentioned case of lying. To will that lying should be universally practiced would be self-contradictory, for if everybody lied the liar would not be believed. Lying tends to undermine itself; it tends to its own defeat. It is parasitic upon truth-telling; if it were universalized, there would not be any truth to lie about. Or suppose that you are thinking of making a promise that you do not intend to keep. It is clear that the maxim of your action could not be universalized.

For supposing it to be a universal law that everyone when he thinks himself in a difficulty should be able to promise whatever he pleases, with the purpose of not keeping his promise, the promise itself would become impossible, as well as the end that one might have in view in it, since no one would consider that anything was promised to him, but would ridicule all such statements as vain pretences.[16]

The principle that one should lie, or that one should make promises with the intention of breaking them, cannot be *thought* as holding universally. It is somewhat different with certain other types of immorality, which can be *conceived* as holding universally but cannot be *willed* as universal. Take for example the refusal to help others in need of aid.

Now no doubt if such a mode of thinking were a universal law, the human race might very well subsist. . . . But although it is possible that a universal law of nature might exist in accordance with that maxim, it is impossible to will that such a principle should have the universal validity of a law of nature. For a will which resolved this would contradict itself, inasmuch as many cases might occur in which one would have need of the love and sympathy of others, and in which, by such a law of nature, sprung from his own will, he would deprive himself of all hope of the aid he desires.[17]

What Kant is proposing is a kind of thought-experiment. Any conduct that you cannot will as universal is immoral—therefore, you must imagine that the maxim of your contemplated act (for example, that you should break a promise) will become an absolutely universal practice. This means that you should ask yourself, "What would happen if *everybody* acted that way?" Now Kant, as we have seen, distinguished two tests to be met in this thought-experiment. First, you must ask yourself, "Is it *possible* that the maxim be universalized?" Certain types of acts, if universalized, would be self-eliminating, and therefore could not possibly be the universal practice. This would be true of lying, for example, because if everybody lied, no one would believe you. Second, you should ask yourself, "Can I consistently will that the maxim of my act be universalized?" Since no one wishes to be treated inconsiderately, you cannot will that inconsiderateness or unkindness be universal. You would want to make yourself an exception to the rule.

Some acts that pass the first test must be rejected because they fail to pass the second. A duty prescribed by the first test (for example, "do not murder") Kant calls "perfect," and a duty prescribed by the second test only (for example, "do not inflict unnecessary suffering") Kant calls "imperfect." If there is a conflict between perfect and imperfect obligation, the former should be chosen. The duties of perfect obligation, forbidding us to lie, break promises, steal, murder, and so forth, admit of no exception whatever in favor of duties of imperfect obligation.

The second formula. One reason that we cannot universalize the principle of immoral acts is that every man wants to be treated with respect; he does not want to be a victim of wrong action, and therefore he cannot consistently will that this sort of action be universalized. The ultimate reason for this fact is that every man is an end in himself and wants to be so regarded. Therefore Kant was led to his second formulation of the principle of the categorical imperative: "Act so that you always treat humanity, whether in your own person or in that of another, always as an end and never as a means only." Treat everyone as a spiritual being having intrinsic value, never as merely a means, a tool, as a thing with only instrumental value. This principle follows from the fact that man as rational and moral, and as capable of happiness, possesses dignity and inner worth. When applied to conduct, it rules out all forms of selfishness, for the essence of selfishness is the employment of someone as a mere tool without proper respect for him as a person. Every sort of vengeance, exploitation, aggression, or gratification of sadistic impulses must be considered immoral, because it involves the use of someone as a mere means.

Kant interpreted this second formula in a broad way. In declaring that every person should be treated as an end in himself, he maintained that everyone should perfect his own rational nature, by cultivating both his intellectual faculties and his moral disposition, and that he should at the same time promote the happiness of others. In a later work, *The Metaphysics of Morals,* he laid down the rule of life, "Promote perfection in yourself and happiness in others." As Ross points out:

One might be inclined to say: "If we are bound to promote capacities of greater perfection in ourselves, why not in others? If we are bound to promote happiness in others, why not in ourselves?" But Kant's view is quite intelligible, on his own premises. He is too deeply committed to anti-egoism to say that we have a direct duty to promote happiness for ourselves (though he holds that there is a derivative duty to do so, since "adversity, pain, and want are great temptations to transgression of one's duty"); he is too deeply convinced of the inwardness of virtue to admit a duty, incumbent on one man, to promote virtue in others.[18]

The third formula. The characteristic that makes a person an end-in-himself is above all his freedom, and accordingly Kant put a great deal of emphasis upon this attribute. Dare to be free, and respect the freedom of others—this is the spirit of his ethics. Because *compulsory* obligation is a contradiction in terms, there can be no meaning in moral obligation without freedom of choice. *Ought* implies *can* and is incompatible with *must.* Hence Kant is led to a third formulation of the principle of the categorical imperative, namely, insistence that every man should act as a free moral agent, himself willing the moral law and willingly submitting himself to it. This is "the idea of the will of every rational being as a will which makes universal law":

By this principle all maxims are repudiated which cannot accord with the will's own enactment of universal law. The will is therefore not merely subject to the law, but is so subject that it must be considered as also *making the law* for itself and precisely on this account as first of all subject to the law (of which it can regard itself as the author).[19]

"Making the law" does not mean creating it. Since moral laws are as objective and universal as the truths of mathematics, they are not created by human beings, either individually or collectively. "Making" means freely willing the law, so that it is no longer external and alien to the mind of the moral agent.

This formulation leads to a closely connected and very fruitful concept—that of "a kingdom of ends." This concept means that every man should unite with others in a society in which each freely realizes his own good in promoting that of others, and in which he is both subject and sovereign. As sovereign, he should exercise his freedom; he should will the right; he should develop and exercise his capacity for rational choice. As member, he should exhibit moral responsibility, willing his own obedience to moral law. The result of thus exercising both freedom and responsibility is to unite with others in a self-governing society of rational agents, each one of whom is an end in himself and a means to the ends of others:

For all rational beings come under the law that each of them must treat itself and all others *never merely as means,* but in every case *at the same time as ends in themselves.* Hence results a systematic union of rational beings by common objective laws, i.e., a kingdom which may be called a kingdom of ends, since what these laws have in view is just the relation of these beings to one another as ends and means. . . . A rational being belongs as a *member* to the kingdom of ends when, although giving universal laws in it, he is also himself subject to these laws. He belongs to it *as sovereign* when, while giving laws, he is not subject to the will of another.[20]

Kant explained that this "kingdom"—which might better be called a "republic of ends"—is "certainly only an ideal," but it is none the less a valid norm for human conduct.

In the final section of his book, Kant discussed the epistemological and metaphysical implications of his theory of moral freedom. In essence, he argued that it is impossible to *prove* that man is either free or unfree, but that obligation implies freedom of the will. There is no sense in saying that one *ought* to do something if one is bound by sheer necessity to do it or not to do it. Hence we are justified in believing in free will as an article of moral faith. Kant went on to interpret freedom as the action of a "noumenal" self. This conception of noumenal freedom is very difficult to make intelligible, and few philosophers would accept it. I shall not discuss it here.

In his political writings, Kant applied his moral principles to society. Especially important, in this connection, is his emphasis upon the a priori universal character of morality, his conception of the human being as an end in himself, and his conviction that freedom is indispensable to the good life.

The ideal of the political state, he believed, is to embody universal moral law. The moral law that should serve as the basis of the state is determined by the categorical imperative rather than by utilitarian considerations. Although Kant recognized that a good government promotes the welfare of the people, he insisted that "by this is not to be understood the individual well-being and happiness of the citizens of the state. . . . The welfare of the state as its own highest good signifies that condition in which the greatest harmony is attained between the constitution and the principle of right."[21] Law should be essentially an application of the categorical imperative, and as such it should be obligatory upon all rational beings, irrespective of their class, sex, race, nationality, or personal peculiarities. With this conception of universal law, Kant was impelled to reject the ideal of quite separate and independent states, since these represent only a halfway stage in the realization of the universality of law and morality. Only a world-wide legal order can embody the idea of universal law, and hence Kant was an ardent advocate of an international confederation or world state, capable of expressing universal laws and securing eternal peace. All history, he believed, is the checkered story of human progress, and progress is essentially the movement of humanity toward this ultimate ideal.

Kant's conception of the human being as an end in himself underlies his democratic convictions. The democratic idea that all men are created equal implies that all men have the same basic right to be considered as ends in themselves and not as mere means. If no man is a mere tool, to be exploited for the benefit of others, it is immoral for any class to live off the sweat of another, or for any individual to rule over others for the sake of his personal aggrandizement. The state, likewise, is not entitled to use its citizens as mere tools. Hence the state is made for man, not man for the state. A human being, in other words, is not a mere ant in a social ant heap: he is an end and is entitled to be treated as such. To deny this is to blaspheme against the essential dignity of man and to degrade him to the status of a machine or a slave. Kant is here expressing the fundamental moral basis of democracy.

Kant's emphasis upon freedom underlies his liberalism. The best constitution, he declared, allows "the greatest possible human freedom in accordance with laws by which the freedom of each is made to be consistent with that of all others."[22] Man as free should be subject and sovereign in both the moral and the political sphere. As subject, he must freely accept the law of the state if it truly embodies moral principles; a social return is to be demanded of all; there are to be no parasites. Freedom entails responsibility, and duties are correlative with rights. As sovereign, man is free; he has the right to legislate over himself; he has the right to participate in the decisions of the community; he cannot legitimately be the pawn of any dictatorship.

5. A CRITICISM OF KANT'S ETHICS AND POLITICS

It is time to turn from an exposition to a critical evaluation of Kant's ethical principles. The criticism of Kant opens a vast field for discussion, and what I shall say merely touches upon the controversial questions involved.

First of all, we must grant that there is much in his thought that is extremely valuable. No one can read him understandingly without being impressed by his high seriousness and deep insight. Whatever may be his mistakes, he has performed a great service in formulating his basic principles, such as the central importance of good will, the impartiality and universality of duty, the clear-cut distinction between a hypothetical and a categorical imperative, the recognition that "I ought" implies "I can," and the insistence that everyone should be treated as an end in himself. In applying his principles to society, Kant provided a strong moral foundation for democracy, liberalism, and internationalism. No doubt there is much to quarrel with here, and some of his more valuable principles, such as the concept of a categorical imperative, need to be fundamentally reinterpreted; but as C. D. Broad remarked, "Kant's failures are more important than most men's successes."[23] Nevertheless, it is worthwhile to see in what respects he does fail.

The principal weakness of his moral philosophy is its excessive abstractness and formalism. He declared that morality can be determined only by universal moral rule irrespective of inclinations and consequences. It is immoral to violate a universal rule even for the sake of very good consequences. It is this view that I wish to challenge.

Let us consider his first formula of the categorical imperative: "Act only on that maxim through which you can at the same time will that it should become a universal law." Now in practice we often apply this type of formula. For example, in reference to a certain election I may ask myself, "Should I vote?" I may reason that my vote is insignificant in comparison with the many votes cast, and that in all probability it will decide nothing. But then I think to myself, "What if all people should think similarly and abstain from voting?" I cannot *will* that this should be so: if nonvoting were universalized the effect would be disastrous; indeed there would not even be any elections and so no chance to refrain from voting; and the realization that this would be the case helps to make clear to me that I have a real obligation as a citizen to vote.

Yet this mode of reasoning involves a tacit appeal to consequences. Why *not* will that nobody should vote? Similarly, why not will that every man should break his promises, steal his neighbor's goods, commit adultery with his neighbors' wives, or murder his friends and associates? It is because we value human life that we would not care to have it thus completely undermined. To a complete amoralist or cynic or pessimist, who puts no value at all upon life, there would be nothing repugnant to reason in the universalization of some or all of these forms of wrongdoing. Some anarchists have advocated the view that nobody should ever vote; and if we disagree, it is surely because we think that voting does some good.

Without such an appeal to consequences, there is nothing plausible about Kant's formula. His attempt to derive his rules upon the basis of pure logical consistency is specious. We can no more derive moral truth from a formal logical law than we can derive scientific truth from such a law. No juggling of the principle of contradiction will ever give us a particular law of nature, such as Boyle's law of the behavior of gases. Similarly no manipulation of the principle of contradiction can ever yield a particular moral truth, such as that we ought to vote.

Let us assume, however, that the rule that one should vote is morally justified. Should it ever admit of exceptions? Kant would apparently have to say no, because he insisted in the very strongest language that moral rules do not permit exceptions. Yet I might have a very weighty reason for not voting. I might be ill, or I might be needed to tend someone who is ill, or there might be some other special circumstance that would justify my decision not to vote. To say that no consideration of welfare, no view of consequences, could possibly justify my failure to vote would be fanatical. In opposition to Kant, any reasonable person is prepared to admit some philanthropic exceptions.

In Kant's defense it might be argued that one maxim of duty must be limited by another maxim of duty: the duty to vote, for example, must sometimes be limited by the duty to tend someone in distress. If duties conflict with and limit one another, however, they must necessarily have a relative and tentative character, and not the absolute, unconditional, a priori character which Kant ascribes to them. Moreover, when duty conflicts with duty, it is difficult to see how Kant could decide which duty takes precedence except in so far as he prefers "perfect" to "imperfect" duties. Unlike a utilitarian, he could not say that we have the stronger obligation to perform the act that would bring about the greater welfare.

Despite the fact that in real life duties often do conflict, he apparently adheres to the position that morality should be utterly uncompromising and that a "perfect duty," such as telling the truth, holds in all circumstances. At least he is almost always so interpreted, and it is difficult to see how some of his statements could mean anything else.

The need for a more flexible ethics can be illustrated from his own life. As a number of writers have pointed out, universal celibacy would be self-contradictory because it would wipe out the human race; Kant, as a bachelor, was celibate; therefore he is condemned by his own principles. It is not a sufficient answer to point out, as Marcus Singer does in his *Generalization in Ethics* (pages 151–152), that it would likewise be disastrous to universalize the principle that *everybody* should have children, for the dangers and evils of overpopulation are as great as those of underpopulation. The point, that Singer seems to miss, is that *neither* principle—to have children or *not* to have children—should be universalized. Some people, but not everyone, ought to have children, and the decision (if it is not just a matter of accident) should be determined in the light of particular circumstances. There is also the question of how many children to have—one, two, three, four, or more? How can one universalize such decisions as these?

Or consider this example:

Kant was . . . very fond of dried fruits and used to have them especially imported for him by his friend Motherby. "At one time he was eagerly expecting a vessel with French fruits which he had ordered, and he had already invited some friends to a dinner at which they were to be served. The vessel, however, was delayed a number of days by a storm. When it arrived, Kant was informed that the provisions had become short on account of the delay, and that the crew had eaten his fruit. Kant was so angry that he declared they ought to have starved rather than to have touched it. Surprised at this irritation, Motherby said, 'Professor, you cannot be in earnest.' Kant answered, 'I am really in earnest.' Afterwards he was sorry." [Quoted from Stuckenberg, *The Life of Kant,* p. 138.] But still it was quite in accordance with Kantian morality that the sailors should have starved.[24]

It might be argued that, with suitable qualifications, Kant's universalization formula can be made flexible enough to meet such objections. For example, we could universalize the principle that men should steal rather than starve to death. But if we begin to admit qualifications and exceptions, it becomes very difficult on the basis of a priori reason to judge where to draw the line. For instance, should we universalize the principle that men should starve rather than suffer acute pangs of hunger, and if so, just how acute must the pangs be? We cannot reasonably answer questions of this sort without a more empirical approach to ethics than Kant was prepared to admit.

As a final example, let us consider Kant's controversy with Benjamin Constant, a French philosopher. Constant argued that it is right to lie to a would-be murderer in order to save his intended victim. A man bent on murder, Constant insisted, has forfeited all right to a truth that would abet his plot. To this contention Kant replied, "The duty of truthfulness makes no distinction between persons to whom one has this duty and to whom one can exempt himself from this duty; rather, it is an unconditional duty which holds in all circumstances."[25] Hence, we are duty bound to tell the truth even in this extreme instance. Very few philosophers or laymen would agree with Kant.

In defense of his theory, it can be argued that he misapplied his own principle, and that the principle is sound even if his application is not. Marcus Singer suggests that Kant should have answered Constant differently. The question that Constant raised is this, "Is it right to save an innocent man by telling a lie to a would-be murderer?" To apply the criterion of universality, one should ask, "Could it be willed as a universal law that everyone should lie in order to save an innocent man from murder?" There is no difficulty at all in conceiving and willing *this* law as universal.[26]

Singer's defense of Kant does not eliminate the difficulty. As Ross has pointed out, "Any individual act is an instance of a class of acts which is a species of a class of acts which is a species of a still wider class."[27] In the case that we are considering, we have (1) "lies told to would-be murderers of *innocent* persons," (2) "lies told to would-be murderers," (3) "lies told to persons who intend harm," (4) "lies," (5) "statements." Kant evidently pitches upon the fourth class, and since lies cannot be universalized, he concludes that the particular lie is wrong. Singer chooses to universalize the first class, and since this can be done without contradiction, he concludes that the lie is right. Almost everyone would admit that Singer's is the more reasonable procedure, but it is not the way Kant interpreted his own principle. He declared flatly that "the duty of veracity . . . is an *unconditional duty* which holds in all circumstances." He argued that the rule of truthfulness "does not permit any exception," since the exception would involve a "contradiction" and "nullify the universality" of the rule.[28] To reinterpret Kant's first formula of the categorical imperative as Singer does, is not to defend the formula as Kant himself understood and espoused it.

If we begin to qualify the formula as Singer proposes, there is no limit to the qualifications that can be introduced. The formula loses its abstract and a priori character and becomes specific and empirical. Singer is prepared to universalize the class of acts, "Lies told to would-be murderers of *innocent* persons." But the qualification introduced by the word "innocent" needs to be interpreted in the light of the specific instance. Suppose that a member of the German underground during World War II were trying to kill Hitler in order to bring the war to a close and free the German people. Here the intended victim was scarcely "innocent" and immense good might result from killing him. The assassination of Huey Long, the demagogic senator from Louisiana in the Depression period, was likewise motivated by the desire to kill a "guilty" man. Booth's assassination of Lincoln had the same motivation. Probably most people would *approve* the killing of Hitler, would be very *reluctant* to approve the killing of Long, and would *disapprove* the killing of Lincoln. Innocence and guilt are a matter of degree, and the determination of the exact degree in a particular case may be a very delicate matter. When is a person sufficiently guilty that one should tell the truth at the cost of his life? When is he sufficiently innocent so that his life should be spared? It is impossible to say in advance of a careful inspection of the facts. But if we *do* look at the act in all its specific details, and decide upon its rightness in *these* terms, we have abandoned the criterion of universality —at least as Kant understood it.

If this criterion merely means that we should be fair and impartial in our moral judgments, it is not opposed to a utilitarian and empirical approach. Even utilitarians, such as Bentham and Sidgwick, declare that similar cases should be treated similarly, identical cases should be treated identically. But the respects in which two or more cases are similar or identical can be determined only by a study of the facts, including the morally relevant *consequences* of acts. I do not see how Kant could take adequate account of these empirical details without abandoning the a priori and formal character of his universality principle.

If his first formula is interpreted as abstractly and rigorously as he interpreted it, then it is inconsistent with his *second* formula, "Always treat every human being as an end, never as a means only." This second formula, if it signifies anything, surely signifies a respect for the intrinsic value of personality, but such respect is inconsistent with a willingness to sacrifice human life and its values for the sake of abstract moral law. A story has been told about the philosopher Fichte which illustrates the point I am making. He was once asked the question, "What would you do if your wife were very ill and to tell the truth to her, when the truth is very shocking, would kill her?" Now like Kant, Fichte would not admit that a person is ever justified in saying to himself: "It is almost always better to tell the truth, but in this case I shall do much more good by telling a lie; and therefore I had better lie." Instead he is said to have replied, "If my wife must die by the truth, let her die."[29] Surely in so responding Fichte was not treating his wife as intrinsically precious, as an end in herself. Kant's formula that we should never treat anyone as a mere means implies, among other things, that a person is not to be used as a mere means for the carrying into effect of an abstract moral code.

If Kant had interpreted his second formula in a narrow, deontological way, there would be no necessary conflict between it and his first formula. But, in expounding the second formula in *The Metaphysics of Morals*, he insisted that everyone should not only cultivate his own moral and rational nature, but also promote the happiness of others. So interpreted, the second formula is teleological in spirit. The first formula is a right for right's sake principle, and the second is a right for good's sake principle.

The conflict between the first and second formulas can be expressed in still another way. The first formula insists upon strict moral universality, admitting of no exceptions. This insistence is not consistent with the second formula, that every person is to be treated as an end in himself; because every person is a concrete individual, and he must be dealt with individually if he is to be treated as an end. As Master Eckhart, the German mystic has said:

That I am a man, this I share with other men. That I see and hear and that I eat and drink is what all animals do likewise. But that I am I is only mine and belongs to me and to nobody else; to no other man nor to an angel nor to God—except inasmuch as I am one with Him.[30]

Every man is an individual: he is "man" in the singular: he is not the abstraction "mankind." He shares many characteristics with other animals and with other men; but there is always a peculiar temperament, a unique blend of talents, a separate and distinctive consciousness. Just as there are no two fingerprints exactly alike, so there are no two personalities exactly alike. There is always something about me that is never common to you and me. Respect for a person includes respect for this core of individuality. It means appreciation of the real man of flesh and blood—the individual and human *me*—not just a grammatical abstraction. Kant never sufficiently appreciated this fact.

If he had put more emphasis upon the value of love and less emphasis upon abstract duty, he would not be so open to the criticism that I have been urging. Despite some implications to the contrary, there is scant recognition in his ethics of the importance of love toward the individual human being. He talks about duty far more than he speaks of love. But unless reverence for duty is touched by love, it will be too cold to possess much driving force and to do justice to the individual. Although the sense of duty is necessary to put iron in the human constitution, love is the more creative and elemental force. It is not just an additional value, on a par with the others: it transforms other values, lending them its own beauty and warmth. Many psychologists maintain that love is the root impulse and primary motivation of life. In its wide meaning, moreover, it stands not only for the sexual bond between man and woman but for the diverse and innumerable ties of affection without which life is a sad affair.

We have observed inconsistencies in Kant's argument. In his first formula of the categorical imperative, he based morality entirely upon universal rule, with too little respect for the uniqueness of human personality. In his second formula, on the other hand, he declared that every human being must be treated as an end in himself, thus implying respect and affection for every person as distinct from other persons. Thus he was inconsistent in combining the first and second formulas.

His third formula, that one should join others in a "kingdom" of free and responsible moral agents, likewise implies an individuation of morality. There can be no real freedom except in so far as the individual expresses himself. Freedom surely does not mean reducing all human beings to a common denominator: it means releasing and asserting the individuality in every man. Freedom without self-realization is impossible. Self-realization, of course, is not selfish realization, and individuality is not the same as individualism. Perhaps maximum freedom for the individual can be realized in a cooperative or socialist society. Freedom necessarily involves, however, the autonomy and expression of the real concrete individual.

Kant did not perceive all the implications of his own doctrines. He did not clearly realize that only an individual, expressing his individuality, can be free and an end in himself. He supposed that a man is free only when he is following the dictates of universal abstract reason, and that a man is being treated as an end in himself whenever his "good will," as the embodiment of abstract moral law, is exalted as the highest of values. In maintaining that morality is exclusively obedience to universal law, without regard to the individual and his peculiar circumstances, Kant dissolved the individual personality in an ocean of ethical abstraction, like an individual grain of sand dissolved in a vast sea.

The philosophical movement called Existentialism is in great measure a protest against such an abstract and inadequate view of man and of human values. Such Existentialists as Sören Kierkegaard and Jean-Paul Sartre have insisted upon the reality of the individual, the particularity of his plight, and the impossibility of expressing the concrete truth of existence in abstract, universal terms. Some philosophers have gone to the opposite extreme from Kant's and have denied to the individual any significance beyond the momentary state. Man is both individual and universal—an individual being with universal qualities—and the whole truth about him emphasizes both aspects of his nature.

The insistence upon the reality of the individual is one of the main tenets of liberalism. It is because Kant slights this side of the truth that he is not always a liberal. Unlike ordinary liberals, he does not emphasize the importance of protecting the individual from the encroachment of state power. Good government for him means the application of a rational system of law, which must, in turn, rest upon the universal rules of morality rather than upon the interests or rights of individuals. The essential question is whether the law does or does not agree with a priori principles of right; the question whether it serves the public interest or corresponds to the wishes of the people or protects the civil liberties of individuals is not paramount. Slighting in

this way the consideration of welfare and of individual rights, Kant denied
to the individual the right to rebel under the most tyrannical of governments.
He went so far as to declare:

> Resistance on the part of the people to the supreme legislative power of the state
> is in no case legitimate. . . . There is no right of sedition and still less of rebellion
> belonging to the people. . . . It is the duty of the people to bear any abuse of the
> supreme power, even though it should be considered unbearable.[31]

The weakest part of Kant's ethical and political philosophy is his formalism. This leads him to neglect considerations of welfare and the rights of the
individual. It is ultimately inconsistent with his belief in freedom and in man
as an end in himself.

6. PRIMA-FACIE DUTIES

Since the time of Kant, a new influential school of deontologists has arisen
in England. Its most prominent representatives have been H. A. Prichard,
E. F. Carritt, C. D. Broad, and William David Ross. The theory of Ross
(for many years the Provost of Oriel College, Oxford) is the most interesting
for our purposes.

Ross tried to reach a satisfactory compromise between the deontological
doctrine of Kant and the "ideal utilitarianism" of G. E. Moore (whose ideas
I shall discuss in the next chapter). He rejected the doctrine of Kant that
there are duties which admit of no exceptions, believing as almost everyone
does, that we are justified in telling an untruth or breaking a promise when
the benefit in doing so is very great. A person is justified, for example, in
telling a lie to save a life. Ross agreed with Kant, however, in maintaining
that we must have some principle of obligation other than benefit. He thus
admitted a duality of moral standards: first, production of welfare and, second, intuited obligation independent of the welfare or harm produced.

He introduced the conception of "prima-facie duties" to explain his view
that there are conditional yet non-utilitarian obligations. Literally "prima-
facie" means "at first sight." A prima-facie duty appears *on the face of it* to be
our duty, and it *is* our duty unless there are overriding considerations to the
contrary. It is an obligation which holds in the absence of a stronger obligation. Other things being equal, we have, for example, a duty to keep a
promise; but it may be that a stronger and conflicting obligation should have
the right of way. Sometimes the duty of keeping a promise, however, is
stronger than any conflicting duty, even the duty of maximizing the good.
The duty of producing the greatest good, in fact, is only one duty among a
number, and it has no necessary priority over other duties.

Ross argued that the main defect of the utilitarian theory is "that it ignores,
or at least does not do full justice to, the highly personal character of duty."

If the only duty is to produce the maximum of good, the question who is to have the good—whether it is myself, or my benefactor, or a person to whom I have made a promise to confer that good on him, or a mere fellow man to whom I stand in no such special relation—should make no difference to my having a duty to produce that good. But we are all in fact sure that it makes a vast difference.[32]

According to Ross, utilitarianism simplifies unduly our moral relations to our fellows.

It says, in effect, that the only morally significant relation in which my neighbors stand to me is that of being possible beneficiaries by my action. They do stand in this relation to me, and this relation is morally significant. But they also stand to me in the relation of promisee to promiser, of creditor to debtor, of wife to husband, of child to parent, of friend to friend, of fellow countryman to fellow countryman, and the like; and each of these relations is the foundation of a prima-facie duty, which is more or less incumbent upon me according to the circumstances of the case.[33]

Another important mistake of the utilitarian theory, according to Ross, is that it bases right too exclusively on *future* results. Duty is retrospective as well as prospective. I should keep a promise not just to produce good in the future, but because the promise was made. I should repay a benefactor, not just to promote his welfare, but because he has helped me in the past.

Reasoning in this manner, Ross offered the following list of prima-facie duties as a first approximation to a complete list:

1. The obligation of fidelity, that is, of keeping our promises or engagements. This includes the obligation not to tell lies, since by tacit understanding we commit ourselves to tell the truth whenever we use language that appears to be informative.

2. The obligation to make restitution for injuries we may wrongfully have caused others.

3. The obligation to render services to others in return for services they have rendered to us.

4. The obligation to distribute rewards and punishments in accordance with merit.

5. The obligation to do good to others.

6. The obligation to improve ourselves with respect to virtue and intelligence.

7. The obligation not to injure others.

Ross maintained that a person has no direct duty to promote his own happiness, and that the duty to abstain from injuring others is more stringent than the obligation to do them good. With these qualifications, the last three duties can be considered utilitarian. The fourth duty, that of "justice," is considered by Broad, Prichard, and Carritt to be deontological, but Ross disagrees. Justice, he thinks, is intrinsically good, and our duty to promote it is explicable on utilitarian grounds. The duties of fidelity, reparation, and gratitude (the first three in the above list) he regards as deontological. It is on these duties that he rests his case against utilitarianism.

He believes that we intuitively recognize that something is a prima-facie duty, and that we also intuitively estimate which duty is the stronger when there is a conflict of duties. The prima-facie obligations, taken one by one, are as self-evident as mathematical axioms. "In both cases we are dealing with propositions that cannot be proved, but that just as certainly need no proof."[34] The estimate of which duty takes precedence when there is a conflict of duties is much less evident. For this estimation "no general rules can be laid down." The best that we can do is carefully to intuit which act would be most "suitable" in the light of all pertinent considerations.

But Ross does indicate certain priorities. As I have already mentioned, he thinks that the duty not to injure others is more stringent than the obligation to help them. He also maintains that the first three duties (fidelity, reparation, and gratitude), which he calls "the duties of perfect obligation," are the most stringent of all, and that utilitarian considerations must be very strong if these deontological duties are to be overriden. To this degree, he subordinates utilitarian to deontological duties.

Since he makes intuition the final court of appeal, it is appropriate to reply that I do not find his "intuitions" self-evident. I do not intuit that fidelity, reparation, and gratitude are "duties of perfect obligation," more stringent than all the others. Unlike Ross, I find it difficult to believe that something is our duty when there is no good in it at all, or when the balance is on the side of evil rather than of good. Good, being good, ought to be maximized and evil, being evil, ought to be minimized, and we therefore ought to act in such a way as to achieve the maximum surplus of ultimate good over ultimate evil. Our duty is to help people and not to hurt them—and the more we help them and the less we hurt them the better. None of Ross's deontological principles seems to me so evidently true as this principle.

The point of my disagreement with Ross may need to be clarified. He maintains that the deontological duties are especially stringent, and that they should ordinarily take precedence over utilitarian duties. He thus affirms the independence of rightness from goodness, maintaining that an act may be right, hence one's duty, even though it "detracts from the balance of values in the universe." This means that it may be our duty to make the world *worse* rather than better. It would be theoretically possible, through nothing but *right* acts, gradually to reduce the goodness in the world until it is completely gone. Now this is surely not a reasonable position. I agree with the comment of Professor Oliver O. Johnson:

If we appeal to the deontologists' own standard for the judgment of theories in ethics—moral insight—the answer seems inescapable: Their theory must be rejected. Rather than elucidating our non-theoretical moral convictions, this theory, I should contend, would render these convictions finally meaningless. For if one can fulfill his duty in the full meaning of that term and yet through his action leave the world in a worse condition than had he not acted at all, what significance can the notion of duty or moral obligation have? If such an action could be right, would we not have just as much reason for urging people to act wrongly as rightly? And if this be true, can any meaningful distinction be drawn between right and wrong?[35]

A more detailed answer to Ross will have to be postponed until we consider utilitarianism in the next chapter. We shall then be in a position to compare his deontological principles with the principles of utilitarianism. In the light of the latter, we can reconsider the prima-facie duties, and examine Ross's arguments for the deontological view. I shall maintain that the prima-facie duties, including the so-called "duties of perfect obligation," are in general obligatory, but obligatory *because* they further ends that are good. This explanation would provide us with a single ground of duty, the rule of the greatest good, rather than a heap of heterogeneous duties. It may be that we can never find a common ground that makes right acts right, but we should not abandon the attempt before we try. As for myself, I still cling to the view that the sole aim of morals should be to enrich life, our own and other people's. But I realize that it will be necessary to answer Ross's objections to utilitarianism, and this I shall endeavor to do.

We have now reviewed several attempts to base action upon the laws or dictates of duty. First, we have briefly considered the doctrine that conscience provides a decision for each new occasion, commanding or forbidding a specific act without regard to rules or principles; and we have concluded that conscience thus described is so unprincipled, so without guiding ideas, that it cannot serve as a basis for individual or social morality. Second, we have pondered the doctrine that conscience supplies us with immediate unreasoned knowledge of many independent ethical rules, for example, that one ought to keep promises, or that one ought not to murder; and we have seen that conscience so interpreted cannot be justified rationally and is not an adequate guide to action. Third, we have discussed the doctrine of Kant that ethical rules can be reduced to a few universal a priori principles which duty unconditionally prescribes; and we have seen that his theory is inconsistent and too inflexible. Fourth, we have examined the conception of intuited prima-facie duties as advanced by Ross, and we have not found his "intuitions" self-evident.

NOTES

1. Hastings Rashdall, *The Theory of Good and Evil*. London and New York: Oxford University Press, 1924, I, pp. 82–83.
2. Cf., Henry Sidgwick, *The Methods of Ethics*. London: Macmillan & Co., Ltd., 1922, Book III, Chapter XI.
3. Thomas Reid, *Essays on the Intellectual Powers of Man*. London: Macmillan & Co., Ltd., 1941, Essay VI, Chapter IV.
4. Erich Fromm, *Man for Himself*. New York: Holt, Rinehart and Winston, Inc., 1947, p. 144.

5. Claude Eatherly and Günther Anders, *Burning Conscience*. New York: Monthly Review Press, 1962, p. 52.

6. *The Manchester Guardian*, April 22, 1954. The reference is to Dr. P. W. Bridgman, the famous physicist.

7. For an account of the scientific atrocities of the Nazi physicians, see Alexander Mitscherlich and Fred Mielke, *Doctors of Infamy*. New York: Henry Schuman, Inc., 1949.

8. *In the Matter of J. Robert Oppenheimer*, Transcript of the Hearing Before the Personnel Security Board, Washington, D.C., 1954, p. 6.

9. "Let Us Pledge Not to Use the H-Bomb First!", *Bulletin of the Atomic Scientists*, vol. 6 (March 1950), p. 75. Signed by twelve eminent American scientists. There have been many similar declarations since the date of this statement.

10. *Life* (January 1961); quoted by Anders, *Burning Conscience, op. cit.*, p. 108.

11. *Burning Conscience*, p. 109.

12. *Ibid.*, p. 6.

13. H. J. Paton, *The Categorical Imperative*. London: Hutchinson & Co., Ltd., 1947, p. 198.

14. Immanuel Kant, *Fundamental Principles of the Metaphysics of Ethics* (translated by Thomas Kingswill Abbott). New York: David McKay Company, Inc., 1916, p. 41.

15. *Ibid.*, p. 4.

16. *Ibid.*, p. 48.

17. *Ibid.*, p. 49.

18. Sir William David Ross, *Kant's Ethical Theory*. London and New York: Oxford University Press, 1954, p. 56.

19. H. J. Paton, *The Moral Law*. London: Hutchinson & Co., Ltd., 1947, pp. 98–99. (In this instance, I have preferred Paton's translation because of its greater clarity.)

20. Immanual Kant, *Fundamental Principles of the Metaphysics of Ethics, op. cit.*, pp. 61–62.

21. Kant, *Philosophy of Law*. Edinburgh: T. and T. Clark, 1887, p. 173.

22. Kant, *Critique of Pure Reason* (translated by Norman Kemp Smith). London: Macmillan & Co., 1933, p. 312.

23. C. D. Broad, *Five Types of Ethical Theory*. New York: Harcourt, Brace and World, Inc., 1930, p. 11.

24. Havelock Ellis, *The Dance of Life*. Boston: Houghton Mifflin Company, 1923, pp. 245–246.

25. Immanuel Kant, "On a Supposed Right to Lie from Altruistic Motives," *Critique of Practical Reason and Other Writings in Moral Philosophy* (translated by Lewis W. Beck). Chicago: University of Chicago Press, 1949, p. 349.

26. *Cf.*, Marcus George Singer, *Generalization in Ethics*. New York: Alfred A. Knopf, Inc., 1961, pp. 228–233.

27. W. D. Ross, *Kant's Ethical Theory, op. cit.*, p. 32.

28. Kant, "On a Supposed Right to Lie from Altruistic Motives," *op. cit.*, pp. 349–350.

29. *Cf.*, Wilbur Marshall Urban, *Fundamentals of Ethics*. New York: Holt, Rinehart & Winston, Inc., 1930, p. 40.

30. Master Eckhart, *Fragments*. Quoted by Erich Fromm, *Man for Himself, op. cit.*, p. 38.

31. Immanuel Kant, *Philosophy of Law, op. cit.*, pp. 176–177.

32. W. D. Ross, *The Right and the Good*. New York and London: Oxford University Press, 1930, p. 22.

33. *Ibid.*, p. 19.

34. *Ibid.*, p. 30.

35. Oliver O. Johnson, *Rightness and Goodness*. The Hague: Martinus Nijhoff, 1959, pp. 128–129.

CHAPTER VII

Utilitarianism

I. THE BASIC TENETS OF UTILITARIANISM

We have come to a critical point in our argument. It appears from the last chapter that deontological ethics, whether that of Kant or Ross, cannot be accepted. At the same time, Ross's objections to utilitarianism are weighty. Can we explain on utilitarian grounds the obligation to keep our promises, to tell the truth, to make restitution for injuries, to repay debts of gratitude, and to deal justly with our fellowmen? Does utilitarianism underestimate the highly personal character of duty? Does it oversimplify our moral relations to our fellows? Does it base right too exclusively on future results rather than past performances? All of these questions are raised by Ross and other deontologists, and they are difficult to answer. If no satisfactory utilitarian answers can be found, we shall have reached an impasse, since neither utilitarianism, nor its opposite, deontology, would appear to be true.

I shall set forth the basic utilitarian theory and try to answer briefly the objections raised by Ross and others. Because of limitations of space, the issues cannot be discussed as fully as their complexity warrants, but I can indicate answers that seem to me cogent.

Utilitarianism is often defined as the doctrine that the rightness of actions is to be judged by their consequences. What do we mean by "actions"? Do we mean particular actions or do we mean classes of actions? According to which way we interpret the word "actions" we get two different theories, both of which can be called "utilitarian." The one theory is "act-utilitarianism" and the other is "rule-utilitariansm." We shall distinguish these theories and consider the merits of each.

The word "consequences" also requires explanation. On a strict interpretation, it means only future results. This would imply that, in judging the rightness of an act, we would take no account of the *immediate* values and disvalues of the act itself, and would consider only what follows from the act. I doubt if any utilitarian has ever intended so narrow a view. Even Bentham, who was about as strict as any utilitarian can be, rejected this kind of utilitarianism. He realized that an act may be pleasant or unpleasant, and he counted this immediate pleasure or unpleasure along with the results. I do not agree with his pure hedonism, but I agree that we should count present as well as future goods. The utilitarian standard, as I understand it, is the principle of *the greatest net good,* not leaving out of account the intrinsic values or disvalues of the act itself. When I use shorthand expressions, such as "best results" or "good consequences," I wish to be understood as counting the results plus the intrinsic good or evil in the action itself.

By the "greatest net good" I mean the greatest balance of good over evil. Just as we subtract the losses from the gains in calculating the net profits from a business, so we subtract the evils from the goods in estimating the net good of a course of action. This standard of net good is accepted by utilitarianism. If it appears that two or more alternatives would *equally* produce the maximum net good, the agent's duty is to choose *one* of the alternatives, but it does not matter which one. Otherwise his duty is to choose that single alternative that will yield the greatest net good. Even this way of stating the utilitarian standard is too simple to define the nature of right. Consider the following example:

Suppose that a mother, living with her husband and child in a part of the country generally considered to be attractive, healthful, and comparatively free from natural catastrophes, decides to sit outside with her infant child in order to give the child the benefit of the air and sunlight. As she sits in a chair with the infant on her lap, an earthquake occurs, splitting the earth beneath her chair. Both mother and child fall to their deaths. The house is undisturbed.[1]

The mother's act was catastrophic, but not morally wrong. An act may be as rational as it is well intentioned, and yet turn out to be disastrous. All that we can fairly demand is that a person should do the very best he knows and can. We cannot insist that he be omniscient; only God can be that. In judging human motives, we must take account of probabilities and intentions and not simply actual consequences. No man can take credit for a good which he did not intend and could not foresee, and no man should be blamed for an evil which he did not and could not know would result.

In reply, the utilitarian can make a very sharp distinction between the act and the motive, and maintain that the rightness of the act is entirely distinct from the rightness of the motive. In the words of Mill, "The motive has nothing to do with the morality of the action, though much with the worth of the agent."[2] More consistently than Mill, Bentham took this view because he was interested not in motives but in the improvement of the world. He noted that hell is paved with good intentions, and that what matters is good or bad results. But when we are judging the rightness of acts, motivation is not irrelevant. "It was right to *try*," we remark, "even though the attempt did not turn out well."

To think clearly about these issues, we must distinguish between *objective* and *subjective* rightness. The motive of an act may be *subjectively* right, in the sense of being well intentioned, and yet the act may not be *objectively* right, in terms of good results. An *act,* and not merely a motive, can be called subjectively right. It is subjectively right if it is deliberately directed to a conscientiously chosen end, even though, through no moral fault of the agent, it turns out badly. We can distinguish two senses of objective rightness. In the first sense, an act can be called objectively right if, according to all available evidence and foreseeable consequences, it is right. The choice of the act would then be wholly justified in terms of objective probabilities, even though it later turned out badly. In the example of the mother and the earthquake, the mother was *cognitively* justified in what she did, since the act was right when assessed by the logic of rational probability. Her act was the *wisest* but not the most fortunate. In a second sense, an act can be called objectively right if and only if it *is* the most fortunate act. The test here is not probabilities but *actual* consequences. If the mother had considered taking the infant to the same outdoor location, and because of laziness had chosen to stay indoors instead, her act would have been the most fortunate but not the wisest.

Thus a utilitarian may define rightness in terms of three different sorts of consequences: *intended* consequences, *probable* consequences, and *actual* consequences. People talk about rightness in all three ways. When they are assigning praise or blame to motives and intentions, or when they are considering an act in relation to its motivation, they will be most concerned with intended consequences. When they are judging which act is wisest *before* it is performed, they will be intent upon the most probable consequences. When they are judging whether a past act was most fortunate after its consequences are known, they will be intent upon the actual consequences. To be *wholly* right in *every* sense, an act must combine best intentions, best probable results, and best actual results. It must be blameless, wisest, and most fortunate.

2. TYPES OF UTILITARIANISM

As I have pointed out in the preceding chapter, utilitarianism is a theory about the nature of right—not a theory about the nature of good. Right depends upon good—whatever it be. Hence hedonistic utilitarianism is only one type of utilitarianism, and the tendency to identify utilitarianism with hedonism alone is unjustified.

To illustrate the possible varieties of utilitarianism, it will be helpful to cite examples. Oliver A. Johnson, in *Rightness and Goodness,* has advanced an interesting theory. He spurns the name "utilitarianism," since he identifies it with the notion that right depends only upon results exclusive of immediate values. I have maintained, on the contrary, that this kind of utilitarianism is a straw man, and that the meaning of "utilitarianism" should not be so restricted. Johnson is, according to my terminology, a "utilitarian." "As moral agents," he declares, "we have finally only one duty, to maximize goodness." He rejects the contention of Ross that "one can be morally obliged to choose the lesser rather than the greater good," maintaining that "such a position . . . drains the notion of duty of its moral significance."[3] But he interprets intrinsic goodness much more broadly than does the ordinary utilitarian. He regards not only justice as intrinsically good but also certain moral "ways of life." Other things being equal, a way of life which exhibits faithfulness and gratitude is intrinsically better than a way of life that exhibits ingratitude and unfaithfulness.

A. C. Ewing, in his *Ethics*, adopts a similar position. He maintains that it is always our duty to promote the most intrinsic good, while contending that keeping promises, repairing injuries, dealing justly with our fellows, and displaying gratitude toward our benefactors, are all intrinsically good.

This would indeed imply a considerable transformation in [the utilitarian] view as most usually understood, for it involves the admission that the rightness or wrongness of acts is not always dependent on consequences over and above the acts. But it would be by no means incompatible with the fundamental utilitarian principle that rightness depends on the balance of good over evil produced. For if anything is good-in-itself other than pleasure, or bad-in-itself other than pain, it is only reasonable to suppose that certain morally significant acts are, and if this is so we must before we can determine whether an act is right on utilitarian principles consider its own value or disvalue as well as that of its consequences.[4]

The effect of theories like those of Ewing and Johnson is to undercut the entire deontological position. If we accept their wide concept of intrinsic goodness, we can admit the validity of Ross's prima-facie duties while interpreting that validity by a utilitarian standard.

Another interesting type of utilitarianism is to be found in the ethics of G. E. Moore. Although he is a sharp critic of hedonism, he defines right in utilitarian terms. "Right conduct," he declares, "is universally conduct conducive to the good," and "no action which is not justified by its results can be right." It is such conduct "that more good or less evil will exist in the world if it be adopted than if anything else be done instead."[5] These and similar statements of Moore imply a utilitarian approach to ethics. His view is sometimes called "ideal utilitarianism" to distinguish it from hedonistic utilitarianism. He holds that knowledge, virtue, personal affections, and esthetic enjoyments are among the ultimate goods of life. Although in his *Ethics* he suggests that all intrinsic goods may contain some pleasure, he denies that good is reducible to pleasure alone. This kind of utilitarianism has the advantage over Kant of emphasizing consequences, while including the intrinsic good of moral character upon which Kant so strongly insisted. It has the advantage over hedonism of recognizing other goods besides pleasure, such as the goods of human love and intellectual and esthetic experience. At the same time it retains the basic utilitarian principle that we should act to promote good and to lessen or prevent evil.

The theory of Ralph Barton Perry will serve as another example of utilitarianism. In Chapter IV, I have characterized Perry's theory, and I now wish only to emphasize its relation to utilitarianism. He believes that the proper goal of life is a harmony of choiceworthy interests, representing a maximum of good achieved by the reduction of conflicts. He terms this good the "moral good" or the good of "harmonious happiness." "An act is right," he declares, "when it conduces . . . to harmonious happiness; and it is wrong when it conduces to disharmony."[6] Perry notes that we generally think of right as conformity to rules, but he is opposed to rules merely for the sake of rules. "If an act is to be morally right," he declares, "the rule to which it conforms must be a morally right rule, that is, a rule the observance of which conduces to moral goodness."[7] Thus right is interpreted teleologically, and the basic point of view is utilitarian.

I mention Perry's theory partly because it is akin to my own doctrine. In Chapter IV, I described the highest good, or the *summum bonum,* as "the full expression and realization of human nature as a dynamic organization of interests." Although no brief formula is sufficient to describe the range of human values, this way of phrasing the goal of human conduct seems to me relatively adequate. I believe that right action is most conducive to the good as so conceived.

Most of the classical theories of ethics, from Plato to Moore, are utilitarian, maintaining that the moral justification of actions must be in terms of results. Many of these writers have refused to call their theories "utilitarian," because they have interpreted this term hedonistically or in some other narrow sense. What I am concerned with is a type of theory, not a mere word to label it. If someone chooses to call this type of theory "teleological" or "axiological" rather than "utilitarian," I have no objection. But I shall continue to use the words "utilitarian" and "utilitarianism" throughout this chapter, and if the reader will bear in mind my explanation of their meaning, there should be no misunderstanding.

3. ACT-UTILITARIANISM AND RULE-UTILITARIANISM

As I noted earlier, there are two kinds of utilitarianism. When we say that an action is right, we may mean that an individual action is right, or we may mean that a class of actions is right. Act-utilitarianism judges rightness in terms of the consequences of individual acts; rule-utilitarianism judges rightness in terms of the consequences of the *rule* under which the particular act falls. By "rule" I mean a statement such as "It is wrong to steal" or "Do not break promises"—not a general principle, such as Kant's formula of the categorical imperative, or Bentham's "greatest happiness principle."

Act-utilitarianism. Perhaps the clearest advocate of act-utilitarianism is G. E. Moore. According to his theory, the rightness of an act depends, not on its being a certain *type* of action, such as the keeping of a promise, but on the consequences of this particular act. The total results of the act are the test, and the only ultimate test, of whether it is right or wrong. Moore declares "that the assertion 'I am morally bound to perform this action' is identical with the assertion '*This* action will produce the greatest possible amount of good in the Universe.' "[8] He recognizes the practical usefulness of moral rules, but as guides to the probable results of *particular* acts. "In cases of doubt," he maintains, "instead of following rules, of which he is unable to see the good effects in his particular case, the individual should rather guide his choice by a direct consideration of the intrinsic value or vileness of the effects which his action may produce."[9]

According to Moore, we can say of a particular act that it is either right or wrong, but we cannot speak in this unqualified way of a whole class of acts, because there are bound to be exceptions.

For instance, however we define "murder," it is unlikely that absolutely *no* case will ever occur in which it would be right to commit a murder; and, however we define "justice," it is unlikely that *no* case will ever occur in which it would be right to do an injustice. No doubt it may be possible to define actions of which it is true that, in an *immense* majority of cases, it is right or wrong to perform them; and perhaps *some* rules of this kind might be found to which there are really *no* exceptions. But in the case of most of the ordinary moral rules, it seems extremely unlikely that obedience to them will *absolutely always* produce the best possible results.[10]

If breaking the rule *does* produce the best possible consequences, then the rule ought to be broken. The right is always the very best that can be realized in the particular circumstances. It may be inconvenient or difficult or impossible to estimate the consequences of the particular act—so we are forced to fall back upon the rule. But the rightness or wrongness of obeying the rule against stealing, for example, depends solely on the goodness or badness of stealing on *that* occasion. It seemed to Moore that knowingly to choose the worse results when one might choose the better is always wrong, and that if this be admitted, "then it absolutely disposes of the view that there are any kinds of action whatever, which it *would* always be our duty to do or to avoid, *whatever* the consequences might be."[11] The utility of the act and not of the rule, according to Moore, is the ultimate standard of right.

If we accept the general premise of utilitarianism, there is much to be said for Moore's point of view. Many of the objections against Kantian formalism, or against any inflexible adherence to rules, would appear to be pertinent in defense of act-utilitarianism. If a person carefully and con-scientiously reaches the conclusion that breaking the rule will do more good than harm, what sound reason has he for keeping it? One cannot answer that the rule *in general* is justified, because the point is that following the rule is *not* justified in this instance. The act-utilitarian, in seeking to help and not injure his fellowman, is basing his action upon the principle of benevolence. What better basis can there be? To argue that rules are so sacrosanct that they should take precedence over kindness is to resort to superstition. Rules are made for men, not men for rules. Let us be done with this worship of rules and be mindful of the human person. So the argument runs.

In Marlowe's play, *Doctor Faustus,* it is the Devil who uses the abstract title, "Doctor," and it is God who calls Faust by his individual and proper name. If we are to do justice to the matchless individuality of human beings, we must follow the example of God and not the Devil. Every man is a unique person, and his predicament is likewise unique. When two individuals differ greatly in personality or life-situation the same rule may not serve for both. A single invariant code for the weak and the strong, the healthy and the neurotic, the practical man and the artist, the introvert and the extrovert, the emotionalist and the intellectualist, the mystic and the man about town, is not well designed to secure the happy release of energies and the accommodation to basic differences in situation and character. Insofar as rules repress the rich ferment of contrasting individualities, they make impossible the open, free, spontaneous society that has a real capacity for growth and improvement. The interaction of diverse, creative individuals, each expressing his own bent, is a prime condition of any higher culture. While admitting the limited value of rules, we must take care that they do not fence in the human spirit.

Not only may rules do violence to human individuality, but strict adher-ence to them may lead to a complete impasse. If, for example, the rule not to lie conflicts with the rule not to sacrifice human life, one *cannot* obey both. It is not morally edifying to say that one should live according to absolute moral rules; it is to demand the impossible. Because conflicts between rules can always arise, there is no substitute for responsible individual decision.

Henry Sidgwick, in his *Methods of Ethics,* examines the rule that we should keep our promises, and he finds that it must be hedged by many qualifications. He finally restates the rule in a form that is relatively adequate:

. . . A promise, express or tacit, is binding, if a number of conditions are ful-filled: viz. if the promiser has a clear belief as to the sense in which it was understood by the promisee, and if the latter is still in a position to grant release from it but unwilling to do so, if it was not obtained by force or fraud, if it does not conflict with definite prior obligations, if we do not believe that it will be harm-ful to the promisee, or will inflict a disproportionate sacrifice on the promiser, and if circumstances have not materially changed since it was made.[12]

Even this cumbersome rule will not cover particular exigencies. Each qualifi-cation has to be interpreted in the light of the particular circumstances, and the question whether it is applicable in the instant case cannot itself be decided by rule. Let us consider, for example, Sidgwick's qualification that a promise is not binding if it was obtained by fraud. As Leonard Miller has written:

We do not agree with each other as to what constitutes fraud, we may find it difficult to make up our own minds about what shall be called "fraud," and we may disagree among ourselves or be unsure ourselves as to what degree of fraud is permissible. In short, it is possible for all sorts of situations to occur where it would be extremely difficult to say whether or not this exempting condition was satisfied and therefore whether or not the rule should be followed.[13]

The contention of the act-utilitarian, that the rule is only a tentative guide, and that utility in the particular case must finally be decisive, appears reasonable in a great many circumstances.

Rule-utilitarianism. The concept of rule-utilitarianism, as a definite alternative to act-utilitarianism, has emerged clearly only in recent ethical theory. Nevertheless, we can find this view expressed with some degree of consistency by such classical utilitarians as David Hume, John Austin, and John Stuart Mill. Since Austin writes very clearly, I shall use his phrasing as illustrative.

. . . According to [the] theory, our conduct would conform to *rules* inferred from the tendencies of actions, but would not be determined by a direct resort to the principle of general utility. Utility would be the test of our conduct, ultimately, but not immediately: the immediate test of the rules to which our conduct would conform, but not the immediate test of specific or individual actions. Our rules would be fashioned on utility; our conduct on our rules. . . . If we would try the tendency of a specific or individual act, we must not contemplate the act as if it were single and insulated, but must look at the class of acts to which it belongs. We must suppose that acts of the class were generally done or omitted, and consider the probable effect upon the general happiness or good. . . . The *particular* conclusion which we draw, with regard to the single act, implies a *general* conclusion embracing all similar acts.[14]

Austin has here stated the essentials of rule-utilitarianism. Acts are to be tested by rules and rules by consequences. The only exceptions are when rules conflict, or when the particular act falls under no rule.

Austin cites a number of examples of the application of his theory. If a poor man should steal from his rich neighbor, his act might well be justified in terms of its particular utility; but if stealing were general, the effect would be disastrous. Hence the rule against stealing is justified, and the poor thief like the rich thief should be condemned. Or to take a second example, if I should evade the payment of a tax and devote the money to some excellent purpose, more good than harm might result from my individual act. "But the regular payment of taxes is necessary to the existence of the government. And I, and the rest of the community, enjoy the security which it gives, because the payment of taxes is rarely evaded."[15] Hence my evasion is not justified.

Similarly, the punishment of an individual, as a solitary thing, may do more harm than good. "But, considered as part of a system, a punishment is useful or beneficent. By a dozen or score of punishments, thousands of crimes are prevented."[16] Hence the individual punishment is justified by the results of the general practice.

To take a modern example, the question whether traffic regulations should be obeyed is similar. The law specifies that an automobile driver should not cross a street intersection if the traffic signal light is red. Yet it may seem highly desirable to the driver in certain circumstances to cross despite the red signal. But he might validly reason that the law in general should be obeyed, and obeyed in this instance, even though in the specific case a substantial advantage is to be gained by breaking it. The law should be obeyed because it is important that laws be maintained and because there should be a general respect for law. It is better to have traffic regulations, even though they are often inconvenient, than to have no regulations; and it is better, for the sake of the general practice, to obey the regulations even when it is quite inconvenient to do so. The advantage in strictly maintaining the general rule is greater than the advantage to be gained from particular infractions.

We can judge the value of moral rules only if we appraise them from a social and not merely individual standpoint. Arthur Koestler, in his *Insight and Outlook,* cites an instructive example. During World War II, there was a very serious fuel shortage in England, and to save fuel the government imposed regulations upon the use of hot water. One rule was that bathtubs should be filled to a maximum limit of five inches. As Koestler pointed out, "the temptation on a cold winter morning, particularly after a night spent at an air-raid post, to add two more inches was strong." From the standpoint of enlightened self-interest, there would seem to be no reason to resist the temptation.

Behind the locked door of one's bathroom the contravention would remain undetected; the quantity of water used was so negligible that in itself it could not harm the community; it could only do so if others were encouraged by the bad example to act in the same way; but as nobody would know, there was no question of giving a bad example.[17]

Yet as Koestler said, the welfare of the people of England depended upon the "self-imposed observation of the law by millions of individuals in the privacy of their bathrooms." He cites this example to show the "fallacy of utilitarian ethics," but the illustration merely shows the fallacy of a particular kind of utilitarianism. An individualistic utilitarian standard would excuse the infraction of the rule, but a social utilitarianism would recognize that a rule that is of great benefit to society should be maintained, even though individuals, taken severally, find it to their advantage to break it. An ethics of welfare cannot validly be based merely upon the individual decisions of separate persons, each regarding the utility of the particular act.

It is sometimes supposed that what is a good rule for individuals taken severally is a good rule for society. But to leap to this conclusion is as illogical as to suppose that, since all the notes in a symphony are short in duration, the symphony must be short in duration. Reasoning of this type commits what logicians call "the fallacy of composition," namely, the fallacy of supposing that what is true of the parts of a whole must be true of the whole. To return to our earlier example of voting, it scarcely pays for individuals, as mere individuals, to take the trouble to cast their ballots in a national election, since the voting of any single individual in such an election is very unlikely to affect the outcome; but it is nevertheless very important for a democratic society that its members vote, and the members therefore have a real obligation to vote. Consequently, we cannot judge what is our duty simply by calculating the utility of our acts taken separately and severally. We have many duties to society that are based upon social welfare, and that cannot be determined upon the basis of merely individual welfare. It is true that social welfare is realized in the lives of individuals; but the individuals function within a social whole that has its own distinct characteristics and institutions, and these must be taken into account in judging the duties of individuals. This is one of the reasons why *social* ethics is not identical with *individual* ethics.

But even if we are considering the welfare of individuals, the question of obligation must be answered in terms of the utility of the general rule or practice and not simply in terms of the utility of the individual act. A rule such as "Do not murder" or "Do not steal" represents the collective judgment of innumerable generations of men. Individual judgment, in contrast, is based upon a much narrower range of experience, and is notoriously fallible. Hence the legitimacy of the particular act is generally, and quite properly, decided by reference to the rule.

An act-utilitarian, such as G. E. Moore, may be prepared to grant this latter point. He was keenly aware of the practical difficulties of his theory, believing that the moral rules most universally recognized by common sense are likely to be more correct than our particular calculations. Since the remote effects of actions are generally undetectable, and even the more immediate effects are exceedingly difficult to estimate, "it seems doubtful whether the individual's judgment that the effects will probably be good in his case can ever be set against the general probability that that kind of action is wrong." Moore goes so far as to suggest that we ought never to break well established and tested rules:

It seems . . . that with regard to any rule which is *generally* useful we may assert that it ought *always* to be observed, not on the ground that in *every* particular case it will be useful, but on the ground that in *any* particular case the probability of its being so is greater than that of our being likely to decide rightly that we have before us an instance of its disutility. In short, though we may be sure that there are cases where the rule should be broken, we can never know which those cases are, and ought, therefore, never to break it.[18]

Moore restricts this conclusion to rules that are both generally useful and generally practiced. When rules are generally *un*useful or seldom obeyed, the best course is to be guided by the estimated utility of the individual act. With these exceptions, Moore tends in practice to agree with Austin, however much he differs in theory. Thus the practical difference between a *careful* act-utilitarianism and a similarly careful rule-utilitarianism may be very slight.

We have found that there are good reasons for both act-utilitarianism and rule-utilitarianism. Perhaps both are valid within restricted limits, act-utilitarianism applying at certain levels of moral decision, and rule-utilitarianism applying at other levels. Before we consider whether this is the case, it will be helpful to define the meaning of moral rules more precisely.

4. TWO CONCEPTS OF MORAL RULES

John Rawls has called attention to two different concepts of moral rules, "the summary concept" and "the practice concept."[19] According to the summary concept, a moral rule is a generalization from particular instances. Experience has taught us that certain ways of behaving usually produce good results. Telling the truth, for example, has good consequences and lying does not. Hence truthfulness is "made the rule." As a summary or report of what has been found valid in many instances, the rule is a guide to future decisions. Since there must first be decisions before a rule can summarize their results, the decisions are logically prior to the rules. Hence it is possible to challenge the validity of the rule by charging that it is a false generalization; or if the rule is accepted, it is possible to question whether it should be followed in a particular case.

The utilitarian moralist may insist that, once the summary rule has become well established, it is better to be governed by it. As Mill argued, the rule embodies the stored wisdom of generations of men, and hence it is likely to be more sound than a particular decision. Resort to the rule is also a great convenience. There may be no time to consider the consequences of particular acts; or the calculation of net good may be so difficult as to be unfeasible; or the individual conclusion may be so uncertain as to be unreliable. Keeping to the rule, rather than making an exception, will do indirect good in two ways: first, by strengthening in the agent the habit of keeping the rule, and second, by encouraging a general respect for moral principles. Conversely, violation of the rule has bad side effects. I may weaken my own character as a rule-keeper, and I may weaken the general faith in the rule. As Aristotle said, virtue is a habit or settled disposition, and it is important not to weaken or undermine it.

The theory of act-utilitarianism is logically compatible with a considerable reliance on summary rules. Moore, as we have seen, accepts act-utilitarianism in theory, but generally follows rules. When we turn to the practice concept of rules, however, the rules are so binding as to exclude act-utilitarianism even in theory. According to this concept, the rules are logically prior to the particular actions, since the nature of the actions is *defined* by the practice. As Rawls declares:

> In the case of actions specified by practices it is logically impossible to perform them outside of the stage-setting provided by those practices, for unless there is the practice, and unless the requisite proprieties are fulfilled, whatever one does, whatever movements one makes, will fail to count as a form of action which the practice specifies. . . . Only by reference to the practice can one *say* what one is doing. To explain or defend one's own action, as a particular action, one fits it into the practice which defines it. . . . When the challenge is to the practice, citing the rules (saying what the practice is) is naturally of no avail. But when the challenge is to the particular action defined by the practice, there is nothing that one can do but refer to the rules.[20]

Since the practice defines the form of action, it is absurd to raise the question whether the rule ought to be followed in the particular case. The only relevant question is whether one is "playing the game" faithfully and well.

This comparison of moral rules to the rules of a game brings out the force of the practice concept. In baseball, the various actions, such as stealing a base, striking out, or drawing a walk, have their point and meaning only within the context of the game. Hence the rules of the game determine what is permissible. When the umpire yells, "Strike three, you're out!" it would be absurd for the batter to plead with the umpire, "Can't I have four strikes just this once?" So long as we are playing the game of baseball, a fourth strike is not permissible. The batter has no choice but to abide by the rules.

The comparison of moral rules to the rules of a game makes clear the meaning of a practice, but it is misleading if taken literally. Moral rules, or laws setting forth moral principles, have a seriousness and obligatory character that the rules of a game lack, and hence there is something frivolous about the comparison. Consider, for example, the following passage from a book by the Oxford philosopher, T. D. Weldon:

> Let us . . . ask what it means to say that someone has a right to do something. . . . The simple answer which is also the correct one is "Because there is a law in this country to that effect." . . . Suppose however the objector goes on to say "Even if it is the law, I don't see why I should obey it." The only further comment is "Well, this is Great Britain, isn't it?" The position indeed is exactly parallel to that of the cricketer who asks "Why should I obey the umpire? What right has he to give me out?" One can answer only by expounding the rules of cricket. . . . Beyond that there is nothing to be done except to say, "This is a game of cricket, isn't it?" I believe that this is the answer and the complete answer to "What does it mean to say that A has a right to do X?"[21]

If the intent of this passage, as would appear from its context, is to characterize laws enforcing *moral* rights, the analysis is superficial and misleading.

Weldon blithely overlooks the fact that a game, with its defining rules, is designed mainly for entertainment, whereas laws setting forth human rights and obligations are designed for quite other and weighty reasons. If it is more fun for all concerned, a cricketer is morally free to violate a rule of cricket, but he is not morally free to violate the law of Great Britain against murder, however much fun he or others might find in doing so. Also moral activity is not nearly so conventional and formalized as chess or tennis or baseball. There are very definite rules about how to move a knight or a queen in chess, but ethical problems are often baffling because of the lack of precise or consistent rules.

Englishmen are especially fond of the comparison of moral rules with the rules of a game, and it is also characteristic of American philosophers who have been educated in British schools. There seems to be something characteristically English about the notion that being moral is "playing the rules of the game." It goes along with the Englishman's respect for "good form" and "fair play."

These notions have a moral connotation, and they extend beyond the sphere of games to legal procedures. Still more illuminating and profound than the comparison of moral rules with game-rules is the comparison of moral rules with "due process" and other closely related legal rules or principles, such as the Fifth Amendment privilege against self-incrimination. The root idea of due process is that of fair and regular procedure. This is evident in the stipulations of due process in a criminal trial. An accused person has the right to know the charges against him and to confront his accusers. He must have the opportunity to collect his evidence and to present it fairly and adequately. He is entitled to be represented by counsel, and he or his counsel has the right to cross-examine witnesses and to plead in his defense. The judge and jury who hear his case must be attentive and unbiased. The questioning of witnesses and the admission of evidence must exclude hearsay and forced confessions. If the accused is found innocent, he cannot be tried again for the same crime. Even if he is found guilty, there must be remedial procedure to uncover and correct any serious error that may have been committed in the trial of his case. Finally, the punishment must not be "cruel and unusual." These rules are important both to guarantee the objectivity of the fact-finding and guilt-affixing process and to respect the rights and dignity of the accused. They constitute fair and impartial procedure in the court-room.

The rules of due process are quasi-moral and not merely legal. They are rules of practice and not just summary rules. The practice is logically prior to the individual action, since it is for the sake of "due process" that the action is demanded. In isolation, an action that violates fair play or due process may have a great deal to recommend it, but it is rejected for the sake of the practice.

This fact is made clear by a consideration of the much disputed privilege against self-incrimination (which technically is not considered a rule of "due process" but is closely related). In the famous words of the Fifth Amendment: "No person . . . shall be compelled in any criminal case to be a witness against himself." This rule, as its critics point out, is often invoked by individuals accused of heinous crimes. In some instances, gangsters have successfully invoked the rule to escape conviction. The high court has reversed the conviction of notorious criminals on the ground of forced confession. Many political conservatives have denounced the rule as a shield to "subversives" who refuse to testify before legislative committees. As the Council of the Star Chamber, Britain's historic high court, declared in 1637, the result of the privilege is that many grave offenses go "undiscovered and unpunished."

How can one defend a rule that may thus protect the disloyal or the guilty? Not by citing the particular case, for the rule in the individual instance may *not* be justified. The justification is the value of the general practice. To understand this justification we must know something about the historical derivation of the Fifth Amendment rule.

Historians trace the origin of the rule back to the early Middle Ages, but is was not until the sixteenth century that the idea had been reduced to a Latin maxim, *Nemo tenetur prodere se ipsum*—or, in translation, "No one should be required to accuse himself." As early as 1589, Sir Edward Coke, the great English jurist, obtained a writ of prohibition against self-incrimination, although he himself participated at times in the administration of torture to extort confessions. In 1637, a stubborn and heretical fellow named John Lilburne refused to testify against himself, whereupon the Star Chamber sentenced him to be whipped and pilloried. Although the sentence was carried out, Lilburne appealed to Parliament, and the House of Commons voted that the sentence was "illegal and against the liberty of the subject," and the House of Lords, concurring, ordered that an indemnity of three thousand pounds (a lot of money in those days) be paid Lilburne. This famous case established the privilege as a part of English common law, and in this form it was transplanted to the American colonies. It was finally incorporated in the Bill of Rights and included in the constitution of nearly every state. In wording the rule is limited to criminal cases, but the courts have held the privilege also extends to a civil trial or legislative investigation, since any incriminating testimony may later be used to prosecute or convict in a criminal court.

The historical record shows that the rule was developed as a safeguard against torture and threat. Although torture was once accepted as a standard method of extorting evidence, the conscience of mankind finally condemned this sort of procedure. Dean Griswold of the Harvard Law School has pointed out:

For a very similar reason, we do not make even the most hardened criminal sign his own death warrant, or dig his own grave, or pull the lever that springs the trap on which he stands. We have through the course of history developed a considerable feeling of the dignity and intrinsic importance of the individual man. Even the evil man is a human being. . . . Neither torture nor an oath nor the threat of punishment should be used to compel him to provide the evidence to accuse or to convict himself. . . . As that old tartar Mr. Justice Stephen J. Field said, "The essential and inherent cruelty of compelling a man to expose his own guilt is obvious to every one, and needs no illustration." And in words that he approved, the privilege is the "result of the long struggle between the opposing forces of the spirit of individual liberty on the one hand and the collective power of the State on the other." Brown v. Walker, 161 U.S. 591, 637 (1896).[22]

History shows that the privilege has been invoked frequently in resisting prosecution for heresy or political offenses, and has served to protect freedom of thought and association.

It may also protect the innocent in ordinary criminal trials—for the truth, as well as falsehood, may incriminate an innocent man. To take a concrete example, suppose that a husband is falsely accused of murdering his wife, and that he is asked by the prosecutor if he had been alone with his wife in the murder room on the night of the crime. Let us suppose that he *had*. A truthful answer might send him to the gallows. As readers of mystery novels know, innocent persons often look guilty, and truthful disclosures may count heavily against them.

In the absence of the privilege against self-incrimination, very grave evils are possible. In the great Russian purge trials of the thirties, Pyatakov, Radek, Bukharin and numerous fellow "conspirators" confessed to terrorist plans and acts, and were forthwith condemned and executed. It is now generally recognized, even in the Soviet Union, that these confessions were spurious, and that they were secured by threats, brainwashing, and torture—the evil methods depicted by Arthur Koestler in *Darkness at Noon*. Similar abuses have occurred in Red China and in fascist states such as Nazi Germany. They are the standard operating procedures of police-states, whether of the right or the left. The privilege against self-incrimination, which bars such "third degree" methods, is an important bulwark against tyranny, and a great landmark in man's struggle to be dignified and free.

If the rule does far more good than harm, as I believe it does, its justification is the utility of the general practice and not the utility of the individual application. Rather than weaken and undermine the privilege, the courts will deliberately allow guilty men to escape—for if the rule is to have all the force and majesty of law, it must not waver under the pressures of public opinion, nor be subject to the whims and idiosyncrasies of judges, nor the temptations of police and prosecutors who want to get people to talk. Only if the rule stands firm, a sure rock in a time of storm, will it be a dependable defense against indignity and injustice.

This rule has been discussed here at some length because it illustrates the practice concept. It has emerged gradually from centuries of human experience, and in that sense is like a summary rule; but its usefulness depends upon the regularity of its application, and hence it is a rule of practice and not just a summary report of individual decisions.

5. WHAT DECISION-PROCEDURE SHOULD WE USE?

I am suggesting that a person may be a utilitarian without being *exclusively* an act-utilitarian or a rule-utilitarian, and without clinging to a single concept of rules. We need criteria for mediating between alternative justificatory principles. There should be some way to determine what kind of rule, summary or practice, is applicable, and whether the instant case should be decided by act-utilitarian considerations rather than by rule-utilitarian considerations.

It should be admitted at once that no perfectly clearcut criterion can be found for distinguishing between summary rules and practice rules, and for deciding which should apply in the particular case. "Practice" is an ambiguous term, referring to various kinds and degrees of practice, some of which are akin to the employment of summary rules. As Rawls has wisely commented:

> There will be many borderline cases about which it will be difficult, if not impossible, to decide which conception of rules is applicable. One expects borderline cases with any concept, and they are especially likely in connection with such involved concepts as those of a practice, institution, game, rule, and so on. Wittgenstein has shown how fluid these notions are.[23]

Because "practice" is a matter of degree, the looser sort of practice may permit exceptions. The rule of practice that defines how a rook may move in chess does not permit an exception, for if it *were* an exception to a rook move it would not conform to the game of chess. But the rules of moral practice ordinarily permit leeway and are seldom so definite as the defining rules of a game. They bear a closer analogy to flexible rules of strategy, which are modifiable if the goal of winning the game so requires. Even the defining rules of a game are not absolutely fixed; the rules of football, for example, are revised somewhat from season to season.

The good of a moral practice may be realized if there is a *general,* but not an absolutely universal, application of the rule. To suppose that the utility of a practice rule must be destroyed or greatly diminished by failure to apply it in every instance is a mistake. If the occasions are rare enough, a practice rule of justice, for example, can be set aside in the interests of benevolence without undermining the rule. Far from weakening the rule, a wise exception may strengthen it, for the exception is a device for preserving the rule essentially intact when there is some valid objection to following it. Rules with exceptions can still be practice rules, in the sense that the utility of the practice ordinarily takes precedence over the utility of the individual act. There is a strong prima-facie presumption, but not an absolute prohibition, against granting an exception.

Here I think we have to modify Rawl's contention that the practice defines and determines the act. The extent to which this is the case varies with the nature of the practice. According to the legal principles of due process, for example, the protection of the laws must be "equal"; but the concept of "equality before the law" is vague, and it must be construed differently in various circumstances. It is clear only as long as we do not apply it to individuals and concrete situations. All sorts of puzzles have to be faced and distinctions have to be made when it is so applied. The United States Supreme Court has refused again and again to define such standards as "due process" or "equality before the law," because what the standard requires in one set of circumstances may be different from what it requires in another set, for example, in an emergency. Precise definition would prevent the law from being a living and changing thing, dealing justly with the many cases that are not specifiable in advance. Most moral rules of practice are similarly problematical.

The error of formalism is the failure to realize that the letter of the law, being inflexible, does not guide men wisely in the novel and changing encounters of life. When the circumstances have so changed that the rule is an anachronism, unfitly surviving in an altered environment, it can no longer be justified. In dealing with very novel or complex situations, practice rules may be quite inapplicable, and even summary rules, if applicable at all, may be very tentative rules of thumb.

The practice concept of rules is most applicable to those fields that have become highly institutionalized, with offices and officers, established rules and regulations, penalties for breach of rules, and so on. It fits the rules of an army, or a court, or a legislative body, or a monastic order, or a profession governed by a definite code of ethics. It also fits situations in which uniformity and dependability are important, for instance, in establishing relations of trust by contracts or promises. But many fields are not thus formalized —the conditions are too uncertain and variable, and no relation of trust is at stake. The best guide one can hope for under these circumstances may be a summary rule.

Rules, whether practice or summary, are most suitable in associations in which human beings never get to know each other well. In some relations, people remain strangers, or without intimate personal contacts. They have been brought together by some external circumstance or abstract function, and their only intimacies are with persons *outside* of the association. Since decision on the basis of intimate knowledge is then out of the question, impersonal rules are generally indispensable, although if the circumstances are novel, no rule may be applicable. In addition to impersonal relations, there are bonds and fellowships based on personal affinity, which may range from casual friendship to the deepest love. Here personal decisions are required. Especially when the relation is one of profound love and intimate understanding, abstract rules are too cold and impersonal and undiscriminating. You cannot map in advance the ripening of a friendship, or regulate by formulae the intimacies among unique individuals. What is required is an intuitive sensitivity to the nuances of the particular case.

It must be admitted that practices are sometimes desirable in the most intimate human relations, as, for example, between man and wife. A marriage ceremony, with its vow, "For richer or poorer, in sickness and in health, until death do us part . . . ," makes conduct more dependable by cutting it off to some extent from consideration of consequences. Marriage as an institution depends for its existence upon such stabilization of conduct, the husband and wife each having a role that is faithfully sustained over the years, regardless of the particular temptations or consequences. The values thus conserved are those of a kind of rule-utilitarianism. But the practice of matrimony would be a stale affair if it were not kept fresh by "little, nameless, unremembered acts of kindness and of love." These acts are spontaneous and fall outside the scope of rules or practices.

To summarize, we need criteria to mediate between act-utilitarianism and rule-utilitarianism and between practice and summary rules. The ultimate criterion is the over-all utilitarian consideration, "What standard of justification in the given area of decision will yield the greatest net good (all things considered and in the long run)?" Different standards fit different situations, and the choice will depend upon the nature of the area with which we are dealing. The standard of rule-utilitarianism is usually more applicable to impersonal associations than to intimate personal relations. Practice rules are indispensable when much is to be gained by uniformity and human relations have become highly formal and institutionalized. But summary rules may be more suitable than practice rules in complex and variable situations. Rare exceptions may have to be made even to practice rules, but they should be based upon a wise discretion, such as that exercised by an able judge in a court of law.

With this flexible conception of utilitarianism in mind, we can more easily defend it against attack. I shall state the most important objections and briefly indicate what can be said in reply.

6. THE OBJECTION THAT THE
END DOES NOT JUSTIFY THE MEANS

The idea that the end justifies the means seems to be implicit in utilitarianism. "What I wish to point out," said G. E. Moore, "is that 'right' does and can mean nothing but 'cause of a good result,' and is thus identical with 'useful'; whence it follows that the end always will justify the means, and that no action which is not justified by its results can be right."[24] The utilitarian doctrine, stated in this way, has been subject to a great deal of attack. How can such qualities as truthfulness and fidelity retain any vestige of moral dignity if they are valued for their utility alone? How can we retain our moral integrity if we are prepared to use lying or theft or violence as means to our ends? In maintaining that we are justified in doing evil that good may come, utilitarianism degrades ethics to the level of mere expediency.

Answer. This criticism is justified when directed against certain crude forms of utilitarianism, such as the cynical advice of Machiavelli to the Prince, or the rationalization of vicious means by modern fascists or communists. In these instances, there is grave question whether the end sought is really good and whether the means chosen are really necessary. The saying that "the end justifies the means" can never excuse the use of objectionable means to even the best of ends if less objectionable ones might be chosen. We are not justified in doing evil so that good may come, if the evil outweighs the good or if the good could be achieved at less cost.

The crude utilitarian makes a fundamental mistake in supposing that right is a mere instrument to good, neglecting entirely its intrinsic values. Where love of the good is present in the performance of duties, it cannot be denied that the state of a man's mind, in performing them, contains something intrinsically good. The goodness of a general ideal pattern of living is partially realized at the point of right action—not just at the point of subsequent consequences. Also the means tend to carry over to and infect the end, so that the goodness of the end is compromised and degraded when the means are evil.

Whether "the end justifies the means" depends upon its meaning. It is false if ends and means are regarded as quite external to one another. Even if the end is good, the means may pervert and corrupt the end, or the evil of the means may outweigh the good end, or the means may be unnecessarily bad. But a good end may justify an intrinsically bad but *necessary* means to that end, as for example, the defeat of the fascist powers may have justified our waging of war, terribly evil though that was. Although evil means usually infect the goal, the end may have a relative independence and stability, and consequently we cannot say that the qualitative character of the means must *always* carry over to, and determine, the qualitative character of the end. It does not follow that, because a medical operation is painful, the consequent state of health is also painful, or that the American republic was doomed to be a regime of violence because it was created by violent revolution. Also if ends are degraded by bad means it is equally true that means are elevated by good ends. Christ drove the money changers out of the temple, but Christians do not regard this violent act as reprehensible.

The relation between means and ends is too complex to be understood in terms of any simple or inflexible formula. The end *sometimes* justifies the means, but not always; and either the end or the means can be overempha-sized at the expense of the other. The only safe generalization is that we should estimate very carefully the values and disvalues involved in both act and consequences, in both means and end, and that we should choose, to the best of our ability, the course of action which yields most value and least disvalue when *all* things are considered. If the utilitarian doctrine is phrased in this way, there is nothing morally callous or irresponsible about it.

7. THE OBJECTION THAT UTILITARIANISM CANNOT ACCOUNT FOR THE MOST STRINGENT OBLIGATIONS

Ross maintains that very stringent duties cannot be adequately explained on utilitarian grounds. The obligation to keep a promise is an example. Having made a solemn promise, a person has an obligation to keep it even though purely utilitarian considerations would require breaking the promise. According to Ross:

To make a promise is not merely to adopt an ingenious device for promoting the general wellbeing; it is to put oneself in a new relation to one person in particular, a relation which creates a specifically new prima-facie duty to him, not reducible to the duty of promoting the general wellbeing of society.[25]

This non-utilitarian duty may clash with other prima-facie duties and is not necessarily paramount; but at least it is a prima-facie duty that cannot be ex-plained on exclusively utilitarian grounds. According to Ross, the obligation not to tell lies, to make restitution for harm done, and to return benefit to one's benefactors, are other examples. There seems to be more than a utili-tarian obligation in these cases.

Answer. I have already pointed out that there is a method of undercutting the whole deontological argument. If we can show that right thinking and acting involve *intrinsic* values, we will not have to explain their rightness simply in terms of their consequences. We can maintain that a moral way of life is intrinsically good and an immoral way of life is intrinsically evil. We can still cling to the essential thesis of utilitarianism—that our sole duty is to maximize net-good—but we will insist that the goodness of right action must be counted and not merely the goodness of its consequences. In this way we can explain the stringency of the obligation, and thus undermine the deontological position.

I agree with those philosophers, such as Moore and Ewing and Johnson, who maintain that there are intrinsic values in moral ways of thinking and acting. The good is ingredient in right and not something altogether separate and foreign. There is a kind of health and happiness of the soul in doing right that there is not in doing wrong. Love, generosity, fidelity, fairness, and similar traits are characteristic of right action, and these are good in themselves. Also cruelty, selfishness, infidelity, unfairness, and similar traits are characteristic of wrong action, and these are intrinsically evil. In calculating net-good, we should of course not leave out of account these immediate goods and evils.

One way of putting this point is to say that a moral way of life *satisfies* us, not just in the long run, but in the very act of doing right. Rightness has an inner cleanness and beauty and healthiness about it that is savored in direct experience. As Louis Arnaud Reid has said:

> Greed, cruelty, oppression, it seems, do not . . . satisfy, socially or individually. Generosity, kindness, mercy, do. And if we look at the great moral figures of history, we might say that they were deeply satisfied people (which is not contradicted by the fact that they may have suffered greatly and in some cases were martyred), and that the kind of satisfaction they enjoyed is just what we mean by morally good satisfaction.[26]

The immediate satisfactions involved in virtue are part of the end or ideal life, and not merely a means to a good other than themselves.

We must not overlook another important consideration. According to rule-utilitarianism, there is a strong reason for disapproving such acts as breaking promises or telling lies even when the consequences to the persons directly involved are quite good. Considered as an individual act, a lie may be justified, yet it may be better to tell the truth for the sake of maintaining the general rule of truth-telling. It is better for mankind in general to follow the rule that one should tell the truth, even if in specific instances truth-telling imposes hardships, than to allow individual taste and judgment to decide in each particular instance what ought to be done and thus to weaken and undermine the rule.

This consideration is especially strong when the rule is derived from a practice, as in the case of promises. That promising is a practice and the rule derived from it is a practice rule is beyond question. This is shown by the meaning of the words, "I promise," when used in the transaction of giving and accepting a promise. These words are understood to imply, "I commit myself to carry out my promise, and you can trust me to do it." They create a relation of trust between the promiser and the promisee. But no such relation of trust can be established unless there is already the practice of making and keeping promises. As Rawls has written:

> . . . "I promise" is a performatory utterance which presupposes the stage-setting of the practice and the proprieties defined by it. Saying the words "I promise" will only be promising given the existence of the practice. It would be absurd to interpret the rules about promising in accordance with the summary conception. It is absurd to say, for example, that the rule that promises should be kept could have arisen from its being found in past cases to be best on the whole to keep one's promises; for unless there were already the understanding that one keeps one's promises as part of the practice itself, there could not have been any cases of promising.[27]

The freedom to decide particular cases on utilitarian grounds is incompatible with the concept of a practice. Since it is the practice that is justified on utilitarian grounds and not the particular act, the utilitarian defense for the act of breaking a promise is not available to the promiser.

We have stated two strong reasons for keeping a promise that are usually overlooked by the critics of utilitarianism. First, there are intrinsic values in this act. Faithfulness is the very crux of a promise, for without the guarantee of good faith the promise cannot be made. The keeping of the promise is being true to your word; it is maintaining your faithfulness and integrity, and these qualities of character surely have intrinsic value. Here, as in other instances, the good is ingredient in the right, and this good should be counted as much as any other. Second, it is a practice that is justified on utilitarian grounds, and in the light of the practice, we require the faithful observance of the rule, and disapprove its violation in the particular instance. These two reasons are sufficient to account for the stringency of the obligation without resort to a deontological ethics.

The opponent of utilitarianism may still not be satisfied. He may cite the case of a "solemn promise" made without any witness being present. For example, two men, one dying and the other well, have conversed in solitude; and the survivor has made a solemn promise to the dying man to see to it that the latter's son receives a good education. In a case of this sort, there can be no question of undermining the rule by providing a bad example. All that the survivor has to do is to keep the promise a secret, and then no one else will know about his breaking the promise. If utilitarianism were correct, says the deontologist, the survivor ought to ignore the promise if he can find any way to spend his money that would produce more net good; but this conclusion does violence to our moral sensibilities.

Two points can be made in reply. First, the fact that the promise is kept a secret does not dispose of the argument of the rule-utilitarian. The person who *breaks* the promise knows that he is doing so. In violating a "solemn promise," he is setting a bad precedent for *himself,* quite apart from any example to others. The effect may be seriously to weaken his own character as a promise-keeper, just as his honesty would be impaired if he should feel free to steal whenever it appears expedient and he is safe from detection. From the standpoint of social wellbeing, moreover, a practice rule may be morally binding when its violation is undetectable. To make this point clear, let us recall Koestler's example of the wartime regulation to economize strictly in the use of hot water. In this case, the rule was rightly observed by millions of individuals in the privacy of their bathrooms, where an infraction would remain undetected and there could be no question of providing a bad example. The important consideration was the social utility of the entire *class* of acts as defined by the regulation, and this utility was unaffected by the fact that particular infractions would be undetected. Similar considerations apply to promise-keeping. If individuals in general should feel at liberty to break

promises *when no one is aware,* the effect would be to weaken and undermine the whole institution of promise-keeping. The utilitarian moralist can
here avail himself of Kant's principle of universalization, while interpreting it
on a rule-utilitarian basis.

Second, the intrinsic value of faithfulness remains in this case as in others.
Let us remember that a "solemn promise" has been made. The use of the
word "solemn" implies a kind of ritualistic sanctity attaching to the promise.
Keeping the promise, like the act of putting flowers on a grave, is a way of
being "true" to one's departed friend. The story of a dispute between an
American and a Chinese will illustrate this point. The American chides the
Chinese for placing a bowl of rice on the grave of his loved one. "You silly
fellow," says the American. "You surely don't suppose that the dead will rise
up and eat the rice." In reply, the Chinese chides the American for placing
flowers on the grave of *his* beloved. "You silly man," says the Chinese. "You
surely don't think that the dead will rise up and sniff the flowers." In both
cases, the value of the act is ritualistic; it is a way of keeping fresh the cherished memory of the departed, of commemorating his worth as a human
being, and of celebrating the value of love. Especially is this true when the
dead person has been a close relative or a dear old friend. On the other
hand, a violation of the promise is an act of desecration and infidelity. The
values here at stake are partly esthetic and religious, but they are none the
less intrinsic and substantial. We must take human beings as we find them,
and these "sentimental values," as a cynic might call them, are an important
part of the intrinsic good of human living. They are no more to be scoffed
at than our feelings at a birthday party, which is also a kind of celebration.

I have dealt with the example of promises because it is the favorite among
deontologists. The answer that I would give in other test-cases is similar to the
answer that I have given in this instance. A full discussion would have to be
very lengthy.

8. THE OBJECTION THAT UTILITARIANISM
IS IRRECONCILABLE WITH JUSTICE

This objection can be stated as follows. The sole injunction of utilitarianism
is to produce the greatest possible net-good. According to the utilitarian
standard, any distribution of goods and evils, however unjust, ought to be
preferred to any other distribution, however just, if it would yield the slightest additional net good. To maintain such a view is shockingly to neglect
the right of every man to fair treatment. Slavery might yield the greatest
net good, yet it would be unjust and immoral. Punishment of the innocent
is always wrong, regardless of how much net good may accrue. Even if the
balance of good could be increased by the lonely and undeserved torture
of a single individual, the injustice to him would morally outweigh the
greater good achieved.

Answer. To reply to this criticism, we must clarify the meaning of "justice." Without undertaking an exhaustive analysis, we can say that justice is the virtue of reaching an equitable settlement among competing interests. Seeking a proper balance between conflicting rights or claims, the just decision excludes arbitary bias or favoritism. It is a principle of justice, for example, that no man shall be judge in his own cause lest the decision be prejudiced. Basic to the concept of justice is the idea of *fairness,* as for example, in the distribution of rewards and penalties according to merit. When justice is personified in sculpture, it is commonly represented as a blindfolded figure holding a scale. The symbolism is obvious—the lady is blind to any distinction between persons that is not subject to an objective determination. Sidgwick formulates the principle of justice in the "axiom" that "similar cases should be treated similarly," or stated more fully: "It can not be right for A to treat B in a manner in which it would be wrong for B to treat A, merely on the ground that they are two different individuals, and without there being any difference between the natures or circumstances of the two which can be stated as reasonable grounds for difference of treatment."[28]

This axiom of justice is implied by the principle of utilitarianism, for if it is my duty to promote the greatest net good, then I should not be drawn aside by nonrelevant differences between persons. I should not be swayed by callousness or favoritism with the result that I choose the lesser good when I might choose the greater. I should not make an exception in my own behalf, or in behalf of anyone I favor, unless I can give some objective and sufficient reason for doing so.

With a similar thought in mind, Bentham maintains that everyone should count for one and no one for more than one. As I have already pointed out, this formula is ambiguous, but it *can* mean that the happiness of any man is as intrinsically good, and hence as worthy of respect, as the quantitatively equal happiness of any other. Bentham declares:

> The happiness of the most helpless pauper constitutes as large a portion of the universal happiness, as does that of the most powerful, the most opulent member of the community. Therefore the happines of the most helpless and indigent has as much title to regard at the hands of the legislator as that of the most powerful and opulent.[29]

Hedonistic utilitarianism, as Bentham points out, demands an equal recognition of human pleasure in identical amount wherever and in whomsoever found. In this sense, it is fundamentally democratic, since the variation among people in the capacity for pleasure is much less than the variation in their capacity for intellectual or spiritual development. If we should identify justice with the democratic ideal of equality, then there is a kind of justice implicit in the purest sort of quantitative hedonism.

Another consideration recognized by Bentham that implies a democratic concept of justice is "the law of diminishing utility." This is the common-

sense principle that, as men become more affluent, there is a diminishing return in human happiness for every unit of money or resources expended. For
example, if you give a quarter to a poor and hungry man for a bowl of soup,
you will contribute more to human satisfaction, than if you give an equivalent
sum to a wealthy man. In the words of a distinguished economist:

> . . . It is evident that any transference of income from a relatively rich man
> to a relatively poor man of similar temperament, since it enables more intense
> wants to be satisfied at the expense of less intense wants, must increase the ag-
> gregate sum of satisfaction.[30]

This is a powerful reason for coming to the aid of the more destitute, especially if the beneficiaries of this aid are given a good sound education, so
that their choice of goods will be wise and informed. It is also a reason for a
more equitable distribution of income, limiting the maximum as well as
raising the minimum.

There are other strong utilitarian reasons to favor a policy of spreading happiness as widely as possible. A farmer cannot hope to raise a bumper crop by
cultivating only a portion of his fertile land; likewise a statesman cannot
hope to raise a bumper crop of happiness by cultivating only a portion of
the population. The wide sharing of happiness almost invariably produces
more happiness, first, because more people are happy, and second, because
sharing yields a bonus in additional happiness. What Shelley, in "Epipsy-
chidion," said about the sharing of mental goods applies in this instance:

> True Love in this differs from gold and clay,
> That to divide is not to take away. . . .
> If you divide suffering and dross, you may
> Diminish till it is consumed away;
> If you divide pleasure and love and thought,
> Each part exceeds the whole; and we know not
> How much, while any yet remains unshared
> Of pleasure may be gained, of sorrow spared.

Used as a defense of free love, Shelley's reasoning may leave much to be desired, but otherwise it expresses a profound truth. For a bonus quantity of
happiness is created through the good will and friendly feelings generated by
sharing and fair play. Conversely, the unfair distribution of happiness, or of
the means thereto, results in the considerable diminution of net good, since the
slighted individuals and groups will feel unfairly treated, and this will cause
additional suffering among them. Hence, for a utilitarian of Bentham's stripe,
restrictive policies are to be condemned, but condemned *because* they would
decrease the total net good.

According to utilitarianism, we are never justified in imposing an evil not
compensated by good results. Every man, being capable of enjoyment and
suffering, is a locus of ultimate values, and is to be respected and treated as
such. This means that every person is entitled to as much good and as little
evil as possible, so long as this does not interfere with the greater net-good of

others. Bentham, with these principles in mind, could agree with his critics that it is wrong to distribute goods arbitrarily or unfairly, but he would say that it is not arbitrary or unfair to be governed by best results to all concerned.

To the objection that it is morally wrong to achieve a greater good by the suffering of a single lonely soul, the utilitarian can argue that the common sense of mankind is to the contrary. As a matter of fact, we exact this kind of sacrifice from many lonely souls in prison or on the battlefield. A military commander may realize that he is dispatching men to almost certain wounding or death, yet if he has made a correct military judgment in a sufficiently good cause, we do not blame him for his decision. All that can reasonably be demanded is that he should make the best of a bad situation. No one is ever justified on utilitarian grounds in imposing or permitting *any* gratuitous suffering. The utilitarian, more than his formalistic critic, endeavors to be kind and considerate, and if it is necessary to impose sacrifices, he does it with a heavy heart.

This sort of defense is available to a quantitative utilitarian. A "qualitative utilitarian," such as John Stuart Mill, or an "ideal utilitarian," such as G. E. Moore, can fall back upon additional defenses.

Mill maintains that a merely quantitative approach neglects the qualities of the goods in question, and that in estimating best results, we should consider not only the quantity but the quality of the good-making property. Now the quality of the good may depend in part upon moral characteristics. States of experience that involve fairness may be qualitatively superior (other things being equal) to states that involve unfairness. Mill could thus have dealt with the cases in which the principle of utility seems to sanction injustice. He could say that the pleasures involving injustice are qualitatively inferior to the pleasures free from this taint, although the latter may rank lower by purely quantitative standards. If so, it would be consistent with utilitarianism to prefer the pleasures of justice on the grounds of their qualitative superiority, and the conflict of justice with utility could be avoided. A similar answer can be made by the adherent of an "interest theory" if he recognizes qualitative differences among interests and satisfactions.

An ideal utilitarian, such as Moore, can include the fairness of distribution among the intrinsic goods to be promoted. Ross, on this point, agrees with the ideal utilitarian. He contends that justice is intrinsically good, and that our duty to promote it should be explained on utilitarian grounds. If we concur, we can add to the good to be distributed the good of distributing it fairly and set both goods against the evil of distributing it unfairly. This solution would undermine the deontologist's objection, while preserving the utilitarian conviction that we should leave the world better than we found it, and as much better as we can.

Now it does seem fairly clear that justice *is* intrinsically good. Other things being equal, a just social order is intrinsically better than an unjust one. Justice can be conceived as a way of life, and a just way of life may be considered intrinsically better than an unjust way. Or justice may be interpreted as

the fulfillment of human rights, and if so, there is intrinsic value in this fulfillment. The dignity of the human spirit, as expressed in the rights of man,
is surely one of the ultimate goods of life.

The rule-utilitarian can defend justice on still another ground. Many forms
of justice are like the legal justice of "due process." They pertain to *practices*
that are justifiable as such and not simply to individual acts. Both the deontologist and the rule-utilitarian can agree that the rightness or wrongness of
an act is *not* determined solely by the intrinsic value of the consequences of
that act. Hence they may equally condemn an unjust *act,* even though the
act, when considered in isolation from the practice, may seem to be justified
on utilitarian grounds. Thus deontological formalism and rule-utilitarianism
are in many ways closely related. If the deontologist fails to recognize this
fact, he will greatly underestimate the strength of the utilitarian position.

Take, for example, the matter of punishment. "If some kind of very cruel
crime becomes common, and none of the criminals can be caught," remarks
E. F. Carritt, "it might be highly expedient, as an example, to hang an
innocent man, if a charge against him could be so framed that he were
universally thought guilty."[31] Carritt concludes that a utilitarian would be
logically bound in this instance to approve the "punishment" of an innocent
person. But he overlooks the fact that punishment is a practice, and that in
a civilized society this practice is highly institutionalized. Rawls defines the
institution of punishment as follows:

A person is said to suffer punishment whenever he is legally deprived of some
of the normal rights of a citizen on the ground that he has violated a rule of law,
the violation having been established by trial according to the due process of law,
provided that the deprivation is carried out by the recognized legal authorities of
the state, that the rule of law clearly specifies both the offense and the attached
penalty, that the courts construe statutes strictly, and that the statute was on the
books prior to the time of the offense.[32]

For a judge or jury to condemn a man known to be innocent, even though
there is some substantial advantage in doing so, is to violate the whole concept of punishment as a practice. The safeguards against such miscarriage
of justice are built-in features of the institution of punishment. If the institution is justified on utilitarian grounds, so are these safeguards. Moreover,
if *right,* as the utilitarian contends, means doing most good, we must include in "most good" not merely the results of the isolated act, but the good
produced by the carrying out of just principles and practices as such.

We must also include the moral effect on the judge or the jury that deliberately reaches an unjust verdict. Injustice itself is an evil, and the willing
of it is an evil too. Even if the good produced in a particular case seems less
if the just verdict is imposed than if it is not imposed, justice should still be
done, first, because the habit and institution of justice is good as a practice,
and second, because the realization of a generally good motive in an agent is
itself an intrinsic good of fundamental importance.

It may be said by the deontologist that such utilitarian considerations are largely irrelevant, and that the necessary and sufficient reason to punish anybody is that he deserves it. This conviction has had a profound influence upon the theory and practice of criminal justice. As F. H. Bradley points out, it represents the belief of most men:

> If there is any opinion to which the man of uncultivated morals is attached, it is the belief in the necessary connection of punishment and guilt. Punishment is punishment, only where it is deserved. We pay the penalty, because we owe it, and for no other reasons; and if punishment is inflicted for any other reason whatever than because it is merited by wrong, it is a gross immorality, a crying injustice, an abominable crime, and not what it pretends to be.[33]

This view has been championed by many sophisticated philosophers, such as Kant and Hegel, or more recently, by C. D. Broad. Kant warns us against being misled by utilitarian considerations. "The penal law," he writes, "is a categorical imperative; and woe to him who creeps through the serpent-windings of utilitarianism to discover some advantage that may discharge him from the justice of punishment, or even from the due measure of it."[34]

Unquestionably it is plausible to maintain that good men are more deserving of happiness than bad men, and that bad men are more deserving of unhappiness than good men, and that we should therefore aim at a "just" distribution of happiness and unhappiness, rewarding the virtuous and punishing the wicked. Even God has supposedly been motivated in this way, elevating good men into a never-ending heaven and casting bad men into a never-ceasing hell. Apart from theological doctrines, most people would maintain that punishment should be based upon justice rather than upon utility, and that utility and justice are quite different.

What can the utilitarian say in reply? First, he can point out that utilitarianism does not necessarily condemn rewards and punishments. If goodness is rewarded with happiness, goodness will be encouraged, and men will tend more often to serve their fellows; and if moral badness is punished by unhappiness, badness will be discouraged, and men will tend less often to injure their fellows. To this extent, a utilitarian can be as much in favor of punishment as anyone else. What he condemns is gratuitous increase of misery, without compensatory gain.

Second, he can approve "retribution" in one quite proper meaning of the word, namely, in the sense of *reprobation*. By reprobation I mean the stigmatizing of a crime as reprehensible, as for example, when the Nazi war criminals were condemned, in the Nuremberg trials, for their "crimes against humanity." In this sense, retribution is an emphatic way of telling a man that he has done wrong, being much more impressive and difficult to forget than verbal scolding. At the same time, it is a way of sharpening the conscience of the community.

Without a sense of retribution we may lose our sense of wrong. Retribution in punishment is an expression of the community's disapproval of crime, and if this retribution is not given recognition then the disapproval may also disappear. A community which is too ready to forgive the wrongdoer may end by condoning the crime.[35]

Indignation at wrongdoing is a very healthy attitude, but in proportion to its disinterestedness and the excellence of its consequences.

But if "retribution" means hitting back in a spirit of vengeance, then utilitarianism is not alone in condemning it. It is contrary to the teachings of the greatest moral and religious leaders of mankind. It is a relic of primitive moral systems, such as "an eye for an eye, a tooth for a tooth." Being motivated by hatred, it is always and necessarily bad. In this sense of retribution, it should be expunged from our moral code.

Having reached this point, I must confess that there are still residual doubts in my mind. Perhaps justice cannot be fully explained on utilitarian grounds. To make the question more vivid, let me cite a grisly case in the English courts (Queen v. Dudley, 1884).

Dudley, Stephens, and Brooks, three seamen, and a boy named Richard Parker were the crew of an English yacht which was caught in a storm 1,600 miles from the Cape of Good Hope. As they drifted on the ocean, their meager supply of food, including a turtle which they caught, lasted barely twelve days. By the twentieth day, all of them were in a state of extreme weakness and prostration. There was still no sail in sight nor any prospect of relief. And so, with the approval of Stephens but not of Brooks, Dudley dragged himself over to where Richard Parker lay and stuck a knife into the throat of the helpless boy. The three men fed on the body for four days. On the fourth day, they were picked up by a passing vessel. Dudley and Stephens were tried and both were found guilty of murder.[36]

In this case, three persons were kept alive by the slaughter of an unoffending human being. The moral question is whether their action was right. For an act-utilitarian, the killing would seem to be justifiable. For a rule-utilitarian, the decision is not so clear, but it is arguable that the rule against murder is inapplicable, and that the act should be classified as justifiable homicide.

The jury decided on the verdict of murder. Perhaps they would not have done so if the circumstances of the case were somewhat altered. Suppose that the starving men had agreed that they would all die if someone were not to be sacrificed, and that they should draw straws to determine which one should be the victim. Either *someone,* or everyone, would have to die, and the selection of the victim was devised so as to be unmalicious and as nondiscriminatory as possible. Under these nightmarish circumstances, the procedure would have been fair, and the verdict of the court might have been quite different. The concept of fairness in an instance of this sort is difficult to reduce to utilitarian criteria, *unless we admit that fairness itself has intrinsic value and include it among the goods to be maximized.*

Utilitarianism may have to be qualified but surely not altogether abandoned. If we should decide that justice cannot be wholly explained on utilitarian grounds, our *principal* duty may still be to achieve the most good, subject only to the constraint that justice should not be violated.

9. OTHER OBJECTIONS

Lest this chapter continue to interminable length, I shall briefly consider only
four additional objections.

The argument based on freedom. A number of writers contend that freedom
is irreconcilable with utilitarianism. The right to be free should be cate-
gorically respected, even though it may be possible to create a society of
happy, carefree human-robots. This objection seems to me fatal to hedonism
but not to other kinds of utilitarianism. Aldous Huxley's *Brave New World*
depicts an imaginary state of society which is hedonistically very satisfactory,
and yet is ethically revolting because of its very lack of freedom. Freedom is
part of the essential good of life, being immensely valuable both as means and
end. An adequate utilitarianism, not bound by the limits of hedonism, would
recognize the basic imperfection of an unfree society.

The argument based on the personal nature of obligation. Advancing one of
his most forceful arguments, Ross maintains that the essential defect of the
utilitarian theory is that it ignores or underestimates the highly personal
character of duty. We have special obligations to friends, relatives, benefactors, or others with whom we have personal dealings. Ross contends that we
should choose the lesser good of the person to whom we are specially obliged
rather than the greater good of the stranger toward whom we have no such
obligation. This conclusion, it is said, contradicts the utilitarian rule of the
greatest good.

How can the utilitarian answer this argument? He will reply that people
usually produce more good when they fulfill their special obligations to the
best of their ability than when they aim indiscriminately at the general good;
but he will also insist that we should be kind even to strangers. My own
answer is implied by much that I have written in the present book about the
nature and value of the intimate community. I believe that the deepest
human values inhere in these intimate associations. Where there is such
intimacy, there must be a very special mutual concern, and therefore a recognition of special obligations. The intimate community would quickly disinte-
grate if its members were to recognize no more obligation to one another than
to perfect strangers. Because of the prime importance of personal relations,
Ross is correct in stressing them. But a utilitarian can take this view quite as
consistently as a deontologist. In *The Methods of Ethics,* Henry Sidgwick

examines the duties of personal obligation, and argues convincingly that they have a firm utilitarian basis.

Nevertheless, I do not believe that personal duties *necessarily* take precedence over impersonal ones. The duty of disinterested good will or impartial justice may override personal considerations. The very concept of the moral "ought," as I shall maintain in the next chapter, requires a certain disinterestedness and detachment from personal ties. If we approach the question from a religious standpoint the conclusion will be similar. The all-encircling love of the religious spirit is not limited by personal and group loyalty. The basic moral injunction of Christianity is the principle of love to one's neighbor as to oneself—in the sense that *every* person who can be affected by our actions is our neighbor. This is the implication of the story of the good Samaritan and of much else in the New Testament. In Buddhism, there is a similar doctrine of infinite compassion. Love is rooted in the intimate community, but in its highest manifestations, it is projected beyond all narrow limits.

The argument based upon the retrospective character of obligation. Ross argues that duties are retrospective and not simply prospective. They depend upon obligations contracted in the past, and not simply upon future results. He maintains that the utilitarian moralist, with his eyes fixed upon consequences, neglects the retrospective basis of obligation.

It is true that we are morally bound by past actions, for example, by the signing of a contract. But why honor these "prima-facie obligations"? Because it will do some good? If so, we are agreeing with the utilitarians. Because it is self-evidently our duty? But this is the very question under dispute.

Duties may be retrospective, and still be based upon utilitarian grounds. These special obligations, such as the duty to pay our debts or to keep our promises, imply some sort of practice or institutional framework. For instance, the obligation to respect one's marriage vow involves the whole institution of the family. In general, the duties of fidelity, reparation, or gratitude—the kinds of duties that have a firm basis in the past—form an integral part of the *system* of reciprocity and mutual aid by which the normal functioning of society is maintained. As contributory to this system, these retrospective duties cannot be understood apart from the institutions and practices to which they contribute. They belong, in the famous phrase of F. H. Bradley, to "my station and its duties." Being essential to the social order, they are frequently enforced by law—for instance, through the legal requirements that contracts be kept, that damages be compensated, that debts be paid, or that services be exchanged.

But if laws and practices are involved, there is clearly more at stake, from a utilitarian standpoint, than the results of individual acts. Rule-utilitarianism is here more applicable than act-utilitarianism, and practice rules more applicable than summary rules. But rules and practices *do* have a foundation in tradition and precedent and prior commitments; they are retrospective and not just prospective. Hence the objection of Ross applies only against a limited sort of act-utilitarianism.

The argument based on the incommensurability of values. One of the most common objections to utilitarianism is that values cannot be accurately measured, and that utilitarianism is consequently unworkable as a theory. This objection was noted in Chapter III, and we will return to it in the next chapter. At present, I will merely remark that the eclectic theory of Ross, because it combines the difficulties of both utilitarian and deontological ethics, offers no more practicable alternative. So far as we accept his utilitarian duties, we are confronted by the same problem of calculation that any utilitarian faces; and insofar as we accept his deontological duties, we are confronted by all the uncertainties of intuitionism. Not only must we accept certain general intuitions (for example, that lying, quite apart from utilitarian considerations, is wrong), but we must also intuit the relative stringencies of prima-facie deontological duties whenever they conflict with one another. Finally, we must wrestle with the difficulty of weighing utilitarian considerations against deontological considerations whenever there is a conflict between the two sorts of duty. How can such disparate kinds of consideration be intelligently balanced against one another? Utilitarianism is comparatively simple in its demands.

In this chapter, I have tried to show that a thoughtful reformulation of utilitarianism can meet the objections of Ross and other deontologists. This reformulation involves (1) a wide, nonhedonistic concept of intrinsic goodness, including the intrinsic good of moral character and right action, (2) a subtle combination of act-utilitarianism and rule-utilitarianism, and (3) a distinction between summary rules and practice rules, each having its proper sphere of application. In interpreting and qualifying utilitarianism in this way, we have pretty fundamentally transformed it. The sharp dualism between right and good is broken down, new emphasis is put upon the intrinsic values of intention and motive, and the *consequences* of our acts, as distinguished from the immediate values and disvalues of the acts themselves, are not judged to be of *exclusive* moral importance. To produce net good, nevertheless, remains the end and aim of the moral life, and all duties are interpreted as forms of this endeavor. When utilitarianism is thus reformulated, it appears to be confirmed to a greater extent than any alternative view, and to present less difficulty than its rivals. It may not be completely adequate as an ethical theory, but at least it takes us a long way toward our goal of moral insight.

NOTES

1. Ian McGreal, *The Art of Making Choices*. Dallas: Southern Methodist University Press, 1953, p. 62.

2. John Stuart Mill, *Utilitarianism*. New York: E. P. Dutton & Co., Inc., 1910, p. 17.

3. Oliver A. Johnson, *Rightness and Goodness*. The Hague: Martinus Nijhoff, 1959, p. 141.
4. Alfred Cyril Ewing, *Ethics*. New York: The Macmillan Company, 1953, p. 83.
5. G. E. Moore, *Principia Ethica*. New York and London: Cambridge University Press, 1922, pp. 20, 25, 147.
6. Ralph Barton Perry, *Realms of Value*. Cambridge, Mass.: Harvard University Press, 1954, p. 107.
7. *Ibid.*, p. 108.
8. Moore, *Principia Ethica, op. cit.*, p. 147. My italics.
9. *Ibid.*, p. 166.
10. G. E. Moore, *Ethics*. London and New York: Oxford University Press, 1912 (reprint of 1944), pp. 178–179.
11. *Ibid.*, p. 181.
12. Henry Sidgwick, *The Methods of Ethics*. London: Macmillan & Co., Ltd., 1922, p. 311.
13. Leonard G. Miller, "Rules and Exceptions," *Ethics*, vol. 46 (1956), p. 267.
14. John Austin, *The Province of Jurisprudence Determined*. London: Weidenfeld and Nicolson, Ltd., 1954, pp. 47–48. (First published in 1832.)
15. *Ibid.*, p. 39.
16. *Ibid.*, p. 40.
17. Arthur Koestler, *Insight and Outlook*. New York: The Macmillan Company, 1949, pp. 230–231.
18. Moore, *Principia Ethica, op. cit.*, pp. 162–163.
19. John Rawls, "Two Concepts of Rules," *Philosophical Review*, vol. 64 (1955).
20. *Ibid.*, pp. 25, 27.
21. T. D. Weldon, *The Vocabulary of Politics*. Baltimore: Penguin Books, Inc., 1953, p. 57.
22. Erwin N. Griswold, *The Fifth Amendment Today*. Cambridge, Mass.: Harvard University Press, 1955, pp. 7–8.
23. Rawls, "Two Concepts of Rules," *op. cit.*, p. 29. *Cf.*, Ludwig Wittgenstein, *Philosophical Investigations*. Oxford: B. H. Blackwell, Ltd., 1953, I, pars. 65–71.
24. Moore, *Principia Ethica, op. cit.*, p. 147.
25. W. D. Ross, *The Right and the Good*. London and New York: Oxford University Press, 1930, p. 38.
26. Louis Arnaud Reid, *Philosophy and Education*. London: William Heinemann, Ltd., 1962, pp. 46–47.
27. Rawls, "Two Concepts of Rules," *op. cit.*, p. 30.
28. Sidgwick, *The Methods of Ethics, op. cit.*, p. 380.
29. Jeremy Bentham, *Constitutional Code*, I, xv. 7, in *The Works of Jeremy Bentham*. Edinburgh: W. Tait, 1843, vol. 9, p. 107.
30. A. C. Pigou, *The Economics of Welfare*. New York: The Macmillan Company, 1920, p. 89.
31. E. F. Carritt, *Ethical and Political Thinking*. London and New York: Oxford University Press, 1947, p. 65.
32. Rawls, "Two Concepts of Rules," *op. cit.*, p. 10.
33. F. H. Bradley, *Ethical Studies*. London and New York: Oxford University Press, 1927, pp. 26–27.
34. Immanuel Kant, *The Philosophy of Law*. Edinburgh: T. and T. Clark, 1887, pp. 194–195.
35. A. L. Goodhart, *English Law and the Moral Law*. London: Stevens & Sons, Ltd., 1953, p. 93.
36. Edmond N. Cahn, *The Sense of Injustice*. New York: New York University Press, 1949, p. 29.

CHAPTER VIII

Bias and obligation

I. TWO MEANINGS OF OUGHT

This book is mainly concerned with two great questions, "What is good?" and "What is right?" I have maintained that they are not independent questions—the test of rightness is productivity of good. But the meaning of neither good nor right is complete apart from the concept of "ought." The good is what ought to exist, and the right is what ought to be done.

There is always an implicit "oughtness" in value judgments. Hence there is a "naturalistic fallacy" in simply identifying good with a factual quality or characteristic, such as pleasure, or the satisfaction of desire. As G. E. Moore pointed out, we must distinguish between good and the things or qualities that are good. We may agree with the hedonist that pleasure is good, but this is not to say that good and pleasure are one and the same. If pleasure were the same as good, then to say *Pleasure is good* would mean the very same thing as *Pleasure is pleasure*. To avoid such empty tautologies, we must recognize, according to Moore, a "non-naturalistic" meaning of good.[1] In my opinion, this meaning is to be found in the concept of "ought." Good is what ought to exist. Its existence is better than its nonexistence.

H. A. Prichard, in a famous essay, denies that "ought" can ever have this meaning. "The word 'ought' refers to actions and to actions alone. The proper language is never 'So and so ought to be,' but 'I ought to do so and so.' " Prichard is apparently using the test of ordinary usage. "When we speak of anything . . . as good," he remarks, "we never dream in our ordinary consciousness of going on to say that therefore it ought to be."[2] I doubt that anything can be proved by this appeal to ordinary meaning. In the first place, there is the question whether common usage is so restricted as Prichard supposes. If "so and so ought to be" sounds strange, this is not the case with a number of synonymous expressions. We often say, for example, that something ought to exist, or ought not to be destroyed. In the second place, even if such usages were rare, they might express our considered judgment when we stop and reflect. If we do try to make explicit to ourselves what we mean by ultimate good, we are surely impelled to speak in this way. If something is ultimately good, its existence is worthwhile, it ought to exist. I cannot understand what "good" can mean if all such expressions are inadmissible.

The utilitarian view is that what we ought to do is to bring about what is worthwhile. Well-doing is the production of well-being. This view can not be refuted by a verbal argument, such as Prichard employs. On the contrary, it appears quite sensible to say that, if something ought to exist, and we can bring it into existence, we ought to do so.

The concept of "what ought to be" is a combination of the idea of *value* and the idea of *existence* or *nonexistence*. When we say that something *non-actual* ought to exist, we are ascribing value to a potentially existing content —as when, in anticipation—we attribute deliciousness to the mature stage of a peach that has not yet ripened. If we thus evaluate things in terms of possibilities, we see that many unrealized qualities ought to be or ought not to be. The case is similar when we say that something *actual* ought to be. We are thinking of its nonexistence as a possibility, and we are judging that it is better for it to exist than not to exist. A kindly act or a beautiful painting, for example, ought to be, in the sense that its existence is better than its nonexistence. We can call this kind of "ought" the "ought of worth."

Closely related to the ought of worth is the second kind of ought, which we can call the "ought of duty." Here again there is a combination of the idea of value and the idea of existence and nonexistence, but these ideas are now related to human striving. The vision of what ought to exist or ought not to exist excites the will to act, and moral obligation is the imperative that arises from this volitional excitation.

All cases of an ought of duty find their ultimate justification in the ought of worth. If it is not worthwhile to do something, then there is no sense in doing it. What we "ought to do" is a subdivision of what "ought to exist"— for, if we have a duty to act, we should bring an act into existence.

From the standpoint of a utilitarian ethics, "X ought to exist" entails, "If X were to exist, there would be more net good in the world." Similarly, "Y ought to be done" entails, "Since there would be more net good in the world if Y were done (Y being the most efficient way to maximize net good), Y ought to be done." For a utilitarian moralist, the ought of/duty is thus derivative from the ought of worth.

We owe to Kant, more than to any other thinker, the recognition that the ought of duty is a crucial ethical concept. But as we have seen in Chapter V, his attempt to derive the binding force of the ought from the logical principle of noncontradiction is a failure, and his abstract formalistic interpretation of obligation does far less than justice to the ethical importance of consequences and individual differences. I agree with Kant that the "ought" of duty is distinct from the "is" of fact, but what is thus distinguishable is not separate. The rational demands of obligation must have something to do with the nature of society and the way we are built. Also, if utilitarianism is true, there is a different and much closer relation between the two meanings of ought ("the ought of worth" and "the ought of duty") than Kant supposed.

2. THE BASIS OF MORAL OBLIGATION

It is commonly said that obligation represents the "pull" of society upon the individual. This interpretation means that a human being, in his innermost nature, is social, and feels the tug of society as the internalized "voice" of conscience. All men are involved in a complex network of social forces; these gradually build up within each one of us a social ego, the accumulation and internal deposit of innumerable social attitudes and emotions, which are absorbed into the deep unconscious layers of the mind. When we have an impulse to act in harmony with these social forces, we feel the strong inner support of the social ego; when we have an impulse to act in a contrary manner, we feel its curb and restraint. "To cultivate this social ego," declares Bergson, "is the essence of our obligation to society. Were there not some part of society in us, it would have no hold on us."[3]

This is a partial but not a complete explanation of obligation. The "ought" is to be explained primarily by a combination of two factors: first, the influence of society; and second, the attempt to escape bias and to attain moral objectivity. Both of these factors are included in the interpretation of right that we find in Adam Smith's *Theory of Moral Sentiments* and in David Hume's *Treatise of Human Nature* and *Enquiry Concerning the Principles of Morals*. Although they seldom use the word ought, they provide the basis for a clear and cogent doctrine of obligation.

These two fast friends, who agreed in many of the essentials of their ethical doctrines, believed that the spring of the moral life is sympathy. All of us, to some degree, have a "fellow feeling" for the weal and woe of others. Through such means as pity and kindness and imagination, we come to understand, and to be affected by, what others feel. Emotions and feelings are infectious and tend to flow, in a sense, from person to person. When someone is in agony, for example, we suffer at the very sight and thought of his suffering.

By the imagination [writes Smith] we place ourselves in his situation, we conceive ourselves enduring all the same torments, we enter as it were into his body, and become in some measure the same person with him, and thence form some idea of his sensations, and even feel something which, though weaker in degree, is not altogether unlike them. His agonies, when they are thus brought home to ourselves, when we have thus adopted them and made them our own, begin at last to affect us, and we then tremble and shudder at the thought of what he feels. For as to be in pain or distress of any kind excites the most excessive sorrow, so to conceive or to imagine that we are in it, excites some degree of the same emotion, in proportion to the vivacity or dullness of the conception.[4]

Sympathy is the main basis of our moral concern for others; and it is because of innumerable sympathetic experiences that altruistic dispositions are built up within the mind. These dispositions, along with other social attitudes, coalesce to form the social ego whose voice is conscience. (Hume and Smith do not bring in the concept of the "social ego," and the present use of the term therefore represents an extension of their theory.)

Sympathy, however, needs to be controlled by critical intelligence. It is most intense toward our intimates and our own kind, and it fades or vanishes when distance, prejudice, or unfamiliarity blunts our feelings. Hence reason is morally necessary to correct our biases and to extend the range of our moral concern. To quote Hume:

Sympathy, we shall allow, is much fainter than our concern for ourselves, and sympathy with persons remote from us much fainter than that with persons near and contiguous; but for this very reason it is necessary for us, in our calm judgment and discourse concerning the characters of men, to neglect all these differences, and render our sentiments more public and social.[5]

Since everyone is strongly influenced by the accidents and perspectives of his own experience, he should try to attain a more objective point of view. According to Hume:

Every particular man has a peculiar position with regard to others; and 'tis impossible we could ever converse together on any reasonable terms, were each of us to consider characters and persons, only as they appear from his peculiar point of view. In order, therefore, to prevent these continual *contradictions,* and arrive at a more *stable* judgment of things, we fix on some *steady* and *general* points of view; and always, in our thoughts, place ourselves in them, whatever may be our present situation.[6]

Similarly Adam Smith recognizes that sympathy is very often distorted by favoritism or callousness, and that we must therefore achieve a more fair and unbiased basis for moral choice. He suggests that this higher standard is to be found in the point of view of the "supposed well-informed and impartial spectator," who considers the total effect of each alternative and decides upon the best course of action with a just regard for all the parties concerned. Such a completely wise and unprejudiced judge does not exist; but as an imaginary being, he represents an ideal or standard that we should try to attain. Insofar as our action conforms to what he would recommend, we may be said to act rightly.

Now I believe that these theories of Smith and Hume provide the necessary clues for an accurate interpretation of moral obligation. The "ought," as a moral imperative, is both a rational and a social demand—the internalized pull of society regulated by reason. I shall now define a little more precisely the two aspects of obligation: the social and the rational.

The social pull of obligation characteristically arises when a person feels that he should relinquish his own lesser good for the sake of the greater good of others, or that he should sacrifice the lesser good of some restricted group for the sake of the greater good of some wider group. The interests of society are pulling a man away from something good toward something better.

Suppose a person is taking a stroll in the woods upon some fine summer day. He happens to be walking past a pond when he suddenly sees a child floundering in the water and in danger of drowning. He at once sympathizes with the plight of the child, and at the cost of sacrificing a carefree stroll and wetting his clothes, he plunges into the water to save the youngster. Can we say that the sympathy of the moment impels him to act, and that obligation means no more than this? The matter is by no means so simple! The man's feeling that he ought to rescue the child is called into play by the momentary sympathy; but the present and particular sympathy is merely the nucleus around which gravitate feelings and attitudes implanted in the mind by many past experiences of a kindred sort. All these experiences have left memories and traces that have long since united to form the social ego, a fusion and organization of countless sympathetic attitudes. It is this whole complex that is called into play by the sight of the child in distress; the pressure of the immediate sympathy is reinforced by the cumulative pressure of innumerable past sympathies. This pressure is felt as duty or obligation; and it arises whenever a person is being internally influenced toward an objective that seems not to be his own but to which he responds because something arouses the social ego within him.

The emotions and attitudes that coalesce to form the social ego and thus to constitute the sense of obligation are no doubt of composite origin. Following the lead of Hume and Smith, I have put special emphasis upon sympathy, but there are many diverse reactions that result from social command and prohibition, praise and blame, taboo and charm, punishment and reward. Such attitudes as disapproval, abhorrence, guilt, dread, shame, a sense of constraint, or their opposites, are aroused within the mind. By accretion and fusion, these attitudes are finally synthesized into the dynamic psychological complex that Freud calls the superego and that I have called the social ego. It is the internal pressure from this ego that primarily constitutes the sense of obligation.

This way of putting the matter is not so different from the theory of Hume as might be supposed at first glance. He recognized that there are other important elements besides sympathy that form the psychological core of a sense of obligation. Our spontaneous emotional reactions, he maintained, must be chastened and reinforced by "artificial" attitudes instilled in us by society. The sense of obligation is thus partly "natural" and partly "artificial." It is *natural* to the extent that it is based upon original passions and dispositions characteristic of the human species. Among these natural propensities, sympathy is of prime, but not exclusive, importance. The sense of obligation is *artificial* to the extent that these original sentiments are transformed and fixated by habits, customs, parental discipline, education, political indoctrination, and other such influences. To become a morally responsible human being, a person must not only be motivated by sympathy and other natural feelings, but must be "trained up according to a certain discipline and education."[7] For Hume, as well as for a modern social psychologist, obligation is a complex social product, the result of innumerable forces and influences. But perhaps a present-day psychologist would be more wary of speaking about "original" or "natural" dispositions and would be more inclined to think of sympathy as emerging gradually in the process of maturing and acculturation.

Yet even this is not the whole story. Our feelings of obligation, whether they be natural or artificial, may be wrongly directed: they may be excessive, inadequate, or misplaced; they may be confined within too narrow limits; they may be distorted by bias or based upon misconceptions. The reinforcement provided by the social ego, moreover, is no guarantee against misdirection, since it increases the pressure rather than guarantees its right application. Hence feelings need to be regulated and supplemented by reason in the sense of thoughtful and unbiased moral judgment.

Let us return to our illustration. Suppose the child who is in danger of drowning is a Negro, and the stroller who sees him is a white man with a strong racial prejudice against Negroes. In these circumstances so little sympathy may be aroused that the man may callously walk past. Or if he does stop to rescue the child, it may be because reason checks his spontaneous emotional reaction.

Let us again alter the illustration. Suppose that the man cannot swim and that the attempt at rescue will endanger his life. Suppose also that he is an important public official, whose life is not only precious to himself but highly valuable to others. Then the decision whether to risk his own life in the hope of saving the child might require intense reasoning.

In these instances, there is a need to control emotion by judgment. So it is in the many situations in life requiring moral choice. If sensibly employed, rules assist us in attaining a more steady and impartial point of view, and reason intervenes to broaden and regulate our sympathies and correct our biases. It is thus that action ceases to be merely sentimental and becomes principled.

If the only problem were to exercise sympathy or *feel* conscientious, any action so motivated would be right. But the motive may be *inwardly* or *subjectively* right, in the sense of being well intentioned, and yet the act not *outwardly* or *objectively* right. This is strikingly so in the case of the fanatic, but any sincere person can fall into error. Therefore it is not enough to be motivated by a feeling of obligation: it is important to act without bias, with a keen appreciation of ends, with adequate knowledge of means, with a clear understanding of the relevant circumstances, so that the act will be objectively right. "Ought" expresses the demand for moral objectivity and not simply the subjective feeling of obligation. When we say that a certain act ought to be performed, we mean that it is objectively the best choice.

These characteristics of a mature sense of obligation do not spring into existence all at once. As an individual grows into adulthood, there is a gradual shift from authority to reason and from egocentricity to social concern. The child's first reaction to commands, admonitions, scoldings, and punishments is to develop a sense of "must." He *must* wash his face, he *must* be careful of matches, he *must* not break dishes. Only gradually does he acquire a sense of "ought," and at first this sense is scarcely distinguishable from the "must." It is simply the voice of authority internalized as conscience, reflecting the rewards and punishments administered by adults. At this stage, acts are evaluated in terms of literal conformity with rules. But as the youngster develops, he ceases to interpret obligation as obedience to adult rules and commands. Gradually his own ideals of self-development and social responsibility crystallize, replacing habits of blind obedience and fear of punishment. There is less self-centeredness and more self-guidance: interests are wider, intentions are directed towards other people, right and wrong are seen as expressive of social relationships. Many people, adult in years but not in ethical maturity, have never successfully achieved these transformations. They cling to an authoritarian conscience throughout their lifetime, and never advance to the more creative and enlightened outlook of the humanistic conscience.[8]

To sum up, the sense of obligation involves two elements. First, the emotions and volitional attitudes that become crystallized in the social ego and give one, on occasion, such a strong *feeling* of obligation. Among these emotions sympathy is of great importance. Second, the rational aversion from an act which is judged to be immoral. This rational factor in obligation is expressed in the demand to escape from bias and to achieve moral objectivity. As the child grows into maturity, he becomes both more social and more rational. The ideal climax of this process is enlightened love.

The merit of this conception of moral obligation is that it permits one's head and heart to be in harmony. Without sympathy the moral life has no spring and motivation, without reason it lacks true direction. Only an ethics that combines the two satisfies equally our intelligence and our feelings.

3. OBJECTIVITY AND BIAS

Just as the ideal of objective truth is a regulative principle in the field of ethics, so the ideal of moral objectivity is a regulative principle in the field of ethics. In both cases, objectivity requires an escape from bias and a facing-up to actualities. A man exhibits *scientific* bias when, as a consequence of preconception or prejudice, he distorts or neglects the facts. If an astrophysicist were to cling stubbornly to the theories of Newton when astronomical observations verify the contrary theories of Einstein, he could be said to display scientific bias. This sort of bias is refutable, since it contradicts the evidence. A person exhibits *moral* bias when, as a consequence of some prejudice or inclination, he is cruel or callous toward some and partial towards others. The result is a narrow or perverse choice of values, as shown, for example, in the harsh treatment of Jews by an anti-Semite. Unlike scientific bias, moral bias is not refutable, but sympathy and understanding can be brought to bear against it. The two kinds of bias are frequently interdependent. Moral bias against Jews, for example, may be connected with false ideas about anthropology, as in the fantastic racialist theories of the Nazis.

Objectivity, whether scientific or moral, is the opposite of bias. Scientific objectivity consists in the disinterested search for truth, with its impartial weighing of evidence. Similarly moral objectivity requires that one be fair and disinterested. It is akin to "due process" in legal procedure, which I have discussed in the preceding chapter. F. C. Sharp has formulated the principle of moral objectivity as follows:

> That conduct is right which a judge would desire who was able to put himself completely in the position of each and every person making up the situation, and thus to realize to the full precisely what the proposed course of action would mean to all.[9]

Or in the words of C. I. Lewis: "The basic imperative is . . . that of governing oneself by the advice of cognition, in contravention, if need be, to impulsions and inclinations of feeling."[10] It is to weigh goods and evils in their full-size and objective actuality, resisting any bias that would cause a misapprehension of the worth of an object, or that would lead to the choice of the worse when one might choose the better.

But it might be asked, why should either an individual or a group be bound by what is morally the best choice? Why not yield to bias? Why not prefer our own lesser good to the greater good of society? Why not choose the lesser good of our own little group to the greater good of some other group?

A partial answer is to be found in the fact that morality is a fundamental part of our nature. Society is too much with us, the social ego is too much an essential part of ourselves, flagrantly to deny its claims; or if we *can* override the claims of sociality, we may do so only by suppressing an essential part of ourselves. As Walt Whitman said: "Whoever walks a furlong without sympathy walks to his own funeral dressed in a shroud."[11]

But to some extent morality consists in going against the grain of human nature or habit. It consists in curbing our inclinations, resisting our biases, rooting out evil habits, inuring ourselves to difficult tasks. If we are to have any strength of character, we must learn to do things that we would much rather not do. We must train ourselves in habits of self-denial and energetic volition and disciplined concentration. On occasion, we shall need to resist the pressure of the social ego, since the voice of society is far from infallible. Like the hero of Ibsen's play, *The Enemy of the People,* the man of moral courage will do what he believes to be right even when it is highly unpopular.

The ultimate justification for such action is that there is a sufficient moral reason for doing it. A moral reason is a consideration that justifies a moral act. The best of moral reasons for performing an act is that its total content and consequences stand higher in the scale of intrinsic value than those of any other act which might have been chosen. Suppose someone asks, "Why ought you to perform this act?" A proper reply would be, "Because it is unprejudiced conduct for the sake of the greatest value." An act ought to be done if it meets this criterion of moral objectivity.

On the other hand, a biassed act is to be rejected precisely because it *is* biassed. As we expand our sympathies and attain a livelier realization of the values of diverse individuals, as we approach a complete knowledge and a perfect realization of the weal and woe of everybody concerned, we can find less and less excuse to confine our "moral code" within prejudiced and narrow bounds. If it be reasonable to act upon the clearest realization of the effects of action, then bias must be regarded as unreasonable; since it prevents men from reaching out, in imagination and sympathy, to comprehend the joys and sufferings of others.

There will always be a certain number of people who will cling to their biases. There will be men of prejudice, men of ill will, men with moral blind spots. On the other hand, there are human beings who are gifted with a special moral sensitiveness and breadth of vision, and they gradually win a reputation for their insight. Men like Buddha, Socrates, and Confucius, in ancient times, and Lincoln, Gandhi, and Schweitzer, in modern times, are recognized as having unusually pure motives, unbiassed outlook, and keen ethical insight; and they eventually win the names of saints and sages. No one can study the opinions of these men without discovering a very considerable measure of agreement in their ethical outlook. They agree upon the widest community of good: they not only recognize that there are moral obligations, but they turn away from the multiple forms of intolerance and exclusion. They emphasize the common life of which all men are members.

Let us now turn to an analysis of some of the forms of moral bias. I shall discuss selfishness, group-egoism, retributive bias, and the bias of love and imagination.

4. SELFISHNESS

A selfish person will deliberately choose his own lesser good in preference to the greater good of another person—simply because it is *his own* good. He uses other people as mere means to his own ends. An unselfish person, on the other hand, aims at being impartial between himself and others. He does not regard a good as more worthy of choice simply because it is his own. He acknowledges that others are ends in themselves and treats them kindly.

Selfishness is difficult but not impossible to avoid. Every man is, in a sense, the center of his own little world. He lives within his own skin, sees with his own eyes, feels with his own feelings. Unless we suppose that he has the power of mind reading, he never *directly* experiences anyone's enjoyments and sufferings but his own. As everybody is in this egocentric predicament, it is natural to be selfish. Yet it is no less natural to be sympathetic, and, in this sense, to be unselfish. Sympathy and love break down the walls between human beings and thus are the great solvents of conflict and selfishness. "Love consists in this," Rainer Maria Rilke has written, "that two solitudes protect and touch and greet each other."[12] To this extent people *do* transcend the egocentric predicament.

Far from selfishness being an unalterable human trait, its incidence is a function of social conditions. It is fostered by the predatory and acquisitive features of a social order, and it is comparatively rare in highly cooperative groups such as the Pueblo among primitive societies, or the Quakers among more civilized peoples. Describing the Arapesh tribe of New Guinea, Dr. Margaret Mead points out that "the system is run upon tenets of happy cooperation. . . . The whole conception of human nature is strongly in contrast with that of those cultures which conceive men as working most willingly for self-centered ends."[13] Altruistic patterns of behavior have likewise become institutionalized in highly literate communities, such as the Kibutzim in Israel. The findings of sociology and anthropology conclusively prove that egoistic behavior is not a fixed human trait.

The main question that is relevant to ethics is whether selfishness is morally justifiable. Its value has been asserted most vigorously by Nietzsche. An aristocratic selfishness or egoism, he declares, "belongs to the essence of a noble soul." Fulfillment for the born aristocrat is achieved through power and domination, through the exploitation and subjugation of his "inferiors." The "master morality" is entirely different from the "slave morality" of the masses. The master says to himself, "What is injurious to me is injurious in itself." It is only among the slave-minded "that sympathy, the kind helping hand, the warm heart, patience, diligence, humility, and friendliness attain to honor."[14] But even among the "slaves" these virtues have mainly extrinsic worth; they are weapons of the weak, said Nietzsche, in the struggle for power.

There is something admirable in his frank and honest avowal of an egoistic ethics. Like Freud, he detected attitudes of petty envy and resentment and cowardice under the show of altruism. In modern life he saw a levelling tendency—a sheepish predisposition toward mediocrity and conformity. Defending the intrepid egoist as a rebel against mass vulgarity and tyranny, he maintained that man has an unlimited capacity to surpass himself, and that a new morality of self-assertion is required to scale the heights. His mistake was to suppose that one must adopt egoism in order to be free from conventional hypocrisy and to attain a noble stature.

As an ethical theory, egoism is irrational. In some versions, it amounts to saying that *each* man's good is the *sole* good; but since there are many men, this is to assert that there are *many* sole goods—which is an absolute contradiction. In other versions, egoism asserts that every man ought to promote his own intrinsic good as the sole end worth achieving, and that he ought never to promote the good of others except as a mere means of promoting his own good. This formula is an unreasonable limitation upon the concept of duty. There is nothing peculiar about you or me that makes enjoyment worthwhile if it occurs in *my* experience, and worthless if it occurs in *your* experience. If my good ought to be promoted, by the same token your good ought to be promoted. Good, being good, ought to be promoted, wherever it occurs. This appears unreasonable only when we *are* overmastered by selfishness. As we expand our sympathies, as we attain a livelier appreciation of the weal and woe of others, it seems more and more unreasonable to harden our hearts and to confine our ethical aspirations within the narrow limits of selfhood.

The reasonable way to avoid selfishness is not to crush or harass the self, but to expand it until the good of oneself and others coincide. As Spinoza maintained, a person is as great as his interests, and mere self-seeking, because it narrows the range of interests, impoverishes the self. Like pleasure, self-realization is elusive. Unless you approach it indirectly, it will change and vanish, like the princess of the fairy tale who, when "caught," turns into a deer. The "hedonistic paradox," that "to get pleasure one must forget it," is matched by the "self-realizationist paradox," that "to find the self one must lose it." The ethically wise man will broaden and enrich his life by developing self-transcending interests, first, so that he may enjoy an abundant life, and second, so that he can give to others out of the richness of his being.

As the individual develops from childhood to maturity, egocentricity gradually gives way to the principles of reciprocity and inclusion. To obstruct this process, and to cling to infantile self-centeredness, is one of the surest marks of neurosis. The problem of social control, no less than the problem of psychotherapy, is to eliminate the conflict between self-interest and social interest. This is to be done by changing both the self and society; by making society more cooperative, and the individual more unselfish and far-ranging in his interests.

I do not mean to suggest that there is a perfect coincidence between the good of oneself and the good of others. In a bad social order, such as the Nazi, a kind man is likely to suffer more than the unkind. Even in the best of societies a person may have to choose between his own good and the general good. His sacrifice will then be morally justifiable if the value to be gained, objectively viewed, is greater than the value to be surrendered by the self. To sacrifice oneself needlessly, or for no sufficient purpose, is both foolish and immoral.

Ordinarily we do not expect or require superlative sacrifice even for a very good cause. We distinguish between the faithful performance of duties that can reasonably be demanded of human beings, and the acts of supreme sacrifice that are always bound to be rare. When we meet the saint or the hero, we may admire him intensely, but we say that "he acted above and beyond the call of duty." This does not mean that we have abandoned the utilitarian standard of maximum good. It means that human beings are not angels, and that we are charitable enough to realize this fact.

While seeking to eliminate the conflict between self and society, we should distinguish between selfishness and self-love. Selfishness is a type of bias, but self-love, when not of an obsessive Narcissistic type, may be reasonable and unbiassed. If self-love means the affirmation of one's own growth, freedom, and happiness, if it means a robust sense of one's own integrity and worth, it helps one to live joyfully and affectionately. Incapacity to love and respect human nature in oneself is linked with incapacity to enjoy life and to love others. As Meister Eckhart said, "He is a great and righteous person who, loving himself, loves all others equally."[15] This, rather than self-depreciation, is the meaning of the golden rule.

5. IN-GROUP VERSUS OUT-GROUP

When Huckleberry Finn was asked whether the explosion of a steamboat boiler had hurt anyone, he replied, "No'm: killed a nigger." Aunt Sally remarked, "Well it's lucky because sometimes people do get hurt."[16] This conversation illustrates the callousness that has often characterized the attitude of one group toward another.

In the case of Aunt Sally, the feeling was one of indifference rather than malevolence, but active hostility is also characteristic of group-bias. Favor toward the in-group is combined with *disfavor* toward the out-group. The racist not only favors the members of his own "race," but tramples upon the members of the "inferior races." Likewise bias in favor of one's own nation is combined with bias *against* other nations; or bias in favor of one's class or caste or creed is combined with bias against other classes or castes or creeds. Hence group wars with group, cause with cause, loyalty with loyalty. History has been replete with such bitter antagonisms. The fascists carried their prejudices to mad extremes of sadism and xenophobia, yet we need to pluck the motes from our own eyes and to see how deeply the cancer of racialism and nationalism has eaten into the healthy tissue of the democratic organism.

The defenders of "white supremacy" have sought to justify their position by a theory of innate differences. But anthropologists can find no scientific basis for separating off colored people, as if they lacked the human nature shared by the rest of us. Pigmentation is a superficial trait that has nothing to do with inner worth or capacity. Under favorable conditions, a race may achieve a very high cultural level, but under unfavorable conditions, the very same race may attain to only a low level. Human nature, without undergoing biological transformation, has been molded to a great number of contrasting modes of expression. These facts have driven anthropologists to conclude that the decisive factor in determining the quality of a civilization is not racial stock but historical and environmental circumstances. Men can hardly grow larger than the crevices in which they live, and most colored people have been living in pretty narrow crevices. To assume that their limitations are racially innate is to be guilty of a very hasty inference.

The defenders of "white supremacy" may reply that none of the twenty-one civilizations studied by Arnold Toynbee, in his comprehensive survey of all the major civilizations, was the creation of Negroes, and that this fact is evidence of the congenital incapacity of "black" peoples. But as Toynbee points out, the non-Negroid races existed for millennia without emerging from barbarism. When they finally produced the ancient civilizations, they did so within a relatively brief period of time, with no fundamental change in the biological stock—their cultural spurt, in each instance, being the result of a creative response to some great challenge. It thus appears to be an "accident of history," as Raymond Leslie Buell has said, that the Negroes did not awaken to the "need for progress" as soon as the white man. Now, however, the Negroes all over the earth's surface are on the move, responding creatively to the mighty challenges of the twentieth century. More than any other "race" in the whole world, they represent the struggle for primary human rights. As Martin Luther King Jr. has declared:

This is a great hour for the Negro. The challenge is here. To become the instruments of a great idea is a privilege that history gives only occasionally. Arnold Toynbee says in A Study of History that it may be the Negro who will give the new spiritual dynamic to Western civilization that it so desperately needs to survive. I hope this is possible.[17]

But to reinvigorate Western civilization, and to dispel the clouds of racial prejudice is no easy task.

As part of the folklore of a people, the doctrine of racial differences is very difficult to dispel. There must be a change in fundamental beliefs and mores and not merely in laws and institutions. These changes can be expedited if men recognize the nature of their biases and seek a more objective and disinterested approach to racial questions.

Nationalistic chauvinism, like racial prejudice, has not been confined to the totalitarian states. The slogans that have led to bloody conflict are familiar: "Brittania rules the waves!" "Deutschland über alles!" "France d'abord!" "America first!" "My country, right or wrong!" The human race has paid a dreadful price for rampant nationalism, but the price it has paid in the past is no more than a token of the price it may pay in the future. If we are to avoid ultimate catastrophe, we must stop the fanatical massing of power by the forces of nationalism. We must find reasonable grounds for our faith in the unity of man, and embody this faith in a viable world order.

Bias may take other forms. Class bias, for example, is historically not less important than racial and nationalistic bias. Likewise, creedal differences, as those between Moslem and Christian, Jew and Gentile, Protestant and Roman Catholic, have excited innumerable prejudices and violent clashes. Sex differences have also been perennial sources of friction. Since most societies have been patriarchal, masculine bias has been more oppressive than feminine bias. The result has been the oldest form of tyranny—the subjection of women.

The argument against all these forms of bias is fundamentally the same. Prejudice divides human beings who should be able to work together in peace and amity for the common good. It distorts and perverts moral choice; it perpetuates the cruelty of man toward man; it has brought the world to the brink of ultimate catastrophe.

Just as there is nothing wrong with self-interest if it is not a barrier to social interest, so there is nothing wrong with group-interest if it is not an obstacle to still wider interests. The rich and multifarious growth of human associations, with all the various forms of love and loyalty that they evoke, is a prime requisite of any vital civilization. It is only when loyalty turns into group egoism, or worse still, into group aggressiveness, that it is immoral. What we need, as Josiah Royce maintained, is loyalty that is deeply tolerant, loyalty that respects the loyalties of others, loyalty that is thus "loyal to loyalty."[18] Conflicts of value are usually to be solved, not by direct collision, nor by surrendering basic allegiances, but through a process of inclusion and recentering. Larger loyalties must allow for the maximum inclusion of smaller loyalties, and conflicts be resolved by the enlargement of interests.

There will always be some distinction between the in-group and the out-group. Even if the brotherhood of man should finally be realized, there will remain a fundamental division between human beings and animals. Men may still eat animal flesh, they may still hunt and kill for sport, they may still destroy snakes without compunction. But we should not draw a hard and fast line even here. It is morally irresponsible to allow a fox slowly to starve to death in a trap. It is immoral wantonly to torture a dog or even a reptile. The principle of reverence for life—the principle of Mahavira, St. Francis, and Schweitzer—is a wider principle than the brotherhood of man. This principle, and none narrower, can claim to be unprejudiced. There are objective grounds for maintaining that human beings have capacities that raise them above the level of animals, but there are no objective grounds for maintaining that we have the moral right to treat any sentient creature inconsiderately and cruelly. So long as animals can suffer and enjoy, they are entitled to respect.

6. THE BIAS AGAINST ONE'S ENEMY

Corresponding to the division between in-group and out-group is the conflict between friend and foe. Its psychological expression is the desire to harm. In the more vicious types of gangs, this desire manifests itself in the most abandoned types of retaliation, not stopping short of murder; but it is by no means confined to gangland. It reaches a fierce crescendo in war, and even in peacetime, it blocks disarmament and reasonable compromise. It has had a profound influence upon our whole system of criminal justice, producing the barbarous conditions that prevail in most of the prisons of the world. It inspires the plots of innumerable plays, novels, moving pictures, and television shows, in which the "villains" are killed or severely chastised, to the evident satisfaction of the readers or the audience. It is linked to the psychological attitudes that underlie most human neuroses.

With these deep roots in human nature, the bias against one's "enemy" is the most inveterate form of prejudice. Yet even when faced by an enemy, it is possible to be objective and unbiassed. As David Hume wrote:

> The good qualities of an enemy are hurtful to us; but may still command our esteem and respect. . . . It seldom happens that we do not think an enemy vicious, and can distinguish betwixt his opposition to our interest and real villainy or baseness. But this hinders not, but that the sentiments are, in themselves, distinct; and a man of temper and judgment may preserve himself from these illusions. In like manner, tho' 'tis certain a musical voice is nothing but one that naturally gives a *particular* kind of pleasure; yet 'tis difficult for a man to be sensible, that the voice of an enemy is agreeable, or to allow it to be musical. But a person of a fine ear, who has the command of himself, can separate these feelings, and give praise to what deserves it.[19]

Unfortunately such objectivity is rare. If, instead of resisting our natural bias, we surrender to it, our position will coincide with that of Polemarchus, that "justice" requires us to "do good to our friends and harm to our enemies."[20] This position is rejected, in Plato's *Republic*, by the character Socrates, who maintains that it is wrong to harm anyone, friend or foe; and it is contrary to Christ's injunction to return good for evil.

The desire to harm, Freud has contended (see Chapter II above), is one of the deepest impulses of human life: love and hatred, creation and destruction represent the instinctual dualism of all life. Civilization, he argued, requires that unruly instincts be severely curbed, but men cannot tolerate the instinctual privation that results from this repression and inevitably become neurotic. Thus civilization is inseparable from a vast load of misery.

Other psychoanalysts, such as Ian Suttie and Melanie Klein, have maintained a less pessimistic view of human life. They believe that hate, far from being an innate tendency toward destruction, is a reaction to repression and anxiety. It results from the frustration of a drive rather than from an ineradicable propensity. As Carl Jung remarked concerning Nazi sadism, diabolical cruelty indicates that the perpetrators themselves are suffering deeply. When the need for love and security is severely rebuffed, especially in early life, human beings become "inferior caricatures of what they might have been." To the evidence from the psychologists we can add a great deal of new evidence from social scientists. If aggressiveness is innate, how do we explain the lack of it in such primitive tribes as the Arapesh in New Guinea, described by Margaret Mead, or in the cooperative communities described by Claire Huchet Bishop?[21]

We need not rush to the opposite extreme from the bleak pessimism of Freud, lulling our brains with an insipid lullaby of sweetness and light, to recognize that he has exaggerated the inevitability of human neurosis. To say that hostility is a natural result of frustration is not to say that it can be easily eliminated, yet our better understanding of the social and psychological roots of neurosis is beginning to have its effect. Not only psychoanalysts but behavioristic psychologists, such as E. L. Thorndike and B. F. Skinner, have demonstrated that punishment, not to mention more vicious kinds of retaliation, has very unfortunate by-products, such as disabling anxieties.[22]

In Samuel Butler's satirical utopia, *Erewhon*, physicians of the mind, called "straighteners," try impartially to understand and eliminate the causes of crime rather than to make people suffer. This approach is sometimes adopted in our society toward juvenile delinquents, and in consequence, considerable progress has been made. In some cases, the treatment has resulted from a careful scientific study. The child's difficulties have been expertly diagnosed as a result of searching investigation and analysis of his intelligence, physical disabilities, character traits, psychological conflicts and abnormalities, and the manifold aspects of his environment. Upon the basis of the knowledge thus gleaned, a prescription—as scientific as a physician's prescription—is written out for his care, and this prescription by no means always advocates "punishment." Painstaking study is made of the effectiveness of the treatment thus prescribed, and a different treatment is undertaken if the first fails. This procedure employs the manifold resources of social, psychological, and medical science and brings great benefit to both the individual and society. It seems to me that such humane and scientific methods should be extended not only to youthful offenders but also to adults. We should endeavor scientifically to discover the causes of crime, both in the individual case and in society at large, and we should carry out a well-considered plan for the elimination of crime and the reformation of the criminal. The effect of this rational approach, I am confident, would be to increase greatly the sum of human happiness; and in the long run it would be far less expensive even financially than our present crude methods of dealing with crime.

Education, as distinguished from the treatment of delinquency, has not wholly abandoned the birch rod, but the change is considerable. Claude Colman has written a grimly amusing account of the older practices. He tells of a school master who kept a conscientious account of his services during fifty years of teaching, during which he administered "911,527 blows with a cane: 124,010 with a rod; 20,939 with a ruler; 136,715 with the hand; 10,295 over the mouth; 7,905 boxes on the ear; 1,115,800 slaps on the head."[23]

Beginning with Rousseau, philosophers and psychologists have denounced such punitive methods, revolutionizing the rearing of children in both the school and the home.

The larger problem is to extend this type of reform to the whole gamut of human affairs. We should investigate the possibility of substituting *positive* in place of *negative* reinforcements, stressing reward instead of punishment, love instead of hate, freedom instead of repression, understanding instead of bias. There should be far greater emphasis upon the humanistic arts and sciences (psychology, anthropology, urban planning, and so forth) with a view to discovering better methods of cooperation and conflict resolution. We have employed the utmost of our intelligence and resources to develop the means of total war, but we have devoted comparatively little research and experiment to the problem of social harmony. To remedy this unbalance, an immense redirection of intellectual energies is required. There must also be a change of heart.

7. LOVE, IMAGINATION, AND MORAL BIAS

To avoid bias and act rightly, we must estimate distant goods or evils with something of the poignancy of the here and now, weighing the alien or the absent in the full scale of its objective actuality. This we cannot do without imaginative identification with others, grasping their sufferings and enjoyments as if they were our own. As Shelley declared in his *Defence of Poetry,* "the great secret of morals is love," and the principal means of exciting love is imagination.

When combined with deeply imaginative perception, love imparts vision and intensity to the moral life. Under its spur, we leap out of the pit of selfishness, and identify another's good with our own. Love transforms other values, giving them new zest and worth, which they do not possess by themselves. Duty is comparatively dull and pedestrian without its warmth and inspiration. Just as the privation of love is the main cause of crime and mental disorders, so the ability to love and be loved is the sign of mental health. It is also a means of apprehending and appreciating the innermost core of personality. The individuality of the loved one, his virtues and unique traits, are sensed by the lover as by no one else.

There is a natural affinity between love and imagination. As Shelley wrote: "A man, to be greatly good, must imagine intensely and comprehensively; he must put himself in the place of another and many others; the pains and pleasures of his species must become his own."[24] This sort of imagination is difficult to attain, and no one attains it perfectly. But art can strengthen the power of imagination and immensely widen its scope. In reading a great novel, like Tolstoy's *War and Peace,* all the joys and griefs of life seem to lay hold of our hearts. By means of art and imaginative perception, we are in touch with other people and things, knowing them appreciatively in their vividness and unique qualities. What sets each person apart, what is most precious and distinctive about him, is his inner life, his appreciation, his sense of values. Art objectifies and communicates this subjective core of life. It conveys the sense of a living presence rather than a dead set of abstractions. It can thus help immensely to create that community of feeling without which a deep and vital morality is impossible.

I would not deny that love and imagination may exhibit their own forms of bias. Just as sympathy, itself a kind of love, may be distorted by favoritism, so love in general may be blind and cruel and selfish. Freud as a psychologist and Dostoevsky as a novelist have shown how complex and ambivalent love is. It may be unrequited, or dissipated by inner conflicts, or twisted by sadism and masochism. That love may tragically conflict with prudence or honor or duty is the theme of nine-tenths of the novels of the world. Two people in love with each other may love no one else—their's is merely an egotism multiplied by two. Likewise there is a streak of selfishness in the doting parent, who may, for example, stuff a child with unwholesome sweets rather than deny him anything. The unduly possessive father of Elizabeth Barrett, to cite another example, preferred to ruin his daughter's happiness rather than give her in marriage to Robert Browning. Akin to bias in leading to undiscriminating choice is a merely sentimental eroticism. There are those who are in love with love, preferring an indiscriminate feeling rather than a discerning appreciation. Although sex is a source of the headiest joys of life, it may be a traitor to one's long-range interests, or if not a traitor, a very unruly ally.

We should avoid not only erotic but esthetic bias. In saying this, I am using "bias" in the very wide sense of the word. A biased act, understood in this broad way, is one in which the values which determine choice are *not* seen steadily and completely: the will is controlled by the relatively less important aspects of the situation, and hence chooses a lesser good or a positive evil in place of the greater good. Our moral job is to keep *all* the important factors before our mind's eye, not being distracted by the spotlight effects of the more striking good. We are thus distracted when we narrow our attention to esthetic appearances, like the lover who is so entranced by physical beauty that he is blind to defects of mind and character. In love affairs, women are less prone to this kind of bias than men, but all human beings may be overimpressed by esthetic glitter.

The taste for the vivid and the dramatic is a principal source of moral bias. In seeing a play, we enjoy a dashing villain, although he may bring great suffering to the other characters. When confined to the theater, this pleasure is innocent enough, but the stage view of life influences us on innumerable other occasions. Many a bad public servant has succeeded at the polls because he has had a picturesque character. Half of the popular appeal of Hitler or Mussolini was the result of cheap melodramatic effects. The spectacular party congresses, the fanfare of militarism, the fervid nationalistic myths, the dramatic threats and "heroic" postures, brought color and excitement to millions of jaded lives. Men are more likely to be swayed by these great shows of force and grandeur than by abstract moral conceptions of reason, such as the idea of justice.

Even in the ordinary affairs of life, sympathy is aroused by the striking individual case more than by the abstract idea of mass misery.

> The red haired child
> Sick in a fever, if you touch him once
> Though but so little as a finger tip,
> Will set us weeping; but a million sick. . . .
> You could as well weep for the rule of three
> Or compound fractions.[25]

We sympathize with whatever strikes our imagination most intensely—hence the onesided or fitful play of the imagination can wreak havoc with our moral judgments.

If imagination could be a great floodlight, lighting up the alien and the distant as vividly as the immediate and the striking, it would not lead to subjective and biassed choice.

8. THE OBJECTIVE STANDARDS OF CHOICE

I have been interpreting "ought" as expressing the demand for objective rightness as distinguished from bias and the merely subjective *feeling* of obligation. The demand for unbiassed decision can have no meaning unless there *are* objective standards of moral choice. In this final section of the present chapter, I will suggest the nature of these standards, and in the next two chapters, I will criticize the relativist and subjective theories that deny the objectivity of moral judgment.

There would be no need for a rational estimation of values if the mere play of impulse could solve our problems. But interests get in one another's way, and to avoid chaos we must combine thoughtfulness with sensitivity. We must ponder the lessons of the past, choose with an eye to the future, and consider the interests of our neighbors, so that conflicts can be resolved by a working harmony. Choice is made simpler for us by the fact that we live in an organized society, with customs, rules, laws, and institutions based upon long and varied experience. That kindness is better than unkindness; that lying is a poor practice; that one ought not to steal; that one ought in general to keep one's promises—these and kindred conceptions we imbibe in childhood. As we grow older, we become aware that certain sources of happiness have been accepted by the common sense of mankind; that such goods as health, security, knowledge, freedom, love, beauty, and fine workmanship are, by common consent, the principal sources of human happiness; and that their opposites, ill health, insecurity, ignorance, tyranny, hate, ugliness, and drudgery, are, by common consent, the principal sources of unhappiness. In addition, we can deepen and extend this table of values by reflecting upon the opinions of ancient thinkers and recent experts.[26]

Nevertheless, we ourselves must choose among various and conflicting values. Every value is subject to criticism in the light of its intrinsic merit and its consistency or inconsistency with other values. How shall we determine which values are choiceworthy? What are the principles whereby we may construct our moral economy?

One of the classical attempts to answer such questions is to be found in the "hedonic calculus" of Jeremy Bentham, which we examined in Chapter III. His "calculus" has frequently been attacked as impractical; and no doubt it is impossible to calculate with arithmetical precision the surplus of pleasure over pain or of pain over pleasure resulting from any act. But we can often judge that one pleasure (or pain) is greater in duration or intensity than another, and we can roughly estimate the consequences that will ensue. Some such weighing of values and consequences is required for any teleological ethics, and Bentham at least deserves credit for recognizing the nature of the problem and trying to solve it.

If we should attempt to formulate standards not for a hedonistic ethics such as Bentham's but for an ethics based upon the broader concept of the cultivation and fulfillment of interests, our problem is even more complex. Nevertheless, the following standards are suggested:

The Standard of Duration. President Charles W. Eliot of Harvard University (1834–1926) was fond of the phrase, "the durable satisfactions of life." He was pointing to an important standard—the temporal span of value.

Other things remaining equal, satisfactions or enjoyments that are durable —that do not, for example, quickly turn to the dust and ashes of boredom— are to be preferred; and the interests that yield such satisfactions are to be cultivated. Such interests are those that are deeply based, that express major rather than minor cravings, and that are supplied with the instrumentalities necessary for their realization and maintenance. An interest that is superficial or unrealistic soon lapses or turns to aversion.

The Standard of Intensity. Other things remaining equal, the more intense enjoyments and satisfactions are to be preferred to the less intense. Intensities cannot be exactly measured, but we can sometimes confidently say that one enjoyment is more intense than another, and still more intense than a third. They can thus be ranked in an order of intensive magnitudes, each separated from the next in the hierarchy by some noticeable difference.

Just as profound interests generally yield more durable enjoyments, so they likewise yield more intense enjoyments. When such fundamental interests are frustrated, the resulting misery is correspondingly intense and prolonged. We already have enough psychological data, gathered by such psychologists as Sigmund Freud, Harry Stack Sullivan, Carl Rogers, and E. C. Tolman, to conclude that certain interests are extremely fundamental, and that these include the interest in love and friendship, in security, in productive occupation, in constructive expression of one's talents, in status and good repute, in freedom of expression, and in a considerable variety of stimulation. To realize intense happiness, and to avoid intense unhappiness, it is particularly important to satisfy major cravings.

The Standard of Quality. John Stuart Mill invoked this standard when he maintained that some kinds of pleasure are preferable to others quite apart from the question of intensity or duration. We have already pointed out certain inconsistencies in Mill's argument, but what now concerns us is simply the contention that qualitatively higher enjoyments are to be preferred to qualitatively lower.

In judging quality, we must distinguish between the preferred and the preferable. There are passionate and irrational cravings, such as masochistic and sadistic desires, that are not objective measures or determinants of value-quality. "To crave that which is harmful," as Erich Fromm has said, "is the very essence of mental sickness."[27] The preferences of a diseased, superficial, or ignorant mind are not necessarily indicative of higher quality. Any preference, since it is a form of interest, involves *some* value, but not necessarily a value that is choiceworthy or morally permissible; nor is the *object* of that preference, if it be itself an intrinsic value, necessarily of a qualitatively superior or choiceworthy type.

How then can we judge what is qualitatively superior? This is a difficult question. It may be that the standard of quality will turn out, upon adequate analysis, to be ultimately reducible to quantitative standards, such as intensity. Nevertheless, it is a widely held belief that certain types of satisfactions and enjoyments, such as the values of art, of science, of philosophy, of religion, of love and friendship, are qualitatively higher than purely bodily or sensual enjoyments. Perhaps the main justification for this belief is that the "higher" values represent the mind as a whole, and thus more nearly express the essence and totality of a man's personality, whereas the "lower" values are less rich, complex, full-bodied, integral to the whole self, resonant of every corner of the personality. For example erotic love, at its best, is not only an intense sensual experience but an emotional, imaginative, and intellectual experience as well, and hence it concentrates within it the flavor of the whole personality, whereas mere physical lust, though perhaps yielding enjoyments as intense, expresses only one isolated side of a man's nature, his bodily appetite. It is this kind of standard that DeWitt Parker has in mind when he declares:

That interest is higher which is a better representative of the value of the self as a whole, giving to the whole what the whole wants. The claim of any one of the major interests to be superior to the others can be established, therefore, only by showing that it is more adequate to the value of the self as a whole.[28]

If this be correct, the higher interest is the more inclusive, expressing a larger segment of the self or even the self as a whole. Inclusiveness might appear to be purely quantitative, and therefore reducible to the quantitative standards of duration, intensity, and number. But when we examine the higher values, such as love or beauty or nobility of character, there seems to be a qualitative difference, too.

In his ethical writings, G. E. Moore subscribed to a doctrine which he called that of "organic wholes." This is the idea that a whole may have more value than the sum of its parts—as suggested in the famous lines from Robert Browning's poem *Abt Vogler*, which tells the story of a musician who out of three sounds framed, not a fourth sound but a star! I similarly believe that new and higher value-qualities are the result of a kind of creative synthesis. The qualitative superiority of great esthetic experience is to be found in its blending of contrasting modes of experience. As I have said elsewhere, art is the great reconciler of opposite poles which, in our practical life, ordinarily exclude each other. More than any other form of human experience, it combines such contrasting moments as variety and unity, familiarity and strangeness, repose and stimulation, order and spontaneity, the Apollonian and Dionysian moods. In great tragedy, for example, the extreme intensification of emotions, far from excluding a sense of repose, produces the dynamic calmness which Aristotle terms "catharsis." Likewise, as Freud points out, art involves the harmonious interplay of the conscious and the subconscious: the dream is inserted into the texture of waking life; the phantasmal and the real are fused. Or, again as Friedrich Schiller indicates, art is the reconciliation of law and impulse: the form, the pattern, the "lawfulness" of the experience becomes the expression, not the repression, of impulse. Or, as Theodor Lipps observes, the images of esthetic experience are seemingly objective and yet are colored by the emotion and sensibility of the beholder: the duality of subject and object disappears: the work of art is, in a sense, myself, and I am the object, since I project myself into it. Or, as Hegel understands, the universal essence merges into the specific image; and the more seamless is the unity, the more perfect is the esthetic moment. I wish to emphasize the point that we can extend this principle of dialectical unity beyond the sphere of esthetic experience. The best experiences of life are the ones that are most inclusive without being less harmonious.

If this theory be correct, we must reject the classical doctrine of higher and lower qualities that stems from Plato. According to his doctrine of Eros, as expressed in the *Symposium,* the lover rises ever higher in the scale of values as he moves from the sensuously concrete to the abstract and universal:

> The true order of going, or being led by another, to the things of love, is to begin from the beauties of earth and mount upward for the sake of that other

beauty, using these as steps only, and from one going on to two, and from two to all fair forms, and from fair forms to fair practices, and from fair practices to fair notions, until from fair notions he arrives at the notion of absolute beauty, and at last knows what the essence of beauty is.[29]

This ascent is likewise implied by the doctrine expressed in the *Phaedo*, that the body is the prison of the soul, and that we reach upward in the hierarchy of values as we more and more transcend the things of sense. Similarly in the educational scheme outlined in the *Republic*, we rise from the sensuously rich objects to their sheer forms, then on to pure mathematical form itself, and then on to the high abstractions of philosophical discourse. Plato's doctrine of sublimation and transcendence fitted in with the ascetic tendencies of medieval Christianity, and it has dominated Western thought for many centuries. Opposed to it is the dialectical conception of the unity of opposites, the highest values being not the most abstract but the most inclusively harmonious. This conception opens up the prospect of resolving the dualism of the Apollonian and the Dionysian, the classical and the romantic, reason and impulse, body and soul, id and ego. It suggests the possibility of a nonrepressive culture, such as that envisaged in Herbert Marcuse's profound book, *Eros and Civilization*.

On this dialectical basis, we can develop a concept of values that no longer pits the spiritual as higher against the sensual as lower. The virtue of sex at its best, as D. H. Lawrence has contended, is that it "involves the whole of a human being."

If only our civilization had taught us . . . how to keep the fire of sex clear and alive, flickering or glowing or blazing in all its varying degrees of strength and communication, we might, all of us, have lived all our lives in love, which means we should be kindled and full of zest in all kinds of ways and for all kinds of things.[30]

Instead "our civilization . . . has almost destroyed the natural flow of common sympathy between men and men, and men and women." And it was this that Lawrence wanted "to restore into life."[31] The ideal, more broadly stated by Dewey, is to regain "consciously, and thus on the plane of meaning, the union of sense, need, impulse, and action characteristic of the live creature."[32] The body, with its vivid sensuous experience, is indispensable to "the actual living quick" of human existence in its highest culmination.

If we combine the standard of quality with the standard of intensity, we have a composite standard that can be called that of the peak experiences. In life at its very best, there are experiences of absolute delight, perfect in themselves. They are moments of tremendous intensification of the very highest of values. The only words to express these mountain-peaks of value are like those of Shakespeare: "O wonderful, wonderful, and most wonderful wonderful! And yet again wonderful . . . !"[33]

Although we should certainly bear in mind these summits, we should also remember Sir Philip Sydney's remark, that the good is not the less good because the better is the better. The ordinary enjoyments of life, of eating and drinking, of conversation, of games and amusements, of relaxing in the sun, of enjoying a walk in the woods, are staple satisfactions that no one should despise. Men cannot always "burn with a gemlike flame"; they must fall back, for rest and sustenance, on the little things. These latter are just as necessary in their way as the great moments, and there need be no opposition between them and the best that life has to offer.

The Standard of Number. Other things remaining equal, an aggregate of many values is better than an aggregate of few values. In general, a life in which there are many joys is better than a life in which there are few joys, and a society in which there are many happy people is better than a society in which there are few happy people.

One of the implications of this standard is that one should prefer concordant rather than discordant interests. The effect of discord is to decrease the number of enjoyments and increase the number of miseries. As Bertrand Russell has wittily remarked, love is better than murder because love suits both parties whereas murder suits only one. Selfish, greedy, predatory, sadistic, or intemperate interests breed conflict, whereas unselfish, generous, noncompetitive, and temperate interests produce harmony. Moreover, costly social conflicts should be avoided; from the standpoint of internal harmony, the best of all groups is the community in which the good of each is the good of all.

Another implication of the standard of number is that the good things of life should be extended to as many people as possible. This means that wide democratic sharing is better than narrow exclusiveness.

The Standard of Fruitfulness. Values must be judged not only in terms of their immediate worth but in terms of their instrumental value, or fruitfulness in producing future values or disvalues. Upon this basis, certain external goods, which are of little or no value intrinsically, may be judged choiceworthy. This consideration, for example, justifies us in putting a great deal of emphasis upon the basic essentials of life, such as food, clothing, and shelter. As Helen Lynd has remarked: "Decent food and decent housing do not give men spiritual life, but they are a better basis for it than starvation."[34] For similar reasons, health and good education deserve great emphasis, because without them men are fettered in all their pursuits. The first charge upon any society should be to supply these five essentials to its citizens—food, housing, clothing, health services, education. Similarly fundamental is the achievement of an economic and social system that will avoid the terrible waste of economic depression and war.

In considering instrumental values, we must take account of the factor of risk. In general, the more probable satisfactions and enjoyments are to be preferred to the less probable. Therefore, we must ask, to what extent is it probable that the future values that we aim to achieve will actually be realized. This consideration justifies a certain preference for values near us in time and space, because temporal and spatial distance renders more obscure and uncertain the effects of our actions. But there is a marked tendency in human nature to overrate this factor—the bias in favor of the near is one of the most mischievous forms of bias. For example, like spendthrift children, Americans have denuded forests, exhausted soil, and wasted mineral supplies to the tune of colossal loss. One of the main values of social planning, especially if based upon the careful estimates provided by social scientists, is that it can greatly reduce such waste.

On the other hand, a person is simply cheating himself if he aims only at *future* satisfactions. As John Maynard Keynes has said, this sort of man "does not love his cat, but his cat's kittens; nor, in truth, the kittens, but only the kittens' kittens, and so on forward for ever to the end of cat-dom. For him jam is not jam unless it is a case of jam tomorrow and never jam today."[35] The inveterate tendency to postpone enjoyments, to regard concrete things in the present as merely instrumental to goods in the future, destroys the joy of carefree living. Far better is the advice, "Take no thought for the morrow. . . . Sufficient unto the day is the evil thereof." Half of the art of happiness is to learn when to look ahead and when to find repose in the present moment.

As we have seen, values may differ as more or less durable, more or less intense, more or less high in quality, more or less numerous, and more or less fruitful. It is difficult to assess the worth of alternatives in terms of any or all of these standards, and more difficult to balance these standards against one another. Indeed, the latter problem, how to compare standards, is very difficult indeed. For example, let us suppose that we are considering which of three alternatives to choose when the first is preferable in terms of the standard of intensity; the second, in terms of the standard of duration; and the third, in terms of the standard of quality. How can we compare these standards and decide which should be given priority in the given situation? Much would depend, of course, upon the extent to which each alternative is superior or inferior to the others in respect to each standard. If one alternative, for example, is *greatly* superior in intensity and *very slightly* inferior in duration and quality, it would seem to be, so far as these three criteria are concerned, the best alternative. But if there is no such decisive superiority in favor of any one alternative, and each is superior in some different respect, it may be impossible to choose upon the basis of any clear or rational grounds. In these circumstances we might as well flip a coin. I would like to say much more about the problem, but it is so difficult and involved that I have chosen not to discuss it except in this brief paragraph.

If the worth of alternatives is hard to assess for a single life, it is even harder to assess for the many lives that comprise a society. Social morality is a subtle and difficult art that cannot be reduced to rote; yet if men take time and care, they can at least make their choices much more intelligent and, on the average, much more fruitful of good consequences.

NOTES

1. Moore's "non-naturalism" will be discussed in Chapter IX.
2. H. A. Prichard, "Does Moral Philosophy Rest on a Mistake," *Moral Obligation*. London and New York: Oxford University Press, 1949, p. 4.
3. Henri Bergson, *The Two Sources of Morality and Religion*. New York: Holt, Rinehart and Winston, Inc., 1935, p. 7.
4. Adam Smith, *The Theory of the Moral Sentiments*. London: Cadell and Davies, 1804, p. 3.
5. David Hume, *An Enquiry Concerning the Principles of Morals* (edited by L. A. Selby-Bigge). London and New York: Oxford University Press, 1902, p. 229.
6. David Hume, *A Treatise of Human Nature* (edited by L. A. Selby-Bigge). London and New York: Oxford University Press, 1896, pp. 581–582. See also pages 536 and 591.
7. *Ibid.*, p. 479.
8. *Cf.* Jean Piaget, *The Moral Judgment of the Child*. New York: The Free Press of Glencoe, Inc., 1948. Also Gordon W. Allport, *Pattern and Growth in Personality*. New York: Holt, Rinehart and Winston, Inc., 1961, especially pp. 134–137.
9. F. C. Sharp, *Ethics*. New York: Appleton-Century-Crofts, Inc., 1928, pp. 140–141.
10. C. I. Lewis, "The Rational Imperatives," in Sidney Ratner (editor), *Vision and Action*. New Brunswick, N.J.: Rutgers University Press, 1952, p. 158.
11. Walt Whitman, "Song of Myself."
12. Quoted by Walter De La Mare in *Love*. New York: William Morrow & Company, Inc., 1946, p. 11.
13. Margaret Mead, "Primitive Society," in Findlay Mackenzie (editor), *Planned Society*. Englewood Cliffs, N.J.: Prentice-Hall, Inc., 1937, pp. 23–24. Also Margaret Mead, *Sex and Temperament in Three Primitive Societies*. New York: William Morrow & Company, Inc., 1935, Part I.
14. Friedrich Nietzsche, *Beyond Good and Evil*. New York: The Macmillan Company, 1924, section 260. See also Walter Kaufmann, *The Portable Nietzsche*. New York: Viking Press, 1954, pp. 128, 302.
15. R. B. Blakney, *Meister Eckhart*. New York: Harper & Row, Publishers, Inc., 1941, p. 204.
16. Mark Twain, *Huckleberry Finn*. This novel is, among other things, a profound study of the conflict between sympathy and racial bias.
17. Martin Luther King, Jr., *Stride toward Freedom*. New York: Harper & Row, Publishers, Inc., 1958, p. 224.
18. *Cf.* Josiah Royce, *The Philosophy of Loyalty*. New York: The Macmillan Company, 1909, especially Chapter III.
19. David Hume, *A Treatise of Human Nature, op. cit.*, p. 472.
20. Plato, *Republic*, Book I.
21. *Cf.* Margaret Mead, *Cooperation and Competition Among Primitive Peoples*. New York: McGraw-Hill Book Company, Inc., 1937. Also Claire Huchet Bishop, *All Things Common*, New York: Harper & Row, Publishers, Inc., 1950; and A. H. Maslow, *Motivation and Personality*. New York: Harper & Row, Publishers, Inc., 1954, Ch. 10.
22. *Cf.* B. F. Skinner, *Science and Hu-*

man Behavior. New York: The Macmillan Company, 1953, Chapter XII.

23. Claude Colman, "The Hickory Stick," *Bulletin of the American Association of University Professors*, vol. 39 (1953), p. 464. This report of a Swabian schoolmaster named Hauberle goes back to the eighteenth century.

24. Shelley, *A Defence of Poetry*.

25. Quoted from Elizabeth Barrett Browning by F. C. Sharp, *Good Will and Ill Will*. Chicago: University of Chicago Press, 1950, p. 148.

26. For a summary of expert psychological opinion on the basic values of life, see Marie Jahoda, *Current Concepts of Positive Mental Health*. New York: Basic Books, Inc., 1958. Also Peter A. Bertocci and Richard M. Millard, *Personality and the Good*. New York: David McKay Company, Inc., 1963, Parts I and II.

27. Erich Fromm, *Man for Himself*. New York: Holt, Rinehart and Winston, Inc., 1947, p. 179.

28. DeWitt H. Parker, *Human Values*. New York: Harper & Row, Publishers, Inc., 1931, p. 97.

29. Plato, *Symposium* (Jowett's translation).

30. D. H. Lawrence, "Sex versus Loneliness," *Selected Essays*. Harmondsworth, Middlesex: Penguin Books, 1950, p. 18.

31. D. H. Lawrence, "The State of Funk," *ibid.*, pp. 100–101.

32. John Dewey, *Art as Experience*. New York: Minton, Balch & Co., 1934, p. 25.

33. Shakespeare, *As You Like It*, Act III, Scene 2. For a description of these supreme moments, see A. H. Maslow, "Cognition of Being in the Peak Experiences," *Journal of Genetic Psychology*, vol. 94 (1954), pp. 43–66.

34. Helen Lynd, *England in the Eighteen-Eighties*. London and New York: Oxford University Press, 1945, p. 424.

35. John Maynard Keynes, *Essays in Persuasion*. New York: Harcourt Brace & World, Inc., 1932, p. 370.

PART THREE

Skeptical theories

CHAPTER IX

Cultural relativism

I. THE MEANING OF CULTURAL RELATIVISM

In Parts One and Two, we tried to present an objective interpretation of basic ethical concepts, such as "good," "right," and "ought." In Part Three (Chapters IX and X), we shall turn to relativist and subjective doctrines which deny the cognitive basis for such an objective and universal ethics.

In the present chapter, we shall consider the relativist doctrine that each society and each age can lay claim to its own virtue and its own standard. If men are reared in one culture, they will adhere to one set of moral norms; if reared in another culture, they will adhere to a different set. There is no standard common to all cultures and all ages, and there is nothing outside of the cultures that can serve as a standard. The culture of a period or a group is therefore the *ultimate* frame of reference. Moral judgments always depend for their validity upon relation to this frame. What is right when related to one cultural frame is wrong when related to another. This type of theory I shall call cultural relativism.

"The culture of a people is its total equipment of ideas and institutions and conventionalized activities."[1] It includes arts, sciences, languages, tools, techniques, utensils, customs, sentiments, and mores. It can be studied piecemeal or as a whole. To the extent that it is unified, it exhibits a total structure and internal coherence: changes in one part have reverberations in other parts of the culture. Many cultural traits are passed down from one generation to another, or borrowed from other peoples; but the culture is always developing and changing and it takes on a particular color and configuration. As the man-made part of the environment, it is distinguished from the innate biological makeup of human beings and their purely physical environment. It is transmitted not by physical inheritance but by learning and conditioning. More than any biological characteristic, it is what differentiates one society or civilization from another.

According to the cultural relativist, the culture determines the moral standards of the society, and no cross-cultural standards are admissible. There can be no legitimate rating of cultures in importance or in worth. Values in the respective cultures are incommensurable. We can say, "This is right according to the present culture of Pakistan," but we cannot say, "This is right according to an absolute or universal standard."

The meaning of cultural relativism is clarified by contrasting it with absolutism. An absolutist maintains that certain ideals or moral standards are unconditionally valid, good in any time and any place, eternal and immutable. This view is frequently associated with the view that there is one God ruling over the entire universe and determining, by an unvarying will and wisdom, what is valid for all peoples in all ages. It may also be associated with other philosophical theories, such as the view that all reality is one—a single unity —or that ideals are abstract universals, like Plato's "ideas" or forms, existing independently of any exemplification—or that fixed values are discoverable by pure a priori reason apart from the changing content of experience. Whatever may be its religious or philosophical basis, absolutism insists that the most basic ethical standards are unconditional and invariable. Relativism denies that there are any such unconditional, universal, and objective standards of right and good.

We may distinguish between two aspects of cultural relativism. First, relativism insists that standards necessarily vary *from place to place*. Each society has its own ethical standards, and there is no possibility of finding any ideal that is common and valid among all societies. Second, relativism insists that standards necessarily vary *from time to time*. Each age has its standards, and there are no enduring ethical principles which transcend these temporal limitations.

This denial of enduring and universal norms has a considerable shock-value. When the relativist tells us, for example, that cannibalism is right in a cannibal culture, or that sexual promiscuity is right in a promiscuous age, we are impelled to take a new hard look at the foundations of ethics.

2. SOME ANCIENT AND MODERN
REPRESENTATIVES OF RELATIVISM

The revolt of the relativists against absolutism tends to occur in every revolutionary era. It occurred, for example, in the "age of the Sophists" in ancient Greece, a period when the traditional Hellenic culture was rent by class struggle and war. The effects of the economic revolution, which began in the period of Solon (*circa* 639–559 B.C.), were profoundly disturbing to the structure of Greek life. The early basis of Greek economic life had been primarily subsistence farming; but, in a manner analogous to our modern "industrial revolution," it changed to a more advanced type of cash-crop farming and to commerce and industry. In a little more than a century, this great economic transformation brought into existence a commercial and industrial middle class and a new "proletarian" class of industrial and maritime work-ers. It destroyed the old isolation of the traditional Greek city-states, drew the cities into commercial and imperialistic conflict with one another, and sharpened the clash between the Greek states and surrounding empires such as the Persian. As a result, Greek culture was churned to its depths, and a series of wars and revolutions ensued. The climax of these developments has never been narrated more vividly than by the Greek historian, Thucydides, who described not only the great catastrophe of the Peloponnesian War but the class conflicts that preceded and accompanied it.

Revolution thus ran its course from city to city and the places which it arrived at last, from having heard what had been done before, carried to a still greater excess the refinements of their inventions, as manifested in the cunning of their enterprises and the atrocity of their reprisals. . . . Thus every form of iniquity took root in the Hellenic countries by reason of the troubles. The ancient simplicity into which honor so largely entered was laughed down and disappeared; and society became divided into camps in which no man trusted his fellow.[2]

The Sophists were philosophic representatives of this age of unrest. They belonged to a generation which had seen a great many laws in the making, revolutions, and counterrevolutions, and they reflected the disillusionment and uncertainty of a period when traditions and customs were being fre-quently violated. As wandering teachers, traveling from city to city, they were acutely conscious of both the variety and the instability of moral codes. With a skeptical and predominantly practical attitude, they were also re-acting against abstract science and philosophy. It seemed to them very plain that the answers to philosophical problems vary from thinker to thinker, from city to city, and that no universal truth can be established. In these circum-stances, it was natural for them to conclude that truth and value are relative.

The most famous of the Sophists was Protagoras (481?–411 B.C.), who was an old man when Socrates was young and who died in the early years of the Peloponnesian War. Except for a few brief fragments, his own words have perished, but we can determine his teaching by what Plato and others have said about him. His essential doctrine was that "man is the measure of all things." By this he did not mean that universal humanity is the standard whereby truth and goodness can be judged. According to Plato's dialogue, the *Theaetetus,* he meant by "man" the individual man. Things are to me as they appear to me and to you as they appear to you. There is no *common* real world that can be known by two or more percipients. Every object is relative to the point of view in perception, to a momentary, fleeting act of sensation. The man who is color blind, or who differs otherwise in his per-ceptions or beliefs, can never be proved wrong.

Protagoras maintained that relativity applies also in the sphere of morals and politics. He represented himself as a "physician of the soul": he could not induce truer beliefs about virtue or vice, since no belief is any more objective or "true" than any other, but he could implant healthier and more useful beliefs. In place of judgments of truth he wished to substitute judgments of worth; but here too a relativistic interpretation entered, although not of a purely individualistic sort. He took the view that moral and political values vary from city to city, that these values are embodied in the local customs and traditions, and that the wise and morally healthy man acquiesces in the prevailing standards. His view is stated in the *Theaetetus*: "Whatever appears to a state to be just and fair, so long as it is regarded as such, is just and fair to it."[3]

In Plato's dialogue, the *Protagoras*, he is represented as telling a myth which expresses his fundamental relativism: When the world was very young, Prometheus stole the secret of fire and of the mechanical arts from the gods and bestowed them upon mankind; but men were still unable successfully to cope with other animals and with the rigors of nature, for they lacked political cohesion and the strength that comes from unity. Zeus, fearing that the entire human race would be exterminated, sent Hermes to bestow upon all men the sense of right and justice, necessary if they were to combine for mutual defense. Thenceforward all men, possessing this knowledge, were teachers of virtue to each new generation. According to this interpretation, goodness is to be identified with the mores and conventions of the given community, and the child merely picks up from his elders whatever familiarity with "virtue" he may need. Thus morality is entirely relative, since there is no moral standard more ultimate than whatever is current in a given society.

In comparison with some of the younger Sophists, Protagoras was a conservative. The more radical Sophistic point of view is expressed by Thrasymachus, a character in Book I of Plato's *Republic*. His theory is that right is determined by the laws and conventions of each society, and that these in turn are determined by the ruling class. The group that dominates every state acts in its own interests. As the strongest party in the state, it ordains the ruling ideas of the society, and these ideas determine what is right and just for that society. Hence might is right, and "justice" (a term used in the wide sense of moral goodness) is determined only by force and self-interest. "Justice," Thrasymachus said, "is the interest of the stronger." But not all cultural relativism is thus tied to the concept of power.

We are living in a period analogous to "the age of the Sophists," except that now the forces arrayed against one another are of vastly greater scope. In our time as in the Greek period, relativism has been a reflection of widespread uncertainties. When we no longer listen to the oracles of the past, and when we hear so many new and contradictory voices, we are inclined to suppose that there is no way of discovering any common and objective standard. The causes of the resurgence of ethical relativism are numerous and complicated, but among the major causes are the conflicts, confusions, and revolutionary tendencies of our era.

Another main cause is the increase of knowledge. The fact of cultural variation has been recognized since the *History* of Herodotus in the fifth century B.C., but modern scholarship has supplied a massive documentation. Anthropologists and historians have disclosed "relativism" everywhere in the world of cultures. They have revealed the "irreducible" diversity of human societies, each with its unique "configuration" and "cultural patterns," each with its own kind of religion, science, art, and morality in flux. The relativist concludes that there is no standard of truth or value that runs through all the centuries and all the cultures.

Oswald Spengler, the famous German historian, compares the emergence of cultural relativism to the Copernican revolution in astronomy. The geocentric "universe" of Ptolemy was small and cozy—very much simpler, more stable, more synoptic, than our universe of countless galaxies and inconceivable distances. The Copernican revolution changed all this. Men had to reckon with a boundless cosmos: everywhere there were worlds, everywhere there was the center of things, everywhere and nowhere. A similar reorientation has occurred among historians.

In the "universe" of cultures, Spengler declares, we grow up with a kind of "Ptolemaic" orientation. The ideas and beliefs of our own culture seem to reflect the very nature of things, and the standards of that culture seem the ultimate criteria of right and wrong. This point of view, Spengler argues, is an illusion due to the fact that we have been completely immersed in our own culture. It has been controlling our thoughts and activities since the date of our birth. The new "Copernican revolution" to which Spengler refers means the abandonment of this kind of cultural provincialism and the substitution of a radically different orientation. It implies a great widening of horizons and an escape from ethnocentrism (the point of view that our own cultural way of life is necessarily best).

According to Spengler, we must purge our minds of two pernicious illusions. The *first* is "the illusion of position": the notion that our civilization is the hub and center of the cultural universe. To destroy this illusion we must give up the "empty figment of *one* linear history," centering in our Western culture, and substitute "the drama of a *number* of mighty cultures, . . . each stamping its material, its mankind, in its own image; each having its own idea, its own passions, its own life, will, and feeling, its own death."[4] The *second* is "the illusion of progress"—the conventional interpretation of history as conforming to the "ancient-medieval-modern" scheme, which minimizes the autonomous contributions of non-Western cultures and depicts historical trends as leading up to, and culminating in, modern progress.

The consequence of destroying both of these illusions, Spengler believes, is to leave us with a completely relativistic point of view. "Mankind," he tells us, "has no aim, no idea, no plan"—it is just "a zoological expression," an "empty word." There is no one art, or science, or ethics, but many, "each in its deepest essence different from the others, each limited in duration and self-contained."[5] Humanistic morality is discarded and a relativistic ethical creed is substituted. "We are not human beings *per se*. . . . World citizenship is a wretched phrase. We are human beings of a century, of a nation, of a circle, of a type."[6]

The American anthropologist, Ruth Benedict, has hailed Spengler's work as a great contribution to modern thought, but she speaks of the "confused impression" that results when Spengler characterizes such complex civilizations as the Graeco-Roman and the present-day Western. These variegated and stratified societies lack "the essential homogeneity of a folk culture." Although cultural configurations are as "compelling" and "significant" in these civilized societies as in any other, the material is too intricate to permit a very clear and cogent analysis.

To apply the Spenglerian approach to simpler materials, Benedict minutely describes three primitive societies, the Zuñi Indians in the pueblos of New Mexico, the Dobus on an island north of the eastern end of New Guinea, and the Kwakiutls as they lived a century ago on Vancouver Island in British Columbia. She chose these particular cultures because they sharply contrast with one another. The Zunis love peace and order; they feel at one with the universe; they delight in formality and ritual, in measure and sobriety; they know nothing of strenuous rivalry or individual heroism, the struggle for wealth, power, and reputation. The Dobus are suspicious, treacherous, cruel; they have an intense fear of nature, they live out "without repression man's worst nightmares of the ill-will of the universe," venting "the malignancy" which they attribute "alike to human society and to the powers of nature." The Kwakiutls fiercely compete for wealth and power; they indulge in delusions of grandeur; they prize a "megalomaniac paranoid trend" as "the essential attribute of ideal man," and display a Dionysian preference for intense and ecstatic experiences.

Some of the terms that Ruth Benedict employs to characterize the Dobus and Kwakiutls seem to imply pathological defects in their cultures. But as a relativist, she concludes that these societies merely evince clinical deviations from *our* norms. Behavior which *we* deem pathological may be perfectly normal and healthy according to *their* standards. In every society, normality and virtue consist in exhibiting the dominant cultural patterns of behavior. Cultures cannot be objectively rated as superior or inferior. All cultures should be regarded as "coexisting and equally valid patterns of life."[7]

In certain other passages, Benedict appears to contradict this extreme relativistic position. All of mankind, she has said, has a moral sense, and "it is quite possible that a modicum of what is considered right and what is considered wrong could be disentangled that is shared by the whole human race."[8] At times she seems to be making objective moral judgments—for example, when she declares that "Kwakiutl rivalry produces a waste of material goods" and that such waste "ranks low in the scale of human values." She admits that "it is possible to scrutinize different institutions and cast up their cost in terms of social capital, in terms of the less desirable traits they stimulate, and in terms of human suffering and frustration."[9] These admissions on the part of Ruth Benedict illustrate the inconsistencies that almost invariably crop up in treatises favoring cultural relativism. Very few anthropologists or historians would consistently deny *all* objectivity or universality in the sphere of values.

This admission of universality is also illustrated in the "cultural relativism" of Melville Herskovits, one of America's most distinguished anthropologists. "The very core of cultural relativism," he has declared, "is the social discipline that comes of respect for differences—of mutual respect. Emphasis on the worth of many ways of life, not one, is an affirmation of the values in each culture."[10] He denies that it is possible to evaluate cultures by a supercultural set of norms, and insists that each society should be understood sympathetically in its own unique terms. But he does not deny that there are also cultural universals. "Ideas of right and wrong, good and evil, are found in all societies," he remarks, and "the hard core of similarities *between* cultures" should not be overlooked:

Viewed at a given moment, the cultures of men present a range of infinite variety. On the closest scrutiny, however, they prove to be but intricate variations on a number of basic themes. . . . These unities encompass the satisfaction of the demands made by the physical organism, the perpetuation of the group, the achievement of a sanctioned order of living, adjustment to the universe, and the fulfillment of aesthetic impulses.[11]

He also speaks of "the full development of the individual personality" as a universal value, while insisting that "the individual realizes his personality through his culture."[12] He concludes that "morality is universal, and so is the enjoyment of beauty, and some standard of truth."[13]

While thus admitting that there are cultural "universals," Herskovits denies that there are "absolutes." He defines these terms as follows:

Absolutes are fixed, and, as far as convention is concerned, are not admitted to have variation, to differ from culture to culture, from epoch to epoch. *Universals,* on the other hand, are those least common denominators to be extracted from the range of variation that all phenomena of the natural or cultural world manifest.[14]

Not only does Herskovits admit universals in culture, but he devotes a great deal of attention to them. He seems to be mainly intent upon a kind of orchestration of diversity:

Such emphasis seeks to understand and to harmonize goals, not to judge and destroy those that do not dovetail with our own. Cultural history teaches that, important as it is to discern and study the parallelisms in human civilizations, it is no less important to discern and study the different ways man has devised to fulfill his needs.[15]

In denying absolutes while admitting universals, Herskovits is advancing a position that is not substantially different from my own.

In view of the fact that Herskovits has been widely heralded as the "high priest" of relativism, his recognition of the universality of certain cultural values and traits raises the question whether the main core of anthropology has ever represented the extreme cultural relativism of which Protagoras, in ancient Greece, and Spengler, in modern times, may be taken as representative. No one can read the more eminent authorities, such as Boas, Wissler, Malinowski, Linton, Kluckhohn, and Murdock, without discovering fundamental similarities among all the cultures.

Especially at the present time there is reluctance to espouse an unqualified relativism. This is partly because the relativist position is no longer as fashionable in anthropology as it was a few years ago, but also because it is now realized that early formulations were unguarded. Benedict is presently regarded more as a respected pioneer than as a thinker who immediately contributes to development in the field. Her ideas are widely seen as oversimplifications, and each of her descriptions of particular cultures has received some criticism on empirical grounds. Among historians, Spengler is usually regarded as much too extreme. Even less than Benedict could he be considered typical of present-day opinion.

The critics of these thinkers might still call themselves relativists, or maintain that there is merit in the relativist position. Some would argue that relativism has important heuristic utility (akin to the shock value that I have referred to) but would claim no more for it. Others would say that relativism provides a useful basis for methodological approaches and theoretical formulations, but would profess no interest in its implications for value questions. Certainly, many anthropologists assert the empirical validity of relativism without drawing any ethical conclusions at all.

In the beginning of this chapter, I deliberately set forth the ethical doctrine of relativism in sharp and uncompromising terms, because it is most clear and challenging in this unqualified form. Throughout the following critique, I shall be referring to the simon-pure doctrine, and my remarks will apply to other forms of relativism only to the extent that they approximate this extreme.

3. A CRITIQUE OF RELATIVISM

The "evidence" for relativism, as I have remarked, has been mounting ever since the time of Herodotus and the Sophists. As early as the Seventeenth Century, John Locke characterized the nature of this evidence in his *Essay Concerning Human Understanding*:

> He that will carefully peruse the history of mankind and look abroad into the several tribes of men, and with indifferency survey their actions, will be able to satisfy himself, that there is scarce that principle of morality to be named, or rule of virtue to be thought on (those only excepted that are absolutely necessary to hold society together, which commonly too are neglected betwixt distinct

societies), which is not, somewhere or other, slighted and condemned by the general fashion of whole societies of men, governed by practical opinions and rules of living quite opposite to others.[16]

The evidence of modern anthropology has greatly reinforced Locke's opinion, but not without the recognition of some cultural universals.

Even if cultural differences are as great as the most extreme relativists allege, the *ethical* conclusions of relativism would not logically follow. Whatever else the facts about cultural variations may establish, they do not imply any particular ethical theory. The variability of standards at the *descriptive* level has never been a philosophical bone of contention. Plato and Aristotle were quite as aware as the Sophists that moral standards vary. They concluded that most people, the Sophists included, do not know what is really good. Similarly the data presented by Ruth Benedict will not daunt a philosophical opponent. Walter T. Stace has written:

> Miss Ruth Benedict . . . tells us that the Dobu Islanders disagree with [the] advice of Jesus Christ about loving your neighbor. They found their culture on treachery and ill-will. . . . Miss Benedict seems to conclude that treachery and ill-will *are*, for the Dobu Islanders, good. My own conclusion is that the Dobu Islanders are simply mistaken. . . . People are often mistaken about what is good for the health of their bodies. That is why we have doctors. And people are just as likely to be mistaken about what will be good for the happiness of their souls. That is why we have moralists. The Dobu Islanders need someone to correct their . . . moral mistakes.[17]

The question at issue is not whether moral opinions differ but whether they *ought* to differ. A moral ideal or standard may be objectively valid even though unenlightened societies do not accept this ideal. Just as Einstein's theory of gravitation may be objectively true although many people do not understand or believe it, so a certain norm or ideal may be objectively true or valid even though many people do not grasp or accept it. Moral beliefs vary —this fact cannot be denied. The relativist says that the variation is to be explained by the absence of any valid universal ideal or moral standard. His opponent, with equal consistency, says that the variation is to be explained by moral immaturities and mistakes.

The term "moral standard" has two different meanings. In one sense, standards are indisputably relative. We often speak of judging a man by the standards of his time or place. This implies that different times and places have different standards. Now this is perfectly true—*if* by "moral standards" we mean the ideas that people happen to have about right and wrong. For it is obvious that moral ideas differ from country to country and from age to age. But we also use the term "moral standards" in quite a different sense. Instead of referring to what people *think* is right, we may be referring to what is *really* right. When the absolutist denies that moral standards are relative, he is using the term in this latter sense.[18]

If the relativist is to establish his case, he must do more than present factual evidence that standards, in the *first* sense of the word, vary from one culture to another. He must demonstrate that the criteria of validity by which we accept or reject moral judgments are entirely internal to the culture. He must show that there is no objective way of evaluating cultures, and that consequently the standards of each culture must be regarded as ethically ultimate. According to Herskovits, most American anthropologists are agreed "that objective indices of cultural inferiority and superiority cannot be established."[19] Perhaps so. But the question at issue is a philosophical problem, and perhaps philosophers are best qualified to answer it.

The ethical beliefs of most anthropologists have been strongly influenced by their methodological approach to primitive cultures. As scientists they are trying to be as unbiased as possible. This requires that they should make a very determined effort to surmount deeply inculcated, even subconscious, ethnocentrisms. They must refrain from making judgments or interpretations that arise from a preconceived frame of reference. They must not force the criteria and patterns of their own culture upon those of another. Instead, they must try to grasp the alien culture sympathetically in its own terms. This requires empathy and projective imagination on the part of the anthropologist, who must see the members of alien cultures as they see themselves.

This "methodological relativism" (if that is the right term for it) is necessary and salutary. A knowledge of varying cultural forms is essential for realistic social thought. The anthropologist, like the historian, must escape from "the illusion of position." He must not judge all cultures in terms of his own society. But this "relativism" of *method* should be distinguished from relativism as a philosophical doctrine. A person may practice the method of empathic understanding, and yet in his moral philosophy assert some reasonable and objective basis for preferring one moral principle to another. If the method has ethical implications at all (which in strict logic it does not have), it would *not* favor intolerant cultures such as the Nazi or the Dobu. It makes for the widening of human sympathy. It places us on the side of mankind rather than on the side of bigotry and intolerance. In this sense, it favors ethical universalism rather than an indiscriminate ethical relativism.

There is a kind of incongruity in combining the two kinds of relativism. The methodological type requires tolerance and sympathetic understanding; the ethical type condones the most intolerant of societies. When the two are combined, we are asked in one breath to renounce ethnocentrism, and in the next breath, to respect the narrow standards of highly ethnocentric cultures. In the name of tolerance, we are asked to be tolerant of intolerance. It is not difficult to tolerate comparatively innocent institutions such as polygamy. But it is not as easy, and not as consistent with a creed of tolerance, to respect and tolerate cannibalism, slavery, genocide, and Blitzkriegs. If we are called upon to tolerate a demented cult of racism, a raucous jingoism, a systematic sadism, I for one would draw the line.

There is an even deeper and more subtle inconsistency in the argument of the extreme cultural relativist. He usually defends a relativistic theory of knowledge as well as a relativistic ethics. Spengler, for example, maintains that there is no such thing as "absolute truth" any more than there is "absolute good." Truth, like value, is relative to particular cultural perspectives, and hence no judgment, whether moral, scientific, or philosophical, can have objective or universal validity. Yet Spengler's "Copernican revolution" in the interpretation of cultures demands the very transcendence of culture-bound thinking which he tells us is impossible. In the Preface to the revised edition of *The Decline of the West*, he seems to recognize this contradiction. He says that his theory is true for him as a Westerner, but "not true in itself as dissociated from the conditions imposed by blood and by history, for that is impossible." This admission greatly weakens the significance of his "Copernican revolution" and detracts from the force of his whole argument.

There appears to be a similar inconsistency in the argument of Melville Herskovits. He cites with approval the contention of Ernst Cassirer, the eminent philosopher, that all reality as known is *cultural* reality. Declares Cassirer:

Instead of dealing with the things themselves, man is in a sense constantly conversing with himself. He has so enveloped himself in linguistic forms, in artistic images, in mythical symbols or religious rites that he cannot see or know anything except by the interposition of this artificial medium. His situation is the same in the theoretical as in the practical sphere. Even here man does not live in a world of hard facts, or according to his immediate needs and desires. He lives rather in the midst of imaginary emotions, in hopes and fears, in illusions and disillusions, in his fantasies and dreams.[20]

Herskovits argues similarly that man is a "cultural animal." In knowing as well as in doing, he is many and manifold, changing as the culture changes. The very meaning and character of his environment, his "truths" as well as his "values," are determined by the cultural "frame of reference." "Judgments are based on experience," Herskovits tells us, "and experience is interpreted by each individual in terms of his own enculturation. . . . Even the facts of the physical world are discerned through the enculturative screen, so that the perception of time, distance, weight, size, and other 'realities' is mediated by the conventions of any given group."[21]

If our thinking to an extreme degree is culture-bound, it is difficult to understand how we can have a *science* of cultural anthropology, or a genuine science of any sort. It is nonsense to say that science is true or logic valid only from a particular cultural perspective. Herskovits, in the spirit of science, would be among the first to denounce the concept of a "Nazi anthropology," a "communist biology," or a "Jewish physics." Our *beliefs* may be determined by our culture, but not the truth or falsity of what we believe in. The validity or invalidity of ideas, their truth or falsity, is completely independent of any cultural bias or perspective. That there are polar bears in Alaska is true for anyone who cares to ascertain the facts, whatever his cultural background. So it is with any verifiable hypothesis. At times, Herskovits seems to be prepared to admit this, but such an admission is inconsistent with his remark that all "facts" are discerned through the distorting medium of an "enculturative screen."

There is still another inconsistency, or at least a surprising paradox, in the relativistic theory. The odd consequence follows from its premises that he who acts in accordance with the cultural patterns of his society can do no wrong. The rightness of his act cannot even be questioned, since to ask such a question would be to imply some other criterion of right than the relativistic one. This amounts to saying that the cultural way of life is ultimate and sacrosanct. If witch-burning or Jew-baiting is characteristic of the culture, it is right by definition. The cultural relativist thus proposes to treat relative values as if they were absolute. The plausibility of relativism is due largely to its opposition to an unrealistic absolutism, but now we can see that it involves a peculiar "absolutism" of its own. It demands an acceptance of the cultural patterns of the society, even if these patterns are based upon superstition or prejudice, or represent a "cultural lag."

Not even uncivilized men are prepared to go this far. Franz Boas and Bronislaw Malinowski have pointed out that primitive people often reflect and deviate from custom on the ground of reason and conscience. Robert Redfield mentions a Pawnee Indian, who in defiance of the culture of his tribe, rescued a woman prisoner about to be put to death ceremonially, and strove to end human sacrifice among his people.[22] In civilized society, moral choice is determined with considerable frequency by independent critical judgment. The great moral reformers, such as Buddha, Socrates, and Jesus, rejected the ordinary standards of their societies. George Orwell has praised the lonely dissenters in cruel totalitarian regimes. "There was truth and there was untruth, and if you clung to the truth even against the whole world, you were not mad."[23]

To deny that there is any such objective standard is to cut the heart out of morality. Consider what extreme relativism means. The British, French, Russian, Chinese, and American people spent untold treasures in blood and wealth defeating the fascist-nazi system in World War II. Most of these people believed that they were fighting against a vicious system and for a just cause. They believed that "our side is right." The relativist in effect tells them that this belief is sheer illusion; that there is no objectively valid ideal; that there are only conflicting cultural patterns, each one equally "right," each one right according to its own cultural point of view. In the future, men will be called upon to make many fresh efforts in the interests of a better life. Again the relativist will say that the effort can be based only on illusion. There is no objective meaning in saying that one culture's goal is better than another's. There is also no meaning in improving the moral state of one's own culture for, by definition, the cultural pattern is right and the dissenter is wrong. Very few people will accept this view when they really understand it.

The relativist may deny that we have correctly stated the implications of his position, but it is difficult to see on what grounds he can do so. Of course, many relativists are inconsistent; they shrink from the implications of their own position. This is because extreme relativism conflicts with the deepest moral convictions of mankind.

The position of the relativist is ambiguous when confronted by the vexing problem of subcultures. A great society such as the American nation is not culturally homogeneous. There is a very great contrast, for example, between our liberals and fundamentalists, our Bohemians and straight-laced Puritans. There are also criminal subcultures, such as the gang culture of racketeers. If right is always relative to the cultural frame of reference, it would seem to require conformity to each subculture as well as to the main culture. In fact, the main culture may be so intricate that no one, not even a Gallup pollster, can be sure of its dominant traits. Surely we do not intend that our moral standards should be undefined until we can figure out the nature of the main cultural configuration, or so uncertain that they will shift with every change in cultural group or subgroup. There must be some more universal and objective ethical criterion.

4. ON BEING HUMAN

That there is such a criterion is the thesis of one of the greatest of philosophical traditions. This is the tradition of humanism which has its roots in the philosophy of Plato, Aristotle, and the Stoics. It found expression in the ideas of "natural law" and "natural rights" which we have examined in Chapter I. A similar Chinese tradition is to be found in Confucius, Mencius, and other Chinese sages. Morally, it means the cultivation of human excellence. Logically, it refers to the unity of mankind.

A humanistic ethics is opposed to an absolutism which would deny the realistic basis of ethics in human needs and circumstances; but it is equally opposed to a relativism which would deny the ethical significance of our common humanity. Good is the affirmation of human life, the unfolding of man's powers. Evil is the negation of life, the frustration of human needs and capacities.

Human nature is more than an empty term. No one would deny that the human body has a basic structure—that Chinamen have hearts and livers as do also Americans—and that therefore the science of medicine, the science of physical health and wellbeing, is applicable to all men. Similarly, the human mind is not an utterly amorphous thing: it too has its structure of thought, passion, appetite, emotion, and sensation; its laws of operation, its conscious and subconscious levels. If it were not so there could be no science of psychology, no science of *mental* health such as psychiatry. No doubt the mind is more profoundly conditioned and modified by varying cultural environments than is the body, yet there is no good evidence that either the mind or the body is absolutely characterless.

As Erich Fromm has well said:

. . . Man, in contrast to the animal, shows an almost infinite malleability. . . . He can live free, and as a slave. Rich and in luxury, and under conditions of half-starvation. He can live as a warrior, and peaceably; as an exploiter and robber, and as a member of a co-operating and loving fellowship. There is hardly a psychic state in which man cannot live, and hardly anything which cannot be done with him, and for which he cannot be used. . . . Yet, in spite of all this evidence, the history of man shows that we have omitted one fact. Despots and ruling cliques can succeed in dominating and exploiting their fellow man, but they cannot prevent *reactions* to this inhuman treatment. Their subjects become frightened, suspicious, lonely and, if not due to external reasons, their systems collapse at some point because fears, suspicions and loneliness eventually incapacitate the majority to function effectively and intelligently. Whole nations, or social groups within them, can be subjugated and exploited for a long time, but they *react*. They react with apathy or such impairment of intelligence, initiative and skills that they gradually fail to perform the functions which should serve their rulers. Or they react by the accumulation of such hate and destructiveness as to bring about an end to themselves, their rulers and their system. . . . But whatever the reactions are, the statement that man can live under almost any condition is only half true; it must be supplemented by the other statement, that if he lives under conditions which are contrary to his nature and to the basic requirements for human growth and sanity, he cannot help reacting; he must either deteriorate and perish, or bring about conditions which are more in accordance with his needs.[24]

Health and disease in the personality are quite as amenable to study as health and disease in the human body. We can discover what human needs are so basic that their repression leads to mental and social breakdown: to neurosis, insanity, and suicide in the individual personality; to crime, depression, war and revolution in society. We can define man's aim as the unfolding of his basic powers according to the laws of his nature, and we can use our humanistic sciences to investigate these laws. A good beginning of such research has already been made by psychologists and sociologists. Morality should have a sound basis in such known facts about human beings. Admittedly, we have less accurate knowledge about human personality than about physical matter; but there is no reason for declaring that knowledge of human nature is impossible, or for neglecting the knowledge that we already have.

Some anthropologists would object at this point that I have gone beyond the limits of verifiable knowledge in conceiving psychological health and illness in terms of universal criteria. This is a problem area in which the question of the empirical validity of norms still gives social scientists great difficulty in discovering convincing cross-cultural formulations. Perhaps most specialists, at least among anthropologists, would insist that the problem of universal criteria for psychological normality and abnormality, or of health and illness, is not yet solved satisfactorily. According to some experts, the formulations of our psychiatrists and psychologists are narrowly culture-bound, and neither psychiatry nor social science has yet found an effective way out of this impasse. My own feeling is that the quotation from Erich Fromm, cited above, is a reasonable statement of the limits of cultural relativism, borne out by a vast body of evidence. I grant that the conditions of psychological health and ill health will vary significantly from culture to culture, but I would insist that these conditions, including the ethical standards which they sustain, are not utterly various.

We already know enough to discern some of the universal requirements of morality. Every society, at the very least, *is* a society. Within it, human beings meet together, live together, and are faced with the need of getting along together. A universal requirement of morality is a code which will enable the society to function as a viable social system. The essential maxims of morality—be kind, be considerate, be fair—are reasonable human responses to this universal need. So long as human beings are human, and so long as they live together in societies, there will be certain universal elements in morality.[25] There will be the ideal of satisfying their common human nature and the moral imperative to avoid a suicidal war of each against all. Morality, at the universal level, enjoins men to live with that degree of wisdom and justice and kindliness without which life, in any age or in any society, is intolerable.

The recognition of such universal values is the more necessary in view of the new technological basis of human life. Because we are now living in "one world," because the various nations and cultures are now articulated and enmeshed within a world pattern, it is anachronistic and suicidal to live in terms of exclusive particularisms. Not only do our technical instruments for the conquest of space and time create an interdependent world, but these same instruments, combined with the world-wide ramifications of industrialism, add a common human nurture to the factor of a common human nature. The environmental factors, the types of stimuli, are becoming more and more alike the world over. Almost everywhere human beings must adjust themselves to the modern instruments of production, transport, communication, to modern administrative techniques, to modern types of social organization, to the promise and the threat of atomic power. As these factors in man's environment become increasingly widespread, there is an ever-more-imperative need of a moral universality to match a technological universality. It has become tragically clear that if well-intentioned men fail to grasp this moral imperative, evil-minded men will employ these technical instruments of universality to heighten the destructiveness of warring particularisms. What will then be universalized is death and anarchy. A thousand writers have warned us of the disasters that impend if we do not embrace the moral imperatives of our world, but so long as we continue to tremble on the verge of the abyss, the warning must be repeated again and again.

We do not need to rely on vague "intuitions" in meeting this challenge. We can proceed empirically in working out our plans for a world-wide community. We can define a good civilization as one in which the basic wants and needs of human nature are most fully satisfied, and by studying man and society, we can find out the nature of those needs and wants. We can then make a scientific inventory of available resources for meeting fundamental human needs, and, finally, by means of social science and engineering, we can achieve a planned use of these resources on a world-wide basis.

5. AN INTERMEDIATE POSITION

The position that I am advocating is intermediate between absolutism and relativism. In the initial section of this chapter, I pointed out that there are two kinds of relativism, and by implication, two kinds of contrasting absolutism. First, there is the relativism of the historical moment as contrasted with the absolutism of the timeless creed. Second, there is the relativism of diverse coexisting cultural norms as contrasted with the absolutism of a single universal code. I shall discuss each of these in turn, and indicate the humanistic alternative to each kind of relativism.

In its more exclusive and extreme form, temporal relativism denies enduring moral standards or ideals. Extreme temporal absolutism not only asserts such standards and ideals but denies any change in respect to them. The fallacy, in each case, lies in the extremism and the exclusiveness. The realistic alternative both to a static absolutism and a mercurial relativism is to shun these extremes, to avoid the conception of relativism and absolutism as indissoluble opposites and to recognize *both* the old and the new, the tradition and the innovation. As Whitehead points out:

There are two principles inherent in the very nature of things, recurring in some particular embodiments in whatever field we explore—the spirit of change, and the spirit of conservation. There can be nothing real without both. Mere change without conservation is a passage from nothing to nothing. Its final integration yields mere transient nonentity. Mere conservation without change cannot conserve. For after all, there is a flux of circumstance, and the freshness of being evaporates under mere repetition. . . . A static value, however serious and important, becomes unendurable by its appalling monotony of endurance. The soul cries aloud for release into change. It suffers the agonies of claustrophobia.[26]

If we endeavor, in the spirit of Whitehead, to unite conservatism and innovation, we can find instruction in ancient Chinese civilization. As William Ernest Hocking has pointed out, Chinese sages such as Confucius and Mencius realized that we must push thought and action above and beyond existing formulas, not to escape the rules but to revise them. There is no such thing as being above reason and order, nor even above conceptions, ideas, principles, laws, but every wise man sits loose from his definitions for the sake of better principles and laws. Out of respect for "the latent lawfulness of the future," the sage criticizes "the sufficiency of the lawfulness of the past. . . . The way out of a misfit formula is not a policy of no formula, but one of better formula."[27] Such readiness to find a superior lawfulness in the new and experimental, an attitude which Confucius called "mental hospitality," is quite different from the hostility to lawfulness per se. This combination of adaptability and respect for principle is needed in a disturbed and transitional age such as the present.

If we are to escape moral chaos and anarchy, we must realize that life is more than "a bagatelle of transient experience." We must recognize that the essential values of civilization, such as truth, beauty, courage, and love, are as valid as ever they were. We must sense the continuity in history and establish contact with the best minds of the past. Thus only can we rise above the shifting multiplicity of standards and find a binding power more rational than prejudice and less brutal than force. Yet we must also recognize that enduring values are, like the themes of music, endlessly varied. We must resist the reactionary demand to return to the "eternal verities" and "absolutes" of medievalism or any other vanishing or vanished social system. We must recognize that an "atomic age" requires fresh solutions and insights, not an abandonment of ancient ideals but an ever-new embodiment. To fix our minds upon the past alone, to seek only to repeat or prolong the past, is to stunt our creative energy. It is the way of death rather than of life.

Just as we must avoid the extremes of temporal relativism and absolutism, so we must avoid the extremes of cultural pluralism and monism. As opposed to a pluralistic relativism, we must uphold the ideal of universality. The very possibility of an enduring peace depends upon the organization of an international community upon the basis of a common humanity and a common justice. Such universalism, however, must avoid the rigid and unempirical doctrines of a monistic absolutism.

Although the world must be unified if we are to avoid terrible catastrophe, it should be a unity in variety and not a monotonous uniformity. Americans are all too prone to think of world unification as the Americanization of the world, just as every nation tends to consider its own norms absolute and universal. World unification based upon ethnocentrism—upon the cultural standards of a single nation or race—is but a form of totalitarian domination. It means the ruthless stamping out of many rich cultural traditions in favor of a single peremptory pattern of life.

A world government or a world culture of whatever sort should not take the place of restricted loyalties and regional differentiations. A world state is too colossal, remote, impersonal—too monotonous in its universal sway—for the innumerable human beings on this planet by its means to achieve social unity in ways that are intimate, spontaneous, homelike. To do justice to human nature, we must recognize both the universal and the particular, the parochial and the catholic, the local community and the family of nations.

Human beings are alike, but they are also different. They are alike in requiring food, but they differ in their tastes. They are alike in needing clothing, but they want individuality in their costumes. They are alike in demanding shelter, but they do not wish to live in identical houses. They are alike in needing love and sexual expression, but they love different objects and in different ways. They are alike in enjoying beauty and the play of the imagination, but they differ in their arts. They are alike in needing some creative expression of their talents, but they do not have the same talents. They are alike in possessing some religious impulse, but they satisfy that impulse through different symbols. They are alike in their need to reason and understand nature, but they differ in their thoughts and beliefs. Only a stupid and debased totalitarianism would try to suppress these differences. A society of identical twins, whether in mind or body, is not the *summum bonum,* and a world-wide uniformity is but a nightmare.

In thinking out the moral basis of world peace, therefore, we need to appreciate both the universal and the particular elements in culture. In the first place, we must recognize that, at a certain level, all the peoples in the world have much in common. As the ancient Chinese sage Mencius declared: "The heart of mercy is in all men; the sense of shame is in all men; the sense of courtesy and respect is in all men; the sense of right and wrong is in all men."[28] If human beings at times become so unnatural and dehumanized that they lack these things, it is necessary to restore them by proper education. In the second place, we should recognize that cultures, societies, communities, and individuals differ in their emphases, cherish certain values more than others, enjoy values that others lack. Men must learn to understand and respect these fluctuations. Tolerance is one of the great qualities of civilization; and if we are ever to achieve a lasting peace, we must learn to believe less in self-assertion or group righteousness and more in tolerance.

Universalism and particularism, local and general culture, so far from being in conflict, are truly necessary to each other. A general culture, without local differentiations, soon becomes stale and dies, because it lacks any vital interplay among its parts, and hence any creative ferment and spontaneity. On the other hand, a self-sufficient parochialism is too smug and constricted to achieve a rich cultural life. Therefore, the ideal of complete local autarchy and the ideal of an undifferentiated universalism must be abandoned in favor of an interpenetration of "opposites": the universal lending breadth to the particular and the particular lending concreteness to the universal. The valid solution is to unite the wider with the narrower loyalties, to encourage a varied and decentralized articulation of cultural interests but to eliminate the injustices and predatory biases that interfere with the more universal loyalty. We cannot otherwise peacefully enclose within a single world framework national cultures so diverse as the Chinese, the Russian, the German, and the American; nor can we do justice to the rich local variations within each of these cultures.

Relativism, if not pushed too far, liberates the mind from dogmatic narrowness. Awareness of different points of view widens our vision, and enables us to confront problems, old and new, with greater freedom and creativity. The recognition that obligation does not arise in a historical no-man's land, or a cultural void, lends an element of wholesome realism to moral deliberation. But relativism serves us ill if it *is* pushed too far, if it excludes all humanistic values, all values that transcend time and place, all values based upon the more enduring nature of man.

To conclude, neither relativism nor absolutism, as an *extreme* or *exclusive* theory, meets the world's needs. We need ideals flexibly applied yet wide in scope. We need to combine the universal and the particular, the changeless and the changing.

NOTES

1. Robert Redfield, *The Primitive World and Its Transformations*. Ithaca: Cornell University Press, 1953, p. 85.
2. Thucydides, *The Peloponnesian War*. New York: Modern Library, Inc., 1934, pp. 189, 191.
3. Plato, *Theaetetus*, in *The Dialogues of Plato* (translated by Benjamin Jowett). London and New York: Oxford University Press, 1924, IV, p. 224.
4. Oswald Spengler, *The Decline of the West*. New York: Alfred A. Knopf, Inc., 1926, I, p. 21. (I have omitted italics in the original.)
5. *Ibid.*
6. Oswald Spengler, *Politische Schriften*. Munich: C. H. Beck, 1934, p. 85.
7. Ruth Benedict, *Patterns of Culture*. Baltimore: Penguin Books, 1946, pp. 116–119, 159, 203–205. (First published by Houghton Mifflin Company, Boston, 1934.)
8. Ruth Benedict, "Anthropology and the Abnormal," *Journal of General Psychology*, vol. 10 (1934), p. 79.
9. Ruth Benedict, *Patterns of Culture, op. cit.*, pp. 227–231.
10. Melville J. Herskovits, *Cultural Anthropology*. New York: Alfred A. Knopf, Inc., 1955, p. 365.
11. "Statement on Human Rights Submitted to the Commission on Human Rights, United Nations" (drafted by Herskovits on behalf of the Executive Board of the American Anthropological Society), *American Anthropologist*, vol. 49 (1947), pp. 539–543.
12. Melville J. Herskovits, "The Processes of Cultural Change" in Ralph Linton (editor), *The Science of Man in the World Crisis*. New York: Columbia University Press, 1945, especially p. 144.
13. Melville J. Herskovits, *Cultural Anthropology, op. cit.*, p. 364.
14. *Ibid.*
15. *Ibid.*, pp. 365–366.
16. John Locke, *Essay Concerning Human Understanding*, I, Ch. 3, sec. 10.
17. W. T. Stace, "Science and Faith," in John Ely Burchard (editor), *Mid-Century: The Social Implications of Scientific Progress*. New York: John Wiley & Sons, Inc., 1950, pp. 217–218.
18. *Cf.* W. T. Stace, *The Concept of Morals*. New York: The Macmillan Company, 1937, pp. 8–10.
19. Melville Herskovits, "Tender and Tough-Minded Anthropology and the Study of Values in Culture," *South-*

western Journal of Anthropology, vol. 7 (1951), p. 22.

20. Ernst Cassirer, *An Essay on Man*. New Haven: Yale University Press, 1944, p. 25.

21. Melville Herskovits, *Cultural Anthropology*, *op. cit.*, p. 351.

22. Robert Redfield, *The Primitive World and Its Transformations*. Ithaca: Cornell University Press, 1957, pp. 136–140.

23. George Orwell, *Nineteen Eighty-Four*. New York: Harcourt, Brace & World, Inc., 1949, p. 219.

24. Erich Fromm, *The Sane Society*. New York: Holt, Rinehart and Winston, Inc., 1955, pp. 18–19.

25. *Cf.* Clyde Kluckhohn, "Values and Value-Orientation," in Talcott Parsons and Edward A. Shils (editors), *Toward a General Theory of Action*. Cambridge, Mass.: Harvard University Press, 1954, pp. 417–419. Also consult Kluckhohn, "Universal Categories of Culture," in A. L. Kroeber (editor), *Anthropology Today*. Chicago: University of Chicago Press, 1953, pp. 507–523.

26. Alfred North Whitehead, *Science and the Modern World*. New York: The Macmillan Company, 1925, pp. 289–290.

27. William Ernest Hocking, "A New East in a New World," *Fortune* (August, 1942), pp. 124–126.

28. Lin Yutang, *The Wisdom of India and China*. New York: Random House, Inc., 1942, p. 774.

CHAPTER X

Subjectivism, old and new

1. KINDS OF LANGUAGE

In the preceding chapter, we examined the contention of cultural relativism, that goodness varies as the culture varies, whether in time or place. Such a theory, as pointed out, is at the opposite pole from absolutism, which maintains that ethical standards are unconditional and invariable.

The position I have advocated is a mean between the extremes of relativism and absolutism, combining the old and the new, the universal and the particular, the enduring ideal and the changing applications. This intermediate position is based upon the nature of man. Human beings are neither utterly changeable nor completely fixed and static, neither merely alike nor merely different. They share basic needs, but express them in different ways.

This is an empirical approach to ethical problems. One would naturally expect this sort of view in the present age of science. Yet it is in this age that the possibility of an empirical ethics has been most stoutly denied. Scientific-minded philosophers, such as Rudolf Carnap and Bertrand Russell, have maintained that ethical statements are expressions of desire or emotion, not of intellectual judgments or inductive generalizations from matters of fact. Russell, for instance, has concluded that "science cannot decide questions of value," since these questions "cannot be intellectually decided at all, and lie outside the realm of truth and falsehood."[1] This type of theory I shall call subjectivism, and I shall examine its grounds in the present chapter.

Subjectivism can be contrasted with its opposite, objectivism. When we speak of the "objectivity" of ethical judgments, we do not mean that they ascribe value-properties to physical objects. Most philosophers, including the ethical objectivists, do not believe that values exist independently of experience. When we assert the objectivity of an ethical judgment, we mean (a) that there is good reason to suppose that it is true (truth and falsity being applicable to ethical statements), and (b) that the judgment is not merely a report of the psychological state of the speaker. The contention that an ethical sentence is *subjective* means that it is incapable of being true or false (such as the exclamation "ouch!"), *or* that it merely reports the state of mind of the speaker. Ethical subjectivism denies that values can represent anything more than the subjective feelings and reactions of individual minds, and it contends that ethical discourse has no truth status independently of such reactions. It is a form of ethical scepticism.

Before we turn to particular advocates of subjectivism, we will find it helpful to consider the uses of language. The arguments for and against subjectivism depend in part upon the meaning of words. The subjectivist maintains that ethical terms, such as *good, right,* and *ought,* when employed in moral discourse, do not describe anything at all. The ethical use of language, we are told, is entirely different from its ordinary factual use, not because it points to uniquely different facts, as the "non-naturalists" contend, but because its import is not factual. A strictly ethical statement, being nondescriptive, is neither true nor false. Its function is practical, not theoretical. It serves to move or incite, not to inform; it appeals to the heart, not to the head. It may be used for a variety of purposes: to express feelings, to persuade or prescribe, to recommend or command, and so on—but *not* to describe matters of fact. If I say, "That man is six feet tall," I am making a statement that is descriptive, and hence verifiable or disverifiable. But if I say, "He is a good man," I am expressing an emotional or practical attitude, and objective verification is out of the question.

Now the subjectivist, who argues in this way, will readily admit that ethical sentences may *appear* to be factual. The sentence, "Hitler was immoral," seems to have the same grammatical form as the sentence, "Hitler was unmarried." But an expression may be grammatically similar and yet logically different. A number of logicians, such as Frege and Russell, have shown that the apparent form of a proposition may not be its real form. Hence the grammatical appearance of a sentence is not a safe guide to its linguistic function. One cannot infer from the mere fact that an ethical sentence is formulated in the indicative mood that it is being used to *describe* a state of affairs and hence is either true or false. For example, when a person says, "That man is a Nigger," he is not saying the same thing as, "That man is a Negro." Although both are declarative sentences, the first is emotive, and the second is descriptive. Confusion will arise unless we learn to distinguish between meanings that are really different although, grammatically or logically, they appear to be identical.

Words are used in sentences, and we must consider the function of sentences in determining meaning. I shall employ "language" as an inclusive designation for meaningful utterance, embracing both words and sentences. We can distinguish between different kinds of language by considering the uses they are put to. Some of these kinds are as follows:

Descriptive language. Informative statements comprise this category. Their characteristic grammatical form is the indicative mood, but as we have already remarked, the form may be deceptive. The function of a descriptive sentence is to say what is true about some matter of fact. If I say, "The United States Supreme Court consists of nine justices," that is a descriptive statement, and it can be judged either true or false. Whether ethical sentences are descriptive or nondescriptive is one of the most crucial questions in ethical theory. The subjectivist position, as we have seen, is that ethical statements are not descriptive of natural facts, nor of an alleged non-natural sphere of values; they are not descriptive of anything at all. They are disguised imperatives, or expressions of emotion, or something of this sort.

Emotive language. Language of this kind expresses or evokes emotional attitudes. The function of poetry is not so much to assert a fact as to express a mood. So likewise in common speech, I may be expressing my emotional state of mind. If I say that a certain movie is fascinating, or that it is boring, the effect may be to report my subjective reaction rather than objectively to characterize the movie. In the case of propaganda, the intent is not to present an objective body of fact but emotionally to incite. According to the "emotive theory" of ethics, ethical judgments, while not exactly like emotional ejaculations or propagandistic appeals, resemble them more closely than they resemble factual statements. Their function is to express or motivate, rather than to describe matters of fact.

Prescriptive language. Commands or instructions for behavior constitute this category. Ethical statements sometimes take an imperative form, for example, "Thou shalt not kill." Or, like a doctor's prescription, they may tell us what we ought to do. "You ought to tell the truth" is similar in form to "You ought to take Vitamin C tablets." Some philosophers maintain that, even when ethical sentences *appear* to be descriptive, they are really imperative or prescriptive.

Evaluative language. Language of this type is used in the process of grading. A teacher uses such language when he labels student papers as excellent, good, fair, or poor; or a judge at a County Fair uses similar designations when he grades, for example, the ears of corn displayed by competing farmers. A person may be engaged in moral grading when he assigns evaluative adjectives to actions, motives, or states of mind. For example, the members of a jury, pondering the degree of guilt of a number of accomplices in a crime, are involved in such grading. This process requires a grasp of the qualities being graded, but it is not the same as describing. In grading, a person is approving or disapproving, choosing or selecting or scoring, rather than merely reporting what is the case.

Performatory language. Language of this kind is used in accomplishing an action. When a person makes a promise, he is using language in this way. He is not describing a previously existing state of affairs, but is performing an action by speaking certain words, such as "I promise." Similarly when a groom says, "With this ring I thee wed," he is binding himself in wedlock, and thus is acting in a specified way. Since the words are essential to the action, much depends upon just what the words are. Hence their form is frequently prescribed by law, custom, or ritual. There may be a prescribed form of language in making one's will, in baptizing a child, in conferring a medal, in giving a military order, and so forth. Performatory language may have important ethical consequences, for example, in creating rights and obligations, as when marriage vows are exchanged, or a contract is negotiated.

Language is also used in many other ways, for example, to interrogate, propose, encourage, warn, or clarify. Adding to the complexity, words or sentences may be simultaneously used in more than one way. Emotive words, for example, usually have some descriptive import, and vice versa. Lincoln's Gettysburg Address, for example, has both a descriptive and an emotive meaning. Even a flagrantly emotive word, such as "Nigger," has some descriptive import—in this instance, it designates a person with dark pigmentation. Such words as "courage," "selfishness," "honesty," "murder," and "rape" are used not only to describe but to condemn or approve; and the two sorts of meaning are almost inextricable. We should not conclude that such words are necessarily improper. The words of Lincoln at Gettysburg were fit for the occasion, even though they combined emotive and descriptive meanings. However, "mixed words"—words simultaneously serving multiple functions—are apt to be deceptive or confusing. In arguments about what is good and bad, we are likely to employ a great many mixed words of this kind. The effect is often to beg the question at issue, since the very use of the word implies condemnation or approval.

Noting the prevalence of nondescriptive meanings in ethical discussion, the subjectivist concludes that the descriptive import of ethical language is either absent, or so small as to be negligible, or not pertinent to the *normative* core of meaning. If he is to be proved wrong, it will be necessary to show that some ethical statements have descriptive meanings or can be logically derived therefrom. In addition, it will be necessary to show that there is a way to verify these descriptions, and thereby to establish ethical judgments on an objective basis. But first we must consider what sort of argument can be advanced for the subjectivist position.

2. THE LIMITED SUBJECTIVISM OF HUME

Although David Hume (1711–1776) was not a complete subjectivist, he contributed very substantially to the subjectivist argument. This canny Scot, with his mild and kindly disposition, has been generally considered the arch-destroyer in modern philosophy. He is known as the most sceptical of that great sequence of British empiricists, which includes Bacon, Locke, Berkeley, and Mill. To philosophers he is best known for his critical analysis of the idea of causation and the logical foundations of induction, but to the general public he is better known for his "scandalous" criticisms of traditional religious beliefs. Less famous but no less significant is his attack upon rationalism in ethics.

There are two different senses in which Hume used the term "reason." All reasoning, he pointed out, can be divided into two kinds, demonstrative reasoning, concerning "relations of ideas," and empirical reasoning, concerning "matters of fact and existence." Hume cited as examples of demonstrative reasoning the mathematical propositions that two times two is equal to four, and that the three angles of a triangle are equal to two right ones. The province of demonstrative reasoning is the world of abstract ideas, as in pure mathematics or formal logic, rather than the world of concrete matters of fact.

An example of empirical reasoning is any generalization based upon experience, for example, that cigarette smoking is a cause of lung cancer. The mark of valid propositions of this type is their *factual truth*, established by empirical verification. It is *logically* possible for these propositions to be false, since their denial involves no contradiction. They are confirmed not by formal logic but by observable matters of fact.

Hume admitted no other ways of establishing the truth of propositions, and he proposed to eliminate all else as trash:

> When we run over libraries, persuaded of these principles, what havoc must we make? If we take in our hand any volume, of divinity or school metaphysics, for instance, let us ask, *Does it contain any abstract reasoning concerning quantity or number?* No. *Does it contain any experimental reasoning concerning matter of fact and existence?* No. Commit it then to the flames: for it can contain nothing but sophistry and illusion.[2]

Should books on ethics be cast to the flames?

Hume was convinced that they contain no valid demonstrative reasoning. The essence of an immoral act, he maintained, never consists in a merely logical relation discovered by reason. We do not establish that a crime has been committed by finding a formal contradiction. It might be argued, for example, that the man who returns evil for good is being logically inconsistent, and hence immoral. But, strictly speaking, there is no logical contradiction involved. There is only a contrast between positive and negative value. On the ground of such contrariety, we should equally disapprove of returning good for evil, and this a morally sensitive person refuses to do. By a number of such examples, Hume drove home the point that ethics is based not upon the relations among abstract ideas but upon the concrete data of moral experience. The approach to the subject should be not a priori or speculative but factual:

Men are now cured of their passion for hypotheses and systems in natural philosophy, and will hearken to no arguments but those which are derived from experience. It is full time they should attempt a like reformation in all moral disquisitions; and reject every system of ethics, however subtle or ingenious, which is not founded on fact and observation.[3]

Although most philosophers would question details in Hume's argument, few would reject his conclusion that ethics cannot be established by demonstrative reasoning.

The really crucial question is whether the truth of ethical propositions can be established by *empirical* reasoning. Hume's answer was a carefully qualified one. He denied that ethical characteristics are objective and independent features of actions, characters, or situations, and he maintained that moral distinctions are ultimately based upon subjective attitudes of approval or disapproval. Yet he believed that these attitudes and their objects should be studied empirically, and that men should guard against whim and prejudice in their moral judgments. Let us consider his main arguments.

The argument based on the "ought." No one will deny the distinction between *what is* and *what ought to be*. If the mere fact that something occurs is sufficient to justify it, we would have to approve all the crimes and calamities of history. What happens is one thing, and what ought to happen is often another. Hence the fact that something is, or was, or will be the case, is never a ground for saying that it ought to exist. There is no logical bridge between the realm of facts and the realm of values. Therefore, we cannot use the method of experience, which is adapted to the study of facts, in an effort to determine norms or ideals. In a famous passage Hume declared:

In every system of morality, which I have hitherto met with, I have always remarked, that the author proceeds for some time in the ordinary way of reasoning, and establishes the being of a God, or makes observations concerning human affairs; when of a sudden I am surprized to find, that instead of the usual copulations of propositions, *is,* and *is not,* I meet with no proposition that is not connected with an *ought,* or an *ought not.* This change is imperceptible; but is, however, of the last consequence. For as this *ought,* or *ought not,* expresses some new relation or affirmation, it is necessary that it should be observed and explained; and at the same time that a reason should be given, for what seems altogether inconceivable, how this new relation can be a deduction from others, which are entirely different from it. But as authors do not commonly use this precaution, I shall presume to recommend it to the readers; and am persuaded, that this small attention would subvert all the vulgar systems of morality, and let us see, that the distinction of vice and virtue is not founded merely on the relations of objects, nor is perceived by reason.[4]

Since Hume speaks of "deduction," he appears to be arguing that there must be a *logical* connection between factual statements and moral judgments if the latter are to be derived from the former, and that no such logical connection is discoverable. Evidently the point of his remarks is that you cannot get "ought" (or, by implication, any other ethical concept) into your conclusion unless you already have it in your premises. You cannot argue validly from factual premises to ethical conclusions.

The argument that values are not intrinsic and observable properties. Hume denied that good (or right) was objective and observable. He pointed out that it is neither a sensible quality, such as a color or a sound, nor a configurational property, such as circularity. In this respect *good* is akin to *beauty*:

Euclid has fully explained all the qualities of the circle; but has not in any proposition said a word of its beauty. The reason is evident. The beauty is not a quality of the circle. . . . It is only the effect which that figure produces upon the mind. . . . In vain would you look for [beauty] in the circle, or seek it, either by your senses or by mathematical reasoning, in all the properties of that figure. . . . Till . . . a spectator appear, there is nothing but a figure of such particular dimensions and proportions: from his sentiments alone arise its elegance and beauty.[5]

It is the same with moral qualities, such as virtue or vice. They are matters of feeling, not of objective fact:

Take any action allowed to be vicious: Wilful murder, for instance. Examine it in all lights and see if you can find that matter of fact, or real existence, which you call *vice*. In whichever way you take it, you find only certain passions, motives, volitions, and thoughts. There is no other matter of fact in the case. The vice entirely escapes you as long as you consider the object. You never can find it till you turn your reflection into your own breast, and find a sentiment of disapprobation which arises in you towards this action. . . . It lies in yourself, not in the object. So that when you pronounce any action or character to be vicious, you mean nothing but that from the constitution of your nature you have a feeling or sentiment of blame from the contemplation of it.[6]

Such a moral judgment, being expressive of feeling rather than descriptive of matters of fact, can be neither true nor false. In a moral situation, empirical reason enables us to inform ourselves as to the facts, but it can do no more. The ultimate verdict, pronouncing something good or bad, is left to our appetites, desires, emotions, or sentiments. These "passions," as Hume chooses to call them, arise from instinctive sources. Reason does not produce them, and is incapable of governing and judging them except so far as a passion may be aroused by a mistaken belief. If there is no such mistake to be corrected, reason has nothing to do with the matter. Reason is the discovery of truth or falsehood, and no passion can be true or false. Hence it cannot be regarded as either reasonable or unreasonable.

It is not contrary to reason to prefer the destruction of the whole world to the scratching of my finger. It is not contrary to reason for me to choose my total ruin to prevent the least uneasiness of an Indian or person wholly unknown to me. . . . In short, a passion must be accompanied with some false judgment in order to its being unreasonable; and even then it is not the passion, properly speaking, which is unreasonable, but the judgment.[7]

The argument that reason cannot provide a motive. It is passion alone that can move us to act, and reason can do no more than assist passion. Hume admitted the importance of reason in marshalling evidence (for example, that a murder has been committed) and in judging that means are more or less effective in achieving a given end. But it is passion, not reason, that finally commits us to the ends, and that provides the motivation for action.

We speak not strictly and philosophically when we talk of the combat of passion and of reason. Reason is, and ought only to be the slave of the passions, and can never pretend to any other office than to serve and obey them.[8]

To review Hume's reasons for this opinion would take more space than we can afford. Others besides Hume have argued that feeling and desire move us, not reason. What is distinctive in his discussion is its application to morals. If reason cannot move us, he argued, it cannot be the basis of morality.

Since morals . . . have an influence on the actions and affections, it follows, that they cannot be derived from reason; and that because reason alone, as we have already proved, can never have any such influence. Morals excite passions, and produce or prevent actions. Reason of itself is utterly impotent in this particular. The rules of morality, therefore, are not conclusions of our reason.[9]

In short, morality is essentially practical and devoted to action; and since reason cannot contribute to action, it cannot be the foundation of morals.

There are other arguments advanced by Hume, but I think I have stated the most telling ones. Do these arguments mean that morality is completely irrational and subjective? At times Hume comes close to saying this. But he admitted that reason can *indirectly* excite a passion by informing us of the existence of something which is a proper object of it. He likewise admitted the indispensable function of reason in selecting *means* to ends, and in quenching the desire for impossible ends by showing the impossibility. Also in discussing the relation of justice and other virtues to utility, he reasoned in much the same fashion as the later utilitarians, such as Bentham and Mill.

In Chapter VIII, we considered a phase of Hume's ethics that greatly qualified his subjectivism. He argued that we are too partial toward our intimates and our own kind and too cold toward strangers. Favoritism and callousness play the devil with our sense of justice. Such moral aberrations cannot, strictly speaking, be refuted, but it is possible to attain a "steady and general" point of view—a point of view undistorted by the particularities of circumstance or by the whims and biases of the individual and the circumscribed group. In achieving such moral impartiality, the agent detaches himself from the party of prejudice and attaches himself to "the party of humankind." Hume thus distinguished between factual descriptions and normative judgments without wholly abandoning the concept of moral objectivity.

3. THE NATURALISTIC FALLACY AND ITS SUBJECTIVIST SEQUEL

Hume's contention that there is no easy bridge between factual descriptions and ethical judgments has received powerful support from G. E. Moore, whose *Principia Ethica* (1903) has been the most discussed work in ethics published in this century. Moore was no subjectivist, but his theory of "the naturalistic fallacy" has been used to bolster the subjectivist cause.

The basic problem of ethics, he believed, is to determine the meaning of "intrinsic good" (good as an end in itself) as distinguished from "instrumental good" (good as a means). He maintained that good in this sense has no definition. It is an ultimate and indefinable property that we grasp by intuition.

The question that Moore raised was not a verbal one; he was not asking how the *word* "good" is used in common speech. Nor was he trying to decide what *things* have the property of intrinsic good. Just as a number of things are yellow, so a number of things are good. Good, he believed, is a property common to these good things, just as yellow is a property common to yellow things—and the question is whether this common property (and *not* the things to which it attaches) can be defined.

Naturalists seek to define intrinsic good in terms of some natural property, usually a psychological datum. No one would identify good with blue, or loud, or round, but many have identified it with pleasure, or the satisfaction of desire. Moore (as we have already remarked in Chapter VIII) argued that such attempts can be refuted. To identify good with such a natural property would entail the trivialization of non-trivial statements. For example, if good were the very same quality as pleasure, then the manifestly non-trivial statement, "Pleasure is good," would be equivalent to the trivial statement, "Pleasure is pleasure." To identify good with satisfaction would likewise imply that the proposition, "Good is satisfaction," is equivalent to the tautology, "Satisfaction is satisfaction," when obviously the two statements are not equivalent. Good *must* have an essence of its own if such empty tautologies are to be avoided.

Moore reinforced this logical argument by an appeal to intuition. He maintained that we are intuitively aware that "good" means something different from, or more than, any such property as pleasantness.

. . . Whoever will attentively consider with himself what is actually before his mind when he asks the question "Is pleasure (or whatever it may be) after all good?" can easily satisfy himself that he is not merely wondering whether pleasure is pleasant. And if he will try this experiment with each suggested definition in succession, he may become expert enough to recognize that in every case he has before his mind a unique object, with regard to the connection of which with any other object, a distinct question may be asked. Every one does in fact understand the question "Is this good?" When he thinks of it, his state of mind is different from what it would be, were he asked "Is this pleasant, or desired, or approved?" It has a distinct meaning for him, even though he may not recognize in what respect it is distinct.[10]

Moore concluded that we are aware, at least confusedly, of a unique ethical property, intrinsic good, that is not the datum of any natural science, such as psychology or biology. No one can "find" it merely by inspecting his sense data or introspecting his mental states.

Moore went on to argue that good, as a nonnatural property, cannot be defined. One common sort of definition is the analysis of something into its components, as for instance, the chemical definition of water as two parts hydrogen and one part oxygen. Moore frequently used the word "definable" as equivalent to "analyzable," and when he denied that good is definable, he meant that it is a simple and unanalyzable quality like blue (except that it is nonnatural). Nowhere did he argue the point; he apparently held that the simplicity of good is self-evident. Those who try to define good fall into the error of identifying the simple with the complex—and this they do because they do not attend to what is revealed in intuition.

In maintaining that good is distinct from any natural property, Moore was arguing, somewhat as Hume had done, that values are irreducible to non-values. From this standpoint, "the naturalistic fallacy" can be characterized as the attempt to define an ethical property in nonethical terms. It is this specific "fallacy" that deserves the name "naturalistic":

When a man confuses two natural objects with one another, defining the one by the other . . . then there is no reason to call the fallacy naturalistic. But if he confuses "good," which is not in the same sense a natural object, with any natural object whatever, then there is a reason for calling that a naturalistic fallacy; its being made with regard to "good" marks it as something quite specific, and this specific mistake deserves a name because it is so common.[11]

Unfortunately, Moore did not make very clear just what the "non-natural-ness" of good consists in. Perhaps, as Brand Blanshard has suggested, the best analogy is with a relational property such as similarity. No one fails to recognize that certain things are similar, but similarity is not itself sensed, and is clearly distinguishable from the *things* that are similar. A dozen apples are similar, but similarity is not a *quality* of the apples, as roundness is. Moore apparently wanted to maintain that good, like similarity, is not directly grasped in sensory or introspective experience, but is intellectually intuited as a highly abstract and unanalyzable property attaching to good things.

Actually Moore discussed two distinguishable fallacies, which he blanketed under the single name "the naturalistic fallacy." The first fallacy is the attempt to define the indefinable. Such a fallacy can be committed even when there is no ethical characteristic involved. Whenever there is a simple and unique quality (such as sour), it cannot be analytically defined because it cannot be analyzed into parts. Moreover, to identify such a quality with something else, as might be done in a so-called definition, is to confuse two distinct objects. As Bishop Butler declared, "Everything is what it is, and not another thing." It follows that good is what it is and not another thing. To seek to define good, *either* (a) in the sense of analysis, or (b) in the sense of identifying it with something else, is to commit "the definist fallacy." (Note that there are two ways of committing this fallacy.)

Another fallacy, as we have seen, is the attempt to reduce the ethical to the nonethical. This fallacy entails nothing about the indefinability of good in ethical terms. Even if good were so definable, it would still be a fallacy to reduce it to any nonethical property. There is a distinction between a value and a bare matter of fact—to neglect this distinction is to be guilty of "the factualist fallacy" (a term suggested by Philip Wheelwright). It is unfortunate that these two fallacies, the "definist" and the "factualist," were not more clearly distinguished by Moore.

His conclusion was that good is a simple, indefinable, non-natural, and intuited property. It is simple and indefinable like yellow, but it is not a natural quality discovered in direct experience, as yellow is. Moore claimed not only to intuit good as a unique property, but to know intuitively that certain things—love, knowledge, happiness, beauty, and virtue—exhibit this property.

The subjectivists acknowledged the force of Moore's argument against naturalism while rejecting his intuitionism. They agreed that we cannot identify good with a natural property such as pleasure; hence, we cannot observe good, either in introspective or sensory experience, in the way in which we observe a natural property. In opposition to Moore, however, they denied that we can intuit a unique value property, or that we can know by intuition that certain things are good. They pointed out that the intuitionists do not agree among themselves, and that their alleged "intuitions" are not supported by a "consensus of experts." Moore, in their opinion, should have concluded that "good" (and so too with "right" and "ought") does not describe anything at all. What he mistook for a non-natural property is actually the motivational force of a subjective attitude. He reified as the non-natural property of an object what is only a state of mind in the person who pronounces the judgment. Whenever a value judgment is treated as a claim to knowledge, rather than as the expression of an emotion or desire, its distinctive normative force is lost. The naturalistic fallacy, when thus reinterpreted by the subjectivists, becomes in effect "the cognitivist fallacy": the fallacy of interpreting a subjective expression as a claim to objective knowledge.

4. THE ETHICAL THEORIES OF THE LOGICAL POSITIVISTS

The rise of the Vienna Circle and the spread of logical positivism brought subjectivism to a head. The positivists enunciated a theory of verification and meaning that provided a strong foundation for the subjectivist position. According to this school of thinkers, every statement that is capable of being true is one or other of two kinds. First, it may be an a priori statement, and in that case it is true analytically, that is to say, it would be self-contradictory to deny it. Examples would be the statements of pure mathematics and formal logic. Likewise included are tautologies, such as "All bachelors are unmarried," in which the predicate merely states the meaning of the subject. To say that bachelors are married men would be inconsistent and therefore false. Second, a true statement may be empirical, and then it is a statement of fact that can be verified, at least in principle, by means of perception. Unless some test of observation can be made, a statement cannot be empirically true or false. This is essentially the doctrine of Hume, elaborated in terms of modern logic and epistemology.

A doctrine of meaning was tied to this theory of truth. For a statement to have cognitive meaning it must be either analytic or empirically testable. If the statement is analytic, it can be confirmed or disconfirmed by the test of logical consistency, and it then has *logical* meaning. If the statement is empirical, it can be verified or disverified by observation, and it then has *factual* meaning. To understand a factual statement means to know how to obtain evidence for or against it. When there is no conceivable way to find such evidence, the statement has no factual meaning. For example, if the allegedly factual statement, "God exists," cannot be tested by any conceivable observation, it is nonsensical.

The application of this theory to ethics was most clearly stated by A. J. Ayer, Professor of Philosophy at Oxford University, in his famous little book, *Language, Truth, and Logic* (1936). According to the verifiability theory of meaning as advocated by Ayer, purely ethical statements have no factual meaning at all. They cannot be tested by observation, and hence they are nonsense from an empirical point of view.

Ayer did not deny that some statements about ethical matters may be meaningful. He had no objection to definitions that specify or analyze the meaning of ethical terms without asserting the objective existence of ethical properties. Such analytical sentences have logical meaning, and may be useful for the purposes of clarification. Also Ayer did not object to descriptions of social mores or the psychological phenomena of moral experience. Such factual statements belong to the science of psychology or sociology and not to ethics proper. The statements that Ayer questioned are "actual moral judgments," such as "murder is wrong" or "pleasure is good." These are allegedly factual statements about things that are right or wrong, good or evil. They are irreducibly normative and yet appear to be descriptive.

Ayer's thesis is that such statements have no cognitive meaning because they cannot be stated in verifiable terms. They should be classified with ejaculations or exhortations, as mere expressions or excitants of feeling, none of them either true or false.

Accepting Moore's concept of the naturalistic fallacy, Ayer insisted that "good," "right," "ought," and the like—words used in ethical discourse—are indefinable in factual terms. But he rejected Moore's appeal to intuition and the concept of good as a nonnatural property. His alternative view is summed up in an oft-quoted passage:

> The presence of an ethical symbol in a proposition adds nothing to its factual content. Thus if I say to someone, "You acted wrongly in stealing that money," I am not stating anything more than if I had simply said, "You stole that money." In adding that this action is wrong I am not making any further statement about it. I am simply evincing my moral disapproval of it. It is as if I had said, "You stole that money," in a peculiar tone of horror, or written it with the addition of some special exclamation marks. The tone, or the exclamation marks, adds nothing to the literal meaning of the sentence. It merely serves to show that the expression of it is attended by certain feelings in the speaker.[12]

Because assertions of value are not descriptive but "emotive," they are unverifiable and factually nonsensical. "They are unverifiable for the same reason as a cry of pain or a word of command is unverifiable—because they do not express genuine propositions."[13] At this point, there is a duality in Ayer's doctrine. He likened ethical statements to "a cry of pain" and also to "a word of command." These functions are different and should be distinguished. A cry of pain expresses the feeling of the person who utters it. If an ethical statement is expressive in this sense, it is like an ejaculation, such as "Hurrah!" or "Boo!" Some critics of the theory, by way of booing it, have labelled it "the Boo-Hurrah theory of ethics." But Ayer also likened an ethical statement to "a word of command," or on other occasions, to an "exhortation." On this interpretation, the function of an ethical statement is to arouse emotion in the listener and thus to incite to action. But both functions fall outside the scope of argument. Whether ethical statements express feelings or excite emotional dispositions, they have no cognitive meaning.

If this theory be correct, it is impossible to argue about purely ethical matters. There is a clash of subjective attitudes but no logical contradiction of assertions. Yet people *seem* to engage in ethical disputes, to advance arguments pro and con. How can this be explained upon the basis of Ayer's theory? The answer is that we may argue about factual matters that are related, in some way, to ethical attitudes.

We do this in the hope that we have only to get our opponent to agree with us about the nature of the empirical facts for him to adopt the same moral attitude towards them as we do. And as the people with whom we argue have generally received the same moral education as ourselves, and live in the same social order, our expectation is usually justified. But if our opponent happens to have undergone a different process of moral "conditioning" from ourselves, so that, even when he acknowledges all the facts, he still disagrees with us about the moral value of the actions under discussion, then we abandon the attempt to convince him by argument. . . . It is because argument fails us when we come to pure questions of value, as distinct from questions of fact, that we finally resort to mere abuse.[14]

In later formulations, Ayer softened and modified his argument, admitting that his original theory was an "oversimplication." In effect he agreed with Charles L. Stevenson, Professor of Philosophy at the University of Michigan, whose views we shall now turn to.

Educated in America at Yale and Harvard and in England at Cambridge, Stevenson was deeply impressed by positivist currents at all three Universities. Like Ayer and other positivists, he excluded from the realm of knowledge everything except the logical truths of a priori statements and the factual truths of empirically verifiable propositions. Many ethical sentences, he believed, contain verifiable references to matters of fact, and to this extent they are true or false. What is distinctive about them, however, is their "normative" meaning, involving references to "good," "right," "ought," "valuable," and so forth. These ethical terms have an emotive or imperative force that cannot be analyzed as cognitively significant. They are used dynamically, rather than descriptively. According to Stevenson, the basic failure of all cognitivist theories of ethics, whether naturalistic or non-naturalistic, is that they neglect this dynamic usage of ethical language.

Stevenson began his analysis of ethical sentences by calling attention to the distinction between two kinds of disagreement.

The difference between the two senses of "disagreement" is essentially this: the first involves an opposition of beliefs, both of which cannot be true, and the second involves an opposition of attitudes, both of which cannot be satisfied.[15]

The first kind of disagreement is illustrated by a scientific dispute. In this case the disputants are chiefly concerned with how certain matters are to be truthfully described and explained, and the argument may be settled by reasoning and evidence. The second kind of disagreement is illustrated by the clash of preferences apart from disagreement about matters of fact. This sort of clash cannot be settled merely by argument, for what is required is a change of attitude rather than belief.

An ethical dispute may involve both types of disagreement. Let us suppose for example that two people disagree about the justification of "euthanasia" (legalized "mercy-killing"). The person who favors euthanasia maintains that certain diseases are known to be incurable, that the patient in these instances carries a great load of suffering, that the pain cannot be effectively curtailed without the administration of morphine in lethal doses, and that a panel of physicians can be relied upon to avoid mistakes. The opponent of euthanasia argues that many diseases thought to be incurable have turned out not to be so, that one can never be sure that a new discovery (such as insulin in the treatment of diabetes) will not be discovered in time to save the patient, that control of pain has now advanced to the point of being very effective, and that adequate safeguards cannot be set up to prevent mistakes or abuses. Here the disagreement concerns primarily matters of fact, and it may be settled by more accurate information on the subject.

Now let us suppose that the opponents finally reach an agreement on the questions of fact, but still disagree in their attitudes. One person still maintains that euthanasia is justified on the basis of simple humanitarian considerations, and the other person still contends that the deliberate taking of a human life is immoral. Each has different scruples and neither can agree with the other. Argument fails at this point, because the question is not one of truth or falsity but of ultimate moral commitment. There could still be an attempt to change attitudes by irrational means, such as emotional exhortation, but *rational* persuasion is out of the question.

The difference at this level is a purely ethical one, and Stevenson analyzed it as follows. (He admitted that his analysis is only approximate, for ethical meanings cannot be exactly paraphrased.) When the proponent of the action says, "This is right," the meaning of his statement is, "I approve of this; do so as well." When his opponent says, "This is wrong," the meaning is, "I disapprove of this; do so as well." Similarly if a person says, "He ought to do this," the meaning is, "I disapprove of his leaving this undone; do so as well." The meaning in each case has two components, first a declarative statement ("I approve" or "I disapprove"), which describes the attitude of the speaker, and second an imperative statement ("do so as well"), urging others to adopt the same attitude. It is this imperative part that constitutes the peculiarly normative character of ethical statements.

In this analysis there is no explicit reference to the questions of objective fact which, as in the dispute about euthanasia, may be an important factor in the clash of ethical opinion. To remedy this omission Stevenson suggested a "second pattern of analysis," according to which "This is good" has the meaning, "This has qualities x, y, z . . . , except that 'good' has as well a laudatory emotive meaning which permits it to express the speaker's approval, and tends to evoke the approval of the hearer."[16] The letters x, y, and z symbolize such possible expressions as "universal love," or "integration of interests," or "the greatest happiness of the greatest number." This second pattern incorporates the features of the first pattern while admitting descriptive references that are not limited to the speaker's attitudes. But these references, according to Stevenson, are not *purely* descriptive. The terms used in the definition of "good," or any other ethical word, have an emotive as well as a descriptive force. "Ethical definitions," Stevenson explained, "involve a wedding of descriptive and emotive meaning, and accordingly have a frequent use in redirecting and intensifying attitudes." Since "to choose a definition is to plead a cause," the result is what Stevenson called a "persuasive definition."[17]

We can now sum up his conclusions. The function of ethical discussions is to change *attitudes* rather than *beliefs*. To a degree, our attitudes depend upon our beliefs and our beliefs can be influenced by rational arguments. If we could be sure that all disagreements in attitude are rooted in disagreements in belief, we could hope to resolve our ethical differences by rational means. But of this we cannot be sure; indeed, the contrary often seems to be the case. When rational considerations fail to change a man's attitude, then resort is had to nonrational methods, such as "rhetorical cadence, apt metaphor, stentorian, stimulating, or pleading tones of voice, dramatic gestures, care in establishing *rapport* with the hearer or audience, and so on."[18] Even the rational reasons have no ethical function except to change the hearer's attitude to agree with the speaker's. This ultimate nonrationality is the Achilles' heel that dooms all cognitive theories of ethics.

Just as Ayer softened his original doctrine, so Stevenson has qualified his theory. Of "the so-called noncognitive view," he now remarks:

> No one, I suppose, continues to hold this view just as it stands. It was once defended . . . by Russell, Carnap, Ayer, and myself; but the need of qualifying it—and always in a direction that takes account of the flexibilities of our language—has since been evident. My *Ethics and Language* made a beginning of these qualifications by introducing a "second pattern of analysis"; and since the war a number of writers, notably Hare, Nowell-Smith, and Urmson, have felt the need of further qualifications, some of which I am prepared to accept.

Stevenson still believes that the relation between factual reasons and evaluative conclusions cannot be judged by the rules of deductive or inductive logic.

> That is precluded by the very notion of reasons for approving, which fall outside logic simply because they require inferences (if I may call them that) from belief-expressing to attitude-expressing sentences. The truth of the reasons themselves can be tested by logic; but their bearing on the evaluative conclusion is neither logical nor illogical. It is simply non-logical.

But he goes on to insist that "all of us, in commonsense discussions, accept certain reasons as justifying an evaluative conclusion and reject certain others as failing to justify such a conclusion." Even though we cannot logically verify or disverify our moral attitudes, this should not lead us into wholesale scepticism. "Why can't we start as we do in ordinary life?" Stevenson asks. "There we have attitudes that we initially trust, and we proceed to express them. Reasons serve not to bring our attitudes into being, but only to redirect them. . . . If we initially distrust all our attitudes, . . . our reasons will not *give* us attitudes; but an initial distrust of all our attitudes is so fantastic that we need not, surely, take it seriously."[19]

Stevenson's early doctrine, as here described, remains his most fully developed theory. Although it does not exactly represent his present convictions, it remains an illuminating statement of the noncognitivist doctrine. Rather than examine his reformulated theory in greater detail, we shall turn to another treatment of the problem.

5. THE PRESCRIPTIVE THEORY OF HARE

A less subjectivist theory of ethics than that originally advanced by Ayer and Stevenson has been propounded by R. M. Hare of Oxford University in an important book, *The Language of Morals* (1952). It can be considered an intermediate theory between objectivism and subjectivism. Although it denies that ethical statements are true or false, it admits that there are good reasons for accepting or rejecting them.

Hare agreed with Moore and the logical positivists that value-concepts are indefinable in terms of purely descriptive meanings. No *ought* follows from an *is*—one premise at least must be normative. Also no purely descriptive definition squares with the commending, or condemning, function of ethical utterances. Hare did not deny that a word such as "good" can be used merely to convey information (as when a person speaks of a "good example" of a disease, that is, an example that clearly exhibits the type-characteristics), but such usage empties the word of its ethical import. The language of morals is irreducibly "imperative" rather than descriptive. While recognizing "the naturalistic fallacy," Hare differed from Moore in rejecting the notion of good as an intuited non-natural property.

Down to this point Hare was in substantial agreement with Ayer and Stevenson, but here the agreement ended. Unlike his predecessors, Hare argued that the function of an ethical utterance is to tell someone to *do* something, rather than to express or influence emotional attitudes. The excitation or expression of emotions is no proper answer to the ethical problem, "What shall I do?" Ethical discourse is "prescriptive" rather than "emotive." The effect of the emotivist theory is to confuse ethical statements with propaganda or other nonrational forms of expression.

Hare wished to defend "the rationality of moral discourse" by a "middle way" in ethics, avoiding the "extremes" of a descriptive or emotive theory. As against the descriptivists, he maintained that ethical judgments are not factual statements, and that their function is practical rather than informative. They are not true or false strictly speaking. As against the emotivists, he held that there may be good reasons for ethical conclusions. They may be valid or invalid, wise or foolish. They form a unique class of prescriptive statements, having reasons of their own as valid in the ethical sphere as the reasons of science in the descriptive sphere. There may be good reasons for *doing* something, just as there may be good reasons for *believing* something. Ethics is concerned with reasons for doing, not for believing in the scientific sense. On this view, moral discourse has a quite distinct "logic" of its own.

According to Hare, the function of ethical language is to guide choices. When I say "X is right," I am uttering a kind of recommendation that X should be chosen. Or if I say, "You ought not to do X," I am warning or instructing someone *not* to choose X. The judgment of "good," as well as of "right" or "ought," is prescriptive. Hare accepted the definition of the *Oxford English Dictionary* that "good" is "the most general adjective of commendation." The constant function of "good" is this one of commending, and "to commend is to guide choices." When I say that something is good I am saying that it is choiceworthy.

Although this commendatory meaning of good is fairly constant, the characteristics of things by virtue of which we judge them commendable are quite various. If we speak of such diverse things as a "good automobile," "good fertilizer," "good fire-extinguisher," "good symphony," and "good man," the criteria for applying the word good vary from case to case. The criteria are the factual grounds for our value-judgments. For example, when I call strawberries good, I justify my judgment by saying, "These strawberries are large, red, juicy, and sweet." Similarly there are factual criteria for moral judgments—for example, when we cite acts of kindliness as a justification of moral praise. So long as the criteria are agreed upon, the only question at issue is whether the objects or persons exhibit these criteria.

When applied to strawberries, the word "good" is being used in a normative ("commendatory") but nonethical sense. Hare maintained that the ethical and nonethical uses of the term are alike in implying commendation. What, then, is the difference? Since the primary function of a value-term is to guide choice, there is always the implication that one kind of thing or action ought to be chosen rather than another. In the case of nonmoral choices, the "ought" implied is a hypothetical one. When I say that "these strawberries are good," I am implying that they are choiceworthy under certain conditions. I would not attach moral blame to a prospective buyer who replies, "Yes, they are good strawberries, but I would rather have something else to eat." The implication of my original statement was, "*If* you want to buy strawberries, these are an excellent choice." There is no such limiting if-clause in the case of a moral judgment. For example, when I say, "It is bad to torture a human being for torture's sake," I mean that it is bad for anybody at any time to do this. "The complete universality of the moral judgment," Hare explained, "means that we cannot 'get away from it'; and therefore its acceptance is a much more serious matter than the acceptance of an imperative from whose range we can escape."[20]

This statement of Hare's is similar to the "categorical imperative" of Immanuel Kant, which we have examined in Chapter VI. Hare also strongly espoused the Kantian principle that the exercise of freedom and responsibility is the core of morality. But in one very fundamental respect he disagreed with Kant—he believed in an ultimate relativism rather than in absolutism, as the following résumé of his argument indicates.

Given certain ethical principles, we choose upon the basis of reason and evidence which are the best means to carry them out. Rational deliberation is quite possible in this application of our ethical standards. As we meet exceptional circumstances, we revise and broaden our principles. Thus, when particular principles are in question, we can appeal to wider and wider principles. Finally we come to a "way of life," the most inclusive organization of principles, and at this point there is an ultimate relativism.

Thus, if pressed to justify a decision completely, we have to give a complete specification of the way of life of which it is a part. This complete specification it is impossible in practice to give; the nearest attempts are those given by the great religions. . . . Suppose, however, that we can give it. If the inquirer still goes on asking "But why *should* I live like that?" then there is no further answer to give him. . . . We can only ask him to make up his own mind which way he ought to live; for in the end everything rests upon such a decision of principle.[21]

Hare's contention is more understandable if we consider the circumstances under which he formulated his theory. As a result of his capture and imprisonment by Japanese soldiers in World War II, he became sharply aware of the clash between the democratic-Christian principles of his own moral background and the Bushido principles of his Japanese captors. American prisoners who were "brain-washed" by the Chinese Communists in the wake of the Korean War were confronted by a similar clash of principles. Some of them renounced their Western way of life and embraced the Communist way. In quite a different manner, Hare reacted by reformulating the tenets of his ethical philosophy. The final decisive step in each instance was a commitment to a way of life. In Hare's case, this meant a rededication to the Christian and democratic style of living. This is the point where argument ceases.

To sum up Hare's view, we reason from principles, and we revise and broaden our principles as we go along. If we are able to reason comprehensively, we can see how these principles hang together in some inclusive way of life. When we are confronted by a conflict between this way and other ways of life, there is the necessity of final choice. We can clarify the meaning of this choice by a clear and detailed recognition of what is at stake. But reason can go no further. The final option is an act of will—an ultimate, nonrational commitment.

6. THE ORDINARY LANGUAGE APPROACH

Like most of the philosophers at Oxford, Hare was much influenced by Ludwig Wittgenstein's theory of "ordinary language." Characteristic of this theory is Hare's remark:

A logician cannot do justice to the infinite subtlety of language; all he can do is to point out some of the main features of our use of a word, and thereby put people on their guard against the main dangers. A full understanding of the logic of value-terms can only be achieved by continual and sensitive attention to the way we use them.[22]

"The meaning is the use," according to Wittgenstein's famous slogan—and the uses of words are various. Words are like tools that can be used for many different purposes.

Think of the tools in a tool-box; there is a hammer, pliers, a saw, a screwdriver, a rule, a glue-pot, glue, nails and screws.—The functions of words are as diverse as the functions of these objects.[23]

Even a single word, such as "justice," has a wide spectrum of meanings, each serving a different use.

The meaning of an ethical concept, such as "good" or "right," can best be determined by studying the actual usages of human beings as they go about the business of living. Wittgenstein offered the following advice:

Look at the sentence as an instrument, and at its sense as its employment . . . . Ask yourself: On what occasion, for what purpose, do we say this? What kind of actions accompany these words? (Think of a greeting.) In what scenes will they be used; and what for?[24]

When words or sentences are studied in this way, it is found that they have no fixed meanings and sharp edges. There is no mark or characteristic, no "essence" that is common to all uses of the word, or to all properties or things that the word denotes. The many diverse employments of the word constitute a kind of "family resemblance" rather than a single invariant usage. "We see a complicated network of similarities overlapping and criss-crossing."[25] Wittgenstein did not deny that we may precisely define a word with a view to a particular purpose, but this precise meaning, he said, is not the one and only signification of the term. Such a neat demarcation is deceptive if interpreted as the only correct usage or as excluding fresh usages in the future.

P. H. Nowell-Smith, an Oxford philosopher, has pointed out the application of this theory to ethics:

The words with which moral philosophers have especially to do, which are usually called "value-words," play many different parts. They are used to express tastes and preferences, to express decisions and choice, to criticize, grade, and evaluate, to advise, admonish, warn, persuade and dissuade, to praise, encourage and reprove, to promulgate and draw attention to rules; and doubtless for other purposes also. These activities form the complex web of moral discourse and our problem is to trace the connections between them and to come to understand how it is that the same word can be used in all these different ways.[26]

According to Nowell-Smith, it is quite as mistaken to suppose that there is *no* similarity between these diverse uses as to suppose that the same word can be used to do only one job.

The "informalists" (to use a term applied to the followers of Wittgenstein) have differed among themselves, each pointing out distinctive uses of ethical terms. H. L. A. Hart has emphasized the overlapping zone between law and ethics. Both legal and ethical language, for example, ascribe to someone responsibility for past conduct or obligation to perform future acts. J. L. Austin has stressed the "performatory" use of ethical language, as for example, in the promise to pay a debt—the words themselves being a part of the action which creates a new state of affairs. Margaret Macdonald has called attention to the similarity between ethical statements and ceremonial utterances, such as those of religious ritual, which sanctify some common task, purpose, or belief. J. O. Urmson has maintained that to call things good or bad is to grade them, moral grading being analogous, for example, to sorting and grading apples as "fancy," "super," etc. Stephen Toulmin has argued that ethical terms mean "worthy of something-or-other," in this respect resembling the class of "gerundives" in Latin grammar—for example, *amandus*, "worthy of love," or *laudanus*, "worthy of praise." Nowell-Smith has emphasized both the "gerundive" use of ethical language, after the manner of Toulmin, and the "commendatory" function of ethical terms, after the manner of Hare. Some of the disciples of Wittgenstein have pointed to a rather bewildering plurality of value-meanings, the broad definitions of traditional ethical theory being dissipated into innumerable distinctions.

The result of this multifunctional theory of language is to deny that ethical terms have clearcut meanings. The word "good" does not mean "A," it means "either A or B or C etc." The many things that "good" can mean have only a "family resemblance," since there is no common essence with respect to which they are called good. This theory should not be labelled "subjectivist," since it admits a wide plurality of meanings, some of which are non-subjective.

Perhaps the most interesting characteristic of the movement, which we have already discovered in the work of Hare, is the attempt to formulate a "middle way" in ethics, intermediate between subjectivism and objectivism. Most informalists reject the view that ethical sentences are purely descriptive statements, true or false in a strict scientific sense; but they also reject the opposite view that there is a wide and impassable gulf between normative judgments and factual descriptions. On their interpretation, ethics is not primarily cognitive but practical, and practical considerations have a kind of "logic" of their own. Since there may be good reasons for moral decisions, we should regard some ethical judgments as not true but still valid. They are sustained by facts, but are not reducible to descriptions. The informalists

have taken a long step toward the view that ethical statements may be
rationally justifiable.

7. THE SUBJECTIVIST-OBJECTIVIST DISPUTE

Among the philosophers considered in this chapter, those who seek a "middle
way" seem to me closest to the truth. Both the subjectivists and the objectivists are too extreme. Hence an intermediate position, like that of Hare, is
highly plausible. I shall consider the truth to be found in subjectivism and
its opposite, objectivism, and then what sort of compromise is tenable.

The subjectivists are right in connecting values with people's desires, emotions, interests, and preferences. There could be no good or bad if the world
were utterly neutral, so that nothing would make *any* difference. Now the
world, it seems to me, *would* be utterly neutral if it never aroused the slightest glimmer of liking or disliking in any creature whatsoever, beast or man
or god. Whenever I imagine that every sentient being in the universe has
been completely annihilated, or has been turned into some kind of automaton
without the least spark of feeling, desire, or interest, I find that all value
is, in my imaginary world, destroyed. In removing emotion and desire, I have
removed the possibility of worth.

The subjectivists are right in refusing to commit "the fallacy of factualism."
Given the factual proposition, X *is* (or *was, or will be*) *the case,* those who
commit the fallacy conclude that X *is good* or X *ought to be.* But the fact
that something is or was or will be the case is never a sufficient ground for
asserting that it is valuable or obligatory, since the whole tragedy of existence
is to be found in the disparity between *fact* and *value.*

The subjectivists are also right in rejecting the non-naturalism of Moore.
The great majority of philosophers have been unable to detect a simple
non-natural quality of good, and the others have been very doubtful whether
they could discover it. Even Moore eventually abandoned his early view. He
was correct, it seems to me, in not identifying good with a natural property,
but he wrongly identified it with a non-natural property.

The reason for the irreducibly ethical character of good is to be found in
its normative character. It involves not simply *what is* but *what ought to be.*
The ought is not identical with what is; hence, if good involves an "ought,"
it cannot be detected by a mere inspection of what is. Intrinsic good, I believe, is meaningless apart from the "ought to be," just as right is meaningless apart from the "ought to do." The nondescriptive, specifically ethical factor in good and right comes in with the "ought" and only with it. Hare, with
his prescriptive theory, grasped this point, and thereby avoided the fallacy
of factualism.

Unlike Hare, the logical positivists went too far in maintaining that
normative statements are factually nonsensical. The effect of the positivist

doctrines was to limit unduly the province of empirical reason. Normative judgments involve much more than bare cognition, but this does not mean that they are exempt from intellectual criticism. It is one thing to prize, and quite another thing to discover reasons why the object should be prized or why, perchance, the prizing is misdirected. I may love, but to reflect upon that love, and to determine its validity, is not in itself an act of loving. The solution of life's problems requires such critical evaluation and not just irrational liking or disliking. As A. I. Melden has written:

We are familiar with the challenging query, "How can reason be practical?" Should we not also face up to its counterpart—those of us at any rate who deny that *ought* can be derived from an *is*—"how can practice be reasonable?" For the practices of human beings may be right or wrong no less than fortunate or unfortunate. If right, they are surely reasonable; and, if so, often at least, reasons for them can be given that establish that they are reasonable and right. But anything that is a reason must surely refer us to some factual matter.[27]

In insisting upon a factual basis for ethics, the objectivists were more nearly correct than their opponents, the extreme subjectivists.

The mistake of the objectivists (and ethical naturalists in general) was not in supposing that ethical propositions follow from factual, but in *reducing* ethical propositions to factual. Although not descriptions, ethical judgments obliquely refer to, and are validated by, facts. A valid ideal is a plan of action for the satisfaction of genuine needs, and as such refers to what exists. Hume in the Eighteenth Century, and the logical positivists in recent years, did not take sufficient account of these objective factors.

Ayer's identification of moral judgments with emotional ejaculations or exhortations is clearly inadequate, and Stevenson's suggested model of analysis for normative statements, "I like X, do so as well," is almost as implausible. According to Stevenson's view, ethical discourse merely reports subjective likings and seeks to entice others to like in the same manner. But surely, when I condemn Hitler for exterminating millions of Jews, I am not merely talking about my own feelings. It is *really true* that he acted badly, and this quite independently of my subjective attitudes. Moreover, I am not merely trying to entice others to feel as I do. My purpose may be to arouse sober thought rather than to stir up emotion. Stevenson's theory makes no clear distinction between rational argument in ethics and mere "propaganda." This is a fatal defect.

His answer, which I regard as inadequate, is that our attitudes often depend upon our beliefs, and our beliefs are often verifiable. On this view, "ethical judgments" are in part statements about matters of fact and in part expressions of emotional attitude. But neither the statements of fact nor the expressions of attitude, as he interpreted them, are properly speaking ethical judgments. The factual statements are merely factual statements and therefore not ethical (being concerned with the "is" rather than the "ought"), and the expressions of attitude are merely expressions of attitude and therefore not objective, as a real judgment must be. The connection between the factual considerations and the ethical attitudes was conceived as nonlogical. "The supporting [factual] reasons," Stevenson declared, "have no sort of *logical* compulsion, and are related to the judgment psychologically rather than logically. They do not strictly imply the judgment in the way that axioms imply theorems; nor are they related to the judgment inductively, as statements describing observations are related to scientific laws."[28] The aim of ethical argument is persuasion only; and in its moral function, rational persuasion is no different from irrational persuasion. On this view, the distinction between ethical argument and propaganda, and between right approval and mere liking, remains a hazy one at best.

Why were the logical positivists, at least in their more extreme statements, loath to admit that there may be good reasons for ethical judgments? Having decided in advance that all knowledge must be fitted into the rubric of natural science, they proceeded to lay down a formula for what constitutes scientific verification, and then to test all existing disciplines by their ability to fit this Procrustes' bed. Some fields, such as metaphysics and theology, were said to consist of nonsense-propositions; ethics was treated a little more deferentially, but still in a rather highhanded way.

The positivist conception of method, derived from sciences such as physics, is too narrow. Much of our most important insight, particularly in the sphere of human values, depends upon knowledge of mental processes or of cultural and social factors. We must be wary of judging ethics in terms of a scientific tradition which, as Whitehead argued in *Science and the Modern World*, is too narrow for its own good. Ethical judgments have their own criteria, and reason in ethics, although different from reason in natural science, is not absent.

Neither objectivism nor subjectivism is entirely satisfactory. Extreme objectivism emphasizes only the factual insights and falsely concludes that ethical judgments are purely descriptive. Extreme subjectivism emphasizes only the nonintellectual attitudes and falsely supposes that normative statements are incorrigible. Both extremes need to be corrected by a more comprehensive interpretation which would recognize that normative statements are complex and mixed, and therefore never purely descriptive nor, if valid, arbitrary. A well-grounded normative principle expresses (a) certain insights into human needs and potentialities and other ethically relevant facts, and (b) volitional and passional attitudes that are not capricious and are sustained by such insights. It thus combines both cognitive and noncognitive factors.

The informalists come close to this kind of intermediate theory, but are still too subjective or relativistic. They direct attention more to the characteristics of language than to the objective facts of human experience. Frequently there is a failure to pass beyond the linguistic expressions to the facts of action, choice, satisfaction and frustration. Ethics is treated as a study of language rather than a study which must take into account, among other things, the factual data of morals. For example, an ethical judgment is interpreted as a non-declarative sentence, rather than as an act of decision. The linguistic form is worthy of analysis, but the act, which is subject to cognitive description, should not be lost to sight.

A sophisticated informalist, such as Hare or Toulmin or Urmson, will admit that a moral judgment may be justified, but he will contend that its justification does not lie in its truth. The judgment, he will say, is practical, and a practical judgment is prescriptive rather than descriptive—"valid" but not "true." This scrupulousness in the use of "true" departs from the standard of ordinary language which the informalists otherwise espouse, for ethical statements are called true or false in ordinary speech. Also, it is difficult to see how our moral judgments can be justified unless they are, somehow, true. I should have no good reasons for doing something, any more than I would have good reasons for believing something, if the reasons turned out to be false or had nothing to do with truth. As Melden has remarked:

> Instead of speaking about good reasons for doing X we can speak, equivalently, about good reasons for believing that X should be done. . . . Something is a reason for acting precisely because and just to the extent that it refers us to a matter of relevant fact.[29]

Finally, I question the relativism in Hare's theory. He maintains, as we have seen, that there are different "ways of life," and that relativism is unavoidable at this level. Although I would reject an extreme absolutism, I think that we can discriminate between life styles and judge some to be superior to others. It is difficult indeed to compare and evaluate ways of life, but it is possible to do so. Since I have already discussed this question in Chapter IX, I need not go over the ground again.

8. ON THE USES OF REASON AND EVIDENCE IN ETHICS

In arguing as I have in the preceding section, I have not committed the factualist fallacy. I have recognized that ethical norms involve the concept of "ought," and that they are not reducible to mere descriptions. Moral deliberation is to a great extent concerned with ideal possibilities rather than actualities. The moralist, like the poet, can say:

> I dwell in Possibility,
> A fairer House than Prose,
> More numerous of windows,
> Superior—for Doors.[30]

Since ideals are desirable possibilities, they are never mere factual descriptions.

But valid ethical ideals are derived from a consideration of facts, just as the medical ideal of good health is derived from an understanding of actual health and disease. The expert, with a detailed knowledge of relevant facts, is able to formulate a much more precise and valid norm than the ignorant man. This implies that valid norms are sustained by factual insights, even though, strictly speaking, they describe no actual entities. As Stephen Toulmin has pointed out, factual statements are not equivalent to normative judgments, but they may provide a perfectly reasonable basis for such judgments:

> Of course, "This practice would involve the least conflict of interests attainable under the circumstances" does not *mean* the same as "This would be the right practice"; nor does "This way of life would be more harmoniously satisfying" *mean* the same as "This would be better." But in each case, the first statement is a *good reason* for the second: the "ethically neutral" fact is *a good reason* for the "gerundive" moral judgment. If the adoption of the practice would genuinely reduce conflicts of interest, it is a practice *worthy of adoption,* and if the way of life would genuinely lead to deeper and more consistent happiness, it is one *worthy of pursuit.* And this seems so natural and intelligible, when one bears in mind the function of ethical judgments, that, if anyone asks me *why* they are "good reasons," I can only reply by asking in return, "What better kinds of reason could you want?"[31]

It is therefore a great mistake to suppose that factual data and logical inference are irrelevant to moral deliberation. In a sense, good-making qualities are quite as much open to inspection as indifferent qualities, and they are of great interest to the moralist. Such states as love, humor, frustration, delight, consolation, despair, and the enjoyment of beauty, are just as real and subject to inquiry as shapes, colors, sounds, weights, and motions. Human likings and dislikings and their corresponding objects can be described quite as truly as the properties of a hydrogen atom. Human beings are essentially goal-seeking creatures, and their teleological propensities—their needs, capacities, aspirations, and purposive endeavors—are as much subject to scientific study as any other aspects of their nature. An ethically responsible person is not disdainful of such knowledge. He does not wildly cruise in the seas of possibility with no regard for the shores of fact.

He distinguishes between *bare* possibilities and real possibilities. A bare possibility is *logically* possible but is not *really* possible. To aim at that which is not really possible is human folly, frittering away precious energies and resources and risking heartbreak. Real possibility, however, can be determined only in the light of facts. Whether we are thinking of an individual or a society, there are physical, mental, and technological limitations upon human potentialities. Just as we may need to know the weight, horsepower, gear-ratio, fuel supply, and so on of an automobile before we can calculate whether it can climb a certain very steep grade, so we may need to know the constitution and resources of a human being before we can judge whether he can realize a certain difficult goal. Moreover, intelligent experiment is often necessary to determine capacity. In many instances, we cannot know what we can do without trying, and such experiments often disclose pertinent information for judging *other* possibilities. Sometimes, as in the social field, the experiment cannot be made by the immediate investigator; but he can critically evaluate social movements as they emerge, stage by stage, in various parts of the world. Thus what has happened in the Soviet Union or in semisocialist Sweden, Israel, or Britain may cast a great deal of light upon what we as citizens ought to do here in America.

We need to know, so far as we can, *all* of the significant possibilities and not just some of them. Especially in a scientific and technological age such as ours, we are in danger of overlooking real and desirable possibilities that our expanded resources make possible. Many of the people in the Tennessee Valley, before the great TVA project was begun, did not realize that there was a real possibility to escape from poverty. Eventually they were taught, by instruction and experiment, that modern technology has provided vastly increased opportunities. Before democratic social ideals can be realistic, the common people must know what the experts have discovered—what modern science and technology can achieve for human welfare. Actually, the advance of science has led to an enormous elaboration of purposes, disclosing hundreds of thousands of possible objectives that before were utterly unknown, and providing the efficient means for the realization of ends that would otherwise be utterly Utopian.

We need to analyze the implications and consequences of the alternative *real* possibilities. These possibilities are not logically or causally isolated from one another. By logical reflection, we can pass from possible to possible so as to realize the innumerable logical interconnections of human norms. By causal analysis based upon observation and experiment, we judge what will probably happen in consequence of our embracing one possibility rather than another. We are able to say, "If this, *then* that," or "If not this, *then* not that." Possibilities will be hazy, choices will be blind, ideals will be inconsequential, to the extent that implications, whether logical or causal, are left unexplored.

We need to understand our own natures, including the values of human experience, before we can judge which possibilities are most choiceworthy. A detailed knowledge of the telic nature of man—his needs, satisfactions, and potentialities—is indispensable to the responsible exercise of moral choice. There is often a vast difference between what a person *thinks* he wants and what he *really* wants, and between what he wants if he does not know himself and what he wants if he truly understands his own nature. Apart from self-knowledge and social understanding, ideals are so vague and capricious as to be almost meaningless. With the development of psychological and social science, plans for the betterment of human life can be worked out upon the basis of definite knowledge of the major human cravings and capacities and the efficient means to satisfy or cultivate them. That human nature is no mere nominal essence, that human beings are a good deal alike the world over, is a premise of our argument. If human beings are inordinately swayed by some pathological motivation such as a guilt complex, death instinct, sadistic bent, or psychotic compulsion, or if their actions are determined by fanaticism, stupidity, or perverse cultural conditioning, they may divorce themselves from the human community. The invalidity of their responses will then be revealed by such consequences as crime, suicide, insanity, social hysteria, sadism, and war. On the other hand, if they are morally responsible, if they are motivated by good will and guided by intelligence, they will participate with others of like mind in reaching a moral consensus. The norms which they choose will then be sustained by a clear and dispassionate insight into the needs, potentialities, and telic nature of man, and will be tested by the collective judgments of many "experts," such as the physician, the hygienist, the psychologist, the educator, the social scientist, and the community planner. If these norms are indeed well chosen and effectively applied, their validity will be revealed in such consequences as the freedom from irreconcilable conflicts and frustrations, the presence of enjoyable and gratifying experiences, the predominance of interest over satiety, of love over hate, of satisfaction over dissatisfaction. There are no better indications that norms are valid.

The validity of norms is thus to be judged by informed insight. A valid norm is a *real* and not a *bare* possibility; it is chosen not blindly but with a view to *all* the significant alternatives that can be known; it is rationally conceived in terms of its logical and causal implications; and it is soberly appraised in the light of the real needs, potentialities, satisfactions, and enjoyments of the human beings concerned. Here, then, is a set of criteria for determining the validity of norms and avoiding moral subjectivity. If we are debarred from being completely rational, we are not barred from being as rational as possible.

NOTES

1. Bertrand Russell, *Religion and Science.* London and New York: Oxford University Press, 1935, p. 227. Russell has confessed himself discontented with his ethical theory, and in view of the intensity of his moral concern over public issues, one cannot wonder.

2. David Hume, *An Enquiry Concerning Human Understanding* (edited by L. A. Selby-Bigge). London and New York: Oxford University Press, 1902, p. 165.

3. David Hume, *An Enquiry Concerning the Principles of Morals* (edited by Selby-Bigge). London and New York: Oxford University Press, 1902, pp. 174–175.

4. David Hume, *A Treatise of Human Nature* (edited by Selby-Bigge). London and New York: Oxford University Press, 1896, p. 469.

5. Hume, *An Enquiry Concerning the Principles of Morals, op. cit.,* pp. 291–292.

6. Hume, *Treatise*, *op. cit.*, pp. 468–469.
7. *Ibid.*, p. 416.
8. *Ibid.*, p. 415.
9. *Ibid.*, p. 457.
10. G. E. Moore, *Principia Ethica*. Cambridge and New York: Cambridge University Press, 1903 (reprinted 1929), pp. 16–17.
11. *Ibid.*, p. 13.
12. A. J. Ayer, *Language, Truth and Logic*. London: Victor Gollancz, Ltd., 1958 (first edition, 1936; revised, 1946), p. 107.
13. *Ibid.*, pp. 108–109.
14. *Ibid.*, p. 111.
15. Charles L. Stevenson, "The Nature of Ethical Disagreement," Centro di Metodologia, Milan, Italy. Reprinted in Melvin Rader, *The Enduring Questions*. New York: Holt, Rinehart and Winston, Inc., 1956, p. 437.
16. Charles L. Stevenson, *Ethics and Language*. New Haven: Yale University Press, 1944, p. 207.
17. *Ibid.*, p. 210.
18. *Ibid.*, p. 139.
19. *Cf.*, Charles L. Stevenson, "Relativism and Non-Relativism in Value Theory," *Proceedings and Addresses of the American Philosophical Association, 1961–1962*. Yellow Springs, Ohio: Antioch Press, 1962, pp. 32–33, 37, 41.
20. R. M. Hare, *The Language of Morals*. London and New York: Oxford University Press, 1952, p. 178.
21. *Ibid.*, p. 69.
22. *Ibid.*, p. 126.
23. Ludwig Wittgenstein, *Philosophical Investigations*. New York: The Macmillan Company, 1953, p. 6.
24. *Ibid.*, pp. 126, 137.
25. *Ibid.*, pp. 31–32.
26. P. H. Nowell-Smith, *Ethics*. Baltimore: Penguin Books, 1954, p. 98.
27. A. I. Melden, "Reasons for Action and Matters of Fact," *Proceedings and Addresses of the American Philosophical Association, 1961–1962*, *op. cit.*, p. 46.
28. Charles L. Stevenson, *Ethics and Language*, *op. cit.*, pp. 30, 113.
29. A. I. Melden, "Reasons for Action and Matters of Fact," *op. cit.*, pp. 53, 58.
30. From *The Complete Poems of Emily Dickinson*, edited by Thomas H. Johnson. Boston: Little, Brown & Company, 1960, p. 327. Copyright © 1929, 1957 by Mary L. Hampson. By permission of Little, Brown & Company.
31. Stephen Toulmin, *The Place of Reason in Ethics*. Cambridge: Cambridge University Press, 1950, p. 224.

PART FOUR

Social ideals

CHAPTER XI

The group and the individual

I. A STATEMENT OF THE ISSUES

In the preceding Parts of this book, we have been more concerned with the meaning of the basic ethical concepts, such as "good," "right," and "duty," than with their application to rival social orders. Part Four will have a different emphasis and will deal mainly with values in the field of social action. The importance of the task need not be emphasized: it is unlikely that we can avoid social catastrophe in this critical period of history if we have no clear objectives or well-conceived plans. Social intelligence depends upon our capacity to know both the proper goals of our social order and how we ought to achieve them. Ethical issues are as relevant in this area as in private life. The question whether a man ought to join the Communist party, or the John Birch Society, is as much an ethical problem as the question whether he ought to keep a promise.

In principle, I have already indicated the criterion for judging whether a social order is good or bad. I have characterized ultimate good in terms of the cultivation and fulfillment of interests, especially those interests that represent what is deepest in human nature and that blend harmoniously with other fundamental interests. The good of achievement is the harmonious satisfaction of these basic drives, but this good is incomplete unless it includes the good of enjoyment. Hence the volitional "dimension" of good (the fulfillment of desire) must be supplemented by the affective dimension (pleasure and enjoyable emotions). As I have defined "interest," it combines both of these dimensions, being essentially an affective-volitional state of mind. Reason, although it qualifies interest, does not constitute its core. Nevertheless, a rational interest is almost invariably better than an irrational one. Without intellectual judgment directing our interests, life would not be distinguished from madness; and knowledge is rightfully one of the supreme objects of interest. When I speak of the good as the cultivation and fulfillment of interests, therefore, I am implying that it is the comprehensive attainment of human excellence, the realization of the whole man, as feeling-striving-thinking.

I maintain that the ultimate test of any social order is its efficacy in promoting such goodness among its members. This test can be applied not only to the social order as a whole but to its main parts. An economy, or polity, or legal system that unnecessarily thwarts interests, or that favors the interests of the few rather than the many, or that favors interests that are superficial rather than profound, cannot, in these respects, be justified.

Let us consider, as an example, the question of the proper balance between work and leisure. The longer men work, with no resultant slowdown or increase in unemployment, the greater will be the volume of goods and services; but the advantages that would accrue from this increased production must be balanced against the disadvantages that would result from diminished leisure. To maximize good, men should work as long as each added increment of work would contribute, directly or indirectly, to the fulfillment rather than the frustration of human interests as I have characterized them. They should cease work when they have reached the point at which an added increment of work would diminish rather than increase this fulfillment. In practice, it might be impossible to determine with any degree of exactitude whether the men in a certain industry should work eight hours a day, or more, or less; but the principle for judging the issue is clear and would serve to guide social policy.

If we deal not with a single issue such as the proper length of the working day but with the evaluation of a comprehensive social ideal, the problem is more complicated. But the *principle* for determining social policy remains the same. We must inquire what kind of social order *is* best fitted to cultivate and fulfill human interests. The answers currently given to this question differ fundamentally, and the differences depend in great measure upon competing sets of values. A communist and a democrat, for example, differ in their interpretations of freedom, in their concepts of equality, and in their estimates of the state as an instrument of social policy. Most of these differences probably resolve themselves into questions of means, but some of the differences may involve questions of ends or ultimate goals. Social intelligence depends upon our capacity to know both the proper goals of our social order and how we ought to seek them.

Part Four will examine a number of social ideals, such as the aristocracy of Plato, the communism of Marx, the democracy of Rousseau, and the liberalism of Mill. This section shall be concerned most of all with "the ideal of community," which is one of the *leitmotifs* of the present book. Community involves a person-taken-as-person relation, a mutual regard and respect, among free individuals; it thus stands in contrast to the relation that exists when one person, or group, oppresses or exploits another. I regard this ideal as the heart and soul of liberal democracy.

If we are to use interest-fulfillment as our ethical touchstone, it is important to ask where interests are to be found. The answer appears to be obvious. An interest, including the good of its fulfillment, is to be found only in the individual. There is no intrinsic value where there is no interest and no interest where there is no mind. Hence the locus of intrinsic value is in the individual who has a mind, and not in the group which has none except the minds of its individual members. Interests, as Ralph Barton Perry has said, "are found, and found only, in individuals; that is, in one or more of those beings enclosed within a skin, born of woman, subject to natural death after a period approximating three-score and ten years, denominated by a proper name, and numerable in the census."[1]

We might unhesitatingly agree with Perry if it were not for the opposite contention that a group may have an interest that is quite different from the sum of interests of its individual members. Rousseau expresses this latter point of view in his famous doctrine of "the general will." He points out that "the body politic," like the individual human body, has a kind of internal coherence and organic interrelatedness of all its parts, and he concludes that it therefore has a self and is a moral being with a will of its own.

The body politic, taken individually, may be considered as an organized, living body, resembling that of man. . . . The life of both bodies is the self common to the whole, the reciprocal sensibility and internal correspondence of all the parts. . . . The body politic, therefore, is also a moral being possessed of a will; and this general will, which tends always to the preservation and welfare of the whole and of every part, and is the source of the law, constitutes for all the members of the State, in their relations to one another, and to it, the rule of what is just or unjust.[2]

Rousseau clearly and emphatically distinguishes between the general will and the sum of particular wills:

There is often a great deal of difference between the *will of all* and the *general will;* the latter considers only the common interest, while the former takes private interest into account, and is no more than a sum of particular wills.[3]

Thus is the issue joined. On the one hand, we have the theory that the locus of goodness is always the individual, and that the good of the group or society is never more than the sum of the individual goods. My good is one thing, your good is another, and there is never a common good that fuses them into a single whole or that exists in addition to the separate goods of you and me and of other individuals. On the other hand, we have the theory that there is a general or common interest of the group, and that the fulfillment of this interest constitutes a distinct good that is not the sum of the goods of individuals.

Let us now consider each of these views in turn. We shall discover, I believe, that Perry's view is essentially correct; but we shall find enough truth in Rousseau's point of view to warrant a rejection of extreme individualism.

2. THE INDIVIDUAL AS THE LOCUS OF VALUE

The ethics of extreme individualism can perhaps best be illustrated by expounding the relevant theories of one of its principal representatives, Thomas Hobbes (1588–1679). It is easier to understand Hobbes if we know something about his personality and his times. "Fear and I were twins," he declared, blaming his abnormal fearfulness upon the coincidence that his birth occurred when the Spanish Armada threatened England with disaster. Although it is very unlikely that this is a correct explanation, fear was one of the strongest motives of his life. This temperamental tendency was reinforced by the character of his age, a time of civil war when Charles I lost his head and the nation was thrown into a panic. In his *Behemoth,* Hobbes depicted the civil war as a terrible state of lawlessness, disorder, and anarchy; in his more famous book, *Leviathan,* he described the extreme measures necessary to quell anarchy, fend off disaster, and guarantee security to each individual.

Equal to fear as a motive in his life was Hobbes' determination to discover the real facts about existence. He was resolved to be utterly unsentimental, to let not feelings but only reason and evidence determine his beliefs. As a friend of Francis Bacon, as a contemporary and acquaintance of Descartes, as an admirer of Kepler, Galileo, and Harvey, he was impelled to study the new developments of natural science and to import its methods into the philosophical and political spheres. Leo Strauss, in *The Political Philosophy of Hobbes,* has argued that the essence of Hobbes' ethical and social philosophy was formulated *before* his detailed study of natural science. But the broad presuppositions of natural science were an inescapable part of the "mental climate" of the age and required no special study to absorb. These presuppositions, if not the more detailed conclusions of the sciences, were reflected in the ethics of Hobbes.

It was a very common view among scientists that any material whole is an aggregate of atoms, each one of which, as Newton later expressed it, is a "solid, massy, hard, impenetrable, movable particle."[4] There was also a very widespread tendency exhibited by both scientists and philosophers to think of the world as a mechanism or as made up of mechanisms. Now a mechanism is put together out of separate parts, and those parts, although perhaps geared together, always retain their separate identity. For example, a tire can be taken off an automobile, and it still remains a tire; but a heart cannot be plucked out of a biological organism without ceasing to be a real heart and, indeed, without soon decaying. A part of a mechanism, therefore, is much more of an "individual" than is a part of an organism. Influenced by the science of his day, Hobbes was prone to think of any whole as made of atomic isolates, or of individual parts like those of a mechanism; and he proceeded to describe man and society after this manner.

The economic forces of the time reinforced these ideas. It was the age of early capitalism when "individual enterprise" was being defended against feudal collectivism and monarchical absolutism. The businessmen wished to substitute a relationship of free contract in place of a relationship of enforced status. They insisted upon the right of the enterprising individual, conceived as separate and self-seeking, to carve out his own economic destiny. These capitalistic developments were just beginning in the lifetime of Hobbes, but they no doubt influenced him to some degree.

Upon these foundations Hobbes reared a materialistic and mechanistic theory of reality and an individualistic theory of man and society. I shall mention only those parts of his philosophy that throw light upon his ethical individualism.

The general foundation of his individualistic doctrines is the view that a whole is simply the additive sum of distinct parts, a theory implied, as we have seen, by his atomism and mechanism. He believed that all reasoning is a kind of addition and subtraction of discrete elements.

When a man *reasoneth,* he does nothing else but conceive a sum total, from *addition* of parcels; or conceive a remainder, from *subtraction* of one sum from another. . . . These operations are not incident to numbers only, but to all manner of things that can be added together, and taken one out of another. . . . In sum, in what matter soever there is place for *addition* and *subtraction,* there also is place for *reason;* and where these have no place, there *reason* has nothing at all to do.[5]

This view of the reasoning process implies that a whole made up of parts is not an organic unity but an aggregate of discrete elements which can be freely added and subtracted. It was a short step from this reasoning to the conception of society as merely an aggregate of egoistic individuals.

This atomistic point of view was reinforced by Hobbes' denial of the validity of universal ideas. He believed that the particular, not the universal, is real. The so-called universal is simply a name to refer to many individuals: thus "man" has no meaning except as a name—the reality is always the particular man. From this position, Hobbes worked out a nominalistic interpretation of groups and organizations including the state. He called them "artificial bodies"—fictions of a sort—and thought of them as mechanisms to serve individuals, in whom reality ultimately dwells.

The world, he believed, consists of extended bodies in motion, and a human being is a material body—a kind of elaborate machine, separate and distinct from other machines. When acted upon by other bodies, this machine responds with a motion of its own, which takes the form of sensation. A sensation is a vibratory motion of particles—"only a motion in the organs of sense." "Imagination is decaying sense," and "memory" is another form of the same. "Endeavor," "will," and "desire" are just motions within the nervous system. A man calls a thing "good" when it is an object of desire or motion toward; and "evil" when it is an object of aversion or motion away from. Good and evil are always relative to the motions or volitions of the individual, and there is no suggestion of any objective social good.

According to this point of view, every person is motivated solely by egoistic drives. In a characteristic passage, Hobbes compares life to a race.

This *race* we must suppose to have no other *goal*, nor other *garland*, but being foremost, and in it: To endeavour, is *appetite*. To be remiss, is *sensuality*. To consider them behind, is *glory*. To consider them before, is *humility*. . . . To fall on the sudden, is disposition to *weep*. To see another fall, is disposition to *laugh*. To see one out-gone whom we would not, is *pity*. To see one out-go whom we would not, is *indignation*. To hold fast by another, is to *love*. To carry him on that so holdeth, is *charity*. To hurt one's-self for haste, is *shame*. Continually to be out-gone, is *misery*. Continually to out-go the next before, is *felicity*. And to forsake the course, is to *die*.[6]

Each person, motivated by self-interest, comes into conflict with every other. "If any two men desire the same thing, which nevertheless they cannot both enjoy," declares Hobbes, "they become enemies, and . . . endeavor to destroy or subdue one another."[7] Human desire is insatiable: every man is driven by "a perpetual and restless desire of power after power, that ceaseth only in death."[8] Thus impelled, everyone will naturally prey upon his fellows, and be preyed upon in turn. The consequence is "such a war as is of every man against every man"—a state of anarchy described in a very famous passage:

In such condition there is no place for industry, because the fruit thereof is uncertain: and consequently no culture of the earth; no navigation, nor use of the commodities that may be imported by sea; no commodious building; no instruments of moving, and removing, such things as require much force; no knowledge of the face of the earth; no account of time; no arts; no letters; no society; and which is worst of all, continual fear, and danger of violent death; and the life of man, solitary, poor, nasty, brutish, and short.[9]

This is the intolerable condition of men before they have created a civil state; and to end this condition men band together to establish a sovereign who shall have absolute power to enforce peace. The "social contract," which establishes the unlimited power of the sovereign, is an agreement among asocial, self-seeking individuals in the interests of self-preservation. Only the naked force of the sovereign power, set up expressly for the purpose, can compel egocentric human beings to live peacefully together, for "covenants, without the sword, are but words, and of no strength to secure a man at all."[10] Without the force of the state to compel men to civil obedience, they would relapse into the state of anarchy. Believing that the only possible choice is between extremes, men have preferred the whips of tyranny to the scorpions of anarchy. They have surrendered anarchic liberty for the sake of iron-clad security.

It is obvious that Hobbes is here stating an extreme form of individualism: man's basic nature is antisocial; social relations are merely artificial; the state is simply a contrivance invoked by fear and maintained by force. The ethics of Hobbes fits this individualistic scheme of things. Good and evil are relative to the emotions and volitions of the individual. "Of the voluntary acts of every man," declared Hobbes, "the object is some good to himself."[11] Ethics is based upon rational self-interest rather than benevolence.

In the state of nature men have the right of self-preservation and the need to secure it. The fundamental conditions of security, such as the keeping of covenants, are the dictates of a far-sighted prudence. Hobbes called them "the laws of nature." These laws oblige in reason always, but in effect only when there is power to enforce them.

For the laws of nature, which consist in equity, justice, gratitude, and other moral virtues on these depending, in the condition of mere nature, . . . are not properly laws, but qualities that dispose men to peace and obedience. When a commonwealth is once settled, then are they actually laws, and not before.[12]

According to Howard Warrender in *The Political Philosophy of Hobbes*, these laws of nature are commandments of God even when they are not commanded by the state. To this extent, Hobbes' ethics would have an eternal foundation in God's will. But unlike St. Thomas Aquinas, Hobbes derived the force of God's commandments from His power, not from His reason or goodness. He also thought that few men in the state of nature would be restrained by the fear of God's fiery furnace. Whether the force be that of God or the state, men are united in society by an external power which counteracts their tendency as aggressive egocentric individuals to destroy one another.

An ethical individualist need not agree with all the opinions of Hobbes—indeed, some of these opinions are obsolete and many are extreme. Jeremy Bentham, who was likewise an extreme individualist, had a much higher opinion of human nature than Hobbes, and did not believe that a strong state is essential to security. Like Bentham and unlike Hobbes, most individualists have been opposed to political absolutism. Yet the doctrines of Hobbes serve to throw into bold relief the thesis of ethical individualism that value is relative to the self-seeking individual. Let us now turn to the opposite point of view.

3. THE GROUP AS THE LOCUS OF VALUE

The ethical theory of extreme collectivism has evolved over a long period of time and has been expressed by innumerable writers. To a certain extent, Plato contributed to this theory; it was widely current in the Middle Ages;

Rousseau, Hegel, Durkheim, Bosanquet, Gentile, and many other modern thinkers have, in greater or lesser measure, promulgated it. It has been influential in the formulation of fascist ideology and has tinged communist doctrine. Its outstanding representative is Georg Wilhelm Friedrich Hegel (1770–1831), perhaps the greatest German philosopher since Kant. Not only is he the most devoted and articulate spokesman of social organicism, but he is also the most influential. Before Hegel, philosophers had concerned themselves with practical affairs, and a few of them had made some little stir. Plato had a finger in the political intrigues of Syracuse; Hobbes' *Leviathan* was dangerous enough to arouse the ire of both Cromwell and Charles the Second; Locke did much to inspire the American Revolution, and Rousseau to inspire the French Revolution. But the influence of all these thinkers has been exceeded by that of Hegel. As Ernst Cassirer has remarked:

All our modern political ideologies show us the strength, the durability and permanence of the principles that were first introduced and defended in Hegel's philosophy of right and in his philosophy of history. . . . A historian recently raised the question whether the struggle of the Russians and the invading Germans in 1943 was not, at bottom, a conflict between the Left and Right wings of Hegel's school. That may seem to be an exaggerated statement of the problem but it contains a nucleus of truth.[13]

Hegel's philosophy is called "idealism," but he was not an idealist in the ordinary philosophical sense of the term. He did not maintain with Berkeley that the whole of reality consists of minds and their ideas, nor with Royce that a single Infinite Mind contains us and all our experiences and all things besides.[14] Rather he was an "idealist" in holding that "ideas" provide a pattern, a kind of conceptual blueprint, for interpreting human life and the natural world. All things are developing in accordance with a logical scheme. The processes of nature and the stages of history are the acting out, the making explicit, of a latent rationality. Every spirit, and every thing, is part of a single vast web of logically interrelated entities—nothing is really separate, like a hard impenetrable atom or an enclosed self-subsistent mind. In expressing these views Hegel was giving voice, in a quite original way, to the dominant philosophical movement of the Germany of his day.

He was also influenced by the expanding knowledge of organisms. Biological science was beginning to develop rapidly, and Buffon, Erasmus Darwin, Lamarck, and Goethe had supplied much new insight into the structures and functions of organic life. In his *Critique of Judgment*, Kant had pointed out the distinctive characteristics of an organism as involving a systematic interdependence of its parts, which are thus the causes and effects of each other and of the whole—the leaves of a tree, for example, depending upon the trunk; the trunk, in turn, depending upon the leaves; and both the leaves and trunk contributing to and being governed by the dynamic equilibrium of the whole.

This doctrine of organic part-whole relationships is fundamental in Hegel's philosophy. The universe, he believes, is an immense organic unity made up of component organic unities. In any organic unity, each part is through and through relational; it cannot be isolated without altering its character or destroying it; its value and character are like those of a single musical phrase in a sonata, dependent upon and derivative from its relations to the whole. The pattern of the whole is prior to and immanent in the parts, just as the plan of the whole human body dwells within and governs all its parts.

Since things are essentially related to one another, they cannot be understood truly apart from such relationships. The truth is a whole, each integral part of which is mutilated when considered in isolation. To see things together, therefore, is to enrich vision, to see things apart is to impoverish it. No proposition taken in isolation is wholly true because no thing taken in isolation is wholly real.

This point of view is basic in Hegel's social philosophy. He believes that individualism is false because separate individuals are unreal. Apart from their social relations, human beings are as artificial and insubstantial as the personifications in an allegory. They are shaped and constituted by the social forces penetrating into them—by the customs, traditions, institutions, and cultural life of the society.

A social group is more than a mere aggregate, an arithmetical sum total of its parts. The mark of an aggregate is that its parts can be joined or separated without essential change in their internal characteristics. No genuine social group is such an aggregate—its members are too interdependent; they are sustained in their activity by one another and by the whole. The group has a total character impressed on every member—a concrete and ineluctable unity of its own, with an organized social structure and distinctive social functions. The common interests of a group regarded as a single individual, therefore, cannot be identified with the several interests of its members. A mob, acting as no individual would act, is simply the more pathological embodiment of a basic and universal fact: that every coherent group has an *esprit de corps*, a common interest, a collective will, a kind of group mind. All of us have experienced such group feeling and group thought, the experience of being merged in something greater than ourselves, the experience of being dominated by the group spirit.

Hegel's sense of interrelatedness was reinforced by his theory of a new kind of logic, which would take account of the continuities and gradations of reality. He had noticed that there is a characteristic pattern of thought in the give-and-take of fruitful argument. The first stage tends to be that of unqualified assertion (the thesis), an idea being advanced as unqualifiedly true and intelligible in and of itself. The second stage is a sceptical rejoinder (the antithesis); the original idea, opposed by a counter notion, is shown to be false and incomplete when taken in its initial and unqualified form. As the argument proceeds each person is made to see the strength in the opposing position, and the disputants, if the outcome is fruitful, finally reach an agreement involving a more inclusive organization of thought (the synthesis). Thus a larger truth emerges from the strife of partisan views.

Hegel believed that this concrete movement of thought differs from the abstract character of formal logic. The traditional logic, following the theory of Aristotle, conceived opposition as the contradiction of a positive and a negative: "X is Y" being opposed by "X is not Y." From this opposition no new synthesis can spring. Thinking of the characteristic way in which arguments develop, Hegel conceived of opposition, not as the juxtaposition of a positive and a negative, but as the opposition of two *positive* terms, the thesis and antithesis, which implicate and yet in a sense negate each other, their mutuality and opposition forcing us to reconcile them in a wider thought-construct (the synthesis). In turn, the synthesis tends to become a new thesis, and the process begins anew. Thus each new idea, not being the whole truth, is inevitably tainted with falsehood, and must be gathered up and transformed in a more comprehensive whole.

Contradiction and its resolution in the realm of thought are paralleled by a similar movement in the field of human affairs. Here, too, there are antithetical tendencies, each bent upon destroying its opposite, and producing a kind of crisis by its inordinate one-sidedness. The clash of these tendencies exposes the logical ridiculousness of each factor taken in isolation, and thus releases corrective forces which restore the balance. In this way the whole process leads on to more coherent and comprehensive states of equilibrium.

It must not be supposed that all development can be fitted into a neat, triadic pattern. The terms "thesis," "antithesis," and "synthesis" have been used much more frequently by expositors of Hegel than by Hegel himself. In his Preface to *The Phenomenology of the Spirit*, he warns against a violent forcing of any and every sort of material into the triadic pattern. His own philosophical thinking, although predominantly "dialectical," is too rich and various to reduce to any simple scheme.

Applied to problems of ethics, the dialectical approach implies that the good life is "a unity of the multiform and an accord of the discordant." The proper reconciliation of ethical conflicts is to be found, not in exalting one set of ideas or values at the expense of another, but in the creative interpenetration and reconciliation of "opposites." So it is with the great antinomies that plague and yet enrich men's experience: growth and order, impulse and rationality, breadth and specialization, practicality and idealism. In dealing with each of these polarities, we should seek no one-sided or fragmentary solution but a happy union of the apparently incompatible. So it is with the antinomy between the individual and the community. Only folly and disaster can result from denying either of these antithetical modes. Individuality, if pitted against community, is a dangerous half-truth, while community, if considered total and absolute, is no less delusory. The only happy solution is to recognize that the full development of individuality requires identification with the community, just as the rich unfolding of community requires the cultivation of individuality.

From these premises, Hegel derives a doctrine of freedom. He rejects the view that freedom could be anything merely negative, such as an absence of restraint. We cannot find freedom in detachment from all connections that make demands upon us. Such freedom is illusory, because the detached individual is lonely, empty, unreal. Nor can we find freedom in self-assertion. A man is as big as his interests; if he asserts only his own worth, he shrinks to the vanishing point. Nor can we find freedom in capricious interests, because then we garner no coherent happiness. Freedom requires organization and discipline, a coherence of personality that expresses itself in coherent action and striving. The only real freedom is to be found in social participation. The way for a man to become free is to achieve a deep and comprehensive self through many sympathetic relations to other things, other people, and the institutions which embody their collective life.

Hegel distinguishes three stages in the realization of freedom. The first stage is the participation of the individual in the family. By living in the family circle, individuals lose their stultifying independence and participate in a wider and deeper whole. Every family has its distinctive character and atmosphere: no two homes are exactly alike. The union of its members creates a little social organism, a kind of collective personality, an *esprit de corps*. By sharing in this common life, each member learns the meaning of love as a loosening of the bands of selfhood. Declares Hegel:

> Love means in general the consciousness of my unity with another, such that I am not isolated from myself, but win my self-consciousness only by giving up my explicit being or independence, and thereby know myself as the unity of myself with the other and the other with me.[15]

The freedom of each member of the family lies in just this differentiation and union within the common life.

The second stage is the participation of the individual in civil society. This is the realm of institutions wider than the family but narrower than the state. It includes school and church and economic group and cultural association. Within its wide ambit, the individual finds less intimacy but a larger scope than in the circle of the family. Hegel's analysis of civil society, in which he is especially concerned with economic activities and property rights, is characterized by his unsparing recognition of anarchic tendencies—the conflict of private interests, the clash of economic groups, and the welter of competing institutions. Yet all is not anarchy; each individual or group, in pursuing its private or particular interest, helps to create a system of social interdependence, as embodied, for example, in the division of labor. In so doing, it enlarges the area of freedom and rational association. Because of the anarchic tendency within society, however, it is necessary to achieve a binding force or synthesis which will integrate all divergent individuals and institutions into a supreme social organism. This unification is achieved in and through the state.

The third stage of freedom, therefore, is the participation of the individual in the state. It is here that the culmination of freedom is reached, because the state, in providing the widest and deepest integration of interests, supplies the individual with the richest form of social participation. Hence its claim upon the individual is higher than that of civil society. Hegel explains:

> Were the state to be considered as exchangeable with the civil society, and were its decisive features to be regarded as the security and protection of property and personal freedom, the interest of the individual as such would be the ultimate purpose of the social union. It would then be at one's option to be a member of the state. But the state has a totally different relation to the individual. It is the objective spirit, and he has his truth, real existence, and ethical status only in being a member of it. Union, as such, is itself the true content and end, since the individual is intended to pass a universal life. His particular satisfactions, activities, and way of life have in this authenticated substantive principle their origin and result.[16]

In the ideal state, Hegel goes on to explain, "the private interest of its citizens is one with the common interest of the state," and "the one finds its gratification and realization in the other."[17] Although the ideal has not been fully attained, the actual state provides its individual citizens with their essential values.

> The state, its laws, its arrangements, constitute the rights of its members; its natural features, its mountains, air, and water, are *their* country, their fatherland, their outward material property; the history of this state, *their* deeds; what their ancestors have produced, belongs to them and lives in their memory. All is their possession, just as they are possessed by it; for it constitutes their existence, their being.[18]

The worth of the state, according to Hegel, is not merely that it affords a better life for its citizens, but that it has a supreme intrinsic value. In rhapsodic language, he extols the state as "the march of God in the world" and as the "absolute, stable, end-for-itself."[19] He describes it as an organism, attributes to it will and thought, and reveres it as a thing divine.

> No predicate, principles, and the like suffice to express the nature of the state; it must be comprehended as an organism. . . . To the complete state belongs, essentially, consciousness and thought. The state knows thus what it wills, and it knows it under the form of thought. . . . We must therefore worship the state as the manifestation of the divine on earth.[20]

"This final end" of the state, Hegel explains, "has the supreme right against individuals, whose supreme duty it is to be members of the state."[21]

Although he thus apotheosizes the state, he does not seek to abolish individual distinctions. Unlike a modern fascist, he believed that freedom requires the differentiation of the parts.

The one essential canon to make liberty deep and real is to give every business belonging to the general interests of the state a separate organization wherever they are essentially distinct. Such real division must be: for liberty is only deep when it is differentiated in all its fullness and these differences manifested in existence.[22]

Hegel even reserved to the individual a sphere of private conscience "which as such does not come within the sphere of the state."[23] In the Hegelian system the state belongs to the realm of "the objective Spirit," and this realm is transcended by art, religion, and philosophy—the three forms of the Absolute Spirit. These spheres of culture have an independent meaning and value, and do not exist for the enhancement and glorification of the state. Hegel thus refused to countenance the subordination of culture to politics. He would have rejected the famous slogan of Mussolini: "All within the state, nothing outside the state, nothing against the state."

At his best, Hegel expressed a valid insight: that freedom and organization should not be pitted against one another as irreconcilable opposites but should be reconciled and synthesized in a free and organized community. Unfortunately, he betrayed this insight in his excessive glorification of the nation-state. He remains the supreme representative in modern philosophy of the theory that values are essentially social and that the group, rather than the detached individual, is the locus of value.

4. THE THEORY OF INTEGRATIVE LEVELS

In the light of what we know about human nature, we should avoid an exaggerated individualism such as that of Hobbes and an overpowering collectivism such as that of Hegel in his more extreme doctrines. Society should be conceived neither as a monstrous superorganism of which individuals are but cells, nor as a mere arithmetical sum of self-enclosed egoists. We should reject the concept of a "state organism," "race soul," or "group mind" but should also reject the concept of independent selfish individuals, connected by no real ties to one another. We should try to do justice to both sides of human nature, the individual and the social.

A third view, that will avoid the pitfalls of both social atomism and social organicism, is therefore required. Such a view will carefully distinguish between the various types and grades of integration and will point out the kinds of unity that characterize human groups and the kinds that do not. In the light of this analysis, it will be possible to indicate the fundamental errors of extreme individualists such as Hobbes and extreme collectivists such as Hegel. This alternative view I shall call the theory of integrative levels.

In the first place, this theory points out that unity permits of infinite degrees. If by unity we mean, as I shall mean, the integration of parts within a whole, the unity may be very slight or very intense. Any quality can thus vary from little to great. For example, there may be a very faint degree of light, so faint as to be scarcely distinguishable from total darkness; or there may be a brilliant intensity of light, blinding in its terrific luminosity. In between these two extremes are infinite gradations of intensity from least to greatest. Similarly, there may be a very slight degree of unity, so slight that one may hesitate to say that the parts are joined together at all; and at the opposite extreme, there may be a very intense and tight coherence. In between these extremes, there are again infinite gradations, and any given group may be low or intermediate or high on the scale. The mere fact that a group is a group indicates very little concerning the degree of its integration.

In the second place, it is important to remember that there are different kinds of integration. The integration that an organism or a mind exhibits is not the only kind, and it may not be the kind that a group or society exhibits. Let us now consider different kinds of unity, ranged in a scale of intensity. As we consider these kinds, we should remember that they are not mutually exclusive, and that the intenser kinds of unity may include the less intense. Moreover, within each kind there are infinite gradations in degree of integration, so that the lowest degree of one kind may be no more intense than the highest degree of the kind immediately preceding.

Mere Adjacency. Things may form a group in the sense that they are juxtaposed in time and space. A pile of miscellaneous rubbish forms a group in this sense: there is no real connection between the objects except that they are heaped together. A merely accidental and heterogeneous collection of individuals, indifferent to one another, is a human group of this type. A number of people, for example, may happen to be passing each other on some busy streetcorner. In such a casual group, each person is going his own separate way and is very slightly affected by the other people in the immediate vicinity. Such a group has a very low level of integration, so low that we hesitate to call it a group at all: it is a mere aggregate or collection.

External Association. Things may be grouped together, not because they are related to each other, but because they are all related to something outside the group. The pieces of driftwood that litter a beach, for example, are grouped together, not because they are interrelated, but because they have all been cast there by the ocean tide. Similarly human beings may be held together, not because they have any concern for each other, but because they are all related to some common external factor. For example, the crowd that sits in a moving picture theater forms a group of this sort. With the exception of friends or lovers in the audience, who go less to see the show than to enjoy each other's company, the bulk of the onlookers ordinarily do not know or care about one another; but they are held together because they are all interested in a common object, the story on the screen.

Mechanical Interdependence. At this level of integration, there is no mere relation to an external factor but a functional interaction of parts. In an engine, for example, cylinder, piston, connecting rod, flywheel, and shaft act upon one another and "cooperate." Part acts and reacts upon part, directly or through some transmission mechanism. Now such a part is, in one sense, *more,* and in another sense, *less* of an "individual" than is the part of an organism. It is more of an individual in the sense that it is more independent: it has a certain determinate shape and composition that remains relatively unaltered when it is added to or subtracted from the machine. A gear, for example, can be taken out of a machine, and it still remains substantially the same gear; but a foot cannot be cut off a human body without ceasing to be a foot. On the other hand, the gear is less of an "individual" in the sense that it is standardized and replaceable, whereas the foot is unique and irreplaceable. It is characteristic of a machine part that it is made in accordance with exact specifications; it can usually be ordered by number from a catalogue; and it can be replaced by another part made according to the same precise specifications.

Human beings are never exactly like the parts of a machine, but they sometimes function mechanically. For example, a Roman galley slave pulling his oar in monotonous rhythm, was picked and trained essentially for this machine-like function and quickly replaced by another galley slave if he failed to perform according to specifications. Likewise acting mechanically are the modern workers on an assembly line, each performing some minute, monotonous task over and over again, day in and day out. From the standpoint of the "scientific manager," the inner life of the worker does not matter: all that matters is his external function and his externalistic relations to the other workers on the assembly line. If he breaks down, he is quickly replaced by another human robot who carries out the same monotonous motion in the same precise manner.

Essential or "Organic" Interdependence. At this level, there is not only an interaction of parts, but the essential characteristics of the parts are modified by the interaction. The relations between the parts, therefore, are not external but internal. A relation is internal if it substantially influences the nature of the things which it relates. Such internal or essential relations, as opposed to merely external and inessential, are often called "organic"; but it should be remembered that individuals can be thus related without constituting an "organism" in the literal sense of that term.

Everything is probably related to everything else—every time you nod your head, for example, you affect every star in the universe, but the relation, in this case, is so slight that it is negligible. Human relations, however, are very often not of this superficial character. A person is a son, a brother, a husband, a friend, an enemy, a citizen, a trade unionist, a church member, etc.; and stripped of all such relations, he would not be a human being. Some of these relations are so essential to his personality that they can properly be called internal. You do not greatly change a bolt when you destroy the machine from which you have removed it, but you do profoundly change a person when you destroy his family.

Existential Interdependence. At this level, the parts depend upon one another not only for their functions but for their very existence. The parts of an organism are usually related in this manner. (Alexis Carrel managed to keep a chicken's heart beating for several years after he removed it from the chicken's body, but this feat is the exception.) Existential interdependence, however, is not limited to the parts of an organism. A very young animal, for example, may depend for its life upon its relations to its family, but this does not mean that it is not a separate organism. Or again, a soldier may lose his life if he becomes separated from his regiment, but this does not indicate that the regiment is a single organism. Generally, if the members of a group are existentially dependent upon one another, there is a fairly high degree of integration.

Configurational Unity. The term *configuration* is now commonly used to designate a unity in which the parts are not merely interdependent but are determined by the character of the whole. We owe particularly to the Gestalt psychologists the insistence that oftentimes the whole determines the existence and nature of the parts: the parts do not simply combine to make a whole, but the whole expresses itself in and through the parts. In this sense, the whole is prior to, immanent in, and more than the sum of the parts.

Any well-composed work of art is such a unity. Some of the details may seem to precede the whole, but the total effect determines whether they will have to be altered or omitted. Every inconsistent detail, as for example an inappropriate chord in a musical composition, cries out for change or elimination; if it is finally included, the structure of the composition must be re-adjusted so as to achieve a consistent effect. The chord, when fitted into this new context, sounds different than it did before: it is not heard as a detached set of tones but as an integral part of the total composition. Once the total form is perfected, moreover, it has a certain relative independence of its constituents. A melody, for example, can be transposed into a different key, as from C to C sharp, even though not a single tone of the original arrangement recurs. Therefore the form, or configuration, is not simply the arithmetical sum of the constituents.

Likewise in the case of human groups, there exist more or less well-defined wholes and characteristics of wholes, and these are impressed upon the parts. The parts are therefore to be conceived as parts within the configuration of the whole. Moreover, as in the case of a melody, the parts can change and the form remain fairly constant. A national culture, for example, is such a configuration: it is the common possession of all the individuals within the nation but is relatively independent of any of them. It is a unique pattern of religion, art, language, morality, ideology, history, etc., embodied in customs, traditions, institutions, and such artifacts as books, laws and works of art. Impressed upon individuals, it pervasively molds their mentality and behavior; but it endures and develops, even though individuals come and go. "Americanism," for example, is something relatively independent of any one individual or any single generation. Moreover, no person is merely an American: he participates in other cultural configurations, perhaps in what we call Christianity. Every individual is at the focal point of various social patterns or systems of culture, each contributing to his personality.

Corporate Unity. This type of unity is "configurational" with the added characteristic that it is constituted by statute or charter granted by the state. A corporation, as an organized group whose structure is defined and sanctioned by law, can carry on enterprise, hold and manage property, distribute profits, sue and be sued in the courts. Its "life" is independent of the lives of its individual officers and members, in the sense that no single individual is responsible for its acts; it may be legally dissolved at any time or may outlast any individual. Although the most familiar type is that engaged in business enterprise, corporations may also be the vehicles for charitable activities or other cooperative non-profit functions. The corporation is an ancient institution, sanctioned under Roman law, but the modern business corporation has received its chief impetus from the industrial revolution, providing the large capital and complex administration for massive business operations. As a party to legal transactions, it may be said to possess "legal personality"; but it is not literally a person, for as the old saying goes, "it has neither a body to be kicked nor a soul to be damned." While it establishes a legally created capacity for the sharing of rights and duties, it has no moral identity apart from its members: its purposes must always be entertained by living minds, and its values realized only in the lives of individuals.

Biological Unity. A relatively intense degree of integration is achieved at the level of the biological organism. By an organism I mean a unity composed of a number of cooperative and mutually dependent parts constituted for subserving vital processes. Thus there is a single unity, the life of the whole, which is the end of its parts. It involves the organic and existential interdependence of the parts and the configurational unity of the whole. But it involves something more: the intense degree of integration that is realized in the unity of a life, though perhaps only the life of a vegetable or a very simple animal.

For reasons that I shall indicate, I do not believe that a group of human beings attains this level of integration.

Psychological Unity. A higher animal is not only organic after the manner of a vegetable or a very simple animal, but is *consciously* organized, with a core of self-identity. It has a mind that expresses itself through what it experiences and what it does. Animals probably have experiences without being aware that they have them; but a man is aware of himself as the subject of experiences; he can consider himself as himself, the same thinking being, in different times and places. He thereby attains a capacity for self-direction and self-criticism.

As I shall later contend, a group does not attain the level of integration represented by a mind. In a group, there are the minds of the individual members, but no other mind.

In the light of this theory of integrative levels, we can now expose the fundamental fallacies of both extreme individualism and extreme collectivism.

5. THE REFUTATION OF EXTREME INDIVIDUALISM

The basic fallacy of individualists such as Hobbes is that they deny that groups can be characterized in terms of any of the higher and intenser levels of integration. They represent a reductive or *leveling down* type of theory: they interpret groups in terms of mere adjacency or external association or mechanical interdependence, to the neglect or exclusion of higher types of unity.

This failure to recognize the intenser forms of integration is a necessary consequence of extreme individualism. In its very nature, this type of theory exaggerates the independence of individuals. It supposes that individuality largely excludes sociality, that each human being is self-centered and self-seeking. Anyone who, in contrast, emphasizes the intenser types of social integration is by reason of that very emphasis not an extreme individualist.

At times the individualist may speak as if human groups are mere fortuitous collections, the members of which are connected by nothing more than temporal and spatial adjacency. Although this interpretation may more or less apply to very casual groups, it is obviously inadequate when applied to organized groups. Consequently the individualist must rely upon some other kind of explanation.

This he can find in the second type of integration, which I have called external association. In this type of group, as the reader will recall, the members are no more than superficially related to one another, but they are nevertheless bound together by their common relation to some external factor. For example, according to the philosophy of Leibniz, all finite beings have no direct relations to one another but nevertheless fit together into a harmonious whole, because they are all related to a common external factor, God, who predetermines each of them to be in harmony with every other. Somewhat similarly, Hobbes maintains that human beings within a state are all self-centered egoists, without any deep intrinsic relations to one another, but they manage to live together with a fair degree of peace and security, because they are all related to a common external factor, the absolute sovereign set up by the "Social Contract." Other individualists fall back upon similar mechanisms to hold together their separate human atoms. Turgot and Quesnay, for example, speak of the "laws of nature" that promote and maintain a harmony of egoisms; Adam Smith writes about the "invisible hand" of economic competition that reconciles the gain of each self-seeking individual with the gain of every other; Jeremy Bentham discusses the system of "sanctions," of rewards and punishments, that induces unmitigated egoists to work together harmoniously; and Friedrich Hayek maintains that the separate efforts of individuals are harmoniously coordinated by the self-equilibrating mechanism of the market system. In each instance, there is some common external force or agency that brings about an artificial harmony among self-centered individuals.

Extreme individualists also tend to interpret human relations in terms of mechanical interdependence. They admit that human beings functionally interact, but they think that the interaction is like that of the parts of a machine, which are not essentially altered by their interconnections. This view has traditionally been expressed by the myth of the "state of nature": individuals are said to have inherited their fundamental characteristics from a primeval, precivilized state, and these characteristics are thought to be constants throughout the social process. Each human being, like a hard impenetrable atom or a cog in a machine, remains fundamentally the same whether he is fitted into or is removed from a particular social mechanism. This theory of the obdurate natural man—as promulgated in the works of Hobbes, Locke, Paine, Godwin, and the earlier books of Rousseau—had a profound influence upon the development of individualistic liberalism.

In economic theory of this type, the mechanistic nature of the doctrine becomes more obvious. Again there is a myth—the myth of the "economic man," an abstract, artificial, dehumanized individual, concerned solely with economic gain and controlled by impersonal economic forces. From this point of view, human beings are judged all alike; their individual emotions and aspirations do not matter; the difference between them is reduced to a merely quantitative difference, expressed in terms of their cash value. As Hobbes unsentimentally noted:

The *value,* or worth of a man, is as of all other things, his price; that is to say, so much as would be given for the use of his power; and therefore is not absolute; but a thing dependent on the need and judgment of another.[24]

From this standpoint, workers are commodities, and value is determined by the impersonal mechanism of the market.

Like the economic theories to which it has been linked, modern industry has been individualistic, externalistic, and mechanical in its mode of organization. Technology, with its tendency toward mechanical "rationalization," and finance capitalism, with its development of credits and abstract expense accounting, have too often depersonalized human relationships. The tendency of capitalism has been to exalt acquisitive above creative and sympathetic impulses, and to develop a narrow self-seeking, a hard, grasping egoism. The impersonal cash nexus has tended to replace the intimate human community. Here we discover the same tendency as in mechanistic philosophy, to dissolve wholes into self-enclosed monads, into "atoms" related externally without any deep internal connections. Extreme individualism has reflected these tendencies and has thus expressed some of the fundamental aspects of modern life. If it recognizes any higher types of integration, such as intimate communities, it does so only inadequately and grudgingly.

Now it must be said emphatically that this is an inadequate interpretation of human nature. Men and women are not mechanisms nor parts of mechanisms. As William Ellery Channing, one of the great New England preachers of the early nineteenth century, declared:

I do not look on a human being as a machine, made to be kept in action by a foreign force, to accomplish an unvarying succession of motions, to do a fixed amount of work, and then to fall to pieces at death.[25]

Workers must not be conceived *abstractly* as *machines* or commodities but concretely as persons, who bleed when they are pricked, who dream and love and suffer. Human beings must not be regarded as social atoms, as isolated, egocentric individuals, each going his solitary way, but as members one of another. Individuals they are, and as individuals they are ends in themselves; but they are effective and happy only in relation to one another and to the social wholes of which they are members. The notion that an individual is complete in himself, and that the relationship between individuals is necessarily external—the notion of Hobbes and Bentham—is inadequate and erroneous.

When these philosophers wrote, the implications of science seemed to bear out their extreme individualism, but this is not the case in recent decades. As far back as the Victorian period, the discovery by Maxwell and Faraday of the electromagnetic field represented a fundamental departure from the older physical notions of relatively unchanging particles and external relations. Subsequently, physical scientists have built up a new type of "field physics" in which atoms or electrons are conceived to be interdependent events functionally dependent upon their spatio-temporal environment. Similarly, in biology there has been an increasing emphasis upon part-whole relationships, upon the idea of the organism, in which the whole in a sense is prior to and determines its parts; the idea of the ecological community, in which organisms socially live and function; and the idea of emergent stages of evolution, in which there are real creative syntheses and not mere additive resultants. Likewise, social science and psychology no longer employ the notion of a self-enclosed and self-sufficient individual. There has been an increasing tendency (represented by many besides the Gestalt psychologists and the cultural anthropologists) to think in terms of organic wholes and structural relationships. This increasing recognition of the interrelational nature of things constitute a profound revolution in human thought which has been extended to almost every field of human investigation. Extreme individualism has thus been undermined by the advances of modern science. A positivist may protest that the content of science has no bearing on moral questions, but inevitably the mental climate of the age influences ethical theory. At the level of psychology and social science, moreover, the facts of interpersonal relatedness are by no means irrelevant to moral discourse. An ethics out of touch with reality has little to be said for it.

As long as antiquated individualistic notions prevail, it is impossible to explain why human beings continually gather in societies. The extreme individualist tries to explain the formation of groups by the self-interest of each member. The group, he says, is only an artificial contrivance created by a "social contract" or similar agreement among self-seeking individuals. Now some groups, of course, are formed in this way; but other groups, and indeed most groups, arise out of the fundamental and essential nature of man as a social being. Men often are born into a group—into a family, tribe, clan, nation, etc.—and even when they join a group voluntarily, they may be impelled by their social nature and not simply by individual selfish calculations. Sociality is an essential human trait, and if it were not for man's social propensities, it would be impossible to account for that degree of trust and cooperation necessary for the formation and functioning of most human groups.

We are here touching upon the very essence of the human. Aristotle defined the essential nature of man as rationality; but more profoundly human, because more integral to man's whole nature, is the capacity for self-transcendence, of which reason is but a part. In his challenging book, *Man the Measure*, Erich Kahler gives the name of "spirit" to this faculty of going beyond oneself. It is the faculty, he says, of "detaching and discerning a definite non-self from a definite self," and of identifying oneself, in sympathy and understanding, with the non-self.

Thus spirit is not only the faculty of discerning and detaching but, at the same time, of establishing a relation between a self and a non-self, the faculty of overstepping the limits of the self. It is discerning and uniting in one. It is the very essence of a being concerned with more than itself. A person leads a spiritual life in so far as he rises above his personal "practical" interests, as he is able to detach himself from his own and conceived self and to grow more and more objective, to integrate himself in a higher, comprehending objective.[26]

Absorbed in himself and in the present moment, a man is just a transient flash of consciousness; but in so far as he transcends himself, he escapes from the petty compass of his own momentary identity and lives in the ample world that is brought into view by love, imagination, knowledge, and foresight. The *human* world, above all, emancipates the spirit. As David Hume wrote:

> Let all the powers and elements of nature conspire to serve and obey one man: Let the sun rise and set at his command: The sea and rivers roll as he pleases, and the earth furnish spontaneously whatever may be useful or agreeable to him: He will still be miserable, till you give him some one person at least, with whom he may share his happiness, and whose esteem and friendship he may enjoy.[27]

Jailers have learned how important man is to his fellow man—they know that one of the most exquisite forms of torture is prolonged solitary confinement.

The effect of the inability to make sympathetic contact with other people is illustrated by an interesting type of neurosis which psychologists call "depersonalization." A neurotic of this type finds it very difficult to experience other human beings as real personalities; they seem to be mere automatons, toward whom he can feel no personal warmth. Moreover, he has the odd impression that his own personality has become purely mechanical. He seems to himself a puppet, a soulless automaton; he cannot find or acknowledge his own personality; there is no "real me." All things, including his own nature, seem to belong to the kind of depersonalized world so profoundly depicted in the novels of Franz Kafka. This type of mental illness illustrates the fact that no one can be fully a person unless he acknowledges others as persons. Full personality requires self-transcendence, appreciative awareness of other things and especially other people.

Morality, too, requires that the individual should overstep the boundaries of self. If all of us were sealed within ourselves we could not comprehend or respond to the moral injunction: "Be unselfish." If we did not feel the ties that bind us to others, we would not feel a sense of social obligation. The essential reason that a person feels obligated to others is that he is part of a larger whole. He is committed by his social nature to moral obligation, and he cannot deny the claims of social morality without denying an essential part of himself and without violating the society of which he is a constituent. Deep down in his mind he realizes the truth of Donne's oft-quoted words:

> No man is an Iland, intire to it selfe; every man is a peece of the Continent, a part of the maine. . . . any mans death diminishes me, because I am involved in Mankinde; and therefore never send to know for whom the bell tolls; It tolls for thee.[28]

As I have tried to make clear in Chapter VII, the sense of duty is the internalized "voice" of society exercising a "pull" or inner compulsion upon the individual. This explains why it is felt as a kind of external influence, yet as also internal. Some such theory must be accepted if we are to explain moral obligation. It cannot be explained upon the basis of extreme individualism. Jeremy Bentham, who denied that society was much more than a fiction and conceived of individuals as entirely egoistic, drew the correct implication from his own doctrine when he declared that *ought*, if it has any meaning at all, ought to be expunged from the dictionary.

Our criticism of extreme individualism amounts to this: it tries to explain social life in terms of only the relatively low forms of integration—mere adjacency or external association or mechanical interdependence—and in so doing it fails adequately to explain why men congregate in societies, why men are so necessary to one another, and why men are moral.

6. THE REFUTATION OF EXTREME COLLECTIVISM

Whereas extreme individualism is a *leveling down* theory, extreme collectivism is a *leveling up* theory. Just as the individualist insists upon interpreting groups in terms of the low levels of integration, so the extreme collectivist insists upon interpreting groups in terms of the high levels of integration. Some of these levels—organic interdependence, existential interdependence, configurational unity, and legal or corporate "personality"—really do apply to human groups. In emphasizing this fact, collectivists have corrected the errors of extreme individualism. But other more intense forms of integration—the forms that characterize a living body and a mind—do not apply to groups; and extreme collectivism commits a fundamental mistake in supposing that they do apply.

To discover the nature of this error, let us consider the family, which is a relatively simple group and therefore less difficult to analyze than the state, nation, or race. Each member of the family is an organism, mind, or personality, but this does not mean that the family is an organism, mind, or personality. A group, in many respects, does not have the same characteristics as its members; a pile of bricks, for example, may be six feet high but no individual brick is that high. Likewise a human group is made up of organisms, but this does not make *it* an organism.

The term "organic" is so loaded with biological connotations that we must use it with extreme caution in applying it to a human social organization. A coherent society is not literally a biological organism, but it is an integrative structure the members of which are bound together by social relations which determine their essential personalities. Outside of these relations, they would be very different, if indeed they could even exist. Such internal and essential relations, as opposed to merely external and inessential, are often called "organic," and there can be no valid objection to the term if the reader clearly understands that groups without being literally organisms may have a touch of the organic, some more and some less.

In this limited sense, there are "organic" relations among the members of a family. A husband, a wife, a son, or a daughter is affected through and through by family relations and would be a very different being apart from them. These relations may involve not merely functional but existential dependence or interdependence. The children, at least, would not have come into existence apart from the family relations, and while they are still infants, they might not continue to exist if separated from the family. But there may be organic or existential relations between the members of a group, without the group being an organism. The father is an organism, the mother is an organism, and each of the children is an organism, and there are organic interrelations between them; but there is no group organism over and above the individual, or as the result of any fusion of individuals. To speak of a "family organism" is to use a metaphor.

It is also true that the family has a kind of configurational unity: it is not a mere sum of individuals but a synthesis, a *Gestalt,* a unique form or pattern. Every well-knit family is bound together by common goods, common memories, common hopes, common ideals, and common deeds. These coalesce into an *esprit de corps,* a kind of spirit that impresses itself upon each of its members and that gives a spiritual significance to the home. In these respects, the family has some sort of corporate character. The social organicists, such as Hegel, have performed a real service in emphasizing this fact, but they have not correctly analyzed what it means.

It does not imply that there is literally a family mind or a family personality. Even a work of art, as we have pointed out, has a *Gestalt* or configuration; but this does not imply that it has a life, a mind, or a personality. Of course, in the case of the family the constituents are minds or personalities, but this does not mean that the *configuration* of the family is a personality or a mind. The extreme collectivists have muddled their heads into supposing that the organization of individuals is itself an individual, that the organization of minds is itself a mind, that the organization of personalities is itself a personality. Admitting that the organization has configurational characteristics, we must still reject the mystical theory that there are group minds and collective souls, equipped with interests of their own.

Nothing can literally have an interest except an individual. Within the family, each member has interests, and these interests are affected by the family *esprit de corps* and by the relations between the members of the family. But the interests of the family are nevertheless the interests of the father, the mother, and each of the children—these and nothing more. There are no family interests over and above these individual interests. And what is true of a group of a few members is also true of a group of many members, even a vast nation. It too has no interests that are not the interests of its members, because it has no mind apart from the minds of its members.

Certain philosophers, such as Emile Durkheim, have argued that it is impossible to explain the moral and religious life without supposing that society is an actual organism or group mind. They argue that religious and moral experience represents the pull of society upon the individual, and that society must be a real agency with objectives of its own to exert such a pull. Now I have contended that neither morality nor religion can be adequately explained in terms of extreme individualism, but I think that we need not fly to the opposite extreme and assume that society is an organism or a mind. The moral and religious pull of society upon the individual can be explained if we recognize that individuals are internally related to one another, that they can feel and enjoy and celebrate these intimate relations, and that society has a pattern of organization, a real configuration, that deeply impresses itself upon its members. All this can be recognized without assuming that society is literally a superorganism or group mind; and to make the assumption is to "multiply entities beyond necessity."

If a group cannot literally have a mind, it cannot be said to have intrinsic value. As we have said, there can be no intrinsic value where there is no interest, and there can be no interest where there is no mind. It follows that the locus of intrinsic value is the individual because the individual, after all, is the seat of interest. The group exists for the sake of the individual, and not the individual for the sake of the group. The welfare of human beings, therefore, is what counts, and not the "good" of the state, the nation, the race, or the "working class."

I do not deny that a group may be an *object* of interest, and in that sense the cause or occasion of intrinsic goodness. It is a familiar fact that a group, whether large or small, may be an object of human affection. We may love individuals not only for themselves but as members and representatives of a group; and, what is more to the point, we can love the group as having characteristics not to be found in the individuals taken severally. Affection toward the group, such as patriotism, can extend to its traditions, institutions, and symbols. As objects of intrinsic satisfaction some groups rank among the very highest of human values. I am, therefore, not denying for an instant that they are *objects* of value, but I am denying that they are *subjects* of value. No group, as distinguished from its members, can have an interest; and since I maintain that the seat of intrinsic value is interest, I deny that groups have intrinsic value. My position is different from that of Perry, because he speaks of intrinsic value as the object of interest. A group is often an object of interest, and hence on Perry's definition, it would possess intrinsic value, not independently of individuals, of course, but relative to the interest of individuals. My own view is different: I have argued that intrinsic value resides in interest, primarily in the fulfillment of interest, rather than in the *object* of interest; and hence, as I see it, no group can have intrinsic value.

It is of course true that a group has intrinsic value, if we mean that its *members* have; but it is false to say that a group as such has intrinsic value. It is also true that the interests of the group should take precedence over the interests of the individual, if we mean that the interests of the *many* individuals in a group should take precedence over the interests of *one* individual; but this is because they are many *individuals* as opposed to one. The group as such is not intrinsically higher than the individual; it has no intrinsic value at all except within the *individuals* that comprise it. Hence the tendency to worship the state or the race or any other group, large or small, is a form of idolatry. As the philosopher McTaggart has declared:

> A religion which fastens itself on a means has not risen above fetish-worship. Compared with worship of the state, zoolatry is rational and dignified. A bull or a crocodile may not have great intrinsic value, but it has some, for it is a conscious being. The state has none. It would be as reasonable to worship a sewage pipe, which also has considerable value as a means.[29]

The state may have a vast amount of instrumental and terminal value, but its value is that of a means and not that of an end.

This conclusion is worth emphasizing, because the contrary view has had great influence. The notion that a race or a class or a state or a society can have intrinsic value is one of the great social myths—a myth that has had a terrific impact upon mankind. We need only remember that it is the myth of Mussolini and Hitler to realize what a stupendous role it has played. More or less unconsciously, it appears to have been the myth of a good many communists. But all of us, even in a democracy, tend to personify groups: we think of the United States as Uncle Sam, of England as John Bull, of Russia as a bewhiskered Bolshevik. Cartoons and political speeches reinforce these images, interpreting races or nations or classes as real personalities, loving, hating, quarreling, fighting, winning, and losing. It is altogether too easy to forget that these personifications are fictitious—that they inevitably distort and misrepresent. The ingrained human propensity to think in terms of such images is one of the principal causes of war, threatening the destruction of the whole civilized world. It is high time that we think cooly and clearly about these matters. A group or organization is not an organism, not a mind, not a person—it is a structure of individuals, playing certain roles and tied together by communication. It has no ultimate value except in the individuals that comprise it.

In rejecting the myth of extreme collectivism, we must not embrace its opposite—the myth of extreme individualism—the myth of the isolated, egocentric, self-sufficient man. The real individual is a profoundly social being: it is he alone, and not his mythical counterpart, that is the locus of value. It is only a false individualism and a false collectivism that are pitted against one another. Individuality and sociality, instead of being incompatible, are necessary to one another. The more men are truly united the more they respect each other's differences. People who are in love treasure each other's individualities. Human beings should be both more differentiated and more united than they are now; and the unity that is the legitimate goal of human aspiration is the unity of difference. This sort of relatedness I call "community," and the main purpose of the remaining chapters is to explore its meaning and its relation to communism and democracy.

NOTES

1. Ralph Barton Perry, *Puritanism and Democracy*. New York: Vanguard Press, Inc., 1944, p. 441.
2. Jean Jacques Rousseau, *Discourse on Political Economy*, in *The Social Contract and Other Discourses*, translated by G. D. H. Cole. Everyman's Library. London: J. M. Dent & Sons, Ltd. New York: E. P. Dutton & Co., Inc., 1913, p. 253. Reprinted by permission of the publishers.
3. Rousseau, *Social Contract*, in *ibid.*, p. 25.
4. Isaac Newton, *Opticks*, 2nd ed. London: W. and J. Innys, 1717, p. 375.
5. Thomas Hobbes, *Leviathan*, in *The English Works of Thomas Hobbes*. London: Bohn, 1839, III, pp. 29–30.
6. Hobbes, *Human Nature*, in *ibid.*, IV, p. 53.
7. Hobbes, *Leviathan*, *op. cit.*, p. 111.
8. *Ibid.*, pp. 85–86.
9. *Ibid.*, p. 113.
10. *Ibid.*, p. 154.
11. *Ibid.*, p. 120.
12. *Ibid.*, p. 253.
13. Ernst Cassirer, *The Myth of the State*. New Haven: Yale University Press, 1946, pp. 248–249.
14. *Cf.* J. N. Findlay, *Hegel*. London: George Allen and Unwin Ltd., 1958, especially Chapter One. Hegel is often misinterpreted and I have misconstrued his theory in the past.
15. Hegel, *The Philosophy of Right*, section 158 note. Quoted by Hugh A. Reyburn, *The Ethical Theory of Hegel*. London and New York: Oxford University Press, 1921, p. 208.

16. Hegel, *The Philosophy of Right*, translated by S. W. Dyde. London: G. Bell & Sons, Ltd., 1896, p. 240.
17. Hegel, *The Philosophy of History*, translated by J. Sibree. New York: P. F. Collier, Inc., 1900, p. 70.
18. *Ibid.*, pp. 102–103.
19. J. Macbride Sterrett, *The Ethics of Hegel*. Boston: Ginn & Company, 1893, pp. 189, 245.
20. Hegel, *The Philosophy of Right*, translated by J. Loewenberg, in *Hegel Selections*. New York: Charles Scribner's Sons, 1929, pp. 446–447.
21. J. Macbride Sterrett, *op. cit.*, p. 189.
22. Hegel, *Encyclopaedia of the Philosophical Sciences*, section 541. Quoted by Ernst Cassirer, *op. cit.*, p. 276.
23. Hegel, *The Philosophy of Right*, translated by S. W. Dyde, *op. cit.*, p. 264.
24. Hobbes, *Leviathan*, *op. cit.*, p. 76.
25. William Ellery Channing, "Self Culture," lecture delivered at Boston, September 1838. Quoted in S. Giedion, *Mechanization Takes Command*. London and New York: Oxford University Press, 1948, p. 127.
26. Erich Kahler, *Man the Measure*. New York: Pantheon Books, Inc., 1943, pp. 11–12.
27. David Hume, *A Treatise of Human Nature*. London and New York: Oxford University Press, 1896, p. 363.
28. John Donne, *Complete Poetry and Selected Prose*. New York: Random House, Inc., 1936, p. 538.
29. J. M. E. McTaggart, *Philosophical Studies*. London: Edward Arnold & Company, 1934, p. 109.

CHAPTER XII

The communist ideal

I. MARX AS MAN AND THINKER

In the preceding chapter, I criticized the extremes of ethical individualism and ethical collectivism. I shall now continue the analysis of the issues thus raised, turning to Marxism as the most potent expression of the communist ideal. Since the present book is devoted to ethics, I shall begin with the ethical argument and stress its implications throughout, including the humanistic concepts most evident in Marx's early writings (1844–1845). The question whether the later works conflict with these earlier doctrines will be carefully examined.

The life of Marx may throw light upon his doctrines. Born in Trier, Prussia, in 1818, Karl Marx came from an upper middle-class Jewish family, but his father, a lawyer, abandoned the Jewish faith and joined the state church of Prussia. Karl was sent to the Universities of Bonn and Berlin, where he came into contact with the Young Hegelians, a group of left-wing philosophers and critics who deeply influenced him. After recieving the degree of Doctor of Philosophy, he found that his political ideals were too radical to permit an academic career. In 1842 he entered politics as editor of an opposition newspaper, the *Rheinische Zeitung*, which was soon suppressed by the Prussian government. Accompanied by his aristocratic young wife, Jenny von Westphalen, he chose to live in Paris and Brussels until he was exiled from Belgium in 1848. He then went to Cologne, where he founded a newspaper and participated in the unsuccessful Revolution of 1848–1849. Seeking refuge from the ensuing political reaction, he took his family to London, where they established a permanent home. It was there that he unremittingly toiled as a socialist writer and organizer for the remainder of his lifetime, often collaborating with Friedrich Engels, a socialist of German extraction who worked in the family business of Ermen and Engels, cotton spinners in Manchester. In 1864, the two friends helped to organize the International Workingmen's Association, known later as the First International; and they took an active part in its affairs until it was dissolved in 1872.

During years of laborious research and writing, Marx rarely spared time from his tremendous labors to straighten and air-out his smoke-filled study. With only a meager income as a correspondent for the *New York Daily Tribune*, he could not keep himself and his family supplied with necessities, such as shoes and postage stamps. To the miseries of poverty were added the deaths of three of his children—all because the family could not afford adequate food or medicine. In his later life and until his death in 1883, he himself suffered from a disease of the liver, inflammation of the eyes, hemorrhoids and carbuncles. It is perhaps no wonder that he was a man of great anger—there is holy anger and there is unholy anger, and Marx had his full share of both. But no one can deny the great scope of his learning and the fearless and devoted character of his life.

His strength as a moral philosopher lay in his synthesis of two great traditions. The older tradition was that of the Enlightenment, with its faith in reason and freedom and progress. As a prophet of human emancipation, Marx was a successor of Condorcet, Lessing, and the other great figures of the Enlightenment. But he also participated in a very different tradition—that of "existentialism." The sources of existentialist thought can be traced in the writings of Marx's predecessors, Hegel and Schelling, and his contemporaries, Stirner, Feuerbach, and Kierkegaard. To this existentialist current of thought belong his early writings. They express an idea apparently the very opposite of that of the Enlightenment—the sense that modern existence has become impoverished and rootless—that men are cut off from whatever gives meaning to their lives. In Marx's works, this idea of "alienation" runs alongside of, and in counterpoint to, the idea of progress. His ethical philosophy was mainly an attempt to delineate and reconcile these two powerful ideas. Because they are so different, even antagonistic, the reconciliation was no mean feat.

In addition he wove in other threads, derived from the Utopian socialists, St. Simon, Fourier, and Owen; the British economists, particularly Smith and Ricardo; and the German philosophers, especially Hegel and Feuerbach. Finally he drew from radical sources and his own temperament the proto-totalitarian tendencies that contributed unfortunately to the communist tradition. The result was a subtle and intricate and somewhat inconsistent body of thought. I shall try to expound it as faithfully as possible, reserving criticism for the latter part of the chapter.

2. ALIENATION

Marx's ethical theory sprang from a profound realization of the troubles of civilized man. He was deeply impressed by the concept of spiritual estrangement articulated at length in Hegel's *Phenomenology of Mind* and other works. Human beings, according to this concept, are alienated from themselves and their fellows and enslaved by their own superstitions and unfree institutions. The very things they have created—money and machines, laws and customs, institutions and culture—appear as forces arrayed against them. In a state of alienation, declared Hegel, "there is no living union between the individual and his world; the object, severed from the subject, is dead; and the only love possible is a sort of relationship between the living subject and the dead objects by which he is surrounded."[1] The essence of alienation is this separation between the subject and the object: man finds himself set off from a world that is adverse and alien to his impulses and desires. The basic problem of mankind, Hegel maintained, is to end this alienation and restore the unity of life. The "subjective" sphere of thought must be harmonized with the "objective" sphere of laws, institutions, industry, and culture. This harmonization requires both the transformation of the inner life and the reconstruction of the environment.

Among the "Young Hegelians," with whom Marx initially associated, alienation was interpreted broadly as the loss of man's essential humanity, the deprivation of a full life, of justice, freedom, and self-realization. But in Prussia, where the censorship prevented a frontal attack upon the state and the church was a mainstay of the established order, the more radical Hegelians emphasized religious rather than political alienation. Typical of this emphasis was the work of Ludwig Feuerbach, who influenced Marx more than anyone else in this group.

Feuerbach maintained that traditional religion is based upon a reification of man's own needs and powers. The characteristics attributed to the gods are, in fact, the ideals and capacities of man so disguised and projected as to seem supernatural forces arrayed against him. "The more empty life becomes," declared Feuerbach, "the richer and fuller becomes God. The impoverishing of the real world and the enriching of the Deity is one and the same act. Only an impoverished humanity has a rich God." The object of worship is a fantastic projection of the human essence, but the real human essence can be found only in the unity of man with man. "Only a life in fellowship is truly life, satisfying in itself."[2] This "true" life was interpreted as not so much intellectual as sensuous and passionate. "Love is passion," declared Feuerbach, "and only passion is the mark of existence. . . . Only what is an object of passion—really is."[3]

Although Marx was deeply indebted to Hegel and Feuerbach, he differed significantly from both. Hegelian philosophy, he maintained, is false in its excessive abstractness, and hence it, too, belongs to man's estrangement. The return of man to himself as human, the overcoming of alienation, brings into play the whole man, with his senses and his emotions. This emphasis upon "man in all the plenitude of his being" distinguished Marx from Hegel and allied him with Feuerbach. But Marx derided Feuerbach's religion of love as a sentimental notion, without realistic basis and institutional embodiment. He also rejected Feuerbach's emphasis upon philosophical anthropology and returned to Hegel's stress upon history. In his radical new emphasis upon the economic causes of alienation, he differed from both Hegel and Feuerbach.

He distinguished three interdependent forms of alienation: (1) *objectification*—the alienation of the thing; (2) *dehumanization*—the alienation of the self; (3) *species-alienation*—the alienation of man from his own kind.

Objectification. Human beings cease to own, recognize, and control the things of their own making. "The object produced by labor, its product, now stands opposed to it as an alien being, as a power independent of the producer."[4] Workers produce commodities, give them economic value as the result of their labor; but the commodities, once produced, have a "will" of their own and act as hostile powers. They appear as independent beings endowed with life, and enter into relations both with one another and the human race. Declared Marx:

> The worker is related to the product of his labor as to an alien object. . . . The more the worker expends himself in work the more powerful becomes the world of objects which he creates in face of himself, the poorer he becomes in his inner life and the less he belongs to himself. . . . The worker puts his life into the object, and his life then belongs no longer to himself but to the object.[5]

This "alienation of the thing" is intensified by the superstitious attitude which men assume toward economic commodities. The values of these commodities, which they possess only through their relations to persons, seem to be intrinsic properties exchanging on the market in terms of their fixed objective worth. A diamond, for example, seems *intrinsically* very valuable, whereas, according to Marx's "labor theory of value," it would be as cheap as coal if it should require as little labor to obtain it. Hence the human core and content of exchange values becomes depersonalized and, in consequence, heartless. Both the worker and his employer deal with their fellow men through the impersonal mechanism of the market, where prices appear to be the substantial realities and human beings merely their instruments. These economic quantities "vary continually, independently of the will, foresight and action of the producers. To them, their own social action takes the form of the action of objects, which rule the producers instead of being ruled by them."[6]

This depersonalization of human relations is brought to its highest pitch by a money economy. Apart from money, exchange is in terms of human qualities.

> Let us assume *man* to be *man,* and his relation to the world to be a human one. Then love can only be exchanged for love, trust for trust, etc. If you wish to enjoy art you must be an artistically cultivated person; if you wish to influence other people you must be a person who really has a stimulating and encouraging effect upon others.[7]

What makes things humanly precious are their concrete and various qualities, and to use and appreciate them we must possess corresponding human traits. But in a money economy, concrete use-values are reduced to abstract exchange-values. The worth of a thing is its price, and all prices are expressed in terms of a common denominator, money. Exchange is governed not by the fitness of a product to fulfill anyone's actual needs, but by its abstract commodity-value. To make money, advertisers and salesmen will stimulate any sort of appetite, however depraved, unnatural, or imaginary it may be.

No eunuch flatters his tyrant more shamefully or seeks by more infamous means to stimulate his jaded appetite, in order to gain some favor, than does the eunuch of industry, the entrepreneur, in order to acquire a few silver coins or to charm the gold from the purse of his dearly beloved neighbor.[8]

In such a money-ridden civilization, the individuality of persons and uniqueness of things are alike negated. By reducing all things to a common measure, and by giving inordinate power to the wealthy, money produces a "universal confusion and inversion of things."

What I am and can do is . . . not at all determined by my individuality. I am ugly, but I can buy the most beautiful woman for myself. Consequently, I am not ugly, for the effect of ugliness, its power to repel, is annulled by money. As an individual I am lame, but money provides me with twenty-four legs. Therefore, I am not lame. I am a detestable, dishonorable, unscrupulous and stupid man but money is honored and so also is its possessor. Money is the highest good, and so its possessor is good.[9]

The rule of money, in short, means the tyranny of impersonal forces. There is a basic failure to distinguish things and people; the proper relation between them is inverted. What rightly belongs to the world of people is regarded as if it belonged to the world of things. Human life is treated as other than it is, as nonhuman, and things are no longer subordinated to human uses. Consequently, the products of man's work confront him as hostile, independent forces. In the words of Emerson:

> Things are in the saddle,
> And ride mankind.

Men become enslaved to machines and pecuniary values, and things take on life and dominate people.

Even in primitive life, man stands in an alienated relation to his environment, but in this case it is not so much the man-made environment but wild nature that "appears . . . as a completely alien, all-powerful and unassailable force, with which men's relations are purely animal and by which they are overawed like beasts."[10] In *The Economic and Philosophical Manuscripts,* Marx indicated that alienation toward nature is also a characteristic of modern man. When human beings are dehumanized in the economic process, the effect is to impoverish man's perceptions, and to set him at odds with the whole outer world of sense experience.

Marx primarily emphasized the alienated relation of industrial man toward things of his own making. This alienation is accentuated when the productive forces expand much more rapidly than the corresponding social controls. The economic and political system, thrown out of balance, then begins to run riot, driving men into and out of employment, dragging them through cycles of inflation and depression, casting them into the black hell of war. Nobody intends, plans, or organizes these developments. Consequences quite other than those intended result from "the innumerable intersecting forces."

This process of alienation has reached a fierce crescendo in our own age, when nothing could more drastically prove "to what extent things and circumstances of our own making have become our masters" than two World Wars and the nuclear arms race.[11] Although Marx could not have foreseen these events, he did envisage the tragic paradox of our age:

> At the same pace that mankind masters nature, man seems to become enslaved to other men or to his own infamy. Even the pure light of science seems unable to shine but on the dark background of ignorance. All our inventions and progress seem to result in endowing material forces with intellectual life, and in stultifying human life into a material force.[12]

Dehumanization. Alienation appears not only in the results, but in the very process of production. The worker would not stand in an alienated relation to the things of his own making if he did not alienate himself in his work and daily life. The worker's activity, the process of labor itself, is taken out of his control and dehumanized.

This alienation, Marx contended, reaches its acme under capitalism. In the mechanized industries of capitalist civilization, ordinary workers sell their labor power and are handled as commodities; and the objects they create are not theirs to keep or to market. They work under a routinized system of a minute division of labor which utilizes and develops only a fraction of their potentialities. Hence the worker does not realize himself, does not fulfill his own ends: he is used as a tool by his employer.[13]

Still more dehumanizing is the unemployment and poverty, the waste and decay of manpower, which results when machines compete against human beings, impoverish them, or cast them out of work. "Not having," declared Marx, "is . . . an entire negation of the reality of the human being, a very positive *having*, a having of hunger, of cold, of sickness, of crime, of debasement, of imbecility, of all forms of inhumanity and pathology."[14] In *Capital*, Marx substantiated this indictment with appalling descriptions of life among the poor.

Even the wealthy, we are told, are perverted and dehumanized by the profit system. Their absorption in moneymaking, business in itself, production of goods per se, their obsessive devotion to mammoth, inhuman, impersonal business organizations, stultifies their personalities and robs them of the fruits of any broad and generous culture. "Contempt for theory, for art, for history, for man . . .," declared Marx, "is the real conscious standpoint and the virtue of the monied man."[15] The worker, in a sense, is less dehumanized than his employer, because his dehumanization is a manifest one, against which he consciously struggles. The dehumanization of the monied man, on the other hand, is unconscious, hidden, or, if half-recognized, it is excused and rationalized. The proletarian is *in* the system but not *of* it, whereas the bourgeois is possessed by the system body and soul.

The most crucial alienation, it seemed to Marx, is caused by the division of labor. In the older handicraft industries, a watch or a fine piece of furniture was the individual product of a skilled craftsman. Very different is the work of a modern factory hand, devoting himself hour after hour, day after day, year after year to "the perpetual repetition of one and the same limited operation." These routines "mutilate the laborer into a fragment of a man, degrade him to the level of an appendage of a machine, destroy every remnant of charm in his work and turn it into a hated toil."[16]

Not only the manual worker is mutilated by the division of labor but also the scholar, the intellectual, the artist, the professional or businessman. Few escape the effects of a narrow specialization of thinking at the expense of doing, of "business enterprise" at the expense of culture, or of some special competence at the expense of a great wealth of human potentialities. But Marx's chief concern was to show the much more crippling effect that results from the detail-work of modern industry.

Species-alienation. Objectification and dehumanization entail a third kind of alienation, the estrangement from humanity. As Marx declared:

> One immediate consequence of the fact that man is estranged from the product of his work, from the act of being, from his own essential nature, is the estrangement of man from man. When man stands over against himself, other men stand over against him also. What goes for the relation of man to his labor, to the product of his labor and to himself, is true also of the relation of man to other men, and so to the labor and to the objective form of the labor of other men. In short the estrangement of man from his own essential being means that a man is estranged from others, just as each is estranged from his essential humanity.[17]

Species-alienation involves two phases: First, there is the alienation of man *from his own humanity*. Instead of expressing his essential nature, his social existence becomes a mere means for satisfying the egoistic demands of the monied class. Second, species-alienation also means the estrangement of man *from other men*. Instead of being members of a community, human beings confront one another as enemies.

This kind of alienation cannot be understood apart from Marx's concept of man. By nature, man is social, achieving his individuality through interaction with his fellows. Declared Marx: "It is above all necessary to avoid postulating 'society' once again as an abstraction confronting the individual. The individual *is* the *social being*."[18] Not only man's mind, but the very organs of his body, his senses, are social.

It is evident that the human eye appreciates things in a different way from the crude, non-human eye, the human ear differently from the crude ear. . . . The senses of social man are different from those of non-social man. It is only through the objectively deployed wealth of the human being that the health of subjective human sensibility (a musical ear, an eye which is sensitive to the beauty of form, in short, senses which are capable of human satisfaction and which confirm themselves as human faculties) is cultivated or created. . . . The cultivation of the five senses is the work of all previous history.[19]

This theory, that even sensory experience is a cultural product, is similar to the doctrines of modern anthropologists, such as Benjamin Whorf and Leslie White.

Characteristic of Marx's entire argument is his insistence upon the all-sidedness of human nature. Man realizes "his manifold being in an all-inclusive way, and thus as a whole man," by "seeing, hearing, smelling, tasting, touching, thinking, observing, feeling, desiring, acting, loving."[20] Here Marx took issue with Hegel, whose one-sided emphasis upon logic and rationality he sharply condemned. "Logic is the money of the mind," Marx declared, recalling his characterization of money as a depersonalizing force.[21]

In a different respect he was in agreement with Hegel. The latter had maintained in *The Phenomenology of Mind* that man is, at least potentially, a universal being. When a person is truly himself, when he is human and free, he identifies himself with civic humanity in the universality of the ethical state. Although Marx rejected this idea of reconciliation in and through the state, he believed that a more genuine and inclusive universality could be achieved in the classless society of advanced communism. For both Hegel and Marx, history is the march of man toward freedom, conceived as the unification of self with society, of the individual with the human community. "Man is a species-being," Marx wrote, "not only in the sense that he makes the community . . . his object both practically and theoretically, but also . . . in the sense that he treats himself . . . as a universal and consequently free being."[22] It was this "need for universality" that motivated Marx throughout his life.

The world of freedom and universality, Marx maintained, can be actualized only through labor power. He conceived labor as not only the source of productivity but the expression of the very humanity of man. "The whole of what is called world history," he said, "is nothing but the creation of man by human labor."[23] Thus even at the time that Marx wrote the Paris *Manuscripts* of 1844, he did not believe in a fixed and eternal human essence—a point to which we shall return later. He derived his idea of the self-creation of man from Hegel, but he gave the idea a radical new twist by insisting upon the supreme importance of labor. He defined man as an *animal labor-ans,* the laboring animal, and he conceived labor as the "life-activity" whereby man acquires his species-nature and distinguishes himself from the brute.

A person is alienated from his species-nature whenever his labor is treated as a mere mechanical operation or animal function.

Of course, animals also produce. They construct nests, dwellings, as in the case of bees, ants, etc. But they only produce what is strictly necessary for themselves or their young. They produce only in a single direction, while man produces universally. They produce only under the compulsion of direct physical need, while man produces when he is free from physical need and only truly produces in freedom from such need.[24]

Animals are bound by the immediate physical needs of their species, while man "knows how to apply the appropriate standard to the object," to construct "in accordance with the laws of beauty."[25]

Under the conditions of modern industry, the distinctively *human* character of labor is denied and degraded. The life of the poor wage earner sinks almost below the animal level.

Savages and animals have at least the need for hunting, exercise and companionship. But the simplification of machinery and of work is used to make workers out of those who are just growing up, who are still immature, *children,* while the worker himself has become a child deprived of all care. Machinery is adapted to the weakness of the human being, in order to turn the weak human being into a machine.[26]

The conditions away from the factory are also subhuman. In the industrial slums of the great manufacturing cities, there is a terrible scaling down and simplification of life.

For the worker even the need for fresh air ceases to be a need. Man returns to the cave dwelling again, but it is now poisoned by the pestilential breath of civilization. The worker has only a precarious right to inhabit it, for it has become an alien dwelling which may suddenly not be available, or from which he may be evicted if he does not pay the rent. He has to *pay* for this mortuary. The dwelling full of light which Aeschylus' Prometheus indicates as one of the great gifts by which he has changed savages into men, ceases to exist for the worker. Light, air, and the simplest *animal* cleanliness cease to be human needs. *Filth,* this corruption and putrefaction which runs in the *sewers* of civilization (this is to be taken literally) becomes the *element in which man lives.*[27]

Under these conditions of life and work, man is alienated from all that makes life human—from his freedom, his universality, his civil-mindedness, his wide-ranging capacities. He is also divided against himself and estranged from other men. By "species-alienation" Marx meant not only the degradation of the human essence to a subhuman level but the estrangement of man from man.

He sought to expose the perverse character of modern existence, which pretends to be broadly human but is only limited and particular. Under the conditions of modern capitalism, with its minute division of labor and its exploitation of man by man, there is a great separation of man's private life, his "practical" life, from the life of the community. To end this species-alienation, Marx demands a truly "human" emancipation. Class-man, special-ist-man, must be supplanted by whole-man. There must be a development of the totality of productive powers together with a totality of human faculties. The contradiction between particularity and universality, between private and public life, must be resolved by a classless humanism.

3. MARXIAN ETHICS

We can now understand the best part of Marxian ethics: the demand that human beings be treated as human beings, and things as things. In his own way, Marx was as insistent as Ruskin that the only wealth is life. "In place of the wealth and poverty of political economy," which conceives value only in narrow economic terms, Marx wanted to substitute "the wealthy man and the plenitude of human need. The wealthy man is at the same time one who needs a complex of human manifestations of life, and whose own self-realiza-tion exists as an inner necessity, a need."[28] He is rich in the human sense rather than in mere external goods.

Marx sharply contrasted the goals of a commercial society with the human-istic goals which he had in mind.

Political economy, the science of wealth, is . . . the science of renunciation, of privation and of saving. . . . Its moral ideal is the worker who takes a part of his wages to the savings bank. . . . Its principal thesis is the renunciation of life and of human needs. The less you eat, drink, buy books, go to the theater or to balls, or to the pub, and the less you think, love, theorize, sing, paint, fence, etc. the more you will be able to save and the greater will become your treasure which neither moth nor rust will corrupt—your capital. The less you are, the less you express your life, the more you have, the greater is your alienated life. . . . Thus all passions and activities must be submerged in avarice.[29]

Those who stress "practical" objectives and wish to limit production to "useful" things "forget that the production of too many useful things results in too many useless people."[30] Marx was completely free of the modern delusion that the mere piling up of money or the multiplication of material goods is the proper goal of society.

In a letter written to his friend Ruge in 1843, he called himself an "ideal-ist" who has the "impertinence" to try "to make man a human being." He soon thereafter ceased to label himself an idealist but his humanist objective was never abandoned. Demanding a "radical" theory and practice, he ex-plained that, "to be radical is to grasp the matter by its roots. Now the root for mankind is man himself." Like Feuerbach, he believed that "man is the supreme being for mankind," and he declared that the "categorical imperative" is to abolish all circumstances "in which man is a degraded, servile, neglected, contemptible being."[31] These were declarations of his youth, but even in *Capital,* the last of his major publications, he spoke of the need to produce "fully developed human beings" and to achieve "the full development of the human race."[32] His objective was to end the fundamental discord between the conditions of life and the nature of man.

According to his definition:

Communism is the positive abolition . . . of human self-alienation, and thus, the real appropriation of human nature, through and for man. It is therefore the return of man himself as a social, that is, really human, being, a complete and conscious return which assimilates all the wealth of previous development. . . . It is the definitive resolution of the antagonism between man and nature, and between man and man.[33]

This requires a social system "in which the free development of each is the condition of the free development of all."[34]

Marx confidently looked forward to a higher kind of civilization, where the creative and cooperative impulses would supplant the acquisitive ones, and where the invidious distinctions of class, race, sex, nationality, and creed would no longer divide and bedevil mankind. He wanted to curb the industrial division of labor, which stunts and cripples human capacities, and to restore the wholeness and balance of life. In his vision of the communist society of the future, a man would practice a variety of occupations, without ever being limited to "a particular, exclusive sphere of activity, which is forced upon him and from which he cannot escape." "This is not possible," he declared, "without the community. Only in community with others has each individual the means of cultivating his gifts in all directions; only in the community, therefore, is personal freedom possible."[35]

Marx's conception of advanced communism is fundamentally esthetic in character. Its effect will be "to humanize man's senses, and also to create the human senses corresponding to all the wealth of human and natural being." At this stage, the duality of subject and object disappears:

It is only when objective reality everywhere becomes for man in society the reality of human faculties, human reality, and thus the reality of his own faculties, that all *objects* become for him the *objectification of himself.* The objects then confirm and realize his individuality, they are *his own* objects, i.e., man himself becomes the object.[36]

Marx conceived a good social order as a community of *creative* individuals, whether their creativity be scientific, artistic, or craftsmanlike. This creativity is to be directed toward self-realization and the production of a truly human environment.

Marx's ideal of the comprehensive fulfillment of human nature distinguishes his theory from any narrowly-based ethics, such as the hedonistic utilitarianism of Bentham. Like Aristotle, Marx maintained that what is good for an animal is based upon the animal's nature, and what is good for a man is based upon human nature.

To know what is useful for a dog, one must study dog-nature. This nature itself is not to be deduced from the principle of utility. . . . Applying this to man, he that would criticize all human acts, movements, relations, etc. . . . by the principle of utility, must first deal with human nature in general, and then with human nature as modified in each historical epoch. Bentham makes short work of it. With the dryest naivete he takes the modern shopkeeper, especially the English shopkeeper, as the normal man. Whatever is useful to this queer normal man, and to his world, is absolutely useful. This yard-measure, then, he applies to past, present, and future.[37]

Significant in this quotation is Marx's contrast between "human nature in general" and "human nature as modified in each historical period." Erich Fromm, who quotes the above passage from *Capital*, cites a similar passage from Marx's early work, *The Holy Family*, in which the distinction is drawn between the fixed human drives, such as hunger and love, and the changing appetites, which "owe their origin to certain social structures and certain conditions of production and communication."[38] It is important to note that this distinction occurs both in Marx's early and in his late works.

On this basis, Marx distinguished between an ethics relative to historical circumstances, and a nonrelative humanist ethics which is only now emerging in history. Relative ethics, he believed, is mainly an "ideology," a misleading set of ideas with which men rationalize and excuse their class interests. As Engels explained:

Ideology is a process accomplished by the so-called thinker consciously, indeed, but with a false consciousness. The real motives impelling him remain unknown to him, otherwise it would not be an ideological process at all. Hence he imagines false or apparent motives. . . . He works with mere thought material which he accepts without examination as the product of thought, he does not investigate further for a more remote process independent of thought. . . .[39]

This theory is akin to Freud's theory of rationalization, except that the unconscious motivation and causation are held to be economic rather than instinctive.

Men are loath to recognize the selfish interests and class biases that motivate them, and they disguise their true aims by an appeal to the moral and religious ideals of the past.

. . . Unheroic as [French] bourgeois society is, yet in its birth it had need of heroism and sacrifice in the classically austere traditions of the Roman Republic; its gladiators found the ideals and the art forms, the self-deceptions that they needed, in order to conceal from themselves the bourgeois limitations of the content

of their struggles and to keep their passion at the height of the great historical
tragedy. Similarly, at another stage of development, a century earlier, Cromwell
and the English people had borrowed speech, passions and illusions from the Old
Testament for their bourgeois revolution.[40]

This doctrine of ideology was a critical weapon of devastating force, but
Marx specifically exempted his own revolutionary principles from this type of
criticism.

The social revolution of the nineteenth century cannot draw its poetry from the
past, but only from the future. It cannot make a beginning until it has stripped
off all superstition of the past. Earlier revolutions required world-historical recol-
lections in order to drug themselves concerning their own content. In order to
arrive at its own content, the revolution of the nineteenth century must let the
dead bury their dead. There the phrase went beyond the content; here the content
goes beyond the phrase.[41]

In prophesying the coming social revolution, Marx spoke not in terms of a
relative morality but of a broadly human and universal morality. He reminded the representatives of the First International of "the simple laws of
morals and justice, which ought to govern the relations of private individuals"
and "of nations."[42] He maintained that the proletariat, in emancipating itself,
will emancipate all mankind: ". . . It cannot emancipate itself at all," he declared, "without emancipating itself from all other spheres of society, thus
emancipating them at the same time. In a word, there must be a complete
forfeiture of man as he is, compelling an equally complete rebirth of a new
humanity."[43]

This ethical universalism is sometimes combined with an insistence upon
inward change and active moral effort. Marx, for example, criticized Feuerbach and other materialists who put all their emphasis upon the environment. "The materialist doctrine concerning the changing of circumstances
and education forgets that circumstances are changed by men and that the
educator must himself be educated."[44] Although human beings cannot change
themselves without altering their environments, they cannot alter their environments without changing themselves. Marx adds: "The philosophers
have only *interpreted* the world in different ways; the point is to *change* it."[45]
Such passages imply that the economic determination of morals must be
limited by the moral determination of economics. But Marx's activism is not
entirely consistent with his historical determinism, as K. R. Popper, in *The
Open Society and Its Enemies,* has shown.

Despite inconsistencies, the main tenor of the argument is clear. Marx
believed that it is possible to discover objective norms based on a realistic
knowledge of human nature and a scientific understanding of history. Like
Vico and Hegel, he rejected an antihistorical rationalism, and maintained that
"the nature which is developing in human history . . . is the real nature of
man."[46] He wanted to establish ethics firmly upon human psychology, and

he called for a new kind of psychology based on history—for "no psychology . . . can become a *real* science with a genuine content" if the book of history "remains closed."[47]

In his early writings, he distinguished between the human "essence" and human "existence." By the *essence,* he meant the specific determinate character of man, his underlying nature, and by the *existence,* he meant the changing forms and conditions of human life. In a state of alienation, the existence and the essence are in contradiction; there is a flagrant conflict between the deepest human needs and the inhumanity of man against man. By establishing a communist order, history will resolve this contradiction:

> Communism . . . is the true solution of the conflict between existence and essence, between objectification and self-affirmation, between freedom and necessity, between individual and species. It is the solution of the riddle of history and knows itself to be this solution.[48]

Thus Marx found an ethical pattern, a rationale of progress running within and across the centuries. As Engels pointed out in his *Anti-Dühring,* feudal morality, capitalist morality, and socialist morality have much in common because they represent progressive stages of the same historical development. The climax of this process is a synthesis of contraries: the self and society, freedom and organization, reason and reality, ideal and fact, theory and practice will be brought into working harmony. The fundamental antinomies of human life are not only expressed in history but will ultimately be resolved by historical progress.

Marx's belief in human dignity and worth, his faith in human potentialities, and his ideal of a community of free and many-sided individuals distinguish him sharply from the totalitarians who invoke his name and link him with the great humanists and liberals of Western culture. He was not being perverse when he represented his thought as linked with the Enlightenment, the French Revolution, and German idealism.

What I have been saying appears to be in sharp contradiction with a number of Marxian pronouncements. "Law, morality, religion," Marx and Engels declared in the *Communist Manifesto,* "are so many bourgeois prejudices, behind which lurk in ambush just as many bourgeois interests." In the same work, they ridiculed the German True Socialists, a Utopian sect, for harping on "the alienation of humanity." The True Socialists, they complained, were ready to sacrifice the real "interests of the proletariat" to the imaginary "interests of human nature, of man in general, who belongs to no class, has no reality, who exists only in the misty realm of philosophical fantasy." In later years, Marx denounced twaddle about justice and the modern "goddesses of Justice, Freedom, Equality and Fraternity." Likewise Engels declared that "love" is "cant" and complained that Lasalle still believed in "the idea of justice."[49] Some scholars, impressed by the anti-ethical tone of these passages, and the apparent repudiation of the concepts of alienation and a human essence, have concluded that Marx and Engels wholly abandoned the humanism of their early writings. This conclusion is inconsistent with many passages in the later writings, some of which I have already quoted.

What, then, is the explanation of the apparent contradiction? That there is some difference in tone between the early and the later works is undeniable. After 1846, Marx and Engels discarded much of their earlier Hegelian jargon and were chary of ethical appeals. They hated "preaching" and felt that moral exhortation was more sentimental than scientific. As environmentalists and "materialistic" historians, they emphasized economic and political revolution rather than inward moral transformation. They noted with disdain the hypocritical moralism of apologists for the established order, and they criticized Utopian socialists and visionary reformers. They wanted to demonstrate, not by moral criticism, but by the inexorable "logic" of economic development, that the collapse of capitalism is inevitable. They distinguished between false moralistic ideology and the objectives of the communist movement. It was the false ideology, and not the ideals of advanced communism, that they intended to attack in their polemics. They admitted that in the past all moral theory has been tainted by class bias, but they believed that in the future a really human morality would emerge. In the heat of controversy, their language was immoderate and open to misunderstanding, but they never entirely abandoned their early humanist ideals.

In his later works, Marx seldom used the word "alienation," but his ideas changed less than his terminology. "The alienation of the thing" he later called fetishism; "self-estrangement" he called subjugation to machine-production and the division of labor; the alienation from other men he described in terms of class conflict; the worker's loss of control over his life and products he explained in terms of exploitation. But the *concept* of "alienation," if not the word, remained in many passages. He still thought of man as alienated from himself, from other men, from his work, from his products, from his society, from nature. Inconsistently he tended to limit the concept of alienation to the economic sphere, but this limitation may have been the result of his intense preoccupation with the writing of *Capital,* his major economic work, rather than of a basic change in viewpoint.

The apparent repudiation of the concept of a "human essence" poses a thorny problem for Marx scholarship. Some critics find only residual traces of the naturalistic humanism of the youthful Marx in the later writings. They believe that the doctrine of a human essence was replaced by a historical relativism. Others believe that the idea of an enduring human nature remained with Marx to the end of his life.

This question of interpretation concerns the extent to which Marx can be characterized as an existentialist. William Barrett contends that "existentialism is the counter-Enlightenment come at last to philosophic expression; and it demonstrated beyond anything else that the ideology of the Enlightenment is thin, abstract and therefore dangerous."[50] Marx, he maintains, is a child of the Enlightenment, and stands in opposition to existentialism. This is basically the view of Sidney Hook, except that he has a more favorable opinion of the Enlightenment.

In one respect, Hook and Barrett seem to me demonstrably mistaken. As I have maintained, the theme of alienation is fundamental in both Marxism and existentialism. To dismiss it as characteristic only of the youthful Marx is a misinterpretation. But if we ask if Marx is an existentialist in other respects, our answer will depend on what we understand by existentialism. Jean-Paul Sartre has defined it as the doctrine of the primacy of existence over essence. As he sees man, there is no enduring nature, no underlying core of potentialities. We cannot say that a man "is," that he has an essence, but only that he *tends* to be this or that; he is a radically indeterminate being, his existence is mere possibility. Not all existentialists are prepared to go this far, but they all agree that, in some sense, "existence precedes essence." In the words of Barrett: "There is no prefabricated human nature that freezes human possibilities into a preordained mold; on the contrary, man exists first and makes himself what he is out of the conditions into which he is thrown."[51]

Was the mature Marx an existentialist in this precise sense of the word? Our answer must be carefully qualified. There can be no doubt that he dropped his early Hegelian terminology of "essence" and "existence" and rejected the concept of a *fixed* core of being. "All history," he wrote as early as 1847, "is nothing but the continuous transformation of human nature."[52] But it is questionable if there was any great shift in his point of view. Even in the Paris *Manuscripts* of 1844, the work in which he had most explicitly referred to "the human essence," he characterized man's nature as dynamic and changing. On the other hand, he continued to distinguish in *Capital* between "human nature in general" and "human nature as modified in each historical period." Both early and late, he deplored the "dehumanization" that occurs under capitalism, and prophesied that man, after his long exile in the desert of alienation, would come into his own. Thus he shared with the existentialists a belief in the plasticity of human nature, but he was too much the child of the Enlightenment to embrace an extreme relativism and indeterminism like that of Sartre. The *whole* of human nature, he believed, changes, but the universal, generic core of man's being is *relatively* constant. This core, Marx believed, is the nucleus of that richer and deeper humanity that is emerging in history.

Marx has enriched the humanistic ethics of the Enlightenment with the more romantic ethics of existentialism. Like the existentialists, he rejected the ideal of pure abstract reason and a static human essence; he believed in the importance of human passions and concrete sensuous experience; he maintained that contemporary industrial society has trampled upon the dignity of the human person; he was primarily concerned with the problem of human bondage and human freedom, of alienation and disalienation.[53] But he clung to the belief in reason, science, and progress, in the attainment of a universalist society, in the full rational realization of human potentialities—the basic faith of the Enlightenment.

I would not deny, I would insist, that there are deep contradictions in his argument. Stanley Edgar Hyman, in a detailed study of his imagery and style, has revealed how vitriolic his language often was.[54] This bitter strain in his temperament was intensified by his later sufferings—the abysmal poverty, the death of his children, the carbuncles and the hemorrhoids. The terrible anger of the man occasionally burst forth in violent or cynical remarks. As he grew older, there was some accentuation of the more totalitarian and relativistic aspects of his thought. But in view of the evidence that I have already cited, I cannot believe that there was a complete reversal of his early humanism. He certainly retained his intense faith in human progress—a concept that is meaningless from a completely relativistic or cynical perspective.

His most distinctive ethical contribution was the linking of humanist ends with "materialist" means. The overcoming of alienation, he maintained, is possible only if social relations are fundamentally reorganized to harmonize with the more highly developed productive forces. Under a planned economy for social benefit, the workers must attain mastery over the products of their labor. Real freedom demands liberation from the bondage to material conditions, especially from poverty and excessive toil. Marx insisted:

> Freedom in this field cannot consist of anything else but the fact that socialized mankind, the associated producers, regulate their interchange with nature rationally, bring it under their common control, instead of being ruled by it as by some blind power, and accomplish their task with the least expenditure of energy and under such conditions as are proper and worthy for human beings. Nevertheless, this always remains a realm of necessity. Beyond it begins that development of human potentiality for its own sake, the true realm of freedom, which however can only flourish upon that realm of necessity as its basis.[55]

It is not by turning away from material things, but by mastering them, that the spirit of man is to be freed.

Without this mastery of material forces, Marx believed, the appeal to "human rights" will avail little. While the conditions of human alienation continue, "none of the so-called Rights of Man eliminates the egoist, man as member of bourgeois society—that is, an individual withdrawn into his private interests and arbitrariness, separated from the community."[56] By itself alone, *political* "emancipation" cannot eliminate the contradiction between private interest and public welfare. The basic evils of the modern world, the egoism and alienation engendered by private property, will remain untouched. Hence from Marx's standpoint, the government of the United States belonged in the same category as the Prussian system, despite the great difference in political institutions. Both governments failed to come to grips with the main causes of human alienation.

To achieve the genuine emancipation of mankind we must look to the economic, rather than to the political, sphere.

The fellowship from which the worker is isolated is a fellowship of a scope and order of reality quite different from that of the political fellowship. The fellowship from which his own labor separates the worker is *life* itself, physical and intellectual life, morality and customs, human activity, human satisfaction, being human. Being human is the true fellowship of men. Just as irremediable isolation from this fellowship is incomparably more pervasive, unbearable, horrible and full of contradiction than isolation from the political fellowship, so the dissolution of this isolation from being human, or even a partial reaction or uprising against it, is as much wider in scope as man is wider in scope than the political citizen, as human life is wider in scope than political life. Thus, no matter how sectional an industrial uprising, it carries within it a universal soul; a political uprising, no matter how universal, hides in the hugest form a narrow soul.[57]

When men recognize that the forces that rule their lives are primarily economic, and when they learn to organize and control these forces according to a common plan, then and then only will a truly human emancipation be possible.

4. THE ANALYSIS OF SOCIETY

Marx combined a scathing indictment of things as they are with a rosy vision of things as they will be. How can this chasm be bridged? How can alienated man come into his own?

The answer of Marx is his philosophy of history. Man's goal will be realized—not because it is a worthy ideal, not because it is favored by good men, not because the workers desire it—it will be realized because of inexorable historical laws.

To understand Marx's theory we need to distinguish between various levels within the social order. He analysed society into three main levels: the productive system, with its attendant social institutions; the state and legal order; and "the cultural superstructure." Let us briefly examine each of these.

The Productive System. Marx believed that the way in which a society earns its living will primarily determine its history. There is a very complex interaction of unequal forces of which the economic are by far the most powerful. "Production predominates . . . ," explained Marx. "From it, the process continually recommences . . . but there is interaction between the various elements."[58] This theory, rather than a pure economic determinism, is the authentic Marxian doctrine. As Engels explained:

Marx and I are ourselves partly to blame for the fact that younger writers sometimes lay more stress on the economic side than is due to it. We had to emphasize
this main principle in opposition to our adversaries, who denied it, and we had
not always the time, the place, or the opportunity to allow the other elements involved in the interaction to come into their rights.[59]

The historian should therefore look to the economic system for the *main*,
but not the *exclusive*, causes of historical development. When he does so, he
discovers that there is not just *one* kind of economic system but a succession
of types, such as primitive communism, slavery, feudalism, and capitalism,
with historical forces moving toward socialism. Each stage is marked by a
corresponding level of technological development. "The hand mill," for example, "gives you society with the feudal lord; the steam mill society with the
industrial capitalist."[60]

There is not only a development from stage to stage but a development
within each stage. In the early expanding phases of an economy, the various
interacting factors in a productive system—labor power, natural resources,
instruments, and social relations—are in a state of relative equilibrium and
therefore develop progressively and harmoniously. But sooner or later the
social relations—the class structure and system of property—enter into conflict with labor and technology and the effective use of natural resources.
The cause of this conflict is the incongruous combination of fast and slow
changes: technology, as the main sphere of innovation, develops more rapidly
than the property system, which is the sphere of vested interests and conservatism. This means that the techniques and tools employed on the job
change more quickly than the institutions of property and the distribution
of wealth. Hence, a new system of ownership and relations between classes
must be instituted to match the new productive forces. For example, the
multiplication of inventions, the expansion of trade and manufacture, and
the attendant development of urban life in the late period of feudalism could
not be reconciled with the rigid, hierarchical structure of feudal society; a
profound reorganization, which we call the rise of capitalism, was therefore
necessary. Marx believed that the rapid development of technology in recent
decades similarly necessitates the change from a capitalist to a socialist type
of economy.

Although he believed that technology is the most dynamic factor in historical development, his interpretation of history is not a mere technological
determinism. Not only machines and techniques but class relations are fundamental. The great crises of history, he believed, are mainly the result of the
conflict between rapidly changing techniques and slowly changing class
stratifications. This conflict is not subhuman, automatic: it always involves a
contest of ideas and wills. Above all, it involves a struggle between opposing
classes, such as masters and slaves, feudal lords and serfs, capitalist employers
and workers.

The State and Legal System. To comprehend the effects of this class struggle, we must understand the Marxian doctrine of the state. Marx reacted strongly against the idealistic political theory of Hegel. According to this theory, the state alone provides a just balance between class interests, achieves a synthesis of the forces within society, and gives to all citizens the opportunity for self-realization. Marx and Engels believed that this Hegelian theory is unrealistic. Far from being above class bias, the state "as a rule" is the instrument of "the most powerful economic class that by force of its economic supremacy becomes also the ruling political class, and thus acquires new means of subduing and exploiting the oppressed masses."[61] Since it is thus primarily an instrument of class domination, police and military power are at its very foundation.

Yet Marx and Engels qualified this theory. In the quotation just cited, Engels declared that the state "as a rule" takes the form of class domination. He did not deny that in certain circumstances "the struggling classes balance each other so nearly that the public power gains a certain degree of independence by posing as a mediator between them."[62] Marx indicated, in *The Eighteenth Brumaire of Louis Bonaparte,* for example, that the government of Louis for a time represented such a precarious equilibrium in French society.

He and Engels believed that the economic order, as the more powerful force, determines on the whole the political and legal structure, but that this structure may develop a certain relative independence or may react upon the economic system. Engels explained:

> The reaction of the state power upon economic development can be one of three kinds: it can run in the same direction, and then development is more rapid; it can oppose the line of development, in which case nowadays state power in every great nation will go to pieces in the long run; or it can cut off the economic development from certain paths, and impose on it certain others.[63]

In any of these three ways, political causes may have an important but not a decisive effect upon the economic system. The theory of the primacy of economics over law and politics is never called in question.

The Cultural Superstructure. Not only the political order, but morality, religion, art, philosophy, and science, are predominantly determined by the economic foundation. "What else," wrote Marx, in the *Communist Manifesto,* "does the history of ideas prove, than that intellectual production changes its character in proportion as material production is changed? The ruling ideas of each age have ever been the ideas of its ruling class."[64]

The dependence of ideas and cultural factors upon economic forces can be understood too literally. In many instances, ideas are related not immediately and directly to economic processes but to the ideologies and loyalties of class. Also culture has a certain momentum of its own and may for a time operate in semi-independence of economic forces. In philosophy, for example, economic influences operate "upon the existing philosophic material handed down by predecessors."

Here economy creates nothing absolutely new, but it determines the way in which the existing material of thought is altered and further developed, and that too for the most part indirectly, for it is the political, legal, and moral reflexes which exercise the greatest direct influence upon philosophy.[65]

Likewise in the case of art, religion, morality, and science, the economic causes may operate indirectly and intermittently, and the cultural spheres may react upon the economic order. ". . . Though the material form of existence is the primary agent," Engels explained, "this does not exclude spheres of ideas from reacting upon it in their turn."[66]

Marx did not believe that cultural development is directly proportional to economic development; progress in the latter does not necessarily entail progress in the former. For example, capitalist development in its heyday was inimical to art, because its standards were too quantitative and its division of labor produced "crippled monstrosities" rather than creative craftsmen. Hence we cannot make economic progress a measure of cultural advance.

Religion is *inversely* related to economic improvement. Failing to master the real world, men resort to religious fantasies and consolations.

Religion is the fantastic realization of the human being, inasmuch as the human being has no true reality. . . . Religion is the moan of the oppressed creature, the sentiment of a heartless world, as it is the spirit of spiritless conditions. It is the opium of the people.[67]

In one important sense, Marxism itself is akin to religion. It seeks to realize "the human core of religion . . . in a profane manner," tying its faith to revolutionary deeds and a vision of human progress.

Marx and Engels were, in intention if not always in practice, as favorable toward science as they were hostile toward supernaturalism. But they conceived science, like other forms of culture, as having a close dependence upon the economic order, especially upon technology as a "productive force."

5. A MULTILINEAR THEORY
OF HISTORICAL DEVELOPMENT

History was for Marx the main social science. Even economics, upon which he expended infinite pains, seemed to him less important for its own sake than for the light it threw upon historical development. He sought to disclose the economic forces that were propelling industrial society toward socialism.

In his historical theory, he did not conceive mankind as moving forward "like an escalator, . . . unilineally and irresistibly from a primitive communist society to a slave-holding, feudal, and then capitalist society." Rather, he viewed "the development of societies as a multilinear process which was characterized not only by progress, but also by stagnation and regression."[68] Marx's departure from a unilinear theory has seldom been recognized.

He was influenced in his view of primitive life by the work of Lewis H. Morgan, the American anthropologist. After the death of Marx in 1883, Engels, making use of Marx's notes, wrote *The Origin of the Family, Private Property and the State,* in which he related Morgan's theories to the Marxian conception of history. Morgan had maintained that social cohesion based on kinship groups preceded the rise of the modern type of family, economic classes, and the state, and that the society of the future would resemble the communal institutions of primitive man. "It will be a revival, in a higher form, of the liberty, equality, and fraternity of the ancient gentes."[69] These ideas were developed in Engels' book.

Accepting this theory as a starting point, Marx was aware of various ways in which civilization evolved from its primitive origins. In the south of Europe, primitivism was superseded by the slaveholding societies of Greece and Rome, but in the Germanic north, the tribal "gens" society persisted throughout the Greco-Roman period. The feudal institutions of medieval Europe derived mainly from the kinship societies in the north rather than from the decaying slave system to the south. In Asia, primitivism evolved into a distinctively Asiatic form.

Marx described this Asiatic system in articles he contributed in 1853 to the *New York Daily Tribune.* He found its basis partly in the necessity for large-scale irrigation.

Climate and territorial conditions, especially the vast tracts of desert, extending from the Sahara, through Arabia, Persia, India, and Tartary, to the most elevated Asiatic highlands, constituted artificial irrigation by canals and water-works the basis of Oriental agriculture. . . . This prime necessity of an economical and common use of water, which, in the Occident, drove private enterprise to voluntary association, as in Flanders and Italy, necessitated, in the Orient where civilization was too low and the territorial extent too vast to call into life voluntary association, the interference of the centralizing power of Government.[70]

The despotic control by a central government was combined with a village-system of production. The economic basis of the villages was petty industry and agriculture, with both private and communal use of the soil.

The result was a remarkably static economy and social order. In India, for example, the combination of hand-weaving, hand-spinning, and hand-tilling of the land persisted for innumerable generations. Village isolation, which confined experience within the smallest compass, was heightened and perpetuated by the absence of roads. This isolation left the rural community "almost without intercourse with other villages," and meant "the dissolution of society into stereotyped and disconnected atoms."[71] The population thus divided and pulverized could not withstand the despotic tendencies of the central government. The state was free to impress peasants into gangs for hydraulic and other public works. Marx regarded this constellation of social traits as a distinctive system, and contrasted it with both the slavery of Greece and Rome and the decentralized controls of feudalism.

The "Asiatic" system was, in a sense, a misnomer. Although it embraced the greater part of Asia, it was not limited to this area. It appeared, with certain alterations, in ancient Egypt, Byzantium, and the Aztec, Mayan, and Inca empires. A "semi-Asiatic" society also took root in Russia, where village communities and state despotism appeared without the system of hydraulic public works. Marx and Engels regarded Russia as mainly part of the Eastern and not the Western world.

In Asia, as contrasted with Europe, technology and an industrial middle class played a minor role, and the social order has remained stagnant century after century. The disruptive effect of British imperialism in India, Marx remarked, "produced the greatest and, to speak the truth, the only *social* revolution ever heard of in Asia."[72] Marx looked primarily to outside influences, ultimately socialist, for the liberation of the Orient.

Russia was a special case that fascinated him. In order to estimate its potentialities more realistically, he learned the Russian language and for years studied the original source materials. He concluded that a Russian bourgeois revolution was imminent, that this revolution might help to spark a Western proletarian revolution, and that the Western revolution would then react upon Russia. In the 1882 Preface to a Russian edition of the *Communist Manifesto*, he and Engels declared:

If the Russian revolution becomes the signal for a proletarian revolution in the West, so that each complements the other, the present Russian common ownership of land may serve as the starting point for a communist revolution.[73]

Marx expected that the victorious socialists in the West would be able to show the Russians how to use their old village institutions—their cooperatives and common land—in building a socialist economy.

Despite his far-flung interests, he devoted his main attention to Western capitalism. The wage laborer, he maintained, normally produces more value than is represented by the wages he receives. Labor power is thus a peculiar commodity, since it produces more value than it is worth on the market. If a man works eight hours, for example, he may in the course of six hours produce sufficient to pay the cost of his own wages; and in the next two hours, he will produce "surplus value" for which the employer does not pay him. The workers produce the wealth, Marx contended, but the capitalists appropriate a large part of it.

As surplus value accumulates, wealth and economic value tend to be concentrated in fewer and fewer hands. Great corporations, trusts, associations, cartels develop. Large companies destroy or absorb small companies. Why is this concentration occurring? Marx's answer is that the big companies are more efficient and powerful and can crush their smaller oppcnents. Large-scale production, at a higher technological level, is generally cheaper. But the smaller companies cannot afford mass production and expensive new machinery; hence they are eliminated in the fierce competiticn for profits.

When wealth and economic power become highly concentrated, the crisis of capitalism becomes acute. The wonderful new machines utilized in large-scale production represent an enormously augmented productive potential, but, under capitalism, they compete against the workers, displace and impoverish them. Receiving in wages a diminishing proportion of the wealth produced, the workers do not have the buying power to consume the products that highly mechanized industry can pour forth so plentifully. The result is a constant tendency toward *over*production in relation to effective *demand* and *under*production in relation to human *need* and the *capacity to produce*. As Engels declared:

> Too little is produced. . . . But *why* is too little produced? Not because the [technical] limits of production . . . are exhausted. No, but because the limits of production are determined not by the number of hungry bellies, but by the number of *purses* able to buy and to pay. The moneyless bellies, the labor which cannot be utilized *for profit* and therefore cannot buy, is left to the death-rate.[74]

Here is the source, Marx and Engels asserted, of the modern paradox of poverty in the midst of potential plenty.

It is not only the worker who is squeezed. As mechanized productive power increases and buying power decreases, the rate of profit falls. Less and less labor power is spent on each individual commodity, the creation of surplus value is correspondingly decreased, and the whole basis of profit shrinks. Although the *rate* of profit thus tends to fall, the *mass* of profit, under large-scale production, may rise. Nevertheless, the falling rate of profit, in the long run, is a mortal threat to the capitalist structure. This falling rate and the increasing disparity between the capacity of society to produce and its capacity to consume make the system more and more erratic, and lead to a crazy succession of booms and depressions.

In the effort to counteract these tendencies, employers intensify the dog-eat-dog competition with other employers and the exploitation of their employees. They feverishly attempt to safeguard profits by finding cheaper labor and raw materials and by capturing foreign markets. The nations dominated by capitalist interests are thus driven into commercial rivalry and imperialism, which, in turn, provoke military conflict. War will be spread far and wide by the ramifications of the capitalist system. Engels predicted devastation on a global scale:

> No war is any longer possible . . . except a world war and a world war indeed of an extension and violence hitherto undreamt of. . . . At the end of the

tragedy . . . the victory of the proletariat will either be already achieved, or at any rate inevitable.[75]

The ensuing revolution will be directed not against the techniques and instruments of production but against the social relations that fetter and distort these productive forces. Because the root difficulty is the private ownership of the means of production, *social* ownership must replace private individual ownership. The economic system must be reorganized, not upon the basis of individually directed production for profit, but of socially planned production for use.

Marx apparently believed that the achievement of this goal was inevitable, but that alternative roads may lead thereto. In reply to one critic who spoke of a single route for Russia and the West, Marx denied that there must be "a universal movement necessarily imposed upon all peoples, no matter what the historical circumstances in which they are placed."[76] In his later speculations about the future of the West, he distinguished between the less democratic countries, where violent revolution could be expected, and countries such as the United States and Great Britain, where the workers may be able to achieve their ends by peaceful means. Qualifying his theory of increasing misery, he recognized the possibility of considerable betterment of the workers' lot within the structure of capitalism. For example, in his Inaugural Address to the First International, 1864, he spoke of the "immense physical, moral, and intellectual benefits" of recent ameliorative legislation, such as the Ten Hours' Bill, which he elsewhere called a new "Magna Carta" of labor.

Not only did he envisage various alternatives in the transformation of capitalism, but he recognized divergent possibilities in the future communist order. As early as 1844, he warned that "communism" may be either "democratic or despotic." Referring to some of the radical theories of that period, he deplored a "crude communism" whose hatred of private property would be a morbid, although inverted, addiction to the acquisitive interests of capitalism. "This entirely crude and unreflective communism," he declared, "would negate the personality of man in every sphere. . . . It would be a system in which universal envy sets itself up as a power, and . . . in this form of envy, it would reduce everything to a common level. . . . Crude communism is only the culmination of such envy and levelling down to a preconceived minimum."[77] Increase in wages thus enforced by the state "would be nothing more than a better remuneration of slaves, and would not restore, either to the worker or to the work, their human significance and worth."[78] The state as a superboss is no more acceptable than the private capitalist.

Marx's point here is a very important one. His main objection to capitalist private property is that it invests the few with inordinate power over the many. As long as there exists such "powers *over* individuals," the human problem remains unsolved. To shift the ownership of property to society, leaving power centralized, is simply to make the state an "abstract capitalist." Even to raise wages under state dictatorship would not alleviate human bondage. Hence Marx insisted that "the annulment of private property" is only a *preliminary* stage. It must be superseded by the deeper and more fundamental revolution—the revolution at the point of production, the revolution in the labor and the life conditions of the workers. Without *this* revolution, the nationalized means of production will serve human ends no better than the privately owned means of production.

I have been quoting remarks written in 1844, but in his later works, Marx occasionally recognized the dangers of state collectivism. As we have noted, he wrote articles in 1853 for the *New York Daily Tribune* in which he characterized "Oriental despotism," the state managerialism of the old Asiatic societies, as dooming the masses to a kind of "general slavery." Perhaps he had a secret fear that future collectivism would share these evils. In his Inaugural Address of 1864, he spoke of the great value of cooperatives, as distinguished from state socialism; and again in his comments of 1871 on the Paris Commune, he extolled cooperatives and popular control of the revolutionary government, warning against bureaucracy and militarism. His ultimate ideal was to abolish the coercive state, to organize society on a decentralized basis, and to eliminate the dehumanizing process of mass industry. Dying before communist totalitarianism emerged, he held views that later communists detest. Unfortunately, his position was ambivalent, and Lenin could cite passages of a different tenor. It would be quite inaccurate to say that there was nothing in his values and ideas and acts that led up to Lenin, Stalin, and Mao.

In scattered passages, Marx and Engels outlined the stages in the attainment of communism. Down to the present point man has achieved control only of physical nature. In the control of industry and the making of history, human action has achieved "its desired end only by way of exception and, much more frequently, the exact opposite."[79] "What each individual wills is obstructed by everyone else, and what emerges is something that no one willed."[80] But as a result of the social ownership of the means of production and of planned production for social use, the "*prehistory*" of mankind will come to an end and its *true* history will begin. Man will be the *agent* rather than the *patient* of historical forces. "United cooperative societies" will "regulate the national production under a common plan."[81] The full productive capacity of society, no longer fettered by an obsolete system of property, will be employed to meet essential human needs. The process of production, thus organized and controlled by free men, will create the leisure and the opportunities for the "all-round" cultivation of human personality. The exploitation of man by man will be abolished, and step by step the traces of the old class divisions will disappear. As the new order becomes firmly established, political force will become less and less necessary. Socialism will develop into a cooperative anarchism, and the state, as a coercive organization, will "wither away."

In the first, or "socialist," phase of development, the principle of distribution will be based upon the slogan of St. Simon: "From each according to his ability, to each according to what he produces." There will be differential wages with higher rewards to the more industrious and skillful workers. But when the era of abundance has been established, and the old class antagonisms and the coercive state have disappeared, a more generous system of distribution can be inaugurated. According to Marx:

> In a higher phase of communist society, when the enslaving subordination of the individual to the division of labor, and with it the antithesis between mental and physical labor has vanished; when labor is no longer merely a means of life but has become life's principal need; when the productive forces have also increased with the all-round development of the individual, and all the springs of cooperative wealth flow more abundantly—only then will it be possible completely to transcend the narrow outlook of bourgeois right and only then will society be able to inscribe on its banners: From each according to his ability, to each according to his needs![82]

In his characterization of advanced communism, Marx can be charged with having committed the error that he criticized so harshly in the writings of Hegel and the Utopian socialists: the error of unreal abstraction from the human situation as it is and must be. According to this charge, Marx spun a fanciful Utopia of his own—a purely ideal society, with no poverty, no alienation, no classes, no coercive state, no crippling division of labor, no overcentralization of administrative functions—a society in which economic affairs will be managed by voluntary associations of toilers, employing the most advanced techniques and the most rational plans—a society with abundant leisure, in which art, science, and other creative activities will be joyously pursued for their own sake—a society in which all basic needs will be met, in which human beings, liberated from bread-and-butter cares and the necessity of cringing to the powerful of the earth, will become really free.

The charge that Marx was himself a Utopian is not without basis, but the extent of his unrealism can be exaggerated. He did not believe that advanced communism will be a panacea for all human ills, or the ultimate climax of history. As a young man he declared, "communism is not itself the aim of human development or the final form of human society."[83] Late in his life, he still insisted that men must struggle against "natural necessity" even in the most advanced societies. "Just as the savage must wrestle with nature, in order to satisfy his wants," he wrote, ". . . so civilized man has to do it, and he must do it in all forms of society and under all possible modes of production."[84] Although he looked forward to the time when work will cease to be "something repulsive, as external, forced labor," he did not suppose that it will become "mere fun, mere amusement." On the contrary, it will be "damned serious, . . . the most intensive exertion."[85] The true realm of freedom, he reminded his readers, can flourish only upon the realm of necessity as its basis.

6. CRITICISMS AND CONCLUSIONS

Most evaluations of Marx must be taken with a large grain of salt. Although no social philosopher has been more damned and praised, he has seldom been depicted accurately. Both the huzzas and the boos have been the response to caricature. It is hard to say whether he has been worse served by his "friends" or his "enemies." One remembers his famous quip, "All I know is that I am not a Marxist."[86] I shall try to criticize his theories fairly.

Basic to his philosophy of history is the contention that the technological forces of production change more rapidly than the economic class structure and the institutions of property, and that historical crises are caused primarily by this incongruity between fast and slow changes. It is impossible to deny, now that automation and hydrogen bombs and space rockets have sensationally emphasized the fact, that technology is the greatest dynamic force in the modern world, and that failure to adjust our ideas and institutions to this force imperils the whole fabric of civilization. But Marx's interpretation of history is too narrow.

We come to the central paradox of his philosophy: his "materialistic interpretation of history" is as narrow as his conception of human bondage and emancipation is broad. He maintained that human nature is alienated at all levels and that it must be restored at every level; but he persuaded himself that "all human servitude is involved in the relation of the worker to production," and that "all the types of servitude are only modifications or consequences of this relation."[87] With the same oversimplification, he concluded that "all the conflicts of history have their origin in the contradiction between the productive forces and the mode of intercourse [that is, the class relations]."[88] Hence the radical cure of human ills is economic revolution, bringing the class relations into harmony with the productive forces. This will necessitate the abolition of private property in the means of production and the substitution of social ownership.

In emphasizing the overwhelming importance of property, Marx was at one with the representative thinkers of his age. Lord Macaulay, for example, declared that property is "that great institution to which we owe all knowledge, all commerce, all industry, all civilization, all that makes us differ from the tattooed savages of the Pacific Ocean."[89] Although a Whig, Macaulay was expressing the view of Socialist, Whig, and Tory alike. Marx agreed with Macaulay that private property was the basis of all existing European institutions. In this respect he was the intellectual captive of a materialistic age.

The unequal progress of races, as in South Africa or our Southern states, or of religious and nationalistic groups, as in Algeria and the Near East, may be as disturbing as the unequal development of economic classes. Most disturbing of all is the contrast between advanced and backward peoples. About three quarters of the world's population are Asiatic and African peasants, illiterate, disease-ridden, and near the starvation line. This is not the first time in history that peoples (excepting their privileged minorities) have suffered great deprivation. But it is the first time that hundreds of millions have become convinced that their wretchedness is unnecessary. In Asia, in Africa, in the Middle East, in Latin America, this conviction is growing, and both the communists and the anticommunists are vying for the allegiance of disaffected peoples.

This development is not what Marx expected. He believed that the main revolutionary development would occur in the *most advanced* industrial countries, where capitalism would reach a rotten-ripe maturity. In countries such as Great Britain and Germany, Marx believed, the class conflict would be most severe and the proletariat would revolt. More backward countries such as China and Russia might be swept into the current, but they would not be the spearhead of revolutionary change. Marx did not anticipate what has proved to be the fact, that the main areas of left-wing revolutionary uprising would be in the *least* industrialized countries, and that class differences *within* the mature capitalist nations would be far less disturbing than the social contrasts *between* the advanced and the backward nations.

Marx also wrongly interpreted the role of technology. He underrated the influence of military invention, which has a tremendous momentum semi-independent of the business system. War is a fecund source of technological innovation that ultimately has a very powerful influence upon industry and the whole civilization. Nations are now gripped with terror because the techniques of war have outstripped the skills of peacemaking. As Clemenceau remarked, "The art of massacring human beings is infinitely more easy than that of governing them."[90]

Marxism also failed to anticipate the new forms of *biological, social,* and *psychological* technology. In recent years, there have been important inventions in administrative techniques, in psychological methods of propaganda, and in the methods of our "public relations" experts. All such inventions may disturb the social equilibrium and act as dynamic forces in revolutionary change. The rise of fascist and communist totalitarianism was made possible by new techniques of indoctrination and administration as well as by the older types of physical technology. By cutting down the death rate, the development of medical technology has contributed immensely to an explosive population growth, as well as to other momentous changes. Living when the human sciences were quite immature, Marx was unable to foresee their broad implementation in many areas. He conceived technology too narrowly as the application of *physical* science and technique to *economic* processes. He was not cautious enough in interpreting invention and technology. He tried to extrapolate into the future the technological trends of his own day. As Karl Popper has pointed out, he did not see that these were simply *trends* rather than inexorable historical laws, and that trends can change. He failed to realize that inventions and discoveries, in their very novelty, cannot be anticipated in advance. For example, he could not possibly have predicted the splitting of the atom, with its sensational influence upon history. Hence his predictions have turned out to be wrong as often as they have turned out to be right. His argument is inconsistent because his recognition of the multilinear patterns of history conflicts with his oversimplified doctrine of historical determinism.

He underestimated the independence and importance of basic science. The very rapid expansion of technology would have been impossible without the swift development of pure research. Present-day technology is much more dependent on "pure science" than was the technology of the nineteenth century. As C. P. Snow has said, the old "industrial revolution" was almost entirely the creation of clever mechanics and inventors, with scant knowledge of science. Very different is the new "scientific revolution" of electronics, atomic energy, computers, and synthetics. The new revolution springs directly from quantum mechanics, the physics of relativity, advanced chemical research, and other developments in pure science.[91] Consider that elegant little gadget, the transistor. With all its amazing progeny of electronic devices, it is one of the great revolutionary forces of our age. Yet it is quantum-mechanical in its very essence, and thus originates from the work of the great scientists of quantum physics, such as Planck, Heisenberg, and Schrödinger. The argument of the Marxists that science depends mainly upon the economic system—especially upon industrial technology—is out of date. Even in Marx's lifetime, science floated uncertainly between base and superstructure, being both cause and effect of industrial technology. Now it belongs at the very basis of modern society, and is one of the cardinal "productive forces" of the new age.

Is the disequilibrating effect of science confined to its influence upon technology? I believe not. Even apart from technology, the furious pace of scientific discovery has a profoundly unsettling effect upon modern thought. New scientific discoveries are made much more rapidly than we can spiritually and culturally assimiliate them. Confusion results when the new truth, itself too complex and abstruse for the laity to comprehend, supplants the old truth. If men at times seem to be plunged into intellectual night, one reason is that there has been a very rapid increase in factual knowledge without an equivalent advance in synthesis and a sense of values. We therefore lack an adequate spiritual assimilation of scientific ideas and techniques; our wonderful new resources, for want of this right orientation, are linked to techniques of death rather than to arts of life. Marx's philosophy would have been more adequate if he could have foreseen these developments.

In maintaining the primacy of economics over politics, Marx has underestimated the importance of political factors. To illustrate, let us consider the supreme crisis of Greco-Roman civilization. This crisis was not merely economic but political as well. Economically and technologically the Greek cities became increasingly interdependent, but *political* evolution did not keep pace with these changes. As long as Greece was free and independent, it was not so much a single state as an anarchic bundle of independent city-states. For brief periods, the threat of Persian aggression forced parts of the Greek world into an uneasy alliance, but as soon as the danger subsided, the old economic and military conflicts among Athens, Sparta, Corinth, Syracuse, and other city-states broke out with renewed fierceness. Even when leagues of states were formed, these were pitted against each other, as were the Allies and the Central Powers in World War I or the Axis and the United Nations in World War II. The conflict between the Athenian and the Spartan confederations, growing out of their failure to unite under a common sovereignty, was the principal catastrophe of Greek civilization. Similarly, the conflict between Rome and Carthage was protracted and very costly. Eventually, by grim force of arms, a wider unity was achieved, first and precariously in the Macedonian Empire and later and more permanently in the Roman. Nevertheless, political unification was never attained upon the basis of rational persuasion, and the anachronism of the sovereign city-state persisted until the creative energies of the culture were depleted by war and imperialistic conquest. The failure of political adjustment to keep pace with the development of communication and transport produced a very serious disequilibrium; states that had become interdependent in fact remained disunited in political structure. When political unification was at last superimposed by military might, the decay of the culture was already far advanced.

We are confronted by an analogous crisis. The little city-states of yore have now been replaced by great nation-states, *but even these are not inclusive enough.* The world has become one in danger but not one in government. Transit, communication, and economic ties have developed much more rapidly than political unification. The resulting crisis is made immeasurably more serious by the swift and terrible development of modern technological warfare. As a consequence, the political anachronisms of war and the absolute nation-state are as serious as any economic anachronism could possibly be. The task of disarming and creating a real world government is as urgent as any economic task.

Discounting the importance of political factors in comparison with economic, Marx underestimated the power of the state to control the economic order. What we now call the "welfare state" is a demonstration of the capacity of government to direct and ameliorate the economic system. Marx thought that capitalism was bent on its own destruction, and that nothing could stop it from breaking its silly neck. But the economic theories of men like Keynes and the political experiments of men like Roosevelt proved this view oversimplified. Even in the Soviet Union the *political* direction of the economy has been decisive.

While Marx was aware of the critical importance of the modern organizational revolution in its *economic* aspects, he had little understanding or even awareness of this revolution in its political ramifications. He failed to realize the possibility of new political and social inventions that would humanize and democratize mass-civilization. The notion that democracy, by a series of innovations, would be able to convert "the great society" into an *open society* had not dawned upon him. Hence he concentrated upon the development of capitalism, convinced that its dehumanizing tendencies would work its undoing and that socialism and eventually a nonpolitical and beneficent anarchism would thereafter ensue. But democracy is still in its infancy. It has already created a welfare state such as Marx never envisaged, and it may yet find ways to create a humane, diversified and person-centered society. The growing sense of the importance of human rights and civil liberties is perhaps an earnest of things to come. To this question of the organizational revolution and what can be done about it, we shall return in later chapters.

Marx's one-sided emphasis upon economic factors led him to underestimate the dangers in political rule. Although he recognized the possibility of a "crude communism," he did not keep this danger in the forefront of his mind. He did not *clearly* understand—or if he did he repressed the insight—that the unification of economic, political, and military power within the state can produce an engine of terrible force, and that a new oligarchical class may use this engine for its own aggrandizement and increase in power. If diversity is the salt of freedom, a pluralistic society is far safer than an all-property-owning and all-power-possessing state. Marx had more than an inkling of this truth; it is a pity that he did not emphasize it in his most influential writings.

He was too ready to suppose that human bondage can be resolved by economic revolution, suspending civil liberties while the transition is made. We in this century know better. We have seen the dreadful effects of fascist and communist totalitarianism. We know how terribly basic and how terribly precious is freedom. Socialism is a mask for tyranny unless it is qualified by a stalwart adherence to civil liberties and a decentralization of power. In slighting this fact, Marx's insight, including his moral insight, was defective.

Although I heartily sympathize with Marx's humanist ethics, I am disturbed by his argument that esthetic, moral, and religious values are mainly "reflexes" determined by economic forces. His *tendency*—like that of Marxians at the present time—was to think of ideas and values as merely reflections and rationalizations of events in the economic sphere.

An example of a wider grasp of history may be found in the interpretation by the distinguished English historians, J. L. and Barbara Hammond, of working-class ferment in England during the first half of the nineteenth century. As economic historians, they were dealing with the same phenomena as Marx described in the historical chapters of *Capital,* but the difference in emphasis is illuminating.

The events that they seek to explain are known to every student of British history. The Luddite uprising in the Midlands and the industrial North, the strong popular agitation known as Chartism, the intrepid struggle of the Grand Consolidated Trade Union against the most formidable opposition, and the passionate and widespread enthusiasm evoked by Owen's socialist and cooperative movement were expressions of a great democratic tide of protest and resentment. Marx explained the rise of this unrest in economic terms, but the Hammonds maintained that a purely economic explanation is inadequate.

Inventions had made commodities cheaper; food and clothing were more abundant; the mills increased family incomes; the poorest people wore stockings; and in other respects the humblest person enjoyed advantages out of the reach of the lords and squires of other ages. . . . Statisticians tell us that when they have put in order such data as they can find, they are satisfied that earnings increased and that most men and women were less poor when this discontent was loud and active than they were when the eighteenth century was beginning to grow old in a silence like that of autumn.[92]

Discontent springs from the imagination, and it was the imagination that was chiefly starved. In premechanized England, the peasants and handicraft workers might have been ragged and illiterate, but they had their songs and carols, their Maypole dances and village festivals, pleasant meadows to wander over and the lark to listen to. Among the craftsmen, there was a love of fine workmanship, and among the yeomen, an enjoyment of the pure air and the natural surroundings. Their habits were easy, happy-go-lucky, and their holidays were abundant. In the crowded cities of the Midlands all this was lost. The slums were the foulest and the factories the dreariest that the world had ever known. Even the rich complained of the stench. Torrents of black smoke befouled the air, and water was in such limited supply that cleanliness was out of the question. There were no parks, no playgrounds, no public open spaces, no provisions for exercise and open-air amusements. The Greeks and the Romans, the townsmen of the Middle Ages and the Renaissance, had adorned their cities with the beauty and grace of public buildings, with plazas and statues and colonnades, and even the poorest could witness games, festivals, ceremonies, and theatrical spectacles. As the Hammonds remarked:

The old English towns were often over-crowded, insanitary, honeycombed with alleys and courts that never saw the sun or breathed the air, but the fancy, and emotion, and the skill and craftsmanship of different ages, had made them beautiful and interesting.[93]

Not so in Liverpool, Birmingham, Manchester, or Leeds. Carrying on their daily drudgery in a world of artifacts, the workers in these industrial centers found nature crowded out and beauty absent.

For the new town was not a home where man could find beauty, happiness, leisure, learning, religion, the influences that civilize outlook and habit, but a bare and desolate place, without color, air, or laughter, where man, woman and child worked, ate, and slept.[94]

The facts of injustice and exploitation which the Hammonds recite are as terrible as any in Marxist annals. They point out as emphatically as Marx the tragic consequences of combining rapid technological development with inflexible class rule. But they do not trace all social evils to an economic root, nor exalt economic revolution above all other remedies. Their explanation of the sore condition of British workers emphasizes not so much the imbalance of the economic system as the lack of balance and the incongruity of the civilization as a whole.

In the novel circumstances of rapid scientific and technological advance, men neglected to provide and cultivate the things of the spirit—love, art, recreation, learning, the sense of sacredness, and the feeling for natural beauty. Their *spiritual* poverty, not merely their lack of material goods, rankled within them. The new wealth was shockingly distributed, and the worker's share was often a pittance; but rich and poor alike were cheated by the bleakness of an acquisitive society. Knowledge of the external world and its incessant manipulation, with the piling up of material goods and increase in power, are quite insufficient to create a true civilization. After the fullest satisfaction of the prime, material needs, there remain those of a cultural and spiritual nature, and these are as pressing and decisive as the needs of a lower order. Such are the conclusions of the Hammonds upon the basis of their study of the English industrial revolution. Marx would agree in considerable measure, but there is a crucial difference in his sole emphasis upon *economic* causes.

The issue is relevant to American thought at this critical juncture of history. Our ability to prevail in the face of the communist threat will depend upon our capacity to understand history aright, to measure the strength and weakness of the Marxian creed, and to deepen our attachment to those humane and liberal values that constitute our spiritual resources. We shall be far likelier to succeed if we recognize that the things of the spirit are not only, as Marx visualized them, distant goals to be sought, but also, as the Hammonds realized, very present and potent forces among living men.

We need to be sensitive, as Marx was sensitive, to the enormous burden of human suffering. The humanitarian concern of Marx does honor to him as a man. If we were equally concerned it would be very much to our credit. But Marx, with all his greatness of mind and heart, was too sure about the way history would go, too one-sided in his emphasis upon economic forces,

340 SOCIAL IDEALS

and too ready to accept a powerful state managerialism. With a different
tradition of civil liberties and human rights, we need to cherish the humane
values and the free values of our civilization, and to recognize that man as a
pluralistic being deserves a pluralistic society. And so we have to revise Marx.
But as far as his moral passion is concerned, he was right.

NOTES

1. G. W. F. Hegel, "Love," in *Early
Theological Writings*. Chicago: University of Chicago Press, 1948, p. 303.
2. Ludwig Feuerbach, *The Essence of
Christianity* (abridged). New York:
Frederick Ungar Publishing Co.,
1957, pp. 32–33.
3. Feuerbach, *Grundsätze der Philosophie der Zukunft*. Zürich: 1843, pp.
60, 78.
4. Karl Marx, *Economic and Philosophical Manuscripts* (1844) in Marx,
Early Writings, translated and edited
by T. B. Bottomore. London: C. A.
Watts & Co., Ltd., 1963, p. 122.
Hereafter referred to as EPM. (In
the *Manuscripts*, Marx uses numerous
italics which I have omitted.)
5. *Ibid.*
6. Marx, *Capital*. Chicago: Charles H.
Kerr & Company, 1906–1909, I, p. 86.
(Volume I first appeared in German
in 1867.)
7. EPM, pp. 193–194.
8. *Ibid.*, p. 169.
9. *Ibid.*, p. 191.
10. Karl Marx and Friedrich Engels, *The
German Ideology* (1846). New York:
International Publishers, Inc., 1939,
p. 19.
11. *Cf.*, Erich Fromm, *Marx's Concept of
Man*. New York: Frederick Ungar
Publishing Co., 1961, p. 58.
12. Marx, "Speech at the Anniversary of
the *People's Paper*" (1856) in Marx,
Selected Works. New York: International Publishers, Inc., 1933, II, pp.
427–428.
13 *Cf.*, EPM, pp. 124–125, for an eloquent description of this form of
alienation.
14. Marx and Engels, *Gesamtausgabe*.

Frankfurt-Berlin Moscow: Marx-Eng-
els-Lenin Institute, 1927– , I, iii, p.
212. Hereafter referred to as MEGA.
15. Marx "On the Jewish Question"
(1844), *Early Writings, op. cit.*,
p. 37.
16. Marx, *Capital, op. cit.*, I, p. 708.
17. Marx, *Economic and Philosophical
Manuscripts*, as quoted by Alasdair
MacIntyre, *Marxism*. London: SCM
Press, 1953, pp. 50–51. (In this instance I have preferred MacIntyre's
translation.)
18. EPM, p. 158.
19. *Ibid.*, pp. 160–161.
20. *Ibid.*, p. 159.
21. *Ibid.*, p. 200.
22. *Ibid.*, p. 126.
23. *Ibid.*, p. 166.
24. *Ibid.*, p. 128.
25. *Ibid.*
26. *Ibid.*, p. 170.
27. *Ibid.*, pp. 169–170.
28. *Ibid.*, pp. 164–165.
29. *Ibid.*, pp. 171–172.
30. *Ibid.*, p. 172.
31. Marx, "A Criticism of the Hegelian
Theory of Right" (1844) in Marx,
Selected Essays. New York: International Publishers, Inc., 1926, pp. 26–
27.
32. Marx, *Capital, op. cit.*, I, pp. 530,
555.
33. EPM, p. 155.
34. Marx, "Communist Manifesto" (1848),
Selected Works, op. cit., I, p. 228.
35. Marx and Engels, *The German
Ideology, op. cit.*, pp. 24, 74.
36. EPM, pp. 160–161.
37. Marx, *Capital, op. cit.*, p. 668 footnote.
38. MEGA, I, iii, p. 359, *Cf.*, Erich

Fromm, *Marx's Concept of Man, op. cit.*, p. 25. Of the same import is a draft passage written for *The German Ideology* and omitted before completion. *Cf.*, MEGA, I, v, p. 596.

39. Marx and Engels, *Selected Correspondence*. New York: International Publishers, Inc., 1936, p. 511. For an illuminating discussion of Marx's theory of ideology, see Erich Fromm, *Beyond the Chains of Illusion*. New York: Simon and Schuster, Inc., 1963.

40. Marx, *The Eighteenth Brumaire of Louise Bonaparte* (1852) in Emile Burns, *A Handbook of Marxism*. New York: International Publishers, Inc., 1935, p. 118.

41. *Ibid.*, p. 119.

42. Marx, *Selected Works, op. cit.*, II, p. 442.

43. Marx, "A Criticism of the Hegelian Philosophy of Right," in Franz Mehring, *Karl Marx*. New York: Crown Publishers, Inc., 1935, p. 95.

44. Marx, "Theses on Feuerbach" (1845) in Marx, *Selected Writings in Sociology and Social Philosophy*, edited by T. B. Bottomore and Maximilian Rubel. London: C. A. Watts & Co., Ltd., 1956, p. 67.

45. *Ibid.*, p. 69.

46. MEGA, I, iii, p. 122.

47. EPM, p. 163.

48. *Ibid.*, p. 155.

49. Marx and Engels, *Selected Works, op. cit.*, I, pp. 217, 449, and *Selected Correspondence, op. cit.*, pp. 128, 293, 350.

50. William Barrett, *Irrational Man*. New York: Doubleday & Company, Inc., 1958, p. 244.

51. William Barrett and Henry D. Aiken, *Philosophy in the Twentieth Century*. New York: Random House, Inc., 1962, III, p. 143.

52. Karl Marx, *The Poverty of Philosophy* (1847). New York: International Publishers, Inc., no date, p. 165.

53. For a fuller discussion of Marx's concept of alienation, including abundant evidence that he did not abandon this concept in his later works, see Eugene

Kamenka, *The Ethical Foundations of Marxism*. London: Routledge & Kegan Paul, Ltd., 1962, especially Chapters 7, 8, and 14.

54. *Cf.*, Stanley Edgar Hyman, *The Tangled Bank*. New York: Alfred A. Knopf, Inc., 1962.

55. Marx, *Selected Writings in Sociology and Social Philosophy, op. cit.*, pp. 254–255. (Quoted from *Capital*, III; see page 954 in the Kerr edition.)

56. Marx, "On the Jewish Question," MEGA, I, i, p. 595.

57. Marx, "Critical Glosses on the Article: 'The King of Prussia and Social Reform. By a Prussian,'" *Vorwärts* (Paris), August 7, 1844; as translated by Eugene Kamenka, *The Ethical Foundations of Marxism, op. cit.*, pp. 68–69.

58. Marx, Introduction to *Grundrisse der Kritik der Politischen Ökonomie* (1857), in Marx, *Selected Writings in Sociology and Social Philosophy op. cit.*, p. 18.

59. Marx and Engels, *Selected Correspondence, op. cit.*, p. 477.

60. Marx, *The Poverty of Philosophy, op. cit.*, p. 92.

61. Engels, *The Origin of the Family, Private Property, and the State* (1884). Chicago: Charles H. Kerr & Company, 1902, p. 208.

62. *Ibid.*, p. 209.

63. Marx and Engels, *Selected Correspondence, op. cit.*, pp. 480–481.

64. Marx, *Selected Works, op. cit.*, I, p. 225.

65. Marx and Engels, *Selected Correspondence, op. cit.*, p. 477.

66. *Ibid.*, p. 472.

67. Marx, "A Criticism of the Hegelian Philosophy of Right" (1844), *Selected Essays, op. cit.*, p. 12.

68. Karl A. Wittfogel, *From Marx to Mao* (mimeographed). Seattle: University of Washington, 1960, p. 4. For a very illuminating discussion of Marx's "multilinear theory," see Wittfogel, *Oriental Despotism*, New Haven: Yale University Press, 1957.

69. Lewis H. Morgan, *Ancient Society*.

New York: Holt, Rinehart and Winston, Inc., 1877, p. 552.

70. *New York Daily Tribune,* June 25, 1853, reprinted in Marx and Engels, *On Colonialism.* Moscow: Foreign Languages Publishers House, no date, p. 33.

71. *New York Daily Tribune,* August 8, 1853, in *ibid.,* p. 79.

72. *New York Daily Tribune,* June 25, 1853, in *ibid.,* p. 36. For Marx's similar characterization of traditional Chinese society, see Wittfogel, *Oriental Despotism, op. cit.,* pp. 374–375.

73. Marx, *Selected Works, op. cit.,* I, p. 192.

74. Marx and Engels, *Selected Correspondence, op. cit.,* p. 199.

75. *Ibid.,* pp. 456–457.

76. Marx, *Selected Writings in Sociology and Social Philosophy, op. cit.,* p. 22.

77. EPM, pp. 153–154.

78. *Ibid.,* 132.

79. Engels, *Dialectics of Nature.* New York: International Publishers, Inc., 1940, p. 19.

80. Marx and Engels, *Selected Correspondence, op. cit.,* p. 476.

81. Marx, *The Civil War in France* (1871) in Marx, *Selected Works, op. cit.,* II, p. 474.

82. Marx, "Critique of the Gotha Program" (1875), *Selected Writings in*

Sociology and Social Philosophy, op. cit., p. 258.

83. EPM, as translated in *ibid.,* p. 246.

84. Marx, *Capital, op. cit.,* III, p. 954. (Volume III was published by Engels, 1893–1894.) My italics.

85. Marx, *Grundrisse der Kritik der Politischen Ökonomie* (1857–1858). Berlin: Dietz Verlag, 1953, pp. 504–505.

86. Marx and Engels, *Selected Correspondence, op. cit.,* p. 472.

87. EPM, p. 107.

88. Marx, *Selected Writings in Sociology and Social Philosophy, op. cit.,* p. 247.

89. Lord Macaulay, "Speech on the Reform Bill."

90. Quoted by William L. Shirer in his syndicated column, *Oakland Tribune,* December 29, 1945.

91. *Cf.,* C. P. Snow, *The Two Cultures and the Scientific Revolution.* New York: Cambridge University Press, 1959.

92. J. L. and Barbara Hammond, *The Bleak Age.* Middlesex: Penguin Books, 1947, p. 15.

93. J. L. and Barbara Hammond, *The Town Laborer.* New York: David McKay Company, Inc., 1925, p. 38.

94. J. L. and Barbara Hammond, *The Rise of Modern Industry.* New York: Harcourt, Brace & World, Inc., 1926, p. 232.

CHAPTER XIII

The democratic ideal

I. THE ARISTOCRATIC VERSUS THE DEMOCRATIC IDEAL

In the preceding chapter, we have examined the communist ideal as formulated by Karl Marx. As we have seen, it is not altogether alien to the liberal and humanist tradition of western civilization. But "communism" as practiced in China and the Soviet Union resembles the "crude communism" attacked by Marx in *The Economic and Philosophical Manuscripts*. As a very powerful and expansive state-managerialism, it has challenged democracy more severely than it has ever been challenged before.

The challenge to the democratic ideal is of course not new. One of the classic arguments against democracy was stated in *The Republic* of Plato, whose doctrine we shall now consider. The foundation of his theory was the principle of the right allocation and performance of functions. In tracing the origin and rise of the state, he stressed the natural growth of the division of labor. At first there were only a few farmers, weavers, shoemakers, and builders, but to these were soon added, as the society grew more complex, other kinds of craftsmen and merchants. This specialization made for greater efficiency, the easier production of goods and services. Each worker, mastering the skills of his craft, proved far more useful than the jack-of-all-trades.

In ordinary life we rightly demand this kind of specialized skill. If we have shoes that need fixing, we do not hand them over to anyone who is willing to tinker with them; we take them to a shoe repairman who knows what to do. If we are seriously ill, we are not content to listen to an old wives' tale about remedies; we go to a physician who is wise in these matters. Each man is called upon to do that for which he is best fitted in ability and training. Plato regarded this principle of functional differentiation as the basis of any efficient society. If the shoemaker should stick to his last and master his craft, why should not the statesman stick to his statesmanship and acquire the special skills required for *his* task?

In Athenian democracy, Plato pointed out, things did not work out this way. All of the citizens had the right to sit in the legislative assembly, and the executive officials were selected by lot. Modern democracies are more indirect, but the popular ballot would be condemned unequivocally by Plato. Our politicians, advertisers, publicists, and broadcasters, he would say, have merely mastered the art of the Sophists—to make the worse appear the better cause. They know how to appeal to prejudice and misinformation, how to stupefy and hypnotize the popular mind by endless repetitions, by fomenting extravagant desires, or by creating an atmosphere of delusion. A philosopher who wished to illustrate the nature of logical fallacies could find no end of examples in their outpourings.

There will be no remedy for these evils, Plato maintained, until statesmanship becomes a rational science, demanding careful training and unusual aptitudes. Wisdom and the supreme power of the state must be united in the same persons. An intellectual aristocracy would strenuously guard a high standard of culture. It would insist that only the best representatives of this standard be intrusted with the art of government. Until this change is brought about, democracy will continue to drag all standards down to the cheap mediocre level of the average.

In the Eighth Book of *The Republic*, Plato vividly characterized the foibles and weaknesses of democracy. The typical democrat is guided by no fixed principles or inner discipline. He turns from one interest to another, just as the fancy strikes him.

So he spends his days indulging the pleasure of the moment, now intoxicated with wine and music, and then taking to a spare diet and drinking nothing but water; one day in hard training, the next doing nothing at all, the third apparently immersed in study. Every now and then he takes a part in politics, leaping to his feet to say or do whatever comes into his head. Or he will set out to rival someone he admires, a soldier it may be, or, if the fancy takes him, a man of business. His life is subject to no order or restraint, and he has no wish to change an existence which he calls pleasant, free, and happy.[1]

Democracy is as irresponsible and capricious as its typical citizens. It is indifferent to all distinctions of order and rank, and it will promote to office anyone who calls himself the people's friend. Hence its leaders are demagogues rather than statesmen.

The contrast afforded by aristocracy is a sharp one. The rulers in Plato's aristocratic state are "philosophers" in the broadest sense. They must appreciate the arts and understand the sciences, but they must also know the "form" or essence of goodness—of beauty, wisdom, justice, courage, and temperance. They must know, that is to say, the proper ends of human action, in order that they may direct the activities of the state in the light of a supreme purpose. The state should be guided by the highest and noblest reason which is possible for man.

From this conception of the ruler it follows naturally that he must be very carefully selected and trained. To achieve this end, Plato proposed very sweeping reforms. He advocated a complete comradeship of the sexes in the higher duties of society, women to be given the same opportunities as men. He conceived a bold program of eugenics to improve the blood and bone and brain of the human stock. He wanted to bring together the fittest mates without restriction of monogamous marriage and induce them to multiply. But, above all, he wanted education to revolutionize life and to produce a different and far better world.

Education should use all its resources: the body and character to be trained by gymnastics, the senses and feelings to be cultivated by the arts, the intellect to be developed by the sciences, and the reason to be brought to its peak by philosophical study and dialectic. Those who win highest honors will be given responsible positions to test and train them in practical affairs. Only when tested and trained in every way, intellectually and morally, will the select few be intrusted with the high tasks of statesmanship. Students with lesser ability will be prepared for the vocation of soldiers, while the bulk of the population will receive an education proportioned to their much lower capacities, and will then be occupied with the production of economic goods and services.

Many aspects of Plato's ideal state have turned out to be open to grave objections. His tripartite division of the soul into appetite, spirit, and reason; his corresponding division of the social classes into workers, soldiers, and philosopher-kings; his recommendation that the ruling class should employ myths and "noble lies" to deceive the people; his views about censorship of religion and the arts, about eugenics, about the community of property, or the community of wives and children—all are open to question or severe criticism. The greatness of *The Republic* depends less upon these details than upon its guiding ideal: the cultivation of excellence by the rule of wise men. This ideal has lost none of its vitality.

2. SHARING AND EXCELLENCE

It would be a great mistake to suppose that the democrat must reject the aristocratic ideal of excellence. He is bound to maintain that the aristocratic ideal is not adequate; and he is necessarily opposed to overprivilege and underprivilege. He believes in the equal satisfaction of equal needs, the equal recognition of equal abilities, and an equality of opportunity. But he need not despise excellence in any of its manifestations. He is not compelled by his democratic faith to prefer mediocrity—it would be foolish and vulgar for him to do so—but as a consistent democrat, he cannot be satisfied with excellence alone. He wishes excellence to be widely and equitably shared.

Sharing and excellence—these are the two great values that must be combined and cultivated. The civilized world has experienced much of each individually but not much sharing of excellence. This kind of sharing represents the valid reconciliation of democracy and aristocracy. First, we must share the good things of life, and second, we must make the things shared just as good as possible. If democracy is to be adequate, it must, in this sense, embrace and include the aristocratic ideal.

The timeworn charge against democracy is that it involves sharing without excellence. The impossibility of reconciling excellence and sharing has been asserted, for example, by George Santayana in these words:

Culture is on the horns of this dilemma: if profound and noble it must remain rare, if common it must become mean. These alternatives can never be eluded until some purified and highbred race succeeds the promiscuous bipeds that now blacken the planet.[2]

There is a certain amount of truth in this statement. Many forms of excellence involve such difficulty that they will always be more or less rare. Yet it is doubtful if there is any soil more congenial to high attainment, and certainly to the sharing of its benefits, than a political and social democracy. Wide differentials in opportunity, such as occur in an undemocratic society, prevent the maximum attainment of both sharing and excellence. The underprivileged are seriously handicapped, the overprivileged are preferred to their betters. Only in a democratic society, where opportunity is the heritage of all, can there be the most effective development, and the best use, of talent. As Ralph Barton Perry has well said:

In democracy it is not a question of giving room and authority to the genius which has already declared itself, and of sacrificing thereto the residual mass of mediocrity, but one of tapping new sources, and discovering genius in obscure and unsuspected quarters. By giving light and air to the hitherto buried masses of mankind, democracy hopes to enrich human culture in the qualitative, and not merely in the quantitative sense.[3]

To enrich culture in both a qualitative and quantitative sense—this is indeed the proper goal of a democracy. But such enrichment is possible only if the democracy is of a high type, only if the democratic society itself adopts the aristocratic goal of excellence. It must not sacrifice the choice goods out of love for the common goods; it must not value mere size, speed, and power. If Western democracy is not to go the way of Babylon and Rome, it must cultivate intellectual discrimination, esthetic sensitiveness, and moral refinement.

The nature of the problem—how to combine excellence and sharing—is revealed in the life and correspondence of that brilliant, almost legendary figure, T. E. Lawrence (1888–1935). After his astonishing feats as a leader of the Arabs in World War I, he became profoundly disgusted with the failure of the Allies to fulfill their promises to the Arab people, and in 1922 he sought escape from mental turmoil by enlisting under an assumed name as a mechanic in the Royal Air Force. The following year in a continued attempt to elude publicity, he transferred to the Tank Corps. The ensuing experience as an ordinary enlisted man brought deep anguish, almost to the point of madness and suicide. Being an Oxford graduate, an archeologist, man of letters, and lover of music, he was wounded to the quick by the indifference of his new companions to beauty and wisdom. In a letter to Lionel Curtis, the editor of the quarterly *Review of Politics,* he poured forth his bitter questions and doubts.

Can there be profit, or truth, in all these modes and sciences and arts of ours? The leisured world for hundreds, or perhaps thousands of years has been jealously working and recording the advance of each generation for the starting-point of the next—and here these masses are as animal, as carnal as were their ancestors before Plato and Christ and Shelley and Dostoevsky taught and thought. In this crowd it's made startlingly clear how short is the range of knowledge, and what poor conductors of it ordinary humans are. You and I know: you have tried to tell all whom you can reach: and the end is here, a cimmerian darkness with bog-lights flitting wrongly through its gas.[4]

Lawrence's realization of the pervasive animality of his companions was no more shocking to his personality than the doubts that assailed him as to the role of such artists and intellectuals as himself. Without any deep foundation in the masses, the cultivated élite seemed to him rootless, and therefore lacking the pristine health and virility of his carnal companions. In the same letter from which I have quoted, Lawrence declared:

These fellows are the reality, and you and I, the selves who used to meet in London and talk of fleshless things, are only the outward wrappings of a core like these fellows. They let light and air play always upon their selves, and consequently have grown very lustily, but have at the same time achieved health and strength in their growing. Whereas our wrappings and bandages have stunted and deformed ourselves, and hardened them to an apparent insensitiveness . . . but it's a callousness, a crippling, only to be yea-said by aesthetes who prefer clothes to bodies, surfaces to intentions.[5]

This letter is a vivid presentation of perhaps the supreme problem of human culture: How can the uprooted intelligentsia strike roots in the soil of humanity? How can mankind, split into the élite and the masses, be harmonized and made whole? How can the leaven of culture enter into the lump of common life? How can we attain a culture that is high in its vertical thrust and broad in its horizontal spread?

In Lawrence's letter, we can see him groping toward the combination of excellence and sharing, which is the only valid solution of the problem of aristocracy versus democracy. The first stage of Lawrence's mental history was the experience of the choice goods—the cultivation of excellence in poetry, art, music, and philosophy. This was followed by a shocking reversal: the apparent negation of all that he most valued—the discovery that the com-

mon goods, which lack refinement but have intense vitality, are sharply opposed to his aristocratic values. The resulting conflict forced him to think
back over the whole of his previous experience. His letters written at this
stage implied that mankind must not sacrifice the common goods out of love
for the choice goods, or vice versa; and consequently the goal is neither
excellence alone nor sharing alone, but the sharing *of* excellence. His whole
view of life was being broadened and transformed; he was reaching out toward the ideal of a high yet classless culture.

Such a culture would be a deep organic part of common life and "as wide
and varied as humanity itself." It would not be a toy of the rich and the
sophisticated—"a thing added like a sauce to otherwise unpalatable stale
fish." Culture as a "separate commodity"—"something to be acquired by
superior people with sufficient time and money," and described in the "society section" of our Sunday newspapers—would not even exist in a thoroughly democratic society. To continue in the words of Herbert Read:

> A democratic culture—*that is not the same thing as a democracy plus culture.*
> The first important point that I must make and keep on stressing, is that culture
> in a natural society will not be a separate and distinguishable thing—a body of
> learning that can be put into books and museums and mugged up in your spare
> time. Just because it will not exist as a separate entity, we had better stop using
> the word "culture". . . . To hell with culture![6]

A democratic culture, which is the only kind that we should not consign to
hell, is no mere by-product of democracy. It is democracy itself as a creative
and articulate way of life.

It was toward such a conception of culture that Lawrence was groping. He
was too individualistic and unpolitical in his interests, however, to push the
implications of his thinking very far into the field of fundamental social reconstruction. It was characteristic of him to think in terms of personal action,
such as the attempt, by sharing his phonograph record collection, to stimulate the appreciation of fine music among the enlisted men. But at least *we*
can appreciate the broad implications of his more mature insight; we can
understand that the valid ideal for human culture, in its many diverse
aspects, is the interpenetration of excellence and sharing. This means a culture high in its vertical thrust into excellence and yet broad in its horizontal
spread among the masses.

An undemocratic state, such as Czarist Russia, may be content with a
vertical culture. The old Russian empire achieved a narrow kind of eminence.
Names such as Dostoevsky and Tolstoy in literature, Moussorgsky and
Tschaikowsky in music, Pavlova and Nijinsky in dancing, and the Moscow
Art Theater in drama, testify to the heights of the Russian achievement.
Even in science there were such illustrious figures as Lobatchewsky, the
mathematician, Mendeleef, the chemist, and Pavlov, the physiologist. But
only the few could participate in art and science. The overwhelming mass of

the population was filthy, illiterate, and half starved. The vertical culture was enviably high, but the horizontal culture was insufferably narrow. Similarly wealth and political power were the monopoly of the few.

The United States has yet to achieve a culture as high in some respects as that of Czarist Russia. We likewise have not attained, except in science, to the heights of other historical periods—Athens in the time of Pericles, Florence in the time of the Medicis, London in the time of Queen Elizabeth. The achievement of these ancient societies was high but restricted to narrow limits. We democrats want no such restriction. Ours is a dual demand: give us *both* excellence and sharing.

We should, therefore, encourage the people of unusual ability—the artists and the thinkers—and we should increasingly use our public institutions— schools, forums, libraries, museums, theaters, and concert halls—to diffuse the benefits of this stimulated talent and to evoke the latent talents of the people. Whatever be the form of sharing, there is a corresponding form of excellence—political intelligence, economic efficiency, or cultural eminence. We must strive to achieve and share all of these forms of excellence. These values will thereby be embodied not merely in institutions but in the hearts and minds of the people. Democracy, as a way of life, is the self-realization of cooperative human beings—the interpenetration of excellence and sharing.

To achieve this goal, our nation should fully embrace, and adapt to its own purposes, Plato's ideal of an educational state. Education is at the very heart and core of democracy, and without it civilization cannot survive in a world as complex and dangerous as ours. As Whitehead has said, civilization is "the victory of persuasion over force";[7] and such victory requires, above all, the arts of the teacher. At a time when the capacity both to destroy and to construct has increased by leaps and bounds, we need a gigantic effort at synthesis and liberal education, so that human knowledge can be directed to life enhancement rather than to life destruction, and so that the vast and ever-accumulating mass of scientific information can be integrated into a unified interpretation of nature and man. This great task in itself depends upon a broad community of effort, transcending the specialisms of research, scholarship, and teaching. It calls not only for the expert and the technician but for an open forum of discussion and socially elaborated judgments, to which every man can contribute his little stock of talent and wisdom for the common good. It calls for a juster and wider employment of human resources than any aristocracy can ever boast.

Democracy does not mean that all men will be treated alike: it means that all will be given a chance to prove themselves, and that preference will be given only to those who can contribute most to human well-being. Democracy believes not in the absurd doctrine of an equality of native capacities but in the sensible ideal of an equality of rights and opportunities. The very fact of psychological inequality is all the more reason for equal opportunity, since without it, able men will often be handicapped and the less gifted will often be preferred to their natural betters. A wise democracy will be eager to develop its geniuses, but it will recognize that genius crops up in lowly places.

Jesus was the son of a carpenter and Leonardo da Vinci the illegitimate son of a domestic servant; . . . Shakespeare's father was a butcher and glover; Beethoven's, a "confirmed drunkard"; Schubert's, a peasant; Faraday's, "a poor blacksmith"; Carlyle's, a stone-mason; Lincoln's, a "roving carpenter"—"poor white trash"; Pasteur's, a tanner; Browning's, a clerk; . . . Socrates' mother was a midwife, Beethoven's, the "daughter of a cook"; and Schubert's, "an ignorant drudge."[8]

The democrat's reply to the aristocrat is that he does not want art or science or education for the few any more than government for the few. He recognizes the importance of cultivating intelligence, but he wants it to be social, expressing the interests of the community rather than the interests of privilege.

3. SOCIAL INTELLIGENCE

What is "social intelligence?" Is it something reserved to an élite or something possessed by common men? Can democracy summon the intelligence to set its house in order? Among political philosophers, no one has answered these questions more illuminatingly than Jean Jacques Rousseau (1712–1778). I am thinking less of the earlier Rousseau, who glorified the unspoiled innocence of the primitive natural man, than of the later Rousseau, who envisaged the "freedom under law" enjoyed by the civilized citizen as a responsible member of the body politic. To find the more mature thought of Rousseau we must turn to his Social Contract.

We shall mistake the nature of his theory if we suppose that it is merely another version of the social contract theory, such as that of Locke. The language of Rousseau was in part a carry-over from the tradition of individualistic liberalism, but his basic thought was very different. When he spoke of men entering into a social contract, he did not mean an artificial compact between self-seeking individuals, with certain definite and stipulated conditions agreed to by all the parties concerned. Far from being a deliberate and artificial creation, the state as he conceived it is a spontaneous and natural growth. It is a continuing expression of the common life of its members, the embodiment of "the general will."

Instead of maintaining that there are "natural rights" that exist in a *pre-social* "state of nature," Rousseau contended that all rights are essentially social.

The social order is a sacred right which is the basis of all other rights. Nevertheless, this right does not come from nature, and must therefore be founded on conventions.[9]

As a result of social conventions, a human being ceases to be "a stupid and unimaginative animal" and becomes "an intelligent being and a man."[10]

The fundamental convention, which Rousseau called "the social contract," is that which created the state. The question of its historical origin is unanswerable and irrelevant, and the pertinent question is its legitimacy.

The problem is to find a form of association which will defend and protect with the whole common force the person and goods of each associate, and in which each, while uniting himself with all, may still obey himself alone, and remain as free as before.[11]

To this problem, the social contract provides the solution.

Each of us puts his person and all his power in common under the supreme direction of the general will, and, in our corporate capacity, we receive each member as an indivisible part of the whole.[12]

The body politic thus created is a society of free assent and not of force, and a union of each with all on equal terms for the common welfare. Although individualistic "freedom," the mere isolation and independency of the "natural man," is surrendered to such a union, a far more substantial freedom, the power and prerogative of the citizen, is thereby attained.

Each man, in giving himself to all, gives himself to nobody; and as there is no associate over whom he does not acquire the same right as he yields others over himself, he gains an equivalent for everything he loses, and an increase of force for the preservation of what he has.[13]

Ernest Hunter Wright, in his excellent book, *The Meaning of Rousseau*, supplies a "homely illustration" of the terms of this exchange.

When there was no society, of course I paid no taxes, and now I have to do so. That is my loss. But all the other members also pay taxes, and the amount of their tribute that is used for my benefit should equal the amount I pay to benefit them all. So my gain is equal to my loss. But together we can do things with our taxes that would be impossible in any other way; so by joining forces we have each inherited a power hitherto unknown. Extend the illustration, and the principle would seem to hold. Every duty that I owe the other members of society is balanced by a duty they perform in part for my benefit; and meanwhile we have all gained the strength that comes from union.[14]

Such union creates the democratic state. In the active exercise of its functions, the state is called a sovereign; and the sovereign is the general will, exercised by the single collective body of all the citizens. Law is the voice of the general will, and it alone provides security in human rights. Liberty under law is the only kind that is not illusory.

The general will, which thus expresses itself in law, is "general" in two senses. It is general in its objective: its aim, in the language of the United States Constitution, is "to promote the general welfare." It is also general in expressing the will of all. The Constitution begins: "We, the people of the United States . . . do ordain and establish. . . ." The will of a whole people is being expressed.

The general will is not the sum of particular wills. In so far as a person is expressing only his separate identity, his selfish interest, he is not functioning as a citizen, and no summation of the votes of private self-seeking individuals can speak for the general will. Rousseau insists that a political community is a union that binds men organically together, their wills merged and transformed in a corporate will.

At once in place of the individual personality of each contracting party, this act of association creates a moral and collective body, composed of as many members as the assembly contains votes, and receiving from this act its unity, its common identity, its life and its will. This public person, so formed by the union of all other persons, formerly took the name of City, and now takes that of Republic, or Body Politic.[15]

Just as this corporate personality transcends all purely individual interests, so it transcends all limited group interests. Rousseau rejects the "pressure group" theory of the state no less emphatically than he rejects the purely individualistic theory. A state is not an arena of conflicting groups, each expressing its bias, but an organic body of disinterested citizens intent upon the general welfare.

If the clashing of particular interests made the establishment of societies necessary, the agreement of these very interests made it possible. The common element in these different interests is what forms the social tie; and, were there no point of agreement between them all, no society could exist. It is solely on the basis of this common interest that every society should be governed.[16]

The clear implication of this passage is that there must be no "house divided against itself," no fundamental cleavage into classes or other divisive groups. "If the general will is to be able to express itself," declares Rousseau, "there should be no partial society within the state."[17] The prime requirement for such unity is the abolition of special privilege, and hence the establishment of social equality.

From whatever side we approach our principle, we reach the same conclusion, that the social compact sets up among the citizens an equality of such a kind, that they all bind themselves to observe the same conditions and should therefore all enjoy the same rights.[18]

Long before Marx, Rousseau had sketched the ideal of a classless society. That it is an ideal, and not an actuality, Rousseau would have been the first to admit. He would have agreed with the words of Walt Whitman in his *Democratic Vistas* that

We have frequently printed the word Democracy. Yet I cannot too often repeat that it is a word the real gist of which still sleeps, quite unawakened, notwithstanding the resonance and the many angry tempests out of which its syllables have come, from pen or tongue. It is a great word, whose history, I suppose, remains unwritten, because that history has yet to be enacted.[19]

If the history of democracy remains largely unenacted, can we still say that societies, in so far as they approach the democratic ideal, exhibit social intelligence? The theory of Rousseau will help us to answer this question.

The first point to make is that no other kind of intelligence is truly *social* in the sense of representing a real community of interests. The private interests of individuals, competing in a system of devil-take-the-hindmost, are not in this sense social. Among interests of this sort there can be conflict or domination or compromise but not a real integration and mutual enhancement. Again, the interests of the most powerful class, or of a dominant élite, are not truly social, in the sense of representing the society as a whole. They involve a separation of the part from the whole, and to this extent, they are outside the society, imposing patterns upon it. All such interests, whether of private individuals or of partial groups, are *special* interests seeking *special* privileges. Quite different are the interests involved in and evolved by a community of interacting and interdependent individuals, consciously acknowledging the mutuality of their interests.

If Rousseau's theory be correct, democracy must remain master in its own house. It must not turn the state over to experts, whether they be the philosopher-kings of Plato's *Republic*, or the psychologist-engineers of B. F. Skinner's *Walden Two*, or the industrial technicians of Thornstein Veblen's *The Engineers and the Price System*. But popular self-government will be far more successful if the experts participate in the democratic process. They should help to educate the electorate and enlarge their political choices by revealing what alternatives science and technology make possible. The common people, in turn, should educate the technicians so as to make clear the wants and needs of the community and thus to define the great ends that knowledge should serve. In order to secure this mutual instruction, what is required is not an oligarchy of experts but a vigorous democracy that brings the masses and the experts together in lively communication. The leaders, expert though they be, belong to the people. They are the leaven within the common loaf.

4. FREEDOM AND POLITICAL OBLIGATION

We have been dealing with what seems to me the soundest part of Rousseau's theory of democracy. What is permanently valuable in the *Social Contract* is the theory of "the general will." But there is another strain in Rousseau's thinking—perhaps more profound but less liberal. It leads in the direction of a kind of "totalitarian democracy," that is, a majority government without civil liberties and minority rights. Alexis de Tocqueville, in his famous study of democracy in America, pointed out the popular tendency toward this kind of antiliberalism:

I think that democratic communities have a natural taste for freedom; left to themselves, they will seek it, cherish it, and view any privation of it with regret. But for equality, their passion is ardent, insatiable, incessant, invincible; they call for equality in freedom: and if they cannot obtain that, they still call for equality in slavery.[20]

The older individualistic philosophers, such as Locke, feared the popular demand for equality, and wished to protect individual liberty as a natural right by hedging government with checks and restraints. But Rousseau had a very different approach to the problems of freedom. He conceived of law in a democratic state as springing from the *free* corporate will of the citizens. Hence the law is no alien thing exercising an *external* compulsion. It is the expression, even though imperfect, of the common will of men for the life worth living—the embodiment of their immanent and unquenchable idealism. The state, with its legal system, is not something to be hated and if possible escaped. It should be unleashed as a friend, not tethered and bound as an enemy.

Rousseau was aware of the objection of the nonconformist. Whenever a malefactor or dissenter is punished by the state, it is a shocking paradox to say that the victim himself has willed the chastisement. Here the private will of the individual and the general will of the state appear to be in irreconcilable conflict. But such a view, Rousseau maintained, is superficial. The malefactor *does* will his punishment, the rebel his imprisonment. For the deepest will of each human being is to achieve the best life possible, and *that* life can be achieved only in and through the state. We must distinguish between *two* wills in the recalcitrant individual: first, the particular and private will that is pitted against the state; and second, the deep common will that works in all of us. In breaking the law, the citizen does not extinguish in himself the general will, but only eludes it. For his private antisocial will represents merely the capricious aspect of his nature. It is open to correction in view of the deeper interest and will of the individual and the community. In repressing the wayward anti-social self, the law frees the citizen from the forces that betray him.

In order then that the social compact may not be an empty formula, it tacitly includes the undertaking, which alone can give force to the rest, that whoever refuses to obey the general will shall be compelled to do so by the whole body. This means nothing less than that he shall be forced to be free. . . .[21]

It is not too hard to see an underlying truth in Rousseau's paradox. The "real will" of the individual—his long-range and fundamental will—may be better expressed by the state and the legal order than by his casual, careless, or superficial will. The coercive power of the state, as for example when it requires compulsory school attendance, will be justified as it sets at liberty a growth of mind and spirit that has been struggling to find fulfillment. Such compulsion will eventually reward the individual and the community alike. Even in the extreme case, that of the punishment of crime, the treatment meted out may be in accord with the deeper desire of the criminal. In a sense, the murderer wills that the law against murder shall stand, for although he kills, he wants his own life and the lives of his family and friends secure against the kind of reckless deed that he is committing.

The citizen gives his consent to all the laws, including those which are passed in spite of his opposition, and even those which punish him when he dares to break any of them. The constant will of all the members of the state is the general will; by virtue of it they are citizens and free.[22]

If Rousseau had limited himself to this argument, we might differ with him in details but agree with him in essentials. But his position is more extreme. He argued that no person will oppress himself, and therefore a sovereign people, reflecting the interests of all, will oppress none of its members.

The Sovereign, being formed wholly of the individuals who compose it, neither has nor can have any interest contrary to theirs; and consequently the sovereign power need give no guarantee to its subjects, because it is impossible for the body to wish to hurt all its members. We shall also see later on that it cannot hurt any in particular. The Sovereign, merely by virtue of what it is, is always what it should be.[23]

Rousseau was guilty of what logicians call "the fallacy of composition." He argued that what is true of each member of a group is true of the group as a whole. But the fact that each individual in a group will not tyrannize over himself does not guarantee that the group as a whole will not tyrannize over its members.

Here as elsewhere Rousseau's argument was unrealistic. He assumed that "the general will" is the *actual* sovereign (the supreme governing agency) within the democratic state; and he tended to identify the *general will* with the *good will* and the *actual state* with the *ideal state*. But the plain fact is that the person or party vested with supreme coercive power may or may not express the general will, and the will of a people may or may not be wise and beneficent.

How very far Rousseau's totalitarian tendencies go is indicated by his remarks about "civil religion." He wanted to make the creed of patriotism a compulsory dogma:

There is therefore a purely civil profession of faith of which the Sovereign should fix the articles, not exactly as religious dogmas, but as social sentiments without which a man cannot be a good citizen or a faithful subject. While it can compel no one to believe them, it can banish from the state whoever does not believe them—it can banish him, not for impiety, but as an anti-social being, incapable of truly loving the laws and justice, and of sacrificing, at need, his life to his duty. If any one, after publicly recognizing these dogmas, behaves as if he does not believe them, let him be punished by death: he has committed the worst of all crimes, that of lying before the law.[24]

Rousseau's worship of the state was combined with an attack upon every lesser form of association. The theme of almost all his early writings was the oppressions and corruptions of society. This motif ran through his early *Discourses, Emile,* and the *Confessions.* The one organization that he did not condemn was the state: "It is characteristic of society to breed a ceaseless war among its members," he declared, "and the only way to combat this is to find a form of government which shall set the law above them all."[25] The democratic state, he believed, is the only force strong and disinterested enough to free the individual from the corruptions of society. Hence he proposed to suppress all social ties except that of the unfettered state.

Each citizen would then be completely independent of all his fellow men, and absolutely dependent upon the state . . . ; for it is only by the force of the state that the liberty of its members can be achieved.[26]

Inspired by Rousseau, the French Revolution sought to practice these principles. It prohibited various sorts of religious communities; it forbade every kind of union and association either of workers or employers; and it abolished the corporate independence of hospitals, charities, schools, and learned academies. André de Chénier, a poet who lost his head to the guillotine, expressed the Rousseauistic objective of the Revolution:

Unwise and unhappy is the state where there exist various associations and collective bodies whose members, on entering them, acquire a different spirit and different interests from the general spirit and the general interest! Happy is the land where there is no form of association but the state, no collective body but the country, no interest but the general good![27]

The small scale of the city-state, which Rousseau regarded as ideal, would mitigate evils of this sort of totalitarianism. But when his doctrine, as in the case of the French Revolution, is transposed to the great nation-state, its implications become quite terrifying. Atomized and isolated from one another, robbed of the variety of human associations, the citizens stand defenseless before the massive and all-embracing power of the state.

People are complex creatures with many-sided interests and affiliations. The creed of totalitarianism, "nothing outside the state, nothing against the state, everything within the state," does violence to the richness and diversity of human potentialities. Because the state "represents" the people, any action against the state is automatically an action against the people. The right to strike, for example, would be denied, as it is in present-day totalitarian states; the worker would not be allowed to strike against "his own representatives."

There is here no protection against the tyranny of the majority or the authority of the state.

Despite the totalitarian elements in the concept of "the general will," it would be wrong to dismiss Rousseau as merely one of the forerunners of modern totalitarianism. He was a bundle of contradictions; neither the democratic nor the authoritarian elements in his mind could form an harmonious structure. An individualist and a collectivist, an anarchist and a disciplinarian, a primitivist and defender of social conventions, he defies classification.

5. MILL ON LIBERTY

John Stuart Mill was also a complex and contradictory thinker, but there was nothing of the totalitarian in his make-up. In his classic essay *On Liberty,* he took a position quite different from that of Rousseau. He argued that a democratic government is just as much in need of being curbed as any other type. "The will of the people," he pointed out, "practically means the will of the most numerous or the most active *part* of the people; the majority, or those who succeed in making themselves accepted as a majority; the people, consequently, *may* desire to oppress a part of their number; and precautions are as much needed against this as against any other abuse of power."[28]

Mill here put his finger on the latent danger of democracy, "the tyranny of the majority." He had been shocked by Alexis de Tocqueville's classic study, *Democracy in America,* which decried the illiberalism and crowd pressure of a mass society. Sharing de Tocqueville's alarm, Mill believed that strong safeguards must be erected against mass conformism. His argument was a defense of individuality against public opinion, the despotism of custom, the conventionalities of society, and the overweening power of government. "Protection . . . against the tyranny of the magistrate is not enough," he pointed out. "There needs protection also against the tyranny of prevailing opinion and feeling which would compel all other characters to fashion themselves upon the model of its own." His objective was to create not only a liberal government but a liberal society.

He avowedly based his argument not upon natural rights but upon "utility, in the largest sense, grounded on the permanent interests of man as a social being." Without freedom, he maintained, the individual cannot be happy or society progressive. But there is no trace in his essay of the teaching of Bentham or James Mill that it does not matter what people are like so long as they have as much pleasure and as little pain as possible. "Call them soldiers, call them monks, call them machines," exclaimed Bentham, "so they were but happy ones I should not care." Nowhere in Mill's essay is there approval of happy robots.

The real premise of his argument is indicated by the quotation from Baron von Humboldt's *Sphere and Duties of Government,* with which the essay is prefaced: "The grand, leading principle, towards which every argument unfolded in these pages directly converges, is the absolute essential importance of human development in widest diversity." In Chapter III, Mill quoted the same source. "The end of man," declared Humboldt, "is the highest and most harmonious development of his powers to a complete and consistent whole," and for this there are two requisites, "freedom and variety of situations." From their union arise "individual vigor and manifold diversity," including the "originality" indispensable to every progressive society. In the same vein, Mill declared that the central truth of *On Liberty* is "the importance to man and society, of a large variety in types of character, and of giving full freedom to human nature to expand itself in innumerable and conflicting directions."[29]

Now this standard of self-realization is not so far removed from that of natural rights as might be supposed at first glance. As pointed out in Chapter I, a natural right is an interest or claim that is reasonable in view of the essential characteristics of human nature and its natural environment. What distinguishes Mill's doctrine from most theories of natural right is the strong emphasis upon the diversity of human nature. To live freely is to unfold one's *individual* human capacities. His theory in this sense is complementary rather than contradictory to the natural rights theory. It calls attention to the individual, and not merely the generic, elements in human nature. But even Mill appealed to "the permanent interests of man as a social being," a phrase that could have come out of Cicero or St. Thomas.

One thing that distresses many people when they learn about the theory of "natural law" and "natural rights" is that it appears to deny *individual* self-realization. A basic notion of the theory is that of a *unitary* human nature, and the realization of this generic nature appears to exclude the self-fulfillment of the unique human person. Mill himself apparently believed that his doctrine of the supreme importance of individuality contradicts the natural-law tradition. But this contradiction can be resolved if we recognize that one of the very basic human needs—part of our fundamental human nature—is to actualize our unique potentialities. Each person is a complex unity in which the specific and the generic merge. Any basic manifestation of one's personality —for example, one's sex life—exhibits species-characteristics, but at the same time, it is a unique expression of one's individuality. To deny the instinctively common part of man's nature, *or* to deny the idiosyncratic part, is equally a mistake. One of the generic characteristics of human nature is the need to express individuality, the need to be oneself. This is a profoundly human trait, and it exists in all of us. This trait, when combined with a due regard for the individuality of others, is an affirmation rather than a negation of our common humanity. Mill's argument would have been sounder if he had clearly enunciated this fact.

He was especially anxious to defend the exceptional individual against "the collective mediocrity" of public opinion. He contended that "a State which dwarfs its men in order that they may be more docile instruments in its hands even for beneficial purposes, will find that with small men no great thing can really be accomplished." The progress of society, he maintained, depends upon the creative genius of its rare and noncomformist members. In this respect, there was an aristocratic, as well as an individualistic, cast to his thought.

The initiation of all wise or noble things comes and must come from individuals: generally at first from some one individual. The honour and glory of the average man is that he is capable of following that initiative; that he can respond internally to wise and noble things, and be led to them with his eyes open. . . . It does seem . . . that when the opinions of masses of merely average men are everywhere become or becoming the dominant power, the counterpoise and corrective to that tendency would be the more and more pronounced individuality of those who stand on the higher eminences of thought. It is in these circumstances, most especially, that exceptional individuals, instead of being deterred, should be encouraged in acting differently from the mass.

Mill's essay, as George H. Sabine has well said, "is in a sense a defense of liberty against democracy."[30]

Mill suggested a principle to guide us in this defense: the principle that society ought to interfere in the life of an individual only when his actions harm someone else and not merely himself.

As soon as any part of a person's conduct affects prejudicially the interests of others, society has jurisdiction over it, and the question whether the general welfare will or will not be promoted by interfering with it, becomes open to discussion. But there is no room for entertaining any such question when a person's conduct affects the interests of no persons besides himself, or needs not affect them unless they like (all the persons concerned being of full age, and the ordinary amount of understanding). In all such cases, there should be perfect freedom, legal and social, to do the action and stand the consequences.

All of us accept this kind of principle to some extent. We say, "Let him alone —that's *his* business." Each of us recognizes an area of privacy in which his thoughts and acts are his own, in which he should be safe from snoopers and busybodies. Just as I want my right of privacy and personal decision to be respected, so too I admit that you have the same right. You are you, and I am I, each with something inviolably his own. The acknowledgment of this right to be left alone is one of the clearest demarcations between a liberal democracy and a totalitarian state.

Yet Mill's statement of the principle is defective and needs reformulation. It distinguishes between acts that affect only oneself and acts that affect others, the first class of acts being immune from social control and the second class being subject to it. The difficulty is that almost every act of a person affects both himself and others. His acts have social causes and consequences; his values are bound up with those of his fellows. If personal freedom is to be reserved to acts that affect only oneself, there would seem to be room for a great deal of interference. "Your freedom ends where my nose begins." Very well; but if we are not talking about things so palpable as a fist and a nose, the boundary is hard to draw. Practically, it is impossible to distinguish between that part of a person's behavior that affects himself and that part which affects others. The distinction will be drawn by each man in accordance with his prejudices or predilections.

Mill should have stated his principle more positively. Instead of trying to trace a sharp boundary between self and others, he should have insisted upon the *social* as well as the personal benefits of self-direction and privacy. A democratic society needs men who have a rich inner life, men who amount to something apart from others, who have a capacity to govern themselves and to be responsible for their own decisions. These results will not be achieved if human beings are, like laboratory rats, controlled and "conditioned" and manipulated by others. In things of the spirit, moreover, compulsion is usually out of place. The promotion of righteousness by force is a very questionable procedure. The point that John Locke made about religion extends to any conviction of the spirit, such as loyalty to one's country:

> Although the magistrate's opinion be sound, and the way that he appoints be truly Evangelical, yet, if I be not thoroughly persuaded thereof in my own mind, there will be no safety for me in following it. No way whatsoever that I shall walk in against the dictates of my conscience will ever bring me to the mansions of the blessed. I may grow rich by an art that I take not delight in, I may be cured of some disease by remedies that I have not faith in; but I cannot be saved by a religion that I distrust, and by a worship that I abhor. . . . In a word, whatsoever be doubtful in religion, yet this at least is certain, that no religion which I believe not to be true can be either true or profitable unto me. In vain, therefore, do princes compel their subjects to come into their Church, under pretence of saving their souls. If they believe, they will come of their own accord; if they believe not, their coming will not avail them. However great soever, in fine, may be the pretence of goodwill and charity, and concern for the salvation of men's souls, men cannot be forced to be saved whether they will or no. And therefore, when all is done, they must be left to their own consciences.[31]

Force can compel outward observance but not inner conviction; it will more likely turn the spirit sour than make it sweet. This is the fatal flaw in compulsory religion, or compulsory patriotism, or anything of this sort. If Mill, instead of trying to insulate the individual from his society, had argued in the manner of Locke in the above passage, his position would have been greatly strengthened.

In an essay "On Social Freedom," doubtfully ascribed to Mill, the author abandoned the attempt to distinguish self-serving acts. He denied that "human freedom can be attained by the mere fencing off of human beings, each into his own sphere of activity." "I have not the slightest doubt," he declared, "that the life of each human individual thus penned up in his own 'sphere,' would be a life of continual misery."[32] When Mill wrote *On Liberty*, how-

ever, he was still under the sway of the exaggerated individualism so prominent in the writings of his father and Bentham. He had not fully grasped the
extent of human interdependence, and the fact that (as he declared later)
"association, not isolation of interests, is the school in which excellencies are
nourished."[33] Fortunately this individualistic approach does not entirely pervade *On Liberty*, and much of the time he argued on the ground of social
benefit.

He distinguished between four kinds of freedom: the liberty of thought,
of expression, of association, and of action.

The Freedom of Thought. The right to reflect, to inquire, to learn and to
teach, is basic to every other kind of freedom. There can be no freedom without choice, and there can be no choice without knowledge—at least none that
is not blind. Knowledge cannot flourish if the mind is in chains.

Freedom of thought requires that every man be free to think for himself
and to come to conclusions by the light of his own mind and investigation. It
means freedom to think not only *right* thoughts but *wrong* thoughts. The
freedom to think only "right thoughts" is no freedom at all: it is only the
"freedom" to think as the majority in the church, or the party, or the town, or
the country thinks. It is the freedom to conform. It is the freedom to be an
"organization man" and nothing else. The idea that the truth is already
known, and that the only legitimate freedom is to believe this truth, is the
concept of the police-state. Those who launched the great human adventure
of democracy had another idea in mind. They trusted men to think for themselves, to inquire and to discuss and to differ.

Freedom of thought implies the right to heterodoxy in one's opinions—the
right not to be hostilely interrogated or publicly shamed for one's beliefs. The
power of the state should be used to protect the individual against the pressure of the many rather than as a repressive force. But to insure that this will
happen and dissenters be allowed, a liberal climate of opinion must be created.
The *mores* of the people must be changed by education and thoughtful discussion. They must learn not only to tolerate but to enjoy and cultivate intellectual differences.

Freedom of thought, Mill remarked, is inseparable from freedom of expression. No man can feel free in his thoughts if he dare not express them.
His thoughts come to him in the act of expression—in the struggle to translate
vague and inchoate ideas into clear and articulate speech, in the give and take
of open and informed discussion. The creative mind must not only express
itself but hearken to the free expression of others. There can be no freedom
of thought if facts are withheld, if censorship or propaganda is substituted for
open debate, if there is no opportunity to explore controversial issues without
fear of penalties. The way to starve the human mind is to cut off the stimulation to thought; the way to enslave the mind is to "brain-wash" it by controlling the stimuli.

The Freedom of Expression. Mill's plea for free expression—the liberty of speech and press and every form of communication—is based upon his belief in progress. The progress of mankind is desirable, he maintained, and the suppression of ideas impedes progress. He considered three possibilities: that the suppressed idea may be true; that it may be wholly false; that it may be partly true and partly false.

First, the condemned idea may be true. To assume that this cannot be the case is to assume our own infallibility; and history is replete with examples of ideas which, seemingly absurd or noxious, have turned out to be highly salutary. The great Socrates was condemned to death by the most democratic city-state of ancient Greece, and Jesus was condemned alike by the Jewish community and the Roman authorities. Even the best and wisest of men, such as Marcus Aurelius, who unfortunately tried to suppress Christianity, have been mistaken in what they have regarded as certain.

Mill's point is not that we should lack confidence in our own convictions. It is rather that this confidence is justified only when our convictions have survived the test of free and vigorous discussion.

There is the greatest difference between presuming an opinion to be true, because, with every opportunity for contesting it, it has not been refuted, and assuming its truth for the purpose of not permitting its refutation. Complete liberty of contradicting and disproving our opinion is the very condition which justifies us in assuming its truth for purposes of action; and on no other terms can a being with human faculties have any rational assurance of being right. . . . In the case of any person whose judgment is really deserving of confidence, how has it become so? Because he has kept his mind open to criticism of his opinions and conduct. . . . The steady habit of correcting and completing his own opinion by collating it with those of others, so far from causing doubt and hesitation in carrying it into practice, is the only stable foundation for a just reliance on it. . . .

Almost every truth begins as the opinion of a minority, often a minority of one. The orthodoxy of this generation is the heterodoxy of past generations. We should be eternally wary of assuming that an opinion is false because it is unpopular.

Second, the condemned idea may be wholly false. Even so, it should not be suppressed. If men are allowed to hear only one side of an argument, they can never be *sure* that they are right, and can have no clear and vivid understanding of the arguments pro and con. The truth, if perchance we happen upon it, can be held in the manner of a mere prejudice or lifeless dogma, and it will be so held if it is never challenged.

He who knows only his own side of the case, knows little of that. His reasons may be good, and no one may have been able to refute them. But if he is equally unable to refute the reasons on the opposite side; if he does not so much as know what they are, he has no ground for preferring either opinion. . . . Nor is it enough that he should hear the arguments of adversaries from his own teachers, presented as they state them, and accompanied by what they offer as refutations. That is not the way to do justice to the arguments, or bring them into real contact with his own mind. He must be able to hear them from persons who actually believe them; who defend them in earnest, and do their very most for them. He must know them in their most plausible and persuasive form; he must feel the whole force of the difficulty which the true view of the subject has to encounter and dispose of; else he will never really possess himself of the portion of truth which meets and removes that difficulty. Ninety-nine in a hundred of what are called educated men are in this condition; even of those who can argue fluently for their opinions. Their conclusion may be true, but it might be false for anything they know: they have never thrown themselves into the mental position of those who think differently from them, and considered what such persons may have to say; and consequently they do not, in any proper sense of the word, know the doctrine which they themselves profess.

Without controversy, the very meaning of the truth may be lost, for meaning is best brought out by contrast and debate. Ideas are taken for granted and are never questioned enough to establish their meaning. Many people give lip-service to "democracy" or "Christianity," for example, without any clear understanding of what they stand for.

The words which convey it cease to suggest ideas, or suggest only a small portion of those they were originally employed to communicate. Instead of a vivid conception and a living belief, there remain only a few phrases learned by rote; or, if any part, the shell and husk only of the meaning is retained, the finer essence being lost.

Mill recognized that we need to understand *false* doctrines as well as true ones, and that we have no basis for understanding them if we do not allow them to be expressed. Let us suppose, for example, that communism is a false doctrine. We still have to reckon with it, and this we cannot intelligently do unless we understand it. What is the likelihood that the Russians will truly understand *our* ideas if they never listen to their advocacy? And what is the likelihood that we can understand *their* ideas if we shut our minds in the same fashion?

Third, the condemned idea may be partly true and partly false. Seldom is the truth altogether on one side. Only by the collision between opinions can the whole truth be brought out. Half-truths asserted as dogmas, without the opposition being permitted to speak, are often as deadly as errors.

Let us again apply Mill's point to today's world. As opponents of communism, we are tempted to suppose that its ideas and objectives are entirely false and regressive; yet no significant social doctrine is wholly false: if it were so, it would be merely silly, and hence innocuous. Communist theory has won many adherents that are highly idealistic. Any cause that could have enlisted, even temporarily, such men as Richard Wright, Louis Fischer, Stephen Spender, Pablo Picasso, Romain Rolland, Ignazio Silone, and Jean-Paul Sartre, cannot be dismissed as an *unmitigated* falsehood. The Soviet beliefs and practices, moreover, are in transition, and there are powerful forces that are tending to ameliorate their worst defects.

We shall have a much better chance to achieve East-West peace if we do not allow anxiety to freeze our thinking. In a crisis situation, there is nothing harder to stand than ambiguity, and frightened men tend to think in black and white terms. When both sides engage in such oversimplification, each tends to act in such a way as to justify the other's suspicions. Then neither side will trust the other, and the nuclear holocaust is more likely.

The Freedom of Association. The freedom to unite with others, to associate with whom we please, and to join such organizations as we prefer is the freedom of association. It is scarcely more than mentioned in *On Liberty,* although more is said about it in other works of Mill.

In the *Social Contract,* as we have seen, Rousseau wanted no effective challenge to "the general will" as embodied in the state, and consequently he looked askance at other associations. Mill, in contrast, did not oppose the freedom of association, but neither did he emphasize it. His argument for the freedom of individuals applies, by implication, to any body of individuals who unite, by free choice, for any legitimate end or purpose; but he did not spell out this implication. His reason for this lack of emphasis is at the opposite pole from Rousseau's hostility toward free associations. Mill's approach shows the influence of the traditional doctrine that the individual, as such, is free, and that his freedom will be beneficially exerted if society does not interfere. He primarily defended the individual, as against government and public opinion, in his right to be left alone.

His position would have been greatly strengthened if he had more explicitly defended the freedom of association. The absence of voluntary group activities leaves the individual with a sense of emptiness and estrangement, while it permits the total centraliation of power in the state. By the fostering of voluntary associations, we can prevent the atomization of the social structure, and we can create strong bulwarks against state tyranny. Human beings are social creatures, and their free development requires many and varied ties. Alone and isolated, they cannot withstand the pressures of mass-conformity.

Freedom of Action. Mill vigorously defended the "liberty of tastes and pursuits, of framing the plan of our life to suit our own character; of doing as we like . . . without impediment from our fellow-creatures so long as what we do does not harm them, even though they should think our conduct foolish, perverse, or wrong." He believed that experimentation in many modes of living is socially advantageous; and he had a deep and generous respect for the independent, or even eccentric, personality.

It is not by wearing down into uniformity all that is individual in themselves, but by cultivating it, and calling it forth, within the limits imposed by the rights and interests of others, that human beings become a noble and beautiful object of contemplation; and as the works partake the character of those who do them, by the same process human life also becomes rich, diversified, and animating, furnishing more abundant aliment to high thoughts and elevating feelings, and strengthening the tie which binds every individual to the race, by making the race infinitely better worth belonging to.

Yet even in this passage, Mill recognizes that personal freedom must be limited by "the rights and interests of others," and in another passage, he admits that the freedom of each must be limited so as to avoid "harm to others." Within a complex and highly interdependent society, this limitation may call for a very considerable amount of social control. After writing On Liberty, Mill became increasingly aware of the social context within which human liberties function and the brutalizing effects of gross inequalities in wealth and economic power. In his Autobiography, the last edition of his Principles of Political Economy, and his posthumous work, Socialism, he considerably modified his earlier individualism and even accepted a half-socialistic outlook. He had no sympathy for extreme socialism, with its concentration of almost all powers in the state, but he approved of voluntary cooperation and a very considerable amount of common ownership. The great problem of the future, he declared, is "how to unite the greatest liberty of action, with a common ownership in the raw materials of the globe, and an equal participation of all in the benefits of combined labor."[34]

In discussing all these kinds of freedom, Mill maintained that the permanent welfare of mankind is bound up with the rights of the individual, and that the individual can be happy and progressive only if he be free. Mill was right: freedom is as necessary to man as bread and air. Without civil liberties, such as free speech and assembly, human beings are dehumanized, and a society made up of such ciphers lacks all the essentials of greatness. Without freedom, the methods of persuasion are abrogated, the channels of peaceful adjustment are blocked. No country, in these conditions, is safe; social lags and injustices will pile up, resentments will mount, until violent explosion is inevitable. When the need of adaptation to unprecedented and rapidly changing situations is acute, civil liberties may be a matter of life or death. Without freedom, we cannot achieve the peaceful, orderly, and flexible adjustment to rapid technological change. Without such adjustments, there is little chance to avoid an eventual world war or violent revolution.

Free speech and other basic rights should not be denied to those who do not believe in them. As Ernest Renan declared:

Liberty is the best weapon against the enemies of liberty. Certain fanatics say to us with sincerity, "We take the liberty you give us, because you owe it to us on your principles; but you should not receive it from us, because we do not owe it to you." Very well, let us give them liberty all the same, and do not let us imagine we shall be cheated in the bargain. No; liberty is the great solvent of all fanaticisms. In demanding liberty for my enemy, for him who would suppress me if he had the power to do so, I give him in reality the worst gift he could receive. I compel him to drink a strong beverage, which will turn his head, whilst I shall keep mine steady. Science can endure the virile rule of liberty: fanaticism and superstition cannot endure it.[35]

To be consistent, the advocate of free speech must permit arguments against his own position, for it would be contradictory to exempt his own principles from the free discussion he recommends as the best method of finding, confirming, and elucidating the truth.

Yet I think there are profound crises in human life, such as when powerful antidemocratic cliques threaten to destroy democratic processes, at which times we are justified in suppressing the freedom of some in order to save or regain the freedom of most. A democracy may need to curtail liberty to survive at all; but the policy-makers should be reasonably sure that the crisis is deep enough to justify suppression of the antidemocratic forces, and that these forces really *are* antidemocratic and not merely allegedly so.

If they do not exercise extreme caution, they will, by suppression, create greater evils than those they seek to avoid. As Mr. Justice Oliver Wendell Holmes wrote:

I think we should be eternally vigilant against attempts to check the expression of opinions that we loathe and think to be fraught with death, unless they so imminently threaten interference with the lawful and pressing purposes of the law that an immediate check is required to save the country.[36]

Mill was right in his insistence that liberty should be protected in the democratic state, but I think he was too distrustful of democracy. The issue is whether we are willing to democratize freedom and liberalize democracy. The liberal ideal of freedom and the democratic ideal of equality should be combined. Liberalism, when sundered from democracy, is an upper-class privilege and is far too limited to satisfy the demands of justice. Democracy, when sundered from liberalism, is what I have called "totalitarian democracy"— majority rule without civil liberties. Such rule, tyrannical in itself, may degenerate into the deeper tyranny of totalitarian autocracy. We must, therefore, create a social structure that will ensure the creative interplay of freedom and equality, a society of free men united in a democratic community.

6. FREEDOM AND ORGANIZATION

In a totalitarian dictatorship or a totalitarian democracy, the man of independent opinions and talents is a pariah. Mill, above all, dreaded this type of regime, and it seems to me that he had good reasons for dreading it. But it is important to see that there are two sides to the individual: the side that separates and isolates, and the side that unites. The full development of individuality includes the expression of self-transcending, and not merely self-asserting, interests. Historically, individualistic liberalism has been so intent upon emphasizing the latter type of interest that it has grossly underestimated the importance of the former. It has tended to think of the individual as self-complete, self-enclosed, and self-centered; consequently it has conceived of freedom as inherent in the individual apart from his social relations and has regarded freedom and social organization as antithetical terms. This aspect of liberalism requires careful and extended consideration.

Although such individualistic liberalism contains a precious element of truth, it is inadequate, and, in its traditional insistence that freedom is inconsistent with organization, it survives mainly as an anachronism. It provides the main slogans for those who are endeavoring to divert the people from fundamental social reconstruction. Everywhere they are telling the voting public that "freedom," especially "the freedom of enterprise," is opposed to "the tyranny of planning." They often declare that planning is "un-American" and contrast it with the liberty to which the Founding Fathers of our republic were devoted.

Actually, planning, whether it be by civic groups, business organizations, or governmental bodies, is quite as much a part of the American tradition as individualism. From the time of the Mayflower Compact to the recent reports of our planning boards, our citizens have known how to sit down together, to talk over their mutual problems, to reach intelligent understanding upon the basis of exact information, and to achieve coherent social action which integrates divergent interests and activities in the light of a common knowledge and a common design. Planning, so far from being a new kind of disease imported from Soviet Russia, is American to the core. The sensible attitude is not to flee it as a foreign plague, but to use and control and democratize it.

Freedom without organization is a delusion; organization without freedom is a strait jacket. These two values, instead of being pitted against each other, must be interfused, so that freedom is no longer merely freedom and organization merely organization. There must be a new quality in both and a new ideal as a result of their fusion: *organized* freedom and *free* organization.

Anything so precious as freedom exacts a price—it can be achieved only when we plan and organize to achieve it. Being *legally* "free" to do what we choose and being *actually* free and *able* to do so are not equivalent. We tend to think of freedom abstractly, as mere absence of legal restraint, as "the freedom of both rich and poor to sleep under bridges"; we too seldom think of it concretely and operationally as the opportunity to do what we like, which depends upon planning and organization. In considering a problem of this kind, it is very important that we should get down, as William James would put it, to the pressing concrete particulars of the matter. When we think in these terms—of remunerative work, good food, decent clothing, and adequate shelter, of sufficient rest and carefree holidays, of education sufficient to evoke one's talents, of the right to speak one's mind on the job without fear of economic reprisal, of the right to a happy and secure old age with more than a beggarly pension—we realize that a welter of competing selfishness or mere absence of legal restraint does not constitute a free society.

A more adequate conception of freedom is contained in the definition of Ralph Barton Perry: "the absence of external obstacles which prevent, and the presence of resources and capacities which promote, the power of any individual to realize his desires or execute his will."[37] This definition combines two concepts: negative freedom, the absence of external restraints, and positive freedom, the presence of resources and capacities to effectuate one's choices.

With this definition in mind, we can understand two basic mistakes that many so-called liberals commit. First, they interpret negative freedom too narrowly as involving merely governmental restraint, whereas there are other important forms of restraint, such as physical force, social ostracism, or economic coercion. Whoever wields power can restrain those who lack power. When there are wide class differentials in society, some will possess a greatly disproportionate share of power and will be able to restrain those who lack such power. A government actively devoting itself to the protection of the weak and the removal of these wide differentials may greatly increase the amount of negative freedom even when it sternly restrains unduly powerful members of the society.

Second, "liberals" often stress negative freedom to the relative neglect of positive freedom. They conceive of freedom as consisting almost exclusively of "civil liberties," such as we find stipulated in the first ten amendments to the American Constitution. These rights are necessary to a free society—*there should be no misunderstanding on this point*—but they are not *sufficient* to constitute real freedom. A man is only nominally free if he is "allowed" to make a choice but lacks the instruments to effectuate the choice, or if his personality is so undeveloped that he can make few wise or ample choices. As Helen Lynd has said, in so far as liberalism emphasizes only negative freedom it leaves "men free to live without the material basis of life, free to speak, but with nothing of their own to say, free to believe but with nothing positive to believe in, free to worship but with nothing in which to place their faith."[38] To possess any large measure of positive freedom, men must satisfy fundamental needs, such as for food, shelter, clothing, health, education, security, play and recreation, the creative expression of one's talents, the enjoyment of beauty and art.

Even the traditional civil liberties require positive conditions to realize them. Free speech, for example, demands much besides the legal right to speak. As the Office of War Information declared during World War II:

> The first condition is that the individual have something to say. Literacy is a prerequisite of free speech, and gives it point. Denied education, denied information, suppressed or enslaved, people grow sluggish; their opinions are hardly worth the high privilege of release. Similarly, those who live in terror or in destitution,

even though no specific control is placed upon their speech, are as good as gagged. Another condition necessary for free speech is that the people have access to the means of uttering it—to newspapers, to the radio, the public forum. When power or capital are concentrated, when the press is too closely the property of narrow interests, then freedom suffers. There is no freedom, either, unless facts are within reach, unless information is made available. And a final condition of free speech is that there be no penalties attached to the spread of information and to the expression of opinion, whether those penalties be applied by the Government or by any private interests whatsoever.[39]

Thus supplied with the instrumentalities for their full and effective expression, human rights are very real and precious; but if they are not thus buttressed by the necessary social organization, they may be good as resolutions but barren of results.

The truth is that we cannot achieve a decent measure of individuality, we cannot achieve real, effective, operational freedom, without deep-ranging and far-reaching plans. We know what a vast deal we *can* produce, and we begin to see that it is sheer folly and cruelty to perpetuate poverty when we have the necessary resources to eliminate it. Our planning, of course, must counterbalance directives from the leaders above with initiatives from the masses below. It must unite free men within an organized community.

The fact that real freedom is not inconsistent with organization is indicated by many ordinary activities. Consider, for example, two people dancing together. They move together according to a pattern which is their cooperative deed. They dance in time and in step—the motion of one dancer is continually responsive to the motion of the other. They dance in this manner, not because they are compelled to do so but because they want to move in just this way. Their desires are fulfilled in and through this very pattern. The result is a fusion of law and impulse, a reconciliation of the two fundamental aspects of man's nature, the spontaneous and the orderly, the impulsive and the rational.

True individuality, moreover, is enhanced, not repressed, by the right kind of organization. As Felix Cohen has remarked, there is more true individuality, more scope for diverse talents, in the superb coordination of a baseball team, than in a field of nine runners each pursuing his separate course. "Social harmony," therefore, "no more requires that each individual play a simple tune, much less the same tune, than does orchestral harmony."[40]

It may be objected that in these examples of free organization no restraints are imposed upon the individual, whereas social planning usually requires such restraints. This sort of objection is frequently based upon the assumption that any type of coercion decreases the amount of freedom. If this were the case, there would be little justification for laws with police to enforce them. Traffic regulations, for example, impose curbs and require enforcement, but without them the lives of many people would be less free and more hazardous. Similarly, when a public meeting is governed by Roberts' Rules of Order, it may be necessary to supply the chairman with a gavel and to provide a sergeant at arms, but the effect of such enforcement is usually to expedite the freedom of those who wish to deliberate and vote in a fair, democratic manner. Coercion is often necessary to "keep the peace," without which real freedom is impossible.

It may also be objected that freedom and organization can be reconciled only if the group is small. We must admit that if a large group, instead of a small, move and act together, the problem of reconciling freedom and organization becomes more subtle and complex; but the harmony, when achieved, may be correspondingly richer, the resulting freedom more profound and exhilarating. The concept of free organization I shall call the ideal of community, and I shall devote the remaining chapters to its interpretation and to its relation to the crisis of our age.

NOTES

1. Plato, *Republic*, translated by Francis MacDonald Cornford. New York: Oxford University Press, 1945, p. 286.
2. George Santayana, *Reason in Society*. New York: Charles Scribner's Sons, 1927, p. 111.
3. Ralph Barton Perry, *Puritanism and Democracy*. New York: Vanguard Press, Inc., 1944, p. 453.
4. *The Letters of T. E. Lawrence*. New York: Doubleday & Company, Inc., 1939, p. 413.
5. *Ibid.*, p. 414.
6. Herbert Read, *The Politics of the Unpolitical*. London: Routledge and Kegan Paul, Ltd., 1946, pp. 47, 50–51.
7. Alfred North Whitehead, *Adventures of Ideas*. New York: The Macmillan Company, 1933, p. 105.
8. F. W. Coker, *Recent Political Thought*. New York: Appleton-Century-Crofts, 1934, p. 361.
9. Jean Jacques Rousseau, *The Social Contract*, in *The Social Contract and Other Discourses*, translated by G. D. H. Cole. London: J. M. Dent & Sons, Ltd. and New York: E. P. Dutton & Co., Inc., 1913, p. 6. Reprinted by permission of the publishers.
10. *Ibid.*, p. 19.
11. *Ibid.*, p. 14.
12. *Ibid.*, p. 15.
13. *Ibid.*
14. Ernest Hunter Wright, *The Meaning*

of Rousseau. London and New York: Oxford University Press, 1929, p. 73.
15. Rousseau, *The Social Contract, op. cit.*, pp. 15–16.
16. *Ibid.*, p. 22.
17. *Ibid.*, p. 26.
18. *Ibid.*, p. 28.
19. Walt Whitman, *Democratic Vistas*, in Floyd Stovall, *Walt Whitman: Representative Selections*. New York: American Book Company, 1939, p. 409.
20. Alexis de Tocqueville, *Democracy in America*. London and New York: Oxford University Press, 1947, p. 310.
21. Rousseau, *The Social Contract, op. cit.*, p. 18.
22. *Ibid.*, p. 21.
23. *Ibid.*, p. 17.
24. *Ibid.*, p. 121.
25. *Correspondance Générale de J. J. Rousseau*, Paris, 1932, p. 156. Quoted by Robert A. Nisbet, *The Quest for Community*. London and New York: Oxford University Press, 1953, p. 143.
26. Rousseau, *The Social Contract*, Book II, Chapter 12, as translated by Nisbet, in *ibid.*, p. 143. In this instance I have used Nisbet's translation because of its greater clarity.
27. Quoted by R. R. Palmer, "Man and Citizen: Applications of Individualism in the French Revolution," in Milton R. Konvitz and Arthur E.

Murphy, *Essays in Political Theory*. Ithaca: Cornell University Press, 1948, p. 149.

28. John Stuart Mill, *On Liberty*, Chapter 1. Since there are many editions and the quotations are not too difficult to find, I have omitted footnotes in further citations from this work.

29. John Stuart Mill, *Autobiography*. New York: Columbia University Press, 1924, p. 177.

30. George Sabine, *A History of Political Theory*. New York: Holt, Rinehart and Winston, Inc., 1937, p. 667.

31. John Locke, *A Letter Concerning Toleration*. New York: Appleton-Century-Crofts, Inc., 1937, p. 192.

32. *On Social Freedom*. New York: Columbia University Press, 1941, pp. 41, 46. The evidence submitted by John C. Rees in *Mill and His Early Critics* (Leicester: University College Press, 1956) casts doubt on Mill's authorship of this essay.

33. John Stuart Mill, *The Principles of Political Economy*. London and New York: David McKay Company, Inc., 1940, p. 763.

34. John Stuart Mill, *Autobiography, op. cit.*, p. 162.

35. Ernest Renan, *The Influence of Rome on Christianity* (Hibbert Lectures, 1880), quoted by David G. Ritchie, *Natural Rights*. London: George Allen and Unwin, Ltd., 1916, p. 186.

36. Myer Cohen (editor), *Selected Supreme Court Decisions*. New York: Harper & Row, Publishers, Inc., 1937, p. 9.

37. Ralph Barton Perry, *Puritanism and Democracy, op. cit.*, p. 512.

38. Helen Lynd, *England in the Eighteen-Eighties*. London and New York: Oxford University Press, 1945, p. 348.

39. Quoted by Abraham Edel, *The Theory and Practice of Democracy*. New York: Harcourt, Brace & World, Inc., 1946, p. 261.

40. H. M. Kallen and Sidney Hook (editors), *American Philosophy Today and Tomorrow*. New York: The Citadel Press, 1935, p. 92.

CHAPTER XIV

Crisis

1. MISCONCEPTIONS OF CRISIS

Freedom and organization, as I have been arguing, should not be pitted against one another as opposites. There are out-of-date "liberals" who deny community for the sake of "personality," and up-to-date "totalitarians" who deny personality for the sake of "community"; but the valid ethical solution is to assert their interdependence. Personality shrivels into nothingness when separated from community; community evaporates into monotony when its component personalities are stultified. "The *great* community," as Whitehead has said, "is the community of vivid individualities connected in the unity of a background."[1]

In the present chapter and the next, I shall relate this ideal of the free community to the crisis of our age. First I shall define the general meaning of historical crisis, postponing until the next chapter the discussion of "community."

The problem of social crisis is almost ubiquitous, since no society achieves a perfect equilibrium and every generation feels itself threatened. The Victorian period, which seems to us very calm, was stormy to many then alive. Yet the crises of this century, in comparison, are far-reaching and profound. We have witnessed two world wars, a very severe economic depression, revolutionary movements of terrific scope and fury, and the threat of nuclear holocaust. No less important is the crisis in thought, which penetrates to the very roots of our culture. Taking a large view, we can think of the main critical events of the Twentieth Century as more or less interdependent, and accordingly speak of the "crisis of our age." So extensive and profound a crisis expresses the basic nature of the socio-historic process and hence provides the data for a searching study of modern civilization. I shall be concerned with "crisis" in this sense of an historical period of tensions, rather than a brief and local emergency.

I shall begin by dismissing two misconceptions. The first is that crisis may be identified with such evils as poverty, disease, and injustice; and the second is that it occurs whenever there is rapid transition. In discussing these views, I shall indicate certain features of a sounder interpretation.

First, crisis is not to be equated with mere suffering, such as poverty and disease. Although a primitive society may be poor and wretched, no crisis can be said to exist if it is making full use of the limited techniques and resources at its disposal. Nor is economic exploitation, with its accompanying injustice and conflict, necessarily a sign of crisis, because exploitation is endemic to any higher type of civilization based upon an economy of scarcity. Nor is widespread disease a mark of crisis if the science of medicine has not developed far enough to eliminate it.

Until recently these evils, in view of the technological backwardness of the society, were inevitable. During four thousand years of civilization, the useful arts stagnated, relatively speaking, because the techniques of invention were not sufficiently advanced. In the age of Pericles or Queen Elizabeth or even Napoleon, it was technically impossible to maintain a leisure class, necessary for the cultivation of the arts, sciences and social amenities, without subjecting great masses of human beings to penury and excessive toil. But such evils become indicative of crisis if they reach abnormal and unnecessary proportions. My point is that exploitation, conflict, disease and poverty—weaknesses never wholly transcended in past history—are signs of crisis at certain times and not at others. Crisis in the society occurs when the *amount* of misery, injustice and conflict is no longer reasonably well adjusted to the potentialities of the economy.

"Reasonable adjustment" or "maladjustment" must be regarded as relative to the potentialities present at any given historical stage. A vast amount of *unnecessary* poverty, illness and injustice in a technologically advanced society is a sign of crisis, since it involves a wide disparity between potentialities and achievements, and indicates that some fetter is holding the productive potentials in check. The same amount of suffering at a more primitive stage of society would be normal, since at *that* level, poverty and suffering must be widely prevalent even if the achievements fully measure up to the capabilities of the society.

I am implying that an essential mark of crisis is the fettering of a society's potentialities, so that it is wasting or misdirecting its creative capacities. The essential mark of a satisfactory equilibrium, on the other hand, is the relative absence of such waste and misdirection combined with a tendency in the entire social order to enlarge its creative capacities and transform itself by unceasing growth.

I mention the factor of growth because I wish to eliminate a second misconception of crisis. It is possible to confuse crisis with rapidity of transition, and indeed there is a modicum of truth in this point of view, because crises tend to occur during periods of swift change, as for example, in the transition from feudalism to capitalism. Yet surely rate of change is not a sufficient criterion of crisis. The Dutch historian, Johan Huizinga, remarks that, because of the increasing acceleration of history, the process of change is much more rapid now than during the crisis and downfall of Roman civilization: "Years seem to have replaced centuries as the yardstick of development."[2] This fact, taken by itself, does not prove that the crisis of Roman history was relatively superficial and that our own crisis is relatively profound.

Rapid transition is not necessarily indicative of crisis because *quantity* of change is less significant than *quality* of change. It makes a deal of difference whither the society is bent. Conservatives, who prefer the static to the dynamic, often neglect this fact: they habitually regard a rapid rate of change as evil, regardless of its direction. The conservative sentiment that order is heaven's first law, however, is less wise than the old adage that to conserve one must reform. In addition to order, there must be an element of *adventure* in the good life—a moving equilibrium which creatively resolves conflicts by broadening and deepening the order. Rapid transition, if it results from good will and intelligent foresight, is a sign of health rather than of crisis. *Failure* to make a change may deepen and intensify the crisis, since it may increase the disparity between the society's potentialities and its accomplishments.

It is not so much change that is indicative or productive of crisis as unequal rate of change, with the resultant lack of synchronization between the relatively fast and the relatively slow changes. The *status quo*, in certain fundamental respects, does not change fast enough, and these "lags" act as basic fetters upon development. As a consequence, the potential and the actual, the ideal and the fact, the "ought" and the "is," the ideological verbalization and the actual behavior, are in sharp contrast. To remove the fetters by a thorough reconstruction of the *status quo* is therefore necessary in order to advance to a more complete integration, in which the actual and the potential are no longer fundamentally opposed. Until this reconstruction occurs, very deep and intense conflicts will persist, conflicts between the old and the new, or between the hypertrophied and the atrophied phases of civilization. These conflicts appear in human thought as basic issues and in human behavior as crime, economic depression, war, and revolution.

Within the present century, for example, a terrible world crisis has been produced by a combination of things new and old: by the swift development of superb mechanical efficiency without a correlative advance in morals and social control; by the rapid increase in natural scientific knowledge without an equivalent advance in synthesis and humanistic disciplines; by the enormous expansion of productive capacity without an adequate transformation of class privileges and property relations; by the very rapid development of international mobility, communication, and exchange without sufficient alteration of the institutions and practices of the absolute nation-state. The result has been a great discrepancy between potentialities and accomplishments. At the very time when scientific and material potentialities have increased by leaps and bounds, barbarism and international anarchy have sprung up and multiplied among advanced civilized peoples.

Our concept of crisis begins to emerge. A crisis occurs when a society develops so unevenly as to produce a grave cultural disequilibrium, in which the more static phases act as fetters to prevent the realization of the proper potentialities inherent in the civilization. The existence of these fetters constitutes not merely an evil and a danger but an opportunity—to remove the hindrances and thus to release the potentialities of the society and restore its equilibrium.

2. THE PATTERN OF CRISIS

It may seem that I am exalting equilibrium as an ultimate ideal and that the attempt to do so is unwarranted. Perhaps a society that is always off balance, in which there are ferments and tensions and conflicts, is "better"—more creative, productive, progressive, less flat and jejune—than a completely equilibrated society. Does not equilibrium imply stasis? Are not "dynamic" and "equilibrium" antinomic terms?

The force of this objection is indicated by the historical analysis of Arnold Toynbee. In his study of twenty-one great civilizations, he again and again emphasizes "the sin of Idolatry": the dangerous infatuation with the *status quo*, with the traditional ideals, techniques, and institutions. As a civilization declines, it tends to fall into a more and more rigid pattern of response and the creativity of its earlier phases is replaced by a mimetic regimentation enforced by a "dominant minority." The people, formerly responding flexibly to the inspired leadership of a "creative minority," now settle into a mechanical routine. The change is symbolized by the replacement of Orpheus, the poetic and imaginative leader, by Xerxes, "the drill sergeant with his whip" who enforces a herdlike conformity upon the masses. This gradual onset of a cultural *rigor mortis* is illustrated in Toynbee's pages by many historical examples, such as the self-idolization of Athens as "the Educator of Hellas" in the period of Pericles, or by the more extreme cultural petrifaction of Sparta.

If it be objected that I am exalting such a mechanical order, I would reply that I intend no such implication by my use of the word "equilibrium," and that an equilibrium may be either static or dynamic. A static equilibrium does not eliminate all change because every society is in constant flux, but the changes consist of slight, or limited and temporary, deviations from the *normal* pattern of life. There is no *cumulative* development bringing about *fundamental* change. For example, after an earthquake, flood, epidemic or a brief war involving no very great strain, there is a reaction and a return to a normal balance of forces. If a society, changing in this manner, is so constituted that its component factors are in general harmoniously coordinated with one another, we can say that it exhibits a static equilibrium.

A dynamic social order, as contrasted with a static, is one in which cumulative changes, either progressive or retrogressive, are taking place in important parts of the society. Thus there is no stable, persisting, "normal" equilibrium; and if we can, under these circumstances, speak of equilibrium, it must be *dynamic*. Such an equilibrium occurs when irreversible and fundamental changes take place, yet in balance and harmony with one another, so that, at any point of time, the various phases of development are fairly well coordinated with one another, with an absence of costly unresolved conflicts and frictions.

The norm of social health which I am suggesting is dynamic equilibrium. Its loss means a stasis or a crisis, its reestablishment is the proper aim of reconstruction. I am implying that we should hold fast to two concepts and fuse them together. First, we should recognize that society is, or ought to be, a unity. There should be an interaction and reciprocity of parts; there should be distinctive characteristics attaching to society as a whole; and the parts should, on the whole, contribute to, or be governed by, the total design. Such unity, if not too tight and restrictive, results in more efficiency, fewer disastrous conflicts, greater fulfillment. Second, there should be a continuous *process* of social realization, achieving not merely a greater coherence but a greater comprehensiveness and intensity. In this extending and deepening of civilization, freedom is basic: originality, adventurousness, individuality are no less important than order. Our goal should not be a tidy, rigid, preconceived unity but a rich and changing harmony: a dynamic, unfolding interaction of free personalities.

These two elements, the orderly and the dynamic, should interpenetrate. As in a great work of art, there should be unity and variety, harmony and richness, familiarity and strangeness, repose and stimulation: a harmony in contrariety, a union of opposites. The good society unfolds like a musical composition, with a theme ever varied and enriched. Conflicts, like musical discords, will doubtless occur, but they will either be minimal or be resolved into harmony.

If it be objected that "dynamic equilibrium" is merely an ideal and never an actuality, and that, if crisis means the absence of equilibrium, *dynamic* societies are always in a state of crisis, I should reply that my terms must be understood in a relative sense, and that certain historical periods exhibit relatively little crisis and relatively satisfactory, although mobile, equilibrium. Admitting the improbability of the full attainment or prolonged maintenance of any such changing equilibrium, it can at least be approached, and the concept of such an equilibrium can be employed as a means of visualizing and measuring a social crisis.

I do not mean to suggest that social equilibrium always contributes to tranquility. An equilibrium in one part of the society may create disequilibrium in the society as a whole. An example from economic theory will illustrate this point. According to the American economist, Alvin H. Hansen, it is possible for economic equilibrium to be reached at a point considerably below full employment. In a "mature" capitalistic economy, when there is no longer a frontier and when there is no other special lure for private investors, a condition of "economic stagnation" may develop. There may still be a great need for a higher standard of living on the part of the masses, but if they lack buying power, this need will not stimulate the necessary volume of private investment. The conditions of such a low-level static equilibrium, according to Hansen, were being realized in the 1930s, when the economy was becoming stabilized at a level of mass-unemployment, but the effect upon the *total* society was to heighten disorder and unrest—disequilibrium rather than equilibrium—and thus to aggravate the crisis of these depression years. Large-scale governmental intervention was required to translate the static economic equilibrium into a dynamic economic expansion. An equilibrium in some part of the society, if it is not properly synchronized with other social factors, may throw the society as a whole off balance, and thus cause or intensify a social crisis.

To return to our definition, a crisis is a *dynamic* state, but it differs from a dynamic equilibrium in exhibiting *uncoordinated* rather than *coordinated* development. When there is a *grave* disturbance of equilibrium, such that the various cultural factors develop at different rates and with slight coordination, there is a social crisis. The future is then uncertain and men are challenged by danger and opportunity.

This consequence of dynamic disequilibrium was remarked by Hippocrates, who was the first to introduce "crisis" as a term in medicine. The turning point, when recovery or death hangs in the balance, he called "the crisis"; and he was convinced that a physician should bring all his remedies to bear at this decisive stage. He thus conceived a crisis as not only a present evil but a challenge to action in the light of an uncertain future. It is the point when danger and opportunity are at their maximum. He was mistaken in supposing that the best time to apply the remedy is when the crisis is at its height. Both in medicine and in social therapy this stage is often too late to permit a cure, and it is usually better to begin the treatment before the disease becomes so aggravated. Unlike Hippocrates, I am employing the word "crisis" to denote not merely the climax of the malady but the longer period of increasing and diminishing peril. But we can agree with him that a crisis is a challenge to act in the face of danger and opportunity.

An analogous theory of social crisis has been advanced by Toynbee.[3] According to his interpretation, a crisis occurs when the relatively stable organization of society is shattered by a severe blow or pressure: the result is a labile condition in which future prospects are ambivalent, hovering between disaster and resurgence. If the society can summon enough energy and wisdom to meet the challenge, the result is a new springtime of culture. Toynbee illustrates this pattern of "challenge and response" with many historical examples, and maintains that crisis has precipitated both the great disasters and the great creative moments in history.

The challenge may arise from either external or internal causes or a combination of both. It may be due to the intrusion of human or natural forces arising *outside* of the society, such as a flood or a military invasion by an external power. Or it may arise from within the society, as in the case of a class conflict, an undermining of faith, or an intellectual schism. Or it may result from both internal and external causes, as in the case of France during World War II, when the invasion of Hitler from without coincided with internal stress and weakness. Now that the whole planet is bound together by a web of interdependence, every major crisis tends to involve the totality of world civilization, with causes arising from within rather than simply impinging from without.

3. THE DISPARITY BETWEEN ACHIEVEMENT AND POTENTIALITIES

The opportunity that a crisis presents is based upon the discrepancy between potentialities and achievements. What is being achieved falls far short of what *might* be achieved. There is some fetter that is holding the potentialities in check, with the result that there is a nonuse or misuse of resources. Hence, there is the opportunity to remove the fetter and to realize the potentialities of the society.

The terms "potentiality," "fetter," "nonuse," and "misuse" require further clarification. Potentiality is not a mere privation, the bare absence of a characteristic. It is a *developed capacity* that has not yet found its proper use. The absence of technological development in a primitive society is a mere privation, but millions of idle men and machines, in a period of economic depression, represent developed but unused capacity—something quite different.

A prime mark of crisis is the nonuse or misuse of such developed capacity. Let me illustrate. Imagine a young German student just entering college during the late period of the Weimar Republic. He is trying to decide upon a career. "I wish to be a doctor," he announces. "Sorry. There are already too many doctors," is the immediate response. "I wish to be a teacher, then," the young man declares. "Too bad. There are already more teachers than can find employment," is the inevitable answer. "Well then, I would like to be an engineer," the student insists. "Sorry again. There is no longer any demand for engineers," his advisors reply. Whatever profession the young man considers, he is at once greeted by the response that professionals of that type are too numerous. This situation is a sign of crisis because it indicates that there is a gross failure to employ the human and technical resources of the society.

Now let us imagine that same student a few years later. There is no longer any question of unemployment. He is busy, extremely busy, and as a youth leader in the Nazi movement, he has a vocation he can call his own. He and his fellows are intensely occupied burning books, baiting Jews, liquidating liberals and radicals, and preparing for war. We can no longer speak of nonuse of capacity (except among the Jews, liberals, and radicals) but surely we can speak of misuse; and we can say that the society is still in a condition of crisis, which is actually more intense than before.

Now we have introduced a normative concept. How shall we define "misuse" and how shall we conceive of "proper use"? This question may be answered either in terms of standards relative to the culture or in terms of more universal standards. From an abstract, absolute standpoint, societies almost never make a very "proper use" of their productive potentialities. Thornstein Veblen, in his *Theory of the Leisure Class*, pointed out that "conspicuous waste," with a consequent failure to produce and consume for basic biological human needs, is a general characteristic of human culture. More recently the American anthropologist, Melville Herskovits, has remarked that, in every society of which we have knowledge, there is organized ceremonial waste, often on a great scale.[4] From the standpoint of cultural relativism, this uneconomical lavishness in consumption and honorific destruction of property are not signs of crisis unless they are "abnormal"—unless they considerably exceed the limits deemed "reasonable" by public opinion in that community. When a primitive Melanesian tribe, for example, deliberately destroys a large crop of yams for ends deemed moral or religious, this behavior is not a sign of crisis, since it is a characteristic and socially approved feature of their culture. In contemporary America, the wasteful standards of the leisure class, or the immense amount of waste normally associated with advertising, are not indicative of crisis because, given the mores of our business civilization, such waste is considered normal and even proper. But the waste involved in a vast depression or a world war *is* a sign of crisis because it is not accepted as reasonable and necessary by the conscience of the community, or at least by a very large obstreperous class within that community. We can thus define proper or improper use of resources in terms relative to the mores and public opinion of the given society.

Such a relative standard is not always satisfactory in determining the misuse of resources. If we revert to our previous illustration, the youth leader in the Nazi movement who was burning books, baiting Jews, liquidating liberals and preparing for war, was *not* engaged in improper activity according to the norms that had become predominant in Germany. Sometimes a society becomes deranged: a "national psychosis" may develop in a frustrated and defeated people. The standards of such a society are no longer serviceable in defining the improper use of resources. Unless we are to surrender all rational basis for condemning the society, we must find an independent and less relative standard.

In formulating such a universalist norm of welfare, it is possible to employ a number of ethical alternatives. In Chapter IV, I have characterized human welfare as the satisfaction of basic human interests, with its experience of achievement and enjoyment; and human misery as the frustration of such interests, with the resultant unhappiness. A society can be said to function properly if, *within the necessary limits of its historical situation*, it tends to satisfy fundamental interests, everybody considered and in the long run. The frustration of these interests, estimated thus inclusively, is conversely the sign of a malfunctioning society. *Abnormal* waste, measured in terms of such frustration, can then be regarded as a sign of crisis.

Such an objective standard will have to be applied with discretion. When the Aztecs captured their human victims and tore out their hearts in blood-curdling ceremonies, this was but the normal propitiation of their gods and therefore not a sign of crisis. Yet, at first glance, their behavior would seem to deviate radically from our objective criterion of value. However, the quali-fication italicized in the preceding paragraph, that we must take account of the historical stage of development of a people, must not be forgotten. It would not do to demand the same level of behavior at a primitive level of moral and religious development as we rightly expect at a highly civilized level. Just as the "normality" of childhood differs from that of adulthood, so the "normality" of the primitive differs from that of the civilized. When the Aztecs, still quite primitive in religion and morality, behaved in a savage manner, their actions must be considered normal, but when the Germans, a highly civilized people, acted like savages under Hitler's command, their atrocities were a sign of derangement.

Within every society there are forces that tend toward the cultivation and fulfillment of human interests. If the interests remain uncultivated or unful-filled despite the developed capacity of the society to cultivate and fulfill them, we can speak of a fetter that is holding the potentialities in check. It would be wrong to suppose that this fetter is simply evil. On the contrary, the analysis of Hegel seems to be basically sound, that the thesis fetters the antithesis, the old fetters the new, the tradition fetters the innovation; and that the ideal resolution of the conflict is not the cancellation of either set of values but the conservation of both sets through their translation into a more inclusive organ-ization.

The discrepancy between potentialities and accomplishments is reflected by an inward psychological disparity between thought and being, ideal and fact, the "ought" and the "is." The actual, falling glaringly short of the potential, cannot satisfy human aspirations. Men fear or detest the existing order, and in thought soar beyond it. This tension is reflected in states of alienation and anxiety. To escape from these states, men try to return to an idealized past (archaism) or leap ahead to an idealized future (Utopianism). They may seek escape in religious supernaturalism; or in a dream world of art or neurotic fantasy; or in submission to a "strong man," such as Hitler, or an authoritarian institution, such as the Communist party. Or they may seek refuge in nihilism —the mood of extreme negation expressed by Macbeth:

> From this instant
> There's nothing serious in mortality.
> All is but toys: renown and grace is dead;

The wine of life is drawn, and the mere lees
Is left this vault to brag of.[5]

There have been thinkers in the past, such as Callicles, Machiavelli, and Nietzsche, who have enunciated a semi-nihilistic creed, but it remained for modern totalitarians, the Nazis most shockingly of all, to demonstrate an utterly wild nihilism—a horrible ravening intoxication with death and destruction that drove them to the most fiendish deeds.

Crisis produces not only despair and madness but hope and rational endeavor. The realistic way of dealing with a crisis-situation is by means of social technology: a scientific inventory of actual needs, a scientific inventory of available resources, and a planned use of these resources, under free and democratic auspices, to meet the needs. This is the method advocated by many liberals, such as John Dewey, Karl Mannheim, and Barbara Wooton, or, in a more piecemeal and individualistic fashion, by Karl Popper. If regarded as an *exclusive* method, it partakes of what Peter Drucker, in *The End of Economic Man,* terms "the intellectual myth": the collective illusion that human beings can find the all-sufficient answer to their problems in science or reason. If man could be as rational and objective as this solution demands, the crisis would never have arisen in its present form. The resolution of the crisis demands more than science and social technology—it demands the full resources of humanity, material, intellectual, and spiritual. But the method of social science and technology is at least fundamental.

4. THE CRISIS OF OUR AGE

To sum up, a crisis is a dynamic state of disequilibrium, in which wants are frustrated, resources are unused or misused, potentialities are fettered by the disproportionate development of cultural factors, and thought seeks to transcend or transform the existing order.

This definition is abstract; it tells us nothing concrete about the crisis of our own age. The Marxist interpretation, reviewed in Chapter XII, is an attempt to formulate this more concrete explanation. It finds the essence of historical crisis in the catastrophic conflict between dynamic *forces of production* and static *relations of production.* I too would explain crisis in terms of the incongruous combination of fast and slow changes; but, generalizing the analysis, I would speak of the increasing disparity between the organizational revolution (the dynamic factor) and communal relations (the static factor).

The Organizational Revolution. Within the last five or six decades, a gradual, silent, profound revolution has been taking place—a revolution in ideas, in techniques, in institutions that is carrying our social order from an individualistic way of life to a collective one. This revolution consists primarily in an increase in the number, variety, and scope of organizations. Vast, bureaucratized collectives, such as the business corporation, national farm organization, labor union, professional association, political party, military establishment, and governmental department, are bulking ever larger in the lives of more and more people. Most titanic of all, the nation-state has become increasingly massive, complex, and hierarchical. Even the "intimate" groups, such as the church, school, and fraternal order, have grown big and impersonal.

The trend toward massive organizations has led Roderick Seidenberg, in one of the most provocative books of recent years, *Posthistoric Man*, to predict the total mechanization of society. The organizational revolution, he believes, is only in its beginning phases, and it will move inexorably toward an antlike collectivism as its limit. "Organization breeds organization as a crystal breeds crystals. Such is the inherent law of organization—a principle that we have not yet apprehended clearly, but, which, nonetheless, is transmuting the world of yesterday into that of the future." The machine is the most potent factor in precipitating and accelerating this transmutation. Itself a triumph of organization, it is "the perfect adaptation of means to the achievement of specific and attainable ends." As technology becomes more and more pervasive, the machine "will demand an ever greater degree of integration and coordination in the social aspects of life commensurate with its own perfection." The increasing intricacy of social organization will give rise to administrative problems, but the technical skills that created the machine will likewise be applied to administrative integration and direction. Organizations of ever-increasing scale will be conducted with smooth efficiency. "The mesh of . . . societal relationships will be drawn ever finer and more firmly, reducing the individual to an ever minuter atom within the expanding patterns of his social aggregates."

This change "will unavoidably transmute the basis of his person and his values as he now conceives and understands them." The spontaneous and instinctive aspects of his nature will become increasingly obsolete, and cold intelligence will prevail in one activity after another. Nonadaptable types, dreamers and rebels will be extirpated, and individualistic traits will disappear. Just as the intimate, spiritual communalism of the Middle Ages gave way to the "unleashed ego" and the "atomistic individualism" of modern society, so our individualistic ways and free institutions will give way to "a new collectivism, no longer of the spirit, but of the conscious mind." "It is as though man had achieved for a brief moment, as a transitional being, a perspective of far-off values—a vision of spiritual freedom—only to be swept under by the force of his own numbers . . ." and "the arbitrary, mechanical collectivization of the herd." Man does not lack "within his rich and volatile nature elements presaging another destiny, loftier perhaps, more spiritual and humane;" but "the hope of retaining the machine while avoiding the consequent mechanization of society is wholly wishful and fallacious. For the logic of the machine, repeating always its fixed and predesigned patterns, is a mass logic; and collectivism . . . is inherent in its laws and implicit in its operations."[6] Here is a vision as frightening as Orwell's *1984*, presented not as a piece of fiction but as a sober prediction based upon the manifest forces of our technological age.

The Communal Relations among Human Beings. The organizational revolution has been developing swiftly, but the communal relations have improved little or suffered a decline. For the last three or four centuries, the main impetus of Western civilization has been toward the hypertrophy of self-asserting drives and the corresponding atrophy of self-transcending impulses. The prevailing culture is competitive; economically the individual competes with others for livelihood; socially he competes for prestige. The intimate institutions, such as the family and the small neighborhood, have been weakened or supplanted. Individuals are pressed into groups, and these groups are more and more massive. They tend to be pitted against one another and divided by barriers of class, nationality, race, religion, language, and custom. The resulting conflicts among individuals and groups are potentially so destructive that the survival of civilization is very much in question.

We civilized human beings have fathomed many of the secrets of the universe; we have invented the mechanical means to wipe out poverty and to build a world community; but we have attained no corresponding cultivation of feeling and no adequate spiritual assimilation of the new ideas and techniques. Our "progress" has been far more swift in the techniques of homicide than in the arts of peace. Power has increased so fast and so much; harmony has improved so slowly and so little. Martin Luther predicted:

> Our minds will form a plan
> To draw man unto man.[7]

No effective "plan" has been formed; none is in operation. For want of such a plan, the whole world is trembling on the verge of ultimate catastrophe.

Here, then, as nearly as one can sum it up in a few words, is the essence of the colossal world crisis facing twentieth-century man. The organizational revolution, spearheaded by technology, has developed with extreme and dramatic swiftness. The values and institutions of the free community have in no way kept pace with this revolutionary transformation. The price humanity has paid for this lag is manifest: it includes World Wars, totalitarian regimes, class and racial tensions, anxiety and alienation everywhere spreading, and the possibility of nuclear Armageddon.

> No auguring mind can doubt that deeds which root
> In steadiest purpose only, will effect
> Deliverance from a world-calamity
> As dark as any in the vaults of Time.[8]

The communal lag, so fraught with danger, can be interpreted in either of two ways. First, it can mean that the organizational revolution, in its massive and impersonal character, has dehumanized social relations and has thus perverted community life. The implication is that man, with the communal values inherited from the past, is inevitably pitted against the great society, which must be confined and curbed as much as possible. This first interpretation has some merit: the more impersonal forms of organization have surely had, whether necessarily or inadvertently, very unfortunate consequences. Second, the communal lag can be interpreted as a slowness in making psychological and institutional adjustments to "the great society." What is required is not so much a rear-guard action against the organizational revolution as an adaptation to it. Improvements in organization have been of great importance; they have made large societies possible; they have put the immense resources of modern technology at the disposal of mankind. We must not lose sight of the great variety of organizational inventions in this century and the possibility of future political and social inventions that, with the necessary intellectual and emotional readjustments, will humanize the whole organizational structure.

I believe that we should embrace neither of these interpretations exclusively, since both contain essential elements of truth. Our problem is to eliminate the more dehumanizing forms of organization, thus protecting man against the depredations of mass society, while conserving and mastering its more valuable features. Our objective, as I have said repeatedly, should be the interpenetration of freedom and organization. It is this goal, which I call the ideal of community, to which we shall turn in the remaining chapters.

NOTES

1. Alfred North Whitehead, *The Adventures of Ideas*. New York: The Macmillan Company, 1933, p. 132.
2. Johan Huizinga, *In the Shadow of Tomorrow*. New York: W. W. Norton & Company, Inc., 1936, p. 35.
3. Arnold J. Toynbee, *A Study of History*. London and New York: Oxford University Press, 1934, I, pp. 271–302.
4. Melville Herskovits, *The Economic Life of Primitive Peoples*. New York: Alfred A. Knopf, Inc., 1940, pp. 421–444.
5. *Macbeth*, Act II, Scene III.

6. Roderick Seidenberg, *Posthistoric Man*. Chapel Hill: University of North Carolina Press, 1950, pp. 112, 133–134, 176, 229, 231–232.
7. Martin Luther, "A Mighty Fortress" (hymn), 1529.
8. Thomas Hardy, *The Dynasts*. London: Macmillan & Co., Ltd., 1923, p. 444. Quoted by permission of the Trustees of the Hardy Estate, Macmillan & Co., Ltd., London, and The Macmillan Company of Canada, Limited, and the Macmillan Company, New York.

The basis of renewal

I. THE BRONTOSAURUS PRINCIPLE

I have argued that the prime mark of historical crisis is the incongruous combination of fast and slow changes, with a consequent nonuse or misuse of human resources. In our century, the resolution of social conflicts has lagged far behind the technological and organizational revolution. Although Wendell Willkie told us that there was already One World, the announcement was premature. Hence the development of more harmonious ways of living is the prime need of mankind at this critical juncture of history. But the massive forces of change seem to be moving toward an organizational gigantism and regimentation that will undermine the values of community life.

I doubt that this outcome is foreordained. There are natural limits of growth that may turn history in a new direction. Aristotle, in the *Poetics,* comparing a too-lengthy play with an imaginary animal a mile long, implied that both real animal and good play must have its organic limits. Goethe, in a wise saying quoted by Seidenberg, observed that trees do not reach the sky. D'Arcy Thompson, in *Growth and Form,* has argued that each kind of organism has its upper limit of growth, beyond which it cannot function. In the fossil record of the rocks, as H. G. Wells has noted, it is "always the gigantic individuals who appear at the end of each chapter."[1]

When I first visited the great hall of the Smithsonian Institution and gazed in amazement at the titanic dinosaur skeletons assembled there, it seemed that the law of limits could be overpassed. In the evolution of social organizations, we have entered the Age of Dinosaurs, and the question arises whether there is any limit to growth in the case of organizations as well as organisms.

It may be instructive to take the dinosaur metaphor seriously and to glance at the history of the Mesozoic Era. This was the period when the dinosaurs dominated all the land surface of the globe, and then rather suddenly disappeared. Although the causes of their disappearance are obscure, the ultimate disadvantages of huge scale appear to have outweighed the advantages.

The dinosaurs evidently proved too ponderous and inflexible to cope with their environment. Perhaps the tremendous organizations of the twentieth century will meet with a similar fate. Kenneth Boulding has coined the phrase, "the brontosaurus principle," to label the disadvantages of immense size.[2] Up to a point, there are "increasing returns to scale," but "decreasing returns" in time may predominate.

Huge organizations have a power and striking force that puny organizations lack. If it were not for such increasing returns, big government, big business, and big labor would not have evolved to their present brontosaurian proportions. But the disadvantages are great. The struggle of giants may be very bloody, and the defense of each (as in an armaments race) may contribute to the insecurity of all. The principal disadvantage is the depersonalization and externalization of life. Only small groups can be personal. Members of a massive organization are strangers to one another; the tie that binds them must be impersonal and abstract, such as the fear of the police, or routinized propaganda, or stereotyped administrative techniques, or considerations of financial advantage. As the organization grows larger, its hierarchial structure becomes more elaborate, communication between the various grades becomes difficult, and the managers tend increasingly to regard the rank-and-file as pawns to manipulate.

The great difference between the intimate community and the brontosaurian organization is that the former is concrete and personal and the latter is abstract and impersonal. As Karl Popper remarks:

> This point, which has been rarely understood, may be explained by way of an exaggeration. We could conceive of a society in which men practically never meet face to face—in which all business is conducted by individuals in isolation who communicate by typed letters or by telegrams, and who go about in closed motor cars. (Artificial insemination would allow even propagation without a personal element.) Such a fictitious society might be called a "completely abstract or depersonalized society." Now the interesting point is that our modern society resembles in many of its aspects such a completely abstract society. Although we do not always drive alone in closed motor cars (but meet face to face thousands of men walking past us in the street) the upshot is very nearly the same as if we did—we do not establish as a rule any personal relation with our fellow pedestrians. Similarly, membership in a trade union may not mean more than the possession of a membership card and the payment of a contribution to an unknown secretary. There are many people living in a modern society who have no, or extremely few, intimate personal contacts, who live in anonymity and isolation, and consequently in unhappiness.[3]

The depersonalization of existence is not only a threat but a constant reality in a society dominated by massive organizations. Hence springs the crisis of the human person.

The effect of the organizational revolution on human personality has been dealt with at length by such writers as David Riesman, Erich Fromm, and

William H. Whyte, Jr. In the language of Riesman, the "inner-directed" type of person, whose motivation is provided by his own staunch values and convictions, is being supplanted by the "outer-directed" type, whose mirror-personality has no depth, who merely reflects what is going on around him, who is all things to all people, and who devotes so much attention to "selling" himself that he has no real self to sell.[4] Fromm similarly points out that in large collectivities "people are not able and cannot afford to be concerned with what is unique and 'peculiar' in each other." What matters is not what people *are* but how they *seem*. Hence, they become so intent upon playing roles that their inner life dries up.[5] Whyte sees the consequences in the excessive desire to "belong" and be "together," the repression of individuality, the fear of being different.[6] All three writers present their argument with vigor and intelligence, and with a mass of telling evidence. They are confirming the fears that Alexis de Tocqueville and John Stuart Mill expressed so eloquently one hundred years ago.

The consequences of developing a mechanistic and depersonalized society may be much more pathological than these writers have suggested. There is the possibility of producing an impersonal consciousness that will lack sentiment altogether. Sympathy will give way to indifference, imagination will give way to calculation, warmth will give way to a ghastly coldness. Something of this sort happened under Nazi regimentation. Hitler's sadists impress one not with their hot ferocity but with their frigid detachment. Communist cruelty, perhaps, has been less cold and methodical, and its motivation has been different. As Erich Kahler has written: "The Soviets betrayed their ends by their means; the Nazis betrayed everything human by the insensate criminality of their very ends."[7] Both regimes, however, have displayed too much moral rot to qualify as "the wave of the future." But destructive and dehumanizing tendencies are prevalent even in the Western democracies. The organizational revolution, with its deadening and desensitizing of all things personal, is a main force on both sides of the Iron Curtain. It seems unlikely that these antihuman tendencies can long prevail. They will either reduce the world to a cinder, or there will be a change of direction.

Individualism is on the wane, and there appears to be no prospect of a revival in its old form. Collectivism is waxing, but here and there appear signs of slackening and decay. The "realists" who see no other future for mankind than the accentuation of a dehumanizing collectivism are blind to these signs and have too little faith in the inner resistance and resilience of mankind. Neither the social homelessness of individualism nor the mass anonymity of collectivism can supply any deep and lasting happiness. The false dilemma, "individualism or collectivism," no longer appears so inescapable; and the choice that it presents no longer appears attractive. There is increasing realization that neither horn can provide the genuine freedom and realization that each promises, and that there is a *third* alternative that avoids the extremes and distortions of the other two. "The essential human reality is neither one of individual nor of collective existence," as Martin Buber has written, "but lies in the relation between man and man, and is a matter between me and you."[8] Modern civilization is desperately in need of reorientation, and this reorientation should be around the concept of the human community.

2. "COMMUNITY" AS A NORMATIVE CONCEPT

If we are to use "community" as a basis for human renewal, we must employ the term in a broad and fundamental sense. Any narrow meaning can not serve as an instrument for that new endeavor of critical examination, creative synthesis, and social reconstruction through which alone our civilization can survive and advance.

Baker Brownell, who has reflected deeply upon the subject, employs the term "community" to denote "a group of people who know one another well."

It is a pattern of contact or communication of man with man, where repetition and rhythm have their place, where men meet familiarly face to face, and the contacts between any two of them are numerous, diverse in quality, and functionally significant. . . . It refers, not to the abstract relationships of men with men as functions or elements of a great society, but to the association of whole, concrete, living, breathing persons with each other. Such relationships on the part of any individual are limited to a rather small number of persons. A man is human, and because of inherent human limits cannot know many persons well. Such groups within the range of human acquaintance and only such groups, I think, are communities.[9]

For the purposes of Brownell's argument, the term "community" should be limited in this way. He is concerned with the critical importance of the intimate pattern of living. I share this concern, but I am also greatly concerned with the problem of worldwide unification. If we are to discover a principle broad enough to pervade our culture and to promote world harmony, we cannot limit our key concept to the small, intimate group.

Similar to Brownell's usage is the employment of Gemeinschaft (ordinarily translated "community") by Ferdinand Tönnies, the famous German sociologist. By Gemeinschaft Tönnies means a grouping based upon the "essential will," which embraces all instincts, impulses, and feelings that are part of the organic essence of man. Therefore a community means for Tönnies a social unity of a deeply organic character, arising out of the instinctive and essential nature of human beings. It stands in contrast to Gesellschaft, an association based on the "selectvie will," that is, the deliberate purpose, of its members. A Gesellschaft is an artificial social construction expressing some common function, law, intent, or contract—for example, a political party or a labor union. The distinction that Tönnies draws is very useful for certain purposes, but it narrows the meaning of "community" to a greater extent than is helpful in the present context. A community, as we shall use the term, may be either a *Gemeinschaft* or a *Gesellschaft*: it may be based upon either organic character or deliberate purpose: it may be family-like or contractual.

Robert M. MacIver uses the term "community" to denote a group bound together by common living and a common locality. "At every moment its members occupy together a definite place on the earth's surface;"[10] but there must also be "a social unity whose members recognize as common a sufficiency of interests to allow of the interactivities of common life."[11] This definition is not limited to the small, intimate group; both the village and the nation are cited as examples. But the reference to a geographical area again limits the meaning in a way that is undesirable for my purposes. "Community," as we shall employ it, is a *process* term denoting how human beings under certain conditions interact. Its defining essence is *psychological* rather than *geographical*.

At the opposite extreme from all restrictive definitions is the usage of Josiah Royce (1855–1916), whose mature philosophy is based upon the concept of community. In his idealistic metaphysics, the word takes on cosmic sweep. "The history of the universe," he declares, "the whole order of time, is the history and order and the expression of this Universal Community."[12] It may be that a community is a much better model of the universe than either a mind or a machine: but to assert this, or to assert that the whole of reality is literally a community, is unverifiable and leads us into speculative fields beyond the scope of our present argument. The ideal of community is indeed deeply rooted in the nature of things; but I would not call the universe, except possibly in a metaphorical sense, a "community."

In one of his less metaphysical essays, "The Hope of the Great Community," Royce proposed that the ideal of *human* community be extended to include all mankind. He pleaded for a world order based upon a profound respect for the manifold loyalties and indigenous cultures of the earth's many peoples. Such a pluralistic world order, the richer because of its diversity, is only a hope and an aspiration, but if it should ever be realized, it would deserve the name of "the Great Community." The problem of our age is not simply to rehabilitate the small community but to bring the entire family of man into relations of amity and interchange. Peoples that have been suddenly thrown into point-blank atomic range of one another *must* learn to live together as friends and neighbors.

The right solution is to recognize the interdependence of the great and the small community. It would be vain to attempt a fundamental reconstruction of human life by operating *only* at the local level. Wise national and regional planning is imperative to the welfare of localities. Even the whole international order must be taken into account, for without peace, the development of every community is in question. Also the wide perspectives and the far-flung contacts of the great community will "flow back into local life, keeping it flexible, preventing the stagnancy which has attended stability in the past, and furnishing it with the elements of a variegated and many-hued experience."[13] On the other hand, we cannot create the great community unless we reconstitute and conserve the values of the intimate group—the love that comes only with intimacy, the appreciation of personality in its wholeness and integrity, the sense of mutuality and interdependence. As Dewey points out, there is little chance to cultivate regard for distant peoples "as long as there is no close neighborhood experience to bring with it insight and understanding of neighbors."[14]

The future world order may be either a collective or a community. A collective would be imposed from the top, regimenting the masses to an obedient conformity. One can imagine a bureaucracy swollen to planetary proportions, efficient in giving orders and manipulating minds, and equipped with the secret police and the centralized army to enforce its every decree. A world community, on the other hand, would spring from the intimate cells of social life: the family, the neighborhood, the work group, the circle of friends, the cultural or civic association. It would thus be a community of communities, expressing in its very structure and institutions the cooperative habits of its constituent groups. Only human beings who have acquired the inner disposition of a life in common are fit citizens of the world. Hence they must not lose or forsake their distinct and local communities, in which they learn the ways of fellowship. The community of mankind will be the richer because it is differentiated and the stronger because it sinks its roots deep into the small communities.

We have seen that some writers, such as Brownell, reserve the term "community" for the small intimate, face-to-face group, and that others, such as Royce, use the term to denote any essentially cooperative group, even though world-wide (not to mention cosmic) in scope. I shall argue that we need both the *intensity* of community as insisted upon by Brownell, and the *extensity* of community as envisaged by Royce.

A definition of community that is broad enough to suit our purpose has been supplied by E. C. Lindeman. He distinguishes between a "functional" definition, which emphasizes psychological process, and a "structural" definition, which emphasizes geographical pattern. "A community . . ." he declares in his functional definition, "is any process of social interaction which gives rise to a more intensive or more extensive attitude and practise of interdependence, cooperation, collaboration, and unification."[15] This definition admits both the *intensive* dimension stressed by Brownell and the *extensive* dimension emphasized by Royce. It is a definition based upon attitude and process, not upon the limiting factor of locality specified by MacIver or of organic nature required by Tönnies. My definition of community would be similar to Lindeman's, except that I should like to emphasize the factor of freedom as well as of interdependence. Community, as I use the term, refers to all the ways and means by which human beings *freely* recognize and realize their interdependence. In a family, a neighborhood, a circle of friends, in a free,

cooperative activity of any sort, in relations that are very intimate and in
relations that are far-flung in time and space, men realize the fact of interdependence and mutuality. A community exists when this experience is made
the voluntary basis of social coherence.

This broad meaning is in accordance with Dewey's usage. He sometimes
speaks of "the community" so as to imply a geographical locale, but in many
other passages the term is not so limited. The emphasis is upon participation
and sharing rather than physical proximity. "Associated or joint activity is a
condition of the creation of a community," he points out. "But association
itself is physical and organic; while communal life is moral, that is emotionally,
intellectually, consciously sustained."[16] It develops through the give-and-take
of communication rather than through mere adjacency. In the past, human
associations have been determined chiefly by geographical proximity; but
technology is supplying the means of rapid transit and easy communication,
and the leisure to enjoy them. Human beings can now flock together upon
the basis of friendship and mutual interest rather than accidental juxtaposi-
tions in space. New bonds, functional rather than geographic, can thus be
forged, and the limitations of the immediate locale can be transcended. The
emphasis upon community as a process fits the new age of freer communication and transit.

A community, as a real meeting and interaction, differs from a mere aggrega-
tion of individuals, such as a crowd of people who happen to be passing each
other on some busy street corner. In such a casual group, each person is going
his own separate way, without any true relation, any genuine mutuality. It
is not so in a community: *you* affect *me*, as *I* affect *you*. The members are
raised up and bound up in relation, which stirs in the depths of their being
and constitutes their very nature.

Such unity does not exclude differentiation. If we truly love, we treasure
the other person all the more because of his uniqueness. Concrete individuality
is enhanced, not emasculated and repressed, by fraternal bonds. Each person
steps forth in his singleness to join the other single ones in giving and receiving. The members of a community are able to bridge their differences in
virtue of the things they have in common, but they are able to enrich one
another by the rich ferment of their contrasting individualities. The mark of
a community is not likeness but free mutuality.

A community differs from an association in which some are using others
as mere tools. The relation is between man and man, not between man and
thing, or between man and person regarded as thing. A human being may
look at another and say to himself, "You exist for my use." He then regards the
other as a mere "*it*," not as a subject like himself but as an object to be manipulated. His attitude is quite different when he thinks, "You are a person like
me, and each of us can help the other." The first attitude leads to domination,
the second to fellowship. We Americans are experts in our knowledge and
manipulation of impersonal forces, and we are tempted by that achievement

to try to manipulate men with the same skill and ingenuity as we manipulate machines. But the manipulation of men is the destruction of community.

There is thus a radical distinction, in the language of Martin Buber, between the relation "I-Thou" and the relation "I-it." Not only does the "Thou" differ from the "it," but the "I" in the first relation differs fundamentally from the "I" in the second. The first "I" is a real person in a world of persons; the second is a depersonalized individual in a world of things. A person is fully a person only in relation to other persons. He is not a real person so far as he regards others as things, as mere objects or implements. The real meeting between man and man comes about only when each regards the other as an end. This is not always possible. To live, we need to use things, and what is more to the point, to use human beings. But in a real community, the means-relation between individuals, the "I-it" relation, is subordinated to the ends-relation between persons, the "I-Thou" relation. "Only men who are capable of truly saying *Thou* to one another can truly say *We* with one another."[17]

A community differs from an involuntary association. Robert H. MacIver and Charles H. Page, in their book, *Society,* suggest that even a prison is a community, since it is an "area of social living." This is contrary to my usage. There may, of course, be community feelings among the inmates, but so far as the prison is an embodiment of force, it is the very opposite of a true community. Even if coercion be exercised by organizational pressure or "the force of circumstance" rather than by human beings with weapons, the element of free mutuality, and therefore of community, may be lacking. Community is the meeting of real, authentic persons, and to the extent that individuals are creatures of force, circumstance, or pressure, they lack the essential attribute of personality. Here I agree with the existentialists. "So far as I choose, I am," declares Karl Jaspers. "If I am not, I do not choose."[18] Community, being an associatition of persons, requires the autonomy that is inseparable from genuine personality. A *Gemeinschaft,* admittedly, is not based upon deliberate choice: a person is born into a family or a tribe. But if it be a true community, the members realize themselves in and through it, acknowledging one another's rights because they respect one another's being. Community is the reconciliation of freedom and organization: it cannot exist if the "freedom" is anarchical, or the "organization" is imprisoning.

The mark of community is to be found in the quality and not the quantity of human associations. An indiscriminate passion to "belong" produces the condition which H. G. Wells, in his *New Machiavelli,* attributed to the "progressive" town of Bromstead—"a dull, useless boiling up of human activities, an immense clustering of futilities."[19] Modern technology has already made our lives overcomplicated. There is too much hustle and bustle; too much overcrowding of the surfaces; too rapid a sequence of impressions and events. Life should be less congested; it should be simpler and calmer and deeper, with fewer things to do and time to do them better. Excessive sociability merely adds to the din and confusion of life.

William H. Whyte, Jr. complains that the organization man is "imprisoned in brotherhood," but it is not really brotherhood that is imprisoning him. The passion to dissolve oneself in the group is not a sign of community but of the contrary. As Dewey shrewdly remarks:

We should not be so averse to solitude if we had, when we were alone, the companionship of communal thought built into our mental habits. In the absence of this communion, there is the need for reinforcement by external contact. Our sociability is largely an effort to find substitutes for that normal consciousness of connection and union that proceeds from being a sustained and sustaining member of a social whole.[20]

An indiscriminate togetherness, or lack of reserve, is a violation of community. To cherish another person is not merely to enjoy his company but to respect his privacy: to be sensitive to what is inviolably his own.

According to some critics, the idea of community implies social conservatism and preservation of the *status quo*. This charge can not be levelled against the concept as I have interpreted it. The standardization of thought and behavior are characteristic of collectivism rather than of genuine community. A collective is an organization in which the controlling standards and directives are imposed upon its members *from without*, in disregard or defiance of their wills, needs, interests, and individualities. A community is a free association whose consequences are appreciated as good by all who take part in it and whose functioning promotes not only the common interests but the individualities of all the singular persons who are its members. By its very nature it is not a crowd of unthinking conformists but a union of free and various personalities. Far from being a settled and finished affair, it is perpetually in the making; and the individual's commitment to it is not simply retrospective but dynamic and prospective. Like Socrates' love of Athens, the spirit of community is no mere acceptance of convention, no uncritical or credulous orthodoxy, no buckling under to force or prejudice. It demands courage, independence, free inquiry, and respect for individual rights.

A true community seeks the mutual enrichment and enhancement of its members. This seeking can be exhibited in a number of ways. First, the community can intensify the ties between the persons that compose it. They can learn to know and appreciate one another; they can explore the methods of new and deeper and more delightful intimacies. Second, the community can achieve a richer differentiation. Its members can become more free, more creative, more various, more genuinely individual, finding ways of adjusting, or even enjoying, their differences. Third, the community can cultivate its traditions and extend its temporal span. Through memory, it can reach back into the past, and through expectation, it can reach forward into the future and can thus become, in the words of Edmund Burke, "a partnership . . . between those who are living, those who are dead, and those who are to be born."[21] Fourth, the community can widen its spatial extent and break through the limits of narrow parochialism. Its members can seek ways to transcend the barriers of nationality, race, class, and creed, and to establish the cultural basis of a universal human community.

To sum up, the term "community" refers to a process rather than to a locality. Although it is not limited to the small, intimate group, its roots are personal rather than abstract and impersonal. It is based upon free mutuality rather than like-mindedness. It excludes any relation of dominance or exploitation. Far from being a settled and finished affair, it is perpetually in the making; and the individual's commitment to it is not simply retrospective but dynamic and progressive.

Perhaps there never has been and never will be a full-fledged community as so conceived. In its perfection, it is an ideal and not a present fact. But it is a legitimate ideal, and it is sometimes realized in considerable measure.

3. THE PROBLEM OF COMMUNICATION

If we ask why it is so difficult for the denizens of our cities to know one another well—not merely to meet face to face, eye to eye, but mind to mind—the answer is mainly to be found in the specialization that has become so characteristic of our technological age. It is impossible to produce a real community with partial, arrested, lopsided individuals, hypertrophied in some respects and atrophied in others. Too narrow to intuit what diverse persons are thinking and feeling, they are related only fractionally and not deeply related at all. They may have plenty of technical "know-how," but they lack empathic understanding, the ability to place themselves in the position of the other fellow, to reach out in knowledge and imagination and sensibility to appreciate lives different from their own. Whole man speaks to whole man, not fragment to fragment.

Even when the specialization is that of the highly trained technician, it still may limit and stultify the personality. It may overemphasize and overdevelop a single technical function, while leaving the broader human qualities to atrophy. This breaking down of human beings into fragmental selves is characteristic of modern education: broad and fundamental human culture is being sacrificed to the development of narrow technical aptitudes. The "practical curriculum" tends to crowd out the humanities and even the theoretical sciences.[22] Likewise, in the innumerable specialized organizations of urban life, the segregated function and the fractional contact have become the rule.

Communication is a major human problem because the Tower of Babel situation has become general. Your experience and mine, in their intricate totality, remain largely unexpressed and uncommunicated. The technical vocabularies that have been elaborately developed—vocabularies that permit specialists to communicate with one another—have been refined and developed to a high degree. Anyone with the requisite knowledge, for example, can name the minutest parts of an automobile engine clearly and definitely. But these technical vocabularies are irrelevant when human beings attempt to speak as man to man. On the rare occasions when they try to convey their deepest human feelings they stutter and are tongue-tied.

The task of restoring the integrity of the human being and therewith the possibility of full communication is the deepest problem of culture. As Lewis Mumford has remarked, the old adage that it takes nine tailors to make a man is much too modest: a whole man is made by a whole civilization. It requires the cultivation of a central core of values so that human beings can relate themselves to one another by relating themselves to this core. It also requires the enrichment of the language of interpersonal communication by the cultivation of artistic sensitivity and expressiveness. It means that the limited individual, the mere bearer of a specialized function, should be replaced by the fully developed human being.

There is considerable reason to think that the extreme division of labor is a passing phase. Up to a point, machine technology produces the kind of segmentation that Marx and Ruskin denounced, but beyond this point something quite different happens. When a complex industrial operation has been broken down into minute and repetitive phases, the stage of automation becomes feasible. Then the worker's task is not to adjust a spindle or turn a bolt; it is to keep the automatic system in working order. He needs an intelligent grasp of the entire operation and the skill of an all-round mechanic. Under the conditions of a dynamic, ever-changing technology, men must acquire a new adaptiveness to unprecedented technical problems and processes as they arise. This requires breadth and versatility.

As long ago as the fourth century B.C., Aristotle had some inkling of the changes that "automation" would bring. In a remarkable passage in the *Politics*, he pointed out that "if every instrument could accomplish its work . . . if the shuttle would weave and plectrum touch the lyre without a hand to guide them, chief workmen would not want servants, nor masters slaves."[23] The terrifying notion of robots taking over human functions is at least as old as the medieval myth of the Golem. By the end of the nineteenth century, Oscar Wilde had reinterpreted the robot concept as the key to a practicable Utopia:

Civilization requires slaves. . . . Unless there are slaves to do the ugly, horrible, uninteresting work, culture and contemplation become almost impossible. Human slavery is wrong, insecure, and demoralizing. On mechanical slavery, on the slavery of the machine, the future of the world depends. . . . At present machinery competes against man. Under proper conditions machinery will serve man. . . . The machines will be the new slaves.[24]

Early in this century the gifted electrical engineer, Charles P. Steinmetz, predicted that there would be not only a great multiplication of automatic machinery but of machines to *tend* the machines. He had in mind the basic concept of automation, that of the *control* apparatus, such as the thermostat that regulates a furnace. By application of this principle, a fully automatic and self-correcting mechanical system can be created. The push-button factory is now obsolete; the buttons push themselves!

The immediate effect of these changes is to intensify the problem of unemployment, but society will finally make the necessary readjustments. The worker not only will have a better income but far broader training and much more leisure time. If he learns what to do with his time, he can refresh his spirit and widen his horizons. Aristotle maintained that the "noble employment of leisure" is the highest pursuit of man. In the past, it has been the prerogative of a small leisure class; but in the future, it will be within reach of the common man. There will then be need to work out a pattern of living in accordance with the very different possibilities that have been unfolding. The humiliating idea that man is a working animal will no longer correspond to the facts of life. Men will work, but their labor will not be overlong. There will be far more opportunity for love and play and art, the enjoyment of wild nature, the pleasures of travel, the adventures of the mind, the cultivation of life in its sparkle and diversity. Cultural communities, based upon broad and fundamental human interests, will spring up and multiply.

We all know what the advocate of specialization will say in reply. Such interests and avocations, he will insist, are good enough as marginal activities, but specialization is essential in the main business of living. Emile Durkheim has aptly stated the case for specialization:

. . . It is difficult to see why it would be more in keeping with the logic of human nature to develop superficially rather than profoundly. Why would a more extensive activity, but more dispersed, be superior to a more concentrated, but circumscribed, activity? Why would there be more dignity in being complete and mediocre, rather than living a more specialized, but more intense life . . . ?[25]

Answering his own questions, Durkheim argues that the individual achieves greater profundity, freedom, and individuality by specialization: he develops his own peculiar aptitudes to the highest degree, and attains a mastery that no dilettante could ever achieve.

Durkheim contrasts the "mechanical solidarity" that is exhibited by a preliterate, pretechnological society with the "organic solidarity" of a literate, technological society. The former is based upon the likeness of its members, the latter upon the differences. In the primitive society, social cohesion is founded upon the sway of custom, the enforcement of common mores, the possession of an identical stock of ideas and sentiments. At this level, individuality is nil; personality vanishes because no one is truly himself, but is absorbed and effaced by the collective life. In the advanced, civilized society, cohesion is based upon the division of labor. The binding principle is the reciprocal service rendered by unidentical functions. It is illustrated at the subhuman level by what biologists call "symbiosis," the interdependence and mutual benefit of dissimilar organisms. Ferns, for example, thrive in shade and protect the roots of trees; each type of organism helps the other to flourish. So it is, Durkheim believes, in the functional complementarity and interdependence of human specialists.

The service they can render to one another is proportionate to their individual skills. The doctor cannot be of great service to the lawyer, or vice versa, unless each is a master of his own speciality. By thus specializing, they become more individuated, and thereby more interesting and valuable to one another. Those who object to this process as divisive and who conceive of human community as the relation of like to like, have much too tame and impoverished a notion. The truly vital community is realized through the interaction of diverse individuals, and the division of labor is the great means of bringing about this end.

This argument of Durkheim is a mixture of truth and error. The contrast between primitive and technologically advanced societies is not as sharp as he would lead us to believe. More recent anthropological works, such as Boas' *The Mind of Primitive Man,* indicate a certain amount of complexity, specialization, and individuality even at the primitive level. Glancing at the other side of the coin, we find a good deal of mass-conformity among the most "civilized" peoples. The herd-impulse is the curse of all societies, including our own. The effect of technology and the division of labor have been quite as often to constrict and regiment the personality as to liberate and individualize it. Siegfried Giedion's history of industrial specialization, *Mechanization Takes Command,* recounts a pretty grim story in this respect.

Durkheim is forced to admit that the division of labor will not produce the happy effect of social harmony unless human beings are able to choose occupations that will give scope to their true capacities, and unless they are free from the coercions of poverty, oppression, and class stratification. The ideal conditions which he thus specifies are seldom realized in fact. His famous book, *Suicide,* published a few years after *The Division of Labor in Society,* reveals that personal demoralization and consequent self-destruction are especially prevalent in the more industrialized areas. One of the principal causes of the death wish is the lack of a meaningful social life. "The older social forms of organization . . . have disappeared either through the slow usury of time or through great disturbances," such as the French Revolution.[26] In consequence, the ordinary citizen now lacks strong social allegiances, and society has become "a disorganized dust of individuals." Neither the political state nor the division of labor can take the place of the intimate associations which have so largely disappeared. The state is too massive, remote, and impersonal, and the division of labor does not provide warmth and intimacy. The remedy that Durkheim proposes is a reconstitution of small and intimate groups. He wishes to decentralize and democratize industry, with workers sharing in the direct management. It is clear that he no longer depends upon industrial specialization to establish "organic solidarity."

The argument in his earlier book, *The Division of Labor in Society*, scarcely fits the environment in which we now live. Science and technology have made our world interdependent. The web of interrelations is now wide and dense. If men are to be good citizens and live realistically in this sort of world they must be trained for it. As Norman Cousins has remarked: "It stands to reason that if we are living in an interdependent world, we must educate for interdependent living."[27] Although no one should be jack-of-all-trades, there is a great need for "an integrated approach to knowledge and life." The ideal is to combine intensive mastery of a chosen field with a broad and fundamental human culture.

Durkheim's contention that a true community is a unity of the multiform is in agreement with our definition, but his argument is one-sided. He contrasts, as I have said, a "mechanical" kind of "solidarity," based upon the likenesses of its members, with an "organic" kind, based upon the differences. The contrast that he thus draws is too sharp: there can be no mutual respect for differences where there is no community of values. It is interesting to compare his formulation with Dewey's emphasis upon communication and like-mindedness:

There is more than a verbal tie between the words common, community, and communication. Men live in a community by virtue of the things which they have in common. What they must have in common in order to form a community or society are aims, beliefs, aspirations, knowledge,—a common understanding—like mindedness as the sociologists say. Such things cannot be passed physically from one to another, like bricks; they cannot be shared as persons would share a pie by dividing it into physical pieces. The communication which insures participation in a common understanding is one which secures similar emotional and intellectual dispositions—like ways of responding to expectations and requirements.[28]

Here the emphasis is upon the likenesses that Durkheim believes to be characteristic of a comparatively low state of social cohesion. In later books, Dewey puts greater emphasis upon the values of diversity, but he continues to emphasize communication and common understanding.

One of the merits of his interpretation is that it stresses the morale of consent. When human beings are bound together by common ideas, common feelings, common memories, and common aspirations, they experience the sort of unity for which "we" is the natural expression. Durkheim's emphasis upon symbiosis implies no such spiritual cohesion. Edward Gross, an American sociologist, has pointed out:

What distinguishes symbiosis most clearly is that it implies a segmented relation and is least dependent for its operation on positive feelings. The relation between the shoemaker and the customer is symbiotic: each has something that the other needs—services, on the one hand, and money on the other. As long as those needs persist, and as long as each has no easy alternative way of satisfying those needs, then the two will be linked. This does not mean that they will necessarily like each other; it does mean that they will remain united *whether they like each other or not*.[29]

Likewise the very elaborate system of symbiosis that constitutes the division of labor in a modern factory may involve very little sympathy and mutual identification. The workers are functionally interdependent but may otherwise be strangers to one another. Quite different is the kind of sharing and participative life of which Dewey speaks; this depends on the strength of positive feelings.

Another interpretation of the basis of community is that of Plato in his dialogues on love, the *Lysis* and the *Symposium*. In the latter, he declares that Love is the child of Poverty and Plenty.

On the birthday of Aphrodite there was a feast of the gods, at which the god Poros or Plenty . . . was one of the guests. When the feast was over, Penia or Poverty, as the manner is on such occasions, came about the doors to beg. Now Plenty who was the worse for nectar (there was no wine in those days), went into the garden of Zeus and fell into a heavy sleep; and Poverty considering her own straightened circumstances, plotted to have a child by him, and accordingly she lay down at his side and conceived Love . . .[30]

Insofar as love springs from lack (poverty) it is a yearning for completion; insofar as it springs from communion and shared enjoyment (plenty) it is a present fulfillment. In the *Lysis,* one must read between the lines, but the implication is fairly clear that love is derived from both opposition ("the opposite is the food of the opposite") and sharing ("friends have all things in common"). According to both dialogues, the lover yearns for those goods which he lacks and which his beloved possesses, but he is also in close sympathetic accord with his beloved. In the ideal case, the relation is reciprocal; each of the lovers complements the other, yet they share in common goods. Love thus implies both similarities and dissimilarities—a spiritual kinship, yet a rich diversity.

So it is in the larger community. The members are able to bridge their differences in virtue of the things they have in common, but they are able to enrich one another by a synthesis of complementary traits. The highest type of unity is based upon *both* likeness and difference, each as indispensable as the other. A true community requires that men relate to each other not merely in terms of a division of labor but in a broad and deeply human way.

In this search for a new intellectual synthesis, we must accent the social sciences and techniques, as long as they are not used to regiment and manipulate people. As Elton Mayo, the industrial psychologist, has remarked:

The achievements of physical science, of chemistry, of medicine, in the last century have been very great; but the very dimension of these achievements has thrown society out of balance. . . . If our social skills (that is, our ability to secure cooperation between people) had advanced step by step with our technical skills, there would not have been another [world] war.[31]

We have employed the utmost intelligence to develop the means of total destruction, but we have devoted comparatively little research and experiment to the problems of conflict resolution. To rectify this unbalance, an immense redirection of intellectual energies is required.

The first sentence of the charter of UNESCO reads: "Since wars are made in the minds of men, it is in the minds of men that the foundations of peace must be constructed." This statement points to the overwhelming need for psychological and social skills to create a universal human community.

4. INSTITUTIONAL RECONSTRUCTION

The old slogans ring hollow and the old passions are spent. Among our intellectuals, it is now rather difficult to find an apologist for either *laissez faire* or doctrinaire socialism. Aside from extremist fringes, political ideologies do not divide us as once they did. There is wide agreement about major objectives: a mixed economy, combining private and public enterprise; the decentralization of power; the attainment of welfare in a free and open society. The main political parties have tended to converge. There is no longer so deep a chasm between the Labor and the Conservative parties in Great Britain, or between the social-democratic parties and their principal opponents on the Continent. In a number of countries the socialists have been reformulating their objectives, emphasizing Marx's theme of alienation and its overcoming, rather than mere nationalization of the means of production. In the United States, the liberals in both the Democratic and Republican parties have moved close together, and the socialist parties have all but disappeared.

The situation is different in newly risen countries, where communism has a major appeal. But the idea that really strikes fire among them is that of rapid economic growth. The communist system is defended less as an end in itself than as a means to swift modernization and economic development. This plea cannot be effectively countered without an immense effort upon the part of both the industrially advanced and backward peoples. The idea of the welfare state, as Gunnar Myrdal has argued, will have to be widened and changed into the concept of a welfare world. If, with massive aid from the advanced democratic states, the new societies can grow rapidly by nontotalitarian means, the lure of communism will abate.

The great struggle between community and mass society, between mutuality and conformity, I believe, will ultimately be decided in favor of freedom and community. What impresses me about the modern world is not merely the uncertainty and trouble but the immense hope that thrusts itself up through human suffering. Even the huge scale of modern calamities gives us grounds for hope: it is an indication of an immense tide of change which has been gathering force for more than one hundred years and has been rushing toward a climax. As a recent book states:

Never has the history of civilization reached a more hopeful moment. This may seem an extraordinary statement to make at a time when human affairs appear to be chaotic, both on a domestic and international level. We think that the very chaos, which can be so depressing, is, if rightly understood, a hopeful sign.[32]

The power of turning in a radically new direction never reveals itself outside of crisis. An age of crisis, as I have repeatedly said, is marked by both danger and opportunity.

Out of the brains of scientists and engineers have sprung millions of machines with billions of horsepower. Because this prodigious energy has not been mastered, we have had war, revolution, economic chaos. Nevertheless, technology, if rightly employed can eliminate poverty and the exploitation of man by man. It can bind all parts of the world together by transit and communication and thus create the indispensable basis of a universal community. Our machines, therefore, are too wonderful, too productive, too indispensable for us ever to destroy them. But we must have the will to conquer these mechanical monsters that have been running amuck, running wild. *This* is the great adventure of our age—to master the unlimited potentialities of science and technology—the boldest, the most exhilarating, the most promising and dangerous adventure that ever challenged the spirit and intelligence of man.

Whatever the future may hold, it will be very different from the past. The terrific clash of interests which breeds strikes, riots, wars, and revolutions testifies to the radical nature and immense impetus of the transition. These changes are too pervasive and profound to be dismissed as temporary aberrations. They are clear announcements, so that those who run may read, of a profound alteration in human life. We as individuals cannot prevent the coming of this new order, but we can understand its necessities, appreciate its potentialities, and contribute to its values. If we are guided by understanding and motivated by good will, we not only can mitigate the cruelty of the transition but can help to build a humane and rational society. It will not be easy, but it is not impossible.

A fraternal society cannot be achieved apart from the planned development of free communities, in a cultural, not merely a political, sense. We must have a real working faith in the values of personal communication and interdependence; and these values must be cultivated by morals, religion, technology, science, art, politics, and town planning. There must be a general renewal and decentralization of our culture, putting humanity before machines and considerations of welfare ahead of profits. We must limit the mass standardization so characteristic of the coca-cola-and-television dimension of our civilization. The emphasis should be upon personal creativity and *active* participation in small, friendly, face-to-face groups—religious, scientific, artistic, recreational, and so forth. What is required is a new synthesis that will put *personal* relations at the focus of life while utilizing, selectively, the immense potentialities of a technological and scientific age. Technology can free men from bread-

and-butter cares and supply them with leisure and easy transit. They can then flock together upon the basis of friendship and creative interests.

I do not envisage the return to the old neighborhood life of a previous generation. As Tönnies pointed out, it is impractical to restore *Gemeinschaft* as the dominant form of human association. Humpty Dumpty was a pretty good egg as long as he was on top of the wall, but now that he has tumbled, he can never be set up again. The best hope, Tönnies maintained, is to create a new kind of fraternal society in which the characteristics of *Gemeinschaft* and *Gesellschaft* will be integrated. This requires the strengthening of voluntary associations, whether they be friendship circles, or cultural associations, or producers and consumers cooperatives. These spontaneous groups must be given enough stability and depth to sustain rich and intimate human relations.

If this endeavor is to be successful, it must be integrated with technology and community planning. Enough statistical evidence is already at hand to indicate that technology, in certain areas, is beginning to create a new type of social order—less centralized, less congested, less impersonal and bureaucratic. Under the influence of automobiles and rapid transit, suburban villages and outlying trading centers are multiplying and some of the smaller towns are beginning to revive. There is a relatively new and quite marked tendency to build factories away from congested centers of population. In the United States, these new factories are springing up in little towns in the South and West and in other nonmetropolitan locales. Although the great cities are growing, the population increase in the satellite villages or suburban areas is faster than in the city proper. There are many signs that the metropolis is in process of far-reaching transformation.

The concept of a fluid and decentralized city is beginning to take shape. Heavy traffic will be concentrated along separate arteries that do not traverse residential districts or other areas requiring silence. The cafes, the shops, the clubs, the green plots and walkways, will be off the travelled streets, with their gasoline odors, noise, dust, and dirt. Rapid transit and planned decentralization will reduce automobile congestion and commuting time. The city will be designed so that related activities will be concentrated in functional groupings and these will be spaced so as to avoid overcrowding. The blighted areas will be cleared and rebuilt and even the better areas improved, but not without a sense of historical continuity and the human uses of old familiar places. There will be ample provision for well-planned shopping centers, for recreational, religious, educational, and art centers, for public buildings surrounded by spacious plazas, for boulevards, parks, and parkways. The freshness and natural beauty of the countryside will be brought into the far interior of the city. Architects, engineers, and city planners will be asked to build for vivid human contacts, to design neighborhoods and centers which invite face-to-face meetings and sustain intimate and productive community-activities. These planned neighborhood units will be threaded with pleasant walks and protected from outside encroachment by surrounding parkways.

They will be provided with the facilities that will give them a considerable independence of the larger metropolis. The city will be a differentiated structure of fairly independent cells, and the units of human services, such as the schoolroom or the art-center workshop, will be made smaller, so as to avoid mass-anonymity. Life will be adjusted to a human scale without losing the manifold opportunities of the urban environment. At every stage the planning will be conceived concretely in terms of life values and not abstractly as a drawing-board project. There is scope for thousands or even millions of people in such rebuilding of our cities. Hence, there is no excuse for idle men and idle resources, even if disarmament should vastly augment the forces at our disposal.

An important factor in this rebuilding and decentralization is the exploitation of new sources of power, electric and atomic. The inexpensive conductivity of electric power and the small bulk of material from which atomic energy is derived reduce the difficulties in the distribution of fuel and therefore permit the location of power stations and factories in scattered areas near the consumers. The first great steps have been taken to exploit a superabundant source of fuel, deuterium (heavy hydrogen), which may eventually cost far less than any present source of power. The effect of such a scientific breakthrough can scarcely be exaggerated: it would make for a fundamental restructuralization of industry, and if properly guided, for a much more decentralized system.

The assumption that industrial technology must necessarily contribute to centralization and authoritarianism is quite unwarranted. The technical weakness of monolithic authoritarian structures, whether it be in government or industry, is that the directors are too out of touch with the complex details they are seeking to regulate. There is no effective dialogue between the managers and the managed: orders go out but accurate reports do not return. Hence the sources of information become increasingly unreliable. In the language of engineering, there is an inadequate "feedback" to the control stations.

This may not be a serious defect in a simple and uniform setup, but it is very serious indeed in a highly complex and diversified system. It produces the typical diseases of the brontisaurian organization: apoplexy at the center and anaemia at the extremities. As Kenneth Boulding points out, technological efficiency itself demands greater democracy and decentralization:

It seems likely that authoritarian forms of organizational structure are quite inappropriate in developing the kinds of skill which a highly technological society requires. Within the structure of American business enterprises, for instance, we have seen a marked change in the present generation from highly authoritarian structures toward looser and more democratic ones, with greater decentralization of power and distribution of authority, human relations programs, and the like. In the communist world also, there may be a profound tendency toward the replacement of authoritarian structures by looser and more democratic ones. Because of the imperious demands of the dynamics of skill, we are rapidly approaching the time when labor as brute force, mechanically applied, will become obsolete. As we move forward into the society of the skilled, such a society would seem necessarily to be based on extensive discussion, accurate feedbacks, a network of mutual information channels, and an absence of coercion. This is close to our ideal image of democracy.[33]

Instead of rejecting the organizational revolution *in toto,* we shall find ways of democratizing and decentralizing and humanizing its processes. Democracy is largely a series of political and social inventions: it will yet devise new and better ways of transmitting accurate information, it will create more effective institutions for dialogue and discussion, it will use technology to serve community life rather than cater to big business, big government, or bigness of any sort.

The remedy for the defects of industrialism and democracy is not a return to the older philosophy of *laissez faire.* As history has already taught us, our system will run amuck if it lacks social and moral controls. *Laissez faire* destroys freedom, because it leaves the bullies free to tyrannize over the weak. The power of government, wisely employed, can check the bullies and strengthen individual freedom and voluntary associations. First and foremost, the government should engage in aggressive maintenance of civil liberties: free speech and assembly, the right to dissent, the right to privacy, "due process" and fair trial. In this period of hyperorganization, civil liberties become more necessary and precious than ever before. Second, government can throw its support to underprivileged groups, such as Negroes, slum dwellers, and migrant agricultural workers. A government actively devoting itself to the protection of the weak and unfortunate and the elimination of poverty and unemployment can greatly increase the freedom of its citizens even when it curbs the unduly powerful. Third, the provision by government of better health, education, security, and cultural opportunities, and the right political control of science and technology, can immensely facilitate individual liberties and voluntary associations. But it will be necessary to decentralize governmental services, guard against a top-heavy bureaucracy, and design institutional safeguards to prevent the abuse of power. Fourth, the government can maintain agencies for community development and can enlist the assistance of educational and civic institutions in behalf of community projects. Experiments of this type, in such states as Illinois, Montana, and Washington, have been remarkably successful. Similar community-development projects are now being undertaken in many lands, sometimes by governments, sometimes by private agencies such as the Ford Foundation or the American Friends Service Committee. If such projects are to be successful they must work with local forces and stimulate grass-roots initiatives.

As Dewey declares, the principle of the free community "does not deter political activity from engaging in constructive measures. But it does lay down a criterion by which every political proposal shall be judged: Does it tend definitely in the direction of increase of voluntary free choice and activity on the part of individuals" and autonomous groups?[34] Dewey thus rejected an exclusive emphasis upon the state and political activity as the means to communal living. The principle of "cooperative association" or "shared experience," rather than a mere political program, is the heart of his faith. He looked forward to the development of cooperative voluntary endeavor in innumerable fields—recreational, artistic, religious, scientific, technical, and economic. Any group engaged in valuable activity may become aware of its functions and responsibilities, and may seek to extend its services and to enrich and enhance its members. Dewey thought of a democratic government as largely the servant of such voluntary cooperative groups, with their many and diversified interests. "The state," he declared, "remains highly important—but its significance consists more and more in its power to foster and coordinate the activities of voluntary groupings."[35] Its function is mainly to integrate and augment the various techniques which free associations have at their disposal. Remarked Dewey:

I am not optimistic enough to believe that voluntary associations of individuals, which are even now building up within the cracks of a crumbling social order, will speedily reverse the trend toward political collectivism. But I am confident that the ultimate way out of the present social dead end lies with the movement these associations are initiating. Individuals who have not lost faith in themselves and in other individuals will increasingly ally themselves with these groups.[36]

There is no lack of pilot projects, such as the Peace Corps established by the Kennedy Administration, the Research Center for Conflict Resolution at the University of Michigan, the New Towns in Britain, the innumerable cooperatives in Denmark and Sweden, the "communities of work" in France, and the kibbutzim in Israel. They are not panaceas but ways of discovering new possibilities in human relations. By wise experimentation in many different directions, it may be possible to discover the basic principles of fraternalism. Gradually men may learn how to live together harmoniously, nobody being suppressed and nobody the suppressor, and all developing their basic potentialities.

We must strengthen human fraternity at the two opposite poles—the intimate association and the worldwide federation. Starting at the grass roots of social life, we must cultivate the attitudes of global unity. Success in this endeavor will depend largely upon our ability to respect cultures different from our own. Most people in the West regard themselves as the bearers of human progress, and they fail to understand that there are values in the "backward" cultures that are very much worth preserving. It has been precisely among the least "progressive" peoples—as progress is ordinarily measured—that community spirit has remained most intact. That is why Gandhi said to India's leaders: "Go to the villages and identify yourselves with the people there." The village communities preserve the man-to-manness, the intuitively felt communion of the heart, which Gandhi invoked as a principle of moral and political regeneration. Among a great many sophisticated Westerners this community-spirit has withered:

> The desert is not only around the corner,
> The desert is squeezed into the tube-train next to you,
> The desert is in the heart of your brother.[37]

The hope of the world is that a new synthesis will eventually emerge from the mingling of cultures: that the ancient wisdom of the community will be used to replenish the spiritual desert of our over-mechanized civilization, and that Western scientific and technological skills will simultaneously be used to spread enlightenment and raise living standards among folk communities all over the globe.

Both divisions of mankind would gain immensely by such a synthesis. The folk societies would gain a new sense of the efficacy of human actions; they would no longer feel doomed, as if by inexorable necessity, to a life of grinding labor and bitter poverty. With new hope and understanding, with new energies and powers, they would find themselves on a different and higher level of existence. The highly technical societies could also gain immeasurably by recalling some of the primordial values of human life. They would learn that mechanical civilization, by itself, is radically insufficient to make men happy. They would rediscover the need to sink their roots deep in the contexts of humanity, and to subordinate matter to life, the mechanical to the spiritual, the egocentric to the communal. The ideal of human brotherhood is as old as Isaiah, but now for the first time ethics and vital necessity and technical feasibility coincide.

NOTES

1. H. G. Wells, *Mind at the End of Its Tether*. New York: Didier Publishers, 1946, p. 25.
2. Kenneth E. Boulding, *The Organizational Revolution*. New York: Harper & Row, Publishers, Inc., 1953, *passim*.
3. Karl Popper, *The Open Society and Its Enemies*. Princeton: Princeton University Press, 1950, p. 170.
4. David Riesman, *The Lonely Crowd*. New Haven: Yale University Press, 1950.
5. Erich Fromm, *Man for Himself*. New York: Holt, Rinehart and Winston, Inc., 1947, p. 74.
6. William H. Whyte, Jr., *The Organization Man*. New York: Simon and Schuster, Inc., 1956.

7. Erich Kahler, *The Tower and the Abyss*. New York: George Braziller, Inc., 1957, p. 81. On Nazi cruelty, see Victor H. Bernstein, *Final Judgment*. New York: Gaer Associates, Inc., 1947.
8. From Martin Buber's Foreword to E. A. Gutkind, *Community and Environment*. London: C. A. Watts & Co., Ltd., 1953, p. viii.
9. Baker Brownell, *The Community and the College*. New York: Harper & Row, Publishers, Inc., 1952, pp. 43–44.
10. Robert M. MacIver and Charles H. Page, *Society: An Introductory Analysis*. New York: Holt, Rinehart and Winston, Inc., 1949, pp. 9–10.

11. Robert M. MacIver, *Community*. London: Macmillan & Co., Ltd., 1917, p. 107.
12. Josiah Royce, *The Problem of Christianity*. New York: The Macmillan Company, 1913, II, p. 273.
13. John Dewey, *The Public and Its Problems*. New York: Holt, Rinehart and Winston, Inc., 1927, p. 216.
14. *Ibid.*, p. 213.
15. E. C. Lindeman, "Community," *Encyclopedia of the Social Sciences*. New York: The Macmillan Company, 1930, IV, p. 103.
16. John Dewey, *The Public and Its Problems, op. cit.*, p. 387.
17. Martin Buber, *Between Man and Man*. New York: The Macmillan Company, 1948, p. 176.
18. Karl Jaspers, *Philosophie*. Berlin: Springer-Verlag, 1932, II, p. 182.
19. H. G. Wells, *The New Machiavelli*. London: Collins' Clear-Type Press, no date, p. 41.
20. John Dewey, *Individualism Old and New*. New York: Minton, Balch & Co., 1930, pp. 87–88.
21. Edmund Burke, *Reflections on the French Revolution*. New York: E. P. Dutton & Co., Inc., 1910, p. 93.
22. For a summary of these trends, see William H. Whyte, Jr., *The Organization Man, op. cit.*, Chapter 7.
23. Aristotle, *The Politics*, translated by Benjamin Jowett. London and New York: Oxford University Press, 1938, p. 31.
24. Oscar Wilde, "The Soul of Man Under Socialism" (various editions).
25. Emile Durkheim, *The Division of Labor in Society*. New York: The Free Press of Glencoe, Inc., 1947,

pp. 403–404. (Original French edition, 1893.)
26. Emile Durkheim, *Suicide*. New York: The Free Press of Glencoe, Inc., 1951, p. 388. (Original French edition, 1897.)
27. Norman Cousins, *Modern Man Is Obsolete*. New York: The Viking Press, Inc., 1945, pp. 19–20.
28. John Dewey, *Democracy and Education*. New York: The Macmillan Company, 1916, p. 5.
29. Edward Gross, "Symbiosis and Consensus as Integrative Factors in Small Groups," *American Sociological Review*, Vol. 21, 1956, p. 176.
30. Plato, *Symposium*, #203. (Jowett's translation.)
31. Elton Mayo, *The Social Problems of an Industrial Civilization*. Cambridge, Mass.: Harvard University Press, 1945, p. 33.
32. Richard and Hephzibah Hauser, *The Fraternal Society*. London: The Bodley Head Ltd., 1962, p. 7.
33. Kenneth E. Boulding, *The Image*. Ann Arbor: University of Michigan Press, 1956, pp. 108–109.
34. John Dewey and others, *I Believe*, edited by Clifton Fadiman. New York: Simon and Schuster, Inc., 1939, p. 351.
35. John Dewey, *Reconstruction in Philosophy*. New York: Holt, Rinehart and Winston, Inc., 1920, pp. 203–204.
36. John Dewey, *I Believe, op. cit.*, p. 354.
37. T. S. Eliot, Chorus from "The Rock," *Collected Poems 1909–1962*. London: Faber and Faber, Ltd. New York: Harcourt, Brace & World, Inc., 1963, p. 149.

CHAPTER XVI

The spirit of community

I. THE IMPORTANCE OF RELIGION

The basis of morality is more than a set of concepts. Not only understanding of the good but devotion to it is required. Without this devotion, a person is very likely to think to himself, "Why should I bother about my duty?" His attitude will remain egocentric or his effort will be halfhearted. But when he acquires a profound emotional conviction that his ideals are based upon the nature of things, he may be lifted right out of his listless humdrum self and gain immensely in strength and passion. Such transformation and integration of a whole life can be called, in the wide sense, "religious."

I use this word with some hesitation because of its usual connotations. Most of what passes under the name of "religion" seems to me myth, archaic or decadent. But naturalistic philosophers are not justified in their usual neglect of religion. As Whitehead has said:

> In considering religion, we should not be obsessed by the idea of its necessary goodness. This is a dangerous delusion. The point to notice is its transcendent importance; and the fact of this importance is abundantly made evident by the appeal to history.[1]

The truth of Whitehead's remark came home to me forcefully during a sojourn in Mexico. I was on leave of absence from the University of Washington during the winter season. My family and I were living on the outskirts of Mexico City. From our kitchen window we looked down on the highway to Toluca. The weather was so cold that all records had been broken. On December 13, the thermometer sank to thirteen degrees Fahrenheit—a very chilling temperature for so far south. A few miles from our house, snow was packed on the Toluca–Mexico City highway, which soars to an altitude of over ten thousand feet. Early in the morning I was awakened by the sound of innumerable voices singing in unison. On looking out the kitchen window I saw an almost never-ending train of men, women, and children—the men wearing colorful serapes, the women heavy rebozos, the children sweaters and other thick clothing—many of them barefoot and ragged. Some in the procession were old and infirm, some had crutches, others were carrying infants or heavy bedrolls. But their spirits were high, they chanted together and a number carried colorful banners. This was the annual pilgrimage, when thousands of peasants and townsfolk make the long trek from Toluca, a distance of about thirty miles, to the shrine of the Virgin of Guadalupe.

On this day, December 13, 1958, an estimated 800,000 persons braved the chill temperature to worship the Virgin on the 426th anniversary of her apparition. Many of the pilgrims came from the far interior of the country. A few of the more devout crawled from the Peravillo Circle—a distance of four kilometers—on their knees. Some were unable to endure the cold and exhaustion and collapsed on the way. The Red Cross ambulances picked up hundreds who were injured by exposure or the pressure of the crowd. Inside the Basilica, services began at 5:30 P.M. with solemn Mass and continued for hours. Outside, Indians took turns dancing their strange rituals and the traditional Mañanitas were sung by mariachis and others in the crowd. No one could witness this scene without realizing that religion is a mighty force.

Less dramatic, but equally impressive, is the immense amount of religious art, such as statues, paintings, and church edifices, which confront one in Mexico on every hand. For centuries religion has stirred the Mexican imagination with extraordinary depth and force. The frequently hostile attitudes of the revolutionary governments may have dimmed but certainly have not extinguished the fire of the religious spirit. Although the ordinary Mexican approves governmental curbs upon the political activities of the Church, he is still intensely religious at heart.

Mexico is no great exception in this respect. For most people in the world, religion provides the main cultural basis of a way of life; and this has been the case throughout history. So pervasive and tenacious a form of culture must reflect some genuine need. Although religion has carried over into civilization many of the crudities of barbaric imagination, its very persistence and universality indicate something fundamental, something that may be given a noble and unsuperstitious expression. It is comfortable to the anti-religious to suppose that the deeply religious man is *homo ignorans* or *homo stupidus* rather than *homo sapiens,* but this supposition is not justified.

In this age of crisis we can no longer take any of the basic forms of culture for granted. Human beings must become transparent to themselves: they must understand the passions and institutions that move them; and they must learn to control the deep irrational forces that, when uncontrolled, drive men like autumn leaves in a storm. Only thus can they hope to find a vision deep and realistic enough to guide them safely in an age of monstrous tensions and to make the arts of life prevail over the newfangled techniques of death.

2. THE CULTURAL ROOTS OF RELIGION

We must understand the fundamental nature of religion if we are to grasp its moral import. The clue to this understanding is a very curious fact. The cultural conditions that have given rise to so much great art, science, philosophy, and statesmanship have been unproductive of original religious genius. We can recall scientists such as Archimedes, Newton, Pasteur, Darwin, and Einstein; or artists such as Praxiteles, Michelangelo, Shakespeare, Bach, and Cezanne; or philosophers such as Plato, Descartes, Spinoza, Hume, and Kant; or statesmen such as Pericles, Cromwell, Jefferson, Garibaldi, and Churchill. All of these men flourished in relatively complex civilizations. Many of them lived in great cities such as Paris and London or in sophisticated centers of culture such as Athens and Florence.

We do not look to such cities for the original founders of the world's religions. Not a single major religion has ever been created by any of the myriad human beings in our teeming metropolises or even in our sophisticated towns. The truly commanding figures—men such as Lao-Tse, Confucius, Buddha, Moses, Zarathustra, Jesus, and Mohammed—belong to the much simpler societies of the dim and misty past. We can point to a few relatively minor cults and their founders, but how limited in comparison with the superlative religious geniuses and their world-conquering faiths! We have had our derivative figures, our preachers and theologians aplenty, but no great seminal religious minds. How shall we explain this paradox?

We cannot say that religion, like wine, must be old in order to excel. The immediate followers of Buddha, Jesus, or Mohammed, took no such view. Age may add a certain taste and bouquet to religion but it cannot account for its original tang.

The prevalent psychic atmosphere in these ancient times was one of myth and prophetic vision. This would suggest that religion is more closely allied to poetic intuition than to scientific understanding; but it has been too pervasive a factor in human culture to be dismissed as belonging to humanity's nonage. It *originates* in less sophisticated and complex societies, but it proliferates and spreads over a vastly wider area. Although Christianity sprang up in the villages of Judea, it took the effete civilization of Rome by storm and has exerted a mighty role in the world ever after. Many highly cultivated human geniuses, such as Socrates, Bach, and Einstein, have been intensely, even if unorthodoxly, religious. In this respect, religion is very different from magic, which usually remains local and primitive.

There must be some point of contrast between the ancient, simple, and naïve communities and the relatively modern, complex, and sophisticated societies that will help to explain the fact that religion arises *mainly* in the former but *spreads* in the latter. The essential difference is that the simple community is close, warm, and human whereas the complex society is relatively cold, abstract, and impersonal. In the simple community, men know one another intimately as concrete, vivid, flesh-and-blood personalities within the family, neighborhood, or small circle of friends. In comparison, our modern societies function largely by way of abstract indirect relations such as communication by telephone, radio, printed page, or casual economic transaction.

This contrast between the concrete and abstract society is our clue for the interpretation of religion as a cultural force. In the intimate community, human beings first learned the ways of fellowship. Only within the milieu of personal relations, men like Jesus and Buddha and Lao-Tse came to spiritual maturity. Here they developed the capacity for personal communion and created the religious symbols and myths of the human race. In our abstract, sophisticated societies, where even "charity" is institutionalized and thereby depersonalized, our geniuses are relatively untouched and uninspired by the close communion of persons. They can create great art, science, philosophy, and statecraft but cannot create religion.

A city such as ancient Athens was intermediate between the concrete community and the depersonalized society. Its citizens developed some of the mobility, intellectual detachment, and blasé individualistic attitudes characteristic of modern city dwellers, but without altogether losing the closeness and intimacy of the primitive blood brotherhood. Their dramatists, such as Aeschylus and Sophocles, and their philosophers, such as Socrates and Plato, were still religiously loyal to the community—the sacred city-state. In reading philosophical works such as the *Apology* or plays such as *Oedipus the King,* we feel the conflict and tension between the old ideal of clan-fellowship and the new dawning ideal of free "emancipated" individuality. The communal religious spirit was still creatively at work among the Greeks, but it was not so intense as among the less sophisticated people of Judea. In comparison, the mobile, restless, uprooted denizens of our gigantic modern cities are much farther removed from the spiritual milieu in which the world's religions have originated.

Yet the hunger for communion persists even in the most impersonal societies. Love is too instinctive to be wholly repressed. However depersonalized our human relations become, we try to reach across the abyss that separates man from man and man from the surrounding universe. Here, then, is the secret of religion's power. The impulse of the higher religions is to extend the community-mindedness of the close, intimate, concrete group to the wider sphere of the immense, impersonal, abstract society.

John MacMurray has said that the function of religion is the "extension of family unity of affection to wider groups."[2] This is too narrow a formulation. The sense of communion—which is perhaps the main psychological root of religion—is nourished by all the "I-Thou" relations of life—the unison of lovers, the bond of friends, the spirit of neighborliness, or any other close affectionate ties. The function of religion is not merely to bind together "wider groups" by the extension of these feelings: it is also to achieve an emotional harmony and integration of the individual with the world conceived as a whole. This function demands self-transcendence, a capacity that is originally cultivated and developed in the intimate community. Religion may finally attain to "cosmic consciousness" but it begins with the immediate ties of love.

Hence it naturally uses the language of the face-to-face community: it speaks of love, fellowship, brotherhood, communion, the fatherhood of God. The higher religions seek to project these concepts to their widest possible scope. For this is the meaning of the higher religions: to take the love that is cultivated in the most intimate circles and to extend it to the widest circles that the human imagination can trace.

Primitive religions similarly have expressed the values of the intimate tribal community, but they have failed to project these values beyond their original parochial limits. Likewise the more parochial religions of civilized peoples, such as Japanese Shintoism, have lacked the power to spread. The contagiousness of the higher religions is the result of two factors: first, they have expressed the primordial values of the intimate community and thus have tapped the deepest roots of human feeling; and second, they have sought to extend these values to the widest compass and thus to universalize them.

This escape from parochialism has been discussed by Arnold Toynbee:

> When we mark down the birthplaces of the higher religions on a map, we find them clustering in and round two relatively small patches of the land-surface of the Old World—on the one hand the Oxus-Jaxartes Basin and on the other hand Syria, using that term in its broader sense to cover an area bounded by the North Arabian Steppe, the Mediterranean Sea, and the southern escarpments of the Anatolian and Armenian plateaux.[3]

The Syrian area gave birth to Judaism and Christianity, and the adjacent highlands fringing the Red Sea, to Mohammedanism. The Oxus-Jaxartes Basin, and its adjacent basins of the Indus and the Ganges, gave rise to primitive Buddhism, the later Mahayana Buddhism, post-Buddhaic Hinduism, and, perhaps, Zoroastrianism. Both regions were centers of traffic from various points of the compass and the scene of repeated encounters between different civilizations.

> As a result of these encounters, each of these two peculiarly "numeniferous" [religion-bearing] regions had been included in the universal states of a number of different civilizations, and the exceptionally active intercourse between civilizations in these two areas explains the extraordinary concentration, within these limits, of the birthplaces of higher religions.[4]

The Yellow River valley, which was the birthplace of Confucianism and Taoism, cannot be described in the same terms. It was not at the crossroads of civilizations, and there was not the same need to generalize the precepts of religion to apply to strangers of an alien race. But there were other historical circumstances which required an escape from parochialism. The early history of China is in large measure a struggle for political and cultural unity. During the Chou dynasty, which lasted for 867 years, a well-organized Chinese state was finally achieved. But there followed a long period, still nominally under the Chou dynasty, when this process of unification stopped and there was disorganization. Petty rulers of local areas became practically independent and quarreled violently with one another. The age of militarism and disintegration had already begun when Confucius and Lao-Tse[5] propounded their wisdom of the heart; and it continued for over two centuries following the death of Confucius in 479 B.C. During this long "time of troubles," Taoism and Confucianism were developed into moral and religious systems by their followers. As Arthur Waley has pointed out, the great need was for unification:

To the Chinese of this period the word One [unity, singleness, etc.] had an intensely emotional connotation, reflected equally in political theory and in Taoist metaphysics. And, indeed, the longing—or more accurately, the psychological need —for a fixed standard of belief was profounder, more urgent and more insistent than the longing for governmental unity.[6]

Taoism taught the futility of contention for power, and the importance of harmony with the One behind the mystery of time and change. Confucianism sought to reintegrate Chinese society according to the principles of a moral order having a personal basis but universal scope. As a famous Confucian passage says, "When the personal life is perfected, there will be family harmony. When there is family harmony, there will be national order. And when there is national order, there will be world peace."[7] Thus the historical need for unity in China played a role analogous to the geographical need for unity in Syria and India. In both cases the effect was to lift religion out of its original parochial setting and universalize it.

3. RELIGION AS THE SPIRIT OF COMMUNITY

If religion is rooted in community, this fact must be reflected in its fundamental nature, and this is exactly what we find. A religion such as Hinayana Buddhism (in its pure, original form) can exist without the worship of God; and a profoundly religious man, such as Spinoza, can forego belief in the supernatural; but no religion and no religious individual, I dare say, can exist without the realization, in some form, of the values of community.

There are many definitions of religion and these vary widely. Leo Tolstoy, James Leuba, and others have listed definitions by the score. The definitions stress various factors: feeling, action, belief, cult, art and ritual. All of these factors are involved in religion, but it is necessary to see how they fit together. Most authorities in the field—such as Emile Durkheim, R. R. Marrett, Rudolf Otto, M. E. Crawley, and John MacMurray—agree that the binding force is the sense of sacredness, or as some would prefer to say, of holiness. Principal John Oman has declared: "If we are to have one mark of religion, it could only be the sacred . . . valuation. . . . Everything that is sacred is in the sphere of religion, and everything in the sphere of religion is sacred."[8] The attitude of sacredness is a complex sentiment, something of a blend of wonder, awe, gratitude, and tender admiration. It is as distinctive as the sense of beauty, marking off the field of the religious as definitely as beauty marks off the field of the esthetic. To substitute mere intellectual conviction or moral rectitude is to rob religion of its psychological core.

Robert Lowie, in his book *Primitive Religion*, maintains that the feeling of sacredness is evoked primarily by abnormal stimuli—the mysterious, weird, extraordinary, or supernatural. But even the most common objects can be sensed as wonderful and strange. What could be more mysterious than the universe of Hume, in which one incomprehensible event follows with incomprehensible regularity after another incomprehensible event! But perhaps one must be something of a mystic or poet to *feel*, as Walt Whitman did, the sacred and unutterable mystery of the most common things, such as leaves of grass.

While admitting Lowie's contention that the sense of astonishment is at the heart of religion, I believe that more is involved in religious experience than blank wonder and awe. There is also the feeling that what is deep and mysterious within oneself is akin to what is deep and mysterious in the object. "What is that," St. Augustine asks, "which gleams through me and smites my heart without wounding it? I am both a-shudder and a-glow. A-shudder, in so far as I am unlike it, a-glow in so far as I am like it."[9] The unlikeness lends to religious experience its note of dread, but the likeness lends the note of tender exaltation. This sense of kinship seems to me not the whole of religion but an essential part of it. Toward sacred objects we generally feel a fundamental bond of community.

The need for communion and self-transcendence springs largely from man's solitariness. In the little span between birth and death, each of us experiences the poignant fact of being confined within his own skin and limited by his individual ego. Each of us is curbed and hemmed in by the massive force of human culture, its laws, its taboos, its conventions. Each tends to feel small and insignificant and powerless before the vast indifference and immensity of nature. Especially in moments of crisis, every man, like a shipwrecked Robinson Crusoe, wants to escape from the little island of his own selfhood. Religion is the return from solitariness to community. It is man's endeavor, by an inward personal adjustment, to make himself at home in the world. By cultivating the religious sense of community, he escapes from his loneliness and self-alienation.

The form of this self-transcendence is not necessarily attachment to a *human* community. In the religion of the Crow Indians, for example, the essential quest is to attain, in solitary vigils, communion with a supernatural guardian spirit. Likewise the higher religions have their recluses, each seeking a lonely understanding with his God. Even in the case of the mystic, however, the value of religious withdrawal is never to be found in *mere* isolation, but in the spiritual union of the self with the non-self: "the flight of the alone to the alone." To this extent all religion is social.

Some writers have minimized the social and emphasized the individualistic side of religion. "Religion is what an individual does with his own solitariness," declared Whitehead, denying "that religion is primarily a social fact."[10] William James characterized religion as "the feelings, acts, and experiences of individual men in their solitude."[11] But from the earliest times solitariness has been felt as a deprivation: "Single is each man born into the world;" laments an ancient text, "single he dies; and his body lies like a fallen tree upon the earth."[12] Every man needs to escape from his singleness and isolation and from the self-centeredness that is its consequence. The strength of Buddhism is to be found in its clear and profound expression of these facts. Gautama summed up his teaching in Four Noble Truths. The First Truth is that life is full of suffering and that this suffering is caused by the conditions of individuality ("the aggregates of grasping"). The very conditions that are necessary to make an individual, his solitariness and self-centeredness, are also the conditions that give rise to sorrow. The Second Noble Truth is that suffering is caused by craving, and this, in turn, is based upon error. Every person, being self-centered, tries to bend and appropriate things for his selfish purposes. But self-centeredness is an intellectual error: no human being is in truth the center of the universe, and the very notion of the self, as enclosed and enduring, is illusory. There is really no self, in this sense, to be selfish about. One's life is just an unbroken stream of successive states that are causally connected, and behind this stream there is no permanent ego, no self-contained entity independent of change and independent of one's fellows. Self-centeredness is also a moral error: the inordinate bias of the individual setting himself up as if he were the whole, as if *he* had the right to make all other creatures and things minister to *his* purposes. This is the primal sin and the root moral error of life. The Third Noble Truth is the value of emancipation from selfhood. Selfishness *can* and *should* be abandoned. The consequence of this emancipation is a blessed state called "Nirvana." Negatively, it is the extinction of selfish craving, and positively, it is a deep and abiding peace. The Fourth Noble Truth is the way to remove suffering and achieve Nirvana. The Buddha propounded a comprehensive system of intellectual and moral cultivation, summarized in the Eightfold Path: right understanding, right aspiration, right speech, right conduct, right livelihood, right effort, right thought, and right concentration. In no other religion is there so clear a statement of the root problem of human existence and the need to cope with it. Here is a profounder reading of the riddle of human existence than any doctrine of "the ego and its own."

To reject egoism is not to deny the value of solitude. Withdrawal, such as that of Mohammed into the desert or Jesus into the Garden, is characteristic of deeply religious personalities. The most intense religious experience requires inward concentration and mental detachment. The need for such privacy as a counterweight to the raucous mechanization and crowd pressure of modern life has never been greater than at present. If withdrawal is not a mere perversion, however, it is followed by a return, with the recluse's contribution to society enriched by the clarification of intention and the concentration of power achieved in solitude. Purely individualistic religion cannot succeed in transcending selfishness, nor achieve the deepest self-realization. One realizes oneself by transcendence: "He that loses his life shall find it." But individuality and sociality are not exclusive and ought to enrich one another.

This is the very meaning of community—that both oneself and the other selves are enhanced by mutuality.

Religion, for the most part, is the consecration, generalization, and sublimation of the values of community. If we think of the small, intimate community as the microcosm, we can say that religion tends to interpret nature or supernature as the macrocosm. The microcosm is the community writ small, the macrocosm is the community writ large.

There have been many religious variants of this idea of community. The totemism of primitive religion, for example, springs from the deep communal feeling of the tribe. At this level, man is scarcely aware of his individuality; he conceives of himself as an indivisible part of the cycle of all natural and human forces. Even inorganic objects are conceived of as animate and as having intimate affiliations with the human community. Primitive tribesmen really believe what St. Francis of Assisi taught, that the birds and beasts and fishes are their "little brothers." The tribe, as they conceive it, includes animals as well as human beings. There are other types of primitive religion besides totemism but it is apparently characteristic of all of them to express, in some generalized form, the values of the primordial community.

The older hypothesis, favored by E. B. Tylor in *Primitive Culture* and James Frazer in *The Golden Bough,* interpreted primitive religion in terms of animism, the view that souls are attached to all sorts of things as indwelling spirits. But Lucien Lévy-Bruhl has maintained that there is a still more primitive mentality, which he calls "mystic participation" (using the word "mystic" to imply "belief in forces and influences and actions which, though imperceptible to sense, are nevertheless real").[13] At this stage, there is a nondifferentiation between subject and object; the subjective states of the primitive mind are projected into the object, and the object is introjected into the subject. An example of such participative communion is the widespread primitive custom called *couvade,* according to which the husband behaves, during the pregnancy and birth-labor of his wife, as if *he* were emotionally and physiologically affected in the same way as she. Such communion holds not only between man and wife but between the tribesman and other members of the tribe, or between human beings and the innumerable plants, animals, and natural objects surrounding them. For example, "the Bororos [a tribe of northern Brazil] give one rigidly to understand that they are araras [parakeets] at the present time, just as if a caterpillar declared itself to be a butterfly."[14] In a way that seems contradictory to us, primitive men think that they are themselves and at the same time, for example, tigers, or snakes, or crocodiles. They feel and behave like plants and animals, and plants and animals (it is thought) behave and feel like them. They do not clearly distinguish the animate and the inanimate, the organic and the inorganic, the visible and the invisible, the man and his shadow, the "I" and the "we." What Lévy-Bruhl calls a "mist of unity" envelops all of nature: an occult force or sacred *mana* binds subjects and objects together; human beings directly participate in the inner life of things. This sense of participation is so immediate, so overwhelming, that it is not so much conceived and thought as *lived*, in dance, rite, festival, and symbolic act. It may be, as Paul Radin has maintained in his *Primitive Religion*, that primitive groups are more diverse and capable of logical discrimination than Lévy-Bruhl has supposed. But there is too much corroborative evidence to dismiss the latter's ideas as merely fanciful.

In recognizing the communal nature of native thought, we need not agree with Emile Durkheim, who maintains that primitive religion is the worship of society—the sib, clan, or tribe—in the guise of totemic or other occult symbols. The concept of community is imaginatively projected far beyond the bounds of human society. Religion is frequently "the groping of a lonely-souled gregarious animal to find its herd or its herd leader in the great spaces behind the stars."[15]

The civilized human being, in comparison with primitive man, is more aware of himself as distinct and separate from the surrounding world, and religion assumes the form of man's deliberate attempt to make himself at home in the Universe. By cultivating the religious sense of community, he escapes from his loneliness and self-alienation.

The ancient Egyptian religion was one of the first civilized expressions of this hunger for community, and the main root out of which the Western tradition of human brotherhood has developed. Similar doctrines were current in ancient Babylon and Assyria. James Harvey Breasted has declared:

Our moral heritage . . . derives from a wider human past enormously older than the Hebrews, and it has come to us rather *through* the Hebrews than *from* them. The rise of man to social idealism took place long before the traditional theologians' "age of revelation" began. It was the result of the social experience of *man himself* and was not projected into the world from outside.[16]

We are thus the spiritual heirs, not of any one people such as the Greeks or the Hebrews, but of the early life of man as a whole. The Hellenic and Hebraic civilizations, of course, greatly extended, deepened, and refined this original heritage.

In religions more recent than the ancient Egyptian, there have been many variants of the idea of community: the Confucian doctrine of "human-heartedness" and universal kindness; the Taoist sense of mystic unity with nature; the Buddhist emancipation from selfhood; the Hindu vision of all-encompassing, all-penetrating Spirit; the Moslem idea of One God and One Humanity; the Hebraic devotion to a God of love and justice; and the Christian fellowship of all men in God.

The community-mindedness of all these religions is most clear if we consider their moral implications. Precepts such as we associate with Christianity or Judaism occur in all the great scriptures. For example, among the aphorisms of Confucius we find: "Do not do unto others what you do not want others to do unto you." In the *Tao Te King* of Lao-Tse we read, "Return love for great hatred." In an ancient Buddhist gospel we discover, "Cleanse your heart of malice and cherish no hatred, not even against your enemies, but embrace all living things with kindness." In a Hindu sacred book we are told, "As one's life is dear to himself, so also are those of all beings." In a Mohammedan text we read, "No one of you is a believer until he loves for his brother what he loves for himself."[17] The unity of outlook indicated by these typical passages is an immensely impressive fact—a refutation of the superficial relativism that emphasizes exclusively the differences among the peoples of the earth.

In thus generalizing the moral values of community, religion may appear to make an exaggerated or even nonsensical claim. It may appear to be a meaningless paradox to say that even a stranger should be treated as a friend. Yet this paradox is at the very heart of the moral code of the higher religions. Of course, we cannot love strangers with the same personal intimacy that we feel towards friends. Love, nevertheless, *can* be projected beyond the intimate circle; it can become a very wide encompassing bond; it can become, in a sense, the basis of one's life and the motivation of one's being. Love of this sort is what Buddha had in mind when he said: "All the means that can be used as helps toward doing right avail not the sixteenth part of the emancipation of the heart through love."[18]

There must be some common doctrine that will explain the moral agreement among the world's religions. Aldous Huxley believes that this is to be found in a "perennial philosophy" expressed again and again—by Hindus, Buddhists, Hebrews, Taoists, Christians, Mohammedans, and others. The core of this philosophy is mysticism. Let us consider what it involves.

4. MYSTICISM—NEGATIVE AND POSITIVE

The mystic maintains that it is possible to know the sacred Reality, be it God or Brahman or Tao, not merely discursively but directly and intuitively. "He enjoys," said John of the Cross, "a certain contact of the soul with Divinity, and it is God Himself who is then felt and tasted."[19]

Each mystic has tended to interpret his experience in the light of his cultural and religious background. The more monistic type of interpretation conceives the whole of existence as an ineffable spiritual unity and the deeper self as identical with the Absolute Reality. This creed is stated with great eloquence in the Hindu *Upanishads:*

The intelligent, whose body is spirit, whose form is light, whose thoughts are true, whose nature is like ether, omnipresent and invisible, from whom all works, all desires, all sweet odors and tastes proceed; he who embraces all this, who never speaks, and is never surprised, he is my self within the heart, smaller than a corn of rice, smaller than a corn of barley, smaller than a mustard seed, smaller than a canary seed or the kernel of a canary seed. He also is my self within the heart, greater than the earth, greater than the sky, greater than heaven, greater than all these worlds.[20]

This mystical vision—that all is one and one is all—is likewise expressed in the paradoxical words of Chuang Tse, the ancient Chinese Taoist: "The universe and I came into being together; and I, and everything therein, are One."[21]

Some mystics contend that the One is utterly indivisible and that consequently all discriminations made by the human intellect are false. William Wordsworth, in a manuscript fragment, described an early stage in his mental development in which he regarded all forms, images, and ideas as "the very littleness of life" and as "relapses from the one interior life that lives in all things." All our puny conceptual boundaries are man made and the true reality is a seamless unity:

> In which all beings live with god, themselves
> Are god, Existing in the mighty whole,
> As indistinguishable as the cloudless East
> At noon is from the cloudless west, when all
> The hemisphere is one cerulean blue.[22]

Wordsworth is characterizing a mystical state which he knew in his own experience. In the words of De Selincourt, this state is "the overwhelming consciousness of God," and "the sense that God in Nature is one with God in the soul, so that the soul seems to *be* God or *be* Nature."[23] So absolute is the unity that ideas and images of particular things are dismissed as illusory.

Such mysticism may be called "negative" because its object appears undifferentiated. Carried to its limits, it produces the contention of Oriental pantheism that "the distinction of objects known, knowers, acts of knowledge, etc. . . . is fictiously created by Nescience."[24] Another kind of negativism occurs in the dualistic mysticism that denies all likeness between nature and God and turns away from natural objects to seek identification with a completely transcendent Deity. Its votaries teach the unreality of material things; they often regard the flesh and spirit as at war; they view the ordinary world as a prison or scene of exile; and they reject science as a basis of belief.

There is also a *positive* mysticism, which can be illustrated by a later stage in Wordsworth's mental development. In his famous *Lines* composed near Tintern Abbey, he spoke of an intense and joyous mood in which "we . . . become a living soul" and "see into the life of things." In this passage describing a trance-like state, the unitary "life" does not negate "things" in the plural. There is no turning away from the copious variety of nature. Because of the mystic vision, nature is more precious rather than less. Consequently, Wordsworth is

> A lover of the meadows and the woods,
> And mountains, and of all that we behold
> From this green earth. . . .

There have been many positive mystics, such as Lao-Tse, Jesus, Plotinus, and William Blake. My inclusion of Jesus may call for explanation. So far as

I can judge from the tangled records, he was expressing the fundamental claim of the mystic—the spiritual union of the self with the non-self. He was not literally claiming divinity (this claim, I think, was a misinterpretation among his later followers). There are a number of passages, just as authentic as any in the New Testament, in which he disavows perfection, infallibility, or supernatural origin. "Why callest thou me good?" he asked. "None is good save God only" (*Mark* 10:17). He recognized that he was not able to heal people who did not believe in him (*Mark* 6:5), and his friends on at least one occasion held him to be beside himself (*Mark* 3:21). He admitted that he could not tell when the Messianic realm would be established, insisting that "of that day and of that hour knoweth no one, not even the angels in heaven neither the Son but the Father" (*Mark* 13:32). On the cross, he cried the ancient words of the twenty-second Psalm, "My God, my God, why hast Thou forsaken me?" (*Mark* 15:34 and *Matthew* 27:46), thus voicing a profoundly human sorrow and dismay. When he called himself the Son of God, he was not boasting a unique status, for he taught all men to pray, "*Our* Father who art in Heaven." Rather, he was expressing the old Jewish idea that every man is a child of God. He felt a peculiar identification with the Father, and in that sense he may have regarded himself as unique. His followers were imbued with the Messianic expectation and he apparently regarded himself as chosen to fulfill it.[25] But evidently the main source of his inspiration was inward—the mystic's sense of union with the ultimate spiritual power. He was a mystic of the positive type, mindful that Solomon in all his glory was not arrayed like the lilies of the field and moved by a tender compassion for the stranger, the outcast, the prodigal son, and even the sparrow in the field. When he spoke of the brotherhood of man under the fatherhood of God, he was celebrating not only a God of love but the radical dignity of man. The Kingdom of God, he taught, is not a remote heavenly state. It is within each one of us.

In *The Two Sources of Morality and Religion*, Henri Bergson considers the relatively negative mysticism of India—Brahmanism, Buddhism, and Jainism—as but a halfway stage to the complete and positive mysticism of the great Christian mystics—"a St. Paul, a St. Teresa, a St. Catherine of Sienna, a St. Francis, a Joan of Arc, and how many others besides!"[26] The mysticism of India was too passive and pessimistic; it had too little faith in action; it lacked warmth and glow. The mystic's will was not aroused and committed to the service of his mystical insight. The struggle against drought and famine and blistering heat, against tuberculosis, cholera, dysentery, and diabetes, against a spreading and deepening human poverty, was too bitter and endlessly protracted. Hence the ancient Indian mystics sought escape from "the wheel of birth." The separate self, with all its suffering, must be reabsorbed in the mystic Whole. In preparation for this demolition of the self, the saint must practice renunciation, the quenching of all worldly desires. Very different, Bergson believes, was the burning, active, joyous mysticism of Christ and his followers. Its great impetus was love—a love that had its source in mystic experience and was unchecked by the gloom of Oriental pessimism. It over-leaped the walls of the city, the barriers of caste, class, race, and nationality, and embraced "all humanity in one simple indivisible love." Its ethical function was to raise man to a new and higher level of existence, the life of the "open society," the city without walls. God was experienced as Will-to-Love, and this love knew no bounds. Bergson suggested that the Christian mystics intuited a creative surge at the very heart of life—the *élan vital* interpreted as divine love—and that this intuition transformed them to the very roots of their being. Organized Christianity was merely "the crystallization, brought about by a . . . process of cooling, of what mysticism had poured, while hot, into the soul of man."[27]

But positive mysticism is not necessarily Christian; it can assume quite varied forms. There are at least elements of such mysticism in neo-Platonism, Taoism, Mahayana Buddhism, and the religion of such modern Hindus as Ramakrishna, Vivekananda, Radhakrishnan, and Gandhi. If we think of the less orthodox figures in the Occident, Walt Whitman and D. H. Lawrence spring to mind.

The example of Lawrence seems to me especially interesting. In the last phase of his thought, he called himself "godless" and forswore Christianity and every organized faith, but he expressed as intensely as any other mystic the impulse to unite the me with the non-me, the Self with the Other. With death fast approaching, he wrote a poem to abounding life:

> For man, as for flower and beast and bird, the supreme triumph is to be most vividly, most perfectly alive. Whatever the unborn and the dead may know, they cannot know the beauty, the marvel of being alive in the flesh. The dead may look after the afterwards. But the magnificent here and now of life in the flesh is ours, and ours alone, and ours only for a time. We ought to dance with rapture that we should be alive and in the flesh, and part of the living, incarnate cosmos. I am part of the sun as my eye is part of me. That I am part of the earth my feet know perfectly, and my blood is part of the sea. My soul knows that I am part of the human race, my soul is an organic part of the human soul. . . . I am part of the great whole, and I can never escape. But I *can* deny my connections, break them, and become a fragment. Then I am wretched.[28]

Here is the authentic voice of positive mysticism, insisting on the holiness of the flesh and the joy of earthy connections.

Whereas negative mysticism sacrifices community to other-worldliness or featureless unity, positive mysticism retains the love of individualities which is the distinguishing mark of community. It realizes that the unity of love is higher than the unity of inclusion. Love enjoys the difference between "you" and "me" and hence is the natural bond of community. A positive mystic such as Blake spontaneously employed the language of the intimate community:

> I am not a God afar off, I am a brother and friend;
> Within your bosoms I reside, and you reside in me.[29]

The unity is very close, but it is a unity of distinguishable members, each retaining its peculiar identity:

> He who would see the Divinity must see him in his Children . . .
> . . . he who wishes to see a Vision, a perfect Whole,
> Must see it in its Minute Particulars.[30]

Likewise in the case of another positive mystic, Walt Whitman, the strong feeling of oneness is combined with an equally insistent "thought of identity —yours for you, whoever you are, as mine for me."[31] The *each* is not submerged in the *all*.

It may be that the difference between positive and negative mysticism is not as radical as it appears. In "negativistic" Hindu mysticism, for example, the idea of Brahman as an absolute unity is connected with the practice of "Ahimsa"—noninjury, nonkilling, reverence for life based upon the concept of the oneness and sacredness of all living things. Perhaps the appearance of a sharp contrast between positive and negative mysticism is largely the result of the ineffable character of the mystical vision. Some mystics speak in negative terms because they feel that all positive characterizations are inadequate. Perhaps neither the positive nor negative terms should be taken literally because the "truth" of mysticism cannot be put into words.

The mystics disagree most sharply when they try to give a metaphysical interpretation of their experiences. Then the doctrinal differences among Christians, Buddhists, Hindus, Mohammedans, and other denominations become explicit. Each mystic tends to interpret his mystical experience in the light of his cultural and religious background. This is natural enough, but it should put us on guard against identifying the "truth" of mysticism with any particular creed. As William James, who studied mysticism in detail, remarked:

> The mystical feeling of enlargement, union, and emancipation has no specific intellectual content whatever of its own. It is capable of forming matrimonial alliances with material furnished by the most diverse philosophies and theologies, provided only they can find a place in their framework for its peculiar emotional mood. We have no right, therefore, to invoke its prestige as distinctively in favor of any special belief, such as that in absolute idealism, or in the absolute monistic identity, or in the absolute goodness, of the world.[32]

Mysticism cannot be used as a defense of those beliefs that vary from mystic to mystic, and hence cannot be used as a support for any particular religion.

James nevertheless goes on to suggest an interesting hypothesis: that the conscious person is not only continuous with a wider subconscious self but that this wider self is continuous with a mystic unseen world. Thus the deep subconscious abyss of the human psyche is a well connecting the conscious self with spiritual reality. The religious mind, like that of the artist, draws upon this deep well; but in mystical experiences, it draws upon an even wider and deeper well, a kind of cosmic pool of spirituality. This is a highly speculative hypothesis, and I do not know how to prove or disprove it.

The mystical experience, if freed from unwarranted beliefs, can be of immense value. It has been the source of very intense joy and very profound love. It indicates that ordinary consciousness is only one of a number of possible modes and that the whole tone of living can be lifted up and radically transformed. We have witnessed the most amazing transmutations of matter and energy; there is no reason to think there cannot be equally radical transformations in the mental sphere. As the physiological and psychological factors in mysticism become much better understood, the deep spiritual satisfaction of mystical experience may become widely available to people all over the world.

It is a mistake to think of mysticism as altogether rare and esoteric. Perhaps all men, on occasion, are touched by mystical feeling. The sense of community, I believe, is mystical in essence, although in most men this sense exists in low degree. But ways may be found to tap the deep sources of mystical joy and thus greatly to reinforce the sense of community.

5. HUMANISM VERSUS THEISM

The idea of community may attach to a variety of creeds. Among these doctrines there is no more fundamental contrast than between theism and humanism.

Ludwig Feuerbach (1804–1872) was perhaps the first Western philosopher to formulate the religious idea of community in explicitly humanistic terms. His great insight is summed up in the words, "The meeting place of I and Thou is God."[33] This saying can be interpreted either humanistically or theistically. The humanist interpretation, advanced by Feuerbach himself, is that God is a hypostatization or unconscious symbol of the human community. The theistic interpretation, later formulated by Martin Buber (1878–   ), is that the fulfillment of community requires allegiance to God. Let us consider each of these alternatives.

Feuerbach began his intellectual career as a Hegelian, but he soon abandoned absolute idealism and reinterpreted Hegel's concepts in a naturalistic way. True dialectic, he insisted, is not the conflict and synthesis of abstract ideas, nor the monologue of a solitary thinker with himself: "it is a dialogue between I and Thou." The starting point for a realistic philosophy is the flesh-and-blood human being, not as an isolated individual but as a social person. "The being of a man," Feuerbach declared, "exists only in community, in the unity of man with man—a unity that rests solely on the distinction between I and Thou."[34] Truth and value are to be found in the person-to-person relation:

The other is my *thou*—the relation being reciprocal—my *alter ego*, man objective to me, the revelation of my own nature, the eye seeing itself. In another I first have the consciousness of humanity; through him I first learn, I first feel, that I am a man: in my love for him it is first clear to me that he belongs to me and I to him, that we two cannot be without each other, that only community constitutes humanity. . . . My fellow-man is my objective conscience; he makes my failings a reproach to me; . . . he is my personified feeling of shame. The consciousness of the moral law, of right, of propriety, of truth itself, is indissolubly united with my consciousness of another than myself. That is true in which another agrees with me—agreement is the first criterion of truth. . . . I cannot so abstract myself from myself as to judge myself with perfect freedom and disinterestedness; but another has an impartial judgment; through him I correct, complete, extend my own judgment, my own knowledge.[35]

These truths, Feuerbach maintains, have been obscured by religious mystification. Human beings try to make up for the deficiencies in their lives by imagining a supernatural environment. The powers and capacities they attribute to the gods are, in fact, their own powers and capacities but magnified and ennobled by the religious imagination.

Thou believest in love as a divine attribute because thou thyself lovest; thou believest that God is a wise, benevolent being because thou knowest nothing better in thyself than benevolence and wisdom. . . .[36]

Thus religious ideas embody man's aspirations, his ideas of what he wills or wishes to be, expressed in vivid, emotional imagery. Since statements about the supernatural world are thus disguised statements about human needs and ideals, they reveal genuine insights but in an illusory way. Hence there is both a true and a false side to religion:

Religion is the relation of man to his own nature,—therein lies its truth and its power of moral amelioration;—but to his nature not recognized as his own, but regarded as another nature, separate, nay, contradistinguished from his own; herein lies its untruth, its limitation, its contradiction to reason and morality.[37]

Feuerbach thus denied the "fantastic" projections of the religious imagination in order to affirm the real values of human life.

Religion is the first form of self-consciousness. Religions are sacred because they are the traditions of the primitive self-consciousness. But that which in religion holds the first place—namely, God—is . . . according to truth, the second, for it is only the nature of man regarded objectively; and that which to religion is the second—namely, man—must therefore be constituted and declared the first. Love to man must be no derivative love; it must be original. If human nature is the highest nature to man, then practically also the highest and first law must be the love of man to man.[38]

We have been recreant to natural love because we have been chasing a supernatural rainbow. Love as a *human* bond must now come into its own. This transition from theism to humanism, Feuerbach declared, is destined to be the turning point of world history.

In making community the basis and love the motivating force of our lives, we shall preserve the ideal essence of religion while discarding its obscurantism. "Love is not holy because it is a predicate of God, but it is a predicate of God because it is in itself divine."[39] It is holy in itself and for its own sake. Love, disentangled from superstition, is the only satisfactory answer to the problem of life. This is the conclusion that Feuerbach reaches.

Martin Buber has been greatly influenced by these ideas. He has hailed Feuerbach's doctrine of community as "the Copernican revolution of modern thought," and has declared: "I myself in my youth was given a decisive impetus by Feuerbach."[40] But his thinking led him to theism rather than to humanism. Basic to his thought is the distinction between two types of relation. He states this distinction in enigmatic language:

> To man the world is twofold, in accordance with his twofold attitude. The attitude of man is twofold, in accordance with the twofold nature of the primary words which he speaks. The primary words are not isolated words, but combined words. The one primary word is the combination I-Thou. The other primary word is the combination I-It; wherein, without a change in the primary word, one of the words He and She can replace It. Hence the I of man is also twofold. For the I of the primary word I-Thou is a different I from that of the primary word I-It.[41]

Buber's meaning is this: Man adopts a twofold interpretation of his world, according to the "primary word" that he speaks. To speak the word is not to use one's vocal cords but to stand before existence and to comport oneself in a certain way. In the I-It relation, I regard the object, even if it be a He or a She, as if it were a mere thing. I stand apart from it in order coldly to scrutinize and exploit it: to observe, measure, categorize, and manipulate it—to bend it to my advantage. In this relation there is no reciprocity: the relation is that of master to instrument. If I treat someone as an It, I do not acknowledge his right to treat me as an It in return. In the I-Thou relation, on the other hand, one's essential being is in direct and sympathetic contact with another essential being. The Thou is cherished for what he is in his "singleness"—not as an object but as a presence, not as a type but as an individual, not as a means but as an end. The I-Thou relation is reciprocal: I-Thou implies Thou-I. I not only give but receive; I not only speak but listen; I not only respond but invite response. "My Thou affects me, as I affect it."[42] The I is constituted and remade in this act of meeting: "Through the Thou a man becomes I."[43]

The world of the I-Thou and the world of the I-It are not sharply separated. "Every Thou in our world must become an It."[44] There is nothing wrong with such impersonal relations so long as they remain subordinate to the personal. But "in our age the I-It relation, gigantically swollen, has usurped, practically uncontested, the mastery and the rule. The I of this relation, an I that . . . is unable to say Thou, unable to meet a being essentially, is the lord of the hour."[45]

There can be no recovery from this dread disease without a quickening of love—the love of man for man and the love of man for God. These two kinds of love, Buber believes, are interdependent. "I-Thou finds its highest intensity and transfiguration in religious reality, in which unlimited Being becomes, as absolute person, my partner."[46] Human beings relate themselves most deeply to each other by thus relating themselves to an eternal Thou. But "real relationship with God cannot be achieved on earth if real relationship to the world and mankind are lacking."[47] The meeting with God is direct and mutual; it is a totality act of personality; it requires that we meet human beings and the world in the same total way. "Meet the world with the fullness of your being, and you shall meet God. . . . If you wish to believe, love!"[48]

The dialogue with the Eternal Being is the culmination of all I-Thou relations. It occurs when our ordinary relational capacities have been cultivated and brought to their highest pitch. We then find that God speaks to us through the active, bestowing side of all life and things—not just in the rarity of ecstatic moments, but in the hallowing of everyday perception. The relation to God thus gathers up and includes all others. "For there is no rung of being on which we cannot find the holiness of God everywhere and at all times."[49]

Thus both Feuerbach, the humanist, and Buber, the theist, extol love and develop a theory of community. The contrast between humanism and theism presents one of the great issues in the religious life of mankind, and perhaps this issue will never be resolved. But both sides can agree that community should be the essential basis of human existence, and that love becomes sacred when it is raised to its highest power and consecrated by the deepest feeling.

6. RELIGION'S COMING OF AGE

We can distinguish between the ideal essence of religion and its transient embodiments. The fantasies about the gods, about heaven and hell and grace, about Yahweh and Gilgamesh and Valhalla, are the changing poetic expression of the essential claim of religion: that community is sacred. If we look at nothing but the fantasies, the history of creeds is disillusioning. Religion ordinarily asserts that her imaginings have objective existence, that the God, be it Isis or Apollo or Angra Mainyu, abides in the real world. Time and again men learn that this claim does not correspond with fact, and the human intellect eventually makes a clean sweep of all such fictitious objectivities. But religious fantasy is the bridge by which human beings, generation after generation, pass to a realization of the sacredness of community. Though the gods eventually dissolve like the figments of a dream, the evaluations which they symbolize do not perish.

Yet I have confessed an intense dislike for most of what passes for religion. Searching backward through time for a power and an authority that no longer fit the creative possibilities of the present, religion is more often atavistic than it is progressive. Some would say that it has always been of this questionable character. From Xenophanes to Bertrand Russell, critics have exposed the fanaticism and superstition that have poisoned the wellsprings of religious thought. When human beings feel lonely and impotent and wretched, they may express their hatreds and frustrations in malign myths, such as the doctrine that the damned are everlastingly tortured by reason of man's sin and God's pleasure. Even when religion is not thus perverted, its effect may be like that of an anodyne. Maintaining that the universe is the handiwork of a perfect and omnipotent God, it contends that evil is a good in disguise or a discord resolved into harmony.

Sincere religious idealists, who do not thus minimize evil, may none the less be the victims of a dangerous illusion. This is the notion that we should "save" men by spiritual conversion alone. To affirm spiritual *ends* and to neglect material *means*, to seek to change men's hearts without changing their circumstances, to proclaim "justice and peace" but to disregard the environmental causes of injustice and war, is the main fallacy of traditional religious morality. It will not do to plead that goodness is a state of mind and that its physical embodiment is secondary and incidental. This is a profound error of principle, a false religious idealism. It neglects the constant interplay of mind and nature, spirit and matter, thought and things. It distracts men's attention from the brute material conditions which, in the absence of understanding and control, are left to determine human destiny.

A lack of realism is also to be found in the shaky metaphysical commitments that so frequently characterize religious thought. "Our religion," as Matthew Arnold said, "has materialized itself in the fact, in the supposed fact, it has attached itself to the fact, and now the fact is failing it."[50] Reason has had to wage a long, relentless war against religious superstition.

These defects in the traditional religions can be diminished and perhaps largely eliminated. They betray religion rather than express its innermost essence, which is the sense of sacredness based upon the impulse of self-transcendence and communion. Because all the great denominations share this sentiment, there is, in a sense, but one religion for humanity; the many faiths and creeds are all streams of this one great river. Religions such as Hinduism and Taoism and Christianity should no more be regarded as mutually exclusive than the great philosophies should be so regarded. Just as I recognize the greatness of both Plato and Kant, so I should recognize the greatness of both Buddha and Christ. If what is true in all of the major religions can be admitted, and if superstition can be minimized, there will emerge a sense of the spiritual oneness of all mankind—a world faith to guarantee a world peace.

In any such meeting of religions, we should not ask that all parties unite on some single, eclectic, washed-out formula that covers anything and everything. Without its particularistic elements, a religion is too disembodied and colorless to excite vivid conviction. The concrete image, as in the story of Job or the personality of Buddha, is more unforgettable than the mere abstract precept. Symbolic imagery has always been the content and poetry the language of religious thought. No abstract distillate is a satisfactory or possible substitute. In the very nature of religion the particular must be kept together with the universal, but the image or symbol need not be interpreted with the superstitious literalism of the fundamentalist. When we retain the old language, when we speak, for example, of "the brotherhood of man under the fatherhood of God," we should construe the ancient symbols in terms consistent with modern knowledge.

The concept of brotherhood should be subjected to empirical scrutiny and confirmation. It is far too important an idea to be used without knowledge that it is sound. Because it is a normative rather than a descriptive idea, the question is not whether human beings *do* behave as though they belong to a fellowship but whether they *ought* so to behave. We already have a great deal of evidence that life is happier and healthier and more profoundly satisfying when men treat each other as friends than when they treat each other as enemies. If this fact can be increasingly verified, the psychological and social sciences will lend more and more support to the idea of human brotherhood.

Likewise, if we continue to employ the concept of God, we should interpret it in the light of modern insights. Some people would reject the concept because it is ambiguous and emotionally charged. But, in one sense, the fact that it is heavily laden with meanings and emotions makes it the more indispensable: it has been a main focus of the spiritual life for thousands of years. Many thinkers would prefer to reinterpret rather than reject it.

The facts that are relevant to its reinterpretation can be gleaned from recent science and philosophy. As we now envisage nature, it exhibits levels of increasing complexity and wider integration: electrons, atoms, molecules, simple cells, plants, animals, personalities, and human communities form a mounting series. The higher levels tend to succeed the lower in time: there has been a progression from the amoeba to Neanderthal man, and from the very primitive level of human life to the greatest heroes, artists, thinkers, and saints. The higher we mount in the evolutionary scale, the more richly differentiated and articulated becomes the structure of reality. In the vast upward thrust of life, mutuality is a most important factor; without cooperation, without mutual aid, it is often not possible to live and advance. Psychiatrists have maintained that love is the key to life's riddle, and that when love is frustrated, the personality becomes disordered, morbid, and hostile.

There is bound to be disagreement and there should be debate as to the meaning of these facts. They do not mean that the universe *as a whole* is an organism, or a purposive mind, or is governed by a person, or forms a spiritual community, An idealistic interpretation of *all* reality may ultimately turn out to be correct, but upon the basis of our present knowledge, it would be rash to assert it. But even if the material environment is not purposive, it has proved itself *fit* to produce purposive beings and the higher levels of value. Even if nature is not alive, it enables the development of fullness of life. Even if the universe is not a community, the ideal of fellowship is deeply based upon the nature of things.

If by the concept of God we wish to designate facts of this order, there is a firm empirical basis for its employment. We can mean by God the sweep and force of the cosmos as it pushes on toward higher forms of existence. We can mean the spirit of community emerging out of the mysterious depths of nature and working as a creative nisus in us all. We can believe, in a sense, that God is personal, that His highest manifestation is the infinite worth of personality. There may be still higher forms of spirituality in the vastnesses of space-time, but God has most clearly disclosed Himself as love in the human heart.

There is nothing that requires us to conceive Him exclusively in terms of what is and has been. We can think of Him as "the unity of all ideal ends arousing us to desire and action."[51] Insofar as the ideal has already been actualized, God is a past and present fact, but insofar as He is a hope and an aspiration, His reality lies in the future. This is a conception that demands Promethean creativity and defiance. As André Gide has written:

> The world will be saved, if it can be, only by the *unsubmissive*. Without them it would be all up with our civilization, our culture, what we loved, and what gave to our presence on earth a secret justification. Those unsubmissive ones are the "salt of the earth" and responsible for God. For I am convinced that God is not yet and that we must achieve him. Could there be a nobler, more admirable role, and more worthy of our efforts?[52]

Although I have tried to suggest some of the possibilities in the religion of the future, I can see only a little way in advance, for we do not know how the universe will appear to a scientist or philosopher several centuries from now. It may be that all our present insights are but the pale shadow of the reality yet to be revealed. It may be that existence is infinitely richer and finer than we have guessed, and that the future will be far more majestic than the past. It may be that all that is and has been is but the beginning of the beginning. We move through a little circle of light amid a deep night of mystery, and though modern science has widened the circle, it has increased rather than diminished our wonder and awe. Hope depends upon such realization of the "poetry of life," its depths, its mystery, its wonderful promise.

As human knowledge unfolds, the idea of community will find new unprecedented modes of expression; but it will have a profounder hold upon the human heart if men clearly realize that it is a fresh variation of man's ancient and fundamental religious intuition. The essential problem is to unite genuine feeling and tradition with modern forms of interpretation—to preserve the force of archaic religion while eliminating its obscurantism, to link new idioms and insights with the ancient poetic symbols of the race. Thus we can renew human faith without committing intellectual hara-kiri. We can achieve self-transcendence and the values of community while making a creative and humane use of the miraculous powers of science and technology.

NOTES

1. Alfred North Whitehead, *Religion in the Making*. New York: The Macmillan Company, 1926, p. 18.
2. John MacMurray, *Religious Experience*. New Haven: Yale University Press, 1936, p. 70.
3. Arnold J. Toynbee, *A Study of History* (Abridgment of Volumes VII–X), London and New York: Oxford University Press, 1957, p. 144. The detailed account is to be found in Volume VIII of the unabridged version.
4. *Ibid.*, p. 145.
5. Very little is known about Lao-Tse. According to tradition, he was a contemporary of Confucius, and the *Tao-Te King*, basic scripture of Taoism, is doubtfully attributed to him. It appears to be a composite work, containing old fragments embedded in later contexts.
6. Arthur Waley, *The Way and Its Power*. London: George Allen & Unwin, Ltd., 1942, p. 69.
7. *The Great Learning*, I. Quoted by Wing-Tsit Chan, "Within the Four Seas All Are Brothers," in Robert M. MacIver (editor), *Great Expressions of Human Rights*. New York: Harper & Row, Publishers, Inc., 1950, pp. 23–24.
8. John Oman, *The Natural and the Supernatural*. London: Macmillan & Co., Ltd., 1931, p. 69.
9. St. Augustine, *Confessions*, Book XI, 9. Quoted by Rudolf Otto, *The Idea of the Holy*. London and New York: Oxford University Press, 1950, p. 28.
10. Alfred North Whitehead, *Religion in the Making*, op. cit., pp. 16–17.
11. William James, *The Varieties of Religious Experience*. New York: David McKay Company, Inc., 1902, p. 31.
12. Quoted by Arthur Koestler, *Insight and Outlook*. New York: The Macmillan Company, 1949, p. 235. From the legend of Manu, the first man in Sanskrit mythology.

13. Lucien Lévy-Bruhl, *How Natives Think*. New York: Alfred A. Knopf, Inc., 1926, p. 38.
14. *Ibid.*, p. 77.
15. Gilbert Murray, *The Stoic Philosophy*. London: George Allen & Unwin, Ltd., 1921, p. 42.
16. James Harvey Breasted, *The Dawn of Conscience*. New York: Charles Scribner's Sons, 1934, p. xv.
17. The quotations in this paragraph, in the order in which they occur, are from Lin Yutang, *The Wisdom of Confucius*, New York: Modern Library, Inc., 1938, p. 186; Robert O. Ballou, *The Bible of the World*, New York: The Viking Press, Inc., 1939, p. 504; Paul Carus, *The Gospel of Buddha According to Old Records*, Chicago: The Open Court Publishing Company, 1904, p. 106; Ballou, *The Bible of the World*, op. cit., p. 156; *ibid.*, p. 1337.
18. T. W. Rhys David, "Buddhism," *Encyclopaedia Brittanica*, Eleventh Edition, 1910, p. 744.
19. Quoted by Evelyn Underhill, *Mysticism*. New York: E. P. Dutton & Co., Inc., 1942, p. 73.
20. Robert O. Ballou, *The Bible of the World*, op. cit., p. 60
21. *Ibid.*, p. 508.
22. William Wordsworth, *The Prelude* (edited by Ernest De Selincourt). London and New York: Oxford University Press, 1926, pp. 512–513.
23. *Ibid.*, p. 513.
24. Sankara Acharya (*circa* 789–820 A.D.) in F. Max Müller (editor), *Sacred Books of the East*. London and New York: Oxford University Press, 1890, Vol. XXXIV, pp. 14–15.
25. *Cf.* Albert Schweitzer, *The Quest of the Historical Jesus*. New York: The Macmillan Company, 1948; and A. Powell Davies, *The Meaning of the Dead Sea Scrolls*. New York: New American Library, Inc., 1956.
26. Henri Bergson, *The Two Sources of*

Morality and Religion. New York: Holt, Rinehart and Winston, Inc., 1935, p. 216.

27. *Ibid.*, p. 227.

28. D. H. Lawrence, *Apocalypse*. New York: The Viking Press, Inc., 1932, pp. 199–200.

29. William Blake, *Jerusalem*, in *Poetry and Prose of William Blake*. New York: Random House, Inc., 1927, p. 552.

30. *Ibid.*, p. 737.

31. Walt Whitman, *Democratic Vistas*, in *Leaves of Grass and Selected Prose*. New York: Modern Library, Inc., 1950, p. 487. This thought runs all through Whitman's poetry.

32. William James, *The Varieties of Religious Experience, op. cit.*, pp. 425–426.

33. Ludwig Feuerbach, *Grundsätze der Philosophie der Zukunft*. Stuttgart: Fr. Fromanns Verlag, 1922. *Cf.* sections 33–34, 42, 61, 64–66.

34. *Ibid.*, Section 61.

35. Ludwig Feuerbach, *The Essence of Christianity*. New York: C. Blanchard, 1855, pp. 208–209.

36. *Ibid.*, p. 39.

37. *Ibid.*, p. 254.

38. *Ibid.*, p. 341.

39. *Ibid.*, p. 344.

40. Martin Buber, *Between Man and Man*. Boston: Beacon Press, 1955, p. 148.

41. Martin Buber, *I and Thou*. New York: Charles Scribner's Sons, 1937, p. 3.

42. *Ibid.*, p. 15.

43. *Ibid.*, p. 28.

44. *Ibid.*, p. 16.

45. Martin Buber, *Eclipse of God*. New York: Harper & Row, Publishers, Inc., p. 166.

46. *Ibid.*, p. 61.

47. Martin Buber, *At the Turning*. New York: Farrar, Straus, and Cudahy, Inc., 1952, p. 39.

48. *Ibid.*, p. 44.

49. Martin Buber, *Ten Rungs*. New York: Schocken Books, Inc., 1947.

50. Matthew Arnold, *Essays in Criticism: Second Series*. London: Macmillan & Co., Ltd., 1906, p. 1.

51. John Dewey, *A Common Faith*. New Haven: Yale University Press, 1934, p. 51.

52. André Gide, *The Journals of André Gide*. New York: Alfred A. Knopf, Inc., 1951, Vol. IV, p. 264.

Conclusion

Conclusion

"With everyone engaged everywhere in making things easier," Sören Kierkegaard once remarked, "someone was needed to make them difficult again."[1] Most theories of ethics make things too easy. Relativism emphasizes the differences among human beings and neglects the resemblances; absolutism emphasizes the resemblances and slights the differences. An extreme individualism exalts the individual at the expense of the group; an extreme collectivism exalts the group at the expense of the individual. Hedonism seeks the good in feeling; intellectualism, in reason; voluntarism, in desire. In stressing only one side of human nature, each oversimplifies.

The real subject of value is the person-in-society, and this social personality, as a dynamic focus of interests, is the whole man. Only an ethics that does justice to every essential side of human nature, as both individual and social, as mind and body, as thinking, feeling, and desiring, is complete and complex enough to be the basis of valid ideals. The norm of human well-being is nothing less than the cultivation and fulfillment of the deepest and widest interests of man. "I am well aware that every human being is more or less one-sided," declared Kierkegaard, "and I do not regard it as a fault. But it is a fault when a fashion selects a certain form of one-sidedness and magnifies it into a total norm."[2]

If we turn from the meaning of good to the concept of right, we are again confronted by theories that make things too easy. Cut-and-dried maxims, rigid and inflexible rules, or even the more sophisticated rules of "intuition" and "practical reason" are almost always oversimplified. Kant's principle, that the maxim of conduct should be such that it can be made a universal rule, is no more than a useful guide; we wind up in fanaticism if we take it as absolute. Every sharp moral dilemma is a unique problem to which no moral rule is precisely applicable.

Any theory of right is too narrow if it seeks the good of a race, class, sex, or nation exclusively. Only a universalist conception of right, intent upon avoiding bias and maximizing good, is ample enough to span the wide realm of obligation. If one calls this type of theory "utilitarian," it must be a carefully revised and qualified utilitarianism, borrowing insights from the deontological point of view and subtly combining the utility of acts and the utility of rules. This kind of theory may lack the simplicity of classical utilitarianism, but it is no more complex than life demands. Just as it takes all sorts of men to make a world, so it takes all sorts of ideas to produce a well-rounded theory of right.

I can find no satisfactory escape from these complexities in the stratagems of the linguistic philosophers. Ordinary language embodies the ordinary weaknesses of the ordinary man—the confusions and illogicalities that are altogether too ordinary. Even if the language is extraordinary (as that of the philosophers of "ordinary language" usually is), it is simply a tool for getting at the nub of facts, or else an evasion and distraction. Words, to be apt, must point to things.

Moral judgments therefore represent something more than mere subjective feelings and reactions. Valid ethical ideals are derived from a consideration of facts, even though they are not literally descriptive. Admitting that there has been no satisfactory resolution of the fact-value dichotomy, I veer toward the theory of natural law rather than an extreme subjectivism or antinaturalism.

The main basis upon which ethics should rest is the nature of man. To paraphrase what Enobarbus said about Cleopatra, neither age nor custom can stale the infinite variety of human nature.[3] An ethics that thinks in terms of static qualities belies the dynamic character of human life—the tendency of man to remake both himself and his environment. Hence there is no final and inflexible goal:

> There is no pulling open the buds to see what the blossom will be. Leaves must unroll, buds swell and open, and *then* the blossom. And even after that, when the flower dies and the leaves fall, *still* we shall not know. . . . We know the flower of today, but the flower of tomorrow is all beyond us.[4]

The goal of man is to come into the plentitude of his being and powers, but this goal must be construed historically and dynamically, as in the theory of Vico. To come into full spontaneous being is not easy.

Sensing some of the difficulties, Aristotle defined moral goodness as a disposition to choose a mean between excess and deficiency, a mean adjustable to individuals and particular circumstances. This doctrine, although it avoids a too-easy formalistic approach, is no golden rule that fits all cases. The mean is most applicable, as Aristotle himself remarked, when the extremes are respectively "too much" and "too little," in other words, when they are, as exaggerations, *disvalues* rather than values. If the extreme is a positive value rather than a disvalue, extremism may be precisely what is demanded by the situation.

The idea of dialectical synthesis is subtler than the concept of the mean. This is the notion, as old as Heraclitus, of the creative interpenetration of opposites. When such polar values as we have considered in this book—excellence and sharing, absolutism and relativism, universalism and localism, or mysticism and reason—are thus combined, each of the opposites is enriched by the other. The conflict between freedom and organization demands this sort of creative resolution: the union of strong individualities in a free and organized community. Similarly, the conflict between men and machines requires a new synthesis: not a rejection of either humanism or technology but their creative combination: life the master, the machine the tool. In dealing with such fundamental conflicts, we should try to synthesize conflicting values so as to enhance what is precious in both. But we should not seek to combine *false* values, as in Hitler's "synthesis" of pseudosocialism and depraved nationalism. Nor should we merely combine heterogeneous values in a shallow eclecticism, each value remaining essentially what it was before. In sketching the ideal of a free community, I have tried to avoid this kind of superficiality.

We must not exaggerate the value of dialectical synthesis. The processes of imitation, maturation, adaptation, and cooperation may go on with very little conflict and yet be extremely valuable. Even when two valid principles clash, there is more than one possibility in handling the conflict—for example, the choice of the better, or the sublimation of one or both, or the evasion of the issue to conserve energies for a higher cause. We must not give up the search for unity in our distraught world, but we are more likely to be successful if we realize how intricate are the conflicts and how various must be the resolutions. "Like a dome of many colored glass," life can not be reduced to any simple pattern.

This is the reason that dogmatism is out of place. Oliver Cromwell pled with his enemies before the battle of Dunbar: "I beseech ye in the bowels of Christ, think that ye may be mistaken." A great American jurist, Learned Hand, has quoted these words as the key to his over-all philosophy. He would like them to be written, he has said, "over the portals of every church, every courthouse and at every crossroads in the nation."[5]

Free and democratic methods are imperative if we are to avoid dogmatism. Surrounded by "yes men," the tyrant is in a difficult predicament. He lacks that vital play of criticism and accurate, if adverse, information upon which strength ultimately depends. A liberal democracy has this decisive advantage over tyranny: it can correct its own mistakes. In permitting debate and discussion, in allowing the free play of ideas, in stimulating the expression of popular grievances, in safeguarding the rights of minorities, it supplies the means to eliminate abuses and to respond flexibly to changing needs. Democracy permits basic reform without violence. Dictatorship does not.

It is impossible to sketch in detail the strategy for realizing a more free, democratic, and cooperative society. Great tact and adaptability are required, and unforseeable circumstances must be met as they arise. Freedom we must have, but not the kind of unlimited freedom which means that the strong are free to bully and exploit the weak. Planning we must also have, but not the unlimited planning that gives more and more power to a centralized bureaucracy. Tolerance we must cherish, but not the unlimited tolerance that leaves a democratic society wholly unprotected against the onslaughts of the intolerant. Democracy we must broaden and strengthen, but not the indiscriminate democracy that admits no checks upon the right of the majority to override the civil rights of individuals and minorities. No infallible recipe exists to strike the just right mean between too much and too little freedom, too much and too little planning, too much and too little tolerance, too much and too little democracy. We should recognize that absolutist "solutions," such as full state responsibility for all economic and social activity, are almost certain to prove disastrous.

Cursed by the anachronisms of war and class, this century has been an age of hyperbolic crises. In a crisis situation, there is nothing harder to tolerate than ambiguity, and frightened men tend to think in black-and-white terms. Then it becomes difficult to resist the extremists and hysterics that push us toward violence. In trying to expound Marxism fairly and objectively, I have sought to avoid this kind of blind fear and partisanship.

The choice between individualism and collectivism, I have argued, is a false dilemma: there is a better alternative—the concept of person-to-person relations among free individuals. The third of the great watchwords of the French Revolution, "Liberty, Equality, Fraternity," is the most important and the least regarded. When fully realized, fraternity includes the other two, for men united by mutuality respect one another's freedom and equal rights. Hence we must strengthen both the intimate association and the world-wide federation. What this means in terms of ideas and actions I have tried to explore.

The coming of a fraternal world may be prevented by the hellish fury of scientific warfare, but mankind has exhibited an extraordinary capacity for survival. "It is not probable that war will ever absolutely cease," wrote Winwood Reade in 1872, "until science discovers some destroying force so simple in its administration, so horrible in its effects, that all art, all gallantry, will be at an end, and battles will be massacres which the feeling of mankind will be unable to endure."[6] Such a peak of destructiveness has now been reached, and it is possible that the human will to survival will forever revolt against a thermonuclear holocaust. War may finally be banished to the limbo of dead institutions, like chattel slavery, feudalism, the divine right of kings, and unrestrained *laissez faire*.

In every country and in the interior of every mind, the struggle is continuing between the forces of chaos and the forces that may produce a far better civilization. Despite tragedy and confusion, "the hope of the great community" gives a majestic significance and purposiveness to our age. Those of us who love adventure and desire a better world are not sick before the prospect that looms ahead. If we keep bright the arrows of desire—of Eros and not Thanatos, of love and not death—we may eventually storm and occupy the citadels of power.

NOTES

1. Quoted by William Barrett, "Dialogue on Anxiety," *Partisan Review,* vol. 14 (March-April 1947), p. 152. For the context and a different translation, see Sören Kierkegaard, *Concluding Unscientific Postscript.* Princeton: Princeton University Press, 1941, pp. 164–166.
2. Kierkegaard, *ibid.,* p. 312.
3. Shakespeare, *Antony and Cleopatra,* Act II, Scene 2.
4. D. H. Lawrence, *Selected Essays.* Harmondsworth, Middlesex: Penguin Books, 1950, pp. 91–92.
5. Irving Dilliard (editor), *The Spirit of Liberty: Papers and Addresses of Learned Hand.* New York: Alfred A. Knopf, Inc., 1959, p. xx.
6. Winwood Reade, *The Martyrdom of Man.* London: C. A. Watts & Co., Ltd., 1925, p. 415. (First edition, 1872).

Appendix

Bibliography

Index

Constitutional Protections of Fundamental Rights

Annotated by Arval Morris,
*Professor of Constitutional Law,
University of Washington*

Printed below are the more important protections of freedom found in our United States Constitution. They are accompanied by only the briefest comment on United States Supreme Court opinions interpreting these provisions. The annotations lack the qualifications that a more extended discussion would allow. In addition to the Federal Constitution, there are State Constitutions with various protections at the State level.

THE ORIGINAL CONSTITUTION

(Adopted in 1788)

Article I, Section 9. . . . . *The privilege of the writ of habeas corpus shall not be suspended, unless when in cases of rebellion or invasion the public safety may require it.*

Historically this has been the great writ of freedom. It protects anyone against being deprived of his liberty without constitutional justification. It is used to test the legality of a person's confinement in jail by either state or federal officials.

Article I, Section 9. *No bill of attainder . . . shall be passed.*

A bill of attainder is a legislative finding of misconduct, rather than a court determination, thereby barring the person from enjoying the usual legal rights. An example is a law depriving a person of the right to carry out his profession, e.g. a minister, because he participated in a rebellion.

Article I, Section 9. *No . . . ex post facto law shall be passed.*

An *ex post facto* law is one passed today applying to yesterday's conduct, making an act criminal although it was not criminal when originally committed. The section does not apply to civil matters, and hence, it does not apply to denaturalization and deportation proceedings, which are civil actions. (The last two provisions are made binding on both Congress and the states; see also Article I, Section 10.)

Article III, Section 2. *The trial of all crimes, except in cases of impeachment, shall be by jury; and . . . shall be held in the State where the said crimes shall have been committed.*

Self-explanatory. This provision is binding only on the federal government, and a person may waive these rights if he so chooses.

Article VI. . . . *no religious test shall ever be required as a qualification to any office or public trust under the United States.*

A religious test is one requiring affirmation or repudiation of specific religious beliefs; such tests are disallowed as qualifications for public office. However, certain immoral practices, such as polygamy, have been judged to present a sufficient public evil and may be made a disqualification.

THE BILL OF RIGHTS

(Adopted in 1791)

Amendment I. *Congress shall make no law respecting an establishment of religion, or prohibiting the free exercise thereof;*

The "establishment" and "abridgment" clauses, taken together, mean that government cannot use religion, or a lack thereof, as a standard for action or inaction when it seeks, by law, either to confer a benefit or to impose a burden. For example, the use of public schools for religious instruction during the school day confers a benefit, and is prohibited.

or abridging the freedom of speech,

This provision guarantees freedom of expression and protects against government mutilation of the public thinking process, insuring that citizens will control government, and not vice versa. The government can, however, punish speech that does not receive this protection, e.g. libelous or obscene speech, and all other utterances as well, if there is a "clear and present danger" that they will directly result in harmful activity, such as violent revolution, that government might legitimately suppress.

or of the press,

Leaflet distribution on public streets cannot be prohibited or taxed, and the right to anonymity is safeguarded. Neither the states nor the federal government can censor any printed materials in advance of their publication. However, motion pictures might be required to obtain an identifying permit before their showing, and Congress, perhaps, can deny mailing privileges to certain publications deemed obscene.

or the right of the people peaceably to assemble,

No government can punish anyone for peaceful participation in an assembly, even when the meeting is called by an organization charged with violation of the law.

and to petition the government for a redress of grievances.

Self-explanatory. (The entire First Amendment applies equally to state and federal government.)

Amendment IV. *The right of the people to be secure in their persons, houses, papers, and effects, against unreasonable searches and seizures, shall not be violated.*

This provision applies to federal and state government alike and guarantees a citizen's right to privacy against "unreasonable" searches. Evidence obtained by an "unreasonable" search cannot be used in state or federal courts. Wiretapping is not an "unreasonable" search, and wiretapped evidence may be used in some states, but not in federal courts.

and no warrants shall issue, but upon probable cause, . . .

Among other kinds, searches on a warrant are "reasonable" searches. The warrants must be specific, showing that a crime was committed and describing the nature of the property to be seized.

Amendment V. *No person shall be held to answer to a capital, or otherwise infamous crime, unless on a presentment or indictment of a grand jury . . . ;*

The provision covers only those crimes punishable by hard labor or confinement in a penitentiary.

nor shall any person be subject for the same offense to be twice put in jeopardy of life and limb;

If a person is acquitted on a criminal charge, he cannot be retried, but if his action should give rise to more than one crime, he may be tried for the additional crimes arising from that act.

nor shall be compelled in any criminal case to be a witness against himself,

This provision eliminates the third-degree examination and prohibits the federal government from forcing a person to incriminate himself or produce his private papers, except where documents are required to be kept by law.

nor be deprived of life, liberty or property, without due process of law; . . .

This provision guarantees a fair trial. (In a sharply divided vote, the entire Fifth Amendment has been held to apply only to the federal government and not to the states.)

Amendment VI. *In all criminal prosecutions, the accused shall enjoy the right to a speedy and public trial by an impartial jury . . . and to be informed of the nature of the accusation; to be confronted with the witnesses against him; to have compulsory process for obtaining witnesses in his favor;*

Self-explanatory, except that Congress can allow minor offenses committed in the District of Columbia to be tried without a jury.

and to have the assistance of counsel for his defense.

The denial of an attorney in a federal or state criminal trial nullifies a conviction, but a defendant can waive this right as long as he does so intelligently.

Amendment VII. *In suits at common law, where the value in controversy shall exceed twenty dollars, the right of trial by jury shall be preserved, and no fact tried by a jury shall be otherwise reexamined in any court of the United States, than according to the rules of the common law.*

Self-explanatory.

Amendment VIII. *Excessive bail shall not be required.*

Self-explanatory.

nor excessive fines imposed, nor cruel and unusual punishment inflicted.

Electrocution is not a "cruel or unusual punishment," even where the first attempt fails because of an electric-power blockage. This provision applies to state and federal government alike.

Amendment IX. *The enumeration in the Constitution of certain rights shall not be construed to deny or disparage others retained by the people.*

The purpose of this amendment is obvious.

Amendment X. *The powers not delegated to the United States by the Constitution, nor prohibited by it to the States, are reserved to the States respectively, or to the people.*

The purpose of this amendment is to state the place of residual governmental power. It secures to the states and to the people all those powers not delegated to the federal government, nor prohibited to the states.

THE CIVIL WAR AMENDMENTS

(Amendment XIII adopted 1865)
(Amendment XIV adopted 1868)
(Amendment XV adopted 1870)

Amendment XIII. *Neither slavery nor involuntary servitude, except as a punishment for crime, whereof the party shall have been duly convicted, shall exist within the United States, or any place subject to their jurisdiction.*

The purpose of this provision is obvious, and it applies to individuals as well as to federal and state governments. Except for seamen, it also invalidates forced labor contracts.

Amendment XIV. . . . *No state shall make or enforce any law which shall abridge the privileges or immunities of citizens of the United States;*

This provision prohibits states from abridging the rights of federal citizenship, such as the right to travel, but it does not operate against private persons. The right publicly to discuss problems of national importance is also protected by this section.

nor shall any state deprive any person of life, liberty, or property, without due process of law;

This provision guarantees a fair trial by a state and includes, at least, notice of the charges, an unbiased judge and jury, and an attorney in all capital cases. This provision also incorporates the First and Fourth Amendments, applying them equally to the state and to the federal governments.

nor deny to any person within its jurisdiction the equal protection of the laws.

This provision holds that state government cannot use race or wealth as a classsifying standard for action or inaction when it seeks to confer a benefit or impose a burden. A state may, however, make many reasonable classifications, but it cannot gerrymander its voting districts so as to deny voters fair legislative representation.

Amendment XV. *The right of citizens of the United States to vote shall not be denied or abridged by the United States or by any state on account of race, color or previous condition of servitude.*

Except for "sex" added by the Nineteenth Amendment and the specific criteria enumerated above, the states can impose qualifications on the right to vote. Property and educational qualifications have, for example, been used in such a way as to frustrate the basic purpose of this provision.

Bibliography

The most important reading is in the original sources, from Plato to Freud. As I have indicated these originals in many footnotes, the following list is largely made up of secondary sources. A valuable supplement to this brief bibliography is Ethel M. Albert and Clyde Kluckhohn, *A Selected Bibliography on Values, Ethics, and Esthetics,* New York: The Free Press of Glencoe Inc., 1959.

GENERAL WORKS AND ANTHOLOGIES

Hill, Thomas E., *Contemporary Ethical Theories.* New York: The Macmillan Company, 1950.

Johnson, Oliver A., *Ethics: A Source Book.* New York: Holt, Rinehart and Winston, Inc., 1964.

Melden, A. I., *Ethical Theories: A Book of Readings.* Englewood Cliffs, N.J.: Prentice-Hall, Inc., 1956.

Olafson, Frederick A., *Society, Law, and Morality.* Englewood Cliffs, N.J.: Prentice-Hall, Inc., 1961.

Rand, Benjamin, *The Classical Moralists.* Boston: Houghton Mifflin Company, 1937.

Sellars, Wilfred and John Hospers, *Readings in Ethical Theory.* New York: Appleton-Century-Crofts, Inc., 1952. (Twentieth-century writers, with ample bibliography.)

Sidgwick, Henry and A. G. Widgery, *Outlines of the History of Ethics.* London: Collier-Macmillan, Ltd., 1939.

Taylor, Paul W., *The Moral Judgment: Readings in Contemporary Meta-Ethics.* Englewood Cliffs, N.J.: Prentice-Hall, Inc., 1963.

NATURAL LAW AND RIGHTS

Barker, Ernest, *Traditions of Civility.* New York: Cambridge University Press, 1948.

d'Entreves, A. P., *Natural Law.* London: Hutchinson & Co., Ltd., 1951. (Contains bibliography.)

———, "The Case for Natural Law Examined," *Natural Law Forum,* vol. 1 (1956), pp. 5–52. (There are many other relevant articles in the *Natural Law Forum.*)

Gierke, Otto, *Natural Law and the Theory of Society.* New York: Cambridge University Press, 1934.

Gilson, Étienne, *Medieval Universalism and Its Present Value*. New York: Sheed & Ward, Inc., 1937.

Hart, H. L. A., *The Concept of Law*. New York: Oxford University Press, 1961.

Hawkins, David, *The Language of Nature*. San Francisco: W. H. Freeman and Company, 1963.

Hutchins, Robert M. and others, *Natural Law and Modern Society*. Cleveland: The World Publishing Company, 1963.

Huxley, Thomas Henry and Julian, *Touchstone for Ethics*. New York: Harper & Row, Publishers, Inc., 1947.

Kahler, Erich, *Man the Measure*. New York: Pantheon Books, Inc., 1943.

Kelsen, Hans, *General Theory of Law and State*. Cambridge, Mass.: Harvard University Press, 1949.

Laski, Harold J., *The Rights of Man*. London: Collier-Macmillan, Ltd., 1940.

Lippmann, Walter, *The Public Philosophy*. Boston: Little, Brown & Company, 1956.

Maritain, Jacques, *The Rights of Man and Natural Law*. New York: Charles Scribner's Sons, 1945.

Melden, A. I. *Rights and Right Conduct*. Oxford: Basil Blackwell, Ltd., 1959.

Mill, John Stuart, "Nature" in *Three Essays on Religion*. London: Longmans, Green & Co., Ltd., 1885. (Frequently reprinted.)

Montagu, M. F. Ashley, *The Direction of Human Development*. New York: Harper & Row, Publishers, Inc., 1955.

Murray, Michael V., *Problems in Ethics*. New York: Holt, Rinehart and Winston, Inc., 1960.

Needham, Joseph, *Human Law and the Laws of Nature in China and the West*. New York: Oxford University Press, 1951.

Pollock, Frederick, "The History of the Law of Nature" in *Essays in the Law*. London: Collier-Macmillan, Ltd., 1922.

Ritchie, David G., *Natural Rights*. London: Collier-Macmillan, Ltd., 1903.

Troeltsch, Ernst, *The Social Teaching of the Christian Churches*. New York: The Macmillan Company, 1931.

Strauss, Leo, *Natural Right and History*. Chicago: University of Chicago Press, 1953.

UNESCO, *Human Rights: A Symposium*. London: Alan Wingate, 1949.

Wild, John, *Plato's Modern Enemies and the Theory of Natural Law*. Chicago: University of Chicago Press, 1953.

HEDONISM

Anschutz, Richard P., *The Philosophy of John Stuart Mill*. New York: Oxford University Press, 1953.

Baumgardt, David, *Bentham and the Ethics of Today*. Princeton: Princeton University Press, 1952.

Blake, Ralph M., "Why Not Hedonism?" *Ethics*, vol. 37 (1926), pp. 1–18.

Freud, Sigmund, *Beyond the Pleasure Principle*. New York: Liveright Publishing Company, 1922.

Hilliard, A. L., *The Forms of Value: The Extension of a Hedonistic Axiology*. New York: Columbia University Press, 1950.

Moore, G. E., *Ethics*. New York: Holt, Rinehart and Winston, Inc., 1912. Chs. 1 and 2.
——, *Principia Ethica*. New York: Cambridge University Press, 1903. Sections 36–57.
Ryle, Gilbert, *Dilemmas*. New York: Cambridge University Press, 1956. Ch. 4.
Savery, William, "A Defence of Hedonism," *Ethics*, vol. 45 (1934), pp. 1–26.
Sharp, F. C., *Ethics*. New York: Appleton-Century-Crofts, Inc., 1928. Ch. 19.
Schlick, Moritz, *Problems of Ethics*. Englewood Cliffs, N.J.: Prentice-Hall, Inc., 1939.
Sidgwick, Henry, *The Methods of Ethics*. London: Collier-Macmillan, Ltd., 1922. Especially Bk. III, Ch. 14.

INTEREST AND THEORY OF VALUE

Dewey, John, "Theory of Valuation," *International Encyclopaedia of Unified Science*, Vol. II, No. 4. Chicago: University of Chicago Press, 1939.
——, *The Quest for Certainty*. New York: G. P. Putnam's Sons, 1929. Ch. 10.
Eaton, H. O., *The Austrian Philosophy of Value*. Norman: University of Oklahoma Press, 1930.
Frondizi, Risieri, *What Is Value?* La Salle, Ill.: Open Court Publishing Company, 1963.
Gotshalk, D. W., *Patterns of Good and Evil*. Urbana: University of Illinois Press, 1963.
Hall, Everett W., *The Analysis of Value*. London: Routledge & Kegan Paul, Ltd., 1952.
Hill, Thomas H., *Contemporary Ethical Theories*. New York: The Macmillan Company, 1959. Ch. 14.
Laird, John, *The Idea of Value*. New York: Cambridge University Press, 1929.
Lepley, Ray (editor), *Value: A Cooperative Inquiry*. New York: Columbia University Press, 1949.
Lewis, C. I., *An Analysis of Knowledge and Valuation*. La Salle, Ill.: Open Court Publishing Company, 1946.
Parker, DeWitt H., *Human Values*. New York: Harper & Row, Publishers, Inc., 1931.
——, *The Philosophy of Value*. Ann Arbor: University of Michigan Press, 1957.
Pepper, Stephen C., *The Sources of Value*. Berkeley: University of California Press, 1958.
Perry, Ralph Barton, *The Moral Economy*. New York: Charles Scribner's Sons, 1909.
——, *General Theory of Value*. New York: David McKay Company, Inc., 1926.
——, *Realms of Value*. Cambridge, Mass.: Harvard University Press, 1954.
Prall, D. W., "A Study in the Theory of Value," *University of California Publications in Philosophy*, vol. 3 (1918), pp. 179–290.
Urban, W. M., *Valuation: Its Nature and Laws*. New York: The Macmillan Company, 1909.

RELIGIOUS ETHICS

Ballou, Robert O., *Portable World Bible*. New York: The Viking Press, Inc., 1944.

Barth, Karl, *The Knowledge of God and the Service of God*. New York: Charles Scribner's Sons, 1939.

Bennett, John C., *Christian Ethics and Social Policy*. New York: Charles Scribner's Sons, 1946.

Berdyaev, Nicolas, *The Divine and the Human*. London: Geoffrey Bles, Ltd., 1949.

Bergson, Henri, *The Two Sources of Morality and Religion*. New York: Holt, Rinehart and Winston, Inc., 1935.

Bretall, Robert (editor), *A Kierkegaard Anthology*. Princeton: Princeton University Press, 1947.

Brunner, Emil, *The Divine Imperative*. New York: The Macmillan Company, 1937.

Buber, Martin, *Between Man and Man*. Boston: The Beacon Press, 1955.

————, *I and Thou*. New York: Charles Scribner's Sons, 1937.

Dewey, John, *A Common Faith*. New Haven: Yale University Press, 1934.

Freud, Sigmund, *The Future of an Illusion*. London: The Hogarth Press, Ltd., 1928.

Fromm, Erich, *The Art of Loving*. New York: Harper & Row, Publishers, Inc., 1956.

Kaufmann, Walter, *The Faith of a Heretic*. New York: Doubleday & Company, Inc., 1961.

———— (editor), *Religion from Tolstoy to Camus*. New York: Harper & Row, Publishers, Inc., 1961.

Mumford, Lewis, *The Conduct of Life*. New York: Harcourt, Brace & World, Inc., 1951.

Niebuhr, Reinhold, *An Interpretation of Christian Ethics*. New York: Harper & Row, Publishers, Inc., 1935.

Noss, John B., *Man's Religions*, 3rd ed. New York: The Macmillan Company, 1963.

Otto, Rudolf, *The Idea of the Holy*. New York: Oxford University Press, 1943.

Ramsey, Paul, *Basic Christian Ethics*. New York: Charles Scribner's Sons, 1950.

————, *Nine Modern Moralists*. Englewood Cliffs, N.J.: Prentice-Hall, Inc., 1962.

Reid, Louis Arnaud, *Creative Morality*. London: George Allen & Unwin Ltd., 1937.

Sorley, W. R., *Moral Values and the Idea of God*. Cambridge: Cambridge University Press, 1930.

Tillich, Paul, *The Dynamics of Faith*. New York: Harper & Row, Publishers, Inc., 1957.

————, *The Courage to Be*. New Haven: Yale University Press, 1952.

Toynbee, Arnold J., *An Historian's Approach to Religion*. New York: Oxford University Press, 1956.

DEONTOLOGICAL ETHICS

Broad, C. D. *Ethics and the History of Philosophy*. New York: Humanities Press, Inc., 1952, pp. 244–262.

——, *Five Types of Ethical Theory*. New York: Harcourt, Brace & World, Inc., 1930.

Carritt, E. F., *Ethical and Political Thinking*. New York: Oxford University Press, 1947.

——, *The Theory of Morals*. New York: Oxford University Press, 1928.

Duncan-Jones, Austin, *Butler's Moral Philosophy*. Baltimore: Penguin Books, Inc., 1952.

Ewing, A. C., *Ethics*. London: English Universities Press, 1953. Ch. 4.

Frankena, William, *Ethics*. Englewood Cliffs, N.J.: Prentice-Hall, Inc., 1963. Ch. 2.

Hartmann, Nicolai, *Ethics*, 3 vols. New York: The Macmillan Company, 1932.

Johnson, Oliver, *Rightness and Goodness*. The Hague: M. Nijhoff, 1959. (Criticism.)

Paton, H. J., *The Categorical Imperative*. London: Hutchinson & Co., Ltd., 1947.

Prichard, H. A., *Duty and Interest*. New York: Oxford University Press, 1928.

——, *Moral Obligation*. New York: Oxford University Press, 1950.

Rashdall, Hastings, *Is Conscience an Emotion?* Boston: Houghton Mifflin Company, 1914.

Ross, Sir William David, *Foundations of Ethics*. New York: Oxford University Press, 1939.

——, *Kant's Ethical Theory*. New York: Oxford University Press, 1954.

——, *The Right and the Good*. New York: Oxford University Press, 1930.

Sidgwick, Henry, *The Methods of Ethics*. London: Collier-Macmillan, Ltd., 1922. Book III.

Singer, Marcus, *Generalization in Ethics*. New York: Alfred A. Knopf, Inc., 1961.

Teale, Alfred E., *Kantian Ethics*. New York: Oxford University Press, 1951.

Werkmeister, W. H., *Theories of Ethics*. Lincoln, Neb.: Johnsen Publishing Company, 1961. Chs. 8, 9.

UTILITARIAN AND TELEOLOGICAL THEORIES

Bertocci, Peter A. and Richard M. Millard, *Personality and the Good*. New York: David McKay Company, Inc., 1963.

Blanshard, Brand, *Reason and Goodness*. New York: The Macmillan Company, 1961. Chs. 10, 11, 12.

Bradley, F. H., *Ethical Studies*. New York: Oxford University Press, 1927. (Self-realizationism.)

Brandt, Richard B., *Ethical Theory*. Englewood Cliffs, N.J.: Prentice-Hall, Inc., 1959. Ch. 15. (Contains a valuable bibliography of journal articles on act-utilitarianism and rule-utilitarianism.)

Broad, C. D., *Five Types of Ethical Theory*. New York: Harcourt, Brace & World, Inc., 1930.

Ewing, A. C., *Ethics*. London: English Universities Press, 1953. Ch. 5.

——, *The Definition of Good*. New York: The Macmillan Company, 1947.

Green, Thomas H., *Prolegomena to Ethics*. New York: Oxford University Press, 1890. (Self-realizationism.)

Hospers, John, *Human Conduct*. New York: Harcourt, Brace & World, Inc., 1961. Chs. 5, 7.

Lewis, C. I., *The Ground and Nature of the Right*. New York: Columbia University Press, 1955.

Moore, G. E. *Ethics*. New York: Oxford University Press, 1911.

———, *Principia Ethica*. Cambridge: Cambridge University Press, 1903.

Olafson, Frederick A. (editor), *Justice and Social Policy*. Englewood Cliffs, N.J.: Prentice-Hall, Inc., 1961. (Relevant to the question whether justice is consistent with utilitarianism.)

Plamenatz, John, *The English Utilitarians*. Oxford: Basil Blackwell, Ltd., 1958.

Pratt, James Bissett, *Reason in the Art of Living*. New York: The Macmillan Company, 1949.

Rashdall, Hastings, *The Theory of Good and Evil*. New York: Oxford University Press, 1907. (Ideal utilitarianism.)

Rawls, John B., "Two Concepts of Rules," *Philosophical Review*, vol. 64 (1955), pp. 3–32.

Rice, Philip Blair, *On the Knowledge of Good and Evil*. New York: Random House, Inc., 1955

Santayana, George, *Reason in Morals*. New York: Charles Scribner's Sons, 1905.

Sharp, Frank C., *Ethics*. New York: Appleton-Century-Crofts, 1928.

———, *Good Will and Ill Will*. Chicago: University of Chicago Press, 1950.

Sidgwick, Henry, *The Methods of Ethics*. London: Collier-Macmillan, Ltd., 1922. Book IV.

Smart, J. J. C., *An Outline of a System of Utilitarian Ethics*. Melbourne: Melbourne University Press, 1961.

Stace, Walter T., *The Concept of Morals*. New York: The Macmillan Company, 1937.

CULTURAL RELATIVISM

Asch, S. E., *Social Psychology*. Englewood Cliffs, N.J.: Prentice-Hall, Inc., 1952. Chs. 12, 13.

Benedict, Ruth, *Patterns of Culture*. Boston: Houghton Mifflin Company, 1934.

Brandt, Richard B., *Hopi Ethics*. Chicago: University of Chicago Press, 1954.

Edel, May and Abraham, *Anthropology and Ethics*. Springfield, Ill.: Charles C Thomas, Publisher, 1959.

Herskovits, Melville J., *Cultural Anthropology*. New York: Alfred A. Knopf, Inc., 1955. Ch. 19.

Kluckhohn, Clyde, "Universal Categories of Culture," in A. L. Kroeber (editor), *Anthropology Today*. Chicago: University of Chicago Press, 1953.

Ladd, John, *The Structure of a Moral Code*. Cambridge, Mass.: Harvard University Press, 1957.

Linton, Ralph, "Universal Ethical Principles," in Ruth N. Anshen (editor), *Moral Principles of Action*. New York: Harper & Row, Publishers, 1952.

MacBeath, A., *Experiments in Living*. London: Collier-Macmillan, Ltd., 1952.

Mead, Margaret, *Sex and Temperament in Three Primitive Societies*. New York: William Morrow & Company, Inc., 1935.

Nietzsche, Friedrich, *The Genealogy of Morals*. New York: Modern Library, Inc., 1918.

Stace, Walter T., *The Concept of Morals*. New York: The Macmillan Company, 1937, Chs. 1, 2.

Vivas, Eliseo, *The Moral Life and the Ethical Life*. Chicago: University of Chicago Press, 1950. Ch. 1.

Westermarck, Edward, *Ethical Relativity*. New York: Harcourt, Brace & World, Inc., 1932.

————, *The Origin and Development of Moral Ideas*, 2nd ed. London: Collier-Macmillan, Ltd., 1912.

SUBJECTIVISM, LINGUISTIC THEORY, AND RELATED PROBLEMS

Aiken, Henry D., *Reason and Conduct*. New York: Alfred A. Knopf, Inc., 1962.

Alston, William, *Philosophy of Language*. Englewood Cliffs, N.J.: Prentice-Hall, Inc., 1963.

Ayer, A. J., *Language, Truth and Logic*. London: Victor Gollancz, Ltd., 1958.

Baier, Kurt, *The Moral Point of View*. Ithaca, N.Y.: Cornell University Press, 1958.

Brandt, Richard B., *Ethical Theory*. Englewood Cliffs, N.J.: Prentice-Hall, Inc., 1959. Chs. 8, 9, 10.

Carnap, Rudolf, *Philosophy and Logical Syntax*. New York: Harcourt, Brace & World, Inc., 1937.

Castaneda, Hector-Neri and George Nanhnikian (editors), *Morality and the Language of Conduct*. Detroit: Wayne University Press, 1963.

Edwards, Paul, *The Logic of Moral Discourse*. New York: The Free Press of Glencoe, 1955.

Ewing, A. C., *Second Thoughts in Moral Philosophy*. London: Routledge & Kegan Paul Ltd., 1959.

Findlay, J. N., *Language, Mind, and Value*. London: George Allen & Unwin, Ltd., 1963.

Flew, A. G. N. (ed.), *Logic and Language*. Oxford: Basil Blackwell, Ltd., first series, 1951; second series, 1953.

Gellner, Ernest, *Words and Things*. London: Victor Gollancz, Ltd., 1959.

Hare, R. M., *The Language of Morals*. New York: Oxford University Press, 1952.

————, *Freedom and Reason*. New York: Oxford University Press, 1963.

Mayo, Bernard, *Ethics and the Moral Life*. London: Collier-Macmillan, Ltd., 1958.

Murphy, Arthur E., *An Inquiry Concerning Moral Understanding*, A. I. Melden, (ed.). La Salle, Ill.: Open Court Publishing Company. (Announced for future publication.)

————, *Reason and the Common Good*, William H. Hay and Marcus G. Singer, (eds.). Englewood Cliffs, N.J.: Prentice-Hall, Inc., 1963. (These works by Murphy cover a wide field and are difficult to classify.)

Nowell-Smith, P. H., *Ethics*. Baltimore: Penguin Books, 1954.

Pitcher, George, *The Philosophy of Wittgenstein*. Englewood Cliffs, N.J.: Prentice-Hall, Inc., 1964.

Prior, A. N., *Logic and the Basis of Ethics*. New York: Oxford University Press, 1949.

Russell, Bertrand, *Human Society in Ethics and Politics*. New York: Simon and Schuster, Inc., 1955.

Stevenson, Charles, *Ethics and Language*. New Haven: Yale University Press, 1944.

Taylor, Paul W., *Normative Discourse*. Englewood Cliffs, N.J.: Prentice-Hall, Inc., 1961.

Toulmin, Stephen, *The Place of Reason in Ethics*. Cambridge: Cambridge University Press, 1950.

Urmson, J. O., "On Grading," *Mind*, vol. 59 (1950), pp. 145–169.

Wittgenstein, Ludwig, *Philosophical Investigations*. Oxford: Basil Blackwell, Ltd., 1953.

MARXISM AND COMMUNISM

Adams, H. P., *Karl Marx in His Earlier Writings*. London: George Allen & Unwin, Ltd., 1940.

Berlin, Isaiah, *Karl Marx: His Life and Environment*. New York: Oxford University Press, 1959.

Buber, Martin, *Paths in Utopia*. London: Routledge & Kegan Paul, Ltd., 1949.

Carr, Edward H., *The Soviet Impact on the Western World*. New York: The Macmillan Company, 1946.

Cole, G. D. H., *A History of Socialist Thought*, 3 vols. London: Collier-Macmillan, Ltd., 1953–1955.

Federn, Karl, *The Materialistic Conception of History*. London: Collier-Macmillan, Ltd., 1939.

Fromm, Erich, *Beyond the Chains of Illusion*. New York: Simon and Schuster, Inc., 1962.

————, *Marx's Concept of Man*. New York: Frederick Ungar Publishing Co., 1961.

Hook, Sidney, *From Hegel to Marx*. New York: Reynal & Hitchcock, Inc., 1963.

Kamenka, Eugene, *The Ethical Foundations of Marxism*. London: Routledge & Kegan Paul Ltd., 1962.

MacIntyre, Alasdair C., *Marxism*. London: Student Christian Movement Press, Ltd., 1953.

Marcuse, Herbert, *Reason and Revolution: Hegel and the Rise of Social Theory*, 2nd ed. New York: Humanities Press, 1954.

————, *Soviet Communism*. New York: Columbia University Press, 1958.

Mehring, Franz, *Karl Marx: The Story of His Life*. Ann Arbor: University of Michigan Press, 1962.

Mills, C. Wright, *The Marxists*. New York: Dell Publishing Co., Inc., 1962.

Pappenheim, Fritz, *The Alienation of Modern Man*. New York: Monthly Review Press, 1959.

Popper, Karl R., *The Open Society and Its Enemies*. Princeton, N.J.: Princeton University Press, 1950.

————, *The Poverty of Historicism*. Boston: The Beacon Press, 1957.

Schumpeter, Joseph A., *Capitalism, Socialism, and Democracy*. London: George Allen & Unwin, Ltd., 1959.

Tucker, Robert, *Philosophy and Myth in Karl Marx*. New York: Cambridge University Press, 1961.

Venable, Vernon, *Human Nature: The Marxian View*. New York: Alfred A. Knopf, Inc., 1945.

DEMOCRACY AND LIBERALISM

Acton, Lord, *Essays on Freedom and Power*. New York: The Free Press of Glencoe, 1948.

Adler, Mortimer J., *The Idea of Freedom*. 2 vols. New York: Doubleday & Company, Inc., 1958–1961.

Anshen, Ruth N. (editor), *Freedom: Its Meaning*. New York: Harcourt, Brace & World, Inc., 1940.

Bosanquet, Bernard, *The Philosophical Theory of the State*. London: Collier-Macmillan, Ltd., 1920.

Brandt, Richard (editor), *Social Justice*. Englewood Cliffs, N.J.: Prentice-Hall, Inc., 1962.

Carritt, Edgar F., *Ethical and Political Thinking*. New York: Oxford University Press, 1947.

————, *Morals and Politics*. New York: Oxford University Press, 1935.

Chafee, Zechariah, *Free Speech in the United States*. Cambridge, Mass.: Harvard University Press, 1941.

Dewey, John, *Freedom and Culture*. New York: Minton, Balch & Co., 1939.

————, *Individualism, Old and New*. New York: Minton, Balch & Co., 1930.

————, *Liberalism and Social Action*. New York: G. P. Putnam's Sons, 1935.

————, *The Public and Its Problems*. New York: Holt, Rinehart and Winston, Inc., 1927.

Ewing, Alfred C., *The Individual, the State, and World Government*. New York: The Macmillan Company, 1947.

Fromm, Erich, *Escape from Freedom*. New York: Holt, Rinehart and Winston, Inc., 1942.

————, *The Sane Society*. New York: Holt, Rinehart and Winston, Inc., 1955.

Greene, Theodore M., *Liberalism*. Austin: University of Texas Press, 1957.

Green, Thomas Hill, *Lectures on the Principles of Political Obligation* (1882). New York: David McKay Company, Inc., 1942.

Girvertz, Harry K., *The Evolution of Liberalism*. New York: The Crowell-Collier Publishing Company, 1963.

Hand, Learned, *The Spirit of Liberty*. New York: Random House, Inc., 1959.

Hallowell, John H., *The Moral Foundation of Democracy*. Chicago: University of Chicago Press, 1954.

Hobhouse, L. T., *The Metaphysical Theory of the State*. London: Collier-Macmillan, Ltd., 1918.

Hook, Sidney, *Political Philosophy*. Englewood Cliffs, N.J.: Prentice-Hall, Inc., 1964.

Joad, C. E. M., *Guide to the Philosophy of Morals and Politics*. New York: Random House, Inc., 1938.

Laski, Harold J., *The Rise of Liberalism*. New York: Harper & Row, Publishers, Inc., 1936.

Lippmann, Walter, *The Good Society*. Boston: Little, Brown & Company, 1937.

Mabbott, J. D., *The State and the Citizen*. London: Hutchinson & Co., Ltd., 1948.

Mannheim, Karl, *Freedom, Power, and Democratic Planning*. New York: Oxford University Press, 1950.

Meiklejohn, Alexander, *Free Speech and Its Relation to Self-Government*. New York: Harper & Row, Publishers, Inc., 1948.

Northrop, F. C. S., *The Meeting of East and West*. New York: The Macmillan Company, 1946.

Perry, Ralph Barton, *Puritanism and Democracy*. New York: Vanguard Press, Inc., 1944.

Russell, Bertrand, *Authority and the Individual*. New York: Simon and Schuster, Inc., 1949.

————, *Human Society in Ethics and Politics*. New York: Simon and Schuster, Inc., 1954.

————, *Freedom versus Organization, 1814–1914*. New York: W. W. Norton & Company, Inc., 1934.

————, *Power*. New York: Simon and Schuster, Inc., 1938.

Sabine, George H., *History of Political Theory*, rev. ed. New York: Holt, Rinehart and Winston, Inc., 1950.

Tussman, Joseph, *Obligation and the Body Politic*. New York: Oxford University Press, 1960.

COMMUNITY

Berdyaev, Nicolas, *Solitude and Society*. London: Geoffrey Bles, Ltd., 1938.

Bishop, Claire Huchet, *All Things Common*. New York: Harper & Row, Publishers, Inc., 1950.

Boulding, Kenneth, *The Organizational Revolution*. New York: Harper & Row, Publishers, Inc., 1953.

Brownell, Baker, *The Human Community*. New York: Harper & Row, Publishers, Inc., 1950.

Buber, Martin. *The Writings of Martin Buber*, ed. by Will Herbert. New York: Meridian Books, Inc., 1956.

Cooley, Charles, *Social Organization;* [and] *Human Nature and the Social Order*. New York: The Free Press of Glencoe, 1956.

Darin-Drabkin, H., *The Other Society*. London: Victor Gollancz, Ltd., 1962.

Friedman, Maurice S., *Martin Buber: The Life of Dialogue*. New York: Harper & Row, Publishers, Inc., 1960.

Friedrich, Carl J., *Community*. New York: Liberal Arts Press, 1959.

Fromm, Erich, *The Sane Society*. New York: Holt, Rinehart and Winston, Inc., 1955.

Goodman, Percival and Paul, *Communitas*. Chicago: University of Chicago Press, 1947.

Gotshalk, D. W., *The Promise of Modern Life*. Yellow Springs, Ohio: The Antioch Press, 1958.

Hauser, Richard and Hephzibah, *The Fraternal Society*. London: The Bodley Head Ltd., 1962.

Jacobs, Jane, *The Death and Life of Great American Cities*. New York: Random House, Inc., 1961.

MacMurray, John, *Persons in Relation*. I ʿndon: Faber & Faber, Ltd., 1957.

Marcel, Gabriel, *Man Against Mass Society*. Chicago: Henry Regnery Company, 1962.

Mayo, Elton, *The Human Problems of an Industrial Civilization*, 2nd ed. New York: The Macmillan Company, 1946.

Mead, George Herbert, *Mind, Self, and Society*. Chicago: University of Chicago Press, 1934.

Millis, Walter and James Real, *The Abolition of War*. New York: The Macmillan Company, 1963.

Mumford, Lewis, *The City in History*. New York: Harcourt, Brace & World, Inc., 1961.

————, *The Culture of Cities*. New York: Harcourt, Brace & World, Inc., 1938.

Nisbet, Robert A., *Community and Power*. New York: Oxford University Press, 1962.

Pfuetze, Paul E., *The Social Self*. New York: Bookman Associates, 1954.

Poston, Richard, *Democracy Speaks Many Tongues: Community Development Around the World*. New York: Harper & Row, Publishers, Inc., 1962.

Tönnies, Ferdinand, *Community and Society*. East Lansing: Michigan State University Press, 1957.

Name index

Aeschylus, 411; quoted, 35
Anders, Günther, 143; quoted, 141
Aquinas (see Saint Thomas Aquinas)
Aristotle, 23, 24, 82, 107, 317, 385, 396, 433; compared with Cicero, 20; criticism of his ethics, 63–66; on empirical method, 7; on intellectual goodness, 62, 63; on law, 49–50; on the life of reason, 59–63; on moral goodness, 62–63; on pleasure, 61; quoted, 7, 49–50, 62, 63, 395
Arnold, Matthew, quoted, 427
Aurelius, Marcus, 17, 21, 362; quoted, 18, 19, 78; on Stoic ethics, 18–19
Austin, John, quoted, 49, 171, 172; on rule-utilitarianism, 171–172
Austin, J. L., 267; quoted, 6
Ayer, A. J., 262; emotive theory of, 258–260; quoted, 259, 260

Barrett, William, quoted, 320–321
Benedict, Ruth, 232–233, 234, 235
Bentham, Jeremy, 82, 85, 109, 156, 285, 317; comparison with Mill, 93, 98–103; criticism of his ethics, 99–103; on egoism, 91–92; on the hedonistic calculus, 90, 216; on justice, 187–189; on natural law and rights, 39, 89; on psychological hedonism, 87–88; on punishment, 92; on quantitative hedonism, 86–92; quoted, 87, 89, 90, 92, 357
Bergson, Henri, on mysticism; 420–421; quoted, 199, 421
Blake, William, 419; quoted, 15, 421–422
Blanshard, Brand, 256; quoted, 119
Boulding, Kenneth, 385; quoted, 403–404
Bradley, F. H., 194; quoted, 191
Breasted, James Henry, quoted, 417
Bridgman, P. W., 141
Broad, C. D., 159, 160; quoted, 79, 152

Brownell, Baker, on community, 388, 390; quoted, 388
Browning, Elizabeth Barrett, quoted, 215
Bruno, Giordano, quoted, 36
Buber, Martin, on community, 387–388, 392, 425–426; quoted, 387–388, 423–424, 425, 426; on theism, 425–426
Buddha, Gautama, 415, 418; quoted, 418
Burckhardt, Jacob, quoted, 11–12; on the Renaissance, 11–12
Burke, Edmund, quoted, 393
Butler, Joseph, 99–100; quoted, 99, 257

Carritt, E. F., 159, 160; quoted, 190
Cannon, Walter B., 80
Cassirer, Ernst, quoted, 237, 286
Channing, William Ellery, quoted, 298
Chénier, André, quoted, 356
Christ (see Jesus)
Cicero, Marcus Tullius, 25; compared with Aristotle, 20; on natural law, 19–20; quoted, 19, 20, 21
Cohen, Felix, quoted, 369
Cohen, Morris, quoted, 48
Colman, Claude, quoted, 212–213
Confucius, 242–243; on humanistic ethics, 56–59; quoted, 57–58, 59, 417
Constant, Benjamin, 155
Copernicus, Nicolaus, 35–36, 72
Cousins, Norman, quoted, 398
Croce, Benedetto, 9
Cromwell, Oliver, quoted, 434

Dante Alighieri, quoted, 34–35
Darwin, Charles, 38, 72; on natural selection, 42; quoted, 42
Demos, Raphael, quoted, 75
Descartes, René, 39–40
Dewey, John, 65; on community, 389–

390, 391, 393, 398, 404–405; quoted, 102, 119, 219, 389–390, 391, 393, 398, 404–405, 429
Dixon, W. Macneile, quoted, 51
Donne, John, quoted, 300
Dostoevsky, Feodor, quoted, 143
Durkheim, Emile, 303, 417; on division of labor, 396–399; quoted, 396, 397

Eatherly, Claude, 142–143; quoted, 143
Eckhart, Master, quoted, 157, 208
Eliot, T. S., quoted, 406
Ellis, Havelock, quoted, 154
Emerson, Ralph Waldo, quoted, 310
Engels, Friedrich, 307, 319, 331; on economic factors in history, 323–324, 325–326, 329–330; on ethics, 320; on ideology, 317, 320; on primitive society, 327; quoted, 317, 323–324, 325, 326, 328, 329–330, 331
Epictetus, 17, 21; quoted, 18, 19; on Stoic ethics, 18–19
Epicurus, quoted, 86
Ewing, A. C., 183; on intuition, 9; quoted, 167; on utilitarianism, 167

Feuerbach, Ludwig, on alienation, 308; on humanistic religion, 308, 423–425, 426; and Marx, 308, 316; quoted, 307, 423, 424–425
Fichte, Johann Gottlieb, 156
Freud, Sigmund, 121; on aggressive drives, 76–78, 211–212; criticism of, 78–82, 201; on human nature, 71–78; on morality, 76–78; quoted, 72, 74, 76, 77–78
Fromm, Erich, 317, 386–387; quoted, 139, 217, 240
Fuller, Lon L., 48

Galileo, 37, 40
Gandhi, Mahatma, 405–406
Gide, André, quoted, 429
Gierke, Otto, quoted, 47
Goethe, Johann Wolfgang von, 74
Goodhart, A. L., quoted, 191–192
Gotshalk, D. W., quoted, 78
Green, Thomas Hill, quoted, 31
Griswold, Erwin N., quoted, 177–178
Gross, Edward, quoted, 398–399

Grotius, Hugo, on natural law, 26–27; quoted, 26, 27

Hammond, J. L. and Barbara, on English history, 337–339; quoted, 338, 339
Hand, Learned, quoted, 434
Hardy, Thomas, quoted, 383
Hare, R. M., 95, 267, 268; prescriptive theory of, 263–265; quoted, 264, 265, 266
Hart, H. L. A., 49, 267
Hauser, Richard and Hephzibah, quoted, 401
Hegel, Georg Wilhelm Friedrich, 191, 291–292, 380; on alienation, 307–308; criticism of his ethical collectivism, 300–305; on dialectical logic, 287–289; on ethical collectivism, 286–291; on freedom, 289–290, 291; and Marx, 307–308, 313–314, 318; quoted, 289, 290, 291, 308; on the state, 290–291
Herskovits, Melville, 379; on cultural relativism, 233–234, 237–238; quoted, 233, 237
Hill, Thomas E., quoted, 97
Hippocrates, 377
Hitler, Adolf, quoted, 43, 214, 304, 434
Hobbes, Thomas, 27, 29, 291–292; criticism of his ethical individualism, 296–298; on ethical individualism, 282–285; on materialism, 39–40, 282–284; quoted, 283, 284, 285, 297
Holmes, Oliver Wendell, quoted, 366
Hook, Sidney, 321
Huizinga, Johan, quoted, 373–374
Humboldt, Wilhelm, quoted, 101, 357–358
Hume, David, 86, 131, 171, 256, 258; on bias against one's enemy, 211; on natural law, 49; on obligation and sympathy, 195–201; quoted, 49, 200, 211, 251, 252, 253, 254, 300
Huxley, Aldous, 193, 418; on overpopulation, 46–47; quoted, 20, 21
Hyman, Stanley Edgar, 322

James, William, quoted, 414, 422
Jaspers, Karl, quoted, 392
Jefferson, Thomas, on natural law, 27; on natural rights, 30–31, 33; quoted, 30–31
Jesus, nonformalistic ethics of, 133–135; quoted, 134, 420; religion of, 415, 419–420

Johnson, Oliver O., 166–167, 183; quoted, 161–162
Justinian, 21

Kafka, Franz, 300
Kahler, Erich, quoted, 299–300, 387
Kant, Immanuel, 27, 88, 89, 108, 131, 164, 167, 186, 198–199, 432; on the categorical imperative, 146–152; criticism of his theories, 152–159; on ethics of a priori reason, 143–152; on good will, 145–146; on political ideals, 151–152; quoted, 147, 148, 150–151, 155, 159, 191
Keith, Sir Arthur, quoted, 43
Kepler, Johannes, 37
Keynes, John Maynard, quoted, 221
Kierkegaard, Sören, 130, 158; quoted, 432
King, Martin Luther, Jr., quoted, 209
Koestler, Arthur, 178, 185; quoted, 172
Krueger, Felix, quoted, 101

Lao-Tse, 412; quoted, 417–418
Lawrence, D. H., quoted, 120, 219, 421, 433
Lawrence, T. E., on excellence and sharing, 346–348; quoted, 347
Levy-Bruhl, Lucien, 416, 417
Lewis, C. I., 118; on intrinsic good, 107; quoted, 107, 204
Lilburne, John, 177
Lindeman, E. C., quoted, 390
Lippmann, Walter, 47, 131
Locke, John, 12; on intuition, 8; on natural rights, 29–30, 33; quoted, 8, 234–235, 360; on religious liberty, 360
Lowie, Robert, 413–414
Luther, Martin, quoted, 383
Lynd, Helen, quoted, 220, 368

Macaulay, Thomas Babbington, quoted, 333
McGreal, Ian, quoted, 165
MacIver, Robert M., on community, 389, 390, 392; quoted, 389
Macmurray, John, 411
McTaggart, J. M. E., 131; quoted, 304
Malthus, Thomas Robert, on overpopulation, 41–42, 46; quoted, 41
Maritain, Jacques, quoted, 25
Marshall Alfred, quoted, 4
Marx, Karl, on alienation, 307–315, 320, 321, 400; on communism, 316, 319, 330–333; criticism of theory of, 333–340; on culture, 325–326, 337; on division of labor, 312, 316, 326, 332; on economic factors, 309–315, 323–324, 328–333, 336–337, 339; on ethics, 315–323, 339–340; as an existentialist, 307, 320–321; on history, 324, 326–333; on human nature, 312–314, 316–317, 319, 321; on ideology, 317–318; on law and the state, 325, 327, 331–332, 336–337; quoted, 309, 310, 311, 312, 313, 314, 315, 316, 317, 318, 319, 322, 323, 326, 328, 330, 332, 333
Maupertius, Pierre Louis, quoted, 38
Mayo, Elton, quoted, 399
Mead, Margaret, quoted, 206
Melden, A. I., quoted, 269, 271
Mencius, 242; quoted, 244
Mill, James, 92, 93
Mill, John Stuart, 99, 109, 171; comparison with Bentham, 99–103; criticism of his ethics, 99–103; on liberty, 357–366; on motives, 97–98; on proof of hedonism, 95–97; qualitative hedonism of, 92–103, 107, 213; quoted, 93, 94, 95, 96–97, 98, 118, 165, 359, 362–363, 364–365
Miller, Leonard, quoted, 171
Moore, G. E., 8, 85, 159, 183, 259, 268; on intrinsic good, 2; on naturalistic fallacy, 255–258; quoted, 2, 10, 167, 169, 173, 181–182, 255–256; on utilitarianism, 167–168, 169, 173–174, 181–182
Morgan, Lewis H., quoted, 327
Mumford, Lewis, 395
Murphy, Gardner, quoted, 78
Murray, Gilbert, quoted, 417
Murray, John Courtney, quoted, 28
Mussolini, Benito, 43, 214, 304

Newton, Isaac, 37–38, 282; quoted, 37
Nietzsche, Friedrich, on ethical egoism, 206; quoted, 206; on the will to power, 71
Nowell-Smith, P. H., quoted, 266–267

Oman, John, quoted, 412
Oppenheimer, Robert, 141, 142
Orwell, George, quoted, 238

Page, Charles H., 392

Parker, DeWitt H., quoted, 112, 116, 217–218
Pascal, Blaise, quoted, 36
Paton, H. J., quoted, 143
Perry, Ralph Barton, interest theory of, 112–115, 118–120, 281; quoted, 114, 115, 281, 346, 368; on utilitarianism, 168
Picasso, Pablo, quoted, 73
Plato, 168, 230; on the aristocratic ideal, 343–345; compared with Freud, 75; on democracy, 343–344; on the good soul, 120; on holiness, 128–130; on love, 218–219, 399; quoted, 128, 218–219, 230, 344; on relativism of Sophists, 229–230
Popper, Karl, 81, 318, 335; quoted, 386
Prichard, H. A., 159, 160, 197–198; quoted, 197
Protagoras, 229–230

Rashdall, Hastings, 85; quoted, 136–137
Rawls, John, on moral rules, 174–175, 179, 180, 184; on punishment, 190; quoted, 175, 179, 184, 190
Read, Herbert, quoted, 348
Reade, Winwood, quoted, 435
Redfield, Robert, 238; quoted, 227
Reid, Louis Arnaud, quoted, 184
Reid, Thomas, quoted, 137
Renan, Ernest, quoted, 365–366
Rice, Philip Blair, quoted, 78
Riesman, David, 386–387
Rilke, Rainer Maria, quoted, 206
Rockefeller, John D., quoted, 43
Rogers, Carl, quoted, 5–6
Ross, William David, 3, 8, 144, 164; criticism of his ethics, 161–162, 183–186, 193–195; on prima-facie duties, 159–162, 183; quoted, 149–150, 160
Rousseau, Jean Jacques, on democracy, 350–353, 354–357; on freedom, 354–355; on the general will, 281, 351–352, 354–355; on political obligation, 354–356; quoted, 281, 350, 351, 352, 354, 355–356; on the social contract, 350–351, 354
Royce, Josiah, 210; on community, 389, 390; quoted, 389
Ruskin, John, 315, 395
Russell, Bertrand, 131, 220; quoted, 247

Sabine, George H., quoted, 359
St. Augustine, quoted, 427

St. John of the Cross, quoted, 418
St. Thomas Aquinas, 3, 130; on natural law, 22–25, 26, 35; quoted, 23, 24
Santayana, George, 52; quoted, 5, 66, 346
Sartre, Jean-Paul, 158
Savery, William, quoted, 100, 104
Seidenberg, Roderick, 385; quoted, 382
Shaftesbury, Earl of, quoted, 44
Shakespeare, William, quoted, 106, 219, 380–381
Sharp, F. C., quoted, 204
Shelley, Percy Bysshe, quoted, 188, 213
Sidgwick, Henry, 137, 156; on hedonism, 103, 104; on justice, 187; on promises, 170–171; quoted, 170, 187
Singer, Marcus, 154, 155–156
Smith, Adam, quoted, 29, 199; on sympathy and obligation, 199–201
Snow, C. P., 39, 335
Socrates, 31, 139, 140; on holiness, 128–130
Sophocles, 3, 74
Spencer, Herbert, quoted, 42; on survival of the fittest, 42
Spengler, Oswald, 43; on cultural relativism, 231–232, 234, 237; quoted, 231–232
Spinoza, Baruch, 27, 82, 121; criticism of his ethics, 70–71; ethics of, 66–70; on pleasure, 68–69; quoted, 50, 67, 68–69, 114
Stace, Walter, quoted, 102, 107–108
Stein, Gertrude, 9–10
Steinmetz, Charles P., 395–396
Stevenson, Charles, on the nature of ethical disagreement, 260–263, 269–270; quoted, 260, 261, 262–263, 270
Strauss, Leo, 282
Sumner, William Graham, quoted, 43

Tennyson, Alfred Lord, quoted, 46, 135
Thucydides, quoted, 229
Titchener, Edward, 100–101
Tocqueville, Alexis de, 357; quoted, 353–354
Tönnies, Ferdinand, 388, 390, 402
Toulmin, Stephen, 267, 271; quoted, 272
Toynbee, Arnold J., 209, 375, 377; quoted, 412; on religion, 412
Trilling, Lionel, quoted, 81–82
Twain, Mark, quoted, 138, 208
Tylor, E. B., 416

Urmson, J. O., 267, 271

Vico, Giambattista, on natural law and history, 27–28, 318, 433; quoted, 27–28

Waley, Arthur, quoted, 413
Warrender, Howard, 285
Watson, J. B., quoted, 41
Weldon, T. D., quoted, 175
Wells, H. G., quoted, 385, 392

Wheelwright, Philip, 257
Whitehead, Alfred North, 270; quoted, 45, 242, 349, 372, 408, 414
Whitman, Walt, 421; quoted, 204, 352–353, 422
Whyte, William H., Jr., 386–387
Wilde, Oscar, quoted, 395
Wittgenstein, Ludwig, 267; quoted, 266; theory of meaning, 265–266
Wolfe, W. B., quoted, 100
Wordsworth, William, 93; quoted, 419
Wright, Ernest Hunter, quoted, 351

Subject index

Absolutism, 228, 233, 239, 242–245; *See also* Objectivity; Universality of values

Act-utilitarianism (*see* Utilitarianism)

Aggressiveness, and death-instinct, 75–78, 80–81; as desire to harm, 210–213; non-instinctive, 80–81, 211

Alienation, 307–315, 320, 321, 380, 400; *See also* Depersonalization

Analysis, analytical method, 6, 10; *See also* Language

Aristocracy, and democracy, 344, 345–346, 350, 353, 359; ideal of, 343–345

Art and esthetic experience, 57, 65–66, 73, 213–215, 313, 316

Asceticism, 88

Bias (*see* Moral bias)

Buddhism, 415

Categorical imperatives, 264–265; criticized, 152–158; defined, 146–148; formulas of, 148–151

Catharsis, 74

Civil liberties and rights, 32, 209, 337, 340, 353–354, 361–366, 368–369, 404, 437–441; *See also* Freedom and liberty; Natural rights

Collectivism, in future world order, 387–388, 390; refutation of extreme ethical, 301–305; theory of ethical, 285–291; *See also* Communism; Socialism

Communication, 394–398

Communism, 307; crude form of, 330–331, 343; as ethical goal, 316–323; future stages of, 331–333; lure of, 400; primitive stage of, 327; *See also* Marx

Community, 435; as basis of democracy, 350–353; and communication, 394–400; defined, 280, 394; and institutional reconstruction, 400–406; intimate, 193–194, 386, 388–391, 402, 405–406,

410–412, 416; as normative principle, 388–394; and organization, 370, 372, 381–384, 386–388; *See also* Religion

Conscience, meanings of, 136–137, 139–140; nonreflective, criticized, 137–139, 140–141; reflective, 140–143; as superego, 73, 202; *See also* A priori reason; Duty; Obligation

Cooperation, cooperatives, 331, 404–405; *See also* Community

Crisis, as challenge, 377–378; as communal lag, 381–384; as dynamic disequilibrium, 374–378, 381–384; as fettered potentiality, 378–381; of Greco-Roman civilization, 336; Marxist interpretation of, 324, 329–330, 333, 381; misconceptions of, 372–374; as nonuse or misuse of resources, 378–381; and organizational revolution, 381–384

Cultural relativism, contrasted with absolutism, 228, 242; and crisis, 379–380; criticism of, 234–239, 418; as descriptive or methodological, 235–236; meaning of, 227–228; representatives of, 228–234, 265–266, 271; temporal, 228, 242–243; and truth, 237–238; in various areas, 228, 242, 243–245

Culture, in a democracy, 346–350; Marxian theory of, 325–326, 337; *See also* Cultural relativism

Darwinism and ethics, 42–46

Death instinct (*see* Aggressiveness)

Democracy, based on community, 350–353; culture in, 346–350; and freedom, 353–357, 434–435; meaning of, 115; moral basis of, 151–152; and social intelligence, 350–353; totalitarian, 353–357; *See also* Freedom and Liberty; Liberalism

Deontological ethics, 2–4; as a priori, 143–159; as based on conscience, 136–139; as prima-facie duty, 159–162; as theological, 127–132
Depersonalization, 300, 386–387; See also Alienation
Desire and volition, analysis of, 111–112; Spinoza on, 67–68, 70–71; See also Interest
Determinism (see Free will)
Dialectics, dialectical logic, 287–289, 433–434
Division of labor, and alienation, 312, 316, 326, 332; and aristocratic ideal, 343–344; and communication, 394–400
Due process, 176–179, 190
Duty, duties, as categorical, 145, 149, 153–154, 157; conflicts of, 138, 153–154; of perfect obligation, 149, 153–154, 161; of personal obligation, 193–194; as prima-facie, 159–162; and reflective ethics, 139–143; as retrospective, 160, 194–195; the sense of, 199–203, 301; See also Conscience; Obligation

Education, in aristocratic state, 345; in a democracy, 349–350; need for general education, 398–400
Egoism, 69, 91–92, 97, 205–208, 284–285
Enjoyment, 107–108; See also Happiness; Pleasure
Ethics, 432–433, passim; Biblical conception of, 2–4; Greek conception of, 1–2; methods of, 6–9, 144; and politics, 3–4, 60; as study of good, 1–2; as study of moral law, 2–3; teleological, 2, 134, 168; theological, 2, 134, 168; utilitarian, 2, 164–166; See also Deontological ethics; Utilitarianism
Evil, 73–74, 105–107
Evolution and ethics, 44–46
Excellence (see Sharing and excellence)
Existentialism, 158, 307, 320–321

Fact-value dichotomy, 39–43, 50–52, 78–79, 252–253, 259–262, 268–274, 433
Factualist fallacy (see Fallacy, fallacies)
Fallacy, fallacies, cognitivist, 258; of composition, 97, 355; definist, 257; factualist, 45, 50–51, 96, 257, 268; in Mill's argument for hedonism, 96–97; naturalistic, 120, 197, 255–258, 268

Freedom and liberty, of action, 364–365; of association, 364; and democracy, 357–359; individualistic conception of, 28–30; Marxian theory of, 322–323, 332–333, 337; as natural right, 29–34, 358; and organization, 366–370; and political obligation, 353–357; social conception of, 31, 289–291, 350–353; and the state, 290–291, 351, 353–357; of thought and expression, 361–364, 365–366; and utilitarianism, 193; See also Civil liberties and rights
Free will, 4–7; and determinism, 5–6, 67, 70, 71; in Kantian ethics, 150–151, 158; and responsibility, 4–5

General will, 281, 351–352, 354–355, 357
God, as basis of community, 425–426; duty toward, 128–132; humanistic interpretation of, 423–425; as moral lawgiver, 127–132; mystical concept of, 418–422; and purposive morality, 132–135; reinterpretation of, 428–429
Golden Rule, 58, 208
Good, goodness, as fulfillment of interest, 118, 120–123; instrumental, 2–3, 220–221, 255; intellectual, 62–63; intrinsic, 2–3, 117–118, 255; meaning of, 103–109, 121–123; moral, 62–63, 114; as object of interest, 114; as the ought of worth, 197–199; ultimate, 2; See also Value
Good-reasons approach, 263–264, 267–268
Good social order, criterion of, 279–280, 376
Good will, 89; identified with general will, 355; Kant's interpretation of, 145–146
Group-mind, 296, 303
Group-organism, 295–296, 301–303

Happiness, 60–61, 68–69, 90–91, 93–94, 107–108; See also Enjoyment; Pleasure
Hedonism, criticism of, 103–109; distinguished from utilitarianism, 85; egoistic, 91–92, 97; ethical, 87–88; proof of, 95–97; psychological, 87, 96–97, 99–100; qualitative, 61, 94–95, 100–101; quantitative, 87–92, 100–101; universalistic, 91–92
Hedonistic calculus, 9, 90, 101–103, 216
Hedonistic paradox, 98, 100
History, economic interpretation of, 323–326; Marxian theory of, criticized, 333–

340; multilinear theory of, 326–333; and natural law, 27–28; See also Crisis

Humanism, humanistic ethics, 47, 120–123, 231–232, 239–245, 273–274; Aristotelian, 59–66; Confucian, 56–59; Freudian, 71–82; Marxian, 315–323; Spinozistic, 66–71; and Thomism, 23–24; See also Natural law

Hypothetical imperatives, 146

Ideology, 317–318

Imagination, moral, 199, 213–215

Impartiality (see Objectivity)

Imperatives (see Categorical imperatives; Hypothetical imperatives)

Integrative levels, 291–296; adjacency, 292–293, 296; biological unity, 295–296, 301–303; configurational unity, 294–295, 302; corporate unity, 295, 301; existential interdependence, 294, 301; external association, 292–293, 296–297; mechanical interdependence, 293, 297–298; organic interdependence, 293–294, 301–302; psychological unity, 296, 303

Individualism, defense of, 357–359, 364–365; extreme ethical, theory of, 282–285; and natural rights, 28–34; refutation of extreme, 296–301; See also Freedom and liberty

Individuality, 157–159, 170, 357–358

Interest, 111–123; defined, 113; and good, 114, 121–123, 279–281; Perry's theory of, 112–115, 118–119; and value, 113–120

Intuition, 6, 7–9, 105–106, 255–257

Justice, 160–161, 186–193

Language, 248–250; descriptive, 249; emotive, 249, 259, 260–262, 269; evaluative, 249; multifunctional, 250, 266–267; performatory, 250, 267; prescriptive, 249, 263–264; See also Ordinary language

Law, as fourfold, 22–25; positivistic theory of, 25, 48–50; as standard of right, 2–3; See also Moral law; Natural law

Liberalism, 152, 158–159, 368–369; See also Freedom and liberty; Democracy

Liberty (see Freedom and liberty)

Logical positivism (see Positivism)

Love, 58–59, 75–78, 208, 213–215, 417–418

Mean between extremes, 59, 62–63, 66, 433

Meaning, logical positivist theory of, 258–263; noncognitive, 259, 260–262; See also Language; Ordinary language

Means and ends, 181–183

Methods of ethics (see Ethics)

Moral bias, contrast with objectivity, 199, 200–205; against an enemy, 210–213; as group-prejudice, 208–209; and imagination, 213–215; and love, 213–214; as selfishness, 205–208

Moral law, as a priori, 145–151; ethics as study of, 3; theological interpretation of, 129–132; See also Categorical imperatives; Natural law

Morality, defined, 1, 14; See also Ethics; Moral law

Motives and intentions, 89–90, 97–98, 165–166, 254–255

Natural law, 15–52, 123; common features of theories of, 15–16; historical interpretation of, 27–28; and individual self-realization, 358; and positivism, 48–50; rationalistic theory of, 27; scientific conception of, 34–39; Stoic doctrine of, 17–21; Thomistic theory of, 21–25

Natural rights (see Rights)

Naturalistic fallacy (see Fallacy)

Nature, meanings of, 50–52; state of, 29–30, 33, 284–285, 350

Nazi legal system, 48–49

Non-naturalism, 7–8, 255–258, 268

Norm, normative science, 7–8; See also Fact-value dichotomy

Objectivity, inapplicable to values, 253–254; and moral bias, 199, 200–205, 254–255; opposed to cultural relativity, 238–239; opposed to subjectivity, 247–248; of truth, 237–238, 251–252; See also Universality of values

Obligation, analysis of, 199–205; political, 354–356; See also Ought

Ordinary language, theory of, 265–268, 270–271, 433

Organizational revolution, 337; and brontosaurus principle, 385–388; and crisis, 381–384

Ought, distinguished from "is," 7, 20, 252–253; of duty, 197–199; implies free will, 4, 151; moral basis of, 199–205; of worth, 197–199
Overpopulation, 41–42, 46–47

Peak experiences, 219–220
Planning, social and economic, 331–332, 367, 402–403
Pleasure, 61, 68–69; calculus of, 90, 101–103; displeasure as opposite of, 88; qualities of, 100–101; quantities of, 90–91; See also Happiness; Hedonism
Positivism, ethical, 50, 258–263, 268–270; legal, 48–50; logical, 258–263, 268–270
Prejudice (see Moral bias)
Productive forces and class relations, conflict between, 324, 329–330, 333, 381
Promises, 170–171, 183–186
Punishment, 190–192, 211–212

Reason, good as life of, 60–63, 64–66; in self-fulfillment, 67–68
Reasoning in ethics, 271–274; good-reasons approach, 263–264, 267–268, 270–271; and Humian subjectivism, 251–255; logical positivism on, 258–263, 269–271; See also Methods in ethics
Relativism (see Cultural relativism)
Religion, criticisms of, 426–427; cultural roots of, 409–413; formalistic morality based on, 128–132; humanistic interpretation of, 408–409, 423–425, 426; importance of, 408–409; as mystical, 418–423; primitive, 412, 416–417; reconstruction of, 427–429; sacredness as emotional essence of, 413–414; as spirit of community, 413–418; theistic interpretation of, 425–426
Right, deontological concept of, 2–3, 146–148; good as ingredient in, 183–186; objective, 166, 202; as the ought of duty, 197–199; religious concept of, 129–131, 134–135; subjective, 166, 202; utilitarian concept of, 85, 164–166, 181–186, 198–199; See also Categorical imperatives; Duty
Rights, correlative of duties, 16; individualistic theory of, 28–34; natural or human, 16, 20, 26, 28–34, 89, 350, 358; social conception of, 31–32, 350–351; See also Civil liberties; Freedom and liberty

Rules, and act-utilitarianism, 169–171, 194; of conscience, 136–139; of due process, 176–177, 190; and exceptions, 153–156, 169–171, 179–181; moral, compared with game rules, 175–176; practice concept of, 174–181, 184–185, 190, 194–195; of rule-utilitarianism, 171–174, 194; social basis of moral rules, 172–173; summary concept of, 174, 179–181
Rule-utilitarianism (see Utilitarianism)

Sanctions, 15–16, 92
Science, Marxian theory of, 326, 335–336; and morality, 140–143; See also Technology
Self-incrimination, privilege against, 177–179
Selfishness, 205–208; See also Egoism
Self-knowledge, 72–73
Sex, Freud on, 73, 74–76, 77, 79–80; and moral bias, 214; and the standard of quality, 218–219
Sharing and excellence, 345–350
Social contract, 29, 284–285, 297, 350–351, 354
Socialism, 330–332, 400; See also Collectivism; Communism
Specialization (see Division of labor)
Standards for choice of values, 90, 94–95, 115, 215–222; of duration, 90, 216; of fruitfulness, 220–221; of intensity, 90, 216–217; of number, 90, 220; of quality, 94–95, 217–220
State, freedom under, 290–291, 354–357; as intrinsically good, 290–291; as not intrinsically good, 303–304; Marxian theory of, 325, 327, 331–332, 336–337; role of, in free society, 404–405
State of nature (see Nature, state of)
Stoicism, criticism of, 21; and human brotherhood, 18–20; as type of natural-law ethics, 16–21
Subjectivism, 89, 247–248; criticism of, 268–274; of Hume, 250–255; and language, 248–250, 265–268; of logical positivists, 258–263; modified by Hare, 263–265; modified by the informalists, 267–268; stimulated by Moore's theory, 255–258
Supernaturalism, 24–25; See also Religion

Survival of the fittest, 42–46

Sympathy, 88, 199–205, 206, 213–215

Technology, and communication, 394–400; and community planning, 402–403; and crisis, 382–384; and democratic decentralization, 402–404; Marxian theory of, 324–325, 333–335, 339, 395; and organizational revolution, 381–384; requires reflective ethics, 140–143

Teleological ethics, 1–2, 134, 168; See also Utilitarianism

Totalitarianism, communist, 330–331, 337; and democracy, 353–357, 366; fascist, 251; See also Organizational revolution

Truth, as demonstrable or verifiable, 251–252; and free discussion, 362–364; logical positivist theory of, 258; as non-relativistic, 237–238

Universality of values, 233, 235, 240–242, 243–245, 379–380

Utilitarianism, act-utilitarianism, 169–171, 181; basic tenets of, 2, 164–166; distinguished from hedonism, 85; and prima-facie duties, 159–162; rule-utilitarianism, 171–181, 184–186, 190, 194–195; types of, 166–168

Value, commensurability of, questioned, 101–103, 195; defined, 113; group as locus of, 282–285; individual as locus of, 282–285; instrumental, 220–221; and interest, 113–120, 281; intrinsic, 117–118, 281; terminal, 118; as unobservable, 253; and worthiness, 118–121; See also Good; Standards for choice

Volition (see Desire and volition)

War, 42–43, 140–142, 435

Worthiness, 118–120, 267, 272